本教材受教育部人文社科研究项目"中国林产品贸易潜力、结构重构及相关政策研究"（17YJA790038）和浙江省科技厅软科学项目"进口对浙江农业全要素生产率增长的影响机制研究"（2019C35075）资助出版。

21世纪高等学校国际经济与贸易系列规划教材

International Trade
Practice

# 国际贸易实务
## （中英双语）

主　编　蒋琴儿
副主编　徐　晴

ZHEJIANG UNIVERSITY PRESS
浙江大学出版社
·杭州·

**图书在版编目（CIP）数据**

国际贸易实务 / 蒋琴儿主编. — 杭州：浙江大学出
版社，2021.12
ISBN 978-7-308-20047-9

Ⅰ．①国… Ⅱ．①蒋… Ⅲ．① 国际贸易－贸易实务－
教材 Ⅳ．①F740.4

中国版本图书馆CIP数据核字(2020)第031406号

## 国际贸易实务
GUOJI MAOYI SHIWU

蒋琴儿　主编

| | |
|---|---|
| **责任编辑** | 李　晨 |
| **责任校对** | 宁　檬 |
| **装帧设计** | 春天书装 |
| **出版发行** | 浙江大学出版社 |
| | （杭州市天目山路148号　　邮政编码　310007） |
| | （网址：http://www.zjupress.com） |
| **排　　版** | 杭州林智广告有限公司 |
| **印　　刷** | 杭州高腾印务有限公司 |
| **开　　本** | 787mm×1092mm　1/16 |
| **印　　张** | 28.5 |
| **字　　数** | 760千 |
| **版 印 次** | 2021年12月第1版　2021年12月第1次印刷 |
| **书　　号** | ISBN 978-7-308-20047-9 |
| **定　　价** | 79.80元 |

# 前　言

对外开放是中国的一项基本国策。2018年，全国高校毕业生人数达820万人，再创历史新高，而中国外贸直接或间接带动就业的人数近2亿，每4个就业人口中就有1个从事与外贸相关的工作。因此，深度融入国际生产分工体系，促进外贸稳中提质，加大吸引外资力度，是全面推动经济高质量发展、可持续解决中国巨量人口就业难题的重要举措。

近年来，外国学生来华留学的吸引力与中国的经济实力、综合实力的匹配度进一步提升，来华留学规模持续扩大。中国已成为亚洲最大留学目的国，越来越多的留学生来华学习。高等教育国际化已经成为中国各高校的发展战略之一。2016年，来华留学生人数规模突破44万，比2012年增长了35%，其中学历生人数达21万人，占来华留学生总数的47.4%，比2012年提高了7%。来华留学学历生选读的专业越来越多地从传统的中文、历史和中国文化等专业，转变为经济、金融等社会科学专业。其中，国际经济与贸易是吸引外国来华留学学历生最多的专业之一，这些留学生主要来自非洲和"一带一路"沿线的巴基斯坦、印度、俄罗斯、越南、泰国、印度尼西亚、哈萨克斯坦、乌克兰等广大发展中国家。

"国际贸易实务"课程是一门主要研究国际货物买卖的具体过程、相关活动及其商务运作规范的课程，主要阐述国际货物贸易的基本理论、基本知识和基本技能。教学内容强调符合中国国情，并与世界紧密接轨。通过本课程的学习，学习者能通晓国际通行的贸易惯例与规则，掌握中国对外贸易实践的具体做法，并能结合实际对国际贸易的发展趋势做出预判。本课程是中国高校国际经贸类专业学生必修的专业基础课程，也是经济管理类其他专业、外语类专业开设的限选课或任选课。英语是国际贸易实务中采用的主要语言之一，且大多数来华留学的外国学生很难在短时期内适应专业课程的中文教学，故本教材采用中、英双语编写（中、英双语编写的内容互为补充），以尽可能同时满足中国学生、外国学生学习本课程知识的需要。

本教材由浙江农林大学蒋琴儿教授主编，浙江农林大学的徐晴老师参与了部分章节的英文翻译校对工作。

由于时间及编者水平所限，本教材中的错误和不足之处在所难免，恳切希望同行、专家和广大读者批评指正。

编者

2021年12月

# PREFACE

Opening-up is a basic national policy of China. In 2018, the number of college graduates nationwide reached 8.2 million, a new record high, and the number of employment directly or indirectly driven by China's foreign trade is nearly 200 million, one fourth employees are engaged in the work related to foreign trade. Therefore, to integrate into the international division deeply, promote the stability and quality of foreign trade, and increase the intensity of attracting foreign investment is an important measure to promote high-quality economic development comprehensively and to solve the employment problem of China's huge population in a sustainable way.

In recent years, the attractiveness of foreign students studying in China has been further matched with China's economic capabilities and comprehensive strength. The scale of foreign students studying in China has continued to grow. China has become the largest destination in Asia for foreign students studying. More and more students are coming to China to study for academic programs. Internationalization of higher education has become one of the development strategies of Chinese universities. In 2016, the number of foreign students studying in China exceeded 440,000, an increase of 35% over 2012. Among them, the number of foreign students in academic program reached 210,000, accounting for 47.4% of the total number of foreign students studying in China, an increase of 7% over 2012. The students study in academic, more and more from the traditional majors such as Chinese, history and culture of China, to majors in economic, finance and other social sciences. The major in international economic and trade enjoys great popularity, attracting a lot of foreign students to study in China. The students mainly come from the developing countries including African countries and the countries along "the Belt and Road", such as Pakistan, India, Russia, Vietnam, Thailand, Indonesia, Kazakhstan, and Ukraine.

Practical international trade is a science that mainly studies the specific process, related activities and business operation norms of international merchandise trade. It elaborates the basic theories, knowledge and skills of international merchandise trade. The teaching content emphasizes to conform to China's national conditions and be closely connected with the international standards. Through the study of this course, the learners can be familiar with the international trade practices and rules, master the specific practices of China's foreign trade practice, and make a prediction of the development trend of international trade based on the actual work in the future.This course is a compulsory one for majors in international economic and trade in Chinese universities, and also an optional one for other majors of economic management and foreign languages. English is one of the main languages used in international trade practice, and most foreign students studying in China can hardly adapt to the Chinese teaching of professional courses in a short period. Therefore, this textbook is written in both Chinese and English to meet the needs of Chinese students and foreign students to learn the knowledge of this course.

This texbook is edited by Professor Jiang Qiner of Zhejiang Agriculture and Forestry University, and Xu Qing of Zhejiang Agriculture and Forestry University participated in the English translation and proofreading of some chapters.

Due to the limitation of time and editor's level, the errors and deficiencies in this textbook are inevitable. I sincerely hope that peers, experts, and readers will criticize and correct.

Author

December 2021

Contents **目 录**

# 第一章

# 导　论

## 一、全球经济与贸易发展情况

全球经济贸易格局正发生着深刻变化。伴随经济全球化的纵深发展，全球货物和服务贸易呈现出高速增长态势。发达国家（地区）通过广泛开展区域贸易合作和控制多边贸易体制来主宰国际贸易秩序，在国际交换中获得了大部分贸易利益，占据了世界货物出口70%以上的份额和服务贸易90%以上的份额。尽管美、欧、日三大经济体仍然是世界经济的主要力量，在国际贸易中居于主导地位，但全球各国（地区）的贸易依赖度均有所上升。中国通过全面参与经济全球化和国际合作竞争，国际地位和国际竞争力不断提升，成为全球国际贸易增长最显眼的"亮点"。对外贸易既是中国对外开放的重要载体，也是体制机制改革的前沿领域，为中国经济社会发展做出巨大贡献。外贸新业态以其强劲的发展动能，成为外贸转型升级、实现优进优出、提升开放型经济水平的重要发展方向。根据商务部制定的《对外贸易发展"十三五"规划》，外贸新业态主要包括跨境电子商务、市场采购贸易和外贸综合服务平台。跨境电商是中国外贸发展的新增长点，市场采购贸易方式拓展了传统商品市场的外贸功能，外贸综合服务平台（企业）帮助中小企业实现外贸业务专业化、规范化经营，大幅降低了企业交易成本。

目前，中国有1400个商品的出口份额居全球第一，外贸直接或间接带动就业的人数将近2亿，每4个就业人口中就有1个从事与外贸相关的工作，为促进就业、推动产业升级、平衡国际收支、推动区域发展等做出了积极贡献。据中华人民共和国海关总署2018年年底的数据统计：2018年12月时每5分钟就有约2.9亿元货物进出中国关境，4艘国际船舶离岸或离港，9架国际航线飞机起飞或降落，1120个集装箱、5492个快件、8655件物品离开或到达，206万个集成电路、1.7万块液晶显示板、1万部手机、88台金属加工机床离开中国关境，3.4万件化妆品、1万吨铁矿砂、4300吨原油进入中国国境。中国经济在稳中向好的同时，带动进口持续快速增长，为世界各国提供更广阔的市场和更宝贵的合作契机。2018年11月，中国成功举办了首届中国国际进口博览会，吸引了172个国家、地区和国际组织参会,3617家企业参展，成交额达578亿美元，为各国（地区）出口和共享中国发展红利搭建新平台。

但是，随着国际贸易规模的不断扩大，各国经济景气的不均衡性、区域贸易集团的排他性、贸易分配利益的两极化等成为当今贸易保护主义层出不穷的原因。当前，全球经济格局正发生着深刻变化，并伴随世界贸易进入争端高发期，呈现出以下特点：一是基于战略利益考虑而引发的贸易摩擦增多；二是贸易保护的手段不断翻新，各种技术壁垒成为贸易保护的新式武器，知识产权纠纷成为国际贸易争端的重要方面；三是摩擦从单纯的贸易问题转变为更为综合的问题，社会保障问题、汇率制度问题等已成为产生摩擦的新领域，资源摩擦与贸易摩擦交互作用的趋势越来越明显；四是中国已成为国际贸易保护的最大受害国。从1995年开始，中国已成为遭受反倾销最多的国家。

# 二、国际贸易与国内贸易的相同点与不同点

国际贸易（international trade）俗称通商，是指跨越国境的商品和服务（goods and services）的交换活动，一般由进口贸易和出口贸易组成。如从单个国家或地区的角度出发，一个特定的国家或地区同其他国家或地区之间所进行的商品和劳务的交换活动，则称为对外贸易（foreign trade）。国际贸易与国内贸易都属于商品交换，两者在本质上并无明显不同，但也存在一定程度的差别。

## （一）国际贸易与国内贸易的相同点

①都属于商品和劳务的交换。
②经营目的相同，都是通过交换获取更多的经营利润。
③均受市场规律、供求规律等影响。

## （二）国际贸易与国内贸易的不同点

①在语言、法律、风俗、习惯上，国内贸易可能会遇到的冲突远小于国际贸易。
②国际贸易的商品交换活动及过程远比国内贸易复杂，前者还涉及运输、保险、银行、商检、海关等部门的协作与配合。
③国际贸易的综合风险要高于国内贸易，不论是商业风险、价格风险、汇率风险、运输风险或是政治风险等，前者遇到的概率相比后者更高、更多。
④国际贸易所受的贸易行为约束范围要比国内贸易更广。例如，WTO成员要遵守WTO规则制约，区域贸易协定成员要遵守区域贸易协定规定，等等。

不过，以贸易全球化为首要内容的经济全球化对全球与中国的经济和商务发展产生了深刻影响。国际贸易与国内贸易的差异会随着贸易双方经济自由度水平、贸易便利化水平、贸易开放度水平的提高而逐渐缩小。

# 三、国际贸易分类

国际贸易按照不同的情况拥有诸多分类方法，包括按经济水平、贸易政策、清偿工具、贸易流向、贸易关系、统计制度、商品形态、贸易方式等标准进行分类。以下具体介绍其中的几种。

## （一）贸易流向

按照贸易流向（trade flow），国际贸易可分为出口贸易（export trade）、进口贸易（import trade）、复出口贸易（re-export trade）和复进口贸易（re-import trade）。出口贸易是指一国把自己生产和加工的商品输往国外市场销售；进口贸易是指一国将外国生产和加工的商品输入本国市场销售；复出口贸易是指一国将从外国进口的商品不经任何实质性加工就向外出口；复进口贸易是指一国输往国外的商品未经过加工又输回本国。出口贸易与进口贸易为一次贸易的两个方面，对卖方来说是出口贸易，对买方来说是进口贸易。复出口贸易在很大程度上与过境贸易、转口贸易有关。

## （二）贸易关系

按照生产国（地区）与消费国（地区）之间的贸易关系，国际贸易可分为直接贸易（direct trade）与间接贸易（indirect trade）。直接贸易是指生产国（地区）与消费国（地区）之间直接买卖商品的行为。对生产国（地区）来说属于直接出口，对消费国（地区）来说则是直接进口。直接贸易的买卖双方不通过第三国（地区）商人作为中介来进行贸易。间接贸易是指生产国（地区）与消费国（地区）之间，经由第三国（地区）商人进行买卖商品的行为。间接贸易的双方当事人没有直接关系，而是通过第三国（地区）的商人作为中介来进行贸易。

无论是直接贸易还是间接贸易，贸易双方交易的货物都可以直接从生产国（地区）运输到消费国（地区），也可以通过第三国（地区）的国境转运到消费国（地区）。如果货物运输途经第三国（地区）且未经任何加工，该交易对于第三国（地区）而言就构成了该国（地区）的过境贸易（transit trade），第三国（地区）一般可对该批货物收取一定的费用。生产国（地区）与消费国（地区）通过第三国（地区）商人进行的贸易，对商品生产国（地区）和消费国（地区）来说是间接贸易，而对第三国（地区）来说是转口贸易（entrepot trade）或中转贸易。从事转口贸易的国家（地区）大多数地理位置优越、交通便利，贸易限制较少。

转口贸易与过境贸易是两个容易混淆的概念，两者有显著的区别。转口贸易以盈利为目的，第三国（地区）一般采取正常的商业加价方式来获取贸易利益，属于贸易范畴；而过境贸易一般只收取少量的手续费，属于运输范畴。在转口贸易中，一定有第三国（地区）的商人参与商品的交易过程，不论货物是否经由第三国（地区）运送；而在过境贸易中，可以没有第三国（地区）商人的参与。

### （三）商品形态

国际贸易按照商品形态的不同，可分为货物贸易（merchandise trade）和服务贸易（service trade）。货物贸易又分为有形贸易（visible trade）和有形商品贸易（tangible trade）。国际贸易涉及的有形商品种类繁多，联合国《国际贸易标准分类目录》（SITC）把有形商品分成10类、63章、233组、786个分组和1924个基本项目。其中，10类商品分别为：食品及主要供食用的活动物（0）；饮料及烟类（1）；燃料以外的非食用粗原料（2）；矿物燃料、润滑油及有关原料（3）；动植物油脂及油脂（4）；未列名化学品及有关产品（5）；主要按原料分类的制成品（6）；机械及运输设备（7）；杂项制品（8）；没有分类的其他商品（9）。其中，0—4类商品称为初级产品，5—8类商品称为制成品。

除联合国《国际贸易标准分类目录》（SITC）外，目前使用最广泛的国际贸易统计口径是《商品名称及编码协调制度》（简称《协调制度》，HS）。它是在《海关合作理事会商品分类目录》（CCCN）和《国际贸易标准分类目录》的基础上，协调国际上多种主要的税则、统计、运输等商品分类目录而制定的一部多用途的国际贸易商品目录，是一个完整的、系统的、准确的国际贸易商品分类体系。中国也采用这一分类标准。HS采用6位数编码，将国际贸易商品分为22类、98章，章以下再分目和子目。该编码是国际标准编码，商品编码第1、2位数码代表"章"，第3、4位数码代表"目"（heading），第5、6位数码代表"子目"（subheading）。例如，去壳花生属于初级产品，其HS编码为1202.20。

服务贸易，又被称为无形贸易（invisible trade）、无形商品贸易（intangible trade）或劳务贸易。国际服务贸易是指一切不具备物质自然属性的商品（无形商品）的国际交换活动，包括运输、保险、金融、旅游、技术转让等劳务的提供与接受，以及其他非实物形态的进出口。按照《服务贸易总协定》（GATS）的定义，服务贸易具有4种方式。

①过境交付，即服务消费者和提供者都不跨越国境的服务方式。例如，通过网络进行的国际远程教育、国际医疗等方面的服务。

②境外消费，即服务消费者到服务提供者国内接受服务的方式。例如，中国公民出境旅游、留学等。对于中国来说，是在国外实现服务的进口工作；而对外国来说，是在国内从事服务的出口工作。

③商业存在，即服务企业到国外开办服务场所，提供服务。例如，外国银行到中国开设分行并提供相应的金融服务等。

④自然人移动，即一国的自然人到服务消费者所在国或第三国提供服务。例如，菲律宾女佣到新加坡家庭提供劳务等。

### （四）贸易方式

按贸易方式可分为一般贸易（general trade）和加工贸易（process trade）。一般贸易是指单边进口或单边出口的贸易方式，但设备投资、捐赠除外。加工贸易是指利用本国的人力、物力和技术优势，从国外输入原材料、半成品、样品或图纸等，在国内加工制造或装配成成品以后再向国外输出，以生产加工性质为主的一种贸易方式。它又可以分为来料加工、来样加工、来件装配与协作生产等方式。

# 四、教学章节与内容

## （一）教学章节

国际贸易具有线长、面广、环节多、难度大、变化快的特点。凡从事国际贸易的人员，不仅须掌握国际贸易的基本原理、知识、技能与方法，还应具备分析和处理实际业务问题的能力，以确保社会经济效益的顺利实现。本教材中、英文各10章。除本章作为导论外，第二章介绍贸易术语，第三章介绍国际贸易货物，第四章介绍国际货物运输与保险，第五章介绍国际货物买卖价格，第六章介绍国际货物买卖的货款收付，第七章介绍国际货物买卖争议的预防与处理，第八章介绍国际货物买卖的交易磋商与合同订立，第九章介绍国际货物买卖合同的履行，第十章介绍国际贸易主要方式。

教学内容以贸易术语为主线，以国际货物买卖合同为中心。贸易术语主要讲解卖方在交付货物给买方的过程中贸易双方如何分配任务、风险与费用，但不真正涉及相关任务的具体操作情况，包括如何备货、如何办理国际货物运输与保险、如何规定国际贸易货物的价格、如何支付货款、如何具体处理争议等，因而需要对这些相关问题及其解决方案做出具体的规定。

## （二）教学内容

为充分体现教学内容的集中性、专业性、技能性与复合性等特点，本课程教学内容的逻辑边界设定如下。

### 1. 以货物贸易为主要研究对象

随着国际贸易内涵的不断深化发展，货物贸易与服务贸易关系越来越密切。货物贸易带动了服务贸易，而服务贸易又促进了货物贸易的发展。两者的一个重要区别是：货物进出口要办理海关手续，并体现在海关的贸易统计上，是国际收支的重要组成部分；服务贸易不用办理海关手续，通常不显示在海关的贸易统计上，但也是国际收支的一部分。本教材的教学内容以国际货物贸易为主要研究对象，但货物贸易的基本操作与技能也适用于国际服务贸易。

### 2. 以货物买卖为主要研究内容

本教材的相关教学内容只涉及一次性买卖或链式交易中的上下游企业间的买卖，既不涉及所交付的进出口货物的具体研发、设计、生产及加工等制造环节，也不涉及购买方对货物的后续相关处理（如直接销售、转卖或再加工等）。本教材主要讲解买卖双方如何进行交易磋商，签订相关合同，并成功履行合同。假设的基本前提是买卖双方已各自通过一定的途径获取对方的相关信息，并已开展国际市场行情调研和客户资信调查，初步判定对方是自己所需产品的外国合格供应商（对买方来说）或自己所能提供、生产的产品的拟拓展海外市场中的心仪买家（对卖方来说）。获知对方信息的途径包括互联网、商品交易会、商会、政府、海关、银行、专业调研公司和私人公司等。

**3. 强调线上线下贸易的有机结合**

随着跨境电子商务的发展，本书在加入跨境电商相关内容的同时，也注重将国际贸易中传统经典的做法推广到跨境电商相关内容当中，以推动国际贸易线上线下有机结合。本教材的第二至九章内容中都设计了各章内容与跨境电商结合的相关思考题，以让学生学习跨境电子商务的相关知识。

**4. 反映国内外贸易最新做法和实践**

本教材的教学内容在强调与微观经济学、宏观经济学、管理学、国际贸易理论与政策、国际市场营销、国际运输与保险、国际商务谈判、国际金融、国际结算、跨境电子商务等诸多先修、后续课程教学内容衔接的同时，充分体现国内外进出口贸易最新的做法和实践，理论联系实际，既符合中国国情，又与国际接轨。本教材强调客观性原则，即对任何进出口业务过程中出现的现象必须按它的本来面目加以考察，必须在一定的客观条件下进行研究；同时，注重发展性原则，即国际贸易的任何活动总是处于不断发展变化的过程当中，须贯彻"理论联系实际"原则，从实践中总结、归纳出一定的规律，然后将这些成果应用到实际中指导实践，检验理论的正确性，从而进一步发展和丰富理论。

**5. 强调与法律、法规、国际公约与贸易惯例间的联系**

国际贸易作为一种商事行为，需要遵循各种法律规范，包括国际（商务）条约、国际（商事）惯例和各国商事立法。国际货物买卖合同是对合同当事人双方有约束力的法律文件，必须经过一定的法律步骤才能订立。履行合同是一种法律行为，处理履约当中的争议实际上是解决法律纠纷问题，而且不同法系国家的具体裁决的结果还不一样。国际贸易实务须以国际贸易基本理论和中国对外贸易政策为指导，注重进出口业务与国际上认可度高的法律、法规、国际条约和国际贸易惯例等的联系。

# Chapter 1

# Introduction to the Course

## 1.1 Global Econoic and Trade Development

The global economic and trade landscape is undergoing profound changes. With the in-depth development of economic globalization, the global trade in goods and services shows a high-growth trend. Since the 1990s, the growth rate of international trade has been continuously exceeding that of world production. At the national level, the developed countries (regions) have accounted for more than 70 percent of the world's exports of goods and more than 90 percent of its trade in services. Furthermore, most of the trade benefits from international exchanges is gained by the developed countries (regions) through conducting extensive regional trade cooperation and controlling the multilateral trade system, in order to dominate the international trade order. Although the three major economies including the United States, Europe, and Japan are still the major forces in the world economy and play a dominant role in international trade, the trade dependence of all countries (regions) in the world has increased. China has unswervingly adhered to the basic state policy of opening up to the outside world. It has fully participated in economic globalization and international cooperation and competition. With the rising of China's international status and competitiveness, China has become the most visible "bright spot" in the growth of global trade. Foreign trade is not only an important carrier of China's Reform and Opening-Up, but also a frontier area of institutional reform, making great contributions to China's economic and social development. The new forms of foreign trade have become an important development direction for foreign trade transformation and upgrading, optimal import and export, and improvement of the level of open economy. According to the China's 13th Five-Year Plan for Foreign Trade Development formulated by the Ministry of Commerce, the new forms of foreign trade mainly include cross-border e-commerce, market procurement trade, and foreign trade integrated service platform. Cross-border e-commerce is a new growth point of China's foreign trade development. The way of market procurement trade expands the foreign trade function of the traditional commodity market, and the foreign trade integrated service platform (enterprises) helps small- and medium- sized enterprises to achieve professional and standardized foreign trade business operation, which greatly reduces the transaction cost of enterprises.

At present, China's export share of 1,400 commodities ranks first in the world. Nearly 200 million people are employed directly or indirectly by foreign trade, and 1 out of every 4 employed people is engaged in work related to foreign trade.

According to the data of China's General Administration of Customs on December 2018: Now, in every 5 minutes, there are $290 million of goods in and out of China customs frontier, 4 international ships offshore or departing, 9 international routes aircraft taking off or landing; 1,120 containers, 5,492 expresses, and other 8,655 items leaving or arriving; 2.06 million integrated circuit, 17,000 liquid crystal display panels, 10,000 mobile phones, 88 sets of metal processing machine tools leaving; 34,000 pieces of cosmetics, 10,000 tons of iron ore sand, and 4,300 tons of crude oil entering.

While China is maintaining stability and improving economic performance, China's imports have continued to grow at a rapid pace, providing a broader market and more valuable opportunities for cooperation with other countries (regions).

In November 2018, the first China International Import Expo was successfully held, attracting 172 countries, regions, and international organizations to participate in the expo. 3,617 enterprises participated in the expo, with a total trade volume of 57.8 billion US dollars. Meanwhile, China's domestic demand is growing steadily.

However, with the scale of international trade continuing to expand, trade protectionism emerges in an endless stream as the important reasons, such as the imbalance of economic boom of various countries (regions), exclusivity of regional trade group, the polarization of trade distribution of interests. At present, the world trade has entered a period of high frequency of disputes and has the following characteristics: First, trade frictions caused by strategic interests have increased. Second, the means of trade protection have been constantly updated. Various technical barriers become the new weapons of trade protection. Intellectual property disputes become the important aspects of international trade disputes. Third, frictions have shifted from simple trade issues to more comprehensive areas. Social security issues, exchange rate system issues, and other issues have become new areas of frictions. The interaction between resource frictions and trade frictions has become more and more obvious. Fourth, China has become the biggest victim of international trade protection. Since 1995, China has been subject to anti-dumping for 10 consecutive years.

# 1.2 Similarities and Differences Between Foreign Trade and Domestic Trade

Foreign trade refers to the exchange of goods and services across borders. Becaue it generally consists of import and export, it is also known as import and export trade. From the perspective of a single country or region, the exchange of goods and services between a specific country or region and other countries or regions is called foreign trade. Both foreign trade and domestic trade belong to the scope of commodity exchange. There is no obvious difference between them in essence, but there are some slight differences to some extent.

## 1.2.1 Similarities Between Foreign Trade and Domestic Trade

①They both belong to the exchange of goods and services.

②They have the same business purpose,which is to obtain more operating profits through exchanges.

③Either in foreign trade or domestic trade, the trade activities are affected by market rules, laws as well as of supply and demand.

## 1.2.2 Differences Between Foreign Trade and Domestic Trade

①Due to different languages, laws, customs and habits, domestic trade may face far less conflicts than foreign trade.

② The exchange activities and their processes of foreign are much more complicated than those of domestic trade. Foreign trade also involves the cooperation of departments of transportation, insurance, banking, commodity inspection and customs.

③The comprehensive risk of foreign trade is higher than that of domestic trade. No matter what the risk is, say commercial risk, price risk, exchange rate risk, transportation risk or political risk,  international trade tends to have a higher risk than domestic trade.

④Foreign trade is governed by a wider range of trade practices than domestic trade. For example, WTO members should abide by the WTO rules, and Regional Trade Agreement (RTA) members should abide by the RTA provisions of regional trade agreement.

However, economic globalization, with trade globalization as the primary content, has exerted a profound impact on the economic and commercial development in China and around the world. The differences between foreign trade and domestic trade will gradually converge with the improvement of economic freedom, trade facilitation and trade openness between countries or regions.

# 1.3 Classification of International Trade

International trade has many classifications according to different situations, including national economic level, trade policies, instruments of settlement, trade flows, trade relations, statistical systems, commodity forms and trade modes. Some of the classifications will be explained in cletail.

## 1.3.1 Trade Flows

According to the trade flow, international trade can be divided into export, import, re-export and re-import. Export trade refers to the export of goods produced and processed by a country (region) to foreign markets for sale. Import trade refers to the import of goods produced and processed by foreign countries into the domestic market for sale. Re-export trade means that a country (region) exports the goods imported from foreign countries (regions) without any substantial processing. Re-import trade refers to the import of goods from one country (region) to another country (region) without processing. Export and import are two aspects of a trade, which are export trade for the seller and import trade for the buyer. Re-export trade is related to transit trade and entrepot trade to a great extent.

## 1.3.2 Trade Relations

According to the trade relations between the producing country (region) and consuming country (region), international trade can be divided into direct trade and indirect trade. Direct trade refers to the act of buying and selling commodities directly between the producers and consumers. For the producing country (region) it is direct export, and for the consuming country (region) it is direct import. The buyers and sellers of direct trade do not trade through the intermediary of the merchants in a third country (region). Indirect trade refers to the act of trade by merchants from a third country (region) between producers and consumers of commodities. The two parties involved in indirect trade do not contact directly, for they trade through the intermediary of merchants in a third country (region).

In both direct trade and indirect trade, the goods traded by both parties can be transported directly from the producing country (region) to the consuming country (region), or through the border of a third country (region) to the consuming country (region). If the goods are transported through the territory of a third country (region) without any processing, the transaction constitutes the transit trade of the country (region) to the third country (region) and the third country (region) may generally charge a fee for the goods. The trade between commodity producers and consumers through the merchants of a third country (region) is indirect trade for commodity producers and consumers, while entrepot trade or transit trade is for the third country (region). Most of the countries (regions) engaged in transit trade have advantageous geographical location, convenient transportation and fewer trade restrictions.

Entrepot trade and transit trade are two confusing concepts, with significant differences. The purpose of entrepot trade is to make profits. A third country (region) usually adopts a normal commercial markup to obtain trade benefits, which belongs to the category of trade. Transit trade in general, only a small amount of handling charges, belongs to the scope of transport. In entrepot trade, merchants from a third country (region) participate in the transaction of goods, whether or not the goods are transported through this third country (region). In transit trade, no third country (region) businessmen can participate.

### 1.3.3 Commodity Form

International trade is made by merchandise trade and service trade. Among them, the merchandise trade is also called visible trade or tangible trade. International trade involves a wide variety of tangible commodities. The United Nations International Trade Standard Classification Catalogue (SITC) divides tangible commodities into 10 categories, 63 chapters, 233 groups, 786 subgroups and 1,924 basic items. Among them, 10 categories of commodities are:

Food and main edible live animals (0)

Beverages and cigarettes (1)

Non-edible raw materials other than fuels (2)

Fossil fuels, lubricants and related raw materials (3)

Animal and vegetable fats and oils (4)

Chemicals and related products not listed (5)

Manufactured goods classified mainly by raw material (6)

Machinery and transport equipment (7)

Miscellaneous products (8)

Other goods not classified (9)

Category no.0—4 of commodities are called the primary products and commodities 5—8 are called finished products.

In addition to the catalog of standard international trade classification (SITC) of the United Nations, currently the most widely used international trade statistics caliber is Commodity Name and Code Harmonization System (hereinafter referred to as "harmonization system", the HS). It is in the catalog of classification of goods customs cooperation council (CCCN) and SITC, on the basis of coordination on many major international tariff, statistics, transportation goods classification catalogue for a multi-purpose international trade catalogue, and is a complete, systematic and accurate classification system of international trade goods.

China also uses this classification standard. HS uses a 6-digit code, a code of international standard to classify internationally traded commodities into 22 categories, 98 chapters, sub-headings and headings below chapters. The fist and the second digits of a product code refer to "chapter", the third and the fourth digits refer to "heading", and the fifth and the sixth digits refer to "subheading". For example, the shelled peanuts are a primary product with HS code 1202.20.

Service trade is also known as invisible trade or intangible trade. International trade in services refers to the international exchange activities of the commodities (intangible commodities) without physical nature, including the provision and acceptance of labor services such as transportation, insurance, finance, tourism, and technology transfer, as well as the import and export of other non-physical forms. According to the definition of the General Agreement on Trade in Services (GATS), trade in services has four ways, including transit delivery, overseas consumption, commercial existence and the natural person moves.

### 1.3.4 Mode of Trade

According to the mode of trade, foreign trade can be divided into general trade and processing trade. General trade refers to unilateral import or export, except equipment investment and donation. Processing trade refers to a mode of trade in which raw materials, semi-finished products, samples or drawings are imported from abroad, processed and manufactured in China or assembled into finished products, and then exported to foreign countries (regions) by taking advantage of the manpower, material resources and technical advantages of the country (region). It can be divided into processing with supplied materials, processing with supplied samples, assembling with supplied parts and cooperative production.

## 1.4 Chapters and Teaching Contents

### 1.4.1 Chapters

This textbook has 10 chapters in English and Chinese. In addition to this chapter as an introduction, Chapter 2 is for trade terms, Chapter 3 for international trade goods, Chapter 4 for international transport and insurance, Chapter 5 for the sale price of international goods, Chapter 6 for the receipt and payment of international goods, Chapter 7 for the prevention and settlement of disputes, Chapter 8 for transaction consultation and contract conclusion, and Chapter 9 deals with the performance of contracts for the international sale of goods. Chapter 10 further introduces the common methods and practices of facilitating international trade transactions.Trade term is related to the process of delivery of goods to the buyer trade both sides how to assign tasks, risk and expense, but not really involved in specific operation situation of related tasks, including how to stock up, how to deal with international cargo transportation and insurance, international trade of the goods to the details of price, payment, dispute handling, etc., so need to handle the related problems and made specific provision.

## 1.4.2 Teaching Contents

International trade is characterized by long lines, wide coverage, many links, great difficulties and rapid changes. Those engaged in international trade should not only master the basic principles, knowledge, skills, and modes of international trade, but also learn to analyze and deal with practical business problems, so as to ensure realization of social and economic benefits smoothly. In order to reflect concentration, professional, skills and complexity of the teaching content fully, the logical boundary of the teaching content of this course is set as follows.

### 1. Take Merchandise Trade as the Main Research Object

With the development of international trade, the relationship between merchandise trade and service trade is getting closer. Merchandise trade promotes trade in services, which in turn promotes the development of trade in goods. An important difference between the two is: the import and export of goods goes through the customs procedures, is reflected in the trade statistics of customs and is an important part of the international balance of payments, while the service trade does not go through the customs formalities, usually does not show in the trade statistics of customs, but is also a part of the balance of payments. The teaching content of this textbook takes international merchandise trade as the main research object, but its basic operation and skills are also applicable to international service trade.

### 2. Take the Sale of Goods as the Main Research Content

Related content of the textbook or string trading involves only a one-shot deal between the upstream and downstream enterprises in the business, not involving how to have the specific research and development, design, producing, and processing of the import and export goods, as well as not involving the purchaser how to settle the goods, such as subsequent processing or direct sales. This textbook mainly explains how the buyers and sellers negotiate transactions, sign the relevant contracts and perform the contracts successfully. The hypothesis is that the both parties have their own certain ways to obtain the relevant information of the other party, have finished international market research, customer credit investigation and preliminary judging each other is a foreign qualified supplier or purchaser.

### 3. Emphasize the Organic Combination of Offline and Online Trade

With the development of cross-border e-commerce, this course not only integrates the relevant contents of cross-border e-commerce, but also focuses on promoting traditional and common practices of international trade to cross-border e-commerce, so as to promote the organic combination of online and offline international trade. The relevant thinking exercises on the combination of each chapter's content learning and cross-border e-commerce are proposed to promote the further standardized development of cross-border e-commerce.

### 4. Reflect the Latest Practices in Domestic and Foreign Trade

The teaching content is connected with many prerequisite and subsequent courses, including microeconomics, macroeconomics, management, international trade theory and policy, international marketing, international transport and insurance, international business negotiation, international finance, international settlement, cross-border e-commerce, etc. Simultaneously, the teaching contents reflect the latest theories and practices of domestic trade and foreign trade, in line with international standards and in accordance with China's national conditions.

### 5. Emphasize the Connection with Laws, Regulations, Conventions and Trade Practices

International trade, as a commercial act, needs to follow various legal norms, including international treaties, conventions, trade practices, and commercial legislation of various countries (regions). A contract for international sale of goods must go through certain legal steps before it can be established. The performance of a contract is a legal act, and the handling of disputes in the performance of the contract is actually the solution of legal disputes. Therefore, international trade practice should be guided by the basic theory of international trade and China's foreign trade policy, and pay attention to the connection between import and export business and internationally recognized laws, regulations, international treaties and international trade practices.

# 第二章

# 贸易术语

☞ **案例2.1 出口企业改变贸易术语降低风险与费用**

　　巴西某公司（以下简称买方）与中国浙江某出口企业（以下简称卖方）签订了一份电子配件的长期买卖合同，按月交货，每月的交货时间为当月的15号或之前，贸易条件为"FOB 上海港 INCOTERMS®2020"（FOB Shanghai Seaport INCOTERMS® 2020），由客户指定货运代理。货物经班轮运输从中国上海运往巴西的里奥格兰德（Rio Grande, Brazil）。为避免因到货延误而导致生产线停工，买卖双方在合同中约定：卖方应严格按照合同规定的期限装运，海运费由买方承担；如卖方延期装运1周，卖方应事先告知买方并征求买方同意；如卖方延期装运2周，卖方应采用海空联运方式将货物运往巴西的圣保罗（San Paulo, Brazil），海空联运与全程海运的差额运费由卖方承担；如货物延期装运3周，卖方应采用全程空运方式将货物运往圣保罗，差额运费由卖方承担；如卖方交货延期4周或以上，买方有权提出终止合同并要求损害赔偿。延误时间按周计算，不足一周按整周计算。合同签订后，卖方为了避免延期装运，应客户指定的货运代理要求，一般均提前10天办理订舱。按照上海港的作业习惯，货物一般于班轮开航前3天（截关时间前）运抵上海港指定落箱地点，等待报关完毕后上船。

　　卖方在某月3日向指定的货运代理办理订舱，货运代理当日联系买方并获得运输确认；货运代理于4日告知卖方：已预配本月10日开港班轮，6日将指派集装箱到卖方指定装货点提货。货物装入集装箱后于6日夜晚安全抵达上海港指定装载点落箱。卖方寄送的出口报关单据也于7日送达货运代理指定的接收人员并完成审单。因船公司爆舱，集装箱被抛箱，货物未被装上于10日起航的预配班轮。货运代理分别告知买卖双方，该批货物将改在后一个航班（下一周，即当月的17日）出运，并获得买方认可。然而，实际货物最终是延误2周才装运出去，即实际装运日期为24日，比合同规定时间晚了9天（算2周）。客户得悉后，要求卖方必须在1周内另备一批货物，采用海空联运方式运送货物，额外运费由卖方支付。卖方与买方及其指定货运代理几经交涉，买方的答复是必须按照合同规定履行。按照INCOTERMS®2020的FOB术语规定，卖方应在合同规定的装运日期内将货物在指定的装运港装上买方指派的运输船只，才算完成交货义务。本案中的卖方实际未能在合同规定的装运日期内完成交货。货运代理则是借口船公司原因而非其自身责任，对卖方的要求不予理会。为维持贸易双方的长期关系，卖方无奈不得不按照买方的要求办理了海空联运，承担了差额运费。

卖方在办理上述交涉的同时，也提出了自己的一个特定要求，即希望将买卖合同的贸易条件"FOB Shanghai Seaport INCOTERMS® 2020"改为"FCA Shanghai Seaport INCOTERMS®2020"，买方同意了卖方的要求。过了两个月，相似的情况再次发生。在买方同样的要求下，卖方向买方、货运代理提出了异议。在"FCA Shanghai Seaport INCOTERMS®2020"项下，卖方只要在规定的时间与指定的地点，将货物置于承运人的处置或监管之下，即完成了交货义务。货交承运人后，如货物未能及时装船所产生的风险与卖方无关。买方转而向货运代理索赔。最终，卖方配合买方在短期内赶制了一批货物，并由客户指定的货运代理负责，将该批货物以海空联运的方式运送给买方，海空联运产生的差额运费由该货运代理负责。在本案中，卖方仅仅修改了贸易条件中的两个英文字母，即将贸易术语从"FOB"改为"FCA"，就挽回了巨大的经济损失。在国际货物买卖合同中，采用不同的贸易术语，买卖双方的责任、费用、风险划分是不一样的。因此，国际货物买卖合同中的贸易术语及其选择至关重要。

经济全球化为商业活动进入世界各地市场提供了前所未有的广阔途径。货物正以更大数量、更多种类在更多国家销售。但是，随着全球贸易量的增大与贸易复杂度的提高，买卖合同因起草不当引起误解，导致高成本纠纷的可能性也随之增加。国际贸易流程比较复杂，贸易双方在交接货过程中涉及许多具体问题。货物从出口国的原产地运至进口国的买方所在地，需要经过长途运输并办理相应的进出口手续。运输过程中，可能发生多次转运、装卸和存储，还可能遭受各种风险（如自然灾害、意外事故等），如需要办理与货物进出口相关的运输、保险、报检、申请进出口许可证和清关等手续，并支付相应的运费、装卸费、保险费、检验费、仓储费，以及各种捐税和杂项费用等。这些事务概括起来可称为责任、费用与风险。若买卖双方对每笔进出口交易的上述问题都要进行逐一磋商就显得费时、费力。国际贸易经过长期的实践，逐渐形成了适应各种需要的贸易术语，用以明确买卖双方在货物交接过程中应承担的责任、费用和风险。但是，买卖双方在适用不同贸易术语时需承担的责任、风险和费用规定不同，由其所适用的国际贸易惯例来调整。

# 一、贸易术语的概念与作用

## （一）贸易术语的概念

贸易术语（trade terms）又称价格术语（price terms），是指用一个简短的英文概念或缩写来表明货物的价格构成，明确买卖双方在交接货过程中的责任、费用与风险划分界线。如果买卖双方订立合同时采用了某种贸易术语，如FOB、FCA等，就使该合同具有了一定的特征。例如，以贸易术语FOB、FCA签订的合同，可称为FOB合同、FCA合同。

## （二）贸易术语的作用

贸易术语对简化买卖双方交易磋商的内容、加快交易磋商的进程、促进贸易合同成交、节省业务费用和时间都有积极的作用。贸易术语能产生积极作用的原因如下。

①每种贸易术语都有其特定的含义。买卖双方只要先确定按何种贸易术语成交，即已基本明确了贸易双方在交接货过程中各自应承担的责任、费用和风险，从而可以缩短交易磋商时间，简化交易手续，有利于双方迅速达成交易。

②贸易术语明确了价格的构成要素。买卖双方在确定成交价格时，很容易分析所适用的贸易术语中包含了哪些从属费用，有利于买卖双方进行比价和成本核算。

③买卖双方签订合同时，如对合同的某些条款考虑不周，使某些事项规定不明确或不完备，致使履约产生争议，贸易双方可援引有关贸易术语的一般解释来处理。

④国际贸易活动离不开运输公司、保险公司和商业银行等部门的通力合作，贸易术语及其相关国际惯例为这些业务部门开展相关业务活动提供了客观依据和有利条件。

# 二、与贸易术语相关的国际贸易惯例

19世纪初，国际贸易就已经开始使用贸易术语。因各国法律制度、贸易惯例和习惯做法不同，对贸易术语的理解与运用有一定的差异，容易引起误解、争议和诉讼，浪费时间和费用。为了避免对贸易术语解释不一致所产生的分歧，一些国际组织和商业团体就某些贸易术语做出了统一的解释与规定。目前影响较大的有关贸易术语的国际贸易惯例有以下3个。

## （一）《1932年华沙—牛津规则》

1928年，国际法协会在波兰首都华沙召开会议，制定了关于CIF买卖合同的统一规则，称之为《1928年华沙规则》，共22条。1930年的纽约会议、1931年的巴黎会议和1932年的牛津会议对该规则进行了多次修改，最终将其定名为《1932年华沙—牛津规则》（Warsaw-Oxford Rules 1932）并沿用至今，成为国际贸易中具有一定影响的国际贸易惯例。

《1932年华沙—牛津规则》以英国的贸易习惯和案例为基础，主要就CIF合同双方的权利与义务做出了统一的规定与解释，为以CIF贸易术语成交的买卖双方提供了一套便于使用的统一规则，供买卖双方自愿采用。在买卖双方缺乏标准合同格式或共同交易条件的情况下，买卖双方可以约定采用该规则。该规则在一定程度上反映了各国对CIF合同的一般解释。《1932年华沙—牛津规则》规定，在CIF合同中，货物所有权移转于买方的时间，应当是卖方把装运单据（提单）交给买方的时刻，即以交单时间作为所有权移转的时间。

### （二）《1990年美国对外贸易定义修订本》

在1940年7月30日举行的第27届美国对外贸易会议上，美国商会、美国进口商协会和美国全国对外贸易协会所组成的联合委员对1919年美国九大商业团体制定的《美国出口报价及其缩写》（The U.S. Export Quotations and Abbreviations）进行了修改，并于1941年7月31日将其改名为《1941年美国对外贸易定义修订本》（Revised American Foreign Trade Definitions 1941），后经多次修订，有了1990年的修订本。1990年的修订本中规定和解释的贸易术语有6种：

①ex works，简称 EXW（原产地交货）；

②free along side，简称 FAS（运输工具边交货）；

③free on board，简称 FOB（运输工具上交货）；

④cost and freight，简称 CFR（成本加运费）；

⑤cost, insurance and freight，简称 CIF（成本、运费加保险费）；

⑥delivered ex quay，简称 DEQ（目的港码头交货）。

该规则被美国、加拿大及一些拉丁美洲国家所习惯采用。要注意的是，该规则中的FAS、FOB、CFR、CIF与国际贸易术语解释通则（Incoterms）中相应的贸易术语的解释有很大不同。

### （三）国际贸易术语解释通则

国际贸易术语解释通则（International Rules for the Interpretation of Trade Terms），简称Incoterms，由国际商会（ICC）制定，是当前国际贸易业界使用最广泛、影响最大、使用最广的国际贸易术语解释通则。国际商会于1936年首次公布了一套解释贸易术语的国际规则，定名为《Incoterms 1936》。自1936年国际商会创立Incoterms以来，这套全球普遍接受的合同标准不断进行定期更新以适应国际贸易业务的发展。截至2019年12月，Incoterms已拥有1936、1953、1967、1976、1980、1990、2000、2010与2020等9个版本，且自2020年1月1日起正式适用2020版本（《国际贸易术语解释通则2020》，简称Incoterms®2020）。因Incoterms®2020相比Incoterms®2010所做出的修改内容并不是很多。本教材相关内容以Incoterms®2010为主，Incoterms®2020对应做出的修改将在后续内容中重点涉及。

Incoterms®2020、2010分别在Incoterms®2010、2000版本基础上加以修订。Incoterms®2010的最终版本于2010年9月正式面世，并于2011年1月1日起正式生效。2016年10月14日，在巴黎召开的国际商会商法与惯例委员会会议上决定对Incoterms®2010版本加以修改。其后通过各种途径广泛征求意见，先后形成了三个征求意见稿，收到评论意见3000多份。国际商会商法与惯例委员会（CLP Commission）与海关与贸易便利委员会（Customs and Trade Facilitation Commission）、国际商会各国委员会（NCs）、其他各专门组织（International Federation of Freight Forwarders Associations, International Union of Marine Insurance, European Shippers Council, Senegalese Shippers Council）等通力合作，Incoterms® 2020最终版本于2019年9月10日正式公布，作为向国际商会成立100周年的献礼，于2020年1月1日正式生效。

Incoterms®2020沿用Incoterms®2010的标题，以国际商会出版物编号723E（ICC Publication No.723E）出版。Incoterms®2010考虑了无关税区的不断变化、商业交易中电子信息使用的增加、货物运输中对安全问题的进一步关注以及运输方式的变化等。Incoterms®2020则考虑到了对货物运输中的安全问题的日益关注、根据货物的性质和运输灵活安排保险的需要和FCA规则下银行在特定货物销售融资中对已装船提单的要求。因此，Incoterms是一套顺应国际贸易实践不断发展变化的与时俱进的国际贸易规则，旨在便利全球贸易活动。它是一套由三个字母组成的，反映货物买卖合同中商业实务的贸易术语，主要描述货物由买方交付给买方过程中所涉及的工作、成本和风险。在买卖合同中使用Incoterms®2020或Incoterms®2010术语有利于明确双方当事人的各自义务。

相比Incoterms 2000，Incoterms®2010的内容主要变化主要体现在以下6点。

①贸易术语的数量由13种变为11种，详见表2.1。贸易术语分组从原来的E、F、C、D 4组改为2组，即适用于任何运输方式或多种运输方式的贸易术语和仅适用于海运及内河水运的贸易术语。删去了Incoterms® 2000的4个术语：DAF（delivered at frontier），边境交货；DES（delivered ex ship），目的港船上交货；DEQ（delivered ex quay），目的港码头交货；DDU（delivered duty unpaid），未完税交货。新增了2个术语：DAT（delivered at terminal），在指定目的地或目的港的集散站交货；DAP（delivered at place），在指定目的地交货。DAP取代DAF、DES和DDU3个术语，DAT取代了DEQ。DAP与DAT适用于任何运输方式。

②在适用于海运及内河水运的贸易术语FOB、CFR和CIF中，省略了以"船舷"（ship's rail）作为交货点的描述，取而代之的是货物置于"船上"时构成交货。如选用Incoterms® 2010中的FOB、CFR或CIF贸易术语，卖方承担货物装上船为止的一切风险，而买方承担货物自装运港装上船后的一切风险。这种改变更符合当今商业现实，且能避免那种已经过时的风险在一条假想垂直线上摇摆不定的情形。

③增加了"链式销售"（string sales）的概念和"取得运输中的货物"（by procuring the goods so delivered）的规定，加入了货物在运输过程中被多次转卖（链式销售）的责任义务划分。在商品销售中，货物在运送至销售链终端的过程中常常被多次转卖。当出

现转卖时，处于销售链中端的卖方实际上不运送货物，因为销售链始端的卖方已经安排了运输。因此，处于销售链中端的卖方不是以运送货物的方式，而是以"取得"货物的方式，履行对其买方的义务。为了澄清此问题，Incoterms®2010中加入了"取得运输中货物"的义务，并以其作为相关术语（如FAS、FOB、CFR和CIF）中货物运输义务的替代义务。

④国际贸易术语主要用于货物跨越国界的国际货物买卖合同，而Incoterms®2010以副标题的方式，正式确认其贸易术语对国际和国内货物买卖合同均可适用。修改原因主要有三：一是目前在世界许多地区，一些像欧盟这样的区域经济同盟已使不同成员间的边界形式显得不再重要；二是贸易双方常在国内买卖合同中使用国际贸易术语；三是美国于2004年删除了《美国统一商法典》第二部分的第319—324条有关"运输和交货条款"（UCC Section 2，319—324 "Shipping and Delivery Terms"）的规定，美国国内贸易中出现了更愿意以国际贸易术语取代传统使用的《美国统一商法典》中的运输和交货术语的现象。

⑤Incoterms®2010的每个贸易术语中的买卖双方各项义务，在编排上采用卖方义务与买方义务逐项左右对照排列的方式，在10项义务前分别冠以"A卖方义务，B买方义务"，具体编排方式详见表2.2。Incoterms®2010将"A10""B10"从Incoterms 2000的"其他义务"改为"协助提供信息与相关费用"，明确规定："应对方要求并由其承担风险和费用，买、卖方必须及时向对方提供或协助其取得相关货物出口（进口）和/或将货物运输到最终目的地所需的任何文件和信息，包括安全相关信息。"

⑥除EXW和DDP两个术语外，其他术语都明确规定出口国有关机构强制进行的检验费用由买方承担改为由卖方承担，而买方必须支付除出口国有关机构强制进行的检验费用以外的任何强制性装船前检验费用。当适用EXW术语时，出口国有关机构强制进行的检验费用依然由买方承担。在适用DDP术语时，进、出口国有关机构强制进行的检验费用全部由卖方承担。

表2.1 Incoterms®2010、Incoterms®2020与Incoterms 2000的贸易术语具体情况

| Incoterms 2000 分组 | 缩写 | Incoterms 2000 贸易术语 中英文含义 | Incoterms®2010 分组 | 缩写 | Incoterms®2010 贸易术语 中英文含义 | 缩写 | Incoterms®2020 贸易术语 中英文含义 |
|---|---|---|---|---|---|---|---|
| E组 (Group E) 发货 Departure | EXW | ex works (... named place) 工厂交货 (……指定地点) | 适用于海运和内河水运的术语 Rules for sea and inland waterway mode transport | FAS | free alongside ship 船边交货 FAS(insert named port of shipment) | FAS | free alongside ship 船边交货 FAS(insert named port of shipment) |
| F组 (Group F) 主要运费未付 Main carriage unpaid | FCA | free carrier (... named place) 货交承运人 (……指定地点) | | FOB | free on board 船上交货 FOB(insert named port of shipment) | FOB | free on board 船上交货 FOB(insert named port of shipment) |
| | FAS | free alongside ship (...named port of shipment) 船边交货 (……指定装运港) | | CFR | cost and freight 成本加运费 CFR(insert named port of destination) | CFR | cost and freight 成本加运费 CFR(insert named port of destination) |
| | FOB | free on board(... named port of shipment) 船上交货 (……指定装运港) | | CIF | cost, freight and insurance 成本、保险费加运费 CIF(insert named port of destination) | CIF | cost, freight and insurance 成本、保险费加运费 CIF(insert named port of destination) |
| C组 (Group C) 主要运费已付 Main carriage paid | CFR | cost and freight (...named port of destination) 成本加运费 (……指定目的港) | 适用于任何运输方式或多种运输方式的术语 Rules for any mode or modes of transport | EXW | ex works 工厂交货 EXW (insert named place) | EXW | ex works 工厂交货 EXW (insert named place) |
| | CIF | cost, freight and insurance(... named port of destination) 成本、保险费加运费(……指定目的港) | | FCA | free carrier 货交承运人 FCA (insert named place) | FCA | free carrier 货交承运人 FCA (insert named place) |
| | CPT | carriage paid to (... named place of destination) 运费付至目的地 (……指定目的地) | | CPT | carriage paid to 运费付至 CPT(insert named place of destination) | CPT | carriage paid to 运费付至 CPT(insert named place of destination) |
| | CIP | carriage and insurance paid to (... named place of destination)运费、保险费付至目的地 (……指定目的地) | | CIP | carriage and insurance paid to 运费、保险费付至 CIP (insert named place of destination) | CIP | carriage and insurance paid to 保险费付至 CIP (insert named place of destination) |

续表

| 分组 | Incoterms 2000 贸易术语 | | 分组 | Incoterms 2010 贸易术语 | | Incoterms 2020 贸易术语 | |
|---|---|---|---|---|---|---|---|
| | 缩写 | 中英文含义 | | 缩写 | 中英文含义 | 缩写 | 中英文含义 |
| D组 (Group D) 到达 Arrival | DAF | Delivered at Frontier(... named place) 边境交货（……指定地点） | 适用于任何运输方式或多种运输方式的术语 Rules for any mode or modes of transportl | DAT | delivered at terminal 运输终端交货 DAT (insert named terminal at port or place of destination) | DAP | delivered at place 目的地交货 DAP(insert named place of destination) |
| | DES | delivered ex ship (... named port of destination) 目的港船上交货（……指定目的港） | | DAP | delivered at place 目的地交货 DAP(insert named place of destination) | DPU | delivered at place unloaded 目的地卸货后交货 DPU(insert named place of destination) |
| | DEQ | delivered ex quay (... named port of destination) 目的港码头交货（……指定目的地） | | DDP | delivered duty paid 完税后交货 DDP(insert named place of destination) | DDP | delivered duty paid 完税后交货 DDP(insert named place of destination) |
| | DDU | delivered duty unpaid (... named place of destination) 未完税交货（……指定目的地） | | | | | |
| | DDP | delivered duty paid (... named place of destination) 完税后交货（……指定目的地） | | | | | |

**表2.2 买卖双方义务（Incoterms®2010中的贸易术语）**

| A 卖方义务 The seller's obligations | B 买方义务 The buyer's obligations |
|---|---|
| A1 卖方一般义务 General obligations of the seller | B1 买方一般义务 General obligations of the buyer |
| A2 许可证、授权、安检通关和其他手续 License, authorizations, security clearance and other formalities | B2 许可证、授权、安检通关和其他手续 License, authorizations, security clearance and other formalities |
| A3 运输合同和保险合同 Contract of carriage and insurance | B3 运输合同和保险合同 Contract of carriage and insurance |
| a) 运输合同 Contract of carriage | a) 运输合同 Contract of carriage |
| b) 保险合同 Contract insurance | b) 保险合同 Contract insurance |
| A4 交货 Delivery | B4 收取货物 Taking delivery |
| A5 风险转移 Transfer of risks | B5 风险转移 Transfer of risks |
| A6 费用划分 Allocation of costs | B6 费用划分 Allocation of costs |
| A7 通知买方 Notices to the buyer | B7 通知卖方 Notices to the seller |
| A8 交货凭证 Delivery document | B8 交货证据 Proof of delivery |
| A9 查对—包装—标记 Checking-packing-marking | B9 货物检验 Inspection of goods |
| A10 协助提供信息与相关费用 Assistance with information and related costs | B10 协助提供信息与相关费用 Assistance with information and related costs |

相比Incoterms®2010，Incoterms®2020的实质性变化并不大，内容主要变化主要体现在以下几方面。

① 贸易术语的数量仍然为11种，但将Incoterms®2010中的DAT（delivered at terminal）改为DPU（delivered at place unloaded）。DPU与DAP的唯一不同是使用DPU术语的卖方需要在目的地负责卸货。

② Incoterms®2020最重要的变化聚焦在如何改善呈现方式，以便引导用户针对他们的合同正确地选择Incoterms规则。主要是对引言和解释的扩充、对条款顺序的重新编排，以更好地反映销售交易的逻辑。Incoterms®2020是国际商会Incoterms规则的第一个包含"横向"展示的版本，将所有类似条款集中在一起，使用户清楚地看到11个Incoterms规则在处理特定问题上的差异，使用户使用起来更方便。Incoterms®2020规则的条款顺序编排如下：

A1/B1  一般义务（general obligations）；

A2/B2  交货/提货（delivery/taking delivery）；

A3/B3  风险转移（transfer of risks）；

A4/B4  运输（carriage）；

A5/B5  保险（insurance）；

A6/B6  交货/运输单据（delivery/transport documents）；

A7/B7  出口/进口清关（export/import clearance）；

A8/B8  查对/包装/标记（checking/packaging/marking）；

A9/B9  费用分配（allocation of costs）；

A10/B10  通知（notices）。

③CIP和CIF规则中有关保险的不同要求。Incoterms®2010规定，无论在适用CIF或是CIP术语时，卖方均有义务投保至少最小保障范围的保险险别，如投保伦敦保险协会的ICC（C）险或其他相似条款。但是，根据Incoterms®2020，在CIF和CIP术语下的卖方选择投保险别的最小保障范围规定不一样。当适用CIF术语时，在海运货物贸易中，卖方可默认投保ICC（C）险，但可应买方要求投保更高保障的保险险别。当适用CIP术语时，卖方应默认投保ICC（A）险，但也可应对方同意投保较低水平的保险险别。

④在Incoterms®2010规则中，货物自卖方交付给买方的运输须由第三方运输公司来负责承运。但在Incoterms®2020规则中，明确规定卖方或买方可用自己的运输工具来办理运输，也可与第三方订立运输合同来完成相应的运输义务。例如，当适用CFR、CIF术语时，卖方可派自己的船将货物运输到指定的目的港；当适用FOB时，买方可派自己的船来指定的装运港接货。

⑤当适用FCA术语时，买方可指示承运人签发一份已装船提单给卖方。该规定是一项可选择的安排，需要买卖双方事先就实际业务需要充分沟通，并在合同中予以明确规定。

# 三、常用贸易术语

在实际业务中，以FOB、CIF、CFR、FCA、CIP和CPT这6种贸易术语成交的合同居多。其中，FOB、CFR和CIF适用于海运及内河水运，而FCA、CPT和CIP适用于任何运输方式或多种运输方式。这6种贸易术语均属于象征性交货，运输单据在这类交易中具有特别重要的意义。卖方的"装运期限"就是"交货期限"，运输单据的日期即为"交货日期"，而买方是凭合格单据付款。以这6种术语订立的合同，卖方只负责装运，无须保证货物何时到达或能否到达目的港（地），所以又称为"装运合同"，以区别于"到达合同"。但是，如果卖方交付的货物不符合合同规定，买方可依据买卖合同向卖方索赔。因此，掌握这六种主要贸易术语的含义、买卖双方的义务，以及在使用中应特别注意的问题，非常重要。

## （一）FOB

### 1. FOB术语的内涵、具体适用及买卖双方的基本义务

FOB是free on board的缩写，即"船上交货"。"船上交货"是指卖方以在指定装运港将货物装上买方指派的船舶的方式或通过"取得"已这样交付至船上的货物的方式交货。货物灭失或损坏的风险在货物交到船上时转移，而买方承担自那时起的一切费用。这里的"取得"一词适用于商品交易中常见的交易链中的链式交易（多层销售）。该术语仅用于海运或内河水运。在适用时，应在FOB后面插入"指定装运港"，再加上"Incoterms®2010或Incoterms®2020"，即FOB（inserted named port of shipment）Incoterms®2010（或Incoterms®2020）。该术语要求卖方负责出口清关，但卖方无义务负责

进口清关、支付任何进口税或办理任何进口海关手续。

Incoterms®2010中的FOB术语的买卖双方义务规定如下：A代表卖方义务，B代表买方义务。

**A1 卖方一般义务**

卖方必须提供符合买卖合同约定的货物和商业发票，以及合同可能要求的其他与合同相符的证据。A1—A10中所指的任何单证在双方约定或符合惯例的情况下，可以是同等作用的电子记录或程序。

**B1 买方一般义务**

买方必须按照买卖合同约定支付价款。B1—B10中所指的任何单证在双方约定或符合惯例的情况下，可以是同等作用的电子记录或程序。

**A2 许可证、授权、安检通关和其他手续**

如适用时，卖方必须自担风险和费用，取得所有的出口许可证或其他官方授权，办理货物出口所需的一切海关手续。

**B2 许可证、授权、安检通关和其他手续**

如适用时，买方必须自担风险和费用，取得所有的进口许可证或其他官方授权，办理货物进口和从他国过境运输所需的一切海关手续。

**A3 运输合同和保险合同**

（a）运输合同。卖方对买方无订立运输合同的义务。但若买方要求，或是依商业实践，且买方未适时做出相反指示，卖方可以按照通常条件签订运输合同，由买方负担风险和费用。在以上两种情形下，卖方都可拒绝签订运输合同，如予拒绝，卖方应立即通知买方。

（b）保险合同。卖方对买方无订立保险合同的义务。但应买方要求并由其承担风险和费用（如有的话），卖方必须向买方提供后者取得保险所需的信息。

**B3 运输合同和保险合同**

（a）运输合同。除了卖方按照 A3（a）签订运输合同情形外，买方必须自负费用签订自指定的装运港起运货物的运输合同。

（b）保险合同。买方对卖方无订立保险合同的义务。

**A3 运输合同和保险合同**

（a）运输合同。卖方对买方无订立运输合同的义务。但若买方要求，或是依商业实践，且买方未适时做出相反指示，卖方可以按照通常条件签订运输合同，由买方负担风险和费用。在以上两种情形下，卖方都可拒绝签订运输合同，如予拒绝，卖方应立即通知买方。

（b）保险合同。卖方对买方无订立保险合同的义务。但应买方要求并由其承担风险和费用（如有的话），卖方必须向买方提供后者取得保险所需的信息。

**B3 运输合同和保险合同**

（a）运输合同。除了卖方按照 A3（a）签订运输合同情形外，买方必须自负费用签订自指定的装运港起运货物的运输合同。

（b）保险合同。买方对卖方无订立保险合同的义务。

**A4 交货**

卖方必须在指定的装运港内的装船点（如有的话），以将货物置于买方指定的船舶之上方式，或以取得已在船上交付的货物的方式交货，在其中任何情形下，卖方都必须在约定日期或期限内，按照该港的习惯方式交货。如果买方没有指定特定的装货点，卖方则可在指定装运港选择最合适其目的的装货点。

**B4 收取货物**

当货物按照A4交付时，买方必须收取。

**A5 风险转移**

除按照B5的灭失或损坏情况外，卖方承担按照A4完成交货前货物灭失或损坏的一切风险。

**B5 风险转移**

买方承担按照A4交货时货物灭失或损坏的一切风险。如果：

（a）买方未按照B7通知指定的船舶名称；

（b）买方指定的船舶未准时到达导致卖方未能按A4履行义务，或该船舶不能够装载该货物，或早于B7通知的时间停止装货。

买方则按下列情况承担货物灭失或损坏的一切风险：

(i)自约定之日起，或如没有约定日期的；

(ii)自卖方在约定期限内按照A7通知的日期起，或如买有通知日期的；

(iii)自任何约定交货期限届满之日起。

**A6 费用划分**

卖方必须支付：

（a）按照A4完成交货前与货物相关的一切费用，但按照B6应由买方支付的费用除外；

（b）如适用时，货物出口所需海关手续费用，以及出口应交纳的一切关税、税款和其他费用。

**B6 费用划分**

买方必须支付：

（a）自按照A4交货之时起与货物相关的一切费用，如适用时，按照A6 b)出口所需海关手续的费用，及出口应交纳的一切关税、税款和其他费用除外。

（b）由于以下原因之一发生的任何额外费用：

(i)买方未能按照B7给予卖方相应的通知；

(ii)买方指定的船舶未准时到达，不能装载货物或早于B7通知的时间停止装货。

但以该货物已清楚地确定为合同项下之货物者为限。

（c）如适用时，货物进口应交纳的一切关税、税款和其他费用，以及办理进口海关手续的费用和从他国过境运输费用。

### A7 通知买方

由买方承担风险和费用，卖方必须就其已经按照A4交货或船舶未在约定时间内收取货物给予买方充分的通知。

### B7 通知卖方

买方必须就船舶名称、装船点和其在约定期间内选择的交货时间（如需要时），向卖方发出充分的通知。

### A8 交货凭证

卖方必须自负费用向买方提供已按照A4交货的通常证据。

### B8 交货证据

买方必须接受A8提供的交货凭证。

### A9 查对—包装—标记

卖方必须支付为了按照A4进行交货，所需要进行的查对费用（如查对质量、丈量、过磅、点数的费用），以及出口国有关机构强制进行的装运前检验所发生的费用。

除非在特定贸易中，某类货物的销售通常不用包装，卖方必须自负费用包装货物。除非买方在签订合同前已通知卖方特殊包装要求，卖方可以适用该货物运输的方式对货物进行包装。包装应作适当标记。

### B9 货物检验

买方必须支付任何强制性装船前检验费用，但出口国有关机构强制进行的检验除外。

### A10 协助提供信息与相关费用

如适用时，应买方要求并由其承担风险和费用，卖方必须及时向买方提供或协助其取得相关货物出口和/或将货物运输到最终目的地所需要的任何文件和信息，包括安全相关信息。卖方必须偿付买方按照B10提供或协助取得文件和信息时所发生的所有花销和费用。

### B10 协助提供信息与相关费用

买方必须及时告知卖方任何安全信息要求，以便卖方遵守A10的规定。

买方必须偿付卖方按照A10提供或协助取得文件和信息时发生的所有花销和费用。

如适用时，应卖方要求并由其承担风险和费用，买方必须及时向卖方提供或协助其取得货物运输和出口及从他国过境运输所需要的任何文件和信息，包括安全相关信息收货、付款是买方的基本义务。当卖方按照上述规定履行了交货、交单基本义务后，买方必须收取货物和单证，按照合同约定支付价款，接受卖方提供的交货凭证。对于商业发票或合同可能要求的其他证据，在双方约定或符合惯例的情况下，任何单证都可以采用具有同等作用的电子记录或程序。电子记录或程序是由一条或多条信息组成的整套信息。在适用时与对应的纸质凭证具有同等效力。

### 2.FOB术语运用应注意的问题

**（1）交货、付款义务**

交货、付款是卖方的基本义务。对卖方来说，必须提供符合买卖合同约定的货物和商业发票，以及合同可能要求的其他证据。卖方的交货方式，可以是以下两种方式任选其一：①在指定装运港内的指定装船点（如有的话），将符合合同规定的货物置于买方指定的船舶之上；②取得已这样交付的货物（已装到船上）。无论采用哪种方式，卖方都必须在约定日期或期限内，按照该装运港的习惯方式交货。卖方必须自负费用向买方提供证明其已将货物交至装运港船上的通常证据。在FOB术语下，商业发票是卖方必须交付的单据。

**（2）交货地点的选择**

有关交货地点的选择，Incoterms®2010中使用了不同的表达方法。对只适用于海运和内河水运的术语，包括FAS、FOB、CFR与CIF，使用了"装运港"（port of shipment）和"目的港"（port of destination）的两种描述。对适用于其他运输方式的术语，使用的是"地点"（place）、"目的地"（place of destination）及"目的港或目的地的运输终端"（terminal of port or place of destination）这3种描述。在某些场合，有必要进一步指明这些"港口"（port）、"地点"（place）、"运输终端"（terminal）内的某个具体的"交货点"（point of delivery），因为卖方不仅需要知道他要把货物交至一个特定地区，例如某个城市或某个港口或某个运输终端，而且也要知道在该地区的什么特定地点将货物交给买方处置。FOB术语以"装运港船上"为交货点，卖方必须在指定装运港内的装货点（如有的话），以将货物置于买方指派的船舶之上的方式，或以取得已交付至船上的货物的方式交货。在具体的贸易实践中，经常缺少相应的"装货点"信息。Incoterms®2010规定在适用FOB术语时，如果买方没有指定特定的装货点，卖方可在指定装运港内选择最适合其目的的装货点。

**（3）运输责任及相关费用**

Incoterms®2010有关FOB术语的运输及其相关费用的规定，相比Incoterms 2000更为明确。Incoterms®2010用"卖方对买方无订立运输合同的义务"来代替Incoterms 2000中卖方的"无义务"（no obligation）。同时，Incoterms®2010进一步明确规定：若买方要求，或依商业实践，且买方未适时做出相反指示，卖方可以按照通常条件签订运输合同，并由买方负担风险和费用。但在这两种情形下，卖方都可拒绝签订运输合同，如予拒绝，卖方应立即通知买方。

**（4）保险责任及相关费用**

Incoterms®2010有关FOB术语的运输保险及其相关费用规定，相比Incoterms 2000更为具体。Incoterms 2000有关FOB术语的保险合同的规定，买卖双方均规定为"无义务"。但在实践中，买方一般会为自己要承担的运输风险自行选择办理保险，因此该规定与FOB贸易合同具体实践中一般由买方办理保险的具体做法出入较大。Incoterms®2010有关买方的基本义务为"买方对卖方无订立保险合同的义务"，而有关卖方的基本义务则为"卖方对买方无订立保险合同的义务。但应买方要求并由其承担风险和费用（如有的话），卖方必须向买方提供后者取得保险所需的信息"。因此，Incoterms®2010有关FOB术语的保险责任的关规定，相比Incoterms 2000更为明确与具有可操作性。

（5）许可证、授权、安检通关和其他手续

在适用FOB术语时，卖方必须自担风险和费用，取得所有的出口许可证或其他官方授权，办理货物出口所需的一切海关手续；买方必须自担风险和费用，取得所有的进口许可证或其他官方授权，办理货物进口和从他国过境运输所需的一切海关手续。

（6）双方通知

在适用FOB术语时，一般由买方负责租船订舱，但货物从原产地到装运港的运输由卖方负责，因而存在船货衔接问题。买方应及时租船订舱，并就船舶名称、装船点和其在约定期间内选择的交货时间（如需要时），向卖方发出充分的通知，以便卖方及时备货、安排装船。而卖方必须就其已经按照要求交货或船舶未在约定时间内收取货物给予买方充分通知。

（7）风险转移与费用划分

通常情况下，FOB术语的交货点也是买卖双方风险的划分点（point of risks transfer）和费用分界点（point of costs allocation），即FOB术语只有一个关键点"装运港船上"。买方在货物交至"装运港船上"之时起承担货物灭失或损坏的一切风险，并承担自交货之时起的与货物相关的一切费用，包括货物进口应交纳的一切关税、税款和其他费用，以及办理进口海关手续的费用和从他国过境运输的费用，但不包括出口所需海关手续费用及出口应缴纳的一切关税、税款和其他费用。但因以下原因之一而发生的货物灭失或损坏风险及发生的任何额外费用将由买方承担：①买方未能按照B7给予卖方相应的通知；②买方指定的船舶未准时到达，不能装载货物或早于B7通知的时间停止装货。而买方则按下列情况承担货物灭失或损坏的一切风险：①自约定之日起；②如没有约定日期的，自卖方在约定期限内按照A7通知的日期起；③如有通知日期的，自任何约定交货期限届满之日起。除上述情况下发生的货物灭失或损坏情况外，卖方承担在完成交货前（即交至"装运港船上"之前）货物灭失或损坏的一切风险，但承担的任何额外费用以该货物已清楚地确定为合同项下之货物者为限。因此，签订合同后，买卖双方应加强联系与沟通，防止出现"船、货、期"脱节的情况。

（8）与《1990年美国对外贸易定义修订本》中FOB术语的区别

1990年美国对外贸易定义修订本对FOB术语的解释与运用，与Incoterms®2010的相关规定具有明显的差异，主要表现在：①《1990年美国对外贸易定义修订本》把FOB术语笼统地解释为在某种运输工具上交货，因而适用范围很广。只有"指定装运港船上交货"，即FOB Vessel（... named port of shipment）与Incoterms®2010的FOB相近；②在费用负担上，《1990年美国对外贸易定义修订本》规定FOB Vessel只有在买方提出要求并承担费用时，卖方才有义务协助买方取得出口许可证和其他官方核准文件以及办理出口通关手续，这与Incoterms®2010规定由卖方办理出口清关手续，获得相应出口许可核准证书有较大的不同。因此，在同美国、加拿大等国的商人按FOB术语订立合同时，除必须标明装运港名称外，还必须在FOB后加上"船舶"（Vessel）字样，否则卖方不负责将货物运到装运港交到船上，如FOB Vessel New York；或在合同中直接注明受Incoterms®2010约束，如FOB New York subject to Incoterms®2010（FOB 纽约港交货，有关FOB义务的规定适用Incoterms®2010）。

（9）装船费用及其变通问题

按照Incoterms®2010的惯常规定，FOB术语的买卖双方以"装运港船上"作为交货点、风险划分点和费用分界点，因而惯常情况下在装运港的装船费用应由卖方承担。装船费用包括货物在装运港的吊机费，以及货物装上船后的平舱费、理舱费（如发生的话）等。在采用班轮运输时，班轮运费中包含了装船费用，因而装船费用实际上是由支付运费的一方负担；在采用租船运输时，装船费用由租船人和船东在租船合同中特别约定。因此，FOB术语在具体适用时最好进一步明确装船费用的分摊问题。

因Incoterms®2010属于国际贸易惯例，买卖双方可以变通适用国际贸易术语，而Incoterms®2010也并不禁止此类变通，但是认为这样做是有风险的。为避免歧义，建议缔约方在买卖合同中非常清晰地明确他们希望通过修改达到的效果。在适用FOB术语时，如果买卖双方希望对装船费用分摊的通常规定做出改变，缔约方也应清楚地表明他们是否同时希望改变风险自卖方转移至买方的点。

常见的FOB术语变通有几条。①FOB班轮条件（FOB liner terms）：装船费用由支付运费的一方负担，即由买方承担。②FOB吊钩下交货（FOB under tackle）：卖方负责将货物置于装运港轮船吊钩或码头吊钩可及之处，货物自起吊开始的所有装船费用改由买方负担。③FOB包括理舱（FOB stowed，FOBS）：卖方负责将货物装入船舱，支付包括理舱费在内的装船费用。④FOB包括平舱（FOB trimmed，FOBT）：卖方负责将货物装入船舱，支付包括平舱费在内的装船费用。⑤FOB包括理舱和平舱（FOB stowed & trimmed，FOBST）：卖方负责将货物装入船舱，支付包括平舱费、理舱费在内的装船费用。但应特别注意的是，以上FOB术语变通仅仅改变买卖双方装船费用的划分，但不改变风险的划分点，即风险划分点仍以"装运港船上"为界。

（10）运输方式

FOB术语仅用于海运或内河水运，卖方应将货物在船上交付或者取得已交付在船上的货物。如果货物在上船前已经交给承运人，如采用集装箱运输的货物，通常是在集装箱码头的堆场（CY）、货站（CFS）或出口商指定的门点（DOOR）就置于承运人的处置之下，应当使用FCA术语来替代FOB术语。当适用FCA术语并采用水上运输时，一般不需要涉及装船费用的变通和船舱问题。买卖双方只要按照FCA术语有关装船费用的惯常规定执行即可。在国际贸易实践中，建议扩大FCA术语的使用来替代贸易双方惯常使用的FOB术语。

## （二）CIF

### 1. CIF术语的内涵、具体适用及买卖双方的基本义务

CIF是cost, insurance and freight, 即"成本、保险费加运费"的缩写。在适用时，应在CIF后面插入"指定目的港"和"Incoterms®2010"或"Inwterms®2020"字样，即CIF（insert named port of destination）Incoterms®2010（或Incoterms®2020）。"成本、保险费加运费"是指卖方以将货物交到船上的方式或以取得已这样交付的货物方式交货。此处使用的"取得"一词，适用于商品交易中常见的交易链中的多层销售（链式销售）。

当适用CIF术语时，货物灭失或损坏的风险在货物交到船上时转移。卖方必须签订运输合同，并支付必要的运费，以将货物运往指定的目的港。同时，卖方还要为买方在运输途中货物的灭失或损坏的风险办理保险。但在CIF术语中，卖方仅需投保最低险别。如买方需要更多保险保护的话，则需要与卖方明确达成协议，或者自行做出额外的保险安排。CIF要求卖方办理出口清关，但卖方无义务办理进口清关、支付任何进口税或办理任何进口海关手续。

CIF术语仅适用于海运或内河水上运输。CIF可能不适用于货物在上船前已经交给承运人的情况，例如使用集装箱运输的货物，通常是在装到船上之前就已经装入集装箱内。在此类情况下，应当使用CIP术语。

### 2. CIF术语运用应注意的问题

CIF术语与FOB术语在买卖双方的交货与付款义务，进出口许可证、授权、安检通关和其他手续，风险转移及运输方式等方面的规定相同，但是有关运输、保险和费用转移的规定与FOB术语存在很大差异。

#### （1）交货义务

在使用CIF术语时，尽管卖方需要负责租船订舱和办理运输保险，但卖方只要将货物交至装运港的船上，或取得已这样交付的货物，该船驶往目的港，卖方即完成交货义务。卖方并不需要承担货物抵达目的港的一切风险。自卖方完成交货义务之时起，由买方承担货物灭失或损坏的一切风险。

#### （2）风险转移和费用划分

CIF术语的风险转移地点和费用转移地点不同，因而CIF术语有两个关键点，这与FOB术语只有一个关键点（"装运港船上"）不同。当适用CIF术语时，买卖合同中通常都会指定目的港，但不一定都会指定装运港。"目的港"是买卖双方费用的划分点，卖方要承担将货物运至目的港具体地点的费用，特别建议买卖双方应尽可能确切地在指定目的港内明确该点；"装运港的船上"是卖方将风险转移至买方的地方，因此装运港对买方也具有特殊意义，特别建议买卖双方在合同中尽可能准确地指定装运港。CIF术语下卖方需承担将货物运至目的港的正常运费，但货物在海运或内河水运过程中因意外而产生的额外费用，卖方概不负责。

#### （3）运输责任及费用

按照Incoterms®2010的规定，在适用CIF术语时，卖方必须签订或取得运输合同，

将货物自约定的装运港内某具体地点（如有的话）运至指定的目的港或该目的港内的某具体地点（如有约定的话）。卖方必须按照通常条件订立运输合同，支付通常运费，经由通常航线，由通常运输该类商品的船舶运输。而买方对卖方无订立运输合同的义务。卖方只需按通常条件租船或订舱，买方无权对船籍、船型、船龄、船公司等提出限制。但在实际业务中，如买方提出此类要求，在卖方能够办到，但不增加费用的情况下，一般可以考虑接受。按照Incoterms®2020的规定，卖方也可以用自己的船将货物运送到指定的目的港。

（4）保险责任及费用

按照Incoterms®2010的规定，CIF合同的卖方必须自负费用取得运输保险合同。保险合同应与信誉良好的承保人或保险公司订立，应使买方或其他对货物有可保权益的当事人有权直接向保险人索赔。但是，卖方只需按最低保险险别投保，如投保《协会货物保险条款》（Institute Cargo Clauses）的条款C（Clauses C）或类似条款的最低险别。Incoterms®2020默认卖方可投保最小保障范围的保险险别。但当买方要求，且由买方承担费用，而买方能够提供卖方所需的信息时，卖方应办理任何附加险别，如投保《协会货物保险条款》（Institute Cargo Clauses）的条款A或B（Clauses A or B）或类似条款的险别，或同时或单独办理《协会战争险条款》（Institute War Clauses）和/或《协会罢工险条款》（Institute Strikes Clauses）或其他类似条款的险别。保险最低金额一般按商业发票的CIF金额加收10%（即110%），并采用商业发票的货币。在实际业务中，如买方要求提高保险金额比例（高于10%），或要求指定在目的港（地）的保险勘赔代理，卖方不应贸然同意买方的要求，须在征询承保人或保险公司的意见后加以回复。在适用CIF术语时，买方对卖方无订立保险合同的义务，但买方必须向卖方提供后者按照其要求购买附加险所需的任何信息。

（5）卸货费用及其变通问题

根据Incoterms®2010的规定，CIF术语通常由卖方负责货物在目的港包括驳运费和码头费在内的卸货费用。但CIF合同有时会遇到货物到达目的港后的卸船费用问题。采用班轮运输，因运费中已经包含了装卸费用，卸船费用实际由支付运费的一方即卖方承担。采用租船运输，买卖双方往往采用变通方式对CIF术语的目的港卸船费用加以明确。其常用的变通方式有：① CIF Liner Terms（CIF班轮条件），货物在目的港的卸船费由卖方负担；② CIF Ex Ship's Hold（CIF舱底交货），货物从舱底吊卸到码头的费用由买方负担；③ CIF Landed（CIF卸到岸上），货物从船上卸到目的港岸上的费用，包括驳船费和码头费等由卖方负担。但这些变通方式不改变买卖双方的风险划分点，而只改变目的港卸货费用的划分。根据Incoterms®2010的规定，最好的办法是在合同中详细标明CIF术语后的目的港内的一个特定交付点。

（6）双方通知

在适用CIF术语时，卖方必须向买方发出所需通知，以便买方为收取货物采取通常所必要的措施；当买方有权决定货物运输时间和/或指定目的港内收取货物点时，买方必须向卖方发出充分的通知。

### （三）CFR

**1.CFR术语的内涵、具体适用及买卖双方的基本义务**

CFR是cost and freight即"成本加运费"的缩写。在适用时，应在CFR后面插入"指定目的港"和"Incoterms®2010"或"Incoterms®2020"字样，即CFR（insert named port of destination）Incoterms®2010（或Incoterms®2020），"成本加运费"是指卖方已将货物交到船上的方式或以取得已这样交付的货物的方式交货。此处使用的"取得"一词，适用于商品交易中常见的交易链中的多层销售（链式销售）。CFR术语要求卖方办理出口清关，但卖方无义务办理进口清关、支付任何进口税或办理任何进口海关手续。

CFR术语仅适用于海运或内河水上运输。CFR可能不适用于货物在上船前已经交给承运人的情况，例如使用集装箱运输货物，通常是在装到船上之前货物就已经装入集装箱内。在此类情况下，应当使用CPT术语。

**2.CFR术语运用应注意的问题**

CFR术语与CIF术语在许多方面的规定相同，比如买卖双方的交货与付款义务，进出口许可证、授权、安检通关和其他手续，运输责任及相关费用，风险转移，运输方式，费用转移和卸货费用，等等。有关保险责任的规定与CIF术语存在很大差异，但与FOB术语的规定相同。在适用CFR术语时，卖方给予买方充分的装运通知非常重要，以便买方在合理的时间内取得保险所需的信息，办理相应的运输保险（如买方认为有必要投保），以免造成不必要的可能损失。CFR术语项下卖方给予买方充分的通知，相比CIF、FOB术语项下更为重要。所谓"充分通知"，必须做到及时、详尽。如果卖方未能给予买方充分通知而给买方造成损失，卖方可能承担相应的责任。

### （四）FCA

FCA是free carrier，即"货交承运人"的缩写。在适用时，应在FCA后面插入"指定交货地点"(named place)和"Incoterms®2010"或"Incoterms®2020"字样，即FCA（insert named place）Incoterms®2010（或Incoterms®2020）。"货交承运人"是指卖方在卖方所在地或其他指定地点将货物交给买方指派的承运人或其他人时完成交货。由于风险在交货地点转移至买方，因而特别建议双方尽可能清楚地写明指定地点内的交付点。如果双方希望在卖方所在地交货，则应将卖方所在地的地址明确为指定的交货地点；如果买卖双方希望在其他地点交货，则必须确定不同的特定交货地点。FCA要求卖方办理出口清关手续，但卖方无义务办理进口清关、支付任何进口税或办理任何进口海关手续。

在Incoterms 2000中，"承运人"是指在运输合同中承诺通过铁路、公路、空运、海运、内河运输或上述运输的联合方式履行运输义务或由他人履行运输义务的任何人。如果需使用接运的承运人将货物运至约定目的地，则风险自货物交给第一承运人时转移。在Incoterms®2010中，承运人指签约承担运输责任的一方。

FCA是在FOB的基础上发展起来的。FCA术语与FOB术语在买卖双方的交货与付款义务，进出口许可证、授权、安检通关和其他手续，运输责任及相关费用，保险责任及相关费用和双方通知等方面的规定相同；在运输方式、交货地点、风险转移、费用转移和装货费用等方面的规定有很大不同。使用FCA时，应特别注意以下几点。

（1）运输方式

FCA术语可适用于任何运输方式，也可适用于多种运输方式，尤其是集装箱运输。FOB术语只适用于海运或内河水运。

（2）双方通知

买方必须通知卖方以下内容：①指派的承运人或其他人的姓名，以便卖方有足够时间按照要求交货；②在约定的交付期限内由指派承运人或其他人选取收取货物的时间；③采用的运输方式；④指定地点内的交货点。

卖方须自担风险和费用，就其已经在约定的日期或期限内，在指定地点或指定地点内的约定点（如有的话），将货物交给买方指派的承运人或其他人。如买方指派的承运人或其他人未在约定的时间收取货物，卖方应给予买方充分的通知。

（3）交货地点

在适用FCA术语时，买方必须自负费用，签订自指定的交货地点起运货物的运输合同。卖方按照买方的通知内容，在约定的时间、约定的地点将货物交给买方指派的承运人或其他人。FCA术语的交货地点有两种选择：一是卖方所在地；二是非卖方所在地。若指定地点是卖方所在地，则当货物装上买方指派的运输工具时完成交货。在其他任何情况下，则当货物仍处于卖方的运输工具上，但已准备好卸载，并已交由承运人或买方指派的其他人处置时完成交货。而FOB术语项下的卖方必须将货物置于"装运港的船上"或取得已这样交付至船上的货物完成交货。

（4）风险转移

在适用FCA术语时，风险自卖方在指定地点将货物置于买方指派的承运人或其他人处置之时完成转移。与FOB术语的以"装运港船上"作为风险划分点不同，FCA术语项下的卖方承担的风险较低。如FCA术语后面插入的指定地点为装运港，FCA术语项下的卖方不需要承担货物装到船上的风险，但FOB术语的卖方通常需要承担货物装到船上之前的所有风险。

（5）费用划分

FCA术语以货交承运人作为费用的划分界线。自卖方将货物置于承运人处置时起，由买方承担所有费用。卖方应负责出口应缴纳的关税、税款和其他海关费用。若卖方在其所在地交货，卖方应负责将货物装到买方指派的运输工具上，并承担装货费用；若卖方需要在其他地点完成交货，则在卖方指派的到达运输工具上，并已准备好卸载，货物已交由承运人或买方指派的其他人处置时完成交货，即卖方不负责卸货，也不承担卸货费用。

买方需承担自指定的交货地点起运货物的运输费用，以及进口应缴纳的关税、税款、其他海关手续费用以及从他国过境运输的费用。同时，买方还须承担由于以下原因之一发生的任何额外费用：①买方未能指派承运人或其他人；②买方指派的承运人或其他人未接管货物；③买方未能按照要求给予卖方相应的充分通知。

## （五）CIP

CIP是carriage and insurance paid to，即"运费、保险费付至"的缩写。在适用时，应在CIP后面插入"指定的目的地"和"Incoterms®2010"或"Incoterms®2020"字样，即CIP（insert place of destination）Incoterms®2010（或Incoterms®2020）。"运费、保险费付至"是指卖方在双方约定的地点（如双方约定了地点的话），将货物交给卖方自己指定的承运人或其他人时完成交货。卖方必须签订运输合同并支付将货物运至指定目的地的所需费用；卖方还必须为买方在运输途中货物的灭失或损坏风险签订保险合同并支付相应的保险费用。在使用CIP术语时，卖方在将货物交付给承运人时，而不是当货物到达目的地时，即可完成交货。

CIP术语有关买卖双方交接货的义务、风险转移、进出口报关手续、运输方式等的规定与FCA完全相同。如果货物运输涉及两个或两个以上的承运人，则风险自货物交给第一承运人时转移，但运输、保险的责任规定与FCA很不相同。在适用CIP术语时，由卖方负责运输和保险。但是，买方应注意到，CIP只要求卖方投保最低险别，如买方要求更多保险保护的话，则需与卖方单独商议，或者由买方自行做出额外的保险安排。卖方也只需要按照通常条件订立运输合同，支付通常运费，经由通常路线和习惯方式，将货物运往指定的目的地。如果双方没有约定特别的地点或该地点不能由惯例确定，卖方可选择最适合其目的的交货地点和指定目的地内的具体地点。

CIP术语与CIF术语一样有两个关键点，但两个术语在运输方式、关键点位置上有很大不同。CIP术语的目的是替代CIF术语。CIP术语可适用于任何运输方式，也可适用于多种运输方式。CIP术语的风险转移点和费用转移点不同。特别建议买卖双方尽可能确切地在合同中明确规定交货地点（风险在这里转移至买方），以及指定目的地（卖方必须签订运输合同将货物运到该目的地）。如果运输到约定目的地需要涉及多个承运人，且双方不能就特定的交货地点达成一致时，卖方可以在某个完全由其选择、且买方不能控制的地点将货物交付给第一承运人以完成交货，并将风险转移至买方。因此，如果买方希望将风险晚些转移的话(例如在某海港或机场转移)，需要在买卖合同中特别订明，或改用DAT、DAP术语成交。

## （六）CPT

CPT是carriage paid to，即"运费付至"的缩写。在适用时，应在CPT后面插入"指定目的地"和"Incoterms®2010"或"Incoterms®2020"字样，即CPT（insert place of destination）Incoterms®2010（或Incoterms®2020）。"运输付至"是指卖方在双方约定的地点（如果双方已经约定了地点的话），将货物交给卖方指定的承运人或其他人时完成交货。卖方必须签订运输合同并支付将货物运至指定目的地的所需费用。CPT术语要求卖方办理出口清关手续。该术语适用于各种运输方式，包括多式联运。CPT术语除买卖双方的保险责任规定外，其他规定与CIP术语基本一致；CPT术语的有关买卖双方的保险责任规定与FCA术语相同。但是，在采用CPT贸易术语时，卖方应注意及时向对方发出装运通知，以免造成不必要的损失。

综上所述，在6种象征性交货的贸易术语中，FOB、CFR和CIF属于装运港交货，只适合海洋运输或内河运输；FCA、CPT和CIP适用于各种运输方式，也可适用于多种运输方式，包括集装箱运输。因此，熟悉这6种贸易术语的含义及其买卖双方所对应的权利与义务，以及其在使用中应注意的问题具有十分重要的意义。

# 四、其他贸易术语

除FOB、CIF、CFR、FCA、CIP和CPT这6种象征性交货的贸易术语外，Incoterms®2010或Incoterms®2020还有5种属于实际交货的贸易术语。Incoterms®2010项下分别为EXW、FAS、DAT、DAP和DDP，而在Incoterms®2020项下则将DAT改成了DPU，其余术语不变。这些贸易术语在实践中使用相对较少。

## （一）EXW

EXW是ex works，即"工厂交货"的缩写。在适用时，应在其后插入指定交货地点和"Incoterms®2010"或"Incoterms®2020"字样，即EXW (insert place) Incoterms®2010（或Incoterms®2020）。"工厂交货"是指当卖方在其所在地或其他指定地点（如工厂、车间或仓库等）将货物交由买方处置时，即完成交货。特别建议双方在指定交货地点内尽可能明确指明具体的交货点，因为买方需承担自此指定的交货点（如有的话）收取货物所产生的全部费用和风险。

EXW术语可适用于任何运输方式，也可适用于多种运输方式。该术语与FCA术语相比，在以下方面存在明显区别。

①EXW术语适合于国内贸易，而FCA术语一般更适合于国际贸易。

②EXW术语的交货地点是在卖方所在地或其他指定地点（如工厂、车间或仓库等），而FCA术语的交货地点可以是卖方所在地也可以是非卖方所在地，如集装箱码头、车站、港口、机场等。

③如选择在卖方的所在地交货，EXW术语项下的卖方不需要将货物装上任何前来接收货物的运输工具，而FCA术语项下的卖方则需要负责将货物装上买方派来的运输工具。

④当需要办理出口清关时，EXW术语的卖方无须办理出口清关手续，而FCA术语的卖方需要负责办理出口清关手续。

⑤出口国有关机构强制进行的检验费用（如发生的话），EXW术语项下由买方承担，

而FCA术语项下则由卖方承担。

EXW术语是Incoterms®2010和Incoterms®2020中代表卖方最低义务的贸易术语，在使用时需注意以下方面。

①卖方对买方没有装货义务，即使实际上卖方也许更方便这样操作。如果卖方装货，也是由买方承担相关风险和费用。因此，当卖方更方便装货或买方希望卖方负责装货并承担相应的装货费用时，建议选择FCA术语成交。

②以EXW术语为基础购买出口产品的买方需要特别注意，卖方只有在买方要求时，才有义务协助办理出口，即卖方无义务负责出口清关。因此，在买方不能直接或间接地办理出口清关手续时，也不建议使用EXW术语，建议采用FCA术语。

③买方仅有限度地承担向卖方提供货物出口相关信息的责任。但是，卖方则可能出于缴税或申报等目的，需要这方面的信息。

④卖方必须给予买方其收取货物所需的任何通知。而当买方有权决定在约定期限内的时间和/或在指定地点内的接收点时，买方必须向卖方发出充分的通知。

## （二）FAS

FAS是free alongside ship，即"船边交货"的缩写。在适用时，应在其后插入"指定装运港"和"Incoterms®2010"或"Incoterms®2020"字样，即FAS（insert named part of shipment）Incoterms®2010（或Incoterms®2020）。"船边交货"是指当卖方在指定的装运港将货物交到买方指定的船边（如置于码头或驳船上时）时完成交货。货物灭失或损坏的风险在货物交到船边时发生转移，而买方承担自那时起的一切费用。在适用FAS术语时，应注意以下几点。

①该术语仅适合于海运或内河水运。

②在适用时，FAS要求卖方办理出口清关手续，但卖方无义务办理进口清关、支付任何进口税或办理任何进口海关手续。

③由于卖方需承担在装运港特定地点交货前的风险和费用，而且这些费用和相关作业费可能因各港口管理不同有所差异，特别建议双方尽可能清楚地约定指定装运港内的装货点。

④卖方必须在约定日期或期限内，按照该装运港的习惯方式交货。如果买方没有指定特定的装船点，卖方可在指定的装运港内选择最适合其目的的装货点。如果双方同意在一定期限内交货，买方有权在该期限内选择日期。

⑤卖方应将货物运至船边或取得已这样交付的货物时完成交货。这里的"取得"一词适用于商品交易中常见的交易链中的多层销售（链式销售）。

⑥当货物采用集装箱运输时，卖方通常将货物在集装箱码头交给承运人，而非交到船边。因此，当采用集装箱运输时，选用FAS术语成交不合适，应改用FCA术语。

## （三）DAT或DPU

DAT是delivered at terminal，即"运输终端交货"的缩写。在适用时，应在其后插入"指定港口或目的地的运输终端"和"Incoterms®2010"字样，即DAT（insert named terminal at port or place of destination）Incoterms®2010。"运输终端交货"是指当卖方在指定港口或目的地的指定运输终端将货物从抵达的运输工具上卸下，交由买方处置时完成交货。"运输终端"可为任何地点，不论其是否有遮盖，如码头、仓库、集装箱堆场或公路、铁路、空运货站。

DPU是delivered at place unloaded的缩写。在适用时，应在其后插入指定目的地和"Incoterms®2020"字样，即DPU (insert named place of destination) Incoterms®2020。当卖方在指定目的地将货物从抵达的运输工具上卸下，交由买方处置时完成交货。该术语是唯一需要卖方负责卸货的术语。Incoterms®2020用DPU替代了Incoterms®2010项下的DAT。

在适用DAT、DPU术语时，应注意以下几点。

①该术语可适用于任何运输方式，也可适用于多种运输方式。

②在适用时，DAT、DPU要求卖方办理出口清关手续，但卖方无义务办理进口清关、支付任何进口税或办理任何进口海关手续。

③卖方应承担将货物送至指定港口或目的地的运输终端（DAT）/指定目的地（DPU），并将其卸下的一切风险。

④由于卖方承担在特定地点交货前的风险，特别建议双方尽可能确切地约定运输终端/指定目的地。如果可能的话，最好特别约定在指定港口或目的地运输终端/指定目的地内的特定的点。

⑤卖方必须自负费用签订运输合同，将货物运至约定港口或目的地的指定运输终端/指定目的地。在适用DAT时，如未约定特定的运输终端或该运输终端不能由惯例确定，卖方可在约定港口或目的地选择最适合其目的的运输终端。建议卖方取得完全符合自卖方所在地将货物运至指定港口或目的地的指定运输终端内的特定点的运输合同。在适用DPU时，卖方可用自己的运输工具将货物运抵指定的目的地交由买方处置。

⑥如果双方希望由卖方承担自运输终端到另一地点运送货物的风险和费用，则应当使用DAP或DDP术语；如卖方不愿意在指定的目的地将货物从到达的运输工具上卸下来后交由买方处置的话，则应选择DAP或DDP术语。

## （四）DAP

DAP是delivered at place（目的地交货）的缩写。在适用时，应在DAP后面加"插入指定目的地"insert place of destination和"Incoterms®2010"字样或"Incoterms®2020"，即DAP（insert place of destination）Incoterms®2010（或Incoterms®2020）。"目的地交货"是指当卖方在指定目的地将仍处于抵达的运输工具之上，且已做好卸载准备的货物交由买方处置时完成交货。卖方承担将货物运送到指定地点的一切风险。DAP术语可适用于任何运输方式，也可适用于多种运输方式。在适用DAP时，由于卖方承担在特定地点交货前的风险，特别建议双方尽可能清楚地约定指定目的地内的交货点。建议卖方取得完全符合该选择的运输合同。如果卖方按照运输合同在目的地发生了卸货费用，除非双方另有约定，卖方无权向买方要求偿付。在适用DAP时，该术语要求卖方办理出口清关手续，但卖方无义务办理进口清关、支付任何进口税或办理任何进口海关手续。如果双方希望卖方办理进口清关、支付所有进口关税，并办理所有进口海关手续，则应当使用DDP术语。

## （五）DDP

DDP是delivered duty paid即"完税后交货"的缩写。在适用时，应在DDP后面插入"指定目的地"和"Incoterms®2010"或"Incoterms®2020"字样，即DDP（insert place of destination）Incoterms®2010（或Incoterms®2020）。"完税后交货"是指当卖方在指定目的地将仍处于抵达的运输工具上，但已完成进口清关，且已做好卸载准备的货物交由买方处置时，即为交货。在适用DDP术语时，应注意以下几点。

①该术语可适用于任何运输方式，也可适用于多种运输方式。

②该术语是Incoterms®2010、Incoterms®2020中代表卖方最大责任的贸易术语。

③卖方承担将货物运至目的地的一切风险和费用。由于卖方承担在特定地点交货前的风险和费用，特别建议双方尽可能清楚地约定在指定目的地内的交货点。建议卖方取得完全符合该选择的运输合同。如果按照运输合同，卖方在目的地发生了卸货费用，除非双方另有约定，卖方无权向买方索偿。

④卖方有义务完成货物出口和进口清关，支付所有出口和进口的关税和办理所有海关手续。如卖方不能直接或间接地完成进口清关，则特别建议双方不使用DDP术语。如双方希望买方承担所有进口清关的风险和费用，则应使用DAP术语。

⑤除非买卖合同中另行明确规定，任何增值税或其他应付的进口税款由卖方承担。

# 五、贸易术语的选用及应注意的事项

选用Incoterms®2010或Incoterms®2020的不同贸易术语，买卖双方在交接货物过程中所承担的风险、费用及手续是不同的。FOB、FCA、CFR、CPT、CIF、CIP这6种贸易术语的风险、费用及手续划分较为合理均衡，在实践中被广泛使用，而EXW、FAS、DAT（或DPU）、DAP、DDP这5种贸易术语的风险、费用及手续划分相对不均衡，在实践中较少使用。但要注意的是，在国际货物买卖中，尽管国际贸易惯例在解决贸易纠纷时起到了一定的作用，但应注意以下几个问题。

①Incoterms®2010、Incoterms®2020适用于调整货物买卖合同的双方义务规定和交货有关的事项。应在买卖合同中明确表示适用Incoterms®2010或Incoterms®2020。具体内容应至少包括"所选用的国际贸易术语、指定地点和Incoterms®2010或Incoterms®2020"。鉴于国际贸易术语的不断修改，双方在签订合同时，对所引用的解释贸易术语的国际惯例应注明版别以免引起误解和纠纷。

②由于国际贸易惯例并非"法律"，对买卖双方没有强制约束力，可采用也可不采用。

如果合同中既未对某一问题做出明确规定，也未订明适用某惯例，当发生争议付诸诉讼或提交仲裁时，法庭和仲裁机构可引用惯例作为判决或裁决的依据。如果买卖双方在合同中明确表示采用Incoterms®2020，则该采用的惯例对买卖双方均有约束力。如果合同中明确采用Incoterms®2020，但又在合同中规定与Incoterms®2020相抵触的条款，只要这些条款与本国法律不矛盾，将受到有关国家法律的承认和保护，即以合同条款为准。

③选择合适的国际贸易术语。应根据货物性质和运输方式来选择合适的国际贸易术语。要考虑合同各方是否想给对方增加额外的义务，如安排运输、办理保险、负责装卸、办理清关等。无论选择何种术语，对其合同的解释很可能会受到所使用的港口或地点特有的惯例影响，应尽可能地对地点和港口做出详细说明。只有买卖双方写明港口或地点，所选用的贸易术语才能发挥作用。港口或地点应写得尽量确切，以更能凸显国际贸易术语的作用。

④切记，国际贸易术语并不意味着一个完整的买卖合同。国际贸易术语明确规定了买卖合同中应由哪方安排运输、保险的义务，卖方何时向买方交货及各方应支付的费用。但是，国际贸易术语没有说明应付价格或支付方式，也没有涉及货物所有权的转让或违约后果，这些问题通常依据买卖合同的明确约定或合同的适用法处理。合同双方应当清楚强制适用的本地法可能推翻买卖合同的任何条款，包括所选择的国际贸易术语在内。

⑤Incoterms®2010的11种贸易术语中的A1/B1、A4/B4、A8/B8（即卖方/买方的一般义务、交货/收取货物以及交货凭证/交货证据）形成了严密的逻辑关系。简单地说，对卖方来说，A1规定卖方必须交货和交单，A4是有关交货的规定，而A8是有关交货凭证的规定。交货凭证是运输凭证或对应的电子记录。在使用EXW、FCA、FAS和FOB时，交货凭证可能仅仅是一张收据。交货凭证也会有其他作用，比如支付安排的构成部分，因而非常重要。

⑥Incoterms®2010的A9/B9对卖方的"查对—包装—标记"与买方的"货物检验"做出了规定。其中，每个术语的A9相关义务在前文较少涉及。其规定：卖方必须支付为了按照A4进行交货所需要进行的查对费用（如查对质量、丈量、过磅、点数的费用），以及出口国有关机构强制进行的装运前检验所发生的费用（但EXW术语除外）。除非在特定贸易中，某类货物的销售不需要包装，卖方必须自负费用包装货物。除非买方在签订合同时已通知卖方特殊包装要求，卖方可以采用适合该货物运输的方式对货物进行包装，包装应做适当标记。

包装可适用于不同目的：①为满足买卖合同的要求对货物进行包装；②为适应运输需要对货物进行包装；③在集装箱或其他运输工具中装载包装好的货物。但Incoterms®2010中的术语不涉及各方在集装箱内的装载义务，即包装是指第一种和第二种情况。因此，如需要的话，各方应在买卖合同中特别做出约定。

Incoterms®2010的11种贸易术语的具体相关规定，如表2.3所示。

**思考题**

1. 货物从中国杭州起运，先用集装箱经陆路运输到上海港，再由上海港海运到比利时的安特卫普港，然后经陆路运输到比利时的布鲁塞尔。如果卖方希望在中国完成交货，可选择哪些贸易术语？该如何规定交易条件？

2. 贸易术语CIF Antwerp, Belgium 和贸易术语DAT Antwerp, Belgium有何区别？

3. 贸易术语FOB Shanghai port, China，FCA Shanghai port, China 和 FAS Shanghai port, China有何区别？

4. 跨境电商中的"包邮"和"不包邮"类似于Incoterms®2010或Incoterms®2020中的哪些贸易术语？

表2.3　Incoterms® 2010项下贸易术语中买卖双方的任务、风险与费用分配规定

| 组别 | 术语 | 英文全称 | 中文全称 | 交货方式 | 交货地点 | 风险转移 | 费用划分 | 运输责任及费用 | 保险责任及费用 | 出口清关费用 | 进口清关费用 |
|---|---|---|---|---|---|---|---|---|---|---|---|
| 适合海运或内河水运的术语 | FOB | free on board (insert named port of shipment) | 船上交货(插入指定装运港) | 卖方以在指定装运港将货物装上买方指定的船舶或取得已交付至船上货物的方式交货 | 装运港船上 | 装运港船上 | 指定装运港船上 | 买方 | — | 卖方 | 买方 |
| | CFR | cost and freight (insert named port of destination) | 成本加运费(插入指定目的港) | 卖方在船上交货或取得已经这样交付的货物方式交货 | 装运港船上 | 装运港船上 | 指定目的港 | 买方 | — | 卖方 | 买方 |
| | CIF | cost, insurance and freight (insert named port of destination) | 成本、保险费加运费(插入指定目的港) | 卖方在船上交货或取得已经这样交付的货物方式交货 | 装运港船上 | 装运港船上 | 指定目的港 | 买方 | 卖方 | 卖方 | 买方 |
| | FAS | free alongside ship(insert named port of shipment) | 船边交货(插入指定装运港) | 卖方在指定的装运港将货物交到买方指定的船边(例如,置于码头或驳船上)时,即交货 | 装运港船边 | 装运港船边 | 以装运港船边为界 | 买方 | — | 卖方 | 买方 |
| 适合任何运输方式或多种运输方式的术语 | EXW | ex works(insert named place) | 工厂交货(插入指定交货地点) | 卖方在其所在地或其他指定地点(如工厂、车间或仓库等)将货物交由买方处置时,即完成交货 | 指定交货地点 | 货物交由买方处置 | 货物交由买方处置 | 买方 | — | 买方 | 买方 |
| | FCA | free carrier (insert named place) | 货交承运人(插入指定交货地点) | 卖方在其所在地或其他指定地点将货物交给买方指定的承运人或其他人时,即完成交货 | 卖方所在地或其他指定地点 | 货交承运人 | 货交第一承运人 | 买方 | — | 卖方 | 买方 |
| | CPT | carriage paid to (insert named place of destination) | 运费付至指定目的地 | 卖方将货物在双方约定了地点(如果双方已经约定了地点)交给买方指定的承运人或其他人,即完成交货 | 货交承运人 | 货交承运人 | 指定目的地 | 买方 | — | 卖方 | 买方 |
| | CIP | carriage and insurance paid to (insert named place of Destination) | 运费、保险费付至(插入指定目的地) | 卖方将货物在双方约定了地点(如果双方已经约定了地点)交给买方指定的承运人或其他人,即完成交货 | 货交承运人 | 货交承运人 | 指定目的地 | 买方 | 卖方 | 卖方 | 买方 |
| | DAT | delivered at terminal (insert named terminal at port or place of destination) | 运输终端交货(插入指定港或目的地的运输终端) | 卖方在指定港口或目的地的指定运输终端将货物从抵达的载货运输工具上卸下,交由买方处置时,即完成交货 | 指定港口或目的地的指定运输终端 | 交由买方处置 | 交由买方处置 | 买方 | 买方 | 卖方 | 买方 |
| | DAP | delivered at place (insert named place of destination) | 目的地交货(插入指定目的地) | 卖方在指定目的地将仍处于抵达的运输工具上,且已做好卸载准备的货物交由买方处置时,即完成交货 | 指定目的地的抵达运输工具上 | 交由买方处置 | 交由买方处置 | 买方 | 买方 | 卖方 | 买方 |
| | DDP | delivered duty paid(insert named place of destination) | 完税后交货(插入指定目的地) | 卖方在指定目的地将仍处于抵达的运输工具上,且已做好卸货准备的货物交由买方处置时,已完成进口清关,即为交货 | 指定目的地的抵达运输工具上 | 交由买方处置 | 交由买方处置 | 买方 | 买方 | 卖方 | 买方 |

# Chapter 2

# Trade Terms

☞ Case 2.1

Co. A in China imported equipments from Germany. The trade term of contract was FOB Hamburg subject to Incoterms®2020. When the vessel was arriving at Shanghai port, it was unfortunately sunk and the shipping goods all dropped into the sea. The question was: which of the following party would be responsible for the loss or damage to the goods?

A. The importer                    B. The exporter

C. The insurance company     D. The shipping company

Incoterms means International Rules for the Interpretation of Trade Terms, ICC Official Rules for the Interpretation of Trade Terms. Incoterms®2020 is the latest version that is took effect from Jan. 1, 2020. It is the most widely used international trade practice rules in the world regarding to trade terms. FOB rule is one of trade terms under Incoterms®2020 and must be inserted a nominated port of shipment. In this case, Hamburg is the nominated port of shipment and Shanghai is the port of destination.

FOB is the abbreviation of "free on board". It means that the seller delivers the goods on board the vessel nominated by the Buyer at the named port of shipment or procures the goods already so delivered. The risk of loss of or damage to the goods passes when the goods are on board the vessel, and the buyer bears all the costs from the moment onwards. It is a critical point that the goods is "shipped on board" the vessel nominated by the Buyer at the named port of shipment. The buyer shall bear all the risks of loss of or damage to the goods and all the costs from then on and from that point of place. In this case, as per the stipulation of FOB under Incoterms®2020, the seller had transferred the risk of loss of or damage to the goods to the buyer at the named port of shipment (Hamburg). The buyer shall bear the losses of the goods at the port of destination. If delivery of the seller is completed in this case, the buyer shall make payment to the seller even if the goods are totally lost. So, the best answer of this case is "the buyer".

Maybe you wonder why the insurance company or the shipping company is not the correct answer, as the shipped goods dropped into the sea was caused by the vessel sunk. Either the buyer nor the Seller has no obligation to cover insurance under FOB term as per Incoterms®2020. While, normally, the buyer may cover transport insurance for his own risks at his option. It means that the buyer "may" cover insurance instead of "must". If the buyer covers insurance at his option, he may lodge claim to the insurance company independent of his payment to the seller. If the insurance company made satisfaction to the buyer, the insurance company obtained the right of subrogation to the shipping company. Generally, the shipping company is also worrying about the risk during transportation, and it should cover insurance and finally, the insurance company should bear the losses.

In this chapter, the contents are introduced by the concerning International Trade Practice Rules regarding to trade terms, the function of trade terms and the detailed stipulation of each trade term. The students will learn how to use and select suitable trade term in business transaction, as well as how to grasp the skills to modify the usual terms of trade term in international trade practices.

# 2.1 International Trade Practice Rules

There are three main international trade practice rules regarding to trade terms, including Warsaw-Oxford Rules 1932, Revised American Foreign Trade Definition Interpretation of Trade Terms 1990 and International Rules for the Interpretation of Trade Terms—ICC Official Rules for the Interpretation of Trade (Incoterms) respectively.

## 2.1.1 Warsaw-Oxford Rules 1932

Warsaw-Oxford Rules 1932 has only one trade term, that is CIF. A contract concluded by CIF term can be called as "a CIF contract" generally. Warsaw-Oxford Rules 1932 indicates nature and characteristics of a CIF contract and stipulates responsibilities of Seller and Buyer under a CIF contract in details. Its main adopted countries adopting Warsaw-Oxford Rules 1932 are mainly located in Europe. The responsibilities for seller and buyer of a CIF contract is similar as those of a CIF contract under Incoterms rules.

## 2.1.2 Revised American Foreign Trade Definition 1990

Revised American Foreign Trade Definition 1990 has stipulated six kinds of trade terms, including  EXW, FOB, FAS, CFR, CIF, and DEQ. The stipulation of FOB, FAS, CFR, and CIF term under Revised American Foreign Trade Definition 1990 are quite differently from those in Incoterms® 2020. For example, FOB term under Revised American Foreign Trade Definition Interpretation of Trade Terms 1990 can be divided into the following six kinds, and only FOB Vessel (named port of shipment) is similar as FOB term under Incoterms® 2010.

①FOB(named inland carrier at named inland point of departure).

②FOB (named inland carrier at the named inland point of departure) Freight prepaid to (named point of exportation).

③FOB (named inland carrier at the named inland point of departure) freight allowed to (the named point).

④FOB (the named inland carrier at the named point of exportation).

⑤ FOB Vessel (the named port of shipment).

⑥ FOB ( the named inland point in country of importation).

The countries adopting or representing Revised American Foreign Trade  include the USA, Canada and some South American countries. It should be noticed that different trade countries may apply to different international trade practice rules. The USA deleted UCC (Uniform Commercial Code) section 2-319~324 (shipping and delivery terms) in 2004. It means that incoterms may be widely adopted in the USA.

### 2.1.3 Incoterms® 2010 & Incoterms®2020

Incoterms is the abbreviation of International Rules for the Interpretation of Trade Terms-ICC Official Rules for the Interpretation of Trade Terms. Incoterms rules explain a set of three-letter trade terms reflecting business to business practices in Contracts for the sales of goods. The Incoterms rules describe mainly the tasks, costs and risks involved in the delivery of goods from the seller to the buyer. It is the most commonly used in International trade and adopted by most countries. Till now, it has nine amendments and additions including the versions of 1936, 1953, 1967, 1976, 1980, 1990, 2000, 2010, and 2020. Incoterms ®2020 is the latest version and came into effect on Jan. 01, 2020. Incoterms ®2020 has eleven kinds of trade terms including FAS, FOB, CFR, CIF, EXW, FCA, CPT, CIP, DAT, DAP, and DDP. DAT under Incoterms®2020 is replaced by DPU under Incoterms ®2020. The other 10 terms have not been modified materially.

## 2.2 Function of Trade Terms

International trade is happened between two countries (regions) separated by the sea, inland waterways or land normally. For example, China and the USA are separated by the Pacific Ocean. Cambodia and Vietnam are separated by Mekong River. China and Nepal are connected by land. The distance for the goods transported from the seller to the buyer can be divided into three carriages (see Figure 2.1).

①From points A to B is called as "pre carriage" that covers the place of origin to the place of departure in the exporting country (region).

②From points B to C is called as "main carriage" that covers the place of departure in the exporting country (region) to the place of arrival in the importing country (region).

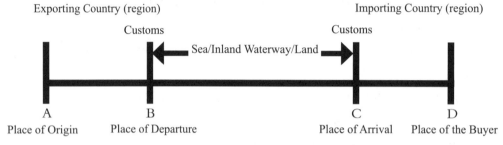

Figure 2.1 Transporting Stages of International Trade

③From points C to D is called as "post carriage" that covers the place of arrival to the place of the buyer in the importing country (region).

For delivery of the goods from the seller to the buyer, the following responsibilities and charges will be allocated between both parties:

①The goods to be loaded on the transport tool in the place of origin and its loading charges.

②The pre carriage from place of origin to place of departure and its charges.

③The storage in the place of departure and its charges.

④The goods to be placed in the dock waiting for on board the vessel and its charges.

⑤Shipment inspection (including or excluding mandated inspection) and its charges.

⑥Export customs formalities, export tariff (if any) and export licenses (if any) and its charges.

⑦Main carriage from place of departure to place of arrival and its charges.

⑧Transport insurance and its premium.

⑨Import customs formalities, import tariff (if any) and import licenses (if any) and its charges.

⑩The goods to be unloaded from the arrival transport tool and its unloading charges.

⑪post carriage from place of arrival to place of the Buyer and its charges.

⑫Other miscellaneous expenses.

If the parties need to discuss the above responsibilities and charges one by one at each negotiation, it is not benefit for the parties to promote transactions smoothly. In practice, the parties just need to decide which trade term be used in the transaction, the above responsibilities and charges are almost set firstly.

The trade term has the following functions.

①To avoid or at least decrease a considerable degree caused by the uncertainties of different interpretations of such terms in different countries.

②To avoid misunderstanding, disputes and litigation with all the waste of time and money for unaware of the different trading practices in their respective countries.

③Simplified to a certain extent, saving negotiation time and expense and benefit for transaction concluded.

From Figure 2.2, you will find if the trade term is selected from the right to the left, the buyer bears more obligations and charges than the seller in delivery of the goods. If the trade term is selected from the left to the right, the seller bears more obligations and charges than the buyer for delivery of the goods.

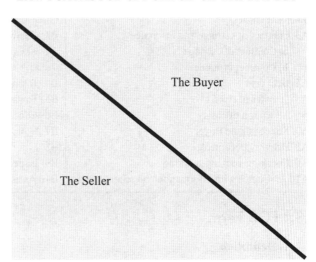

EXW FCA FAS FOB CPT CFR CIP CIF DAT DAP DDP

Loading
Pre-Carriage
Storage
Dock
Inspection
Export tariff
Export licenses
Export formalities
Main freight
Insurance
Import licenses
Import formalities
Import duty
Unloading
Post-Carriage
Other miscellaneous expense

The Buyer

The Seller

Figure 2.2  Responsibilities & Charges & Trade Terms

As per the functions of trade terms, it owns alternative names as:

①Delivery terms. It is on the basis of carriage of the goods from the seller to the buyer and division of costs and risks between the parties.

②Price terms. It is stipulating what are included in the price that the Buyer paid to the seller.

③Delivery obligation. It focuses on what the goods and documents should be provided by the seller, and customs formalities, contract of carriage and contract of insurance should be charged on which party, etc.

# 2.3 Detailed Trade Terms under Incoterms

Trade terms under Incoterms®2020 and Incoterms®2010 are divided into two groups:

① Rules for any mode of transport including EXW, FCA, CPT, CIP, DAT, DAP, DPU (DAT), and DDP.

② Rules for sea and/or inland waterway transport including FAS, FOB, CFR and CIF. Incoterms®2010. Incoterms®2010 sets up the obligations of Seller & Buyer as the following. In Table 2.1, "A" stands for the Seller's obligations, "B" stands for the Buyer's obligations. A and B are arranged in the way of horizontally symmetrical.

Table 2.1 The Obligations of the Seller & the Buyer under Incoterms®2010

| A The Seller's obligations | B The Buyer's obligations |
| --- | --- |
| A1 General obligations of the Seller | B1 General obligations of the Buyer |
| A2 License, authorizations, security clearance and other formalities | B2 License, authorizations, security clearance and other formalities |
| A3 Contract of carriage and insurance<br>　　a) Contract of carriage<br>　　b) Contract insurance | B3 Contract of carriage and insurance<br>　　a) Contract of carriage<br>　　b) Contract insurance |
| A4 Delivery | B4 Taking delivery |
| A5 Transfer of risks | B5 Transfer of risks |
| A6 Allocation of costs | B6 Allocation of costs |
| A7 Notices to the Buyer | B7 Notices to the Seller |
| A8 Delivery document | B8 Proof of delivery |
| A9 Checking-packing-marking | B9 Inspection of goods |
| A10 Assistance with information and related costs | B10 Assistance with information and related costs |

## 2.3.1 FOB Term

### 1. Definition

FOB is the abbreviation of "free on board (Insert named port of shipment)". "Free on board" means that the seller delivers the goods on board the vessel nominated by the buyer at the named port of shipment or procures the goods already so delivered. The risk of loss of or damage to the goods passes when the goods are on board the vessel, and the buyer bears all the costs from the moment onwards.

### 2. Port of Shipment

FOB must be followed by a named port of shipment. As usual, the named port of shipment shall be a seaport/river port in the exporting country. For example, if the goods are exported from China, the trade term in a sales contract may be applied as "FOB Shanghai subject to Incoterms®2010(or Incoterms®2020)", "FOB Ningbo Incoterms®2010(or Incoterms®2020)". If the goods are exported from Ukraine or Nigeria, the trade term in a sales contract may be used as "FOB Odessa, Ukraine subject to Incoterms®2010(or Incoterms®2020)" or "FOB Lagos, Nigeria subject to

Incoterms®2010(or Incoterms®2020)".

### 3. Delivery of the Goods

The seller is required either to deliver the goods "on board the vessel" or to procure the goods already so delivered for shipment. It means that the seller has fulfilled his obligation of delivery after the goods already so delivered. The reference to "procure" here caters for multiple sales down a chain (string sales), which is particularly in the commodity trades.

In the sale of commodities, as opposed to the sale of manufactured goods, cargo is frequently sold several times during transit "down a string". When this happens, a seller in the middle of the string does not "ship" the goods because these have already been shipped by the first seller in the string. The seller in the middle of the string therefore performs its obligations towards its buyer not by shipping the goods, but by "procuring" goods that have been shipped.

For clarification purpose, Incoterms®2010 rules include the obligation to "procure the goods on board the vessel nominated by the buyer at the named port of shipment" as an alternative to the obligation to ship goods in the relevant Incoterms rules. The first seller of string sales or the only seller of non-string sales has fulfilled his obligation of delivery after the goods placed on board the vessel nominated by the buyer at the named port of shipment. While the seller of string sales excluding the first seller has fulfilled his obligation of delivery after he "procures" the goods so delivered by the first seller.

### 4. Critical Point

FOB term under Incoterms has one critical point. The critical point is "on board the vessel nominated by the buyer at the named port of shipment". The seller has fulfilled his obligation of delivery, transfering the risks and allocation of the costs to the buyer from the moment by placing the goods on this critical point. "On board the vessel" means FOB rule is to be used only for sea or inland waterway transport. If the goods are shipped by non-waterway-based transportation, FOB rule may not be applicable. FOB may not be appropriate where the goods are handed over to the carrier before "on board the vessel". For example, the goods are shipped in containers, which are typically delivered at a terminal or premises. In such situations, the FCA rules should be used.

### 5. Obligations

The obligations of the Seller and the Buyer under Incoterms are as following.

(1) General Obligations

The Seller must provide the goods and the commercial invoice in conformity with the contract of sale and/or other evidence of conformity that may be required by the contract. Any documents referred to the Seller's obligations may be an equivalent electronic record or procedure if agreed between the parties or customary. The Buyer must pay the price of the goods as provided in the contract of sale. Any documents referred to the Buyer's obligation may also be an equivalent electronic record or procedure if agreed between the parties or customary.

(2) Licenses, Authorizations, Security Clearances? and Other Formalities

Where Applicable, the Seller must obtain, at its own risk and expense, any export license or other official authorization and carry out all customs formalities necessary for the export of the goods. It is up to the Buyer to obtain, at its own risk and expense, any import license or other official authorization and carry out all customs formalities necessary for the import of the goods and their transport through any country. So, FOB term requires the Seller to clear the goods for export, where applicable. However, the Seller has no obligation to clear the goods for import, pay any import duty or carry out import customs formalities.

(3) Contracts of Carriage and Insurance

① Contract of carriage: The Seller has no obligations to the Buyer to make a contract of carriage. The Buyer must contract, at its own expense for the carriage of the goods from the named port of shipment. However, if requested by the Buyer or if it is commercial practice and the Buyer does not give an instructions to the contrary in due time, the Seller may contract for carriage on usual terms at the Buyer's risk and expense. In either case, the Seller may decline to make the contract of carriage and, if it does, shall promptly notify the Buyer.

② Contract of insurance: The Seller has no obligations to the Buyer to make a contract of insurance. The Buyer has no obligations to the Seller to make a contract of insurance. However, the Seller must provide the Buyer, at the Buyer's request, risk, and expense (if any), with information that the Buyer needs for obtaining insurance.

(4) Delivery & Taking Delivery

The Seller must deliver the goods either by placing them on board the vessel nominated by the buyer at the loading point, if any, indicated by the buyer at the named port of shipment or by procuring the goods so delivered. In either case, the seller must deliver the goods on the agreed date or within the agreed period and in the manner customary at the port. If no specific loading point has been indicated by the Buyer, the seller may select the point within the named port of shipment that best suits its purpose. The buyer must take delivery of the goods when they have been so delivered.

(5) Notices

The buyer must give the seller sufficient notice of the vessel name, loading point and where necessary, the selected delivery time within agreed period. The seller must, at the buyer's risk and expense, give the buyer sufficient notice either that the goods have been placed on board the vessel nominated by the buyer at the loading point, if any, indicated by the buyer at the named port of shipment or that the vessel has failed to take the goods within the time agreed.

(6) Transfer of Risks

As usual, the Seller bears all risks of loss of or damage to the goods until they have been placed on board the vessel nominated by the buyer at the loading point, if any, indicated by the Buyer at the named port of shipment. The buyer bears all risks of loss or damage to the goods from the time they have been delivered. While, the seller has exception of loss or damage in the circumstances described followed, if:

① The buyer fails to notify the nomination of a vessel; or

② The vessel nominated by the buyer fails to arrive on time to enable the seller to place the goods on board the vessel, or is unable to take the goods, or closes for cargo earlier than the time notified by the buyer.

Then, the buyer bears all risks of loss of or damage to the goods from the agreed date, or in the absence of an agreed date; from the date notified by the seller within the agreed period, or, if no such date has been notified; from the expiry date of any agreed period for delivery, Provide that the goods have been clearly identified as the contract goods.

(7) Allocation of Costs

The seller must pay:

① All costs relating to the goods until they have been delivered on board the vessel, other than those payable by the Buyer in the circumstances of exceptions.

② When applicable, the costs of customs formalities necessary for export, as well as all duties, taxes and other charges payable upon export.

The buyer must pay:

① All costs relating to the goods from the time they have been delivered on board the vessel, except, where applicable, the costs of customs formalities necessary for export, as well as all duties, taxes and other charges payable upon export.

② Any additional costs incurred because the buyer has failed to give appropriate notice, or the vessel nominated by the buyer fails to arrive on time, is unable to take the goods, or closes for cargo earlier than the time notified.

③ Where applicable, all duties, taxes and other charges, as well as the costs of carrying out customs formalities payable upon import of the goods and the costs for their transport through any country.

(8) Delivery of Documents and Proof of Delivery

The seller must provide the buyer, at the seller's expense, with the usual proof that the goods have been delivered. Unless such proof is a transport document, the seller must provide assistance to the buyer, at the Buyer's request, risk and expense, in obtaining a transport document, if :

① The buyer fails to notify the nomination of a vessel.

② The vessel nominated by the buyer fails to arrive on time to enable the seller to place the goods on board the vessel, or is unable to take the goods, or closes for cargo earlier than the time notified in the notice.

Then, the buyer bears all risks of loss of or damage to the goods from the agreed date, or in the absence of an agreed date; from the date notified by the seller under A7 within the agreed period, or, if no such date has been notified; from the expiry date of any agreed period for delivery, provide that the goods have been clearly identified as the contract goods. The Buyer must accept the proof of delivery provided as envisaged in A8.

(9) Checking-packaging-marking & Inspection of the Goods

The seller must pay the costs of those checking operations (such as checking quality, measuring, weighting, counting) that are necessary for the purpose of delivering the goods, as well as the costs of any pre-shipment inspection mandated by the authority of the country of export.

The seller must, at its own expense, package the goods, unless it is usual for the particular trade to transport the type of goods sold unpacked. The seller may package the goods in the manner appropriate for their transport, unless the buyer has notified the seller of specific packaging requirements before the contract of sale is concluded. Packaging is to be marked appropriately.

The buyer must pay the costs of any mandatory pre-shipment inspection, including inspection mandated by the authorities of the country of export.

(10) Assistance with Information and Related Costs

The seller must, where applicable, in a timely manner, provide to or render assistance in obtaining for the buyer, at the Buyer's request, risk and expense, any documents and information, including security-related information, that the buyer needs for the export and/ or import of the goods and/or their transport to the final destination. The seller must reimburse the Buyer for all costs and charges incurred by the buyer in providing or rending assistance in obtaining documents and information.

The buyer must, in a timely manner, advise the seller of any security information requirements. The buyer must reimburse the Seller for all costs and charges incurred by the seller in providing or rending assistance in obtaining documents and information. The buyer must, in a timely manner, provide to or render assistance in obtaining for the seller, at the seller's request, risk and expense, any documents and information, including security-related information, that the seller needs for the transport and export of the goods and for their transport through any country.

## 2.3.2 CIF Term

### 1. Definition

CIF is the abbreviation of "cost, insurance and freight (insert named port of destination)". Cost, insurance and freight means that the seller delivers the goods on board the vessel or procures the goods already so delivered. The risk of loss of or damage to the goods passes when the goods are on board the vessel.

The seller must contract for and pay the costs and freight necessary to bring the goods to the named port of destination. The seller also contracts for insurance cover against the buyer's risk of loss of or damage to the goods during the carriage.

The buyer should note that under CIF term, the seller is required to obtain insurance only on a minimum cover. If the buyer wish to have more insurance protection, it will need either to agree as much expressly with the seller or to make its own extra insurance arrangement.

### 2. Mode of Transport & Named Port of Destination

CIF term is only suitable for sea or inland waterway transport. CIF term must be followed by a named port of destination others than FOB term. If the goods are exported from China, the parties may conclude a transaction based on CIF New York, CIF Hamburg, CIF Rio Grande or CIF Cairo, etc. Some ports such as "Port Klang, Malaysia" and "Busan, the Republic of Korea" can be described as "Port Kelang" and "Pusan, the Republic of Korea". It's the same port just with different notations. Some ports have overlapping names, such as Albany, Sydney or Odessa, so it's better to add the country name after the port of destination, such as "CIF Odessa, Ukraine", "CIF Odessa, USA" or "CIF Sydney, Austria" , "CIF Sydney, Canada".

### 3. Delivery of the Goods

When CIF term is applicable, the seller fulfills his obligation to deliver the goods on board the vessel or by procuring the goods so delivered, not when the goods reach the place of destination. The seller delivers the goods on board the vessel at the port of shipment. It means that "the port of shipment" equals to "the place of delivery", where the risks passes from the seller to the buyer.

### 4. Contract of Carriage

The seller must contract for or procure a contract for the carriage of the goods from the agreed point of delivery, if any, at the place of delivery to the named port of destination or, if agreed, at any point on that port. The buyer has no obligation to the seller to contract of carriage.

The contract of carriage must be made on usual terms at the seller's expense and provide for carriage by the usual route in a vessel of the type normally used for the transport of the type of goods sold. The buyer has no right to demand the limitation of vessel's nationality, type, age or shipping company. While in practice, the seller always succumbs to the buyer's demand on the basis of no additional costs occurred.

### 5. Contract of Insurance

The seller must contract for or procure a contract for insurance cover against the Buyer's risk of loss of or damage to the goods during the carriage. The seller must obtain, at its own expense, cargo insurance complying at least with the minimum cover provided by Clauses (C) of the Institute Cargo Clauses (LMA/IUA) or any similar clauses.

At a minimum amount of contract plus 10% and shall be in the currency of the contract. Cover route shall be at least from the point of delivery to at least the named port of destination. The insurance shall be contracted with underwriters or an insurance company of good repute and entitled the buyer, or any other person having an insurable interest in the goods, to claim directly from the insurer. Insurance policy or other evidence of insurance cover shall be provided by the seller to the buyer.

### 6. Critical Points

CIF has two critical points. Risks and costs are transferred at different places. Risks is transferred from the seller to the buyer at the port of shipment, and costs are transferred at the named port of destination.

It is suggested that the parties shall both specify a port of shipment and a port of destination in the contract. The risks passes from the seller to the buyer at the port of shipment and is of particular interest to the buyer. The parties are well advised to identify a port of shipment as precisely as possible in the contract.

The seller must pay:

① all costs relating to the goods until they have been delivered on board the vessel;

② the freight, the costs of loading the goods on board the vessel and any charges for unloading the goods at the agreed port of discharge that are for the Seller's account under the contract of carriage;

③ the costs of insurance;

④ where applicable, the costs of customs formalities necessary for export, as well as all duties, taxes and other charges payable upon export, and the costs for their transport through any country that are for the seller's account under the contract of carriage.

### 7. Delivery of Documents and Proof of Delivery

The seller must, at its own expense, provide the Buyer without delay with the usual transport documents for the agreed port of destination. The transport documents must cover the contract goods, be dated with the period agreed for shipment, enable the buyer to claim the goods from the carrier at the port of destination and, unless otherwise agreed, enable the buyer to sell the goods in transit by the transfer of the documents to the subsequent buyer or by notification to the carrier.

When such a transport document is issued in negotiable form and in several originals, a full set of originals must be presented to the buyer. The buyer must accept the transport document provided by the seller if it is in conformity with the contract.

**8. The Non-applicable of CIF**

If the goods will be shipped by non-water-way based transportation, CIF rules may not be applicable. CIF term may not be appropriate where the goods are handed over to the carrier before "on board the vessel", for example, the goods shipped in containers are typically delivered at a terminal. In such situations, the CIP rules should be used.

## 2.3.3 CFR Term

CFR is the abbreviation of "cost and freight (insert named port of destination)". This term is to be used only for sea or inland waterway transport. "Cost and Freight" means that the seller delivers the goods on board the vessel or procures the goods already so delivered. The risk of loss of or damage to the goods passes when the goods are on board the vessel. The seller must contract for and pay the costs and freight necessary to bring the goods to the named port of destination.

CFR may not be appropriate where goods are handed over to the carrier before they are on board the vessel, for example, goods in containers, which are typically delivered at a terminal. In such circumstances, the CPT rules should be used.

If the goods are exported from China, the parties may conclude a sales contract with CFR term, such as CFR Dubai, CFR London, CFR Karachi.

The main differences and similarities between FOB term, CFR term and CIF term are as follows (see Figure2.3).

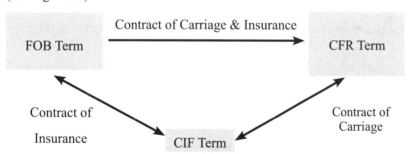

Figure 2.3 The Main Differences and Similarities Between FOB, CFR & CIF

**1. Main Similarities Between FOB, CFR, and CIF**

(1) Delivery of the Goods

When CFR term is applicable, the seller fulfills its obligation to deliver the goods on board the vessel or by procuring the goods so delivered, which is same as FOB term and CIF term, not when the goods reach the place of destination. The seller delivers the goods on board the vessel at the port of shipment. It means that "the port of shipment" equals to "the place of delivery", where the risk passes from the seller to the buyer.

(2) Customs Formalities

CFR, CIF, and FOB terms all require the seller to clear the goods for export, where applicable. However, the seller has no obligation to clear the goods for import, pay any import duty or carry out any import customs formalities.

(3) Mode of Transportation

CFR, CIF and FOB terms are all only suitable for sea or inland waterway transport.

(4) Critical Point for Risk Transfer

The critical point of risk transfer under FOB, CFR, and CIF terms is on board the vessel at the port of shipment.

### 2. Main Difference Between FOB, CFR, and CIF

(1) Contract of Carriage

Under CFR term, the obligations for contract of carriage are same as under CIF term and differ from under FOB term. When CFR term is applicable, the seller must contract for or procure a contract for the carriage of the goods from the agreed point of delivery, if any, at the place of delivery to the named port of destination or, if agreed, any point at that port.

(2) Contract of Insurance

Under CFR term, the obligations for contract of insurance are same as under FOB term and differ from under CIF term. The seller has no obligation to the buyer to make a contract of insurance. However, the seller must provide the buyer, at the buyer's request, risk, and expense (if any), with information that the buyer needs for obtaining insurance. The buyer has no obligation to the seller to make a contract of insurance. While, under CIF term, the seller shall contracts for insurance cover against the buyer's risk of loss of or damage to the goods during the carriage.

(3) Notices

It is necessary and important that the seller gives sufficient notice to the buyer or the buyer gives sufficient notice to the seller. Under FOB term, the buyer must give the seller sufficient notice of the vessel name, loading point and, where necessary, the selected delivery time within the agreed period. The seller must, at the buyer's risk and expense, give the buyer sufficient notice either that the goods have been delivered or that the vessel has failed to take the goods within the time agreed. The seller must provide the buyer, at the buyer's request, risk, and expense (if any), with information that the buyer needs for obtaining insurance.

Under CFR and CIF terms, the Buyer must, whenever it is entitled to determine the time for shipping the goods and/or the point of receiving the goods within the named port of destination, give the seller sufficient notice thereof. The seller must give the buyer any notice needed in order to allow the buyer to take measures that are normally necessary to enable the buyer to take the goods. On the contrary, the notice to the seller for the buyer is much more important under FOB term than under CFR term or CIF term.

The notice to the buyer for the seller under CFR term is most important than FOB term and CIF term because of information asymmetry.

(4) Critical Point for Costs Allocation

The critical point of costs allocation under FOB term is still on board the vessel, while the critical point of costs allocation under CFR and CIF terms is at the port of destination.

## 2.3.4 FCA, CPT, and CIP Term

FCA, CPT, and CIP are usually more appropriate than FOB, CFR, and CIF in international trade. FOB, CIF, and CFR are to be used only for sea or inland waterway transport, while FCA, CIP, and CPT are to be used for any mode of transport selected and may also be used when more than one mode of transport is employed. International Chamber of Commerce (ICC) recommends using FCA term instead of FOB term, CIP term instead of CIF term and CPT term instead of CFR term.

FCA, CPT and CIP may be used irrespective of the mode of transport selected and may also be used where more than one mode of transport is employed, that means any mode of transport and multimodal transport. They require the seller to clear the goods for export, where applicable. However, the seller has no obligation to clear the good for import, pay any import duty or carry out any import customs formalities. When FCA, CPT and CIP are used, the seller fulfills its obligation to deliver when it hands the goods over to the carrier in the manner specified in the chosen rule, not when the goods reach the place of destination.

**1. FCA Term**

(1) Definition

FCA is the abbreviation of free carrier (insert named place of delivery) Incoterms® 2010. "Free carrier" means that the seller delivers the goods to the carrier or another person nominated by the buyer at the seller's premises or another named place. The parties are well advised to specify as clearly as possible the point within the named place of delivery, as the risk passes to the buyer at that point. If the parties intend to deliver the goods at the seller's premises, they should identify the address of those premises as the named place of delivery. If, on the other hand, the parties intend the goods to be delivered at another place, they must identify a different specific place of delivery.

(2) Delivery

The seller must deliver the goods to the carrier or another person nominated by the buyer at the agreed point, if any, at the named place on the agreed date or within the agreed period. Under the following circumstances, delivery is completed: ① if the named place is the seller's premises, when the goods have been loaded by the means of transport provided by the buyer; ② in any other case, when the goods are placed at the disposal of the carrier or another person nominated by the buyer by the seller's means of transport ready for unloading. If no specific point has been notified by the buyer within the named place of delivery, and if there are several points available, the seller may select the point that best suits its purpose.

(3) Notices to the Seller by the Buyer under FCA

The Buyer must notify the Seller of: a) The name of the carrier or another person nominated by the buyer within sufficient time as to enable the seller to deliver the goods in accordance with the contract; b) where necessary, the selected time within the period agreed for delivery when the carrier or person nominated will take the goods; c) the mode of transport to be used by the person nominated; and d) the point of taking delivery with the named place.

(4) The Similarities Between FOB and FCA

① No obligation for contract of carriage. The seller must deliver the goods to the carrier or another person nominated by the buyer if requested by the buyer, or if it is a commercial practice and the buyer does not give an instruction to the contrary in due time, the seller may contract for carriage on usual terms at the buyer's risk and expense. In either case, the seller may decline to make contract of carriage and, if it does, shall promptly notify the buyer.

② No obligations for contract of insurance. The seller has no obligation to the buyer to make a contract of insurance. However, the seller must provide the buyer, at the buyer's request, risk, and expense (if any), with information that the buyer needs for obtaining insurance.

③ Custom formalities. Where applicable, the seller must obtain (it is up to the buyer to obtain), at its own risk and expense, any export/import license or other official authorization and carry out all customs formalities necessary for the export/import of the goods. The buyer shall also carry the transport of the goods through any country or region.

(5) The Differences Between FOB and FCA

① Mode of transport. FCA rule may be used irrespective of the mode of transport selected and may also be used where more than one mode of transport is employed, while FOB rule is to be used only for sea or inland waterway transport.

② Delivery. FCA means the seller delivers the goods to the carrier or another person nominated by the buyer at the seller's premises or another named place. The parties are well advised to specify as clearly as possible the point within the named place of delivery, as the risk passes to the buyer at that point. FOB means that the seller is required either to deliver the goods on board the vessel or to procure goods already so delivered for shipment. The reference to "procure" here caters to multiple sales down a chain ("string sales"), particularly common in the commodity trades.

③Critical point for risk transfer and cost allocation. Under FCA term, the seller must deliver the goods to the carrier and another person nominated by the buyer at the agreed point, if any, at the named place or the agreed date or within the agreed period. From then on, all the risks and expenses pass and to the buyer at that point. While, under FOB term, the buyer must bear all risks of loss or damage to the goods and all costs from the time they have been delivered on board the vessel nominated by the buyer at the named port of shipment, except, where applicable, the costs of customs formalities necessary for export as well as all duties, taxes, and other charges payable upon export.

④Loading charges. Under FCA term, if the named place is the seller's premises, the seller shall load the goods by the means of transport provided by the buyer. In any other case, the goods are placed at the disposal of the carrier or another person nominated by the buyer on the seller's means of transport ready for unloading. Under FOB term, the seller shall normally the in charge of loading the goods on board the vessel at the port of shipment.

**2. CIP Term**

(1) Definition

CIP is the abbreviation of "carriage and insurance paid to" (insert named place of destination). It means that the seller delivers the goods to the carrier or another person nominated by the seller at an agreed place (if any such place is agreed between the parties) and that the seller must contract for and pay the costs of carriage necessary to bring the goods to the named place of destination. The seller also contracts for insurance cover against the buyer's risk of loss of or damage to the goods during the carriage. The buyer should note that under CIP, the Seller is required to obtain insurance only on minimum cover. Should the buyer wish to have more insurance protection, it will need either to agree as much expressly with the seller or to make its own extra insurance arrangement.

(2) The Similarities Between CIP and CIF

The seller must contract for carriage and pay the cost of carriage necessary to bring the goods to the named destination. The seller must also contract of insurance and pays the insurance premium, but the insurance is permitted only on a minimum cover. The greater cover of insurance must either be needed to agree as much expressly with the seller or to make on the buyer's own extra insurance arrangements. Where applicable, the seller must obtain (it is up to the buyer to obtain), at its own risk and expense, any export/import license or other official authorization, and carry out all customs formalities necessary for the export/import of the goods. The buyer shall also carry for transport of the goods through any country or region.

(3) The Differences Between CIP & CIF

By comparison, the difference between CIP and CIF on mode of transport, delivery, and the critical point for risks are same as that between FCA and FOB. The critical point for costs allocation, contract of carriage, contract of insurance of CIP and CIF are different from those of FCA and FOB. The Seller must pay all the costs relating to the goods until they have been handed over to the carrier (CIP) or placed on board the vessel or so delivered (CIF) on the agreed date or within the agreed period. The seller must contract or procure a contract for the carriage of the goods from the agreed point of delivery, if any, at the place of delivery to the named port of destination (CIF)/place of destination (CIP) , or if agreed, any point at that port (CIF)/place(CIP).

**3. CPT Term**

CPT is the abbreviation of "carriage paid to" (insert named place of destination). It means that the Seller delivers the goods to the carrier or another person nominated by the Seller at an agreed place (if any, such place is agreed between the parties) and that the Seller must contract for and pay the costs of carriage necessary to bring the goods to the named place of destination. The Seller has no obligation to the buyer to make a contract of insurance.

However, the seller must provide the buyer, at the buyer's request, risk, and expense (if any), with information that the buyer needs for obtaining insurance. When CPT rule is applicable, it is quite important that the seller shall give sufficient notice to the buyer in reasonable time, because the seller is responsible for transport and the buyer bears the risk of loss of or damage to the goods from the moment that the goods was at disposal of the carrier.

## 2.3.5 Other Trade Terms

Besides FOB, CIF, CFR, FCA, CIP, and CPT, there are other five trade rules under Incoterms®2010, including EXW, FAS, DAT, DAP, and DDP.

**1. EXW Term**

EXW is the abbreviation of "Ex works" (insert named place of delivery) and represents the minimum obligations for the seller. It is suitable for domestic trade. EXW means the seller delivers when it places the goods at the disposal of the buyer at the seller's premises or at another named place (i.e. works, factory, warehouse). The seller does not need to load the goods on any collecting vehicle, nor does it need to clear the goods for export, where such clearance is applicable. Where applicable, the seller has no obligation either to clear the goods for export nor to clear the goods for import. It means that the Buyer is required to clear the goods for both export and import and pay import duties occurred.

The seller shall provide the goods in conformity with the contract and notify the buyer sufficiently where and when the goods will be placed at its disposal. The Buyer must, whenever it is entitled to, determine the time within an agreed period and/or the place of taking delivery, giving the seller sufficient notice thereof. The point within the named place of delivery shall be well advised, as the costs and risks to that point are for the account of the seller. The buyer bears all the costs and risks involved in taking the goods from the agreed point, if any, at the named place of delivery.

**2. FAS Term**

FAS is the abbreviation of "free alongside ship" (insert named port of shipment). It means that the seller delivers when the goods are placed alongside the vessel (e.g. on a quay or a barge) nominated by the buyer at the named port of shipment. The risk of losses of or damage to the goods passes when the goods are alongside the ship, and the buyer bears all the costs from that moment onwards. FAS term is only suitable for sea or waterway transportation. AS term requires the seller to clear the goods for export, where applicable. However, the seller has no obligation to clear the goods for import, pay any import duty or carry out import customs formalities.

**3. DAT Term and DPU Term**

DAT Term under Incoterms®2010 is replaced by DPU under Incotermes®2020.

DAT is the abbreviation of "delivered at terminal" (insert named terminal at port or place of destination ). DAT means that the Seller delivers when the goods, once unloaded from the arriving means of transport, are placed at the disposal of the buyer at a named terminal at the named port or place of destination. The seller bears all the risks involved in bringing the goods to and unloading them at the terminal at the named port or place of destination. Terminal means any place, whether covered or not, such as a quay, warehouse, container yard or road, and rail or air cargo terminal..

DPU is the abbreviation of Delivered at place unloaded (insert named place of destination). DPU means that the Seller delivers when the goods, once unloaded from the arriving means of transport, are placed at the disposal of the buyer at a named place of destination. The seller bears all risks involved in bringing the goods to and unloading them at the named place of destination.

DAT term and DPU term are suitable for any mode of transport including multimodal transport. They require seller to clear the goods for export, where applicable. However, seller has no obligation to clear the goods for import, pay any import duty or carry out import customs formalities.

**4. DAP Term**

DAP is the abbreviation of "delivered at place" (insert named place of destination). It means that the Seller delivers when the goods are placed at the disposal of the buyer on the arriving means of transport ready for unloading by the buyer at the named place of destination. The seller bears all the risks involved in bringing the goods to the named place.

DAT term is suitable for any mode of transport including multimedia transport. DAT term requires the seller to clear the goods for export, where applicable. However, the Seller has no obligation to clear the goods for import, pay any import duty or carry out import customs formalities.

### 5. DDP Term

DDP is the abbreviation of "delivered duty paid" (insert named place of destination). It means the Seller delivers the goods when the goods are placed at the disposal of the Buyer, cleared for import on the arriving means of transport ready for unloading at the named place of destination, and has an obligation to clear the goods not only for export but also for import, to pay any duty for both export and import and to carry out all customs formalities.

DDP term is suitable for any mode of transport including multimedia transport. It represents the minimum obligation for the buyer and the maximum obligation for the seller. The seller charges import customs formalities. If it cannot carry out directly or indirectly, DDP cannot be used. Any VAT or other taxes payable upon import for seller's account unless expressly agreed otherwise in the sale contract. If the seller wishes to exclude VAT, it should be made clear by adding explicit wording in S/C.

# 2.4 Supplements to Incoterms® 2010 and Incoterms® 2020

International Trade Practice Rules do not equal to laws, for they are not binding upon both parties automatically. It can be appointed out use or not use. The court or arbitration agency can apply particular trade practice rules to settling disputes if the particular case isn't stipulated expressly in a contract or isn't stipulated to apply to a certain trade practice rule. If a certain trade practice rule is stipulated in a contract expressly, it is binding upon both parties. If a contract is stipulated to apply one particular trade practice rule but there are discrepancy terms and conditions between trade practice rules and national regulations, these terms and conditions are approved and protected by national regulation based on their conformity with national regulation.

Incoterms is suitable for handle the relative matters relating to responsibilities and delivery of the goods in a sales contract. It is better to stipulate that the sales contract is subject to Incoterms and the applicable trade rule, and nominated place should be contained together. In view of amendments of Incoterms, the parties shall stipulate the specific version referred to applies in order to avoid misunderstanding and disputes.

The tasks, risks, and charges for delivery of the goods from the seller to the buyer that the parties bear are different under different trade rules of Incoterms. FOB, FCA, CFR, CPT, CIF, and CIP are popular in practice as the tasks, risks, and charges distributed are relatively balanced, whereas EXW, FAS, DPU (DAT), DAP, and DDP are the opposite.

It is very important to select the appreciate trade rules in international trades. Factors like nature of the goods, mode of transport, and the extending liabilities should be considered carefully. The extending liabilities are including carriage arrangement, cover insurance, and in charge for loading or unloading, custom formalities, etc.

It is suggested that the parties shall incorporate the Incoterms rules into the contract of sales and choose the appropriate Incoterms rules. When applicable, the parties shall specify the point of place, port, terminal or premises as precisely as possible after trade terms in order for the applicable trade rules to enter into force. The objectives of the Incoterms®2010 rules are to establish clear and binding rules for: ① the division of costs; ② the division of risks; ③ the handling liabilities, such as furnishing of documents, export and import clearance, security related information provided, notification to the parties concerned in delivery of the goods from the seller to the buyer.

While, you should remember that Incoterms rules do not give you a complete contract of sales. Incoterms rules do not deal with the following aspects: ① transfer of property or legal title to the goods; ② breach of contract or deficiency in the merchandise happened; ③ price amount and/or terms of payment; ④ place of jurisdiction. These terms and conditions should be negotiated by the seller and the buyer separately or according to the applicable laws. The parties shall understand clearly that the enforceable domestic laws may overthrow any terms and conditions of the contract, including the applicable trade rules.

See Table 2.2 for specific stipularting of each trade rule under Incoterms®2010.

## Questions

1. For shipment from Hangzhou, China to Brussels, Belgium by container, the main carriage is from Shanghai Port, China to Antewerp, Belgium. If the seller wishes to finish obligation for delivery of the goods in China, which trade terms can be applicable? How to stipulate trade terms?

2. Please make an analysis on the differences between CIF Antwerp, Belgium and DPU Antwerp, Belgium.

3. Please make an analysis on the similarities and differences between FOB Shanghai port, China, FCA Shanghai Port, China, and FAS Shanghai port, China.

4. "Free shipping" and "non-free shipping" in cross-boarder e-commerce are similar to which trade terms under Incoterms® 2010 or Incoterms®2020?

Table 2.2 Specific Stipulating of Each Trade Rule under Incoterms®2010

| Group | Trade Rule Methods of Delivery | | Task, Risk and Charge Allocation | | | | | Customs Formalities | | |
|---|---|---|---|---|---|---|---|---|---|---|
| | | | Delivery Place | Risk Transfer | Cost Allocation | Carriage | Insurance by | Export by | Import by | |
| | F O B | free on board (insert named port of shipment ) | The seller delivers the goods on board the vessel nominated by the buyer at the named port of shipment or procures goods so delivered | On board of the vessel | On board the vessel at the named port of shipment | On board the vessel at the named port of shipment | Buyer | — | Seller | Buyer |
| Suitable for sea or inland waterway transport | C F R | cost and freight (insert named port of destination) | The seller delivers the goods on board the vessel or procures the goods so delivereds. | On board of the vessel | On board the vessel at the named port of shipment | At the named port of destination | Seller | — | Seller | Buyer |
| | C I F | cost, insurance and freight (insert named port of destination) | The seller delivers the goods on board the vessel or procures the goods so delivered | On board of the vessel | On board the vessel at the named port of shipment | At the named port of destination | Seller | Seller | Seller | Buyer |
| | F A S | free alongside ship(insert named port of shipment) | The seller delivers the goods alongside the vessel nominated by the buyer (for example, on the dock or on the lighter) | Alongside the vessel | Alongside the vessel at the named port of shipment | Alongside the vessel at the named port of shipment | Buyer | — | Seller | Buyer |

continued

**Tasks, Risks and Charges allocation**

| Group | Trade Rule / Methods of Delivery | Delivery Place | Risks Transfer | Costs Allocation | Carriage | Insurance | Customs Formalities — Export | Customs Formalities — Import |
|---|---|---|---|---|---|---|---|---|
| | E X W — ex works (insert named place) | The seller delivers the goods by placing them at the disposal of the buyer at the agreed point, if any, and at the named place of delivery, not loaded on any collecting vehicle | At the agreed place | At the disposal of the buyer | At the disposal of the buyer | Buyer | — | Buyer |
| Suitable for any mode of transport or multimodal transport | F C A — free carrier (insert named place) | The seller delivers the goods to the carrier or another person nominated by the buyer at the agreed point, if any, and the named place on the agreed date or within the agreed period. Delivery is completed | At the place of the Seller or another nominated place | Free carrier | Free first carrier | Buyer | — | Seller |
| | C P T — carriage paid to (insert named place of destination) | The seller delivers the goods by handing them over to the carrier on the agreed date or within the agreed period | Free carrier | Free carrier | At the named place of destination | Seller | — | Seller |
| | C I P — carriage and insurance paid to (insert named place of destination) | The seller delivers the goods by handing them over to the carrier on the agreed date or within the agreed period | Free carrier | Free carrier | At the named place of destination | Seller | Seller | Seller |

continued

| Group | Trade Rule Methods of Delivery | | Tasks, Risks and Charges allocation | | | | | Customs Formalities | |
|---|---|---|---|---|---|---|---|---|---|
| | | | Delivery Place | Risks Transfer | Costs Allocation | Carriage | Insurance | Export | Import |
| Suitable for any mode of transport or multimodal transport | delivered at terminal (insert named terminal at port or place of destination) | D A T | The seller must unload the goods from the arriving means of transport and must then deliver them by placing them at the disposal of the buyer at the named terminal at the port or place of destination on the agreed date or within the agreed period | At the named terminal of nominated port or place | At the disposal of the buyer | At the disposal of the buyer | Seller | Seller | Buyer |
| | delivered at place (insert named place of destination) | D A P | The seller must deliver the goods by placing them at the disposal of the buyer on the arriving means of transport ready for unloading at the agreed point, if any, at the named place of destination on the agreed date or within the agreed period | On the arriving means of transport at the named place of destination | At the disposal of the buyer | At the disposal of the buyer | Seller | Seller | Buyer |
| | delivered duty paid (insert named place of destination) | D D P | The seller must deliver the goods by placing them at the disposal of the buyer on the arriving means of transport ready for unloading at the agreed point, if any, at the named place of destination on the agreed date or within the agreed period | On the arriving means of transport at the named place of destination | At the disposal of the buyer | At the disposal of the buyer | Seller | Seller | Seller |

# 第三章

# 国际贸易货物

## 案例3.1

2018年9月19日，深圳大鹏海关发布行政处罚公示，当天一口气处罚了近50家民营企业！这到底是怎么回事？下面以企业A为例说明。

企业A委托某报关服务有限公司持报关单以一般贸易方式向海关申报出口电热水壶（商品编码8516799090）7950个，经海关查验，实际出口水壶（商品编码7323930000）3780个，与申报不符，案值为人民币127.2万元。被罚原因为申报数目不符。根据《中华人民共和国海关行政处罚实施条例》第十五条（五）项、第十七条的规定，决定对当事人作出如下行政处罚：对该报关服务有限公司处以罚款12.7万元整；对企业A处以罚款19.7万元整。

出口企业必须向海关进行如实申报，谎报、瞒报、申报不实或者不申报都是不可取的。在向海关申报时，商品的品名及其对应的海关商品编码、规格型号、数量等必须与报关单、实际出口货物完全一致。表3.1列出了案例3.1中的电热水壶（商品编码8516799090）和水壶（商品编码7323930000）这两种商品在商品描述、申报要素、法定计量单位、进出口税率、海关监管条件、检验检疫、个人行邮税等方面的异同。其中，行邮税是行李和邮递物品进口税的简称，是海关对入境旅客行李物品和个人邮递物品征收的进口税。由于其中包含了进口环节的增值税和消费税，故也为对个人非贸易性入境物品征收的进口关税和进口工商税的总称。课税对象包括入境旅客、运输工具，服务人员携带的应税行李物品、个人邮递物品、馈赠物品以及其他方式入境的个人物品等。行邮税的征管工作是海关征税工作的重要组成部分，也是海关贯彻国家税收政策的一个重要方面——不断通过征收行邮税，对一些国（地区）内外差价较大的重点商品根据不同的监管对象予以必要和适当的调控。另外，GTIN（全球贸易项目代码）、CAS（化学物质登录码）的解释请见本章末的阅读材料。

表3.1 电热水壶和水壶的申报差别

| 商品编码 | 7323930000 | 8516799090 |
|---|---|---|
| 商品描述 | 餐桌、厨房等家用不锈钢器具<br>（包括零件、已搪瓷） | 其他电热器具<br>（电智能马桶盖除外） |
| 申报要素 | 0: 品牌类型<br>1: 出口享惠情况<br>2: 用途（厨房用、餐桌用等）<br>3: 材质（铁、非合金钢、不锈钢、合金钢）<br>4: 种类（水壶、煎锅等）<br>5: 加工方法（已搪瓷、未搪瓷）<br>6: 品牌<br>7: GTIN<br>8: CAS | 0: 品牌类型<br>1: 出口享惠情况<br>2: 用途<br>3: 加热原理<br>4: 品牌<br>5: 型号<br>6: GTIN<br>7: CAS |
| 法定第一计量单位 | 千克 | 个 |
| 法定第二计量单位 | 无 | 无 |
| 最惠国 | 7% | 7% |
| 进口普通 | 80% | 100% |
| 出口从价关税率 | 0% | 0% |
| 增值税率 | 16% | 16% |
| 退税率 | 9% | 16% |
| 消费税率 | – | – |
| 海关监管条件 | A（入境货物通关单） | A（入境货物通关单） |
| 检验检疫 | R/（进口食品卫生监督检验） | L/（入境民用商品认证） |
| 个人行邮（税号） | 11010200 | 无 |
| 行邮名称 | 炊具 | |
| 进口税税款 | 30% | |

　　签订国际货物买卖合同必须首先明确买卖合同的标的物，其内容包括商品的名称、质量、数量与包装。合同标的物的名称与质量不同，不仅商品的用途、运输方式、海关监管条件及其面临的技术性贸易措施不同，而且商品买卖需支付的关税、运输费用和成交价格等也很不相同。合同的标的物必须以一定的数量来表示，数量的约定是国际货物买卖合同不可缺少的内容，没有数量的国际货物买卖合同无法履行。同时，按照一些国家法律的规定，合同中有关包装的规定是构成商品说明的重要组成部分。国际贸易惯例Incoterms®2010也规定：除非在特定贸易中，某类货物的销售不需要包装，卖方必须自付费用包装货物。除非买方在签订合同时已通知卖方特殊包装要求，卖方可以采用适合该货物运输的方式对货物进行包装，包装应作适当标记。在国际贸易中，商品的包装

不容忽视。包装不仅是保护商品在流通过程中品质完好和数量完整的重要条件，而且还会对货物的运输和销售产生影响。因此，国际贸易商品的名称、质量、数量和包装的内容，是国际货物买卖合同的重要内容，必须事先做出明确的具体规定。

# 一、商品的名称及其规定方法

国际货物买卖的双方只有明确了商品的名称，即买卖什么商品，才能进一步确定商品的质量。商品的名称是国际货物买卖合同的基础，是国际货物买卖合同必须具备的内容。

## （一）商品的命名方法

商品的名称，简称"品名"，是指某种商品能区别于其他商品的一种称呼。商品的名称，在一定程度上体现了商品的自然属性、用途及主要的性能特征。加工程度较低的商品，名称一般较多反映商品的自然属性；加工程度较高的商品，名称较多体现出该商品的性能特征。一般说来，商品名称的规定方法有以下7种：①以主要用途命名。突出商品的用途，便于消费者按需购买，如茶叶、按摩仪、浴袍等。②以主要原材料命名。以生产商品所采用的主要原材料并结合主要用途来命名，如全棉布、羊绒衫、玻璃杯等。③以主要成分命名。以商品所含的主要成分命名，既有利于提高商品的价格，又便于消费者了解商品的内涵。适用于大众所熟知的名贵原材料制成的商品，如葡萄籽油、蜂王浆等。④以外观造型命名。有利于消费者从词义上了解该商品的特征，如连衣裤、高跟鞋等。⑤以描述商品的褒义词命名。突出商品的使用效能和特性，提高消费者的购买欲望，如青春宝、美白霜、养颜茶等。⑥以著名的人物、产地命名。突出产品的地方特色，引起消费者注意，如李维斯（Levis）牛仔裤、王老吉凉茶、西湖龙井、祁门红茶等。⑦以制作工艺命名。突出商品的制作工艺，提高商品的吸引力，增强消费者对该商品的信任，如手绘真丝围巾、石磨砂洗牛仔裤、蒸馏水、手工鞋等。

## （二）商品命名应注意的事项

商品名称必须明确、具体，适合商品的特点，避免含糊不清或过于空洞。在选用外文名称时，应做到翻译准确，尽可能使用国际上通用的名称。同一商品如采用不同的名称，其应缴纳的关税、运费和所受的进出口限制可能不同。为降低关税、方便进出口和节省运费，应选用合适的名称。商品名称应能高度概括商品特性，诱发消费者的购买欲望。为了区分不同厂商或销售商的同类产品，商品的名称可与品牌相融合，成为描述、说明货物的重要部分。

☞ **案例3.2**

茶是根据加工过程中的发酵程度不同来进行分类的：绿茶（green tea）的发酵

程度为 0，白茶（white tea）为 5%~10%，乌龙（oolong）为 10%~70%，普洱（Pu-erh）为 50%~80%，红茶（black tea）为 100%。

在销售与统计中，半发酵茶通常归在涵盖范围较大的"绿茶"项下。以 HS 编号为"0902109000"的"每件净重不超过 3 千克的绿茶"（未发酵的，净重指内包装）为例，其对应的法定计量单位为"千克"，增值税率为"10%"，出口退税税率为"6/16%"。绿茶进出口的海关监管条件为"AB"，检验检疫代码为"PR/S"。其中："A"代表入境货物通关单，"B"代表出境货物通关单，"P"代表进境动植物、动植物产品检疫，"R"代表进口食品卫生监督检验，"S"代表出口食品卫生监督检验。

# 二、商品的质量及其描述方法

商品的质量，简称"品质"，是商品的外观形态和内在质量的综合。外观形态包括商品的大小、长短、结构、造型、款式、色泽、光彩、宽窄、轻重、软硬、手感、味道、气味等。内在质量包括商品的物理性能、化学成分、生物特征、技术指标等，一般需借助各种仪器、设备分析测试才能获得，如纺织品的断裂强度、回潮率、缩水率、防雨性能、防火性能、色牢度，化工商品的熔点、沸点、凝固点，机械产品的精密度、光洁度、强度等。

商品质量的高低，不仅关系到商品的使用价值，还直接影响着商品在国际市场上的竞争力。买卖双方都非常重视商品质量，在签订国际货物买卖合同时，必须对商品的质量做出具体的规定。买卖合同中的"品质条款"内容，一般包括：品名、质量的表示方法、品质机动幅度或品质公差、品质增减价条款等。由于各国（地区）贸易摩擦的不断加剧，许多国家（地区）把提高商品质量作为鼓励出口、限制进口的贸易保护手段，提高商品质量也已成为许多生产厂商、销售商冲破质量壁垒、扩大出口的途径和方法。在国际贸易中，商品质量的规定方法多种多样，但归纳起来，主要分为两大类：一是商品质量用文字说明表示；二是商品质量以实物表示。

## （一）以文字说明表示品质

用文字说明表示商品的质量，具体可分为以下 6 种。

### 1．凭规格买卖

商品的规格是指用以反映商品质量的主要指标，如化学成分、含量、纯度、性能、尺寸等。商品不同，规格的内容也不同。用规格来确定商品品质的方法称为"凭规格买卖"。凭规格买卖在国际贸易中应用最广，例如：

①100% cotton denim, 7S × 7S, 140 & 44, width 58/59（全棉牛仔布，规格：经纬向均采用 7 支棉纱，经纬时密 140×44，门幅 58/59 英寸）。

②全棉男衬衣，款号 QWE1102，具体规格与买方 2020 年 12 月 20 日寄来的样品相

似，尺码搭配为XS：S：M：L：XL：XXL=1：2：3：3：2：1（Style No.QWE1102, 100% Men's shirt, detailed specifications are similar as the sample submitted by the buyer on Dec. 20, 2020. Size assortment is XS：S：M：L：XL：XXL=1：2：3：3：2：1）。

在国际市场上买卖有些农副产品时，有时还采用以下两种规格的表示方法。

①"良好平均品质"（fair average quality，简称FAQ），是指由同业公会或检验机构在一定时期或季节，从某地装船的各批货物中分别抽取少量实物加以混合拌制并由该机构封存保管，以此实物所显示的平均品质水平作为该季节同类商品品质的比较标准。良好平均品质的质量一般属于中等，习惯上称为"大路货"。例如：中国鱼粉，蛋白质含量55%以上，脂肪含量最高9%，水分最高11%，盐分最高4%，矿分最高4%（China Fish Meal, Protein 55% Min, Salt 4% Max, Moisture 11% Max, Sand 4% Max）。

②"上好可销品质"（good merchantable quality，GMQ），指卖方所交货物的质量应符合"品质上好，合乎商销"的标准。该标准涵含义模糊，一般不建议采用。

### 2．凭等级买卖

商品的等级是指同一类商品，按其质量、成分、性能、形状、重量等差异，用文字、数字或符号所做的分类。买卖双方对商品等级理解一致时，只需在合同中明确等级即可。但对于双方不熟悉的等级内容，则最好明确每一等级的具体规格。例如：水煮笋，一级品（Boiled Bamboo Shoot, first grade）。

### 3．凭标准买卖

标准是指商品规格的标准化。商品的标准一般由政府、标准化组织、行业团体、商品交易所等机构制定和公布。有些标准具有强制性，不符合标准的商品，一律不准进出口；有些标准不具有强制性，由买卖双方洽商时协商决定。例如：装饰布，日晒牢度4~5级，英国标准（upholstery fabrics, fastness of grade 4—5, British standard）。在国际贸易中，商品的质量标准可分为5类。

①企业标准，指生产企业所制定的标准。

②团体标准，如美国材料试验协会标准等。

③国家（地区）标准，指由国家（地区）指定的标准，如德国国家标准等；

④区域标准，指由区域标准化组织制定的标准，如欧洲标准化委员会制定的标准等。

⑤国际标准，指由国际性机构制定的标准，如国际标准化组织制定的标准。

应注意的是，有些已颁布的标准经常进行修改，因此在援引不同版本的国外标准时，必须标明版本年份。

### 4．凭商标或牌名买卖

对某些质量比较稳定，在市场上已树立了良好信誉的商品，买卖双方在交易洽商与签订合同时，可以这些商品的商标或牌名作为品质依据，如李宁牌跑步鞋（Lining jogging shoes）。当前，牌名或商标已成为强有力的促销手段。在凭牌名或商标买卖时，如同一牌名反映不同型号或规格的商品，须在合同中明确规定牌名或商标及商品型号或规格。因牌名、商标属工业产权，各国（地区）都制定了有关商标法加以保护。在凭牌名或商标买卖时，生产厂商或销售商应注意有关国家（地区）相关法律法规的规定，在进口国（地区）办理登记注册，维护商标专用权。

### 5．凭产地名称买卖

在国际货物买卖中，有些商品特别是农副产品，因产区自然条件、传统加工工艺等因素的影响，在品质方面具有其他产区的同类产品所没有的独特风格和特色。在出口这些产品时，可用产地名称来作为交货品质的依据，如景德镇陶瓷餐具（Jingdezhen ceramic dinner set）、绍兴花雕酒（Shaoxing Hua Tiao Chiew）。

### 6．凭说明书和图样买卖

机电、仪表等技术密集型商品，结构复杂，很难简单地以几项指标来表示品质的全貌，而必须详细说明其构造、用材、性能以及使用方法，必要时还要以图样、照片、分析表及各类数据等加以说明。例如：自行车，款号1205，红色，详细规格见所附文字说明和图样（Art No.1205 bicycle, red, detailed specifications are as per the attached descriptions and illustrations）。

## （二）以实物表示品质

凭实物表示品质，包括看货买卖（sale by actual quality）和凭样品买卖（sale by sample）。

### 1．看货买卖

看货买卖多用于寄售、拍卖和展卖业务。在看货买卖时，买方或其代理人通常先到卖方存放货物的场所验看货物。交易达成后，卖方必须交付验看过的货物。只要卖方交付的是验看过的商品，买方就不得对品质提出异议。

### 2．凭样品买卖

以样品表示商品品质并以此作为交货依据的买卖，称为"凭样品买卖"。样品是指从一批商品中抽取出来的，或由生产、使用部门设计、加工的，足以反映和代表整批商品品质的少量货物。按照样品提供者不同，凭样品成交可分为"凭卖方样品成交"（sale by seller's sample）和"凭买方样品成交"（sale by buyer's sample）。凭样品买卖时，卖方应注意以下事项。

①在凭卖方样品买卖时，卖方选取的样品应具有代表性，品质不应偏高或偏低。如果品质偏高，会造成交货困难；品质偏低，会影响交易达成和成交价格。卖方向外寄出原样（original sample）时，必须留存与原样品质一致的一份或数份复样（duplicate sample），以备日后交货或处理质量争议核对之用。原样和复样上应编上相同的号码，以便日后查找；对于复样应妥善保管，防止变质。特殊情况下，可采用封样（sealed sample），即抽出部分商品，在提供样品时由第三者（如公证机构）或会同买方共同加封，以防交货时复样有变。

②在凭买方样品买卖时，卖方最好制作对等样品。所谓"对等样品"，是指卖方按照买方提供的样品先做一个复制品交买方确认，经买方确认后，以该复制品作为今后交

付货物的品质依据。经确认的复制品，称为"对等样品"或"回样"。该做法，实际上是以卖方样品取代了买方样品，使卖方在交货时取得主动，避免因仿制产品与买方来样不符而招致买方索赔或退货。在凭买方样品成交时，卖方应注意防范侵权行为的发生，比如可在合同中加列保障条款。这样因买方来样而导致侵犯第三者权益，如专利、商标侵权，应由买方负责。

③如卖方寄送的样品不是用以"凭样买卖"，而是为了介绍产品，或是作为交货品质的部分参考（如颜色、花型、款式等），则应在寄送样品时明确"该样品仅供参考"（For reference only），以免与代表交货品质的样品相混淆。

④若今后交付的"货"与提供的"样"难以做到完全一致，应在合同中加列"品质与样品大致相同"（quality shall be about equal to the sample's）的条文，以争取主动。

### （三）条款签订应注意的事项

品质条款是买卖双方交接货物、解决纠纷的依据，是检验机构的检验依据，被称为合同的"奠基石"。按照《联合国国际货物销售合同公约》的规定，卖方所交货物的品质必须与合同规定相符。如果卖方交付的货物不符合合同约定的品质要求，买方有权要求损害赔偿，也可要求修理或交付替代货物，甚至拒收货物或撤销合同。

**1. 正确使用品质的各种表示方法**

质量的表示方法，应根据商品的特点或表示品质的惯例来决定。凡是能用一种方法表示品质的，就不宜用两种或两种以上的方法表示。如必须采用两种或两种以上的方法表示时，应在合同中做出明确的规定。特别应注意的是，凭样品买卖不能与凭规格、等级、标准等表示品质的方法混合使用。如果既凭样品又凭规格买卖，卖方交付的货物质量既要与样品一致又要与规格一致，履约时容易造成产生品质纠纷。同时，品质条款的文字描述应注意科学性、严密性、准确性，尽量避免采用"大约""左右"等词语。

**2. 善用品质机动幅度条款**

对于品质不易做到完全统一的商品，其质量规定要有一定的灵活性，可在合同中规定"品质机动幅度条款"。品质机动幅度的规定方法有：①运用"大约"（about，approximate）字样，如衬衫的规格可大致分特大（XL）、大（L）、中（M）、小（S）4种，每种规格按成交数量，大约按"1：2：2：1"的比例搭配生产；②规定范围，即对某种货物的品质指标规定，允许有一定的差异范围，如"色织牛仔布，门幅58/59英寸"；③规定极限，即对某种货物的品质规定"上限"或"下限"，如"花生的含水量最大不超过13%，含油量最小不低于44%"；④规定上下差异，如"湿度应保持在10% ~ 12%"。

如果货物的品质机动幅度或质量差异被国际所公认，该品质机动幅度称为"品质公差（tolerance）"或"质量公差"。这种误差是绝对的，不可避免的，如圆形产品的直径误差若干毫米，钟表每24小时的走时误差若干秒，等等。在品质机动幅度或品质公差内，一般不另行计算增减价。但是，有些货物如黄金、羊毛、生丝等，必须在合同规定品质加价或减价；另一些货物，经买卖双方同意，也可在合同中规定增减价条款。

# 三、商品的数量及其规定方法

商品的数量是国际货物买卖合同的主要交易条件之一。国际货物买卖合同中的数量条款的内容，一般包括成交商品的具体数量、计量单位。有些合同还需规定确定数量的方法，或卖方交付货物所允许的数量的溢短装条款。为了避免买卖双方日后的争议，合同中的数量条款应当完整准确，对计量单位的实际含义双方应理解一致。在采用对方习惯使用的计量单位时，应注意换算的准确性，以保证实际交货数量与合同数量一致。

在国际贸易中，成交数量一经约定，买卖双方必须按其规定交接货物。《联合国国际货物销售合同公约》规定："卖方必须按合同数量条款的规定如数交付货物。如果卖方交货数量多于约定数量，买方可以全部收取，也可以拒绝收取多交部分货物的全部或一部分；如果卖方实际交货数量少于约定数量，卖方应在规定的交货期届满前补交，但不得使买方遭受不合理的不便或承担不合理的开支，而买方保留要求损害赔偿的任何权利"因世界各国度量衡制度和贸易习惯做法不同，而国际贸易商品种类繁多，不同种类的商品往往采用不同的计量单位和计量方法。因此，买卖双方还应就计量单位和计量方法在合同中加以具体约定。

## （一）商品的计量方法与计量单位

### 1. 计量方法

国际贸易通常的计量方法有公制、英制、美制和国际单位制。各国采用的度量衡制度不同，同一计量单位所表示的商品实际数量也不同。中国采用公制和国际单位制（SI）。国际单位制是国际公认的计量体制。该制度适用7种基本单位、2种辅助单位，所有其他国际单位制均由此7种基本单位导出。中国出口的商品，除照顾对方国家（地区）贸易习惯约定采用公制、英制或美制计量单位外，应使用中国法定计量单位。对于中国进口的商品，应要求使用中国法定计量单位，否则一般不许进口。如有特殊需要，也必须经过有关标准计量管理部门批准。

### 2. 计量单位

国际贸易常用的计量单位有6种：（1）重量（weight），如公吨（metric ton，M/T）、长吨（long ton，L/T）、短吨（short ton，S/T）、千克（kilogram，kg）、磅（pound）、盎司（ounce,oz）等；（2）个数（number），如只（unit）、件（piece,pc）、双（pair）、打（dozen，doz）、罗（gross, gr）、令（ream, RM）、卷（roll, coil）、台或套（set）等；（3）长度（length），如米（meter, m）、英尺（foot, ft）、码（yard）等；（4）面积（area），如平方米（square meter, sqm）、平方英尺（square foot）、平方码（square yard）等；（5）体积（volume），如立方米（cubic meter）、立方英尺（cubic foot）、立方码（cubic yard）等；（6）容积（capacity），如升（litre）、加仑（gallon）、蒲式耳（bushel）等。

在国际贸易中，很多商品按重量计价。在具体业务中，计算重量的方法有下列几种。

（1）**毛重**

毛重（cross weight）是指商品重量加皮重（tare），适用于价值不高的商品。以毛重作为计价单位和交付货物的计量方法，称为"以毛作净"（gross for net）。但是，"以毛作净"应在合同中特别注明。例如：毛重5000公吨，以毛作净，以目的港卸货时重量为准（5,000 M/T，gross weight，gross for net as per landed weight at the port of destination）。

（2）**净重**

净重（net weight）是指商品本身的重量，不包括皮重。在国际贸易中，凡按重量计量的商品，大多数以净重作为计量单位。如合同中未明确规定用毛重还是净重计量、计价的，按惯例应以净重计。国际上计算皮重（包装重量）的方法有：a)按实际皮重（actual tare）计算，实际皮重是对包装逐件过秤后所得的每件包装的重量和所有包装的实际总重量；b)按平均皮重（average tare）计算，随意抽取部分商品，经过秤所得实际皮重，取其平均，再乘以总件数，算出全部皮重；c)按习惯皮重（customary tare）计算，比较规格化的包装，其重量已被公认，可不必过秤，按公认的重量计算；d)按约定皮重（computed tare）计算，即按双方约定的重量计算而不必过称。

（3）**公量**

在计算重量时，用科学仪器抽去商品中的水分，另加标准水分所得的重量称为公量（conditioned weight）。公量通常运用于价值较大，但水分含量极不稳定的商品，如羊毛、生丝、棉花等。公量 = 商品干净重 ×（1+公定回潮率），或者公量=商品净重 ×（1+公定回潮率）/（1+实际回潮率）

（4）**理论重量**

理论重量（theoretical weight）适用于具有固定规格、固定体积的商品。规格一致、体积相同的产品，每件重量也大致相同，如马口铁、规格钢板等。

（5）**法定重量和净净重**

法定重量（legal weight）和净净重（net net weight）是海关在征收从量关税时作为征税基础的重量。法定重量，是指纯商品的重量加上直接接触商品的包装材料（如内包装的重量）。而扣除内包装的重量及其他包含杂物的重量，即为净净重。

## （二）数量溢短装条款

大宗商品如玉米、黄豆、煤炭、矿砂等，成交数量大、不易精确计算，或因受自然条件、包装方式或运输条件的限制，卖方实际交货的数量往往很难符合合同规定的某一确定数量。为方便卖方履行合同，买卖双方可在合同中约定数量机动幅度。在合同中明确规定的数量机动幅度，一般称为"溢短装条款"（more or less clause），即规定允许卖方多装或少装若干数量或成交数量的一定百分比。实际业务中，数量机动幅度的规定方法大致有以下3种情况。

### 1. 在合同中明确规定数量机动幅度

对于允许多装或少装部分的数量，其选择权规定方法一般有3种：①由卖方选择（at seller's option）；②由买方选择（at buyer's option）；③由承运人选择（at carrier's option）。例如：中国大米3000公吨，溢短装2%，选择权归买方（China rice，3,000 metric tons with 2% more or less at buyer's option）。在数量机动幅度范围内，多装或少装的货物，一般都按合同价格计算货款。对于价格波动频繁、幅度较大的商品，为防止当事人利用机动幅度故意增加或减少数量以取得额外利益，可规定增减部分按装运时的市场价格计算。例如：数量1000公吨，为适应舱容需要，卖方有权多装或少装5%，超过或不足部分按合同价格计算（the seller has the option to load 5% more or less than the contracted quantity if is necessary for the purpose to meet the shipping space and each difference shall be settled at the contract price）。

### 2. 在合同中不明确规定数量机动幅度

如合同中未明确规定数量机动幅度，卖方交货数量原则上应与合同规定的数量完全一致。但是，如果是以信用证作为货款支付方式，根据《跟单信用证统一惯例》（UCP600）第三十条b款的规定：在信用证未以包装单位或货物自身件数的方式规定货物数量时，货物数量允许有5%的增减幅度，只要总支取的金额不超过信用证金额。但是，当货物数量是以包装单位或个数计数时，此项增减幅度规定则不适用。

### 3. 在合同数量前出现"约"或"大约"

合同中未明确规定数量机动幅度，但在合同数量前加上"约""大约"的交货数量可以有所机动。但是，因各国（地区）或不同行业对"约""大约"的理解和解释不尽相同，容易引起争议。根据UCP600第三十条a款之规定："约"或"大约"用于信用证金额或信用证所规定的数量或单价时，应解释为允许有关金额或数量或单价有不超过10%的增减幅度。

## 四、商品的包装

包装是商品的必需组成部分，也是商品价值的重要组成部分。按照某些国家或地区的法律法规，如卖方交付的货物未按约定进行包装，或者货物的包装与行业习惯不符，买方有权拒收货物。因此，应在合同中订明包装条款。国际货物买卖合同的包装条款，也是合同的重要贸易条件之一。包装条款内容主要包括包装种类、包装方式、包装材料、包装费用和运输标志等内容。

包装是保护商品在流通过程中数量完整和质量完好的重要措施，而设计新颖、美观、适用的销售包装，不仅能有效地保护商品，还可以起到美化商品、提高商品身价、宣传商品、吸引顾客、扩大销路等作用，增强商品在国际市场上的竞争力。包装在一定程度上反映一国（地区）的科学、文化和艺术发展水平。根据货物贸易价格统计，商品的包装费用一般占商品价格的6%～10%，某些特殊商品如法国香水等，其包装费用可达商品价格的70% ~ 80%。同时，包装可提高商品的附加值。比如中国出口的茶叶，用30千克规格的纸箱装，每公吨为1500美元；如改为铁听装后纸盒装，再箱装，价格将增加到1700美元/公吨，扣除包装材料成本增值依然很可观。

### （一）包装种类

按照商品是否需要包装，可分为散装货物（bulk cargo）和包装货物（packed cargo）。其中，散装货物毋需包装，可直接装于运输工具。散装货物多为不易包装、不值得包装或不需要包装的货物，如小麦、玉米、煤、矿砂及生铁等；包装货物是需经包装的货物，绝大多数的出口货物需加包装。货物的包装，按照包装用途分类，可分为运输包装和销售包装。运输包装又称外包装，它的主要作用是保护商品，便于运输。

**1. 运输包装及其要求**

运输包装可分为单件包装和集合运输包装。其中，集合运输包装是指将一定数量的单件包装组合成一件大的包装或装入一个大的包装容器内，如托盘（pallet）、集装袋（flexible container）和集装箱等。而单件运输包装的种类很多，分为：①箱（case）。如木箱（wooden case）、板条箱（crate）、纸箱（carton）、瓦楞纸箱（corrugated carton）和漏孔箱（skeleton case）等。②包（bundle，bale）。羽毛、羊毛、棉花、布匹和生丝等货物，可以先经机压打包，压缩体积，然后再以棉布、麻布包裹，外加塑料带，捆包成件。③袋（bag）。粉状、颗粒状和块状的农产品及化学原料，常用袋装。袋又可分为麻袋（gunny bag）、布袋（cloth bag）、塑料袋（plastic bag）、纸袋（paper bag）等。为加强包装牢度，现多采用纸塑复合、多层塑料复合和编织袋等。④桶（drum，cask）。液体、半液体以及粉状、粒状货物，可用桶装。桶有木桶（wooden cask）、铁桶（lron drum）、塑料桶（plastic cask）等。此外，运输包装还有瓶（bottle）、罐（can）、坛（demijohn，carboy）和篓（basket）、瓿（Jar）、钢瓶（cylinder）等。

因国际货物运输距离较长、中间环节较多，遭遇风险的可能性也较大。出口商品运输包装应符合下列要求：①坚固，包装结构要合理，能够充分保护商品品质的完好和数量的完整。②科学，应方便运输、装卸、储存、保管、清点和查验，并适合各种不同运输方式的要求。③适销，应充分考虑有关国家（地区）的法律法规或客户的要求，符合进口国（地区）有关法律法规的要求或客户的偏好。④经济，注意节约包装材料、节省运输费用。⑤标准化，运输包装的类型、规格、容量、材料、造型结构、印刷标志以及商品的放置、衬垫、封装方法、名词术语、检验要求等内容规定统一标准，作为各方共同遵守的技术依据。以统一材料、统一规格、统一容量、统一标志和统一封装方法为主。

**2. 销售包装及其要求**

销售包装（selling packing），又称小包装（small packing）、内包装（inner packing）或直接包装（immediate packing），是在商品制造出来以后以适当的材料或容器所进行的初次包装。有些商品如罐头食品，只有进行了销售包装，生产才真正完成。销售包装除了保护商品外，还有促进销售、提高商品价值的作用。销售包装按照包装材料不同，可分为纸制包装、金属包装、木制包装、塑料包装、麻制品包装、陶瓷包装、玻璃制品包装等。

### （二）包装方式与包装材料

合理的包装不仅能够保护货物在长时间和远距离的运输过程中不被损坏和散失，而且还可以方便货物的搬运、储运以及降低运输成本等。在国际运输中，一般以货物体积或重量计算运费。通过改变包装方式，往往可以缩小货物体积。改变包装材料或方法，可以降低包装材料或容器的重量，显著节省运费支出。例如，中国出口的某羽绒被原本是14条羽绒被装一纸箱，体积为0.3513立方米；采用真空包装袋，14条羽绒被只有0.181立方米，可减少运费近50%。另外，包装会影响客户对商品的信任。某些货物如包装不当，会导致商品在储运过程中质量下降或不方便外国（地区）运输，导致最终失去国外（地区）市场。例如：中国出口英国的某蜂蜜。原来用镀锌铁桶装，因内层涂料质量差，铁元素渗入蜂蜜中，导致金属含量偏高，从而失去英国市场；后改为黑铁皮桶加新型内层涂料，经检测金属含量合格，恢复了市场的信任。

包装材料与包装方式一般有2种规定方法：①明确规定包装方式及所用材料，包括用料、尺寸、大小、每件重量、包装数量以及填充物和加固条件等。例如"麻袋装，每袋净重60千克"（in gunny bags of 60 kg net each）。②采用某种包装术语，如"按习惯包装"（customary packing）、"适合海运包装"（seaworthy packing）、"卖方惯用包装"（seller's usual packing）等。这种规定方法内容不明确，各国（地区）理解不同，应避免使用；若非要使用，应明确规定使用何种材料。若包装材料由买方提供，必须在合同中就有关事宜做出明确的规定。

### （三）包装费用

假如合同中未明确说明包装费用归谁承担，则包装费用一般含在货价内。买方如对包装材料或包装形式有特殊要求，额外产生的费用应由买方承担，但须在合同中注明。例如，买方要求采用托盘包装。托盘是按一定规格形成的单层或双层平板载货工具，在平板上集装一定数量的单件货物后捆扎加固，组成一个运输单位，便于运输过程中使用机械进行装卸、搬运和堆存。托盘按结构不同，可分为平板托盘、箱形托盘和柱形托盘。采用托盘运输，运输单位增大，适合机械化操作。托盘包装有利于降低运输成本，因此托盘费用一般应由买方承担。

### （四）运输包装标志

运输包装标志是指为了方便货物运输、装卸及储存保管，便于识别货物和防止货物损坏，在商品外包装上刷写的标志。按其作用分为运输标志（shipping mark）、指示性标志（indicative mark）、警告性标志（warning mark）、其他标志和条形码等。买方如对运输标志没有特殊要求，可不列入合同，或只订明"卖方标志"，然后由卖方自行设计、刷制；若买方要求订立"买方标志"，应在合同中明确规定，卖方也可以接受。

### 1. 运输标志

运输标志俗称"唛头"，通常印刷在运输包装明显的部位，由一些字母、数字及简单的文字组成。运输标志内容应包括4个要素：（1）收货人或买方的名称字首或简称。（2）目的港或目的地名称。如货物运输的目的港或目的地有重名时，还应注明目的港或目的地所在国家或地区的名称；如货物在运输途中需经转运，还须标明转运地或转运港名称；（3）件号。每件货物的顺序号和总件数。（4）业务参考号。如合同号、发票号、信用证号、进口许可证号和货物的花色号、型号、色泽等。运输标志主要便于运输过程中的有关人员辨认货物、核对单证，避免货物在运输途中发生混乱或延误，从而使货物顺利和平安运抵目的地。

### 2. 指示性标志

指示性标志是根据商品的特性，对一些容易破碎、残损、变质的商品，在搬运装卸操作和存放保管方面将所提出的要求和注意事项用图形或文字表示的标志，如，"怕湿""向上""小心轻放"和"禁用手钩"等。为了统一各国(地区)运输包装中指示标志的图形与文字，国际标准化组织（ISO）、国际航空运输协会（IATA）和国际铁路货运会议（RID）等分别制定了包装储运指示性标志，并建议各会员国予以采纳。中国有专门的运输包装指示性标志国家标准，所用图形与国际上通用的图形基本一致。

### 3. 警告性标志

警告性标志又称危险品标志（dangerous cargo mark），是指在装有爆炸品、易燃物品、腐蚀物品、氧化剂和放射物质等危险货物的运输包装上，用图形或文字表示各种危险品的标志，目的是警告有关装卸、运输和保管环节的相关人员须按货物特性采取相应的措施，保障人身和物资的安全。为保证国际危险货物运输的安全，联合国、国际海事组织、国际铁路合作组织和国际民航组织分别制定了国际海上、铁路、航空危险货物运输规则。

### 4. 其他标志

除上述包装标志外，商品的运输包装上一般还刷上包件的毛重、净重、体积尺码和商品的生产国别或地区等，这些标志习惯上称作其他标志。许可证号、信用证号、型号、色泽等内容，有时构成运输标志的组成部分，有时作为其他标志的内容。其他标志一般刷印在外包装的非唛头部位的空白位置。

### 5. 条形码

商品包装上的条形码是国际通用的"身份证"，也可以说是国际市场的"入场券"。国际上通用的条形码标志有两种：①由美国、加拿大统一编码委员会（Universal Code Council，UCC）编制的UPC（universal product code）码。对于出口到北美地区的商品，必须申请使用UPC码。②欧共体的欧洲物品编码协会（European Article Number Association）负责编制的国际物品编码协会（International Article Number Association），其使用的物品标识符号为EAN（European article number）码。为了与国际市场接轨和进一步扩大出口，中国于1991年加入国际物品编码协会，该协会分配给中国的国别号为"690"，即凡是标有"690"条形码的商品都表示是中国出产的商品。

包装条款举例：①木箱装，每箱30匹，每匹40码（in wooden cases, each packing 30 pcs, piece length 40 yds）。②麻袋装，每袋净重60千克（in gunny bags of 60 kg net each）。③布袋装，内衬聚乙烯袋，每袋净重25千克（in cloth bags, lined with polythene bags of 25 kg net each）。④每台装1个出口纸箱，810纸箱装1只40英尺集装箱（each set packed in one export carton, 810 cartons in one 40 ft container）。⑤聚乙烯袋包装，每袋毛重25.2千克，净重25.0千克，40袋入一个塑料托盘，14个托盘装入1只20英尺集装箱。塑料托盘费用（每只9.0美元）由买方承担（In polythene bags, each bag with gross weight 25.2 kg, net weight 25.0 kg. 40 bags to be packed in one plastic pallets, 14 pallets in one 20' fcl. Plastic pallets (each unit price USD9.0) are charged at the buyer's account.）。

目前，国际市场竞争日趋激烈，各国（地区）都把改进出口商品包装作为加强对外销售的重要手段。良好的包装，不仅可以保护商品的质量完好和数量完整，便于商品的贮存、保管、装卸、搬运和销售，而且美观的销售包装，还能美化、宣传商品，提高商品身价，吸引顾客，扩大销路和增加售价。因此，出口商品包装用料和设计方面应力求达到科学、经济、牢固、美观、适销等要求。同时，包装设计应考虑贸易国家（地区）的风俗习惯。例如，商品包装设计上如出现六角星图案，会遭到阿拉伯国家的强力反对，原因是六角星图案与以色列国旗图案相似；而出口伊斯兰教国家的商品包装上如出现"+"及其变形的"×"图形，将遭到不满，因其与基督教十字架相似。

☞ 阅读材料

# GTIN和CAS

2017年9月20日，中国海关更新EDI（电子数据交换）系统，要求对每个税号的规范申报新增两项要素，分别为GTIN号（全球贸易项目代码，global trade item number)和CAS号（美国化学文摘服务社为化学物质制定的登记号，the registry number of chemical abstracts service）。即日起，进出口企业需同时提供这两个申报要素。如实际没有，需填报"无GTIN""无CAS"。

GTIN为条形码，即全球贸易项目代码。GTIN被用作识别商品品项的全球性独一编码，是编码系统中应用最广泛的标识代码。GTIN有4种不同的代码结构：GTIN-14、GTIN-13（原称EAN-13）、GTIN-12（原称UPC-12）和GTIN-8（原称EAN-8）。每一个标识代码必须以整体方式使用，完整的标识代码可以保证在相关的应用领域内全球唯一。其中，GTIN-14是非零售商品标识代码，而GTIN-13、GTIN-12、GTIN-8是零售商品标识代码。

GTIN是EAN/UCC-14代码结构，对应ITF-14条码。它的编码规则是单品的EAN/UCC-13代码加包装指示符。例如，某商品的UPC（universal product code）

是812751008507，第一步要先变成EAN-13代码，方法是直接在前面加1位数字0，这样产品的EAN代码就是0 812751 008507。如果同种产品有不同的包装形式，其外箱条码可在EAN-13的基础上，前面再加1位包装指示符，就可用以区别不同的包装级别（大箱套小箱）、不同的包装类型（纸箱、塑料箱），或不同的包装数量（20件一箱、40件一箱）。包装指示的数字可以用1—8。例如，小箱的代码是1 081275 00850 4，大箱的代码为2 081275 00850 1，4和1是校验码，因第一位数字有变化，所以校验码也要改变。

CAS为化学物质登录码，简称化学码。CAS号（CAS registry number或称CAS number, CAS rn, CAS #），又称CAS登录号，是某种物质（化合物、高分子材料、生物序列、混合物或合金）的唯一的数字识别号码。美国化学会下设的组织化学文摘服务社负责为每一种出现在文献中的物质分配一个CAS号，其目的是避免化学物质有多种名称的麻烦，使数据库的检索更为方便。如今几乎所有的化学数据库都允许用CAS号检索。到2012年1月20日，CAS已经登记了64944800余种物质的最新数据，并且以每天4000余种的速度增加。

## 思考题

1. 中国某制鞋企业按照意大利客户来样，与该客户签订了一份买卖10000双鞋子的销售合同。但卖方在采购原材料时突然发现，客户来样的鞋底是采用高科技材料制作的，目前中国国内还无法生产，必须从国外进口，但进口成本较高。卖方如采用进口材料生产必然面临亏损。试问，卖方从本案例中应得到怎样的教训？

2. 中国某出口企业对外成交自行车300辆，合同规定：黄、红、蓝色各100辆，不得分批装运。出口企业发货时，发现黄色只有95辆，而红色、蓝色的货源充足。因考虑到黄色缺口数量不大，出口企业便以黄色95辆、红色105辆、蓝色100辆，合计300辆装运出口。请问，出口企业是否会遭到买方的索赔？

3. 请根据所学的国际贸易商品知识，包括如何描述商品的品名、质量、数量和包装等知识，从跨境电商中选择一个具体的案例，分析该跨境电商案例在产品标题、质量、包装等方面描述的成功之处和存在的问题。

# Chapter 3

# The Subject Matter to a Sales Contract

☞ Case 3.1

United States President Donald Trump has signed an order calling for up to $250 billion in new tariffs on Chinese imports. The order seeks to punish China for intellectual property, including inventions and research. The action also calls for restrictions on the transfer of technology to China. Robert Lighthizer, the U.S. Trade Representative, said that intellectual property is an important part of the trade problem with China. The intellectual property is really the biggest advantage of the American economy. Trump blamed the trade imbalance between the two countries for the loss of American jobs and that is the largest deficit of any country in the history of our world. The largest deficit of China's trade surplus with the U.S. in 2017 was about $375 billion. Trump said that with the increased tariffs, he hopes to cut the trade deficit with China by $100 billion. The U.S. trade office was directed to publish a list of proposed tariffs for public comment. The Treasury department is also come up with a list of restrictions on Chinese investment. China warned to take all necessary measures to defend. The actions raised the possibility of a trade war between the two biggest economies and sent global stock markets lower.

Chinese officials said that the US trade deficit with China is the result of US trade policy. China officials note that the US bars the export of many high-technology products. Chinese Foreign Ministry spokes woman, Hua Chunying said that the products traded have unequal values. She said: "How many soybeans should China buy that are equal to one Boeing aircraft? Or, US agriculture exports to China are almost $20 billion? Or, if China buys a certain number of Boeing aircrafts should the U.S. buy an equal number of C919 (Chinese aircraft)?" Boeing has said it expects China to buy aircraft worth $1.1 trillion by 2036. But China is also developing its own C919 passenger plane. American businesses, including Walmart, Apple, and other technology companies, also oppose a trade conflict. Some American experts think that tariffs will raise the price of goods, hurt jobs and financial market in the short term, but, if such a policy could get China to reduce its barriers to trade, American buyers and businesses would gain and increased trade would also be good for China. Trump said the action would be "one of many". The U.S. recently placed tariffs of 25 percent on steel and 10 percent on aluminum imports.

Some countries, including Canada, Mexico, are not subject to the new taxes.

The focus of Sino-US trade conflict is on trade in goods. The subject matter is the primary consideration of a sales contract. It contains name of the goods and its quality, quantity and packing. Different names of the goods and its quality associate with different functions of the goods, mode of transport, supervision requirement of customs clearance as well as trade policies, different tariffs, carriage charges, transaction value, etc. The subject matter must be indicated by a certain quantity. Quantity of the goods is also one of main terms and conditions of a sales contract. A sales contract cannot be fulfilled without quantity. In addition, the stipulation of packing is important for description of the goods according to the laws and regulations of some certain countries or regions. The package of the goods should not be neglected in international trade. The package is not only important for keeping the goods in good condition and full quantity in circulating, but also influencing on transportation and sales. So, the name of the goods, quality, quantity, and packing are main terms and conditions of a sales contract and must be definitely stipulated in the contract.

# 3.1 Name of the Goods

The parties shall firstly make it clear the name of goods or what to sell/buy, and then state quality of the goods definitely. Name of the goods is the basic condition of a sales contract. It is concerning natural properties, features, and functions of the goods. Generally, the low processing goods are named by their natural properties; the high processing goods are named by their features.

The goods can be named by the following ways:

① Named by primary use, such as tea, massage chair, bathrobe, seed oil, royal jelly.

② Named by raw materials, such as 100% silk bathrobe, flower tea, leather massage chair.

③ Named by main composition, such as grape seed oil, ginseng antler royal jelly.

④ Named by design and appearance, such as one-piece suit, high heeled shoes.

⑤ Named by commendatory terms, such as eight-treasure tea, fashion high heel shoes.

⑥ Named by celebrity or place of origin, such as Levis jean, Qimen Black Tea.

⑦ Named by manufacturing techniques, such as stone and wash jeans, handmade shoes.

Name of the goods should be definite, specific, and suitable. It should avoid any possible ambiguity and vacuous description. It is best to use the popular names in the world.

Each kind of commodity is corresponding to one HS Ccde (Harmonization System code) only. HS code is drafted by International Customs Council and includes 22 categories and 98 chapters. The most popular HS Code consists of two-level codes, four-level codes and six-level codes. Each country or region can set an HS Code to more than 6 level and associat it with the commodity by itself. In addition, each country or region can also set some certain supervision requirements of customs clearance and legal unit of measurement, tariff, value-added tax (VAT) rate, export tax-rebating rate, etc.

If a kind of goods uses different names, the relating tariff, carriage charges, and restrictions of import and export may be different. The goods should be called by an appropriate name with characteristics in order to arouse the purchaser's desire. Name of the goods may be well integrated with the brand name and become a main part of description of the goods.

☞ Case 3.2

## Green Tea and Its Lmport & Export Requirements

As per the degree of ferment, tea can be divided into several kinds. The fermented degree of green tea is 0, of white tea is 5%—10%, Oolong 10%—70%, Pu-erh50%—80%, and black tea 100%. If the fermented degree is lower than 50%, the tea is generally classed as green tea in sales and statistics.

Table 3.1 shows the relative information of China's import and export of green tea. Green tea falls into the list of products to statutory inspection. Supervision requirements of customs clearance, and inspection and quarantine for green tea include:

A. Import Customs Declaration Form

B. Export Customs Declaration Form

R. Hygienic supervision and inspection of import food

S. Hygienic supervision and inspection of export food

P. Quarantine of import animals, plants, and animal products

Table 3.1 Information for China's Import and Export of Green Tea

| HS Code | 0902109000 |
|---|---|
| Description of the Goods | Other green tea (not fermented) in immediate packings of a content not exceeding 3 kg |
| Elements for Customs Declaration | 1. Export preferential situation<br>2. Production or preservation methods (unfermented, semi-fermented, fermented)<br>3. Net weight of each package<br>4. Brand<br>5. GTIN (Global trade item number)<br>6. CAS(Chemical Abstracts Service) |
| Legal First Unit | Kilo |
| Legal Second Unit | / |
| Most Favorite Nation Tariff | 15% |
| Import Ordinary Tariff | 100% |
| Export AD Valorem Tariff | 0% |
| Value Added Taxes (VAT) | 10% |
| Tax Rebate Rate | 6/16% |
| Goods and Service Tax | — |
| Customs Supervision Conditions | AB |
| Inspection and Quarantine | PR/S |
| Passengers and Personal Postal Article (tax code) | 01020100 |

Tax of passengers and personal postal articles is the abbreviation of the import duty on luggage and postal articles. It is the import duty levied by the customs on the luggage and personal postal articles of inbound passengers. Because it includes the value-added tax and consumption tax of the import link, it is also the general name of the import tariff and import industrial and commercial tax levied on individual non-tradable entry articles. The objects of taxation include inbound passengers, means of transport, dutiable luggage and articles carried by service personnel, personal postal articles, gift articles, and other personal articles entering the country or region by other means. The collection and administration of tax of passengers and personal postal articles is an important part of work of the customs, as well as an important aspect of the implementation of national tax policies by the customs. It is necessary that the appropriate regulation should be given to some key commodities with large price difference at home and abroad according to different regulatory objects.

GTIN refers to global trade items code. GTIN is the most widely used identification code in the coding system. There are four different code structures for GTIN, namely GTIN-14, GTIN-13 (formerly EAN-13), GTIN-12 (formerly UPC-12), and GTIN-8 (formerly EAN-8), and each identity code must be used as a whole. A complete identification code ensures global uniqueness in the relevant application domain. Among them, GTIN-14 is the identification code of non-retail commodities, while GTIN-13, GTIN-12 and GTIN-8 are the identification codes of retail commodities.

The Chemical Abstracts Service (CAS) under the American Chemical Society is responsible for assigning a CAS number to each substance that appears in the literature. The purpose is to avoid the trouble of Chemical substances having multiple names and make the retrieval of the database more convenient. CAS numbers are now allowed in almost all chemical databases. As of January 20, 2012, CAS had registered the latest data of 64,944,800 substances, and the number was increasing at the rate of 4,000 substances per day.

# 3.2 Quality of the Goods

Quality refers to the outward appearance and the essential inherent quality of the commodities, such as shape, structure, color, flavor as well as chemical composition, physical and mechanical properties, biological feature. It is the self-evidence that the commodity with superior quality always enjoys a good market. The quality of the goods is one of main trade terms in a sales contract. The quality clause is the cornerstone of a sales contract and becomes the basic condition for delivery of the goods. The quality clause always consists of name of the goods, description of the quality, quality difference allowed or quality tolerance and adjustment clause relating to price & quality difference. Sale by description of the goods and Sale by the physical commodity are the two main ways to describe quality of the goods.

## 3.2.1 Sale by Description of the Goods

There are six ways to describe quality of the goods in words.

**1. Sale by Specification**

Specification refers to the main indicators reflect quality, such as chemical composition, contents, purity, performance, size. Different commodities use different specifications to describe the quality. Sale by specification is widely used in international trade. For example:

① 100% cotton denim, 7S×7S, 140 & 44, width 58/59.

② Style No.QWE110, 100% cotton men's shirt. The detailed specifications are similar as those of the sample submitted by the buyer on Dec. 20, 2020. Size assortment as XS ∶ S ∶ M ∶ L ∶ XL ∶ XXL=1 ∶ 2 ∶ 3 ∶ 3 ∶ 2 ∶ 1.

Quality of agricultural products can be described as fair average quality (FAQ), or good merchantable quality (GMQ), such as China fish meal protein 55% min, moisture 11% max, salt 4% max, sand 4% max.

**2. Sale by Grade**

Grade refers to classification of a certain kind of goods be, which can further divided into categories as per quality difference, such as composition, performance, shape, weight. and be described in words, figures or symbols. It is suggested and better to define the grade of the goods and their specifications in details in a sales contract unless the parties fully understan the grade.

**3. Sale by Standard**

Standard refers to the standardization of the goods specifications. The standards of the goods are generally drawn up and announced by government, organization for standardization, industry organization, commodity exchange, etc. Standard can be divided into compulsory standards and commendatory standards. The compulsory standards must be complied with. The goods aren't permitted to export if it can't meet the requirements of the compulsory standards. The commendatory standard isn't legally binding or enforceable and may be adopted by the parties after negotiation. Standard can also be divided into five kinds: ①enterprise standard, ②community standard, ③national standard, ④regional standard, and ⑤ international standard. Some announced standard is constantly updated. The adopted standard should make clear the version year if it has different versions. For example: upholstery fabrics, color fastness 4—5 grade, British standard.

## ☞ Case 3.3

### Standard of Fresh Cutting Flowers

Cutting flowers is the main kind of flowers trade. The famous standards for cutting flowers include standard of the Economic Commission for Europe (ECE), standard of American Flower Association (SAF), Netherlands norm, and Japanese standard.

(1) ECE: Quality of the flower products, traded between European countries or regions is controlled by ECE. ECE divideds the flowers into three grades: special grade, first grade, and second grade. The cutting flowers with special grade must have the best quality, clear characteristics and without any flaw, plant diseases or insect pests impact on outward appearance. Only 3% of special grade, 5% of first grade and 10% of second grade of cutting flowers are allowed to have slight defect.

(2) SAF: The classification principal of SAF is the same as ECE. SAF pays more attention on the appearance qualities, such as the stems' length and strength, the petals and paddles' color.

(3) Netherlands norm: As the international center of flower producing and trade, besides the performance standard of ECE, Netherland is the most comprehensive nation for assessments of flower quality and pays more attention on inherent quality, such as entertain period, transport features.

(4) Japanese standard: Japan is a major consumer of fresh cutting flower and attaches great importance to quality grades of cutting flower. It takes three years for the Horticulture Bureau of Farming and Mulberry Silk, Ministry of Agriculture, Forestry and Fisheries of Japan to promulgate 13 kinds of quality standards of cutting flowers including Chinese rose, lily, carnation, chrysanthemum, tulip, etc.

### 4. Sale by Trademark or Brand

The goods can be sold by trademark or brand if it owns consistent quality and good reputation in the market, such as Nike brand jogging shoes. The trademark or the brand name becomes the most powerful sales promotion. If different styles or designs of the goods adopt the same brand name or trademark, the design/style of the goods and its associations with brand name/trademark should be stipulated in the contract. As brand name/trademark belongs to industry property rights and is governed by national laws, the manufacturers or the seller shall notice the stipulating of national laws or regional regulations relating to industry property rights. The trademark should be registered in the importing country or region first for the protection of exclusive rights in trademarks.

### 5. Sale by Name of Origin

Some goods especially the agricultural product own unique characteristics/features as to nature condition of origin place and traditional processing technology. The name of origin can be acted as the evidence of the seller's delivery, such as Jingdezhen Ceramic dinner set and Shaoxing Chiew. Geographical indication of agricultural products is an issue of universal concern in the world as protection of agricultural intellectual properties and promotion of agriculture trade. According to the Trips Agreement, geographical indications (GI) fall into the categories of intellectual property as copyrights, trademarks, patents, and industrial designs. Geographical indications refer to quality, reputation, and other characteristics of the goods manifested which are essentially attributable to its geographical origin. GI protection is divided into protection of designations of origin (PDO) and protection of geographical indications (PGI). China Regulation of Geographical Indications Protection was enforced from 2005. From July, 2005 to Dec, 31, 2012, totally 918 of China products had been registered GI in China. Sichuan was the top 1 with 144 GI products (http://kjs.aqsiq.gov.cn/dlbzcpbhwz/bhml/201208/t20120821_229293.htm.).

**6. Sale by Description and Illustrations**

The quality of technology-intensive products such as technological instruments and electric machine can't be described fully by some certain indicators. The structures, materials, performances and usage should be stated in detail and in case of need use pattern, photography, schedule and data for the supplementary explanation. For example: Art No.1201 bicycle, red, detail specifications are as per the attached description and illustrations.

## 3.2.2 Sale by the Physical Commodity

The quality reflected by the physical commodity can be divided into sale by inspection and sale by sample. Sale by inspection is always used under consignment, auction, and exhibition sales. The buyer or its nominated representatives shall go to the storage place and inspect the goods first. The seller must deliver the goods inspected after transaction concluded. If the seller delivers the goods inspected by the buyer, no discrepancy should be raised by the buyer.

A business with the quality reflected by a certain sample and acting as the delivery evidence is called as sale by sample. A sample is a piece of representing goods selected out from a shipment, or designed and produced by the concerned party specially, and can reflect the quality of the goods. If the provider of sample is the seller, the business is called as sale by the seller's sample. If the provider of sample is the buyer, the business is called as sale by the buyer's sample.

Under sale by the seller's sample, the representing sample is as original sample or standard sample and shall be of moderate quality among a large quantity of the actual commodities. The seller shall guatrantee samples of the same quality as the sample given to the buyer. The dispatched sample and the kept sample shall be sealed and marked with the same item code or article number, and handed for quality disputes or future delivery and verification. If the sample is provided by the buyer, the seller is better to consider first the availability of materials and the possibility of providing the processing technology and to make a return sample for the buyer's confirmation. If the return sample is confirmed by the buyer, the business is changed from sale by the buyer's sample to sale by the seller's counter-sample. In addition, the seller shall notice the property right relating to the buyer's sample.

## 3.2.3 Notices to the Quality Clauses

Quality clauses is acted as the cornerstone of a sales contract and becomes the evidence of delivery of the goods for the seller, taking of delivery for the buyer as well as for the inspection authorities. According to the United Nations Convention on the International Sale of Goods, the quality of the goods that the seller delivered must be in conformity with the stipulating in the contract. Whereas, the buyer may be entitled to claim compensation, or require the seller to repair or deliver the substitute goods, or refuse to take delivery of the goods, or decide upon cancellation of the contract.

Quality of the goods shall be stipulated as per the features of goods or practice of quality described. The stipulating of quality shall be definite, clear, and described by one way. It should be avoided to combine sale by sample and sale by specification, grade or standard together. Otherwise, the quality must be in conformity with the sample and description simultaneously, and then disputes will arouse. Description of the quality shall be scientific, strict, normal, and accurate, and avoid using words like "approximately" "bout", etc.

When a sales contract is based on sale by sample, it is necessary to indicate the number of sample and the date of dispatch. Normally, the quality for delivery of the goods shall be strictly the same as that of the sample. If the sample is just for introduction of the goods or as the reference of the goods' part of quality such as color, design or style, it should be stated as "for reference only" or "the sample No... just for color reference". If quality of the goods is difficult to totally conform to the sample provided, it should be stated in the contract "quality is similar to the sample submitted by the seller on… (date)", or "the goods to be delivered shall be about equal to the Seller's sample No..."

If the quality is hard to realize completely, a suitable quality difference can be stipulated in the contract to retain certain flexibility. The quality difference is called as "quality tolerance" if it is internationally recognized. The price of goods would not be increased or decreased within the range of quality difference or quality tolerance except for the goods with high value, such as gold, wool, silk. Some certain goods can be set in price adjustment in the contract.

# 3.3 Quantity of the Goods

Quantity of the goods is also one of main trade terms in a sales contract. The content of quantity clause always includes specific volume of the goods and the calculating unit. Some contracts need to be stipulated in how to determine the volume or the more or less clauses allowed for the seller. In order to avoid any disputes relating to quantity, the quantity clause shall be complete in accuracy and the calculating unit shall be consistently understood by the parties. If the buyer's customary calculating unit is applicable, correct converting should be noticed and necessary.

The seller must deliver the quantity of the goods as per the contract stipulated. Articles 51 and 52 of United Nations Convention on Contracts for the International Sale of Goods stipulates "If the seller delivers only a part of the goods or if only a part of the goods delivered is in conformity with the contract, articles 46 to 50 apply in respect of the part which is missing or which does not conform. The buyer may declare the contract avoided in its entirety only if the failure to make delivery completely or in conformity with the contract amounts to a fundamental breach of the contract. If the seller delivers a quantity of the goods greater than that provided for in the contract, the buyer may take delivery or refuse to take delivery of the excess quantity. If the buyer takes delivery of all or part of the excess quantity, he must pay for it at the contract rate." The parties are recommended to agree on a specific calculating unit and a method of measurement from different measure systems, different customaries for foreign trade as well as varieties of products.

## ☞ Case 3.4

A Jewish merchant signed a contract and would export 30,000 knives and forks to Chicago, the USA. The arriving date should be on/before Sept 1. It meant that the goods should be shipped on board the vessel at the port of shipment on/before Aug 01, so that the goods could  arrive at the port of destination on time. Due to a production accident, the Jewish merchant could only ship 20,000 knives and forks on/before Aug 1. While, without hesitation, he shipped 20,000 knives and forks on/before Aug 1 firstly. Then, he shipped the balance goods by air later. Finally, all of the goods arrived at Chicago on time and the Jewish merchant lost USD10,000 of air-freight costs. As per Jewish traditional laws, it is justified to keep a contract.

### 3.3.1 Methods of Measurement

The popular methods of measurement are including metric system, British system, American system, and international system. China adopts international system. It owns seven basic units and two auxiliary units. Other units can be exported by the seven basic units. Besides the buyer's customary measures such as metric system, British system or American system, the legal measures of China are applicable for China's exportation, China's importation shall use legal measures of China except for the special needs that are approved by the concerning administration.

### 3.3.2 Measure Unit

Six kinds of measure units are commonly used in international trade, which includ: ①Weight, such as metric ton, long ton, short ton, kilogram, pound, ounce. Table 3.2 shows how to convert between different weight units.②Number, such as unit, piece, pair, dozen, gross, ream, roll, coil, set.③Length, such as meter, foot, yard.④Area, such as square meter, square foot, square yard.⑤ Volume, such as cubic meter, cubic foot, cubic yard.⑥ capacity, such as liter, gallon, and bushel.

Table 3.2 Common Conversion Between Different Weight Units

|  | Kilograms | Pounds |
|---|---|---|
| Metric system—Metric ton | 1,000.0 | 2,204.6 |
| British system—Long ton | 1,016.0 | 2,240.0 |
| American system—Short ton | 907.2 | 2,000.0 |
| Remarks: 1 pound=453.6 grams, 1 ounce =28.3 grams | | |

Many of commodities are calculated as per weight. The methods of calculating weight can be divided into gross weight, net weight, conditioned weight, theoretical weight, legal weight, and net net weight. Gross weight refers to the merchandise's own weight plus tare and suitable for low-value goods. "Gross for net" is used if the goods are priced by gross weight and shall be specially expressed in the contract. For example: 5,000 M/T, gross weight gross for net as per the landed weight at the port of destination. Net weight refers to the merchandise's own weight excluding tare. Normally, the goods are priced according to the net weight. Tare can be calculated as per the actual tare, average tare, customary tare, and computed tare. Conditioned weight refers to the weight of the goods extracted moisture firstly and then plus air dry moisture regain. It is suitable for the high-value goods but with unstable moisture, such as wool, silk, and cotton. Theoretical weight is suitable for the goods with fixed specification and volume, such as tin plate, steel with same type. Legal weight and net net weight are the weight for the use of the levy on ad valorem tariff. The legal weight is the pure weight of commodity plus weight of inner packing in direct contact with the commodity. Net net weight is the weight of commodity excluding any inner packing and other stuff.

### 3.3.3 More or Less Clauses

Sometimes, the quantity of the goods that the seller delivers, especially bulk cargo such as maize, soybeans, coal, and ore, is very difficult to be in conformity with the specific volume stipulated in the contract as the restrictions of great quantities, precisely calculating, nature conditions, packing method or transportation, etc.

To fulfill the contract conveniently, a certain of quantity difference allowed (usually called "more or less clauses") can be stipulated in the contract by the parties. It means that the seller is allowed to ship the goods within the scale of a specific volume or percentage more or less than the basic volume stipulated. For example: China rice, 3,000 metric tons with 2% more or less at the buyer's option. The quantity that the Seller shipped more or less can be stipulated as: ① at the seller's option; ② at the buyer's option; ③ at the carrier's option.

The more or less shipped goods are usually calculated as per the contractual price. For example: the seller has the option to load 5% more or less than the contracted quantity. If it is necessary for the purpose to meet the shipping space, each difference shall be settled at the contract price. If the price of the goods is frequently and horrificly fluctuating, the more or less shipped goods can be calculated as per the current market price.

If a sales contract does not stipulate more or less clause on quantity of the goods, it means that the seller shall deliver the goods as per the contract stipulated on principal. However, if the contract stipulates terms of payment as letter of credit, Article 30 b of UCP600 stipulates: A tolerance not to exceed 5% more or 5% less than the quantity of the goods is allowed, provided the credit does not state the quantity in terms of a stipulated number of packing units or individual items and the total amount of the drawing does not exceed the amount of the credit.

If a sales contract stipulates quantity of the goods connecting with about or approximate such as "about 1,000 PCS", a certain quantity difference is allowed for delivery but may with different understandings. Article 30a of UCP600 stipulates: The words "about" or "Approximately" used in connection with the amount of The credit or the quantity or the unit price stated in the credit are to be construed as allowing a tolerance not to exceed 10% more or 10% less than the amount.

## 3.4 Packing of the Goods

Packing is not only necessary as a part of the goods, but also very important for the goods value. As per the legal regulations of some countries or regions, the buyer has the right to refuse taking delivery if the goods orent packed by the seller as per the stipulating of the contract or the package isn't in conformity with trade custom. In addition, the packing design shall consider the traditions and customs of the importing place. Packing clauses shall be stipulated in the contract and also become one of the main trade terms.

The contents of packing clause include kinds of packing, method of packing, packing materials, packing charges, packing marks, etc. Packing is very important to keep the goods in good condition during circulation. Packing with novel and beautiful design can not only protect the goods, but also beautify the goods, improve goods value, publicitize goods, attract customers, broaden sales as well as increase competitiveness of international market.

Packing also demonstrates development of national science, culture, and art to a certain degree. Normally, the packing charge is about 6%—10% of unit price.The packing of some of special commodities like French perfume costs 70%—80% of the unit price.

☞ Case 3.5

A Japanese buyer refused to take delivery of the golf balls imported from China as the goods were packed into boxes with 4 pieces each. "4" is the taboo number of Japanese and regarded as ominous. Although some Chinese don't like the figure "4", 4 pcs in packing is thought as normal. There are two reasons why the golf balls were rejected by the buyer. The first was the seller didn't pack the goods as per the stipulation in the contract or the parties didn't share an understanding of packing. The second was the seller didn't consider the traditions and customs of the importing country.

### 3.4.1 Kinds of Packing

As per packing condition, the goods are divided into bulk cargo and packed cargo. The bulk cargo is without any packing and loaded on the transport tools directly, including maize, wheat, coal, ore, etc. The packing of bulk cargoes is normally inadvisable, unworthy, and unnecessary. Most of exporting commodities are packed cargo. The packing is including transporting package (outer packing) and marketing package (inner packing) as per classification by use.

The transporting package is divided into single packing and collective packing. The collective packing is built up from some certain single packages and becomes a big package or put into a big packaging like pallet and container. As per the packing materials and methods of packing, the single packing includes case (wooden case, crate, carton, corrugated carton, skeleton case, etc.), bundle, bale, bag (gunny bag, cloth bag, plastic bag, paper bag, etc.), drum, cask (wooden cask, iron drum, plastic cask), bottle, can, Demijohn, carboy, basket, jar, cylinder, etc. Either single packing or collective packing, the package must be strong, scientific, marketable, economical, and standarded.

The sales package is also called small packing, inner packing or immediate packing. It shall be easy to display, exhibit, distinguish, carry, and use, and owns artistic attraction as well as being in conformity with the religion, habits, and customs of the importing country (region). The description of the sales package shall not be against the regulations on the labeling administration. More and more countries or regions require the importing goods to be marked with place of origin. The usual inner package for sales promotion includes hanging packing, stacking packing, portable packing, packing for one time, easy open packing, aerosol packing, conveyance packing, and gift-wrap packing.

## 3.4.2 Methods of Packing and Materials of Packing

Reasonable packing can protect the goods in good condition during long time and far-distance transportation, is convenient to carry, store, and decreases freight costs. The freight is generally calculated as per the measurement or weight of the goods. Sometimes changes in packing can save transport costs. To change method of packing can help to reduce or lessen the packing size, and to change materials of packing can decrease the weight of package. For example, if the eiderdown quilts for exportation are packed in cartons, each carton 14 PCS, the measurement of carton is 0.3513CBM. If the eiderdown quilts are packed in vacuum bags, the measurement of 14PCS is 0.181CBM. So the eiderdown quilts packed in vacuum bags can save about 50% of transport cost, compared to those packed in cartons.

In addition, to use appropriate packing is also very important for keeping good quality and maintaining the foreign markets. Recently, some kinds of goods like honey and canned food exported from China were rejected by US Food and Drug Administration (FDA) for the reason of migration of metal coating from the inner packing. To promote development of packing technologies and products is helpful to lower packaging costs and increase production efficiency. It is better to stipulate expressly the definite method of packing and its materials in detail in a contract.

## 3.4.3 Transport Marking

In order to indentify the goods more easily and prevent cargo damage during carrying, loading, unloading, and storing of the goods, transport marking shall be printed or brushed on the outer package. As per the different functions of marking, transport marking is divided into shipping mark, indicative mark, warning mark, additional mark, bar codes, etc. If the buyer hasn't any special requirements on transport marking, it cannot be stipulated in the contract or just stipulated as "at the seller's option". If buyer requires adopt its company's customary marking, it should be stipulated in the contract expressly.

The shipping mark is generally brushed on apparent front sides of the transporting package. Four elements are prerequisites of shipping marks: ①prefix or abbreviation of the consignee or buyer's name, ②name of place or the port of destination and the country (region) name, ③package number, and ④reference number.

If the goods need to be transshipped, the port (place) of transshipment should be marked the same. It's better to show the package number with combination of the sequence number of each package and total packages. The number of contract, invoice, credit, import license, design, style or color can act as a reference number.

Besides the above, the sides of transport package are always brushed with gross weight, net weight, measurement, place of origin, etc., which are called as "additional mark". The number of credit, import license, design, style or color may be brushed as a part of additional mark instead of the shipping mark.

The indicative mark refers to the marks showed as graphics or words in order to remind the concerning requirements and attentions for the goods carrying, storage, loading and unloading according to the features of the goods, such as "keep dry" "this way up" "handle with care" "fragile". For the purpose of unified graphics or words of indicative marks on transporting package, International Organization for Standardization (ISO) and International Air Transport Association (IATA) drafted the packaging-pictorial markings for handling of goods respectively. The warning mark is also called as "dangerous cargo mark". It refers to the graphics or words showed on the outer package of dangerous cargo such as explosives, flammable substance, corrosive materials, oxidizing agents, and radioactive materials. It is used for warning the concerned parties to adopt the suitable measures to ensure personal safety and property safety.

The goods without bar code can't be imported or sold in the supermarket even if they have good quality. The bar code is scanned for automatic settlement in the supermarket. The contents of bar code include the name of producing country (region), the manufacturer, category, specification, style, etc. The bar code on package of the goods is regarded as the identity card in international market. The most popular bar code in international is UPC (Universal Product Code) drafted by the Universal Code Council (UCC) and EAN (European Article Number) drafted by European Article Number Association. UPC must be used for the goods exported to North America. If the bar code of the goods shows "690", it means the goods are made in China.

### 3.4.4 Packing Costs

If a sales contract doesn't stipulate which party should bear the packing cost, it meant that the packing costs are included in the amount of the goods. If the buyer has special requirements on packing materials or packing methods, the extra costs will be on the account of the buyer and shall be stipulated in the contract expressly. For example, the pallet charges are normally borne by the buyer.

# 3.5 Integrated Cases Study

## ☞ Case 3.6

### How to describe upholstery fabrics?

Name of the goods: chenille upholstery fabrics

Description of quality: design·Ritzi, Intimo, Flamenco

Pattern: Jacquard/Stripe/allover/plain

Colorways: gold/champagne/sky/sage/candlelight/antique/taupe/walnut/espresso/forest

Specification: $150D \times 3.5N + 7S$, $162 \times 64$, width·280cm

Composition: 70% of polyester, 30% cotton

Weight: 1080g/square yard

Color fastness: 4—5 grade (BS1954)

Minimum quantities of order: 500 yards per colorway per pattern per design

Packing: Roll packing. Piece length is $(50 \pm 5)$ yards. One piece in an inner woven bag, outer packing is a plastic bag.

Shipping marks:

B. F.

DESIGN:

PATTERN:

COLORWAY:

LENGTH:

MADE IN CHINA

Remarks: The samples No.TS01378 submitted on Aug 10, 2020 are for design, pattern and Colorways references only.

## ☞ Case 3.7

### How to describe dried black fungus?

Name of the goods: Dried Black Fungus

Alias: Auricularia Auricular, Jew's ear, oodear

Brand: Baishanzu

Certification: HACCP (Hazard Analysis and Critical Control Point)

Specification·shape: whole

Size: L, above 22 mm; M, 15—22 mm; S, below12 mm

Packing:  Inner packing, paper box, 100 g/box or 50 g/box

outer packing·aper carton, measurement: 66 cm × 44 cm × 58 cm

80 boxes (100 g/box)/carton, 140 boxes (50 g/box)/carton

Net weight: 8.0 kg/carton, or 7.0 kg/carton

Gross weight: 9.0 kg / carton, or 8.0 kg/carton

1x20' GP: 196 cartons

1x40' GP: 401 cartons

## ☞ Case 3.8

### How to describe Purified Terephthalic Acid

Name of the goods: purified terephthalic acid (PTA)

Manufacturer: Lonza (Singapore) Pte Ltd.

Packing: In polythene bags, each bag are with gross weight 25.2 kg, net weight 25.0 kg. 40 bags to be packed in one plastic pallets with shrink film, 14 pallets in one 20' FCL. Plastic pallets (each unit price USD9.0) charged at the buyer's account and will be collected together with the cargo value. Shipping marks are at the manufacturer's customary packing.

Minimum quantity of order: 1x20' GP

## Questions

1. A Chinese shoemaker signed a contract with an Italian customer to sell 10,000 pairs of shoes. However, when the seller purchases raw materials, it suddenly finds out that the soles of customer's samples are made of high-tech materials. At present, China cannot produce them at home and must import them from abroad, but the import cost is relatively high. If the seller uses the imported material production, it will face the loss inevitably. What should the seller learn from this case?

2. The contract stipulates bicycles each 100 units in yellow, red, and blue specifically and shall not be shipped by installment. Actually, the export firm delivered 95 units in yellow, 105 units in red, and 100 units in blue. Can the export firm obtain payment from the buyer smoothly?

3. Please select a specific case from the cross-border e-commerce based on the knowledge of international trade commodities, including how to describe the name of commodity, quality, quantity and packing of a commodity, and analyze the descripton of product title, quality, and packing in the case you selected.

# 第四章

# 国际货物运输与保险

☞ **案例 4.1**

这是一则飞马峰号及其在它身上所高度浓缩的中美贸易战故事。根据美国行业网站 EdibleGAeography 的介绍，飞马峰号是一艘建造于 2013 年的散货船。与利比里亚的许多商船一样，它长 229.00 米，宽 32.26 米，是巴拿马型，它可以携带并运送超过 82000 吨的货物，其拥有者为摩根大通全球海事公司。这艘船 2018 年的两次航程，戏剧性地遭受了来自贸易战的"嘲笑"和"戏弄"。

2018 年 4 月，飞马峰号载着来自美国得克萨斯州一座谷仓的 58503 吨高粱，出发前往中国广州。航行途中传来消息：北京宣布对美国高粱出口发起反倾销调查，以报复美国对进口中国洗衣机和太阳能电池板征收的新关税。飞马峰号不得不改变方向，转而前往韩国。当时，飞马峰号仅仅是满载高粱前往中国的 12 艘美国货船之一。为赶在 2018 年 7 月 6 日中国对美国大豆加征关税前抵达大连港，飞马峰号曾在黄海上演"生死时速"。然而，这艘装载了 7 万吨大豆的散货船最终没能"闯关"成功，等待它的是高达 600 万美元的关税。

飞马峰号采取的策略是"以拖待变"，一方面寄希望于中国能给予大豆进口商补贴，一方面只能继续漂在海上等待 7 万吨大豆的所有者路易·德雷菲斯公司的进一步指示。对飞马峰号而言，漂着已经是它所能选择的最为省钱的一条路，即便货主每天都要为此支付 1.25 万美元的租赁费用。一个月来，飞马峰号不断绕着中国大连港转圈，其在海上绕圈的每一条航迹都被实时记录下来。2018 年 8 月中旬，在中国海域漂流了 1 个多月的大豆船飞马峰号终于卸货，成为首批被课征新关税的美国大豆之一，中国储备粮管理集团为这批船货支付了 25% 相当于约 600 万美元的进口关税。

# 一、国际货物运输

国际货物运输具有中间环节多、风险大、涉及面广、情况复杂多变、时间性强等特点。国际货物运输具有多种运输方式，不同运输方式出具的运输单据性质差别很大，直接关系到买卖双方的货物交接是否顺利、货款收付是否安全。货物在长途运输和存储过程中，可能遭受灭失或损坏，需要办理货物运输风险的保险。保险（insurance）是指被保险人（insured）根据合同向保险人支付保险费，保险人（insurer）对于合同约定的可能发生的事故因其发生所造成的财产损失承担赔偿保险金责任，或者当被保险人死亡、伤残、患病或者达到合同约定的年龄、期限时承担给予保险金责任的商业保险行为。国际货物运输保险的被保险人（投保人）在货物装运以前，估计一定的投保金额（保险金额），向保险人（承保人），即保险公司投保货物运输险。被保险人按投保金额、投保险别及投保费率，向保险人支付保险费并取得保险单据。被保险货物若在运输过程中遭受保险事故造成损失，保险人负责对属于投保险别的责任范围内的损失，按保险金额及损失程度赔偿给保险单据的持有人。因此，合理选用运输方式、正确规定装运条款与保险条款的具体内容，是国际货物买卖的成功关键所在。

国际货物运输的范围涵盖出口国家（地区）的原产地直至进口国家（地区）的最终的目的地（如买方的工厂仓库、批发仓库、零售仓库等）。运输范围可细分为3段：①出口国（地区）的国内段运输（pre-carriage），即从货物的原产地运到货物的装运港（地）；②主运输（main carriage），即将货物从位于出口国（地区）的装运港（地）运到进口国（地区）的目的港（地）；③进口国（地区）的国内段运输（post-carriage），即将货物从进口国（地区）的目的港（地）运送到买方所在地。国际货物买卖合同中的运输条款内容一般包括运输责任、运输方式、装运时间、交货时间、装运港（地）和目的港（地）、运输单据、分批装运和转运、装运通知等。

## （一）运输责任

在实际业务中，国际货物买卖普遍采用FOB、CFR、CIF、FCA、CPT、CIP这6个象征性交货的贸易术语成交。采用不同的贸易术语，买卖双方承担的运输责任不尽相同。以FOB、CFR、CIF贸易术语成交的合同，第2段运输（②运输）必须是海洋运输或内河水运，而①③段的运输方式没有限制；以FOB贸易术语成交的合同，卖方负责①运输，买方负责②③运输；以CFR、CIF贸易术语成交的合同，卖方负责①②运输，买方负责③运输；FCA、CPT、CIP贸易术语成交的合同，①②③段的运输方式均没有限制。以FCA贸易术语成交的合同，如规定货物的装运地在卖方的工厂所在地，卖方不负责①运输，货物全程运输（①②③运输）全由买方负责；如规定货物的装运地不在卖方的工厂所在地，卖方负责①运输，买方负责②③运输。以CPT、CIP贸易术语成交的合同，如规定货物的目的地就在买方所在地，则卖方负责货物的全程运输（①②③运输）；如规定货物的目的地不为买方所在地，则卖方负责①②运输，买方负责③运输。

### （二）运输方式

运输方式有海洋运输、内河运输、公路运输、铁路运输、航空运输、管道运输、邮政运输等，其中海洋运输又可分为沿海运输、近洋运输和远洋运输。为了方便运输，减少货物灭失或损坏的风险，集装箱运输应运而生。集装箱运输不仅适用于任何运输方式，而且也推动了国际大陆桥运输、国际多式联运等运输方式的发展。

#### 1. 集装箱运输

集装箱运输在国际货物运输中运用较为广泛。因集装箱运输路程远、使用频率高，在运输途中常受各种力的作用和环境的影响，集装箱的制造应尽量采用质量轻、强度高、耐用、维修保养费用低的材料。集装箱的种类、规格很多，按照集装箱的规格、材料和用途不同，可分为干货箱、开顶箱、台架式及平台式箱、通风箱、冷藏箱、散货箱、动物箱、罐式箱、汽车用箱、平台箱等；按其制造的主体材料的不同，可分为钢制集装箱、铝制集装箱、不锈钢制集装箱、玻璃钢制集装箱。

##### （1）集装箱常用规格

目前，使用最多的3种集装箱规格是8英尺×9.6英尺×40英尺（40'HQ，40呎高箱）、8英尺×8.6英尺×40英尺（40'GP，40呎普通箱）、8英尺×8.6英尺×20英尺（20'GP，20呎普通箱）。箱型参数详见英文部分的表4-1。

##### （2）集装箱运输的货物交接方式

集装箱运输可分为整箱运输和拼箱运输。在发货人有足够货物装满一个或数个集装箱时，通常采用整箱运输（full container load，FCL）；当货物数量不足以装满一个集装箱时，可以采用拼箱运输（less than container load，LCL）。按照集装箱运输的不同装箱方式，集装箱货物的交接方式也可相应分为4种。

①整箱装、整箱接（FCL-FCL）。发货人在工厂仓库或集装箱堆场，将货物装入集装箱，以整箱的方式交给承运人，而收货人在目的地以同样整箱的方式接货。这种运输方式，可实现"门到门"运输（Door-Door）、"场到场"运输（CY-CY）、"门到场"运输（Door-CY）、"场到门"运输（CY-Door）。

②拼箱装、拆箱接（LCL-LCL）。在采用拼箱装运的情况下，承运人负责将不同发货人运往同一目的港（地）的货物装入同一个集装箱。集装箱到达目的地后，由承运人负责拆箱，将货物分别交给不同的收货人。这种运输方式，称为"站到站"服务（CFS-CFS）。

③整箱交、拆箱接（FCL-LCL）。在发货人只有一个，但同一目的地的收货人不止一个时，发货人将整箱货物交给承运人。货物运抵目的地后，由承运人负责拆箱后，各收货人凭单接货。这种运输方式，可实现"场到站"（CY-CFS）、"门到站"（Door-CFS）服务。

④拼箱交、整箱接（LCL/FCL）。在发货人不止一个，而收货人只有一个的情况下，承运人将不同发货人的货物进行分类调整，把同一收货人的货物集中拼装成整箱。货

物运抵目的地后，承运人以整箱交，收货人以整箱接。这种方式下可实现"站到门"（CFS-Door）及"站到场"（CFS-CY）服务。

### 2. 海洋运输

75%左右的国际货物是通过海洋运输完成的。按经营方式的不同，海洋运输可分为班轮运输（liner）和租船运输（charter）两大类。班轮运输和租船运输在租船方式、运输手续、计收运费和船货双方的责任与义务等各方面都有较大的区别。

#### （1）租船运输

租船运输又称不定期船（tramp）运输。当要运送的货物数量较多、货值较低时，一般采用租船运输。货主或货运代理人可根据自己的需要，与船东进行洽谈，议定租船运输的条件，并根据货物性质、输送地点、运输路程的远近以及国际租船市场的供求关系等，商定货物的运价。租船人与船东达成协议后，签订租船合同，共同确定船期、航线及港口。根据租船合同，船东将船舶出租给租船人使用，以完成特定的货物运输，租船人按合同规定的运价支付运费。租船方式可以采用包租船舶全部舱位、部分舱位或指定舱位等不同形式。租船运输适用于批量大、货种单一、交货集中的大宗货物运输。目前，世界上主要的船舶市场有4个：伦敦租船市场、纽约租船市场、欧洲大陆及北欧租船市场和香港租船市场。

租船运输的方式主要有3种：定程租船、定期租船和航次期租。其中，定程租船（voyage charter）又称航次租船，船东必须依照租船合同规定的航程完成货物运输，负责船舶的经营管理，支付船舶在航行途中的一切费用。租船人以航程为基础支付运费。定程租船又可分为单航次租船（single voyage charter）、来回航次租船（round trip charter）、连续单程租船（consecutive trip charter）和包运合同租船。定期租船（time charter）指出租人将船舶出租给租船人使用一定期限，在此期限内出租的船舶由租船人自行调度和经营管理。定期租船的租金，可按月（30天）、按每载重吨（DWT）若干金额计算。定期租船还有一种方式叫光船租船（bare boat charter）。它与一般定期租船不同的是，在光船租船的方式下，船东将船舶交给承租方使用，由承租方自行配备船员，负责船舶的经营管理、航行等各项事宜。航次期租（time charter on trip basis，TCT）是一种介于航次租船和定期租船之间的租船方式，以完成一个航次运输为目的，按完成航次所花的时间，依约定的租金率计算租金。

定程租船费用主要包括租船运费、装卸费、滞期费、速遣费等。其中，租船运费是指货物从装运港运至目的港的海上运费。定程租船运费的计算方式与支付时间，需由租船人与船东在所签订的定程租船合同中明确规定。其计算方式主要有2种：一是确定每单位重量或体积应支付的运费，规定按照装船时的货物重量或是卸货时的货物重量来计算总运费；二是整船包价，规定整船运费，船东保证船舶能提供的载货重量和容积，不管承租方实际装货多少，一律照整船包价付。租船运费的高低取决于诸多因素，如租船市场运费水平、货物价值、装卸货物所需设备和劳动力、运费的支付时间、装卸费的负担方法、港口费用高低，以及船舶经纪人的佣金率等。租船运费有预付、到付之分。预付又可分为全部预付、部分预付；到付有船到目的港开始卸货前付、边卸边付、货物卸完后支付3种。

在定程租船运输中，货物的装卸费用由租船人和船东协商后，在租船合同中做出具体规定。租船合同中有关装卸费的负担，一般可分为：船方不负担装卸费（free in and out，FIO）；船方不负担装货费（free in，FI）；船方不负担卸货费（free out，FO）；船方不负担装卸费、理舱费与平舱费（free in and out and stowed and trimmed，FIOST）；船方负担装卸费（berth term，BT/lner term）等。在船方负担装卸费用的条件下，船方的责任以船上吊钩所及之处为界，即所谓"钩至钩"（tackle to tackle）。

买卖大宗商品时，租船合同的双方往往会规定装卸时间和装卸率。装卸率一般根据货物品种和港口的装卸速度来确定。在规定的装卸期限内，如果承租人未能按时完成装卸，为了补偿出租人船舶延迟开航所造成的损失，从原计划规定的装卸完毕时间到全部货物实际装卸完毕的滞期时间，承租人应向出租人支付"滞期费"。相反，如在规定的装卸期内，承租人实际提前完成了装卸，那么出租人应按其节省的时间向承租人支付"速遣费"。滞期费的数额一般低于船舶租金，速遣费通常为滞期费的一半。

**（2）班轮运输**

班轮运输又称为定期船运输，是指船舶在固定的航线和港口间按事先公布的船期表航行，从事客、货方面的运输业务并按事先公布的费率收取运费的运输方式。班轮运输具有4个特点：①班轮运输具有"四固定"，即具有固定航线、固定港口、固定船期和相对固定的费率；②由承运人负责货物配载、装卸，并负担装卸费用，承运人和托运人双方不计算装卸时间、滞期费和速遣费等；③承运人责任以签发的班轮提单条款为依据；④装载数量不受限制。班轮公司承运货物要收取班轮运费，班轮运费在一定时期内相对稳定，它以班轮运费率为基础进行计算。班轮公会、班轮公司会定期公布班轮运价表。班轮运价表由基本费率（basic freight rate）和多种附加费率（surcharges）所构成。班轮基本运费率的计算标准可分为9种类型。

①按货物毛重计收。在运价表中，以字母"W"（英文weight的缩写）表示。一般以1公吨为计算单位，保留2位小数。有些船公司按长吨或短吨计算运费。

②按货物的体积计收。在运价表中，以字母"M"（英文measurement的缩写）表示。一般以1立方米为计算单位，有些船公司按40立方英尺为1尺码公吨计算。

③按货物的毛重或体积计收运费，计收时以其数量较高者为准。在运价表中以"W/M"表示。1重量吨货物的体积，如大于1立方米或40立方英尺按体积计收运费；如小于1立方米或40立方英尺按毛重计收运费。

④从价运费。在运价表中以"adval"表示。一般按商品FOB货价的一定百分比计算运费。按从价标准计算运费的货物，一般都属于价值较高但体积较小、重量较轻的货物。

⑤按货物重量、体积或价值三者中最高的一种计收，在运价表中以"W/M or

adval"表示。

⑥按货物重量、体积从高计收并加收一定百分比的从价运费，在运价表中以"W/M plus adval"表示。

⑦按货物的件数计收。如汽车、火车头、卡车等按辆（per unit）计收运费；活牲畜如牛、羊、猪等按头（per head）计费。

⑧大宗低值货物按议价计收运费（open rate）。如粮食、豆类、煤炭、矿砂等大宗货物，由于其体积大、价值低，一般在班轮费率表内不规定具体费率。在订舱时，由托运人和船公司临时洽商议订。议价运费比按等级运价计算运费。

⑨起码费率（minimum rate）。在运输中，如果按每一提单上所列的重量或体积所计算出的运费尚未达到运价表中规定的最低运费额时，则按最低运费计收。

班轮附加费的种类较多，在不同的情况下，船公司可收取不同种类和数额的附加费。常见的附加费种类有：超重附加费、超长附加费、燃油附加费、港口附加费、港口拥挤附加费、货币贬值附加费、绕航附加费、转船附加费、直航附加费、选港附加费、偏港手续费等。

各种附加费的计算方法主要有两种：一是以百分比表示，即在基本费率的基础上增加一定百分比的数额；二是用绝对数表示，即每运费吨增加若干金额，或每票货物收若干金额。例如，中国去日本偏港的货物另需加手续费USD20/票，其中那坝港（Naha）需收手续费USD70/票。

各种附加费与基本运费直接相加计算班轮运费。班轮运费的计算公式为：$F = F_b + \sum S$。其中F为运费总额；$F_b$为基本运费；$\sum S$为征收的各种附加费之和。

在同一包装内，如果混装有不同种类的商品，全部运费按较高者计收。同一批装运的货物，如包括不同种类的包装，其计费标准及等级也不同。托运人应按不同包装分列毛重及体积，才能分别计收运费，否则全部货物均按较高者收取运费。同一份提单内如有两种或两种以上不同货名的商品，托运人应分别列出不同货名商品的毛量或体积，否则全部将按较高者收取运费。

在班轮运输情况下，如采用集装箱运输，因集装箱运输有整箱与拼箱之分，其整箱运价与拼箱运价的计算依据有所不同。表4.1是分别从上海航交所官方网站和中国运价超市网公布的从上海（外港）起运的美加航线部分港口包箱费率（FAK）和拼箱海运费，表4.2是从广州起运到一些亚洲港口的集装箱拼箱海运费。

**表 4.1 从中国上海港到一些南美、欧洲港口的集装箱整箱海运费**

**（有效期保留至 2018 年 7 月 23 日）**

| 装运港<br>Port of<br>shipment | 目的港<br>Port of<br>destination | 船公司<br>Shipping<br>company | 小柜<br>20GP | 大柜<br>40GP | 高柜<br>40HQ | 船期<br>Sailing<br>date | 航程<br>Voyage<br>period |
|---|---|---|---|---|---|---|---|
| | | | 美元 USD | | | | |
| Shanghai | Puerto Quetzal | EMC | 1860 | 2020 | 2020 | Wed | 27 days |
| | San Juan | MSC | 2360 | 2520 | 2520 | Thu | 30 days |
| | Puerto Cabello | CMA | 3350 | 3820 | 3820 | Thu | 42 days |
| | Lisbon | CMA | 1045 | 1885 | 1935 | Sun | 33 days |
| | Le Havre | EMC | 800 | 1500 | 1550 | Fri | 30 days |

**表 4.2 从中国广州到一些亚洲港口的集装箱拼箱海运费**

| 装运港<br>Port of<br>shipment | 目的港<br>Port of<br>destination | 船公司<br>Shipping<br>company | 尺码吨<br>Measurement<br>(USD/CBM) | 重量吨 Weight<br>(USD/MT) | 航程<br>Sailing<br>period |
|---|---|---|---|---|---|
| Guangzhou | Bangkok | SITC | 30 | 30 | 19 days |
| | Yangon | WHL | 100 | 100 | 23 days |
| | Brunei | TSL | 80 | 80 | 18 days |
| | Muara | TSL | 80 | 80 | 10 days |
| | Colombo | WHL | 80 | 80 | 14 days |
| | Chittagong | MCC | 95 | 95 | 13 days |

备注：①拼箱运费按货物实际体积（立方米）×体积单价，或货物实际毛重（MT）×重量单价，比较后取大值计算，最小计费单位为 1 CBM/MT；②美国、加拿大、墨西哥航线需申报 AMS（AMS 为"9·11"事件后的反恐信息费）；③单票货物超过 5 公吨，单件货物超长、超高、超重，运价另议。危险品不接受。

### 3. 内河运输

在国际上，有些内河途经不同的国家（地区），因而可以用以国际货物运输。其中，比较有名的内河有以下几种。

**（1）亚洲的湄公河**

湄公河发源于中国青海省，流经中国的西藏自治区、云南省后，经过老挝、泰国、柬埔寨与越南，从越南的胡志明市（西贡）流入南海。老挝的首都万象、柬埔寨的首都金边，也都在其岸边。湄公河对中国与下游国家开展货物贸易具有显著的积极意义。

**（2）欧洲的莱茵河**

莱茵河是西欧第一大河，也是欧洲的一条著名国际河流，自 1815 年起就已成为国际航运水道，是世界上最重要的工业运输大动脉之一，也是世界上航运最繁忙的河流之一。它流经列支敦士登、奥地利、法国、德国和荷兰，最后在鹿特丹附近注入北海，全长1390千米，通航里程900千米，其中大约700千米可以行驶万吨货轮。同时，莱茵河还通过一系列运河与其他运河连接，构成了一个四通八达的水网。

内河运输运价低廉、运输方便，但应注意日益严重的污染问题。目前，国际上在有效扩大内河运输的同时，已开始密切关注生态保护问题。

### 4. 航空运输

按空运方式的不同，可分为班机运输、包机运输、集中托运和航空快递等形式。国际航空货物运输具有许多其他运输方式所不能比拟的优越性：首先，航空运输快速、安全、准确；其次，可以不受地面条件的限制，运输可以深入内陆地区；再次，采用航空运输时，货物在途时间短、周转速度快，企业可以相应地减少包装、保险、利息等费用。

### 5. 邮包运输

国际邮政运输（international parcel post transport），又称为邮包运输（parcel post transport）。邮政托运人只要向邮政局照章办理一次托运，一次付清足额邮资，并取得一张包裹收据（parcel post receipt），全部手续即告完成。国际邮包通过一个或几个国家（地区）经转，邮件运送、交接、保管、传递等一切事宜均由各国（地区）邮政局负责办理。因此，国际邮政运输具有"门到门"运输和国际多式联运的性质。邮包在各个国家（地区）之间的相互协作配合下运抵目的地，收件人可凭邮政局"到件通知"或收据向邮政局提取邮包。国际邮包运输一般采用水路、陆路和航空运输，或由两种或两种不同的运输方式结合起来运输。

国际邮政运输按照经营方式的不同，分为函件和包裹两大类；按照邮寄方式不同，分为普通邮包和航空邮包。国际邮政运输对邮件的重量和体积均有限制，如每件包裹重量不得高于20千克，长度不得超过100厘米，但各国（地区）规定不尽相同，可在邮寄包裹时详细咨询邮局。

中国于1972年加入万国邮政联盟（Universal Postal Union），现已与很多国家签订了邮政包裹协定和邮电协议。因此，在中国办理国际邮政运输比较方便。邮政运输一般只适合重量轻、体积小的货物，如精密仪器、机器零配件、药品、样品和生产上急需的物品等。

☞ **案例4.2**

据新华社2018年10月17日报道，美国白宫17日宣布，自即日起启动退出万国邮政联盟的程序，原因竟与中国有关。中国是一个电商大国，在跨境电商快速发展的今天，占据了巨大的世界市场份额，而美国恰好就是中国电商的最大买家之一。2018年，中国电商在美销售额已经达到了800亿美元左右。万国邮政联盟（简称万国邮联）于1874年成立，现归属于联合国系统，总部设在瑞士首都伯尔尼。万国邮联有192个成员，每4年开一次大会，商定终端费（terminal dues），一国一票，投票结束后18个月内实施。何为终端费？从A国往B国邮寄信函或包裹，在A国邮政支付邮费，但需要由B国邮政投递信函或包裹，A国邮政则支付终端费给B国邮政。因终端费的制定采取普惠制而非精英原则，因此终端费的制定并不反映各个国家的经济状况，而是反映普遍意愿。发达国家以支持发展中国家的国际交流为原则，同意长期将终端费保持在较低水平。然而，当今国际邮件中往来的绝大多数已不再是信函，而是网购商品。中国作为发展中国家，享受了较低的终端费，但中国同时又是一个互联网商业大国，因此美国要给中国的终端费涨价。针对寄到美国快递小包数量最多的国家，2017年美国增加了13%的邮费，但美国邮政还是亏损。

### 6. 铁路运输

铁路运输速度快、运量大、成本低、不受气候条件影响，具有安全、准确、连续性强的特点。通过铁路运输完成的货运量仅次于海洋运输，因而铁路运输在国际货物运输中占据着举足轻重的地位。铁路运输按其承担运输的地理位置不同，可以分为国内铁路运输和国际铁路联合运输。国际铁路联合运输是指由两个或两个不同国家（地区）的铁路当局进行联合，使用一份统一的国际联运票据，途经两个或两个以上国家（地区）铁路来完成一笔国际货物运输。国际铁路联合运输所依据的国际条约有《国际货约》和《国际货协》。1890年，欧洲各国在瑞士首都伯尔尼举行各国铁路代表会议，制定了《国际铁路货物运送规则》；1938年修改时，改名为《国际铁路货物运送公约》，简称《国际货约》或《伯尔尼货运公约》。《国际货协》是《国际铁路货物联运协定》的简称。中国在建国初期与苏联签订了《中苏铁路联运协会协定》。1952年，苏联与东欧七国签订《国际铁路货物联运协定》，中国于1954年1月1日加入《国际货协》。

☞ **案例4.3**

郑欧国际铁路货运班列始于郑州，经新疆阿拉山口出境，途经哈萨克斯坦、俄罗斯、白俄罗斯和波兰后到达德国汉堡，全程10214千米。首趟郑欧国际铁路货运班列于2013年07月18日运行，开启了中国与欧洲的"新丝绸之路"。郑欧班列车次为"80001次"，是全国各地发往欧洲货运班列中的"第一号"。全程运行时间11天到15天，比海运节约20天左右，比空运节约资金80%。 2015年，除郑欧货运班列外，郑州还实现了到哈萨克斯坦第一大城市阿拉木图和俄罗斯莫斯科两条铁路货运线路的常态化开行。2016年，郑欧班列开通了经土耳其等国到达卢森堡的南欧线路。2014年5月10日，习近平总书记在河南考察时视察了郑州国际陆港，详细了解了郑欧班列的运行情况和物流状态。2018年10月24日，比利时列日至郑州中欧班列正式开通，这是中国与比利时的第三条中欧班列。

### 7. 公路运输

国际公路运输一般采用汽车运输，以公路为运输线，利用汽车等陆路运输工具将货物从一国（地区）运往另一国（地区）。公路运输是国际货物运输的主要方式之一，具有灵活、简便、快捷的特点，可进行"门到门"运输。公路运输在短途运输中具有更大的优越性。但是，公路运输也具有一定的局限性，如运量不大、费用偏高、容易造成货损货差事故。中国与朝鲜、缅甸、尼泊尔等许多国的货物运输，大多采用公路运输。

### 8. 管道运输

管道运输主要输送原油、各种石油成品、化学品、天然气等液体和气体物品，也可以运送铁矿砂、碎煤浆等颗粒状物品，至今已有一百多年的历史。在管道运输情况下，对特定货物的运输采用专门的封闭管道，可以不受地面气候影响进行连续作业。货物在管道内输送时，遭受货损的风险较少。管道一经铺设，便可连续使用，因此管道运输的费用比较低。货物经由管道运输时，一般不需要经过包装。

☞ **案例4.4**

中俄石油管道是目前中俄最大的经济合作项目，协议书于2012年9月签署。管道全长999.04千米，其中俄罗斯境内72千米、中国境内927.04千米。根据20年协议，俄罗斯将通过这条管道每年向中国提供1500万吨石油。2016年8月13日，中俄石油管道二期工程开工。2018年1月1日，中俄原油管道二线工程在黑龙江省塔河县呼玛河南岸全线贯通一个多月后，正式投入使用，设计产能每年1500万吨。随着中俄原油管道一线二线全部投产，俄罗斯每年可向中国输入的原油量也将增至3000万吨。

### 9. 大陆桥运输

大陆桥运输（land bridge transport），以横贯大陆的铁路、公路运输系统为中间桥梁，把大陆两端的海洋连接起来。目前，全世界的大陆桥主要有西伯利亚大陆桥、北美大陆桥、新亚欧大陆桥等。

西伯利亚大陆桥东起海参崴的纳霍特卡港口，横贯欧亚大陆后至莫斯科，然后分三路：①从莫斯科至波罗的海沿岸的圣彼得堡港，转船运往西欧、北欧港口；②从莫斯科至俄罗斯西部国境站，转欧洲其他国家（地区）铁路（公路）直运欧洲各国（地区）；③从莫斯科至黑海沿岸，转船往中东、地中海沿岸。

北美大陆桥包括美国和加拿大境内的大陆桥，而美国境内有两条大陆桥运输线：①从西部太平洋口岸至东部大西洋口岸的铁路（公路）运输系统，全长约3200千米；②从西部太平洋口岸至南部墨西哥湾口岸的铁路（公路）运输系统，长500—1000千米。

美国对大陆桥运输有运费优惠条款，即OCP（overland common points，内陆地区）运输条款。美国的北达科他州、南达科他州、内布拉斯加州、科罗拉多州、新墨西哥州起以东地区均属OCP地区。按OCP运输条款规定，凡是经由美国西岸港口转往这些内陆地区的货物，如按OCP条款运输，运价比直达西岸港口运价约低3%～5%。从美国内陆地区起运经西岸港口装船出口的货物同样可按OCP运输条款办理，海运费享受每公吨约低3～5美元的优惠。如果从中国出口一批货物去美国，卸货港为美国洛杉矶，最终目的地是芝加哥，因洛杉矶是美国西岸的基本港。而芝加哥属于美国内陆城市，该笔交易符合OCP规定。经买卖双方同意，可采用OCP运输条款。在买卖合同和信用证的目的港处，应填写"洛杉矶（内陆地区）"（CIF Los Angeles，OCP），在海运提单的目的港处填写"港洛杉矶"，目的地填写"内陆地区芝加哥"（OCP Chicago），同时在提单备注栏内及货物唛头上注明"OCP"字样。只有这样，才能享受OCP优惠条款。

新亚欧大陆桥东起中国连云港，西至荷兰鹿特丹，跨亚、欧两大洲，连接太平洋和大西洋，穿越中国、哈萨克斯坦、俄罗斯，经白俄罗斯、波兰、德国到荷兰，辐射20多个国家和地区，全长1.08万千米，其中在中国境内的运输路线长达4134千米。

**10. 国际多式联运**

国际多式联运是指按照多式联运合同，用两种或两种以上不同的运输方式，由多式联运经营人将货物从一国（地区）境内接管货物的地点运至另一国（地区）境内指定交付货物的地点。

国际多式联运是在集装箱运输的基础上发展起来的新型运输方式，不仅在过去的短短几十年中发展迅速，而且在未来的国际货物运输中也有着广阔的发展前景。国际多式联运手续简便，能够把海、陆、空、公路、江河等多种不同方式、多段复杂的运输手续大大简化，发货人只需要办理一次手续就可将全程运输委托给承运人。

国际多式联运采用集装箱运输，能够安全、准确、迅速地将货物运抵目的地，使发货人节省包装费用。在货物装上第一程运输工具后，卖方即可取得联合运输单据，有利于提早收款。目前，中国已分别开设了到日本、美国、加拿大、西欧、澳大利亚、沙特阿拉伯，经肯尼亚的蒙巴隆港至乌干达与卢旺达，经俄罗斯的西伯利亚到中东、欧洲的多式联运线路，等等。

**（三）装运时间和交货时间**

在国际贸易中，"装运"和"交货"的意义有时是相同的，有时却不相同。按照Incoterms®2010的通常规定，在适用FOB、CFR、CIF、FCA、CIP、CPT这6种象征性交货成交的术语时，卖方只需在指定装运港将货物装到船上或者取得已这样交付的货物，或在约定的装运地（如有约定的话）将货物交给承运人，办妥出口清关手续，卖方即完成了交货义务。这时，"装运"与"交货"的意义可理解为是一致的。而以EXW、FAS、DAT、DAP、DDP术语成交的贸易合同，"交货"和"装运"是两个完全不同的概念，属于实际交货（actual delivery）的贸易术语，绝不能将"装运"和"交货"加以混淆或相互替代使用。

由于国际贸易大多是以FOB、CFR、CIF、FCA、CIP、CPT这6种贸易术语成交，其"装运"和"交货"的意义一致。以 FOB、CFR、CIF、FCA、CIP、CPT这6种贸易术语成交的贸易合同中，买卖双方只需在合同中规定"装运时间"即可，毋须规定"到货时间"。如在合同中规定了"到货时间"，对卖方不利。例如，某 CIF 贸易合同规定："货物必须于2017年10月1日前从广州港起运，并于2017年11月15日前到达巴西的里奥格兰德港。"卖方于2017年9月30日将货物装运出口，如船舶正常航行，货物是可以在规定时间之前到达目的港的。然而，因海上飓风影响，船舶中途在避难港停留期间又不幸与其他船只发生碰撞，为了修理船舶，货物还不得不从船上卸下来。等船修好、货物重新上船，船货已在避难港滞留了18天，导致货物实际于2017年12月1日才到目的港。买方以到货延误为由，向卖方索赔，而卖方不得不对买方理赔。

装运时间（time of shipment）是指卖方在指定的装运港（地）将货物越过船舷或货交承运人的规定期限。装运时间的规定方法一般有以下4种。

①明确规定具体的装运日期。例如：2017年10月1日装运（shipment on Nov. 1, 2017）。这种规定方法极不灵活，对卖方来说非常不利。如果卖方不能在该日装运货物，极有可能导致买方索赔。一般情况下，装运时间应规定为一段期限较好。

②明确规定具体装运期限。这类规定方法比较合理，实践中运用较多，可细分为2种。a.规定一段具体期限，如：2017年11月装运（shipment during Nov., 2017），或2017年11/12月份装运（shipment during Nov./Dec., 2017）。b.规定最迟期限，如：2017年11月30日或前装运（shipment on or before Nov. 30, 2017），或装运期最迟不得迟于2017年11月30日（shipment not later than Nov. 30, 2017）。

③规定在收到信用证后若干天装运（shipment made within ___days after receipt of L/C），或收到一定比例的预付款后装运。如：买方须至少在约定的装运日期前10天将30%的款项电汇给卖方，卖方在收到30%预付款后再将货物装运出去（The buyer shall remit 30% payment at least 10 days before the stipulated date of shipment by T/T. The seller will make shipment on the basis of receipt of 30% advanced payment）。在采用信用证或结合一定比例的预付款付款情况下，为防止买方不按期开立信用证或支付，可采用该种规定方法。

④笼统规定方法，如"立即装运"（immediate shipment）、"即刻装运"（prompt shipment）、"尽速装运"（shipment as soon as possible）等。该方法易产生歧义，在实践中最好不要使用。

### （四）装运港（地）和目的港（地）

因FCA、CPT、CIP术语适合多种运输方式，包括多式运输，因而合同的交货地点可规定为港口，也可以是港口以外的其他任何内陆地点，如机场、火车站、汽车站、集装箱码头、卖方所在地等。而FOB、CFR、CIF术语只适合海运或内河运输，因而交货地点必须规定为港口。装运港（地）和目的港（地）的选用，与合同采用的贸易术语相关。下面以海运为例，来说明装运港和目的港规定应注意的事项。

### 1. 装运港（地）

在以 FCA、FOB 术语成交的合同中明确装运港（地）尤为重要，不仅关系到买方安排运输船只，或者指派承运人或其他人到该规定的装运港（地）接收货物，而且买方需要承担自货物在指定装运港装上船后或货交指定承运人或其他人时产生的一切风险。装运港（地）一般由卖方提出，经买方同意后确定。一般情况下，装运港（地）只规定1个；如货源分散在几个不同的地方，也可酌情规定两三个装运港（地），或对装运港（地）做笼统规定。例如：①shipment from Shanghai Pudong International Airport, China(从中国上海浦东国际机场起运)；②from Dalian/Shanghai Seaport, China(从中国大连港或上海港起运)；③from main ports, China(中国基本港)；④the ports along Yangzi River, China(中国长江沿岸码头)。

笼统规定对卖方有利，但可能会给买方造成一定的麻烦。对买方来说，装运港的规定越明确具体越好；对卖方来说，装运港（地）应邻近货源地，并应选择装卸条件好、费用低、适合船舶安全停靠的港口作为装运港。因为卖方必须在合同规定的装运期内，按照买卖双方约定的装运时间（如有特别约定的话），在指定的装运港（地）将货物装上船或交给买方指定的承运人或其他人即完成交货，并承担完成交货前的一切费用与风险。

### 2. 目的港（地）

在以 CFR、CIF、CPT 与 CIP 术语成交的合同中，明确目的港（地）尤为重要，因为卖方必须签订运输合同以将货物运至指定的目的港（地）。目的港一般由买方根据需要提出，经卖方同意后确定。目的港（地）可以只规定一个，也可根据情况酌情规定两三个或做笼统规定。选择目的港（地）时，应注意：①目的港（地）的规定必须明确具体，避免使用"欧洲主要港口""非洲主要港口"等笼统的规定方法。在卖方安排运输的情况下，笼统规定目的港（地）对卖方比较不利。在签订合同时，应力争将1～3个具体港口作为目的港，但尽量不要超过3个，并且在合同中要明确规定"允许分批装运"。②目的港（地）应是可以安全停靠的港口。如果从装运港出发抵达目的港的直达班轮基本没有或很少，应在合同中明确规定"允许转运"，必要时可以规定"选择港"。③应注意目的港（地）的重名问题，例如名为"维多利亚"的港口，在全世界有12个。重名港口的名称后面必须加注国（地区）名，以防发生错运货物的事故，给买卖双方带来损失。④尽量不要接受以进口国（地区）的偏港、内陆小城镇等地作为目的地，因为会可能导致基本运费、附加费、装运期延误等不可控因素的增加。

### （五）运输单据

运输单据是承运人收到承运货物后，签发给出口商的证明文件。它是交接货物、处理索赔与理赔、向银行办理货款收付的重要单据。在国际货物运输中，运输单据的种类很多，包括提单、海运单、铁路运单、承运货物收据、航空运单和邮包收据等。

### 1. 提单

提单（bill of lading，B/L）是船方或其代理人在收到承运货物时签发给托运人的货物收据，也是承运人与托运人之间的运输契约的证明。从法律的角度来说，海运提单是一种物权凭证。收货人在目的港提取货物时，必须提交正本海运提单。提单的种类较多，可以从不同的角度进行划分：①以货物是否已装到船上，分为已装船提单（shipped B/L, on board B/L）和备运提单（received for shipment B/L）；②以提单上是否加注有关货损或包装不良批注，分为清洁提单（clean B/L）和不清洁提单（unclean B/L）；③以提单抬头（收货人栏）的不同记载，分为记名提单（straight B/L）、不记名提单（bearer B/L）和指示提单（order B/L）；④以提单背面是否印就托运人与承运人之间的权利义务说明，分为全式提单（long form B/L）和略式提单（short form B/L）。另外，还有倒签提单、过期提单（stale B/L）、直达提单、联合运输提单和舱面提单（on deck B/L）等。

如以班轮运输货物，班轮提单的内容一般包括正面条款和背面条款两部分。正面条款的内容大体相同，一般包括承运人名称、托运人名称、收货人名称、通知人名称及地址、船名航次、装运港、目的港、目的地、货物名称、包装、唛头、件数、重量或体积、运费和其他费用、运费预付或是到付、货物上船日期，以及提单签发人、签发地点、签发提单正本的份数和签发日期等内容。提单背面的内容，一般是印就的运输条款，作为承运人和托运人、承运人与收货人、提单持有人之间的权利和义务的主要依据。

☞ **案例4.5**

### 不同船公司对货物运往肯尼亚的提单特殊要求

OOCL 关于运往肯尼亚的提单特殊要求：

（1）提单上必须显示肯尼亚收货人的地址、城市、国家和电话。如果是转运提单并且收货人不在肯尼亚，提单的通知方必须为肯尼亚当地的公司，并显示地址、城市、国家和电话在提单上。

（2）经肯尼亚自行转运至其他东非国家的提单，需在提单的货物描述处显示 cargo in-transit to（city name）in ＿＿（country/region name））via Mombasa Port by consignee's own costs and risk。

（3）所有运至肯尼亚和在此中转的货物必须提供8位的 HS 码，并且显示在货物描述处。如为多种货物混装，涉及不同的 HS 码，须按照 HS 码分开发送货物信息。

（4）务必提供净重信息，并显示在提单上。

（5）根据肯尼亚港务局的通知，到蒙巴萨港的货物须在肯尼亚港务局指定的集装箱货运站（CFS）清关。客户不能自行选择集装箱货运站（CFS）或者内陆集装箱货运站（ICD）。因此，所有至蒙巴萨的提单，不接受显示任何"转运至肯尼亚境内集装箱货运站（CFS）"或者"转运至内陆集装箱货运站（ICD）"的条款。

MSK 关于运往肯尼亚的提单特殊要求：

船公司马士基（MSK）2018年9月24日发布公告，所有出口到肯尼亚的货物提单必须显示收货人的联系电话号码，确保可以在整个发货周期的任何时候与货主联系，以保证马士基主动通知相关方货物到达的能力，并避免因此产生的延迟成本。如果在2018年9月24日之后没有提交电话号码，马士基将不予处理通过蒙巴萨港（肯尼亚最大的港口）或通过蒙巴萨港的国际海运业务。

为了统一提单背面的运输条款，1921年欧美26个主要航运国家在海牙集会，签订了《海牙规则草案》，并于1924年正式签署了《统一提单的若干法律规定的国际公约》，简称《海牙规则》（Hague rules）。目前，全世界有80多个国家（地区）接受了这个规则，一些航运公司根据这个规则制订了自己的提单条款。此后，各主要航运国家（地区）签订了《维斯比规则》，并于1977年6月23日正式生效。《维斯比规则》在保留《海牙规则》的基本责任制度的基础上，对其进行了一些重要修改和补充。1978年，联合国国际贸易法委员会经过长期准备，在汉堡召开了由78个国家（地区）的代表参加的联合国海上货物运输会议，正式通过了《1978年联合国海上货物运输公约》，简称《汉堡规则》（Hamburg rules）。《汉堡规则》对《海牙规则》做了本质上的修改和补充，考虑了航运业不发达国家（地区）的利益。由于三项国际公约制订的时间和产生的历史背景不同，故其内容有很大差异，各国（地区）和各船公司对这三项公约的态度也不一致。

### 2. 航空运单

航空运单（airway bill）是航空货物运输的主要单据，是航空承运人与托运人之间签订的运输契约，也是承运人或其代理人签发的货物收据，但不具有物权凭证的性质，因而不能转让。目的地收货人提取货物，不是凭航空运单，而是凭航空公司发出的通知单。航空运单还可作为核收运费的依据和海关查验放行的基本单据。航空运单的正本一般为1式3份，分3种颜色：蓝色交托运人；绿色归承运人留存；粉红色随货同行，在目的地交收货人。航空运单的副本一般至少6份，如需要还可增加份数，分别发给代理人，目的地代理，第一、二、三承运人和用作提货收据。副本除提货收据为黄色，其余均为白色。在航空运单的收货人栏内，必须详细填写收货人的全称和地址，不能做成指示性抬头。

### 3. 铁路运输单据

铁路运单（railway bill）是铁路部门和货主间缔结的运输契约。铁路运输可分为国际铁路联运和国（地区）内铁路运输两种方式。国（地区）内铁路运输和国（地区）际铁路联运使用的运单，其格式和内容有所不同。国（地区）际铁路货物联运使用国际铁路联运运单，国（地区）内铁路货物运输使用国（地区）内铁路运单。中国内地通过铁路对港、澳出口货物时，由于铁路运单不能作为对外结汇的凭证，而使用"承运货物收据"。"承运货物收据"具有物权凭证的性质。

### 4. 邮包收据

邮包收据（parcel post receipt）是邮包运输的主要单据，它既是邮局收到寄件人的邮包后所签发的凭证，也是收件人凭以提取邮件的凭证。当邮包发生损坏或丢失时，它还可以作为索赔和理赔的依据，但邮包收据不是物权凭证。

### 5. 多式联运单据

多式联运单据（combined transport documents, CTD）是由多式联运经营人签发，用以证明多式联运合同以及证明多式联运经营人接管货物并负责按合同条款交付货物的单据。多式联运经营人必须对运输全程负责，无论货物在何种运输方式下发生属于承运人责任范围内的灭失或损毁，多式联运经营人都必须对托运人负赔偿责任。多式联运单据与海运中的联运提单有相似之处，但其性质与联运提单有别。多式联运单据既可用于海运与其他运输方式的联运，也可用于不包括海运的其他运输方式的联运。而海运联运提单仅限于在由海运与其他运输方式所组成的联合运输时使用。

### （六）分批装运与转运

分批装运和转运是货物装运的重要内容，并直接关系到买卖双方的利益。

#### 1. 分批装运

分批装运又称分期装运，即一个合同项下的货物分若干期或若干批装运，但"分批装运"和"分期装运"有一定的区别。"分批装运"的"分批"，强调的是货物具体是分几次装运，是一个运输概念；而"分期装运"的"分期"，不仅关系到货物的运输批次，还关系到货款是否"按批次"支付。对卖方来说，"允许"分批装运比"禁止"分批装运有利。在"允许"分批装运的前提下，给予卖方宽松的、限制少的分批装运比"限时、限批、限量"的分期装运更为有利。分批装运的规定方法一般有3种：①不准分批装运（partial shipment is not allowed），即货物必须一次全部装运，不允许分批装运。②准许分批装运（partial shipment is allowed），但对于分批的具体时间、批次和数量均不做规定。这种规定方法，不仅允许卖方分批装运，而且只要卖方在规定的装运期内完成合同总数量的装运即可。③准许分批装运，但需要限时、限批、限量装运。这种装运方法规定了具体的装运批次规定、每批次的具体装运时间与详细装运数量。这种规定方法留给卖方的机动余地很小。根据《联合国国际货物销售合同公约》第七十三条第一款的规定："对于分批交付货物的合同，如果一方当事人不履行对任何一批货物的业务，便对该批货物构成根本违反合同，另一方当事人可以宣告对该批货物失效。"而根据UCP600第三十二条的规定："如信用证规定在指定的时间段内分期支款或分期发运，任何一期未按信用证规定期限支取或发运时，信用证对该期及以后各期均告失效。"

#### 2. 转运

在实际业务中，在采用集装箱运输或非水上运输情况下，"转运"的概念已不存在。因此，"转运"是一个比较狭窄的概念。只有在同时满足以下3个条件的基础上，即海运或内河运输、非集装箱运输、换船，"转运"才有可能发生。允许"转运"一般对卖方比较有利，但货物在转运时有可能增加损耗或散失，使运程延迟，增加费用支出。根据UCP600第十九条b条款的规定："转运（transshipment）是指在从信用证规定的发送、接管或者发运地点至目的地的运输过程中，从某一运输工具上卸下货物，并装上同另一运输工具的行为（无论其是否为不同的运输方式）。"而UCP600第二十条c（II）条款的规定："即使信用证禁止转运，注明将要或可能发生转运的提单仍可接受，只要其表明货物由集装箱、拖车或子船运输。"

### （七）装运通知

国际货物买卖，不论以哪种贸易术语成交，买卖双方均有相互通知的义务。装运通知的规定，有利于明确买卖双方的责任，促使买卖双方互相配合，共同搞好车、船、货的衔接，并便于办理货物运输保险。因此，国际货物买卖合同中规定装运通知条款，有利于合同履行，避免和减少纠纷的发生。在买卖双方产生纠纷时，也可运用装运通知，作为评判双方责任的依据。在以CFR、CPT贸易术语成交的合同，卖方在合理的时间发送装运通知给买方具有特别重要的意义。采用其他贸易术语成交时，买卖双方都应约定相互给予有关交接货物的通知，以便互相配合，做好及时交接货物的准备，避免不应有的损失。

## 二、国际货物运输保险

保险可分为财产保险、责任保险、信用保险（或称保证保险）和人身保险4类。国际货物运输保险属于财产保险。投保运输保险是国际货物买卖的重要环节。货物运输保险条款的内容必须明确、合理，其主要内容包括：货物运输保险保障的范围、办理保险办理人、保险金额、投保险别、保险索赔与理赔的注意事项等。准确掌握货物运输保险保障的风险、损失以及不同险别的责任范围、保险期限，有利于正确处理货物运输投保和保险索赔。

### （一）保险索赔与理赔的基本原则

不论哪一类保险，投保人与保险人在订立保险合同时应共同遵守以下4个基本原则。

#### 1. 保险利益原则

保险利益（insurable interest）又称可保权益，是指投保人对保险标的具有法律上承认的利益。保险标的（subject matter insured）是保险所要保障的对象，它可以是任何财产及其相关利益、人的寿命或身体等。保险利益原则是指投保人对保险标的的应当具有保险利益，如果投保人对保险标的不具有保险利益，保险合同无效。在国际货物运输保险中，保险利益主要表现为货物本身的价值，也包括与货物本身价值相关的运费、保险费、关税和预期利润等。

#### 2. 近因原则

近因原则（principle of proximate cause）是指保险人只对承保风险与保险标的损失之间有直接因果关系的损失承担赔偿责任，而对保险责任范围外的风险造成的保险标的的损失，不承担赔偿责任。

### 3. 最大诚信原则

最大诚信原则（utmost good faith）是指投保人和保险人在签订保险合同时以及在保险合同的有效期内，必须保持最大限度的诚意，双方互不欺骗隐瞒。保险人应向投保人说明保险合同的条款内容，投保人在投保时应将自己知道的或通常业务中应当知道的保险标的方面的重要事实如实告知保险人，以便保险人判断是否同意承保或决定承保。被保险人还必须在保险合同中承诺"要做"或"不做"某种事情，保证某种情况的"存在"或"不存在"，或保证履行某一条件。例如，被保险人应保证货物不用15年以上船龄的旧船装运等。

### 4. 补偿原则

补偿原则（principle of indemnity），又称损害赔偿原则，是指当保险标的遭受保险责任范围内的损失时，保险人应当按照保险合同的约定履行赔偿义务，但赔偿金额不得超过保险单上的保险金额或被保险人遭受的实际损失。

## （二）货物运输保险保障的范围

国际货物运输保险因运输方式不同，可分为海洋运输货物保险、陆上运输货物保险、航空运输货物保险、邮包运输货物保险。不同运输方式的货物保险，保险公司承保的责任有所不同，但其保障范围相似。货物运输保险保障的范围包括风险、损失和费用等，下面以海洋运输保险为例来加以说明。

### 1. 风险

海洋运输货物保险的风险，分为海上风险和外来风险。

海上风险（peril of the sea）又称海难，是指船舶或货物在海上运输过程中发生的或随附海上运输所发生的风险，包括自然灾害（natural calamity）和意外事故（fortuitous accident）。自然灾害是指不以人的意志为转移的自然界力量所引起的灾害，如恶劣气候、雷电、海啸、洪水、地震、火山爆发、浪击落海等。这些灾害在保险业务中都有其特定的含义，例如，八级以上的海风、三米以上的海浪，才可被称为恶劣气候。意外事故是指由于偶然的、难以预料的原因造成的事故，如船舶搁浅、触礁、沉没、焚毁、互撞、遇流冰、失火、爆炸等原因造成的事故。需要特别说明的是，按照国际保险市场的一般解释，海上风险并不局限于海上发生的灾害和事故，那些与海上航行有关的发生在陆上或海路、海河或与驳船相连接之处的灾害和事故，如地震、洪水、火灾、爆炸、海轮与驳船或码头碰撞，也属于海上风险。外来风险（extraneous risk）是指因海上风险以外其他外来原因引起的风险，包括一般外来风险和特殊外来风险。一般外来风险，包括偷窃、破碎、渗漏、玷污、受潮、受热、串味、生锈、钩损、短量、淡水雨淋等；特殊外来风险，包括战争、罢工、交货不到、拒收等。

海上风险以外的其他外来干涉风险所造成的损失，称为外来风险损失。按其发生的原因不同，可分为一般外来风险的损失和特殊外来风险的损失。一般外来风险的损失是指在运输途中由于偷窃、破碎、渗漏、玷污、受潮、受热、串味、生锈、钩损、短量、淡水雨淋等一般外来风险所造成的损失。特殊外来风险的损失，是指由于军事、政治、国家（地区）政策法令以及行政措施，如战争、罢工、交货不到、拒收等特殊外来风险所造成的损失。

**2. 海上损失和费用**

海上损失和费用是指被保险人因被保险货物在运输途中遭遇海上风险而造成的损失和引起的费用，包括货物本身遭到破坏或灭失的损失和为营救货物而支出的费用。按照国际保险业习惯，海上损失和费用也包括与海运相连接的陆上或内河运输所发生的损失和费用。

**（1）海上损失**

海上运输途中被保险货物本身遭到损坏或灭失的损失，按其损失程度大小可分为全部损失（total loss）或部分损失（partial loss）。

全部损失简称全损，是指整批或不可分割的一批被保险货物在运输途中全部遭受损失。全部损失又分为实际全损（actual total loss）和推定全损（constructive total loss）。实际全损是指该批被保险货物在运输途中全部灭失，或者受到严重损坏完全失去原来的形体、效用，或者不再归被保险人所拥有。例如，载货船舶失踪，经过一定时间（如2个月）后仍没有获知其消息的，视为实际全损。推定全损是指被保险货物在运输途中受损后，实际全损已不可避免，或者为避免发生实际全损所需支付的费用与继续将货物运抵目的地的费用之和超过保险价值，即恢复、修复受损货物并将其运送到原定目的地的费用将超过该目的地的货物价值。被保险货物遭到实际全损时，被保险人可按其投保金额获得保险公司全部损失的赔偿；被保险货物发生推定全损时，被保险人可以要求保险人按部分损失赔偿，也可要求按全部损失赔偿。如果被保险人要求按全部损失赔偿，被保险人必须向保险人发出委付通知（notice of abandonment）。委付的目的，是表明被保险人表示愿意将保险标的的一切权利与义务转移给保险人，并要求保险人按全部损失赔偿。委付必须经保险人同意后才能生效，但被保险人应当在合理的时间内将接受委付或不接受委付的决定通知被保险人。委付一经保险人接受，不得撤回。

部分损失是指不属于实际全损和推定全损的损失，也就是说没有达到全部损失程度的损失。部分损失可分为共同海损和单独海损。共同海损是指在同一海上航程中，船舶、货物和其他财产遭遇共同危险，为了共同安全，有意地合理采取措施所直接造成的特殊牺牲、支付的特殊费用。构成共同海损，必须同时具备4个条件：第一，导致共同海损的危险必须是真实存在或不可避免的。第二，船方所采取的措施，必须是为了解除船、货的共同危险，有意识而且是合理的。第三，所做的牺牲具有特殊性，支出的费用是额外的，是为了解除危险而不是由危险直接造成的。第四，牺牲和费用支出最终必须是有效的，即采取某种措施后，船舶和/或货物的全部或一部分最后安全抵达航程的重点港或目的地，从而避免了船、货同归于尽的局面。根据惯例，共同海损的牺牲和费用，应由船舶、货物和运费三方按最后获救的价值多少，按比例进行分摊。单独海损是指除共同海损以外的部分损失，应由受损方单独承担该部分损失。

（2）费用

海洋运输保险的费用是指为营救被保险货物所支出的费用，包括施救费用（sue and labor expenses）和救助费用（salvage charges）：①施救费用，是指保险标的在遭遇保险责任范围内的灾害事故时，被保险人或其代理人、雇佣人员等对保险标的采取的各种抢救措施，为防止或减少货损而支出的合理费用。保险人对这种施救费用负责赔偿。②救助费用，是指保险标的遭遇保险责任范围内的灾害事故时，由保险人和被保险人以外的第三者采取了施救措施并获得成功而向其支付的报酬，保险人对这种费用也负责赔偿。

☞ **案例4.6**

### 台风"山竹"致使深圳盐田港168艘集装箱船严重延误

据中国国际商会2018年9月17日报道，2018年第22号台风"山竹"（强台风级）于9月16日17时在江门台山海宴镇登陆，登陆时中心附近最大风力14级（45米/秒，相当于162千米/小时）。深圳盐田、蛇口等码头于9月14日晚（周五）左右正式关闭，停止所有交提柜工作。该台风对深圳、香港、广州等港口造成了极为严重的影响，码头系统出现故障，有超过168艘集装箱船因受台风影响面临严重的船期延误，这些船舶的原定预计到港时间为9月15—17日。盐田国际码头堆场、大铲湾码头和招商港部分集装箱被吹倒，金色海岸码头1号泊位浮桥部分断裂，部分码头建筑被掀顶。

### （三）货物运输保险的险别与条款

长期以来，在世界保险业中，英国制定的保险法、保险条款、保险单等对世界各国的影响很大。目前，国际上许多国家和地区的保险公司在国际货物运输业务中直接采用英国保险业协会所制定的"协会货物条款"（Institute Cargo Clauses，ICC），或者在制定本国（地区）保险条款时参考或部分参考ICC。中国进出口货物运输保险最常用的保险条款是"中国保险条款"（China Insurance Clauses，CIC），该条款由中国人民保险公司参照国际保险市场的习惯做法起草，并经中国人民银行及中国保险监督管理委员会审批后颁布。CIC按运输方式分为海洋、陆上、航空和邮包运输保险条款。对某些特殊商品，还配备有海运冷藏货物、陆运冷藏货物、海运散装桐油、活牲畜及家禽的海陆空运输保险条款等，以及适用于上述各种运输方式货物保险的各种附加险条款。中国的进出口货物，如要办理货物运输保险，可以自由选择CIC或ICC加以投保。下面以中国海洋运输货物保险的险别与条款为例进行说明。

**1. 中国海洋运输货物保险的险别与条款**

中国的货物运输保险险别分为基本险和附加险两大类。基本险可单独投保，附加险不可单独投保。按照1981年1月1日修订的《海洋运输货物保险条款》（Ocean Marine Cargo Clauses）规定，中国的海洋运输货物保险的基本险，分为平安险（Free from particular average，FPA）、水渍险（with particular average，WPA）和一切险（all risks）3种，而附加险包括一般附加险（General additional risk）和特殊附加险（Special additional risk）2种。

（1）**基本险的承保责任范围及除外责任**

平安险的承保责任范围包括：①被保险货物在运输过程中由于自然灾害造成整批货物的实际全损或推定全损；②由于运输工具遭受搁浅、触礁、沉没、互撞、与流冰或与其他物体碰撞以及失火、爆炸等意外事故造成货物的全部或部分损失；③在运输工具已经发生搁浅、触礁、沉没、焚毁意外事故的情况下，货物在此前后又在海上遭受恶劣气候、雷电、海啸等自然灾害所造成的部分损失；④在装卸或转运时由于一件或数件整件货物落海造成的全部或部分损失；⑤被保险人对遭受承保责任内遭遇危险的货物采取抢救、防止或减少货损的措施而支付的合理费用，但以不超过该批被救货物的保险金额为限；⑥运输工具遭遇海难后，在避难港由于卸货所引起的损失，以及在中途港、避难港由于卸货、存仓、运送货物所产生的特别费用；⑦共同海损的牺牲、分摊和救助费用；⑧运输契约订有"船舶互撞责任"条款，根据该条款规定应由货方赔偿船方的损失。

水渍险的承保责任范围，除包括上列平安险的各项责任外，还负责被保险货物由于恶劣气候、雷电、海啸、地震、洪水等自然灾害所造成的部分损失。

一切险的承保责任范围，除包括上列平安险和水渍险的各项责任外，还负责货物在运输过程中由于一般外来风险所造成的全部或部分损失。

在平安险、水渍险和一切险的保险条款中，还明确规定了除外责任（exclusion）。所谓除外责任，是指保险公司明确规定不予承保的损失或费用。按照"中国保险条款"，对于3种基本险别，保险公司的除外责任有：①因被保险人的故意行为或过失所造成的损失；②属于发货人责任所引起的损失；③在保险责任开始前，被保险货物已存在的品质不良或数量短差所造成的损失；④被保险货物的自然损耗、本质缺陷、特性以及市价跌落、运输延迟所引起的损失或费用；⑤该公司海洋运输货物战争险条款和货物运输罢工险条款规定的责任范围和除外责任。

（2）**附加险的承保责任范围及除外责任**

附加险是对基本险的补充。投保人只有在投保一种基本险的基础上才可加保一种或数种附加险。《中国保险条款》中的附加险，分为有一般附加险和特殊附加险。应注意的是，一切险的承保责任范围包含一般附加险，但不包含特殊附加险；而平安险、水渍险的承保责任范围既不包含一般附加险，也不包含特殊附加险。

一般附加险有11种：①偷窃、提货不着险（theft, pilferage and non. delivery，TPND）；②淡水雨淋险（fresh water and/or rain damage）；③短量险（shortage）；④混杂沾污险（inter mixture and contamination）；⑤渗漏险（leakage）；⑥碰损、破碎险（clash and Breakage）；⑦串味险（taint of odor）；⑧受热受潮险（sweating and heating）；⑨钩损险（hook damage）；⑩包装破裂险（breakage of packing）；⑪锈损险（rust）。

特殊附加险具体有8种：①战争险（war risk）；②罢工险（strike risk）；③交货不到

险（failure to deliver）；④进口关税险（import duty）；⑤黄曲霉素险（aflatoxin）；⑥舱面险（on deck）；⑦拒收险（rejection）；⑧货物出口到香港（包括九龙）或澳门存仓火险责任扩展条款（fire risk extension clause，FREC — for storage of cargo at destination Hong Kong, including Kowloon or Macao）。由于特殊附加险的保险责任范围，不包括在一切险的责任范围之内。因此，在投保基本险的基础上，如需要取得特殊附加险的险别承保责任保障，必须加保特殊附加险。

战争险、罢工险的除外责任包括：①对使用原子或核武器所致的损失和费用，不负赔偿责任；②对在罢工期间由于劳动力短缺或不能使用劳动力所造成的被保险货物的损失，包括因罢工而引起的动力或燃料缺乏使冷藏机停止工作所致的冷藏货物的损失，以及无劳动力搬运货物使货物堆积在码头淋湿所受的损失，不负赔偿责任。

☞ **案例4.7**

**意大利工会呼吁：在2018年10月25日星期四和10月26日星期五**
**在意大利各地举行交通罢工**

Trenitalia，Italo NTV 和 Trenord 的铁路工人将于 10 月 25 日至 26 日 21:00（当地时间）举行全国运输罢工。10 月 26 日，工会还呼吁意大利各城市的公共交通工人在 10 月 26 日进行 24 小时的罢工。据了解，与运输有关的罢工在意大利很常见，并且可能具有很强的破坏性。但是，根据意大利法律，在所有罢工期间必须保证最低服务水平。建议在这段时间要向意大利出口货物的公司注意罢工事件，做好货物妥善安排，以免造成延误。

### 2. 伦敦保险协会海运货物保险的险别与条款

于1982年1月1日修订完毕，并于1983年4月1日起正式实行的"协会货物条款"，主要有6种险别，分别是：①协会货物（A）险条款［ICC（A）］；②协会货物（B）险条款［ICC（B）］；③协会货物（C）险条款［ICC（C）］；④协会战争险条款（货物）（Institute War Clauses — Cargo，IWCC）；⑤协会罢工险条款（货物）（Institute Strikes Clauses — Cargo，ISCC）；⑥恶意损害险条款（Malicious Damage Clause）。该6种险别，除ICC（A）、ICC（B）、ICC（C）3种基本险别可以单独投保外，战争险和罢工险在需要时也可以独立投保，而恶意损害险条款不能独立投保。恶意损害险条款承保被保险人以外的其他人（如船长、船员等）的故意破坏行动所致被保险货物的灭失或损坏。如果是出于政治动机的人的行动所致被保险货物的灭失或损坏，不属于恶意损害险承保范围。ICC（A）险的承保责任范围中已加入了恶意损害险，但ICC（B）、ICC（C）险却没有加入恶意损害险条款。因此，恶意损害险可在投保ICC（B）、ICC（C）险的基础上加保。

ICC（A）险的承保责任范围最广，它采用"一切风险减除外责任"的方式。即除了在除外责任项下所列风险所致损失不予负责外，其他风险所致损失均予负责。ICC（A）险的除外责任有4类：①一般除外责任条款；②船舶不适航和不适货的除外责任条款；③战争除外责任条款；④罢工除外责任条款。每一类除外责任都有专门的含义。例如，一般除外责任条款，包括：被保险人故意的不法行为所造成的损失或费用；保险标的自然渗漏、重量或容量的自然损耗或自然磨损；由于包装不足或不当所造成的损失或费用；因保险标的的内在缺陷或特征所造成的损失或费用；由于延迟所引起的直接损失或费用；因船舶所有人、经理人、租船人经营破产或不履行债务所造成的损失或费用；等等。

ICC（B）险对承保风险的规定采用"列明风险"的方式，即把所承保的风险一一列明。凡属承保责任范围内的损失，无论是全部损失或部分损失，保险人按损失程度均负责赔偿。ICC（B）险的承保风险规定，货物灭失或损害要合理归因于10种原因中的任何一种：火灾或爆炸；船舶或驳船触礁、沉没或倾覆；陆上运输工具倾覆或出轨；船舶、驳船或其他运输工具同水以外的任何外界物体相碰撞；在避难港卸货；地震、火山爆发或雷电；共同海损的牺牲；抛货；浪击落海；海水、湖水或河水进入船舱、驳船、集装箱、大型海运箱、其他运输工具或储存处所；货物在装卸时落海或跌落造成整件的全损。ICC（B）险的除外责任方面，除对"海盗行为"和恶意损害险的责任不负责外，其余均与ICC（A）险的除外责任相同。

ICC（C）险的风险责任规定，也与（B）险一样，采用"列明风险"的方式，但仅对"重大意外事故"（major casualties）所致损失负责，对非重大意外事故和自然灾害所致损失均不负责。ICC（C）险的承保风险规定，货物灭失或损害要合理归因于7种原因中的任何一种：火灾或爆炸；船舶或驳船触礁、沉没或倾覆；陆上运输工具倾覆或出轨；船舶、驳船或其他运输工具同与水以外的任何外界物体相碰撞；在避难港卸货；共同海损的牺牲；抛货。ICC（C）险的除外责任与ICC（B）险完全相同。

### （四）运输保险条款规定的保险责任起讫期限和索赔时效

与国际保险市场的习惯做法一样，中国的海洋运输保险条款规定的保险责任起讫期限，采用"仓至仓"条款（warehouse to warehouse clause，W/W clause），即保险公司的保险责任自被保险货物运离保险单所载明的起运仓库或储存处所开始运输时生效，包括正常运输过程中的海上、陆上、内河和驳船运输在内，直至该项货物到达保险单所载明的目的地收货人的最后仓库或储存处所或被保险人用作分配、分派或非正常运输的其他储存处所为止。如未抵达上述仓库或储存处所，则以被保险货物在最后卸载港全部卸离海轮后满60天为止。如在上述60天内被保险货物需转运至非保险单所载明的目的地时，则以该项货物开始转运时生效。

罢工险采用"仓至仓"条款。按照国际保险业惯例，已投保战争险后另加保罢工险，不另收保险费；如仅要求加保罢工险，则按战争险费率收取保险费。

战争险的保险责任起讫以"水上危险"（waterborne）为限，即自货物在起运港装上海轮或驳船时开始，直至目的港卸离海轮或驳船时为止。如不卸离海轮或驳船，则从海轮到达目的港的当日午夜起算满15天，保险责任自行终止；如在中途港转船，不论货物是否在当地卸货，保险责任均以海轮到达该港或卸货地点的当日午夜起算满15天为止，待再装上续运海轮时恢复有效。

海运保险索赔时效自被保险货物在最后卸载港全部卸离海轮后起算，最多不超过2年。

### （五）国际货物运输保险的具体办理

办理货物运输保险的基本环节，包括确定投保险别、投保金额、订立保险合同、保险单据、索赔与理赔等。Incoterms®2010的11种贸易术语中，只明确规定适用CIF、CIP2种术语的卖方有义务办理货物运输保险，而适用其他9种贸易术语的卖方对买方无办理运输保险的义务；但适用11种术语的买方对卖方均无办理运输保险的义务。不过在实际业务中，使用EXW、FAS、FOB、FCA、CFR、CPT术语成交的买卖合同，买方为了降低货物运输的风险，一般会自行选择办理保险。而使用DAT、DAP、DDP术语成交的买卖合同，卖方为了降低货物运输的风险，一般也会自行选择办理保险。

#### 1. 确定投保险别

在办理国际货物运输保险时，应注意选择合适的保险险别。不同的险别，保险公司承保的责任范围不同，保险费率也各有差异。一般来说，选择保险险别时，应该考虑的因素有以下几点。①货物的性质和特点。例如，粮食由于容易受潮、受热而发霉，应选择投保一切险或在投保水渍险的基础上加保受潮受热险、短量险。②货物的包装。例如：散装的矿石可能发生短量，故应加保短量险。袋装大米可能被挂钩钩破包装袋，故应加保钩损险。③货物的用途与价值。例如：价值昂贵的金银、珠宝以及贵重的工艺品，应投保一切险来获得全面保障。④运输方式与运输工具。例如：航空运输强制投保航空运输货物战争险。⑤运输线路。例如：海洋运输途经索马里区域或各国海上军演密集的区域，建议投保战争险、交货不到险。⑥运输季节和港口、车站的条件等。例如：冬季运输的货物容易出现冻裂，夏季运送的货物容易出现腐烂现象。车站或港口条件的不同，也会影响货物的装卸和存放，发生不同的风险及损失。因此，投保人应根据不同的情况确定合适的险别。

#### 2. 确定投保金额

投保金额是计收保险费的依据，也是货物发生损失后计算赔偿的依据。按照国际保险市场的惯例，保险金额一般按CIF金额另加10%的投保加成。保险金额计算的公式是：

保险金额＝CIF货值×（1＋投保加成率）

保险费＝保险金额×保险费率

例如，某公司出口一批货物到新加坡，CIF价为10000美元，要求投保海运一切险，按CIF价加成10%，保险费率0.5%，则保险金额为11000美元，保险费为55美元。

### 3. 取得保险单据

国际货物运输保险常用的保险单据主要有保险单（insurance policy）、保险凭证（insurance certificate）和联合凭证等。保险单是被保险人向保险人索赔或对保险人上诉的正式文件，也是保险人理赔的主要依据，俗称"大保单"。它是保险人和被保险人之间保险合同关系的正式凭证，其主要内容包括：被保险人的姓名、发票号码、合同号码、被保险货物的品名、标记、包装数量、保险金额、运输工具名称、航次/航班、开航日期、运输路线、赔款地点、投保险别、投保日期及投保人签章、企业名称、电话、地址等。除此以外，保险单还附有保险人责任范围以及保险人和被保险人权利和义务等方面的详细条款。保险单可转让，通常是被保险人向银行交单的单证之一。在CIF、CIP合同中，保险单是卖方必须向买方提供的单据。

保险凭证俗称"小保单"，它是保险人签发给被保险人，证明货物已经投保和保险合同已经生效的文件。保险凭证具有与保险单同等的效力，但在信用证规定提交保险单时，不能提交保险凭证。联合凭证是一种简化的保险凭证，仅将险别和保险金额加注在出口公司发票上，其他项目以发票所列为准。联合凭证虽然内容比较简单，但具有与保险凭证同样的效用。货物在保险期间内发生的损失，按该保险类别的有关条款办理。

### 4. 保险索赔

被保险货物运抵目的地后，收货人如发现被保险货物发生了损失时，可以首先确定索赔对象，然后提出赔偿要求。例如，买方发现卖方交付的货物品质、规格、包装、重量（数量）不符合合同规定等，可向卖方提出索赔。如发生以下情况，应向承运人提出索赔：①货物短卸，即货物未卸净，或货物误卸在其他港口造成短卸。②货物在运输过程中被盗窃，或因破损撒漏而货物短少。③属于承运人责任的货物损毁，包括破损、毁坏、水渍、污染等。如发生属于保险单承保险别责任范围内的有关损失，应向保险公司索赔。

被保险人向保险公司提出索赔的程序如下。①损失通知。被保险人获悉货损后，应立即通知保险公司或保险单上指明的代理人。后者接到损失通知后，应立即采取相应的措施，如检验损失、提出施救意见、确定保险责任和签发检验报告等。②向承运人等有关方面索赔。被保险人除向保险公司报告损失外，如发现货损、货差，还应立即向承运人或有关当局（如海关、港务局等）索取相应的证明并以书面形式向有关责任方索赔。③采取合理的施救、整理措施。被保险货物受损后，被保险人应及时采取必要的措施以防止损失的扩大，保险公司对此提出处理意见的，应按保险公司的要求处理，所支出的费用可由保险公司负责，但以不超过该批被救货物的保险金额为限。④备妥索赔单证，及时提出索赔。被保险货物的损失经过检验并办妥向承运人等第三责任方的追偿手续后，应立即向保险公司或其代理人提出赔偿要求。索赔单证除正式的索赔函以外，应包括保险单证、运输单据、发票以及检验报告、货损货差证明等。保险索赔的时效一般为2年。⑤代位追偿。在实际业务中，保险人首先向被保险人进行赔付，被保险人在获得赔偿的同时签署一份权益转让书，放弃向第三责任方追偿的权利。保险人则凭此取得代位追偿权，直接向第三责任方进行追偿。

### 5. 保险理赔

保险公司理赔时，首先应确定损失原因，然后再进行责任审定。保险人应根据保险条款中的保险险别及期限等规定，审定是否进行赔偿，最后计算赔偿金额。

### （六）保险条款举例

保险条款是国际货物买卖合同的重要组成部分之一，必须订得明确、合理。保险条款的内容依据选用的贸易术语不同而有所区别。在以CIF、CIP术语成交的贸易合同中，保险条款内容必须明确规定由谁办理保险、投保险别、保险金额的确定方法、按什么保险条款保险，并注明该条款的修订日期。举例如下。

①Insurance to be covered by the seller for 110% of CIF/CIP total invoice value against All Risks and War Risk as per Ocean Marine Cargo Clauses of the China Insurance Clauses dated 1/1/1981（保险由卖方按照CIF/CIP发票金额的110%投保一切险和战争险，以1981年1月1日修订的"中国保险条款"的有关海洋运输保险的条款为准）。该条款适合海洋运输。

②Insurance to be covered by the seller for 110% of CIP total invoice value against Overland Transportation All Risks and All Risks as per Overland Transportation Cargo Clauses "Train, Truck" and Ocean Marine Cargo Clauses of the China Insurance Clauses dated 1/1/1981, including War Risk as per Overland Transportation Cargo War Risk (by train) dated 1/1/1981 and Ocean Marine Cargo War Risks Clauses dated 1/1/1981［（保险由卖方按照CIP发票金额的110%投保陆运（火车、汽车）一切险和海洋运输货物一切险，按照1981年1月1日生效的中国保险条款的有关陆上运输货物保险条款和海洋运输保险条款；加保战争险，按照1981年1月1日修订的陆上运输货物战争险（火车）条款和海洋运输货物战争险条款）］。该条款适用于陆海联运。

③insurance to be covered by the seller for 110% of total invoice value against ICC (A) and IWC (Cargo) as per Institute Cargo Clauses dated 1/1/1982［（保险由卖方按照发票金额的110%投保协会货物（A）险和战争险，以1982年1月1日修订的伦敦保险业条款为准］。该条款适用于任何运输方式。

采用EXW、FAS、CFR、FCA、CPT、FCA术语成交的贸易合同，保险条款可规定为：(a) Insurance to be covered by the buyer（保险由买方负责）; (b) Insurance to be covered at the buyer's option（保险由买方选择是否投保）。

采用DAT、DAP、DDP术语成交的贸易合同，保险条款可规定为：(a) Insurance to be covered by the seller（保险由卖方负责）; (b) Insurance to be covered at the seller's option)（保险由卖方选择是否投保）。

**思考题**

1. 中国某企业出口商品共100箱，每箱体积为30cm×60cm×50cm，每箱毛重为20 kg。根据货物名称，经查船公司的价格表，在货物分级表中查到相应的运费计算标准为W/M，基本运费为每运费吨USD30.00，另收燃油附加费20%、港口拥挤附加费20%，货币贬值附加费为100%，试计算：该批货物的运费是多少？

2. 某批出口货物的CIF总价为20万美元，投保一切险和战争险。已知一切险、战争险的保险费率分别为0.3%、0.2%，投保加成10%。请问，该批货物应缴纳的保险费是多少？

3. 国际货物买卖合同中的"货物交付"条款，具体包含哪些内容？

4. 投保国际货物运输保险的基本险别与附加险别，"中国保险条款"与"协会货物条款"的区别是什么？

5. 根据跨境电商的一个真实案例，来分析该跨境电商运费模板设置的成功或不足之处。

6. 试分析跨境电商中的产品质量保险、运费险与国际货物运输保险间的相同点与不同点。

# Chapter 4

# Transportation of the Goods and Its Insurance

☞ Case 4.1

Co. B exported a batch of silk garments to the west coast of the United States. The outer packing was carton, the inner packing was breathable plastic bag. The goods were transported in containers. After the goods arrived at the destination, more than 100 packing boxes in the container were found to be seriously affected by damp. The buyer had contacted the inspection claim agent appointed by the insurance policy to make the inspection, trough checked and issued the inspection report. The buyer lodged a claim with the insurance company on the basis of the inspection report, but the insurance company refused to settle the claim on the ground that some of the losses caused by the natural disaster were not covered by the FPA insurance. First of all, the loss of the cargo belonged to partial loss. Second, the reason for the damage was that during the ocean transportation, due to the impact of typhoon and rainstorm, water accumulated on the top of the container, and the rain infiltrated into the container from the air hole on the top of the container, resulting in partial loss of the cargo. For the loss in this case, the buyer could not get compensation from the insurance company if the insurance was covered by FPA or WA only. If the insurance is covered by FPA or WA plus rain or fresh water damaged insurance or by direct insurance against all risks, compensation could be obtained from the insurance company. The safeguard of transport insurance under different coverage are different.

Transport of the goods refers to the act of seller transfer title to the goods to the buyer in accordance with the stipulations of contract. International transport has several modes and involves a lot of intermediate links and complex practical situations with high risks and timely work-going. The nature of transport documents of different modes of transport is quite different and directly related to transfering the goods smoothly and settleing payment in safety. The loss or damage to the goods may be occurred due to transport and storage during long distance, and it is necessary to cover transport insurance. Insurance refers to the insured (applicant), according to the contract, pay premium to the insurer (underwriter). If loss of or damage to the goods is caused by the contractual accident during transport, the insurer should compensate to the party with insurable interest as per the degree of loss or damag. It is critical for international trade to select successfully a proper mode of transport and stipulate shipment and insurance clauses correctly.

# 4.1 International Transport

The transport clauses in a sales contract includes transport liabilities, mode, time, port (place) of shipment, port (place) of destination, transport document, partial shipment, transshipment, shipment notice, etc.

## 4.1.1 Transport Obligation

The transport route covers place of origin to destination, such as from the warehouse of premises to the warehouse of wholesale and retail in another country/region. It can be divided into pre-carriage, main carriage, and post-carriage: ① Pre-carriage refers to the transport from original place to port (place) of departure. ② Main carriage is for transport from port (place) of departure to port (place) of destination. ③ Post-carriage is for transport from port (place) of destination to place of the buyer.

Different trade terms associate with different stipulate about transport liabilities. For example, when FOB term is applicable, the seller is responsible for pre-carriage, and the buyer is responsible for main carriage and post-carriage. When DDP rule is applicable, if it is inserted by the place of buyer, the seller is responsible for the whole journey. If a place is inserted other than the buyer's place, the buyer is responsible for the post-carriage.

## 4.1.2 Mode of Transport

Mode of transport includes shipment by sea, inland waterway, rail, air, highway, pipeline, postal/courier, etc. Container is not only suitable for any mode of transport, but also for land bridge transportation and international multimodal transportation. About 75% of international traded goods are shipped by sea. The shipping business of air, postal, rail, pipeline, and courier are developing rapidly. Railway transport all along plays an important role in international transport, and its transport volume is the number two that just less than sea-freight. Air shipping is very important for the goods needed to be delivered "just in time", such as electronic accessories, perishable commodities, and fragmented orders.

### 1. Container Transport

Varieties and specifications of container include dry container, top open container, refrigerated container, garment container, tank container, car container, platform container, etc. As per main materials, the containers are divided into steel, aluminum, stainless steel and glass steel, container. It is frequently, widely, and durably used and suitable for long-distance transportation. The most popular three kinds of containers are 40'HQ (8feet×9.6feet×40feet), 40'GP (8feet×8.6feet×40feet) and 20'GP (8feet×8.6feet×20feet). Table 4.1indicates the size of three popular containers.

Full container loaded (FCL) is called if a consignor can load a container or some containers with full goods, whereas less than container loaded (LCL). FCL-FCL, LCL-LCL, FCL-LCL, and LCL-FCL are four kinds of methods for delivery and receiving of container. Door, CY (container yard), and CFS (container freight station) are three places for delivery and receiving of container. "Door" can be the warehouse or storage place of the goods for consignor and consignee. Door-door, CY-CY, Door-CY, and CY-door are occurred normally under FCL-FCL. CFS-CFS is often occurred under LCL-LCL.

Table 4.1 The Size of Three Popular Containers

| | | | |
|---|---|---|---|
| 20'GP (8feet×8.6feet×20feet) | Inner size | Length | 5.898 meters |
| | | Width | 2.352 meters |
| | | Height | 2.385 meters |
| | Door size | Width | 2.340 meters |
| | | Height | 2.280 meters |
| | Weight | Gross weight, maximum | 30,480 kilograms |
| | | Tare weight | 3,650 kilograms |
| | | Load weight, maximum | 26,830 kilograms |
| | Internal capacity | 33.2 cubic meters | 1,170 cubic feet |
| 40'GP (8feet×8.6feet×40feet) | Inner size | Length | 12.192 meters |
| | | Width | 2.438 meters |
| | | Height | 2.393 meters |
| | Door size | Width | 2.340 meters |
| | | Height | 2.280 meters |
| | Weight | Gross weight, maximum | 30,480 kilograms |
| | | Tare weight | 3,830 kilograms |
| | | Load weight, maximum | 26,650 kilograms |
| | Internal capacity | 67.7 cubic meters | 2,390 cubic feet |

continued

| 40'HQ (8feet×9.6feet×40feet), | Inner size | Length | 12.192 meters |
| | | Width | 2.438 meters |
| | | Height | 2.896 meters |
| | Door size | Width | 2.340 meters |
| | | Height | 2.585 meters |
| | Weight | Gross weight, maximum | 30,480 kilograms |
| | | Tare weight | 3,830 kilograms |
| | | Load weight, maximum | 26,500 kilograms |
| | Internal capacity | 76.4 cubic meters | 2,700 cubic feet |

### 2. Marine Transport

Marine transport is divided into ocean voyage, short-range voyage, and coastal transport. Liner shipping and charter shipping are two completely different ways of shipping business. Charter is also called tramp and suitable for transportation of bulk cargo with large batch, single overall, and collective shipping. The charterer shall sign a charter agreement with the ship-owner and stipulates the sailing date, line, port, freight, loading, unloading, demurrage, dispatch, etc. Charter can be divided into voyage charter, time charter, and time charter on trip basis (TCT), or leasing whole, part or designate of space. The charterer can select single, round or consecutive trip of voyage charter.

Liner shipping refers to the marine transport business sailing on the scheduled line, calling at the fixed port as per the advanced shipment notice and settled by the relative fixed charge rate. It owns four characteristics: ①"Four-fixation" including fixed line, ports, sailing schedule, and relative fixed charged rate. ②The carrier in charge for loading and unloading. The loading and unloading charges are included in the basic freight. Time for loading and unloading, demurrage, and dispatch money are all neglected. ③The liner bill of lading is the evidence of the carrier's liabilities. ④Without limitation on the loaded quantities, how to stipulate and calculate freight of liner shipping and charter shipping will be explained in price of the goods in chapter 5.

### 3. Inland Waterway Transport

The inland rivers like Mekong River, the Rhine, Amazon River, and the Nile River go through two or more countries and can carry international transport. Mekong River is located in Asia. From the source in Qinghai, China and cross Tibet and Yunnan, China and cross-border go through Laos, Thailand and Vietnam and enter into the South Sea in Saigon. Vientiane, the capital of Laos, nestles on the banks of the Mekong River. The dredging of Mekong

River is significant for international trade between China and the downstream countries. The Rhine is the first river in West Europe and is also a famous international river in the world. It became international shipping channel in 1815. It goes through Liechtenstein, Austria, France, Germany, and Netherland and goes into the Sea in Rotterdam. The full length of Rhine is 1,390 kilometers. The length of navigable inland waterways is 900 kilometers; including about 700 kilometers for the vessels loaded 10,000 tons of cargo. The Rhine is crossed with other inland rivers and forms a waterway transport network of all direction extending. The costs of inland river transportation are low and convenience. However, ecological protection of the inland river is an increasing concern about the issue.

### 4. International Air and Postal Transport

The phenomenal growth of cross-border e-business promotes development of postal and air shipping business rapidly. As per the ways of air transport, air transport has regular flight transport, charter flight, centralized shipping, air express, etc. Air transport has more advantages than other modes of transport, such as fastness, safety, accuracy, and arrival of areas further inland. The airfreight carrier or its agent at the place of departure will issue an airway bill to the consignor for the evidence of cargo receipt and shipping contract. The consignee will take the airfreight cargo against a notice of arrival issued by the airfreight carrier or its agent at the place of arrival.

International postal transport is also called parcel post transport. The international parcel goes through one or more countries (regions) and performance of parcel transportation, handover, storage, and delivery are fulfilled by the post offices of the countries (regions). It has the characteristics of "door to door" and international combined transportation. It is always done by the waterway, overland, and air transportation, or combines two or more different modes of transport. The consignor will obtain a parcel post receipt from the post office in the place of departure. The post office will send the parcel to the consignee directly or the consignee can take the parcel against the notification or receipt issued by the post office.

International postal transport has limitations on the weight and measurement of the cargo. Normally, the gross weight of each parcel must be less than 20 kilograms and the length less than 100 cm. While, each country or region may have different stipulations on post. China joined Universal Postal Union in 1972 and has signed "parcel post agreements" and "post and communication agreements" with many countries. Postal transport is suitable for the goods with light weight and small volume, such as precision instruments, machine parts, pharmaceuticals, samples, and items much-needed for production.

### 5. International Railway Transport

Railway transport is divided into national railway transport and international railway combine transport as per geographical position. International railway combine transport refs to the successive railway transport in the use of two or more countries' railway and issue combined transport documents. Its concerning international treaties are International Convention on the Carriage of Goods by Rail (also called Berne Convention on Freight) and International railway Successive Transportation Agreement. China joined Sino-Soviet Association of Railway Transport Protocol in 1952 and joined International railway Successive Transportation Agreement issued by Soviet Union and seven East European countries in 1954.

## ☞ Case 4.2

Railway transport becomes the life blood of economic for China to the world. Depend on the aid of railway as the backbone of the Eurasian economic integration, China had opened at least eight lines of freight train between China and Europe as the implementation achievement of China's "The Belt and Road" Initiative, including :

① Yiwu-Sinkiang-Europe (Madrid, Spain);

② Yiwu-Sinkiang-Europe (London, United Kingdom);

③ Wuhan- Sinkiang-Europe ( Melinke Pardowitz, Czech);

④ Chongqing-Sinkiang-Europe (Duisburg, Germany);

⑤ Hefei-Sinkiang-Europe (Hamburg, Germany);

⑥ Chengdu-Europe (Lodz, Poland);

⑦ Zhengzhou-Europe (Hamburg, Germany);

⑧ Suzhou-Manzouli-Europe (Warsaw, Poland).

For example, "Chongqing-Sinkiang-Europe" railway transport passes through six countries including China, Kazakhstan, Russia, Belarus, Poland and Germany. "Yiwu-Sinkiang-Europe" railway transport passes through eight countries including China, Kazakhstan, Russia, Belarus, Poland, Germany, France and Spain. The performance of Secure and Smart Trade Line Pilot Program (SSTL) makes China-Europe Railway transport in convenience, simply the procedures and low the freight cost. It fixes the origin station, the terminal, the pathway, the schedule and freight.

### 6. International Road Transport

International road transport use trucks or lorry to send the goods from one country/region to another country/region. It is door to door with flexible, simple, convenient and fastness. It is suitable for small-volume cargo, with high freight & risk and easier to cause loss or damage to the goods. Transport from China to many surrounding countries like Nepal, Myanmar, People's Republic of Korea, Mongolia and Kazakhstan, Kyrgyzstan, Turkmenistan use truck widely.

### 7. Pipeline Transport

The pipeline transport is suitable for transportation of large quantity of bulk cargo, such as petroleum, natural gas, ore, coal, building materials, chemicals and grain. It owns features likes continuous, prompt, economical, safe, dependable, smooth and stable as well as less investment, less land, low cost. It can be automatic controlled.

China-Russia oil pipeline is the largest economic cooperation project between China and Russia at present and the agreement was signed in September, 2012. The full length of pipeline is 999.04 kilometers (72 kilometers in Russia and 927.04 kilometers in China). As per the 20-year agreement, Russia will provide oil 15million tons yearly to China through this pipeline

### 8. International Land Bridge Transport

Land bridge transport refers to transport connected with continents and oceans. It is made through a key link between transcontinental railway and highway system. Currently, the Siberian Land Bridge, North American Land bridge and new Eurasian continental bridge are the main three land bridges in the world.

①The Siberian Land Bridge is east from Hult Card Port of Vladivostok and across the Eurasian continent to Moscow. Then, it is divided into three ways: From Moscow to West & North European ports with transshipment at St. Petersburg located in the Baltic port coast. From Moscow to the frontier station in west Russia and arrive at European countries through other European countries' railway or highway. From Moscow to Black Sea Coast and then transship to Middle East or Mediterranean Coast.

②The North American Land Bridge includes the land bridges inside the United States and Canada. There are two landlines of land bridge in the United States: The traffic system of railway (road) with full length about 3,200 kilometers from the western Pacific ports to the eastern Atlantic ports and with full length 500—1,000 kilometers from the western Pacific ports to the gulf ports of Mexico. The land bridge transportation in the USA is preferential. That is OCP (overland common points) and covers North Dakota, South Dakota, Nebraska, New Mexico, Colorado and the east area.

③The new Eurasian continental bridge is east from Lian Yun Gang, China, across Asia and Europe, to Rotterdam, Netherland in the west. It goes through China, Kazakhstan, Russia, Belarus, Poland, Germany and Netherland and radiates more than 20 countries (regions). Its full length is about 10,800 kilometers including 4,134 kilometers in China.

### 9. International Multimode Transport

International multimode transport refers to use two or more different mode of transportation by the multimodal transport operator for delivery of the goods from the receipt place in one country to the nominated place in another country according to the international multimode transport contract. It develops rapidly and has prospect in the future. It can combine modes of transport like sea, land, air and inland waterway, simply procedures of complex transportation and the consignor only need one time of formalities to entrust the entire transport to the carrier.

Normally, international multimode transport uses container and the goods can be arrived at the place of destination in safety, accuracy and prompt. The consignor may save a sum certain packing costs. The Seller can obtain combine or multimode transport documents when the goods is loaded on the transport tool of pre-carriage so that he can receive advance payment.

### 4.1.3 Time of Shipment and Time of Delivery

Sometimes the real implications of shipment and delivery are same, and sometimes not. As per usual stipulating of Incoterms®2010, the seller fulfills his obligations for delivery of the goods on board the vessel at the port of shipment or procure the goods so delivered, or put the goods at disposal of the carrier at the agreed place of shipment (if any) and settled export clearance under a sales contract concluded by trade term belongs to symbolic delivery, such as FOB, CFR, CIF, FCA, CPT or CIP. In this case, shipment and delivery can be interpreted as same. While, if a contract is concluded by trade term belongs to actual delivery, such as EXW, FAS, DAT, DAP or DDP, shipment and delivery shall not be confuse or replaced each other. Most of contracts are concluded by FOB, CFR, CIF, FCA, CPT or CIP; the parties need stipulate time of shipment and shall not stipulate time of arrival in the contract, whereas the seller's liability is extended.

Time of shipment refers to the time limit that the Seller shall deliver the goods to the buyer on board the vessel at the named port of shipment or free carrier at the agreed place of shipment. In practice, the time of shipment may be stipulate a period of shipment, such as Shipment made in Nov, 2021, or in Oct/Nov, 2021, or on/before Nov 30, 2021, or not later than Nov 30, 2021. If the contract is stipulated that payment will be made by a credit or combine a certain proportion of advanced payment, time of shipment can be stipulated as: Shipment made within 15 (30, 45, 60,...) days after receipt of L/C, or The Buyer shall remit 30% payment by T/T at least 10 days before the stipulated date of shipment. The Seller will make shipment on the basis of receipt of 30% advanced payment. It's better not stipulating time of shipment as a specific date (such as shipment made on Nov 30, 2021) or shipment immediately, promptly or as soon as possible as it is easy to cause ambiguity.

### 4.1.4 Port (Place) of Shipment and Destination

Port (place) of shipment and destination is associated with trade term and mode of transport. The place of delivery must be a port if FOB, CFR, CIF or FAS is applicable as it is only suitable for sea or inland waterway transport. While, the place of delivery may be a port or place of inland if FCA, CPT, CIP, EXW, DAT, DAP or DDP is applicable.

For a contract concluded under FCA or FOB term, the port (place) of shipment particularly important, whereas the port (place) of destination is particularly important under CIF, CFR, CPT or CIP term. The former is relating to the buyer's contract of carriage and nominated the vessel or the carrier where to receive the goods, whereas the later is relating to the Seller. In generally, the port (place) of shipment is appointed out by the Seller and confirmed by the Buyer, whereas the port (place) of destination is on the opposite.

It's better to stipulate only one of port (place) of shipment or destination. If the sourcing of goods is dispersed on several places or the port (place) of destination isn't determined when the contract signed, the seller or the buyer may use his discretion to stipulate two or three ports (places) of shipment or destination or in generally in the contract. For example: (1)Shipment from Shanghai Pudong International Airport, China to San Paulo Congonhas International Airport, Brazil. (2) Shipment from Dalian/Shanghai Seaport, China to Los Angeles Seaport, the USA. (3) Shipment from main ports, China to European main ports. (4) Shipment from the ports along Yangzi River, China to the western ports of the USA.

However, stipulation in generally is benefit only for one party, the port (place) of shipment or destination shall be safety docked. If the port (place) of destination is more than one, it's better to stipulate "Partial shipment allowed" in the contract. If the port of destination is a non-base port, it's better to stipulate "transshipment allowed" in the contract. If the name of port (place) is duplicated, it's better to follow the name of country after the name of port (place). In addition, it is better not stipulate desolate port or inland town as port (place) of shipment or delivery as it is easy to cause increasing of basic freight, surcharges and delay of shipment.

## 4.1.5 Partial (installment) Shipment

A certain difference is existed between partial shipment and installment shipment. Partial shipment is relating to transport and refers to the goods under a contract may be shipped by two or more batches (lots). Installment shipment is not only relating to the batches (lots) of shipment, but also to the installment of payment. It is benefit for the Seller to stipulate that partial shipment or installment shipment is allowed in a contract. On the premise of partial shipment or installment shipment is allowed, a contract with loose or less restrictions on partial shipment is better than that with time limited, batches limited and volume limited for the Seller. Regarding to partial shipment, a contract can be stipulated as: ①Partial shipment is not allowed, or②Partial shipment is allowed, or③Partial shipment is allowed by two equal monthly lots in Oct/Nov, 2021.

Article 31b of UCP 600 stipulates: A presentation consisting of more than one set of transport documents evidencing shipment commencing on the same means of conveyance and for the same journey, provided they indicated the same destination, will not be regarded as covering a partial shipment, even they indicated different dates of shipment or different ports of loading, places of taking in charge or dispatch. If the presentation consists of more than one set of transport documents, the latest date of shipment as evidence on any of the sets of transport documents will be regarded as the date of shipment.

As per article 73 of United Nations Convention on Contracts for the International Sale of Goods (1980): In the case of a contract for delivery of goods by installments, if the failure of one party to perform any of his obligations in respect of any installment constitutes a fundamental breach of contract with respect to that installment, the other party may declare the contract avoided with respect to that installment.

If one parties failure to perform any of his obligations in respect of any installment gives the other party good grounds to conclude that a fundamental breach of contract will occur with respect to future installments, he may declare the contract avoided for the future, provided that he does so within are as on able time. A buyer who declares the contract avoided in respect of any delivery may, at the same time, declare it avoided in respect of deliveries already made or of future deliveries if, by reason of their interdependence, those deliveries could not be used for the purpose contemplated by the parties at the time of the conclusion of the contract.

Article 32 of UCP600 stipulates: If a drawing or shipment by installments with given periods is stipulated in the credit and any installment is not drawn or shipped within the period allowed for that installment, the credit ceases to be available for that and any subsequent installment.

## 4.1.6 Transshipment

Transshipment is disappeared under container transport and non-waterway transport. It is benefit for the Seller. While, transshipment may increase losses or damage to the goods in transit and possibilities of delay delivery and extraordinarily costs. Transportation made by sea or inland waterway, non-container transport and change vessel at a transit port are three essentials to transshipment.

Article 19b of UCP 600 stipulates: "transshipment means unloading from one means of conveyance and reloading to another means of conveyance (whether or not in different modes of transport) during the carriage from the place of dispatch, taking in chare or shipment to the place of final destination stated in the credit). and Article 20c(ii) of UCP 600 stipulates: " A bill of lading indicating that transshipment will or may take place is acceptable, even if the credit prohibits transshipment, if the goods have been shipped in a container, trailer or LASH barge as evidenced by the bill of lading."

### 4.1.7 Transport Documents

Transport document is the evidence for the Seller that the carrier has received the goods. The nature of transport documents issued under different mode of transportation is quite different. It is the important document for the Seller to hand over the goods, settle claim and satisfaction as well as payment. There are many kinds of transport documents including bill of lading (B/L), seaway bill, railway bill, cargo receipt, airway bill, postal receipt and combined transport document. All transport documents can act as the evidence of cargo receipt of the goods that the carrier received and the contract of carriage that the shipper and the carrier signed.

If the goods are transported by sea, the relating transport document can be a bill of lading (B/L) or a seaway bill. Moreover, a bill of lading is always the document title to the goods, whereas other transport documents are not. A liner B/L always has 3 originals in a set. The holder takes delivery of the goods at the port of destination against any original bill of lading. If the carrier released the goods to the holder against an original of B/L, the other two originals lost effectiveness automatically. As per mode of marine transport, the B/L is divided into liner B/L and charter B/L. A liner B/L always has face clauses and back clauses.

The face clauses are generally including name and address of the shipper, consignee and notify party, B/L number, vessel & voyage, port of shipment, port of discharge, place of destination, description of the goods, packing, shipping marks, package number, weight, measurement, freight and other charges, freight prepaid or collect, shipped on board date, place and date of issue, original B/Ls number, the carrier or its agent' stamp and signature.

The back clauses are the printed conditions of carriage and can be acted as evidences of rights and obligations between the carrier and shipper, between the carrier, the consignee and the holder. If a B/L with statements of rights and obligations for the shipper and the carried printed on the back of it, it is a long form B/L, whereas it is a short form B/L if the back of B/L is blank. The back clauses is unified under three international conventions including: ① Hague Rules (International Convention for the Unification of Certain Rules of Law Relating to Bills of Lading,1924), ② Hague-Visby Rules (1977), and ③ Hamburg Rules (United Nations Convention on Carriage of Goods by Sea,1978 ). Due to issue time and historical background are different, their contents are quite different. The three conventions are suitable for different countries and shipping companies.

A B/L is further divided into shipped B/L (or on board B/L) and receive for shipment B/L as per the goods shipped on board the vessel or not. Clean B/L and unclean B/L are classified if the B/L has marked any notations regarding to the goods damaged or packing in bad condition. Straight B/L, order B/L and bearer B/L are classified as per the description of consignee on the B/L. Normally, a shipped, clean, order and long form B/L is accepted by the bank or the consignee.

In practice, an order B/L issued with "to order", or "to order of the shipper", or "to order of ×××　bank" is acceptable and safety. The holder of the B/L can transfer the title to the goods through negotiate the original B/L with endorsement. It is a suggestion that the consignor should not accept a straight B/L issued by the carrier if the buyer didn't make 100% payment before shipment. If the freight is paid by the Seller, the B/L shows "Freight Prepaid", others show "Freight Collect".

In addition, ante-dated B/L, advanced B/L, stale B/L, combined transport B/L and direct B/L are appeared always in practice. An ante-dated B/L refers to a B/L that its shipped on board date is earlier than the actual shipped on board date. An advanced B/L refers to a B/L that the holder received the B/L (shows the actual shipment date) earlier than the actual date of shipment. A stale B/L is occurred under two cases: the goods prior to the transport documents arrived at port of destination under short voyage, and the original transport document delivered to the bank later than the issuance date of transport document under long voyage.

The airway bill is the main transport documents by air freight. It isn't the document title to the goods so that it can't be transferred. The consignee of airway bill shall be showed the detailed consignee's full name and address instead of "to order "as bill of lading. The consignee takes the delivery of the goods against notification of arrival issued by the air company instead of the airway bill. The airway bill is also the basic document for freight collect and the customs' examined and released of the goods. In generally, it has three originals in a set. The blue one for shipper, the green for carrier and the pink goes along with the goods and be delivered to the consignee at place of destination. It also has at least six duplicates and to be given to the agents at departure and destination, the first, second, third carrier and as the receipt of taking delivery. The duplicates are white except for the receipt of taking delivery's yellow.

Railway transport is divided into domestic railway transport and international railway transport. Inland railway bill is used for domestic railway transport and combined railway transport document or combined transport document is used for international railway transport. The cargo receipt is used for railway transport from China mainland to Hong Kong and Macao. The postal receipt can be used for evidence of claims and satisfaction when the parcel lost or damaged.

The combined transport documents (CTD) is issued by the combined transport operator and act as the evidence for the combined transport contract, taking over the goods and documents for delivery of the goods as per contract stipulated. The combined transport operator must in charge for the whole journey of the goods and bears losses of damages to the goods caused by the carriage. The combined transport document is similar as the combined bill of lading. While, the later is only for combination of marine and other mode of transport, the former is for combination of any two different mode of transport including marine and non-waterway transport.

### 4.1.8 Notification of Shipment

Notification of shipment is benefit to define clear responsibilities for the parties and their coordinate with each other for the conveyances and the goods as well as covering insurance. A contract under any trade term shall stipulate notification of shipment. The Seller shall send a sufficient shipment notification to the Buyer in reasonable time is significant under CFR or CPT term.

The contents of shipment notice always includes the sender and receiver's name, address & contact, date, reference no.(order no, commercial invoice no, bill of lading/shipment document no, letter of credit no, etc), name of commodity and its description, kind of package and numbers, total gross weight, total net weight, total measurement, shipping marks, total value of amount, shipping company, vessel and voyage number, port (place) of loading, port (place) of destination, estimated date of dispatch (ETD), estimated date of arrival (ETA), etc.

## 4.2 Transport Insurance

Insurance refers to the insured (the applicant), according to the contract, pay insurance premium to the insurer (the underwriter). The insurer undertakes compensation liability for the loss or damage of property caused by the probable accidents, or undertakes payment as agreed for the insured death, disability, illness or reaches the age/tenor contracted. Insurance can be divided into four types including property insurance, liability insurance, credit insurance (or guarantee insurance) and personal insurance. International cargo transport insurance is in the scope of property insurance.

Losses or damage to the goods may be occurred due to long distance transportation and storage, it is necessary to cover insurance against transport risks. The insured of international transport shall estimate a certain amount of insured amount and effect transport insurance to the insurer (the underwriter) before shipment made. The premium is paid by the insured according to the insured amount, insurance coverage and premium rate. The insured obtains transport insurance document from the insurer. If the goods insured was loss or damaged caused by the contractual accident during transport, the insurer should compensate to the holder of insurance document as per the insured amount and degree of loss or damage of the goods.

To cover transport insurance is one of main tasks to carry out international business. The clauses relate to transport insurance in a sales contract shall be definite and reasonable. It shall contain at least the scope cover of cargo transport insurance, which party is liable to cover insurance, the insured amount, insurance coverage(s) and the matters for claim and its satisfy, etc. It is benefit for the parties to settle how to cover transport insurance and how to lodge a claim against insurance company smoothly if the perils, losses, the scope cover of coverage and the insured period are known well.

## 4.2.1 Basic Principles of Insurance Claim & Its Settlement

Whatever which type of insurance, the insured and the insurer shall abide the following four basic principles mutually.

**1. The Principle of Insurable Interest**

The insurable interest refers to the insured must own the legally recognized insured interest of the subject matters. The insured subject matter can be any property and its relating interest, the human longevity or human body. It's the safeguard object of insurance. The principle of insurable interest means that the insured shall have insurable interest on the subject matter; otherwise the insurance contract is invalid. In international cargo transport insurance, the insurable interest is mainly assumed as the cargo value and associated with freight charges, insurance premium, tariffs and the expected profit.

**2. The Principle of Proximate Cause**

The principle of proximate cause refers to the insurer is only liable for the losses caused directly by the risks in the scope cover of coverage risks. The insurer is no liable for compensation if the losses of subject matter are caused by the risks out of the scope cover of coverage risks.

**3. The Principle of Utmost Good Faith**

The principle of utmost good faith refers to the insured and the insurer must keep the utmost sincerity and no cheating or concealing on each other when the insurance contract signed and in the validity period of insurance contract. The insurer shall express the terms and conditions of the insurance contract to the insured. The insured has the responsibility of declaring the facts of subject matter to the insurer for his determination for accept or not. The insured shall promise "to do" or "not to do", ensure "being" or "not being" and guarantee to perform specific condition is an insurance contract. For example, the insured shall guarantee that the goods shall not be shipped by a ship more than 15 years old.

**4. The Principle of Indemnity**

The principle of indemnity is also known as compensation principle for losses or damaged. It refers to the insurer shall fulfill his obligation on compensation according to the provisions of insurance contract when the insured subject matter suffered losses or damaged in the scope cover of coverage risks. The compensate amount shall not exceeding the insured amount on the insurance policy or the actual losses.

## 4.2.2 The Scope Cover of Cargo Transport Insurance

As per mode of transport, transport insurance is classified by marine transport insurance, road transport insurance, air transport insurance and parcel transport insurance. The insurance coverage and liabilities are different under different transport insurance but with similar scope of coverage including perils, losses and charges.

### 1. Marine Transport Risks

To illustrate, marine transport insurance is used for important explain with an example. Marine transport risks are including perils of the sea and extraneous risks. Perils of the sea refer to the risks caused by natural calamity and fortuitous accidents during transportation at sea. Extraneous risks refers the hazards induced by external causes that others than perils of the sea. It includes general extraneous risks and special extraneous risks.

Natural calamity refers to the hazards induced by the natural forces and can't be controlled through man's efforts, such as vile weather, lightning, tsunami, flood, earthquake, volcanic eruption, shooting down the sea by waves. The hazards have particular implications in insurance business. For example, winds of magnitude eight or higher and or waves of three meters or higher becomes vile weather.

Fortuitous accidents refer to failures due to occasional and unexpected accidents, such as stranded, striked, sunk, burned, crashed, ice drift, fired and exploded. It should be expressly stated that perils of the sea isn't limited to the perils and accidents connected with sea and land, sea and river, or, sea and lighter, such as earthquake, flood, explosion and crash of vessel and lighter or wharf.

General extraneous risks is including theft, breakage, leakage, stain, heating, damp, odor, rust, shortage and fresh and rain water damage, etc. Special extraneous risks such as war, strike, non-delivery and rejection occurred because of military, politics, policies and decree, administrative measures.

### 2. Marine transport Losses

Losses on the sea are classified total losses and partial losses.

Total losses refer to a whole batch or an integral batch of goods is all suffered losses during transportation. It can be divided into actual total losses and constructive total losses. Actual total losses means the goods on transportation lost its original form, utility or no longer belong to the insured. Constructive total losses means the total losses can't be avoided or the total costs paid in order to avoid total losses and arrived at destination higher than the insured amount.

Partial losses refer to the losses except for total losses and include general average and partial average. General average is a kind of special expense and sacrifice caused directly by reasonable measures intentionally to release the common danger of ship, goods and other properties on the same voyage. The sacrifice and expenses of general average shall be apportioned as per the percentage of rescued value of ship, cargo and freight. While, particular average is the partial losses excluding general average and the losses is on the account of the damaged party independently. General average muse be constituted by four conditions: ① The danger lead to general average must be really existed or unavoidable. ② The measures applied must be intentionally and reasonable to relieve the common danger of ship and cargo. ③ The sacrifice is specific and the expenses are additional and they are not caused by the hazards. ④ The sacrifice and expenses are effective. The ship and/ or whole or part of the cargo arrived at the port (place) of destination safely.

According to international insurance business practice, losses and charges of marine transport insurance contains losses or damaged to the goods and the rescue expenses occurred on the sea and land or inland waterway connected with sea transportation.

**3. The Rescue Expenses**

The rescue expenses of marine transport insurance refers to the costs to save the insured cargo including sue and labor expenses and salvage charges.

Sue and labor expenses means the reasonable expenses paid for the rescue measures applied by the insured or its agent, employer to prevent or reduce cargo damages when the subject matter suffered calamity and accidents in the scope of insurance coverage. The insurer is responsible for sue and labor expenses.

Salvage charges means the compensation paid to the third party others than the insured and insurer who adopt reasonable measures to save the subject matter suffered the calamity and accidents successfully. The principle of salvage charges paid is "No cure, no paid". The insurer is also responsible for salvage charges.

## 4.2.3 Insurance Clauses and Its Coverage

For a long time, in the insurance industry of world, British Insurance Act, its clauses and insurance policy has a great influence on the other countries. At present, many insurance companies of nations and regions adopt the Institute Cargo Clauses (ICC) issued by Association of British Insurers (ABI) directly, or for reference or part of reference for issuing national insurance clauses.

China Insurance Clauses (CIC) is the most popular used insurance clauses for China's imports and exports. It was issued by the People's Insurance Company of China, referring to the practices of international insurance market and examined and approved by the People's

Bank of China and the China Insurance Regulatory Commission.

As per modes of transport, CIC is divided into marine, land, air and parcel insurance clauses respectively. For some kinds of special commodities, CIC is also equipped with ocean marine refrigerated cargo clauses, ocean marine wood oil bulk clauses, and land, sea and air transportation insurance clauses of livestock and poultry, as well as various additional risks suitable for any mode of transportation insurance. China's importation and exportation, if it is necessary to cover transport insurance, CIC clauses or ICC clauses can be selected freely by the insured.

**1. The Coverage & Clauses of China Ocean Marine Cargo Insurance**

The coverage of China Cargo Transport Insurance Clauses is divided into basic risks and additional risks. The basic risks can be covered independently, while the additional risks can't be covered independently. According to Ocean Marine Cargo Clauses revised on Jan 01, 1981, the basic risks of China Ocean Marine Cargo Insurance Cargo are including:①Free From Particular Average (FPA), With Particular Average (WPA) and③All Risks.

The additional risks are the supplement of basic risks. The insured may cover against one or more the additional risks on the basis of one basic risk covered. The additional risks under CIC are including general additional risks and special additional risks.

(1)The Scope Cover of Insurance and Its Exclusion

The scope of cover under FPA includes:

①Total losses or constructive total losses of the whole consignment insured caused by natural calamities.

②Total or partial losses caused by accidents.

③Losses and expenses incurred as a result of discharge of the vehicle at the port of refuge and the port of midway after a shipwreck.

④Total or partial losses consequent on failing of entire package or package into sea during the process of loading, unloading or transshipment.

⑤Partial losses caused by vile weather, lightning, etc where the conveyance has been grounded, stranded, sunk or burnt, irrespective of the event or events to take place before or after such accidents.

⑥Sacrifice in and contribution to general average, and salvage charges.

⑦Sue and labor charges paid by the insured in order to avoid or decrease losses under covered scope with limitation to the value of cargo.

⑧Such proportion of losses sustained by the ship owner as is to be reimbursed by the cargo owner under the contract of Agreement "Both to blame collision "clauses.

The scope of cover under WA is including partial losses due to natural calamities on the basis of scope cover of FPA. The scope of cover under all risks is including general additional risks on the basis of scope cover of WA. It means that the general additional risks is under the coverage of all risks, whereas the special additional risks are not.

The general additional risks under CIC clauses are including:

①Theft, Pilferage and Non-Delivery (TPND). TPND means that within the validity period of the insurance, the insurance company shall indemnify the insured company for the loss caused by the short delivery of the entire cargo after the theft of the insured cargo or the arrival of the means of transport at the destination.This risk is a kind of general additional risk on the basis of basic risk. TPND covers the loss of short delivery of the entire cargo, which may be caused by negligence of the carrier or other third party liable in the course of transportation, but may be exempted in accordance with the provisions of the transport contract.

②Fresh water and rain damage (FWRD). The insurance companies are liable for all losses sustained in transit by frseh water, rain or snow. Fresh water includes fresh water tanks, leaking pipes and sweat.However, if there should be traces of rain or fresh water on the outside of the package or other appropriate proof, the insured must take delivery of the goods in time and apply for inspection within 10 days after taking delivery of the goods, otherwise, the insurance company shall not be liable for compensation. The main difference between WPA and fresh water drench insurance is that WPA is one of the basic risks of marine cargo, while fresh water and rain damage insurance is one of the general additional risks. WPA is only responsible for losses caused by salt water and not for losses caused by fresh water, while fresh-water rain cover is responsible for losses caused by fresh water (including drinking water on board, leakage of water pipes, dripping of ship's poles, etc.), rainwater and snow melt water.

③Shortage risk. Shortage risk means the insurance covering the loss of a short quantity of goods. For packaged goods, there must be abnormal phenomena such as breakage of the outer package to identify whether it is caused by external factors

④Inter mixture and Contamination. Inter mixture and contamination insurance is to cover the loss of goods in transit due to impurities or soiled oil, soil or color.Some goods, especially grain, ore and granular chemical products in bulk, are prone to be mixed with soil and gravel, thus affecting their quality. And paper, cloth, clothing and food are very likely to come into contact with oil or colored substances and pollution losses. The insurer shall indemnify for any loss of confounders or contamination.

⑤Leakage. Leakage risk means the leakage loss of the insured fluid, half fluid, oil kind goods in carriage process caused by container damaged , or the goods that uses liquid to store because of liquid leakage, make the loss such as goods produces metamorphism, putrefaction.

⑥Crash and Breakage. The risk of crash and breakage is one of the additional risks covered by marine insurance.The insurance covers the loss of concave, slip, paint and scratch caused by vibration, turbulence and extrusion of the goods during transportation, or fragile material due to rough handling, transport means of shock and so on caused by the breakage of the goods themselves, such as broken loss. This insurance, as an additional risk, is mainly for loss caused by the insured cause. Unlike FPA and WPA in Marine cargo transportation, it is only responsible for damage or collision caused by natural calamities or accidents of the means of transport.This additional risk is included in the coverage of "all risks" in marine cargo insurance.This risk may be added to the coverage of other risks.

⑦Odour. Odour risk refers to the insurance that covers the loss of goods in transit caused by the influence of other smelly articles. The general food, traditional Chinese medicine, perfume produces this kind of loss most easily. For example, tea is shipped together with the leather piece, its protected camphor flavour string, and make the tea taste in leather piece and camphor flavour.

⑧Sweating and Heating. The insurance companies are liable for compensation for the losses caused by sudden change of temperature in the course of transportation or condensation, dampness or heat in the cabin caused by failure of ship's ventilation equipment.

⑨Hook damage. Hook damage insurance refers to the insurance that covers the losses caused by hook breakage of bag-loaded and packaging-loaded goods due to improper operation by loading and unloading or handling workers in the process of transportation, including the expenses paid for the replacement of packaging. Goods with such losses often include baled cotton cloth, rolled paper, bag-packed grain, etc.

⑩Loss or Damage Clause by Breakage of Packing. Loss or damage clause by breakage of packing means the loss caused by shortage, contamination or dampness due to careless handling or loading and unloading of the contracted goods during the transportation process. In addition, the cost of repairing or replacing the packaging for the purpose of transportation safety is also responsible.

⑪Rust. The rust risk refers to the insurance covering losses of metals or metal products as a result of rust in the course of transportation.But to the material that rusts very easily naturally in carriage process like iron wire, steel rope, conduit spare parts, and the bare outfit metal plate that can rust necessarily, the underwriter does not protect this risk commonly.

The special additional risks under CIC Clauses are including:

①Failure to delivery. It refers to failure to deliver the goods within six months after shipment, for whatever reason, the insurance company will compensate for total loss. The loss of goods covered by a non-delivery insurance is often caused not by transport but by political reasons.For example, the embargo imposed between Palestine and Israel during the armed conflict, or the forced unloading of cargo by another country at the midway port, shall not be liable for losses under transportation insurance and war risk.

②Import duty risk. After the goods are damaged, they are still dutiable at the value of the good goods. The insurance company is responsible for paying the customs duties on the damaged goods.

③On deck risk. On deck risk is to cover the damage caused by weather and other adverse factors when the goods are loaded on deck.

④Rejection risk. The losses caused by rejection or confiscation of the goods at the destination port by the authorities of the importing country.

⑤Aflatioxin risk. If the goods (grain or food, etc.) are found to have carcinogenic aflatoxin in the inspection by the importing country, they will be refused to import or confiscated, resulting in losses.

⑥Strike, riot and civil commotion (SRCC). The loss or damaged to the goods caused by strikes, riots or uprising .When the insured has covered war risk and has covered strikes, riots or civil commotion, no additional premium will be charged.

⑦War risk. The loss of goods in transit resulting from seizure, detention, prohibition or seizure resulting from war, hostile ACTS or ACTS of piracy.

⑧Fire risk extension clause-for storage of cargo at destination Hong Kong, including Kowloon, or Macao. After the goods are discharged from the means of transport, others must be stored in a designated bank of transfer warehouse, if there is a fire during the storage, the insurance company is responsible for the compensation for the resulting loss.

As the special additional risks are not under the coverage of all risks, the insured want to obtain the protection of special additional risks,if any, shall cover additionally on the basis of basic risks covered.

(2) The Exclusion of Insurance Company

The exclusions, refers to the losses or damaged to the goods will not be covered by the insurance company, which is also specified in the insurance clauses of FPA, WA and All Risks The exclusion of basic risks of the insurance company includes:①the losses or damage caused by international act or fault of the insured;②the losses or damage due to responsibility of the consignor;③inferior quality or shortage in quantity before the commencement of the insurance duty;④natural losses, inherent vice or nature of the insured goods;⑤losses of the market price of the insured goods;⑥losses due to delay in transportation and any expenses arising there from.

The exclusion of war risks and strikes risks includes:①the losses or damaged to the goods caused by the use of atomic or nuclear weapons;②the losses or damaged to the goods caused by labor shortages or labor non-application during strikes, including the losses to the goods refrigerated cargo caused by lacking power or fuel as the refrigerated machine stop work, or the losses to the goods caused by rain as without enough labor force to handle the goods.

## 2. The Coverage of Institute Cargo Clauses & Its Exclusion

Institute Cargo Clauses (ICC) was finished revised on Jan 01, 1982 and officially adopted from April 01, 1983. Six kinds of insurance coverage are included:①I.C.C(A) (Institute Cargo Clauses A);②I.C.C (B) (Institute Cargo Clauses B);③I.C.C (C) (Institute Cargo Clauses C);④IWCC (Institute War Clauses-Cargo);⑤ISCC (Institute Strikes Clauses-Cargo), and⑥Malicious Damage Clause.

ICC(A), ICC (B), and ICC (C) belong to basic risks and can be covered separately. ICC War risks and ICC Strikes can be covered independently in case of necessary. Malicious Damage Clause can't be covered separately.

Malicious Damage Clause refers to the losses or damaged to the goods caused by the vandalism action of a person other than the insured, such as the captain or the crew. The losses or damaged to the goods isn't fallen into the scope of compensation of Malicious Damage Clause if it is caused by the action of a person in a political motive. Malicious Damage Clause is covered under the coverage of ICC (A), while not under the coverage of ICC (B) and ICC (C). It means that it should be covered additionally if the insured want to obtain the additional protection of Malicious Damage Clause under ICC (B) or ICC (C) covered.

The scope cover of ICC (A) is greatest than that of ICC (B) and ICC (C). The scope cover of ICC (A) includes all risks except exclusions, general average & salvage expenses, and proportion of losses under the contract of agreement "Both to Blame Collision" Clause. Its exclusions includes:①general exclusion;②unseaworthy and unfitness of the carrying vessel or lighter, including the containers;③war, capture, hostile behavior, distrain and conventional weapons; and④strike, terrorists.

Meanwhile, the general exclusion includes:①loss or damage due to willful misconduct of the insured;②natural leakage of the subject matter, natural wear and tear, or wastage of the subject matter ,insufficient or improper packing;③delay;④inherent vice of the subject matter;⑤insolvency of the owner of the ship,the carrier or the charter; and⑥Nuclear or atomic weapons.

ICC (B) choose the proper insurance cover as listed below:①fire,explosion;②ship or lighter colliding with rock,running aground, sunk or capsized;③conveyance overturned or derailed;④ship,lighter or other conveyance colliding with any external object excluding water;⑤loss or damage due to unloading at the port of refuge;⑥loss or damage due to earthquake. eruption of volcano, lightening or thunder;⑦sacrifice in general average;⑧loss of the subject matter due to jettison and washing overboard;⑨loss of the subject matter due to being plunged into water by waves;⑩loss of the subject matter insured due to water entering the ship, lighter, conveyance, container or storage place;⑪total loss caused by falling of the entire package or package into sea during the processes of loading and unloading.

The exclusions of ICC (B) is same as ICC Clause A but excluding piracy and malicious damage.ICC(C)only covers major casualties. Its coverage is same as ICC Clause B, but excluding the following:①loss or damage due to earthquake, eruption of volcano, lightening or thunder;②falling of the goods into sea during the processes of loading and unloading, water entering the ship, lighter, conveyance, container, storage plane, etc. Its exclusion is same as Clause B.

## 4.2.4 The Commencement & Termination of Insurance Responsibilities

Warehouse to warehouse clauses (W/W clauses) is adopted by China Ocean Marine Transportation Cargo Clauses as per the regular practices of international insurance market. It means that the responsibilities of insurance company is taking effect when the insured cargo begin to dispatch from the warehouse or storage place at port (place) of shipment indicated on the insurance policy, including normal transportation in the process of sea, land, inland waterway and barge transportation, until the insured goods arrived at the warehouse or storage place of allocation, assignment at port (place) of destination stated on the policy or the other storage place for abnormal transport. If the goods didn't arrive at the warehouse or storage place at port (place) of destination indicated on the insurance policy, the responsibilities of insurance should be terminated on the 60 days from the date that the insured cargo unloaded at the port of discharge. If the goods is transferred to another place other than that indicated on the insurance policy within the above 60 days, the insurance responsibilities is terminated from the time the goods begin to transfer.

W/W clauses are also adopted by the strikes risks. As per the practice of international insurance, on the basis of war risks is covered, if the insured need to cover strikes risks, he need not to pay the premium of strikes risks. If the insured only need to cover strikes risks, the premium is collected as per war risks.

The commencement and termination of responsibilities for war risks is limited on waterborne. It means the responsibilities is taking effect from the moment that the insured cargo shipped on board the vessel or barge at port of shipment and until the goods unloaded from the vessel or barge at port of destination. If the goods didn't unload from the vessel at port of destination, the insurance responsibilities would be terminated in the midnight of the 15th days from the vessel arrived at the port of destination. If the insured cargo was transshipped at the immediate port, whatever the goods is unloaded or not at the immediate port, the responsibilities would be terminated in the midnight of the 15th days from the vessel arrived at the port of destination. When the insured cargo loaded on the forwarding vessel, the responsibilities recover to be effective.

The period for claim is not more than two year from the insured cargo unloaded from the vessel fully at port of discharge.

## 4.2.5 Practice of International Transportation Cargo Insurance

The processing of cover insurance includes how to select insurance coverage, definite insured amount, conclude insurance contract, obtain insurance policy and lodge a claim and settlement of claim, etc. The seller has obligation for the buyer to cover transport insurance under CIF or CIP term as per Incoterms®2010 and has no obligation under other trade terms. While, the buyer has no obligation for the seller to cover transport insurance under any trade terms as per Incoterms®2010. In practice, normally, the buyer will cover insurance at his option to decrease the risks during transportation under EXW, FAS, FOB, FCA, CFR or CPT contract. The seller will cover transport insurance at his option to decrease risks of transportation under DAT, DAP or DDP contract.

**1. How to select insurance coverage**

The following factors shall be considered when choosing the proper insurance coverage: ①Characteristics of the cargo. For example, cereals is easier to be mildew as sweating and heating, it's better to cover all risks or cover the sweating and heating, shortages with WA covered basically. ②Packing of the goods. For example, ore in bulk is easier to be shortage and is better to cover shortage risks additionally. The rice in bags is easy to be hook damaged and is better to cover hook damaged risks additionally. ③Application & value of the goods. The goods with high value, such as gold, silver, jewelry and expensive arts and crafts, it is better to cover all risks to obtain protection fully. ④Mode of transportation and conveyance. For example, the air transport war risks are forced to be covered by the insured for air transport. ⑤The route of transport. If the transport tools need go through Somali area or the ocean area with intensive army practice, it is suggested to cover war risks and failure of non-delivery risks. ⑥Season and condition of port or station. For example, the insured goods are easier to be frozen and broken during transportation in winter, or to be perished during transportation in summer. The conditions of port or station have influence on the loading, unloading and storage of the goods. The insured shall select the suitable insurance coverage as per the different situations.

**2. How to Definite the Insured Amount**

The insured amount is the basis to calculate premium and compensation after the losses or damaged to the goods occurred. As per the practice of international insurance market, the insured amount is normally calculated with a markup percentage of 10% on the CIF invoice value.

The insured amount is: The Insured Amount= CIF Value of Cargo × (1+Markup Percentage)

The premium is: Premium = Insured Amount × Premium Rate

For example, if the cargo CIF value is USD10,000 and need to cover ocean marine cargo all risks.The markup percentage is 10 and the premium rate is 0.5%. So the insured amount is USD 11,000 and the premium is USD55.

### 3. How to Obtain Insurance Documents

The most popular insurance documents are insurance policy and insurance certificate. The insurance policy can replace the insurance certificate, whereas the opposite not. The insurance policy is the formal documents and main evidence for the insured to lodge a claim or appeal to the insurer. The contents of insurance policy include the name of insured, invoice number, the contract number, the description of commodity, shipping marks, kinds of packages and number, the insured amount, the conveyance tool & its voyage, the sailing date, transport route, the place of claim the insured coverage, the insured date and the stamp and signature of insurer, name of entity, telephone number and address, etc., as well as the liabilities of insurer and the details terms and conditions of the insured and the insurer. The insurance policy must be presented by the seller to the buyer under CIF or CIP contract.

### 4. How to Lodge a Claim

The consignee shall definite the party to lodge a claim firstly when he found the losses or damaged to the goods occurred after the goods arrived at destination. The buyer may lodge a claim to the seller if the quality, packing, weight (quantity) of shipped goods isn't conformity with the contract.

Under the following situations, the buyer may lodge a claim to the shipping company:①unloading shortage;②stolen during transportation;③destroyed as the carrier's responsibilities. If the losses or damaged to the goods is under the scope cover of insurance coverage, the buyer shall lodge claim to the insurance company.

When the insured lodge a claim to the insurer, he shall prepare the notification of losses firstly. The insured shall notice the insure agent indicated on the insurance policy when the losses or damaged to the goods occurred. The agent shall apply the proper measures, such as losses inspection, presenting rescue suggestions, definite the insured responsibilities and issue the inspection report. Besides notice the losses to the insurance company, the insured shall ask for the written evidence from the relating carrier or authorities (such as customs, port administration) for the losses or shortage of the goods.

The insured shall apply the proper measure to prevent losses increasing. If the insurance company has comments on settlement, the insured shall keep the requirements of the insurer. The relating reasonable expenses are on the account of the insurer but without exceeding the insured amount of rescue goods. When the insured finished prepare the documents of claim, he shall lodge the claim on time.

The claim documents include insurance documents, transport documents, commercial invoice, and inspection certificate, the certificate of losses or shortage. In practice, the insurer shall compensate to the insured first.

The insured shall sign an assignment agreement of rights and interest when he obtained the compensation and give up the right to recourse the third party. The insured obtain the relating rights and interests and can recourse to the third party.

**5. How to Settle Claim**

When the insurer settle the requirement of claim, he shall definite the reasons caused losses and examine and approve the responsibilities. According to the provision of insurance clauses and the risks coverage & period, the insurer examine and approval the compensation and calculate the amount of compensation.

## 4.2.6 Insurance Clauses in a Sales Contract

The insurance clauses in a sales contract are very important and must be indicated definitely and reasonably. The stipulation of insurance clauses shall be different under different trade terms. If a sales contract is concluded under CIF or CIP term, the insurance clauses can be stipulated as:

① Insurance is to be covered by the seller for 110% of CIF/CIP total invoice value against All Risks and War Risks as per the relevant Ocean Marine Cargo Clauses of the China Insurance Clauses dated 1/1/1981.

② Insurance to be covered by the seller for 110% of CIP total invoice value against Overland Transportation All Risks and All Risks as per Overland Transportation Cargo Clauses "Train, Truck" and Ocean Marine Cargo Clauses of the China Insurance Clauses dated 1/1/1981, including War risks as per Overland Transportation Cargo War Risks (By train) dated 1/1/1981 and Ocean Marine Cargo War Risks Clauses dated1/1/1981.

③ Insurance to be covered by the seller for 110% of total invoice value against ICC(A) and IWC (Cargo)as per Institute cargo Clauses dated 1/1/1982.

If the sales contract is conclude under EXW, FAS, CFR, FCA, CPT or FCA term, its insurance clauses can be stipulated as: Insurance to be covered by the buyer, or insurance to be covered at the buyer's option.

If the sales contract is concluded under DAT, DAP or DDP term, its insurance clauses can be stipulated as: Insurance to be covered by the Seller or at the Seller's option.

# Questions

1. A Chinese firm exports 100 boxes of goods, each box volume is 30 cm $\times$ 60 cm $\times$ 50 cm, each box gross weight is 20 kg. According to the price table of the shipping company, the corresponding freight of calculation standard in the cargo classification table is W/M, the basic freight is USD30.00 per ton, and 20% fuel surcharge, 20% port congestion surcharge and 100% currency depreciation surcharge are also charged. What is the freight of this batch of cargo?

2. For an export consignment, the CIF total price is $200,000, covering all risks and war risk.The premium rate for all risks and war risk is 0.3% and 0.2% respectively, plus 10%. Excuse me, how much is the insurance premium for this consignment?

3. What shall be included in the "delivery clause"of the international sales contract ?

4. What are the difference between the people's insurance clauses of China and the London institute of insurance clauses?

5. Based on a real case of cross-border e-commerce, analyze the success or deficiency of the establishment of the freight template of cross-border e-commerce.

6. Try to analyze the similarities and differences between product quality insurance and freight insurance in cross-border e-commerce and international cargo transportation insurance.

# 第五章

# 国际货物买卖价格

☞ **案例5.1**

根据商务部统计报告数据，2008年1—12月和2016年1—12月中国出口大米的基本情况详见表5.1。从整体看，2016年的中国大米出口数量相比2008年降低了59.25%，出口总额下降27.20%，而出口平均单价提高78.63%。从洲际情况看，中国对亚洲出口大米的表现情况最好，出口数量下降幅度最低（仅下降1.88%），出口平均单价仅提高48.12%，但出口总额提高了45.33%；中国对北美洲出口大米排名第二，尽管出口数量下降34.31%，但出口平均单价、出口总额分别提高了122.13%和45.87%。另外，中国对南美洲、大洋洲出口大米的数量下降幅度高达99%以上；中国对非洲出口大米的平均单价低于总体平均水平。如将2008、2016年的中国大米出口平均单价按照当年美元对人民币的平均汇率进行折算，2008年的美元对人民币平均汇率为6.9451，而2016年12月31日的为6.64。折算后的2008年中国大米出口平均单价为每公吨3454.50元人民币，2016年为每公吨5899.64元人民币，提高了70.78%，低于按照美元计价的价格增长幅度。

表5.1 2008年和2016年的中国大米出口情况

| 洲际 | 指标 | 2008 年 | 2016 年 | 增减百分比（％） |
|---|---|---|---|---|
| 全部出口 | 出口数量（公吨） | 969317.10 | 394979.70 | −59.25 |
| | 出口金额（万美元） | 48210.10 | 35094.80 | −27.20 |
| | 平均单价（美元／公吨） | 497.40 | 888.5 | 78.63 |
| 出口亚洲 | 出口数量（公吨） | 331378.00 | 325149.00 | −1.88 |
| | 出口金额（万美元） | 20571.90 | 29897.10 | 45.33 |
| | 平均单价（美元／公吨） | 620.80 | 919.5 | 48.12 |
| 出口非洲 | 出口数量（公吨） | 446403.30 | 62767.40 | −85.94 |
| | 出口金额（万美元） | 19802.50 | 4619.10 | −76.67 |
| | 平均单价（美元／公吨） | 443.60 | 735.9 | 65.89 |

| 洲际 | 指标 | 2008 年 | 2016 年 | 增减百分比（%） |
|---|---|---|---|---|
| 出口欧洲 | 出口数量（公吨） | 34477.00 | 4323.00 | −87.46 |
| | 出口金额（万美元） | 1501.90 | 322 | −78.56 |
| | 平均单价（美元/公吨） | 435.60 | 744.9 | 71.01 |
| 出口南美洲 | 出口数量（公吨） | 30347.10 | 20.8 | −99.93 |
| | 出口金额（万美元） | 1210.50 | 1.9 | −99.84 |
| | 平均单价（美元/公吨） | 398.90 | 907 | 127.38 |
| 出口北美洲 | 出口数量（公吨） | 2966.50 | 1948.60 | −34.31 |
| | 出口金额（万美元） | 134.30 | 195.9 | 45.87 |
| | 平均单价（美元/公吨） | 452.70 | 1005.60 | 122.13 |
| 出口大洋洲 | 出口数量（公吨） | 123745.30 | 770.8 | −99.38 |
| | 出口金额（万美元） | 4989.00 | 58.8 | −98.82 |
| | 平均单价（美元/公吨） | 403.20 | 763 | 89.24 |

从出口国别看，2008年中国出口大米排名排名前3的国家分别是科特迪瓦、韩国和利比里亚，其中科特迪瓦和利比里亚是非洲国家；2016年大米出口排名前3的国家分别为韩国、巴基斯坦和日本，全部为亚洲国家。因此，综观中国大米2008、2016年的出口情况，除量减价增外，中国大米的出口市场发生了较大变动。不仅于此，中国是稻谷生产大国，但不是大米主要出口国。2012年，中国进口大米235万吨，较2011年的58万吨增加了305%，而相应的出口量仅为28万吨，较2011年减少一半。自2013年起，中国已成为全球大米的最大进口国，中国从大米的净出口国转为净进口国，2016年中国进口大米就超过了500万吨。

价格直接关系到买卖双方的经济利益，是买卖合同中的重要条款，是交易磋商的核心内容。影响国际贸易商品价格的因素很多，而其中最重要的影响因素有：商品的质量、运输距离、交货条件、季节差价、成交数量、汇率风险、客户资信和交货期的急缓等。国际货物买卖合同中的价格条款，一般包括单价和总值。有些国际货物买卖合同还需要明确作价办法、佣金和折扣等内容。单价是指单位货物的价格，总值是单价和数量的乘积，即一批货物的总价值。国际货物买卖合同中的单价条款，应至少包括计量单位、计价货币、单位金额和贸易术语等4个方面的内容，例如：每公吨100美元FOB上海（USD100 per M/T，FOB Shanghai）。在国际贸易中，正确掌握作价原则、选择有利的计价货币、仔细做好成本核算，是买卖双方的重点工作内容。在确定商品的成交价格时，应切实了解该商品在国际市场上的价格走向与供求变化。在此基础上，充分考虑各种影响价格的因素，合理运用各种行之有效的作价办法。

# 一、国际贸易货物的作价方法

在进出口业务中，货物价格的确定方法，通常有以下几种。

## （一）固定价格

在国际货物买卖中，贸易双方在协商一致的基础上，明确规定商品成交的具体价格，这种作价办法称为固定价格。固定价格在国际贸易中采用较多。固定价格具有明确、具体、肯定和便于核算等特点。但是，国际市场价格变化瞬息万变，买卖双方采取固定价格，意味着卖方要承担从订立合同开始，到实际装运、实际收取货款期间的价格变动风险；而买方要承担从订立合同开始，到货款、实际收货期间的价格变动风险。因此，采用固定价格有利有弊。为减少风险，促成交易，提高履约率，在价格的规定方面，除固定价格外，买卖双方也可采取其他一些变通做法。

## （二）暂不固定价格

在国际贸易中，有些货物因国际市场价格变动频繁、幅度较大，或因交货期较远，买卖双方对市场趋势难以预测，但双方有订立合同的意图。针对这种情况，贸易双方可先约定货物的品种、数量、包装、交货和支付等条件，但对价格暂不固定，而是在合同中约定将来如何确定价格的方法。暂不固定价格的作价方法又可分为两种情况：①在价格条款中明确规定定价时间和作价方法，如以将来某一确定日期的某地有关商品交易的收盘价格为基准加（或减）若干美元；②只规定作价时间，如"由双方在某年某月某日协商确定价格"。

## （三）暂定价格

买卖双方在签订国际货物买卖合同时，对合同中的价格注明为"暂定价"，然后规定在交货前的一定时间内，由双方根据当时市场情况确定正式价格。因没有明确规定定价依据，买卖双方在商定价格时可能各持己见，无法达成协议，导致合同无法履行。在实际业务中，暂定价格的定价方法一般只限于关系密切信誉可靠的用户，且应在合同中规定价格的协商条款，并明确规定在协商无结果时采用何种价格。

## （四）滑动价格

对于成套设备、大型机械等出口商品，从合同订立到履行交货完毕，耗时较长。买卖双方需承担因原材料、工资、汇率等变动而带来的较大风险，可采用滑动价格的作价方式来减少风险。所谓滑动价格，是指买卖双方先在合同中规定一个基础价格（basic price），交货时或交货前一定时间，对基础价格按照工资、原材料价格变动指数做相应的调整，以确定最后价格。同时，在合同中具体订明调整价格的办法。

滑动价格的价格调整条款，通常采用下列公式来调整价格：

P=PO（A+BM/MO+CW/WO）。

其中：P代表商品交付时的最后价格；

PO代表签订合同时的初步价格；

A代表经营管理费用和利润在价格中所占的比重；

B代表原料在价格中所占的比重；

M代表计算最后价格时引用的有关原料的平均价格或指数；

MO代表签订合同时引用的有关原料的平均价格或指数：

C代表工资在价格中所占的比重；

W代表计算最后价格时引用的有关工资的平均数或指数；

WO代表签订合同时引用的有关工资的平均数或指数。

A、B、C所分别代表的比例，在合同签订时确定，以后固定不变。

# 二、签订价格条款应注意的事项

## （一）谨慎选择计价货币

计价货币是指国际货物买卖合同中规定用以计算价格的货币。卖方选择计价货币、买方选择支付货币，均应综合考虑交易习惯、购销意图以及市场价格、竞争情况等因素，灵活掌握价格。计价货币一般与支付货币为同一种货币，也可以是与支付货币为不同种类的一种或几种货币。计价货币可以是出口国（地区）货币，也可以是进口国（地区）货币，甚至可以为买卖双方协商确定的第三国（地区）货币。因各国（地区）经济发展不平衡，各国（地区）货币间的汇率经常发生变动。汇率变化对国际市场价格的影响很大。在国际贸易中，卖方、买方必须认真选择计价货币，尽量避免汇率风险可能造成的损失。一般来说，计价货币的选择原则有两条。

### 1. 选择可自由兑换货币作为计价货币

目前，国际市场上可自由兑换的货币通常有美元、英镑、日元、欧元、港币等，其中美元在国际货物贸易中所占的比例较大。我们在确定国际货物买卖的计价货币时，应该选择国际上通用的可自由兑换的货币作为计价货币，以利于规避汇率风险。在国际货物买卖中，常用的计价货币名称及其标准简称如表5.2所示。

表5.2　国际贸易中常用的计价货币名称

| 国家或地区 | 货币中文名称 | 货币简称 |
| --- | --- | --- |
| 美国 | 美元 | USD |
| 日本 | 日元 | JPY |
| 中国 | 人民币 | CNY |
| 欧盟 | 欧元 | EUR |

续表

| 国家或地区 | 货币中文名称 | 货币简称 |
|---|---|---|
| 英国 | 英镑 | GBP |
| 中国香港 | 港币 | HKD |

**2. 对可自由兑换货币，需考虑其稳定性**

选择计价货币时，应充分考虑汇率波动可能带来的风险，尽量选用对自己有利的货币。一般来说，卖方应选择那些币值相对比较稳定或呈上浮趋势的"硬币"，买方应选用币值有下浮趋势的"软币"。

中国人民银行、财政部、商务部、海关总署、国家税务总局、中国银行业监督管理委员会于2009年7月1日联合公布并于当日起实施的《跨境贸易人民币结算试点管理办法》（公告2009年第10号），标志着人民币的国际地位从国内计价货币提升至国际结算货币。在国际货物买卖中，中国进出口企业可以选择人民币作为计价货币。

### （二）采取一定的措施以降低外汇风险

为达成交易，买卖双方有时不得不采用对己方不利的货币作为计价货币或支付货币，此时应争取用一定的方法进行补救，从而保护自己的利益。以下方法，可在一定程度上降低外汇风险。①考虑货币汇率的浮动因素。对卖方来说，应考虑计价货币汇率的下浮因素，可适当抬高出口报价；对买方来说，适当考虑支付货币汇率的上浮因素，可适当压低进口成交价。②在国际金融市场上，两种货币之间的兑换汇率是不断变化的，一种货币汇率的上浮或下浮是相对于另一种货币来说的；而今天汇率上浮的货币，明天可能变成汇率下浮的货币。因此，在不同的合同中，可适当选择运用多种货币来计价或支付，将汇率处于上浮趋势的货币与处于下浮趋势的货币捆绑在一起，以起到降低外汇风险的作用。③签订外汇保值条款。例如，在国际货物买卖合同中订明支付货币与某一种货币之间的汇率，然后在支付时按当日汇率折合成原货币支付。例如，某国际货物销售合同约定以"美元"计价和支付，合同总金额为10万美元，合同中约定美元与日元的兑换汇率为：USD100=JPY95。待付款时，如美元与日元的兑换汇率变为USD100=JPY100，那么买方应付款105263.18美元，而非10万美元。

### （三）计价数量单位的选择

在国际货物买卖合同的价格条款中，除应明确规定作价方法、谨慎选择计价货币和订立外汇保值条款外，还应正确表达计价数量单位。一般说来，计价数量单位应与数量条款中的计量单位相一致。如计价数量单位采用"公吨"，则在数量和单价中也应采用"公吨"，而不能是"长吨"或"短吨"。买卖双方协商一致的价格，应正确填写在国际货物买卖合同中。如果写错，而合同已由双方当事人签署认可，按照国际贸易法律，被视为否定或改变交易磋商时所谈定的条件。

### （四）合理选用贸易术语

贸易术语直接关系到买卖双方的经济利益，因此贸易双方均十分重视贸易术语的选用。一般情况下，贸易术语的选用，应结合以下几方面因素综合考虑。

#### 1. 注意运价、保险费率的变化

例如，当国际市场石油价格上下波动频繁、波幅显著时，会导致燃油附加费水涨船高，将推动国际运价大幅上涨；当国际海运交通枢纽上海盗盛行时，会导致保险公司纷纷提高国际货物运输的保险费率。为规避运价波动的风险、降低保险费用支出，卖方应尽量争取以FOB、FCA贸易术语成交，而买方应争取以CIF、CIP、CFR、CPT贸易术语成交。

#### 2. 选择合适的货物运输方式

各种贸易术语适用的货物运输方式不同。FOB、CFR、CIF仅适用于海洋运输和内河运输，而FCA、CPT、CIP不仅适用于水上运输，还适用于空运、公路和铁路运输与联合运输。目前，集装箱运输与多式运输已被广泛采用。贸易双方要避免在交接货物义务上产生分歧，相对于FOB、CFR 和CIF的使用，应适当扩大FCA、CPT和CIP贸易术语的使用比例。

#### 3. 适当选择使用实际交货的贸易术语

随着对外开放的不断深入和对外贸易的不断发展，中国已经与许多国家（地区）建立了自由贸易区，如东盟自由贸易区、上海经济合作组织等。因此，可以采用更加灵活的贸易方式。采用其他贸易术语如EXW、FAS、DAT、DAP、DDP等，视不同交易的具体情况适当与这些周边国家（地区）开展贸易往来，积累这些术语的使用经验。

### （五）考虑佣金和折扣因素

佣金（commission）是卖方或买方付给中间商的酬金，其原因是该中间商为货物销售或购买提供了中介服务。中间商通常为经纪人或代理人。在实际业务中，凡是为招揽生意、促成交易提供服务的企业或个人，都可能成为佣金商。折扣（discount）是卖方给予买方的一定价格减让。在国际货物买卖中，佣金和折扣的名目繁多，如销售佣金（selling commission）、累计佣金（accumulative commission）、数量折扣（quantity discount）、特别折扣（special discount）等。

一般情况下，国际货物买卖的价格如包含佣金、折扣，则该价格称为"含佣价""含折扣价"。有时，买卖双方会在合同单价中约定不显示佣金或折扣，而按双方单独签署的佣金协议、折扣协议支付，这种佣金与折扣，称为"暗佣"或"暗扣"。"含佣价"可用文字说明，也可用佣金的英文的缩写字母"C"来表示；"含折扣价"一般用文字说明。例如：①USD500 per M/T CIF London including 2% commission（每公吨500美元CIF伦敦包含佣金2%）；②USD500 per M/T CIFC2 London（每公吨500美元CIF伦敦C2%）；③USD50 per case CFR Singapore less 1% discount（每箱50美元CFR新加坡减1%折扣）；④USD500 per M/T CIF London including 2% commission, less 2% discount（每公吨500美元CIF伦敦包含佣金2%，减2%折扣）。在国际贸易中，为了区别"含佣

价""含折扣价",将既不包含佣金也不包含折扣的价格称为"净价"。净价的表示方法是在贸易术语后加注"净价"（net）字样。例如：每打25美元FOB净价天津（USD25 per dozen FOB net Tianjin）。

佣金一般是按交易金额的一定百分比计算，也可按成交的数量来计算（即按每单位的货物收取若干佣金）。百分比佣金的计算公式为：佣金＝含佣价×佣金率；含佣价＝净价÷（1−佣金率）。例如，某笔出口业务的CFR含佣价总金额为20000美元，佣金率6%，则该笔业务应支付的佣金额为1200美元（20000美元×6%），该笔出口业务的CFR净价金额为18800美元（净价＝含佣价−佣金）。

折扣的计算，通常也是按成交金额的一定百分比计算，也可按成交数量计算。扣除折扣的实收价格称为净价。折扣的计算公式为：折扣＝原价×折扣率；折实售价＝原价×（1−折扣率）。例如，某合同出口价格为CIF伦敦1000美元减3%折扣，则该折扣为每单位货物30美元（1000×3%＝30美元），而折实售价为970美元（折实售价＝原价−折扣＝1000−30）。

佣金和折扣的支付方法不同。销售佣金的支付一般是在卖方收到货款后，按事先约定的期限和佣金比率，由卖方另行支付给中间商。折扣通常是由买方在付款时预先扣除。

# 三、价格换算与价格改报

## （一）FOB、CFR与CIF之间的价格换算

不同贸易术语的价格构成因素不同。由于国际货物买卖绝大多数是采用FOB、CFR、CIF、FCA、CPT、CIP成交的，因此明白FOB、CFR、CIF之间的价格换算方法，也可以推定出FCA、CPT与CIP之间的价格换算。FOB、CFR、CIF贸易术语之间价格换算方法如下。

### 1.FOB价换算成CFR价

FOB为装运港船上交货价，卖方负担货物在指定装运港越过船舷前的一切费用和风险，不负担海运费，而CFR为成本加运费价。因此，由FOB价为基准计算CFR价的方法为：CFR价＝FOB价+海运费。例如，假设FOB价为1000美元，每单位货物分摊的海运费为200美元，则CFR价为1200美元（CFR价＝FOB价＋海运费＝1000＋200）。

### 2.FOB价换算成CIF价

CIF价为成本加运费加保险费，而保险费=CIF价×（1+投保加成率）×海上运输保险费率，以FOB价为基准计算的CIF价应为：CIF=FOB+运费+保险费，或者CIF＝（FOB＋F）/[1−保险费率×（1＋加成投保率）]。例如，假定FOB价格为1000美元，每单位货物摊到的海运费200美元，投保海上货物运输一切险的保险费率为0.5%，投保加成10%，则CIF价格为21818美元：CIF＝（1000＋200）/[1−0.5%×（1＋10%）]。

### 3. CFR价换算成FOB、CIF价

反过来，如果知道CFR价，根据CFR价换算FOB、CIF价应为：

FOB价=CFR价–海运费

CIF价=CFR价+海上运输保险费

　　　=CFR/[1–保险费率×（1+加成投保率）]

### 4. CIF价格换算成FOB、CFR价

同样，如果知道CIF价，根据CIF价换算FOB、CFR价应为：

FOB价=（CIF价格–海运费–海上运输保险费）

FOB价=CIF价×[1–保险费率×（1+加成投保率）]–海运费

CFR价=CIF价–海上运输保险费率，或者

　　　=CIF价×[1–保险费率×（1+加成投保率）]

## （二）同一价格的不同货币换算

国际贸易在不同国家（地区）的买卖双方之间进行，会涉及不同种类之间的货币换算问题。不同种类货币之间的换算，要考虑这两种不同货币之间的兑换汇率。以中国境内的人民币与外汇兑换为例，银行的外汇牌价有银行外汇买入价、现钞买入价、外汇卖出价、基准价与中间折算价。例如2021年11月5日（星期一），中国银行美元的当日牌价为每100美元的现汇买入价690.08、现钞买入价685.18、卖出价693.73、中间折算价为689.76。在实际业务中，一般会用到现汇买入价和卖出价；在采用现金支付时，以现钞买入价代替现汇买入价计算；如分不清是采用买入价或卖出价，则可以简单地用中间折算价来代替。下面以中国进出口为例，说明价格改报的具体计算。

### 1. 人民币价格改报某种外币价格

中国的出口商（卖方）报人民币（本币）价格给国（地区）外买方，希望收回人民币金额，而国（地区）外买方要求支付外币。如卖方同意买方的要求，则需将人民币价格改报成外币价格，以收取外币来代替收取人民币。对卖方来说，在保持预期利润不降低的前提下，如果他（她）将收回的外币卖给银行后，换回的人民币金额不小于原希望收回的人民币金额，那价格改报对其是可接受的。卖方将外币卖给银行，银行以外汇买入价进行折算。因此，本币折算外币时，应采用买入价。外币价格=人民币价格/该外汇的买入价。例如，假设中国A出口公司对美国B公司报价为每公吨人民币3000元，而B客户要求改报美元价。按照2021年5月22日的中国银行美元买入价100美元=690.08计算，中国A公司对B公司改报的美元价格至少应为每公吨434.73美元：3000/（690.08/100）。

### 2. 外币价格改报人民币价格

中国的进口商（买方）收到国外出口商（卖方）的外币报价后，在3种情况下，会涉及该外币价格如何换算成人民币价格：①为了核算进口成本，买方会将外币价格折算成人民币价；②付款期限到来后，中国的买方一般需要拿人民币向银行换取外币后，支付给国（地区）外卖方。用人民币向银行买外币，银行以外汇卖出价进行折算；③为了

支付方便，买方要求卖方直接改报人民币价格。这3种情况下的换算方法相同。外币折算成本币时，应采用卖出价。人民币价格=外币价格×外汇卖出价。例如，假设中国C进口公司收到某英国D出口公司的报价为每打20英镑，C公司要求D公司改报人民币价或者C公司要核算支付20英镑的人民币价格。假设，中国银行当日的英镑卖出价为100英镑=1130.22元人民币，那么人民币价格应该是每打226.04元（20×1130.22/100）。

### 3. 一种外币价格改报成另一种外币价格

假设中国的出口商（卖方）报本币1价格给国外买方，而国外买方要求改报外币2。如卖方同意买方的要求，则需将外币1价格换算成外币2的价格，前提是预期利润不变。然而，中国的银行外汇牌价一般公布的是每种外币与人民币之间的兑换汇率，而两种外币之间的兑换汇率不直接公布出来。将外币1价格换算成外币2价格，一般有两种计算方法。

**（1）根据外币1与外币2之间的兑换汇率进行计算**

根据外币1与人民币之间的公布兑换汇率、人民币与外币2之间的公布兑换汇率，计算外币1与外币2之间的套算汇率，然后进行相应的价格改报。但是，套算汇率的计算比较专业、比较复杂，容易搞混，从而引起计算错误。当然，外币1与外币2之间的兑换汇率，也可以从国外金融市场途径去了解。

**（2）不直接计算或了解外币1与外币2之间的兑换（套算）汇率**

以人民币价格为桥梁，先将外币1价格改报成人民币价格，然后将人民币价格改报成外币2价格。计算方法为：人民币价格=外币1价格×外币1的银行卖出价，外币2价格=人民币价格/外币2的银行买入价。等式替换后，得出外币1价格与外币2价格之间的直接关系为：外币2价格=（外币1价格×外币1的银行卖出价）/（外币2的银行买入价）。例如，假设中国E公司对新加坡F公司出口报价每打400港币，但F公司要求改报英镑价。查询中国银行外汇牌价得知：100英镑的买入价为1121.21元、卖出价为1130.22元，而100港币的买入价为87.95元、卖出价为88.29元。因此，中国E出口公司可改报的英镑价为每打31.50英镑：(400×88.29)/1121.21。

# 四、出口成本核算

综上所述，我们知道了FOB、CFR、CIF之间不同贸易术语的价格换算，也了解了本币与外币、外币与外币之间的价格改报。对卖方来说，进行出口成本核算是判定出口报价是否正确、出口盈利有多少的重要途径。一般来说，出口价格=成本+费用+利润，其中：

## （一）成本

成本可以为生产成本或实际采购成本。因中国货物出口采用出口退税制度，而外贸企业与自营出口的生产企业所采用的退税口径是不一样的。对生产企业来说，成本可以是实际生产成本；对外贸企业来说，成本可以是实际采购成本。一般情况下，外贸企业不自己生产货物，而是向生产企业采购，因而采购成本一般会高于生产成本。

实际采购成本＝采购成本－出口退税额

出口退税额＝（采购成本×出口退税税率）/（1+增值税率）

实际采购成本＝采购成本×（1－出口退税税率）/（1+增值税率）。

### （二）费用

费用包括国内环节费用和国外环节费用。国内环节费用，一般包括货物在指定装运港将货物越过船舷之间的所有费用（如国内运费、仓储费、出口报关费、码头费、港口附加费、检验检疫费用、包装费、业务费用等）；国外环节费用，主要包括海运费和保险费。其中，FOB价格不涉及国外环节费用，CFR价格只涉及国外环节费用中的海运费，而CIF价格则要同时涉及海运费和海上货物运输保险费。

### （三）利润

利润可以按出口成交价、采购价、生产成本的一定百分比进行计算，也可以规定每单位货物出口应具有的利润额。一般情况下，利润以出口成交价的一定百分比计算居多，该百分比被称为利润率。出口报价时核定的利润率，称为预期利润率；收款后，出口成本核算后核定的利润率为实际利润率。每笔交易的预期利润率与实际利润率会存在较大差异。实际利润率可以高于或低于预期利润率。如果卖方在履约过程中加强管理，注重节约成本和费用，采取积极有效的方法防范和规避外汇风险、信用风险等，实际利润率有可能会超过预期利润率。例如，按照2018年5月1日1起正式实施的中国2018年最新增值税税率表，中国出口某产品的增值税率为16%，出口退税率为16%。中国A外贸企业向英国B公司出口该产品，出口价格为每件100美元CIF利物浦价，出口数量为1000个。已知：该批出口货物的采购成本为600元人民币/个，国内环节的总费用为40000元，总海运费为1200美元，保险加成为10%，投保一切险，保险费率为0.5%，卖方经营该笔业务的预期利润率为15%。结汇当日中国银行的外汇牌价：人民币/100美元的买入价为690.08，卖出价为693.73。

从以上这些信息，我们可以对该笔出口业务进行成本核算，并计算其实际利润率。

（1）第一步，计算A外贸企业的出口收汇收入。

外汇收入=CIF价格×出口数量×外汇买入价=690080.00元

（2）第二步，计算A外贸企业经营该笔业务所要支出的费用。

费用=国内环节费用+国外环节费用，其中：

国外环节费用=海运费+海上运输保险费（以CIF贸易术语成交）

国内环节费用=40000元

海运费=1200美元 × 外汇卖出价（A企业需要购买外汇支付船公司）

=8324.76元

保险费=CIF总金额 ×（1+投保加成）× 保险费率 × 外汇卖出价（A企业需要购买外汇支付给保险公司）

= CIF价格 x 出口数量 ×(1+投保加成)× 保险费率 × 外汇卖出价

= 3815.52元

（3）第三步，计算A企业的实际采购成本。

实际采购成本=采购成本−出口退税，其中：

采购成本=600 × 1000=600,000.00元

出口退税=出口数量 ×(采购成本 × 出口退税税率)/（1+增值税率）

=82758.62元

（4）第四步，计算实际利润额与实际利润率。

实际利润额=出口收汇收入−实际采购成本−费用=120,698.34元

实际利润率=(实际利润额/出口收汇收入)×100%=17.49%

因此，与预期利润率15%相比，该笔业务最终实现的实际利润率为17.49%。导致利润率提高的原因，有可能是人民币相对于美元贬值引起的（报价日与收汇日期间的汇率变化），也有可能是增值税税率降低和提高出口退税率、降低出口费用等引起的。为了防止汇率变化和经营费用的变化，卖方在对外报价时最好留有适当余地。

## 思考题

1. 一出口企业出口某商品，以FOB贸易术语对外报价为每箱USD100，国外买方要求改报CIF纽约价格。已知该货物每箱尺码为30 cm×40 cm×30 cm，每箱毛重为15千克；运费计费标准为W/M，基本运费为每运费吨USD20，到纽约需加收燃油附加费10%；投保一切险与战争险，保险费率分别为0.3%、0.2%，按CIF价值110%投保。请问：

   （1）该出口企业对外报CIF纽约的价格应是多少？

   （2）如客户希望改报CIFC2纽约价，请问具体报价应是多少？

2. 一出口企业就某款式服装对英国客户报价为每件100元人民币，合同签订后1个月付款。英国客户要求改报外币价格。请问：该出口企业应选择何种外币对外报价最为有利？具体报价是多少？已知：美元、港币、英镑、欧元的即期汇率和远期1个月的汇率中间价请参考英文部分的思考题。

# Chapter 5

# Price of the Goods

☞ Case 5.1

According to the statistical report of China's Ministry of Commerce, the exports of China's rice from January to December 2008 and January to December 2016 was shown in table 5.1 below. Overall, the total quantity of China's rice export in 2016 was 59.25% lower than that in 2008, the total export amount was 27.20% lower, while the average export unit price was 78.63% higher. From the intercontinental perspective, China's rice exports to Asia had the best performance, with the lowest decline in the export quantity (only down 1.88%). The average unit price of exports had only increased by 48.12%, but the total amount of exports had increased by 45.33%. China is the second largest rice exporter to North America. Although the volume of rice exported to North America decreased by 34.31%, the average unit price of rice exported and the total amount of rice exported increased by 122.13% and 45.87% respectively. In addition, China's rice exports to ROK and Oceania dropped by more than 99%. The average unit price of rice exported by China to Africa was lower than the overall average level. If the average unit price of China's rice export in 2008 and 2016 was converted according to the average exchange rate between US dollars and CNY in that year. The averaged rate of USD was 6.9451 against CNY in 2008, compared with 6.64 on December 31, 2016. The average unit price of rice exported in 2008 was CNY3,454.50 per metric ton, up 70.78 per cent from CNY 5,899.64 per metric ton in 2016, lower than the USD price increase.

Table 5.1  The Basic Situation of China's Rice Export in 2008 and 2016

| Continent | Indexes | Year 2008 | Year2016 | Plus or Minus（%） |
|---|---|---|---|---|
| Total exports | Quantity (Metric tons) | 969,317.10 | 394,979.70 | -59.25 |
| | Amount (USD ten thousand) | 48,210.10 | 35,094.80 | -27.20 |
| | Average unit price (USD/metric tons) | 497.40 | 888.5 | 78.63 |
| Export to Asia | Quantity (Metric tons) | 331,378.00 | 325,149.00 | -1.88 |
| | Amount (USD ten thousand) | 20,571.90 | 29,897.10 | 45.33 |
| | Average unit price· (USD/metric tons ) | 620.80 | 919.5 | 48.12 |
| Export to Africa | Quantity (Metric tons) | 446,403.30 | 62,767.40 | -85.94 |
| | Amount (USD ten thousand) | 19,802.50 | 4,619.10 | -76.67 |
| | Average unit price (USD/metric tons) | 443.60 | 735.9 | 65.89 |
| Export to Europe | Quantity (Metric tons) | 34,477.00 | 4,323.00 | -87.46 |
| | Amount (USD ten thousand) | 1,501.90 | 322 | -78.56 |
| | Average unit price (USD/metric tons) | 435.60 | 744.9 | 71.01 |
| Export to South America | Quantity (Metric tons) | 30,347.10 | 20.8 | -99.93 |
| | Amount (USD ten thousand) | 1,210.50 | 1.9 | -99.84 |
| | Average unit price (USD/metric tons) | 398.90 | 907 | 127.38 |
| Export to North America | Quantity (Metric tons) | 2,966.50 | 1,948.60 | -34.31 |
| | Amount (USD ten thousand) | 134.30 | 195.9 | 45.87 |
| | Average unit price (USD/metric tons) | 452.70 | 1,005.60 | 122.13 |
| Export to Oceania | Quantity (Metric tons) | 123,745.30 | 770.8 | -99.38 |
| | Amount (USD ten thousand) | 4,989.00 | 58.8 | -98.82 |
| | Average unit price (USD/metric tons) | 403.20 | 763 | 89.24 |

In 2008, Cote d'Ivoire, ROK and Liberia were the top three rice importers of China's rice exports, among which Cote d'Ivoire and Liberia are African countries. The top three rice importers in 2016 were ROK, Pakistan, and Japan, all of them are Asian countries (see Table 5.2). Therefore, with a comprehensive view of China's rice export in 2008 and 2016, in addition to the volume reduction and price increase, China's rice export market had undergone great changes.

Table 5.2  The Top 3 Importing Countries of China's Rice in 2008 and 2016

| | Rank | 2008 | | 2016 | |
|---|---|---|---|---|---|
| Quantity (Metric tons) | | Cote d'lvoire | 202,064.80 | ROK | 175,547.00 |
| Amount (USD ten thousand) | 1 | | 8,300.90 | | 13,848.90 |
| Average unit price · USD/metric tons · | | | 410.8 | | 788.9 |
| Quantity (Metric tons) | | ROK | 161,721.00 | Pakistan | 9,325.80 |
| Amount (USD ten thousand) | 2 | | 8,078.50 | | 31,211.70 |
| Average unit price (USD/metric tons) | | | 499.5 | | 3,443.90 |
| Quantity (Metric tons) | | Liberia | 146,709.70 | Japan | 37,872.00 |
| Amount (USD ten thousand) | 3 | | 5,528.60 | | 2,999.00 |
| Average unit price (USD/metric tons) | | | 376.8 | | 791.9 |

China is a major rice producer, but not a major rice exporter. In 2012, China imported 2.35 million tons of rice, 305% more than 580,000 tons in 2011. Since 2013, China has become the largest importer of rice in the world. From being a net exporter of rice to a net importer, China imported more than 5 million tons of rice in 2016.

Price concerns to the economic interests of both parties directly and becomes one of the most important terms and conditions of a sales contract. It is the key content of business negotiation. Price is influenced by many factors, such as quality of the goods, transport distance, delivery condition, seasonal price difference, quantity of the goods, exchange rate, the customer's credit standing and requirement of delivery term. The price clause in a sales contract normally includes unit price and total value of the goods. Some contracts need to be expressly stipulated the pricing method, commission and discount, etc. The clause of unit price usually contains calculating unit, pricing currency, the amount of unit and trade term at least, such as USD100.00 per M/T FOB Shanghai Incoterms®2010. Both parties pay more attention on how to understand the principle of pricing correctly, how to select the benefit pricing currency, how to make costs accounting carefully as well as how to master the trend of price change and the situation of supply & demand in international market. Based on above, the influencing factors shall be considered fully and the effective pricing methods shall be rational used.

# 5.1 Pricing Methods

The price can be set in a contract as fixed price, flexible price, provisional price and floating price. Fixed price is that the parties stipulate a specific price of the goods in the contract on the basis of mutual agreement in international trade. It is used widely and specific, definite, sure as well as be easy to account. The fixed price may be stipulated as "USD75.00 per dozen CIF London Incoterms ®2010. Or USD75.00 per dozen CIF London Incoterms ®2010, no price increase (adjustment) shall be allowed after conclusion of this contract. However, the seller may need to bear risks of price change from the contracted signed, the goods delivered and payment made as the constantly changing conditions of international market if the parties adopt the fixed price. The buyer bears risks of price change from the contract signed to take delivery of the goods. There are both advantages and disadvantages if the fixed price adopted.

The parties may take flexible measures other than fixed price in order to reduce risks, facilitate business and increase performance rate. The parties may adopt flexible price in the contract. It means that the price will be set in the future. This pricing method is suitable for the goods with fluctuate market, the price change sharply, or long term of delivery and the parties are difficulty to grasp the market trend but intention to conclude a contract. The parties may set the name of the goods and its specification, quantity, package, delivery and payment term in the contract, whereas the price not. In the contract, the parties stipulate how to set price in the future. Normally, the pricing time and method can be stipulated in the contract as "Unit price shall be increased (decreased) USD xx subject to the closing point dated on_____".

The parties may stipulate provisional price in the contract and specify that the price is non-fixed. The price for payment settled will be confirmed by the parties as per the currently market situation before a certain earlier than the delivery time. As the pricing basis doesn't be stipulated in the contract, the parties may stick to their own view. No mutual agreement will be concluded for the price negotiation and lead to no performance of the contract. In business practice, the pricing method of provisional price is only suitable for the business between the parties with close relations and good credit standing. The method of price negotiation shall be stipulated in the contract and the finally settle price shall be expressly clearly in the contract in case no agreement be concluded in the price negotiation. The provisional price can be stipulated in the contract as "The price will be set on _____ (Date) through the parties negotiated mutually, or USD75.00 per dozen CIF London Incoterms ®2010. It is a provisional price, which shall be determined through negotiation between the buyer and the seller 15 days before the month of shipment."

Floating price can be adopted for exportation of complete equipment and large machinery as long term from the contract concluded to finish the delivery. The parties shall bear risks caused by change of materials, wages and exchange rate, etc. The floating price means that the parties stipulate a basic price in the contract first and adjust the price as per the indexes variation of wage and materials to confirm the final settled price before a certain lead time. The method for adjustment of floating price must be stipulated in the contract, such as P=PO

(A+BM/MO+CW/WO). P represents the final price for settlement and PO for the basis price of contract signed. A for proportion of operate management fees and benefit to the price. B is for proportion of material to price. M for the average price of materials or index applied for the final price calculated. MO for the average price of materials or index applied for the basic price calculated. C is for or the proportion of wage to the price. W for the average price of wage or index applied for the final price calculated. WO for the average price of wage or index for the basic price calculated. The proportion value of A, B, C is confirmed in the contract.

## 5.2 Pricing Currency

The pricing currency must be contained in the contract. Usually, it is selected according to business practice, intention of purchase and sale, market price and competitive condition, etc. The pricing currency is always same as the currency of settlement, but sometimes not. It may be currency of the exporting country, the importing country or the third country agreed by the both parties. The exchange rates between countries are often fluctuating according to conditions of economic development. Exchange rate variation has an effect on the price of international market. The parties shall select the pricing currency carefully in order to avoid the possible losses caused by the risks of exchange rate. Normally, the pricing currency may be a convertible and relative stable one, such as USD, GBP, EUR, HKD. Whatever the seller or the buyer may select the currency be benefit for his own in order to avoid the exchange rate risks. The seller is biased to select the pricing currency which exchange rate is relative stable and/or with trend of appreciation, whereas the buyer is biased to select the currency with depreciation trend.

It should be noticed that the Chinese currency gradually becomes one of popular pricing/settlement currency in the world now. The Chinese parties may select CNY as the pricing/settlement currency to avoid risks of exchange rate. In case of disadvantage currency adopted, the party shall adopt certain remedy measures to avoid the risks of exchange rate to protect his benefit.  The remedy measures may be:① to put factor of exchange rate floating into consideration. The seller may increase properly the quoted price to avoid risks of currency floating downward. The buyer may decrease the price to avoid risks of currency floating upward.② To select multiple pricing currencies. It means that the different currencies with floating upward and downward tied up in a sales contract or different contracts in order to avoid risks of exchange rate. The convert rate between two kinds of currencies is changed frequently. The trend of floating upward/downward for a kind of currency is relatively to the other one. The currency with upward exchange rate today may become to the downward one tomorrow. ③ To sign exchange rate proviso clause in the contract. Normally, the contract will be stated a specific exchange rate between the settlement currency and a certain currency and payment will be made by the settlement currency calculated as per the current rate. For example: the pricing currency of a contract is USD and the contractual amount is USD100, 000.00 based on the exchange rate between USD and CNY is CNY 6.30/USD100. The contract also stipulated that the settled amount shall be re-calculated as per the current rate of payment date. If the reality current rate on the payment date is CNY 6.20/USD100. The buyer shall pay USD (100,000.00 × 6.30/6.20) instead of USD100, 000.00.

## 5.3 Calculating Unit

The calculating unit shall be same as the measuring unit in the quantity clause. If the measuring unit is metric ton, the price calculating unit shall be same and can't use long ton or short ton. The calculating unit included in the price agreed by the parties shall be stated in the contract correctly. If not, it is deemed to be negative or change of condition concluded through business negotiation as per laws of international trade and commerce.

## 5.4 Trade Terms

The parties attach important to select and use trade term. The following factors are considered overall.

① The rate of freight and premium rate changed. The petroleum price of international market fluctuates frequently and makes bunker adjustment surcharge is raised sharply. The insurer's raises premium rate one after another as prevailing of pirate on international main traffic routes. Meanwhile, the volume of world trade is keeping expanding substantially. All of these push the freight and premium increasing sharply. In order to reduce risks of freight and premium changed, the seller may strive for FOB or FCA, whereas the buyer may strive for CIF, CIP, CPT or CFR.

② Mode of transportation. FCA, CIP or CPT shall be used widely instead of FOB, CIF or CFR because of irrespective mode of transportation.

③ Trade terms belongs to actual delivery including EXW, FAS, DAT, DAP and DDP may be used properly. Whatever developed or developing countries currently strengthen economic and trade ties with other countries (regions). Multinational negotiation conducted by WTO was suffered by repeated setbacks. Regional Free Trade Agreements (FTAs) have already become a new trend of world trade liberalization. FTA is deemed as a new platform to further open up to the outside world and to speed up domestic reforms, an effective approach to integrate into global economy and strengthen economic cooperation with other economies, and, particularly, an important supplement to the multilateral trading system. Free trade agreements opened in markets such as Asia, North Europe (Switzerland, Finland, Iceland), Australia, New Zealand,

South America (Chile, Peru, Costa Rica, and Colombia), Pakistan, Sri lanka and Korea, etc and creating more opportunities for China businesses. China can adopt trade terms of actual delivery to develop business with these countries and accumulate experience of these trade terms adopted.

## 5.5 Commission and Discount

Commission is the reward that the seller or buyer paid to the middle man for his/her intermediary service for the goods sold or purchased. The middle man is normally a broker or agent and helps to get orders and contribute to business. He/she also can be called commission merchant. Discount is certain of price concession that the seller provide for the buyer. The names of commission and discount are many and varied, such as selling commission, purchase commission, accumulative commission, quantity discount and special discount. Generally, the parties will state in the contract if the price is including commission and/or discounting or not. Sometimes the commission/ discounting is stipulated by an independent agreement between the broker and the principal instead of being stated in the contract. If the commission/discounting is stipulating in the contract, it can be described as "including commission" or "less discounting". For example: USD500 per M/T CIF London Incoterms®2010. Or USD50 per Case CIP Singapore Incoterms®2010 Less 1% Discount. Or USD500 per M/T CIF London Incoterms®2010 including 2% Commission and Less 1% Discount. Including commission can be instead by "C" in briefly. For example: USD500 per M/T CIFC2 London Incoterms®2010. If the price is excluding commission and/or discount, "net" can be marked after trade term of the price, such as USD 25 per Dozen FCA Tianjin Net Incoterms®2010.

## 5.6 Price Conversion

Price calculating is top important in practical international trade. It is relating to costs, freight, premium, charges, exchange rate, taxes, tax refund, commission, and discount and trade term so on. The flowing calculating will be introduced in this part:  ①How to convert net price and price including commission or discount?②How to convert price in different currencies, such as Chinese currency and foreign currency, two kinds of different currency.③How to convert price under different trade terms, such as price under CIF, CFR and FOB? ④How to calculate price with combine above all.

### 5.6.1 Price Conversion Between Net Price and Price Including Commission/Discount

Generally, commission is expressed by a certain percentage of trade value or a certain amount of unit. For example: The contract's price is at USD5.00 per PC FOBC3 Shanghai Incoterms ®2010. It means that the rate of commission is 3% or USD0.15/PC and the net price is USD4.85 per PC FOB Shanghai Incoterms ®2010. The calculating method is as following:

Price Including Commission= Net Price/ (1−Commission Rate)

Commission Value= Price Including Commission × Rate of Commission

Discount calculated is same as above. If a price includes commission and discount simultaneously, it can be calculated on the basis of price including commission as follows:

Price Including Commission & Discount= [Net Price/ (1−Commission Rate)]/ (1−Rate of Discount)

Commission Value= Price Including Commission & Discount × Rate of Commission

Discount Value=Price Including Commission & Discount × Rate of Discount

The seller settles the total value of commission and discount differently. The seller shall receive the total value of commission from the buyer first and then pay to the broker. It means that the buyer can't deduct the commission by himself. The discount value permits to be deducted directly.

☞ Case5.2

The quantity of a sales contract was 1,000 PCS; the gross price is USD10.00 per PC CIFC5 New York Incoterms ®2010 less 3% of discount. Please calculate:

① The net price.

② The proceed received for the seller from the buyer.

③ The commission that the seller shall pay.

Net Price = The Gross Price × (1−Rate of Commission) × (1−Rate of Discount)

    = USD10.00 × (1−5%) × (1−3%) = USD9.215 /PC

Proceeds Received Amount = Quantity × Gross price × (1−Rate of Discount)

      = 1,000 PCS × USD10.00/PC × (1−3%)

      = USD9, 700.00

Commission = Quantity × Gross Price × Rate of Commission

    = 1,000 PCS × USD10.00/PC × 5% = USD9,500.00

So, if the seller complained that the commission paid was as higher as the commission should be calculated as per the net price instead of price including commission and discount, or as per FOB net price as the CIF price was including freight and premium charges that the seller should pay to the shipping company and the insurer. The freight and premium charges should not be calculated as the commission factors. If the seller wants to pay commission as per FOB net price, the relating contract clause should be stipulated as "Price is USD10.00 per PC CIFC5 New York Incoterms ®2010 less 3% of discount, the commission shall be calculated as per FOB net price."

## 5.6.2 Price Conversion in Different Currencies

A price can be converted between two kinds of different currencies, such as:

① Price in Chinese currency converted to the price in foreign currency

② Price in foreign currency converted to the price in Chinese currency, and

③ Price in one kind of foreign currency converted to another kind of foreign currency.

It is the basic skill of traders for international trade. The exchange rate between two different kinds of currency is the basis of price conversion. The commercial bank offers spot exchange rate and forward exchange rate between home currency and main foreign currencies on working days. The exchange rate between home currency and foreign currency has selling rate, buying rate, middle rate, cash buying rate and cash selling rate.

In practice, the buying rate and selling rate of same kind of foreign exchange is different. The selling rate is higher than the buying rate and the middle rate is in the middle. The buying rates of cash and inward remittance are also difference. While, the selling rate of cash and outward remittance is same. Sometimes, the middle rate can be acted as the exchange rate for calculating price or cost. The followings has an example of spot exchange rate of some main kinds of currency and the forward excahnge rate of USD and JPY published on Aug 24, 2015 (Monday) and Aug 21, 2015 (Friday) specifically (see Table 5.3, Table5.4, and Table 5.5).

Table 5.3　The Spot Exchange Rate of Bank of China, Home Branches

| Currency Name | Buying Rate | Cash Buying Rate | Selling Rate | Cash Selling Rate | Middle Rate | Pub Time |
|---|---|---|---|---|---|---|
| USD | 637.77 | 632.66 | 640.33 | 640.33 | 638.64 | 2015-08-24 8:06 |
| SGD | 450.21 | 436.32 | 453.37 | 453.37 | 454.76 | 2015-08-24 8:06 |
| JPY | 5.2253 | 5.0641 | 5.2621 | 5.2621 | 5.1669 | 2015-08-24 8:06 |
| HKD | 82.28 | 81.62 | 82.59 | 82.59 | 82.39 | 2015-08-24 8:06 |
| GBP | 997.83 | 967.03 | 1004.83 | 1004.83 | 1000.87 | 2015-08-24 8:06 |
| EUR | 723.16 | 700.81 | 730.42 | 730.42 | 717.71 | 2015-08-24 8:06 |

continued

| Currency Name | Buying Rate | Cash Buying Rate | Selling Rate | Cash Selling Rate | Middle Rate | Pub Time |
|---|---|---|---|---|---|---|
| CAD | 481.47 | 466.6 | 485.33 | 485.33 | 488.18 | 2015-08-24 8:06 |
| AUD | 461.57 | 447.31 | 466.21 | 466.21 | 467.54 | 2015-08-24 8:06 |

Table 5.4  USD Forward Exchange Rate of Bank of China, Home Branches

| Currency Name | Transaction period | Buying Rate | Selling Rate | Middle Rate | Date |
|---|---|---|---|---|---|
| USD | One week | 638.08015 | 641.58045 | 639.8303 | 2015-08-21 |
| USD | 20 days | 638.75255 | 642.36365 | 640.5581 | 2015-08-21 |
| USD | 1 month | 639.28575 | 642.95665 | 641.1212 | 2015-08-21 |
| USD | 2 months | 640.9364 | 644.608 | 642.7722 | 2015-08-21 |
| USD | 3 months | 642.362 | 646.0844 | 644.2232 | 2015-08-21 |
| USD | 4 months | 643.74485 | 647.66795 | 645.7064 | 2015-08-21 |
| USD | 5 months | 645.1303 | 649.0539 | 647.0921 | 2015-08-21 |
| USD | 6 months | 646.6639 | 650.5883 | 648.6261 | 2015-08-21 |
| USD | 7 months | 647.9675 | 652.0995 | 650.0335 | 2015-08-21 |
| USD | 8 months | 648.96545 | 653.09075 | 651.0281 | 2015-08-21 |
| USD | 9 months | 650.16585 | 654.29155 | 652.2287 | 2015-08-21 |
| USD | 10 months | 651.79535 | 656.02185 | 653.9086 | 2015-08-21 |
| USD | 11 months | 652.8527 | 657.0797 | 654.9662 | 2015-08-21 |
| USD | 12 months | 654.2469 | 658.4747 | 656.3608 | 2015-08-21 |

Table 5.5  JPY Forward Exchange Rate of Bank of China, Home Branches

| Currency Name | Transaction period | Buying Rate | Selling Rate | Middle Rate | Date |
|---|---|---|---|---|---|
| JPY | 20 days | 5.1615 | 5.2247 | 5.1931 | 2015-08-21 |
| JPY | 1 month | 5.1665 | 5.231 | 5.1987 | 2015-08-21 |
| JPY | 2 months | 5.183 | 5.2476 | 5.2153 | 2015-08-21 |
| JPY | 3 months | 5.1958 | 5.2625 | 5.2291 | 2015-08-21 |
| JPY | 4 months | 5.2115 | 5.2783 | 5.2449 | 2015-08-21 |
| JPY | 5 months | 5.2287 | 5.2956 | 5.2622 | 2015-08-21 |

continued

| Currency Name | Transaction period | Buying Rate | Selling Rate | Middle Rate | Date |
|---|---|---|---|---|---|
| | 6 months | 5.2442 | 5.3111 | 5.2776 | 2015-08-21 |
| JPY | 7 months | 5.2594 | 5.3242 | 5.2918 | 2015-08-21 |
| JPY | 8 months | 5.2728 | 5.3383 | 5.3056 | 2015-08-21 |
| JPY | 9 months | 5.2853 | 5.3531 | 5.3192 | 2015-08-21 |
| JPY | 10 months | 5.3013 | 5.37 | 5.3356 | 2015-08-21 |
| JPY | 11 months | 5.3196 | 5.3884 | 5.354 | 2015-08-21 |
| JPY | 12 months | 5.3318 | 5.4007 | 5.3662 | 2015-08-21 |

**1. Price Conversion in Chinese Currency to Foreign Currency**

For China exports, the seller normally has price in CNY first, while the foreign buyer may ask the seller to offer price in foreign currency. The Chinese seller needs to convert the price in CNY to the price in foreign currency. It is noticed that the seller shall change back at least the same amount of CNY against the received amount of foreign currency if he shall re-offer price in foreign currency. The seller needs to sell foreign currency to the commercial bank. The commercial bank buys the foreign currency as per its buying rate of foreign currency and pay CNY to the seller. According the exchange quotation of Chinese commercial bank, the conversion method of price in CNY to foreign currency as follows:

Price in Foreign Currency=Price in CNY/ (the Buying Rate of Foreign Currency)

☞ Case 5.3

One Chinese seller quoted towels price at CNY 828.62 per dozen CIF New York Incoterms ®2010 on Aug 24, 2015. The U.S. buyer asked him to quote price in USD, how much shall the Seller offer so that he can obtain the same benefit?

Answer: The seller may re-quote price in USD as per the spot or with reference of relating forwarding exchange rate of USD/CNY buying rate. For example: if payment is to be paid within 30 days after actual shipment and the shipment will be made within 30 days after the contract signed, the seller can quote price in USD with reference of forwarding exchange rate of two months. So the price in USD can be quoted as following in this case:

Price in USD = Price in CNY/ The Spot Buying Rate of USD

= CNY828.62/ (CNY637.77/100USD) = USD129.925 (USD129.93), or

Price in USD = Price in CNY/ The Forward Buying Rate of USD (transaction period two months)

$$= CNY828.62/(CNY640.9364/100USD) = USD129.29$$

Table 5.4 shows that the exchange rate of USD/CNY is expected to be appreciated in the near future, it is suggested that the seller quote price in USD to the buyer as " at USD 129.93 per dozen CIF New York Incoterms ®2010" in order to avoid exchange rate of USD depreciated actually on the payment date.

**2. Price Conversion in Foreign Currency to Chinese Currency**

For China imports, the foreign seller may offer price in foreign currency, while the Chinese buyer shall estimate import cost or make payment in foreign currency. The Chinese buyer needs to convert the price in foreign currency to CNY. If the Chinese buyer needs to pay in foreign currency, he/she shall buy the foreign currency from the commercial bank against CNY and pay to the foreign buyer. Relatively, the commercial bank purchases CNY from the buyer and sells the foreign currency to him/her. According the exchange quotation of Chinese home commercial bank, the conversion method of price in foreign currency to CNY as follows:

Price in CNY=Price in Foreign Currency × the Selling Rate of Foreign Currency

☞ Case 5.4

Co. A in China want to import one unit of equipment from Japan and the Japanese exporter offers total price JPY30, 000,000 on Aug 24, 2015. How much shall Co. A pay in CNY?

Answer: The buyer may calculate the total amount in CNY as per the spot or with reference of relating forwarding exchange rate of JPY/CNY selling rate. For example: If the payment is to be paid at sight after shipment and the shipment will be made within 90 days after the contract signed, the buyer can convert price in CNY with reference of forwarding exchange rate of three months. So the amount in CNY can be calculated as following in this case:

Amount in CNY = Amount in JPY × the Spot Selling Rate of JPY

$$= JPY30, 000,000 \times (CNY5.2621/100JPY) = CNY1,578,630$$

Amount in USD = Amount in CNY/ Forward Selling Rate of JPY ( three months)

$$= JPY30, 000,000 \times (CNY5.2625/100JPY) = CNY1, 578,750$$

Table 5.5 shows that the exchange rate of JPY/CNY is expected to be appreciated in the near future. It is suggested that the buyer calculate import cost in CNY 1,578,750 in order to avoid exchange rate of JPY appreciated really on the payment date.

### 3. Price Conversion in Foreign Currency a to Foreign Currency B

Sometimes, the Chinese seller quoted price in foreign currency and need to requote price in another kind of foreign currency. Hypothetically, the expected profit isn't changed; the seller may convert the price in foreign currency A to foreign currency B if he/she has the relating exchange rate of these two kinds of foreign currencies. If he/she hasn't the relating exchange rate information, according to the exchange quotation of Chinese home commercial bank, he/she can convert the price in foreign currency A to price in CNY first, and then change the price in CNY to price in foreign currency B. How to change the price in foreign currency A to foreign currency B is as following:

Price in Foreign Currency B= (Price in Foreign Currency A×the Selling Rate of Currency
A)/(the Buying Rate of Foreign Currency B)

## ☞ Case 5.5

Co A offered price at USD100.00 per set CIF Osaka Incoterms ®2010 to a customer in Japan on Aug 24, 2015, but the Japanese customer needs to pay in JPY, How much shall the price in JPY that Co A offer ?

Answer: Co A may quote price in JPY as per the spot rate or with the reference of relating forwarding JPY/CNY buying rate and USD/CNY selling rate. For example: if the payment is to be paid at 60 days after shipment and the shipment will be made within 30 days after the contract signed, the seller can convert the price in JPY with reference of forwarding exchange rate of three months. So the price in JPY can be calculated as following in this case.

(1) For Spot Exchange Rate

Price in JPY = (Price in USD× the Selling Rate of USD)/ (the Buying Rate of JPY)

= USD100.00×(CNY640.33/100USD)/(CNY5.2253/100JPY)

= JPY12, 254, or

(2) For Forward Exchange Rate

Price in JPY = USD100.00 × (CNY646.0844/100USD)/(CNY5.1958/100JPY)

= JPY12,435

Sometimes, the changing trend of two kinds of foreign .currency are different. Maybe currency A is expected to be appreciated against CNY, whereas currency B is on the opposite. It is suggested that the seller offer price according to the changing trend of exchange rate.

### 5.6.3. Freight & Premium Charges Calculating

Freight charges and premium are the important factors of price. The freight charges are borne by the seller under trade terms except for EXW, FCA, FOB and FAS. The premium must be calculated into the price under CIF and CIP price. Container is popular used in international trade and can be divided into FCL (full container loaded) and LCL(less container loaded). Here mainly introduce ocean marine transport freight charge in container. The shipping companies announce their freight price through mainstream medias. You can find the relating information about freight price adjustment on the homepage of Shanghai Shipping Exchange or the shipping company. You also can consult the forwarding agents about freight information. Table 5.6 is the freight Charges from Shanghai to Miami by 1×40'FCL with different effective date. Table 5.7 is freight charges of Cosco Shipping Lines from Shanghai to ports of east coast in the USA (CY to CY) specially.

Freight charges of marine transportation include ocean freight and additional surcharges. Different shipping company gathers different additional surcharges for the same line. Table 5-5 shows the freight charges of different shipping companies from Shanghai, China to Miami, the USA by 1x40'FCL. It can be found that different ocean freight and additional surcharges with different kinds of cargos of different shipping companies. The ocean freight is normally offered in USD. BAF, CAF, O.THC, D.THC as well as commission in Table 5.6 are additional surcharges.

①BAF means bunker adjustment factors and always shows in USD. The shipping companies such as UASC, ANL, CMA, MSC, ZIM, ITS, EGH, EMS and APL still need to collect BAF in the effective period, while OOCL, HLAG, MSL,HMM and Cosco forgive BAF during the same period.

②CAF means currency adjustment factors and always shows in percentage. For example: CAF 20 means the shipping company will collect 20% of ocean freight or total freight charges (sum total of ocean freight and additional). The former shipping companies all forgive CAF. It implies that the spot or forward exchange rate of USD is strong and expected to be appreciation.

③O.THC is a kind of additional surcharges and means original terminal handling charges and offered in local currency of the seller.

④D.THC means destination terminal handling charges. It is showed in the currency of destination. D.THC value in Table 5.6 is in USD as the port of destination is Miami, the USA.

Table 5.6  The Freight Charges from Shanghai to Miami by 1x40'FCL

| Shipping Company | Classification of the Goods | Ocean Freight | Commission | BAF | CAF | O. THC | D. THC | Effective Date |
|---|---|---|---|---|---|---|---|---|
| UASC | General cargo | 3,114 | | 645 | | 1,155 | 740 | 2015-08-17 |
| ANL | General cargo | 4,800 | | 861 | | 1,155 | 1,070 | 2015-07-05 |
| CMA | Dangerous cargo | 1,825 | | 2,000 | | 1,155 | 600 | 2015-08-01 |
| MSC | Dangerous cargo | 3,004 | 2.50% | 645 | | 1,150 | | 2015-08-01 |
| OOCL | General cargo | 3,684 | | | | 1,181 | | 2015-08-02 |
| OOCL | Dangerous cargo | 4,284 | | | | 1,299 | | 2015-08-02 |
| HLAG | General cargo | 3,750 | | | | 1,120 | 740 | 2015-07-04 |
| MSL | Classification no.1/ 2/3/4/5/6/7/21/ user–defined no.51/52/ Dangerous cargo /chemicals/ General cargo | 6,120 | | | | 1,150 | 390 | 2015-08-01 |
| MSL | Classification no.14 | 5,520 | | | | 1,150 | 390 | 2015-06-01 |
| MSL | Classification no.8 | 4,920 | | | | 1,340 | 390 | 2015-04-02 |
| MSL | Classification no.22/user–defined no.32/36/61/90/ 31/34/33 | 4,525 | | | | 1,150 | 390 | 2015-01-01 |
| MSL | Classification no.9/17/18/19 | 2,725 | | | | 1,150 | 390 | 2014-06-01 |
| HMM | Dangerous cargo | 5,500 | | | | 1,356 | | 2015-08-15 |
| HMM | General cargo | 5,500 | | | | 1,189 | | 2015-08-15 |
| ZIM | Dangerous cargo | 4,210 | | 990 | | 1,134 | | 2014-09-09 |
| ZIM | General cargo | 3,610 | | 990 | | 1,134 | | 2014-09-09 |
| ITS | General cargo | 1,350 | | 980 | | 1,185 | 1,070 | 2015-08-07 |
| EGH | General cargo | 1,350 | | 980 | | 1,185 | 1,070 | 2015-08-07 |

continued

| Shipping Company | Classification of the Goods | Ocean Freight | Commission | BAF | CAF | O. THC | D. THC | Effective Date |
|---|---|---|---|---|---|---|---|---|
| EMS | General cargo | 1,350 | | 980 | | 1,185 | 1,070 | 2015-08-07 |
| COSCO | General cargo | 5,000 | | | | 1,185 | | 2015-08-17 |
| APL | General cargo | 3,116 | | 684 | | 1,140 | 1,070 | 2015-08-01 |
| | Chemicals | 18,600 | | | | 1,140 | | 2014-09-28 |

Table 5.7 Freight Charges of Cosco Shipping Lines From Shanghai to Ports of East Coast in the USA (CY to CY)

| Port of Discharge | Port of Destination | Container Type | Goods Classification | Container Size | Ocean Freight | O. THC | Effective Date |
|---|---|---|---|---|---|---|---|
| Yangshan Port Waigaoqiao | New York | Flat rack | General cargo | 40 | 6,000 | 1,343 | 2015-08-18 |
| | Miami | Refrigeration HQ | General cargo | 40 | 5,800 | 1,343 | 2015-08-18 |
| | Boston, Massachusetts | Refrigeration container | General cargo | 40 | 5,300 | 1,343 | 2015-08-18 |
| | Baltimore, Maryland | Flat rack | General cargo | 20 | 5,000 | 895 | 2015-08-18 |
| Yangshan Port Waigaoqiao | New York | HQ | General cargo | 45 | 6,500 | 1,663 | 2015-08-17 |
| | Miami | HQ | General cargo | 40 | 5,500 | 1,185 | 2015-08-17 |
| | Boston, Massachusetts | Dry van container | General cargo | 40 | 5,000 | 1,185 | 2015-08-17 |
| | Baltimore, Maryland | Dry van container | General cargo | 40 | 4,200 | 790 | 2015-08-17 |

Besides the above, there are many kinds of additional surcharges be collected as per socioeconomic, trade and logistic statues, such as deviation surcharge, Suez Canal surcharge, transshipment surcharge, direct additional, port surcharge, port congestion surcharge (PCS), heavy-lift additional, long length additional, cleaning charge, fumigation charge, ice surcharge, peak season surcharge (PSS), Panama Canal transit fee (PTF), interim fuel additional (IFA), fuel adjustment factor (FAF), general rate increase (GRI), automatic manifest system(AMS), Yen ascend surcharge (YAS) and Alameda corridor surcharge (ACS), equipment re-positioning surcharge (ERS) and inter-modal administration charge (IAC). The additional surcharges can be included in ocean freight or collected separately. The details can be obtained from the forwarding agents before shipment.

### 1. Freight Calculating

If the goods are shipped by FCL, the freight is charged as per box rate. It can be found from Table 5.6 that the total freight charges of 1×40'FCL shipped by COSCO Container Lines from Shanghai to Miami is USD5,000 (ocean freight)+CNY1185 (O.THC) for general cargo.

If the goods is shipped by LCL, the freight is charged as per volume or gross weight of the goods. Heavy-cargo is calculated freight charges as per the total gross weight of the goods and the measuring unit is metric ton. Light-cargo is calculated freight charges as per the total measurement of the goods and the measuring unit is generally cubic meter. The freight charges relating to LCL can be asked to the freight forwarders.

The most popular three kinds of container are 40'HQ (8feet×9.6feet×40feet), 40'GP (8feet×8.6feet×40feet) and 20'GP (8feet×8.6feet×20feet), their inner sizes with height×width×height are 12.192×2.438×2.896, 12.192×2.438×2.393 and 5.898×2.392×2.385 meters respectively. Although their internal capacities are 76.4, 67.7, 33.2 cubic meters, and the maximum land weights are 26,500, 26,650, and 26,830 kilograms respectively, the suggested capacity and land weight are 68CBM/22MTS for 40'HQ, 54CBM/22MTS for 40'GP and 25CBM/17.5MTS for 20'GP respectively because of gap between packages of the goods and or the packages and the internal face of the container. Normally, the quantity of the packages landed into one container can be calculated by putting according to the inner size of container or in practice.

## ☞ Case5.6

The contractual goods are planned to ship from Shanghai to Miami by COSCO Container Lines. It is packed in cartons with 12 pcs each. Gross weight each package is 12.0 kg, net weight of each package is 10.0 kg, and the measurement of carton is 48 cm×28 cm×28 cm. If the goods are shipped by 1×40'GP, the ocean freight is USD5,000 and O.THC is CNY 1,185.00. If the goods are shipped by LCL, the freight rate is USD85.00/cubic meter or USD80.00/ metric ton. The questions are: ① How many cartons can be landed in 1×40'GP? ② If the goods are shipped by 1×40'GP, please calculate the freight charge per unit in USD and CNY. ③ If the ordered quantity is 1,200 pcs, please calculate the freight charges per unit in USD and CNY.

Answer:

The inner size of 40'GP is 12.192 m×2.438 m×2.393 m and the suggested capacity is 54CBM/22MTS. The carton size is 48 cm×28 cm×28 cm, and the gross weight is 12.0 kg each.

According to the suggested capacity, 1×40'GP can land 1,434 cartons as per calculation:

Gross Weight: 22,000 kg / (12.0 kg/carton) = 1833.33 cartons

Volume: 54/ (0.48 × 0.28 × 0.28) = 1434.9 cartons.

According to size assortment, 1x40'GP can land 1,600 cartons (25 × 8 × 8) as per calculation: length 1219.2/48 = 25.4, width 243.8/28 = 8.7 and height 239.3/28 = 8.54. The total gross weight of 1,600 cartons is 19,200 kg (19.2 mts) and less than the suggested weight 22.0 mts.

Based on above, 1,600 cartons can be landed in 1 × 40'GP after comparing. In this case, 1,600 cartons is the best answer for this question. In practice, the parties may decide to ship the goods by FCL with the quantity less than the best answer. As per the above method, it can be found that 768 cartons can be landed in 1 × 20'GP and 2,000 cartons can be landed in 1 × 40'HQ.

The ocean freight is USD5,000 and O.THC is CNY 1,185.00 for 1 × 40'GP. 1 × 40'GP can land 1,600 cartons. Each carton is 12 pcs. In order to calculate the freight charges per unit. As per the exchange rate of CNY/100USD in Table 5.3, the buying rate is CNY637.77/100USD, the selling rate is CNY 640.33/100USD.

Total Quantity of Lx40'GP Landed = 1600 cartons × (12pcs/carton) = 19 × 200PCS

Total Freight Charges of 1 × 40'GP in USD

= USD5,000 + CNY1185

= USD5,000 + USD1,185/ (637.77/100)

= USD5,185.80

Total Freight Charges of 1 × 40'GP in CNY

= CNY (USD5000 × Selling Rate) + CNY1185

= USD5,000 × CNY640.33/100USD + USD1,185

= CNY33,201.50

Freight Charges per Unit in USD = USD5,185.03/19,200PCS = USD0.27/PC

Freight Charges per Unit in CNY = CNY33,201.50/19,200PCS = CNY1.73/PC

If the ordered quantity is 1200 pcs, it will be shipped by LCL.

Total Packages = 1200 pcs / (12pcs/carton) = 100 cartons

Total Measurement = 100 cartons × (0.48 × 0.28 × 0.28) = 3.7632 CBM

Total Gross Weight = 100 cartons × (12 kg/carton) = 1,200 kg (1.2 MTS)

As freight rate is USD85.00/cubic meter or USD80.00/ metric ton, the total freight charges will be calculated as per measurement, as total measurement/total gross weight is 3.7632/1.2 > 1 , the fright rate of measurement is also higher than that of weight ton.

Total Freight Charges = USD85.00/CBM × 3.7632CBM = USD319.872

Freight Charge per Unit = USD319.872/1,200PCS = USD0.27/PC

**2. Premium Calculating**

Premium is generally calculated on the basis of CIF (CIP) value plus a markup percentage. The markup percentage is normally not less than 10%. The calculating is as following:

Insured Amount= CIF (CIP) Value × (1+ Markup Percentage)

Premium=Insured Amount × Premium Rate

## ☞ Case 5.7

1,000 sets of glassware at USD20.00/SET CIF Hamburg Incoterms ®2010.

①Can the seller cover all risks, crash and breakage, war risks, SRCC risks and malicious damage clause in an insurance policy?

②If the premium rate of all risks, crash and breakage, war risks, SRCC risks and malicious damage clause are 0.3%, 0.2%, 0.2%, 0.2% and 0.1% respectively, how many premium shall the seller pay?

Answer: All risks, crash and breakage, war risks, SRCC risks and malicious damage clause can't be covered together in an insurance policy, as malicious damage clause is one kind of additional risks under ICC, and the others are under CIC. Malicious damage clause can't be covered independently.

All risks is a kind of basic insurance coverages and can be covered independently. Crash and breakage is a kind of general additional risks and included in the scope cover of all risks. War risks and SRCC risks are two kinds of special additional risks and can be covered on the basis of a basic insurance coverage insured under CIC.

Meanwhile, if war risks and SRCC risks are covered together, the insured only need to pay the premium of war risks. As crash and breakage is in the scope of all risks coverage, the insured also need not to pay the premium of crash and breakage on condition all risks covered.

In this case, the seller can cover all risks, crash and breakage, war risks and SRCC risks and only pay the premium of all risks and war risks.

The Insured Amount= CIF Value × (1+ Markup Percentage)

= Quantity × Unit Price × (1+ Markup Percentage)

= 1,000 sets × USD20.00/set × (1+10%)

= USD22,000.00

Premium= The Insured Amount × Premium Rate of (All Risks +War Risks)

= USD22,000.00×(0.3%+0.2%)

= USD110.00

### 5.6.4 Price Conversion Between Different Trade Terms

Price under different trade term is influenced by different pricing factors. As the pricing factors changed, the party may adjust price between different trade terms or change price's trade term. As FOB, CFR, CIF, FCA, CPT and CIP are popular used in international business. If it is understand how to convert price between FOB, CFR and CIF, how to convert price between FCA, CPT and CIP can be also constructed. As freight charges per unit and premium calculated are introduced above, we can convert prices between FOB, CFR and CIF easier as following:

CFR=FOB + Freight Charges

CIF=CFR+ Premium

Premium=CIF×(1+Markup Percentage)×Premium Rate

CIF= (FOB+Freight Charges)/ [1-(1+Markup Percentage)×Premium Rate]

☞ Case5.8

Co. A quoted 100% cotton men shirts at USD10.00 per piece FOB Shanghai Incoterms® 2010. The customer asked him to offer price on the basis of CIF Hamburg Incoterms®2010 again. The shirts are packed in cartons, 12pcs per carton, gross weight 16.0 kgs, net weight 14.0 kgs, measurement is 30 cm×30 cm×35 cm. Insurance is to be covered all risks, TPND, war risks and SRCC risks, premium rate is 0.5%, 0.2%,0.2% and 0.2% with 110% of cargo value. The ocean freight and additional charges were as following.

Ocean freight:  LCL: USD90.00/MT or USD95.00/CBM

FCL: USD750/20'GP

Additional charges:

Container loading charges for LCL: CNY60/CBM

Documents (DOC): CNY300/one time exportation

Export clearance:  CNY300 /one time exportation

Seal charges : CNY25.00 /FCL

Entry summary declaration( ENS) : USD25.00 /one time importation

Currency adjustment factors (CAF): 8.6%

Origin terminal handling charges (O.THC) : USD220.00/20FCL

Destination terminal handing charge (D.THC) : USD730.00/20FCL

Int'l ship and port facility security (ISPS) : USD10 /FCL

Bunker adjustment factors (BAF): USD502.00/20FCL

Other additional charges: 70.00/20FCL

Exchange rate: the buying rate is CNY637.77/100USD, selling rate is CNY 640.33/100USD.

Question: if quantity of goods be ordered is 9600PCS or 2400PCS, how about the CIF price in USD?

Answer: The additional charges are complicated. Some charges occurred only under FCL shipment, some charges occurred under LCL shipment only, some of them occurred under both FCL & LCL shipment.

**Step 1:** To judge whether 9,600 PCS or 2,400 PCS is shipped by FCL or LCL, then calculate the freight charges per unit as per the relating freight information.

9,600 PCS:

Total Packages = 9,600 PCS/ (12 pcs/carton) = 800 cartons

Total Gross Weight = 800 cartons × 16.0 kg/carton = 12,800 kg = 12.8 MTS

Total Net Weight = 800 cartons × 14.0 kg/carton = 11,200 kg = 11.2 MTS

Total Measurement = 800 cartons × (0.30 m × 0.30 m × 0.35 m)/carton = 25.2 CBM

As the capacity of 1 × 20'GP suggested is 25 CBM/17.5 MTS and the theoretical volume is 33.2 CBM, 9600 PCS packed in 800 cartons is suggested to be shipped by 1 × 20'GP.

2,400 PCS:

Total Packages = 2,400PCS/ (12pcs/carton) = 200 cartons

Total Gross Weight = 200 cartons × 16.0 kg/carton = 3,200 kg = 3.2 MTS

Total Net Weight = 200 cartons × 14.0 kg/carton = 2,800 kg = 2.8 MTS

Total Measurement = 200 cartons × (0.30 m × 0.30 m × 0.35 m)/carton = 6.3 CBM

As capacity of 1 × 20'GP suggested is 25 CBM/17.5 MTS, 2,400 PCS packed in 200 cartons is suggested to be shipped by LCL and the freight charges will be calculated as per measurement.

$$
\begin{aligned}
\text{Total Freight Charges by } 1 \times 20'GP =\ & \text{Ocean Freight} + \text{Relating Additional Charges} \\
=\ & [\text{USD750} + \text{Seal Charges (CNY25.00 /FCL)} + \text{ENS} \\
& \text{(USD25.00 /one time importation)} + \text{O.THC} \\
& \text{(USD220.00/20FCL)} + \text{D.THC} \\
& \text{(USD730.00/20FCL)} + \text{ISPS} \\
& \text{(USD10/FCL)} + \text{BAF(USD502.00/20FCL)} + \text{Other} \\
& \text{Additional Charges (70.00/20FCL)} + \text{DOC} \\
& \text{(CNY300.00)} + \text{Export Clearance} \\
& \text{(CNY300.00))]} \times (1 + \text{CAF8.6\%})
\end{aligned}
$$

$$= (USD2,307.00 + CNY625.00) \times (1 + 8.6\%)$$
$$= [(USD2,307.00 + USD$$
$$(625.00/640.42/100) \times (1 + 8.6\%)$$
$$= USD2,611.39$$

Please notice here that the local charges may be included in the seller's price at USD10.00 per PC FOB Shanghai Incoterms®2010, such as DOC, Export clearance, seal charges, O.THC, ISPS,USD10 /FCL, other additional charges and part of CAF, the balance freight charges must be included under CIF instead of FOB, such as ocean fright, BAF, ENS, D.THC and CAF.

The principle of price quoted is for up not for down. The seller may calculate freight charges as total for price calculating, or may calculate without repeat charges.

Total Freight Charges by LCL = Ocean Freight + Relating Additional Charges
$$= [USD95.00/CBM \times 6.3\ CBM + Container\ Loading$$
$$Charges\ (CNY60.00/CBM \times 6.3\ CBM) + ENS$$
$$(USD25.00\ /one\ time\ importation) +$$
$$DOC\ (CNY300.00) + Export\ Clearance$$
$$(CNY300.00))] \times (1 + CAF\ 8.6\%)$$
$$= (USD623.50 + CNY978.00) \times (1 + 8.6\%)$$
$$= [(USD623.50 + USD(978.00/640.42/100) \times (1 + 8.6\%)$$
$$= USD842.97$$

Freight Charges per Unit (by 1 × 20'GP) = USD2,611.39/ (9,600 PCS) = USD0.2720/PC
Freight Charges per Unit (by LCL) = USD842.97/ (2,400 PCS) = USD0.3512/PC

**Step 2:** To judge the premium rate. All risks, TPND, war risks and SRCC risks will be covered, but only need to pay premium of all risk s and war risks.with 110% of cargo value.

The Markup Percentage = 10%

Premium Rate = Premium Rate of All Rrisks + Premium Rate of War Risks
$$= 0.7\%\ (remarks:\ TPND\ is\ included\ in\ all\ risks,\ SRCC\ risks\ is\ free$$
charge under WAR risks and SRCC risks covered simultaneously)

**Step 3:** To convert FOB price into CIF price.

CIF = (FOB Freight Charges)/ [1-(1 + Markup Percentage) × Premium Rate]
$$= (USD10.00 + USD0.2720)/[1-(1 + 10\%) \times 0.7\%]\ (by\ 1 \times 20'GP)$$
$$= (USD10.00 + USD0.3512)/[1-(1 + 10\%) \times 0.7\%]\ (by\ LCL)$$
$$= USD10.3518/PC\ (by\ 1 \times 20'GP)\ or\ USD10.4315\ (by\ LCL)$$

Based above, if the customer ordered 9,600 PCS, the price is USD10.35/PC CIF Hamburg Incoterms®2010. If the customer ordered 2,400 PCS, the price is USD10.43/PC

CIF Hamburg Incoterms®2010.

## ☞ Case5.9

Glassware style no.PZ178, packed in cartons with 2 sets each, G.W.11.0kgs, N.W. 10.0kgs and the carton size is $25 \times 25 \times 39$ CBM. Unit price is USD 20.00/SET CIFC2 Hamburg Incoterms®2010. Insurance is covered against all risks, war risks and breakage clauses with premium rate at 0.3%, 0.2% and 0.2% for 110% of cargo CIF value. If a Buyer from UAE asked the seller offer price under CFR C5 Dubai in HKD on the basis of 1x40GP shipment, please provide the price in HKD.

Answer:

**Step 1:** The quantity be contained in 1x40'GP

According to suggested capacity, 1x40'GP can land 4000 sets as per calculation:

Gross Weight: 22,000 kg / (11.0 kg/carton) = 2000 cartons

Volume: 54/ $(0.25 \times 0.25 \times 0.39)$ = 2,215.38 cartons.

Quantity: 2,000 cartons $\times$ 2 sets/carton = 4,000 sets

As per the size assortment, $1 \times 40'$GP can land 2,592 cartons ($48 \times 9 \times 6$) as per calculation.

Length 1219.2/25 = 48.77, width 243.8/25 = 9.75, and height 239.3/39 = 6.14. While, 2,592 cartons' total gross weight is 28.512mts and exceed the suggested weight 22.0MTS and the maximum landed weight 26.0MTS for $1 \times 40'$GP. So the glassware is heavy-cargo.

**Step 2:** The price under CFRC5 Dubai in USD can be settled as per the following working idea.

Premium Rate = Premium Rate of (All Risks + War Risks) = 0.3% + 0.2% = 0.5%

(Remarks: breakage clauses is included in all risks.)

Freight charges: To search the freight charges of $1 \times 40'$GP from a port of discharge such as shanghai to Hamburg and Dubai respectively. It can be asked to freight forwarder. For example: The forwarder offered the freight charges of Maersk Line as showed in Table 5.8.

Table 5.8 Freight and Charges for 1x40'GP from Shanghai to Hamburg and Dubai

| | | Freight to Hamburg by 1×40'GP | Freight to Dubai by 1×40'GP |
|---|---|---|---|
| Ocean freight | O/F | USD2,970/40GP | USD2,532/40GP |

continued

| | | Freight to Hamburg by 1×40'GP | Freight to Dubai by 1×40'GP |
|---|---|---|---|
| Additional surcharges | OTHC | USD237.00/40FCL | USD237.00/40FCL |
| | DTHC | USD1,150.00/40FCL | USD1,080.00/40FCL |
| Additional surcharges | SBF | USD1,030 | USD530 |
| | CSC(Container stuffing charges) | USD 100 | USD 100 |
| Additional surcharges | DOC | CNY300 | CNY300 |
| | Export clearance | CNY300 | CNY300 |
| | ERS (Equip rest surcharge) | USD110.00 | |
| | GRI (General rate increasing) | USD600 | |
| Additional surcharges | ENS | USD25.00 | |
| Sum of Total | | USD6,222.00 CNY600.00 | USD4,470.00 CNY600 |
| Total | | USD6,322.00 | USD4,570.00 |

Remarks: in order to settle easier, we can regard CNY600 be equivalent to USD100 with reference of exchange rate in recent years.

Freight charges per set from Shanghai to Hamburg = USD6322.00/4000sets = USD1.5805/Set

Freight charges per set from Shanghai to Dubai = USD4570.00/4000sets = USD1.1425/Set

CIF Hamburg – CIFC2 Hamburg ×(1–Rate of Commission)

$$= USD20.00/set \times (1-2\%)$$

$$= USD19.60/set$$

FOB Shanghai = CIF Hamburg ×[1–(1 + Markup Percentage)×Premium Rate]– Freight

to Hamburg/set

$$= USD19.60 \times (1-1.10\times0.5\%)-USD1.5805/set = USD17.9117/set$$

CFR Dubai = FOB Shanghai + Freight to Dubai/Set

$$= USD17.9117/Set + USD1.1425/Set$$

$$= USD19.0542/set$$

CFRC5 Dubai = CFR Dubai/ (1–Rate of Commission)

$$= USD19.0542/set/ (1-5\%)$$

$$= USD20.06/Set$$

**Step 3:** To convert price in USD under CFRC5 Dubai to price in HKD under CFRC5 Dubai.

The exchange rate of USD/CNY, HKD/CNY can be founded on the homepage of commercial bank. The relating exchange rate on website of Bank of China on Aug 25, 2015 is as following (see Table 5.9).

Table 5.9 The Relating Exchange Rate of Bank of China

| Currency Name | Buying Rate | Cash Buying Rate | Selling Rate | Cash Selling Rate | Middle Rate | Pub Time |
|---|---|---|---|---|---|---|
| HKD | 82.55 | 81.89 | 82.87 | 82.87 | 82.54 | 2015-08-25  21:21:52 |
| USD | 639.92 | 634.79 | 642.48 | 642.48 | 639.87 | 2015-08-25  21:21:52 |

Price CFRC5 Dubai (HKD) = Price CFRC5 Dubai ( USD) × Selling Rate of USD/

Buying Rate of HKD

= (USD20.06/set × CNY 642.48/100USD)/

(CNY82.55/100HKD)

= HKD156.10/set

So the seller can offer price at HKD156.10/Set CFRC5 Dubai Incoterms ®2010 to the UAE buyer (See Figure 5.1)

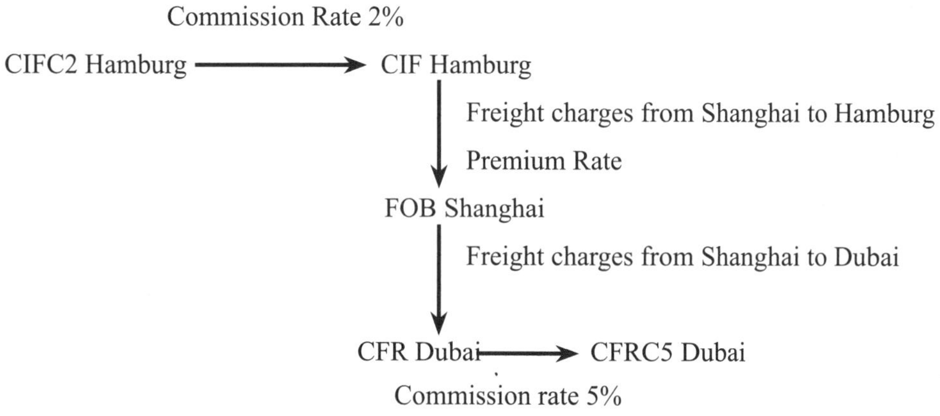

Commission Rate 2%

CIFC2 Hamburg ⟶ CIF Hamburg

　　　　　　　　　　　Freight charges from Shanghai to Hamburg

　　　　　　　　　　　Premium Rate

　　　　　　　　　FOB Shanghai

　　　　　　　　　　　Freight charges from Shanghai to Dubai

　　　　　　CFR Dubai ⟶ CFRC5 Dubai

　　　　　　　Commission rate 5%

Figure 5.1 CIF, FOB, and CFR Prices

# 5.7 Original Price Calculating and Accounting

After introduction of price conversion under different trade terms, such as FOB, CFR and CIF and price conversion between different currencies, such as CNY and foreign currencies. However, where does the price under FOB, CFR, or CIF come from? Is the quoting price correct? How about the benefit if the quoting price is accepted? Can the price be accepted or not? This part introduces how to calculate the original price and how to do price accounting.

## 5.7.1 Original Price Calculating

Generally, the price is calculated as per Price= Cost + Charges +Benefit. In international trade:

① Cost means all the costs occurred before the goods left the sites of production and business operation and prepare to enter into circulation. It includes material cost, producing cost, financing cost, research and development cost, wage, water and electricity, packages, examination, land rent, equipment and its depreciation, marketing costs, taxes, etc.

② Charges includes the relating expenses occurred in the circulation and can be divided into domestic charges and international charges. The domestic charges is containing all the charges occurred before the goods loaded on board the vessel at port of shipment under FOB, CFR, CIF term or before the goods free carrier under FCA, CPT or CIP term, but after departure from the sites of production and business operation, such as relating to local transport, loading and unloading on the conveyance and storage in the exporting country, checking, origin terminal handling charges, export clearance and documentations. The international charges contain international transport and insurance mainly. Normally, FOB and FCA price only relates to local charges. CIF, CIP, CFR and CPT prices relate to both local charges and international charges. CIF and CIP price relates to international freight and premium, while CFR and CPT relates to international freight only.

③ Benefit means the expected interest or earning of the party manages international business.

It is normally expressed by a certain percentage of exporting price.

To combine the situation of international market, the seller may control the price through keeping balance of cost, charges, risks and benefit. For example: If the brand or trade mark of exported goods is well known, the price quoted may be higher. If the seller shall bear high risks or is on account of more responsibilities, the price quoted may be higher. If a new product has good marketing prospect, the seller may raise price through increasing benefit or speed up apportionment of the research and development costs. For a matured product, the seller may decrease benefit, reduce charges or save cost to maintain or improve market share.

For China's export price, the cost means actual cost that is deducted export rebate. Export rebate is popular in the world, China is no exception. Normally, China's trading firms and manufacturing firms share policies of export rebate and the exported goods must be in the scope of levy value-added tax and or consumption tax. The calculating method of export rebate for the trading firm and the manufacturing firm is different. "Refund after collection" is performed by the trading firm. "Exemption, set off and refund" is performed by the manufacturing firm. The trading firm purchases the exporting goods from the manufacturing firm as it does not produce goods by himself. The manufacturing firm generally export goods produced by him. The exporting price of trading firm is normally higher than that of manufacturing firm as it is including benefit of the trading firm and the manufacturing firm. The manufacturing firm may calculate the export price with reference of the method that the trading firm's price calculating but with a higher benefit.

This part introduces export rebate of value-added tax (VAT) mainly as most of Chinese small and medium enterprises (SMEs) only meet export rebate of value-added tax. The manufacturing firm shall issue an invoice of value-added tax to the trading firm for purchasing the exported goods. The invoice is used for the trading firm to make payment of purchase cost to the manufacturing firm and deal with export rebate to the National tax Bureau. The invoice amount is the amount of purchase cost of the trading firm. It contains the sales revenue of manufacturing firm and its relating amount of value-added tax. The following shows how to calculate amount of export rebate amount for the trading firm and the manufacturing firm. The trading firm can calculate amount of export rebate per order. However, as the producing goods of manufacturing firm is provide for domestic & foreign market monthly and the policy of "Exemption, set off and refund" is performed, the manufacturing firm will settle VAT with the local National tax Bureau monthly.

For trading firm:

Amount of Export Rebate = Purchase Cost × Rate of Export/ (1+VAT Rate)　(per order)

For manufacturing firm:

VAT Payable =Sales Revenue × VAT Rate + Total Export Revenue of FOB (converted to CNY) ×VAT Rate － Deductible VAT (VAT paid for purchase materials, electricity, etc) － Export Amount of FOB (converted to CNY) × Rate of Export Rebate (per month)

If the amount of calculated result is greater than zero, it means that the manufacturing firm needs to pay this amount of VAT to the local National tax Bureau this month. If less than zero, it means that the local National tax Bureau needs to return back the absolute amount of VAT to the manufacturing firm (export rebate) this month. If equal to zero, it means that the manufacturing firm need not pay VAT to or hasn't return back VAT from the local National tax Bureau.

Based on above, the trading firm may quote price of FOB, CFR and CIF as following. As actual

FOB Price = Actual Purchase Cost + Domestic Charges + Expected Benefit

Expected Benefit= FOB Price × Rate of Expected Benefit

$$\text{FOB Price} = \frac{\text{Actual Purchase Cost + Domestic Charges}}{\text{1-Rate of Expected Benefit}}$$

CFR Price= Actual Purchase Cost + Domestic Charges + International Freight + Expected Benefit

Expected Benefit= CFR Price × Rate of Expected Benefit

$$\text{CFR price} = \frac{\text{Actual Purchase Cost + Domestic Charges + International Freight}}{1 - \text{Rate of Expected Benefit}}$$

CIF Price =Actual Purchase Cost + Domestic Charges + International Freight + Premium + Expected Benefit

Expected Benefit= CIF Price × Rate of Expected Benefit

Premium=CIF Price ×(1+Markup Percentage)× Premium Rate

$$\text{CIF price} = \frac{\text{Actual Purchase Cost + Domestic Charges + International Freight}}{1 - \text{Rate of Expected Benefit} - (1 + \text{Markup Percentage}) \times \text{Premium Rate}}$$

Export Rebate Amount = Purchase Cost ×Rate of Export Rebate / (1+VAT Rate)

Actual Purchase Cost = Purchase Cost − Export Rebate Amount
    = Purchase Cost×(1 + VAT Rate − Rate of Export Rebate)/ (1+VAT Rate)

Further, as the actual purchase cost and domestic charges are generally calculated in CNY, whereas international freight is always in foreign currency. Meanwhile, the seller always needs to quote price including commission. So, the original price calculating may be changed as following.

FOBC Price in Foreign Currency A=[ (Actual Purchase Cost + Domestic Charges) / Buying Rate of Foreign Currency A]/[(1 − Rate of Expected Benefit) ×(1 − Rate of Commission)]

CFRC Price in Foreign Currency A=[(Actual Purchase Cost + Domestic Charges) /Buying Rate of Foreign Currency A + International Freight]/[(1 − Rate of Expected Benefit)×(1 − Rate of Commission) ]

CIFC Price in Foreign Currency A =[(Actual Purchase Cost + Domestic Charges) / Buying Rate of Foreign Currency A+ International Freight]/ {[1 − Rate of Expected Benefit − (1+Markup Percentage)×Premium Rate)]

## ☞ Case 5.10

Seller: A Import & Export Co. Ltd., Hangzhou

Buyer: Lucy Star Fabrics Inc, New York

Date of Business negotiation: Aug 26, 2015

Payment period: Pay at sight after shipment. Shipment made with 30 days after contract signed.

Commodity: Dyeing cloth, $150D \times 20S$, $122 \times 46$, 58/59", 57% polyester, 43% of rayon

H.S.Code: 5407610042

Purchase cost: CNY13.69/mtr including VAT, VAT rate 17%, rate of export rebate: 16%

Expected profit rate: 10% of unit price

Packing: Rolling with single piece, inner packing with breathing plastic bags,

Outer packing with plastic woven bags, piece length 50mtrs $\pm$ 5mtrs

Measurement per roll: 0.04cbm, gross weight: 15.0kgs

Minimum order: 500 mtrs each colorway, more or less 5% both of quantity & amount permitted

Premium rate: 0.8% for all risks, 0.2% for war risks, markup percentage 10%

Question: If the customer wants to order 28000mtrs, please offer unit price under FOBC5 shanghai Incoterms®2010 and CIFC5 New York Incoterms®2010 in USD & HKD.

Answer: As per the requirement, it needs to know actual purchase cost, domestic charges, international freight, premium rate and exchange rate of USD/CNY and HKD/CNY.

**Step 1:** To calculate actual purchase cost.

Export Rebate = Purchase Cost × Rate of Export Rebate/ (1 + VAT rate)

$\qquad$ = CNY13.69/mtr × 16 %/( 1 + 17%)

$\qquad$ = CNY1.8721/mtr

Actual Purchase Cost = Purchase Cost - Export Rebate

$\qquad$ = CNY13.69/mtr − CNY1.8721/mtr = CNY11.8179/mtr

**Step 2:** To judge mode of container transport for 28,000 mtrs.

Total Packages = 28,000 mtrs/ (50 mtrs/roll) = 560 rolls

Total Measurement = 560 rolls × 0.04 CBM/roll = 22.4 CBM

Total Gross Weight = 560 rolls × 15.0 kg/roll = 8,400 kg = 8.4 MTS

28,000 Mtrs will be shipped by 1 × 20'GP.

**Step 3:** To ask the relating information about domestic charges and international freight from the freight forwarder.

(1) Domestic Charges

Domestic Freight: CNY4875.00 /20GP

DOC: CNY300.00:

Export Clearance: CNY300.00

B/L Charges: CNY 125.00 / BL

(2) International freight

Ocean freight: USD8,090/20'GP

BAF: USD551.00/20'GP

O.THC: USD535.00/20'GP

D.THC: USD66.00/20'GP

Other Additional Surcharges: USD747.00

Total Domestic Charges = CNY4875 + CNY300 + CNY300 + CNY125 = CNY5,600.00

Domestic Charge per Unit = CNY5,600.00/28,000mtrs = CNY0.20/mtr

Total Freight = USD8,090.00 + USD551.00 + USD535.00 + USD66.00 + USD745.00

= USD9,987.00

International Freight per Unit = USD9,987.00/28,000mtrs = USD0.3568/mtr

**Step 4:** To judge the premium rate.

Premium Rate = Rate of All Risks + Rate of War Risks = 0.8% + 0.2% = 1%

**Step 5:** To search for the exchange rate from Bank of China: As payment is to be made at sight after shipment. Shipment made with 30 days after contract signed. The Table 5.10 shows the spot and one month forward exchange rate of USD/CNY and HKD/CNY. As USD and HKD are all expect to appreciate in the near future. The exporting price can be quoted as per the spot rate.

Table 5.10 The Spot and One Month Forward Exchange Rate

| Name of Currency | Spot Buying Rate | Spot Selling Rate | Pub Time | Transaction Period | Forward Buying Rate | Forward Selling Rate | Date |
|---|---|---|---|---|---|---|---|
| HKD | 82.54 | 82.86 | 2015-08-26 18:12:25 | One month | 82.7042 | 83.4988 | 2015-08-25 |
| USD | 639.77 | 642.33 | 2015-08-26 18:12:25 | One Month | 644.4438 | 648.1158 | 2015-08-25 |

**Step 6:** Calculating.

FOBC Price in Foreign Currency A = [ (Actual Purchase Cost + Domestic Charges)/Buying Rate of Foreign Currency A]/[(1−Rate of Expected Benefit) × (1−Rate of Commission)]

= [(CNY11.8179/mtr + CNY0.20/mtr) / (CNY639.77/100USD)]/[(1−10%) × (1−5%)]

= USD2.1970/mtr

CIFC Price in Foreign Currency A = [(Actual Purchase Cost + Domestic Charges)/Buying Rate of Foreign Currency A + International Freight]/ {[1−Rate of Expected Benefit − (1 + Markup

$$\text{Percentage)} \times \text{Premium Rate)}$$
$$= [(CNY11.8179/mtr + CNY0.20/mtr) /$$
$$(CNY639.77/100USD) + USD0.3568/mtr]/$$
$$[1-10\% - (1+10\%)*1\%)]*(1-5\%) ]$$
$$= USD2.6467/mtr$$

$$FOBC5 \text{ in } HKD = FOBC5 \text{ in } USD \times \text{Selling Rate of USD/Buying Rate of HKD}$$
$$= USD2.1970/mtr \times (CNY642.33/100USD)/(CNY82.54/100HKD)$$
$$= HKD17.097/mtr$$

$$CIFC5 \text{ in } HKD = CIFC5 \text{ in } USD \times \text{Selling Rate of USD/Buying Rate of HKD}$$
$$= USD2.6467/mtr \times (CNY642.33/100USD)/ (CNY82.54/100HKD)$$
$$= HKD20.5967/mtr$$

So, if the customer wants to order 28,000mtrs, the seller may offer prices as per requirement:

USD2.20/mtr or HKD17.10/mtr FOBC5 Shanghai Incoterms®2010

USD2.65/mtr or HKD20.60/mtr CIFC5 New York Incoterms®2010

## 5.7.2 Price Accounting

Price accounting is very important to the firm because benefit create is new blood for firm survival and development. Before or during business negotiation, both the parties shall account the price carefully and rational. The price normally shall be profitable. The seller may adjust price through accounting in order to control cost, charges and benefit.

## ☞ Case 5.11

For the above case, the seller wish expected profit rate reaches 10% of the exporting price. If the seller wants to quote USD2.65/mtr CIFC5 New York Incoterms®2010 for 28000 meters of dyeing cloth, did the price really include benefit 10% of the CIFC5 price?

Answer: This question can be settled through the Table 5.11 for price accounting.

Table 5.11 Accounting Table for Exportation

No.:_____          Date: _Aug 26, 2015_____

Name of commodity and Specification: _Dyeing Cloth__   Quantity: _28,000 mtrs__

Price: _USD2.65/MTR CIFC5 New York Incoterms ®2010_____

From: _Shanghai_____  to __New York__  Via _____

The supplier: _____

The buyer: __Lucy Star Fabrics Inc, New York_____

Exchange rate:  USD/CNY:  Buying rate: 639.77    Selling rate: 642.33

| Cost | 1. Purchase Cost (Including VAT) | : | CNY13.69/mtr × 28,000 mtrs=CNY383,320.00 |
|---|---|---|---|
| | VAT Rate | : | 17 % |
| | Consumption Rate | : | 0 % |
| | 2. Export Rebate | : | CNY383,320.00×16%/(1+17%)=CNY52,419.83 |
| | Rate of Export Rebate | : | 16% |
| | 3. Actual Purchase Cost | : | CNY330,900.17 |
| Charges | 1. International Freight (Foreign currency/local currency) | : | =USD9,987×(CNY642.33/USD100)=CNY64,149.50 |
| | Packages | : | =28,000 mtrs/(50 mtrs/roll)=560 rolls |
| | Gross Weight | : | =560 rolls×15.0 kg/roll=8,400 kg=8.4 MTS |
| | Measurement | : | =560 rolls×0.04 CBM/roll=22.4 CBM |
| Charges | Freight Rate | | Shipped by 1×20'GP, total freight USD9,987.00 |
| | 2. Premium (Foreign currency/local currency) | : | =USD2.65/mtr×2,8000 mtrs×(1+10%)×(0.8%+0.2%) =USD816.20 =USD816.20×(CNY642.33/USD100) =CNY5242.70 |
| | Insurance Coverage and Premium Rate | : | All risks  0.8% War risks  0.2% |
| | Markup Percentage | : | 10% |
| | 3.Commission (Foreign currency/local currency) | : | =USD2.65/mtr×28,000 mtrs×5%=USD3,710.00 =USD3,710.00×(CNY642.33/USD100) =CNY23,830.44 |
| | Rate of Commission | : | 5 % |
| | 4.Domestic charges (Foreign currency/local currency) | : | Total CNY5,600.00 |
| | Purchase Expense | : | 0 |
| | Local Freight Expense | : | CNY4,875.00 |
| | Package Expense | : | 0 |
| | Wastage Expense | : | 0 |
| | Storage Expense | : | 0 |
| | Manage and Operation | : | 0 |
| | Other Charges | : | CNY300+CNY300+CNY125=CNY725.00 |

| Benefit | Amount of Benefit (Foreign currency/local currency) | : | =USD2.65/mtr×28,000 mtrs×(CNY639.77/100USD) +Amount of Export Rebate – International Freight – Premium – Commission–Domestic Charges – Purchase Cost =CNY44,986.53 |
| --- | --- | --- | --- |
| | Benefit Rate | : | =CNY44,985.53×100%/[USD2.65/mtr×28,000mtrs× (CNY639.77/100USD)]=9.48% |

We found the real rate of benefit is 9.48% after price accounting which less than the expected rate of 10%. In order to make the real rate of benefit reached 10%, the seller may raise the price, or reduce cost or charges. As the difference is only 0.5% on condition that the other factors never changed, the seller may land not exceeding 10% more of the quantity, such as 30,000 mtrs instead of 28,000 mtrs with the international freight charges same in order to save charges. As total measurement /gross weight of 28,000 mtrs is 22.4 CBM/8.4 mts and less than the suggested capacity of $1 \times 20'$GP. Meanwhile, quantity and amount is allowed more or less 10%.

## Questions

1. An exporter quoted price at USD100 per case under FOB term, and the foreign buyer requested to change the price under CIF New York. The measurement of carton size was 30 cm×40 cm×30 cm, and the gross weight per carton was 15 kg. The freight rate was W/M. The basic freight was USD20 per freight ton and 10 % of BAF was to be charged . The trasport insurance was covered against all risks and war risk at the premium of 0.3% and 0.2% respectively with 110% of CIF cargo value. What price might the exporter quote under CIF New York? If the customer wanted to re-quote price under CIFC2 New York, How about the specific quotation?

2. The price quoted by an exporter to a British customer for a certain style of clothing is RMB 100 per piece, and payment will be made with 30 days after shipment. The British customer asked for a change in the foreign currency price. As per the following information of excahnge rate(see Table 5.12 and Table 5.13), which kind of foreign currency was better for the exporter quoted price?

Table 5.12  The Spot exchange Rate of Bank of China

| Currency Name | Buying Rate | Cash Buying Rate | Selling Rate | Cash Selling Rate | Middle Rate | Pub Time | |
| --- | --- | --- | --- | --- | --- | --- | --- |
| EUR | 785.65 | 761.24 | 791.45 | 793.02 | 786.55 | 2018-11-05 | 16:11:37 |
| GBP | 896.8 | 868.93 | 903.4 | 905.38 | 897.13 | 2018-11-05 | 16:11:37 |
| HKD | 88.22 | 87.52 | 88.58 | 88.58 | 88.15 | 2018-11-05 | 16:11:37 |

continued

| Currency Name | Buying Rate | Cash Buying Rate | Selling Rate | Cash Selling Rate | Middle Rate | Pub Time | |
|---|---|---|---|---|---|---|---|
| USD | 691.35 | 685.72 | 694.28 | 694.28 | 689.76 | 2018-11-05 | 16:11:37 |

Table 5.13  The Forward exchange Rate of Bank of China

| Currency Name | Transaction period | Buying Rate | Selling Rate | Middle Rate | Pub Date | |
|---|---|---|---|---|---|---|
| EUR | EUR | One month | 786.9 | 801.1264 | 794.0832 | 2018-11-02 |
| GBP | GBP | One month | 895.076644 | 910.508744 | 902.792694 | 2018-11-02 |
| USD | USD | One month | 688.98875 | 697.00065 | 692.9947 | 2018-11-02 |
| HKD | HKD | One month | 87.834128 | 89.233128 | 88.533628 | 2018-11-02 |

3. What are the specific factors influencing the free and free postage of cross-border e-commerce?

# 第六章

# 国际货物买卖的货款收付

## ☞ 案例6.1

中国A公司与巴基斯坦B公司签订了一批总值5万多美元的家用缝纫机出口合同，付款方式为：装运前15天电汇30%货款，其余70%货款装运后10天内付款。A公司收到30%预付款后按期装运了货物，并于装运货物后及时将全套单据的复印件传真给了B公司。10多天后，B公司来电称由于缝纫机市场行情急剧下跌，要求A公司降价40%才可以接收货物。A公司不同意B公司的条件，决定将货物运回。然而，A公司联系船公司后被告知无法办妥货物转运，原因是巴基斯坦海关规定，退货必须征得原进口商的同意，否则无法退货。万般无奈之下，A公司同意了B公司的要求。在本案中，导致出口方遭受损失的表面原因是进口国海关的特殊规定，而实质原因是进口商的信用。因此，对与资信不了解的客户或信用较差的客户成交，最好不采用商业信用的货款结算方式。

## ☞ 案例6.2

浙江某出口企业与某美籍华人客商成交了几笔小额贸易，付款方式为预付，交易非常顺利。后来，该客户称已打开销路，数量增加，但是资金周转比较紧张，故而要求出口企业接受付款方式为"D/P AT SIGHT"。出口企业考虑在"D/P at sight"下，买方只有付款赎单才能拿到单据，如其拒绝付款赎单，那货物所有权依然掌握在卖方手中，因而接受了买方的要求，并装运了一个40FCL的货物。装运货物后，买方借口资金紧张，拖延付款赎单。货到目的港10天后，各种费用相继产生。这时，买方提出要求将付款条件从"D/P at sight"更改为"D/A 30天"，否则拒收货物。因考虑这批货物的花色品种是为该客户订制，货物拉回来也是转为库存，因而卖方被迫同意了买方的要求。可是，买方在承兑交单提取货物后就再也没有音信。因此，出口公司要从本案中吸取教训：①在买方市场中，尽管收款方式越来越不利于卖方，但卖方决不应该接受资信不了解的客户提出的高风险结算方式要求，如D/A或O/A（Open Account），除非能够做足风险防范；②买方交易过程中提出更改付款方式的做法，卖方有理由相信其是一个信用欠佳的客户，因此应该对货物最终的出路早做打算；③对于按客户要求订制的产品，卖方不应该接受高风险的收款方式。

☞ **案例6.3**

A出口公司与B进口公司就某种"金鸡牌"货物订立合同，并规定采用信用证结算。但是，B公司通过开证行开出信用证的货物为"金牌"。A公司未仔细审核信用证就办理了交货，制作了全套单据向出口地银行办理交单议付，单据显示为"金鸡牌"。出口地银行审核单据后予以拒付，其理由是单据的货物描述与信用证条款不符合。在本案中，银行拒付合理。在信用证交易中，银行付款的前提是"交单相符"。卖方实际装运的货物是"金鸡牌"，其所做的单据显示"金鸡牌"与合同规定相符，但与信用证规定不符。信用证是独立于买卖合同的文件，不受合同约束。在信用证项下，银行判定是否付款的唯一条件是"交单相符"，即单据表明内容的记载是否与信用证规定相符。假设在本案中，A出口公司实际装运的是"金鸡牌"，但在单据上显示"金牌"。因此，只要交单相符，开证行就会付款。

国际货款收付问题是买卖双方交易磋商的最大难点，因为买卖双方都希望能在货款的收付方面获得较大的保障。对卖方而言，以采用预收货款或取得银行的付款保证为最佳收款方式，以实现收款安全、迅速、及时；就买方而言，最好能够在收取货物或取得物权单据后再付款。因此，买卖双方在交易磋商和订立合同时，都力争对自己有利的收付款条件。货款收付问题很复杂，除涉及买卖双方外，还要涉及买卖双方所在国的金融机构或第三国金融机构，除受所在国外汇法规、金融管制条例以及各种国际通行惯例与规则的约束外，还受世界经济、贸易、金融、货币等因素影响。货款收付磋商的一个重要依据就是"信用"，包括商业信用、银行信用和国家信用。在此基础上，买卖双方就结算货币、信用工具、付款时间、付款方式、付款地点等问题进行洽谈，而洽谈的最终成果将直接影响到买卖双方的资金周转、资金融通、风险和费用的负担。

# 一、信用工具

货款结算方式有现金结算和非现金结算两种。其中，现金结算使用范围很小，一般限于购买样品、预付定金、少量赔款等。当国际结算从现金结算过渡到非现金结算时，其用以清偿买卖双方间债权债务关系的信用工具就是票据。票据是国际贸易中最主要的信用工具，它能将贸易双方的商业信用关系转变为票据的债权债务关系。票据有3种：汇票（draft，bill of exchange）、本票（promissory note）和支票（check / cheque）。

## （一）汇票

根据《英国票据法》的规定："汇票是一人向另一人开出的，由开出人签字，要求收件人对某一特定的人或其指定人或持票来人即期或固定的，或在可以确定的未来某一日期支付一定货币金额的无条件支付命令"（A bill of exchange is an unconditional order of writing, addressed by one person to another, signed by the person give it, requiring the person to whom it is addressed to pay on demand or at a fixed or determinable future time a sum certain in money to or to the order of a specified person or to bearer ）。中国《票据法》第十九条对汇票下的定义为："汇票是由出票人签发的，委托付款人在见票时或者在指定日期无条件支付确定的金额给收款人或者持票人的票据"。

### 1. 汇票的内容

汇票的内容包括绝对必要项目、相对必要项目和任意记载事项。汇票必须要式齐备，即绝对必要项目记载缺一不可，否则汇票无效；汇票的相对必要项目尽管也很重要，但欠缺记载不影响汇票的有效性；而汇票的任意记载事项不重要，有否记载根本不影响汇票的有效性。在国际贸易中，汇票是否有效成立，根据出票地的法律来裁决。值得注意的是，有关汇票的绝对必要项目规定，英美法系的票据法规定与大陆法系的票据法规定有很大的不同。一般来说，大陆法系的票据法规定比较严格，而英美法系的票据法规定比较灵活。

（1）绝对必要项目

以大陆法系的票据法为例，来说明绝对必要项目的具体内容。大陆法系的票据法规定，汇票必须具备7个绝对必要项目。

①标明"汇票"字样。以便区别于"本票"或"支票"，而《英国票据法》无此要求。

②无条件支付命令。汇票是出票人委托付款人支付一定款项给收款人的无条件支付命令。支付不能受到限制，也不能附带任何条件。

③确定的金额,包括"确定的"金额和"可以确定"的金额。例如，汇票记载带有支付利息条款的，其利息支付条款记载要完整，必须有明确的利率和计息起讫时间和终止时间。

④出票人（drawer）签章。出票人是签发汇票的当事人。出票人在交付汇票前，必须在汇票上加具真实签章以明确其票据责任。汇票的签字如果是伪造的，或是由未经授权人签字，则视为无效汇票。

⑤受票人（drawee），它是汇票可能的付款人。如其对远期汇票承兑，作为汇票的承兑人，成为汇票的主债务人；如其对即期汇票或承兑汇票付款，则成为付款人。

⑥收款人（payee），它是汇票的主债权人，必须在汇票上载明。

⑦出票日期。汇票上必须加注出票日期，以便凭以确定出票人在签发汇票时有无行为能力，并凭以确定某些汇票的付款到期日、提示期限、承兑期限、利息起算日等。根据中国《票据法》第二十二条规定，汇票必须记载的具体事项与大陆法系的票据法规定基本一致。

（2）相对必要项目

汇票的相对必要项目有3个：①付款日期，又称付款到期日，是受票人履行付款义务的日期。如未记载，视为"见票即付"。②付款地点，即汇票金额支付地，也是请求付款地或拒绝证书做出地。如未记载，以受票人经常居住地或营业地为准。③出票地点。出票地点通常是在汇票的右上方，常和出票日期连在一起。如汇票没有单独列明出票地点，出票人名字旁边的地点或出票人的经常居住地或营业地视为出票地点。

（3）任意记载事项

汇票除了绝对必要项目和相对必要项目以外，汇票内容还包括一些任意记载事项，有否记载并不影响汇票的有效性，如计息条款、付一不付二或付二不付一、禁止转让、免做拒绝证书或退票通知、汇票编号、出票条款等。

**2. 汇票的分类**

从不同的角度对汇票进行分类，汇票主要有以下几种。

（1）银行汇票和商业汇票

按出票人的不同，可分为银行汇票和商业汇票。银行汇票（banker's draft）的出票人和受票人均为银行。商业汇票（commercial draft）的出票人一般为工商企业或个人，而其受票人可以是工商企业或个人，也可以是银行。

（2）光票和跟单汇票

按汇票是否随附单据，分为光票和跟单汇票。光票（clean bill）是指汇票不随附商业单据，如银行汇票多为光票。跟单汇票（documentary bill）必须随附商业单据。跟单汇票随附的商业单据，包括提单、仓单、保险单、装箱单、商业发票等，商业汇票多为跟单汇票。

（3）即期汇票和远期汇票

按付款时间的不同，可分为即期汇票和远期汇票。即期汇票（sight bill，demand bill）的持票人向受票人提示汇票后，付款人必须立即付款，即"见票即付"。远期汇票（time bill，usance bill），一般规定在出票后一定时间或规定在特定日期付款。

远期汇票的付款日期，常见有4种规定方法：①定日付款，即规定在将来某一特定日期付款。②出票日后若干天付款，如出票日后30天、45天、60天，120天付款。③见票后若干天付款，如见票日后30天、60天、120天付款等。④规定某一特定事件发生后付款，如运输单据签发日后30天付款，等等。

（4）商业承兑汇票和银行承兑汇票

按承兑人不同，可分为商业承兑汇票和银行承兑汇票。远期的商业汇票，如由工商企业或个人加具承兑，则为商业承兑汇票（commercial acceptance bill）；如由银行对汇票加具承兑，则为银行承兑汇票（banker's acceptance bill）。因远期商业汇票是建立在商业信用基础之上，其出票人是工商企业或个人。因此，商业承兑汇票可以理解为"在商业信用的基础上再加上了商业信用"，而银行承兑汇票可以理解为"在商业信用的基础上加上了银行信用"。一份远期商业汇票，在获得承兑前，出票人是汇票的主债务人。

在承兑后，承兑人成为汇票的主债务人，而出票人退居成为次债务人。因此，相比商业承兑汇票，银行承兑汇票更易在金融市场上进行流通。

（5）限制性抬头的汇票、指示性抬头的汇票和来人抬头的汇票

按照汇票抬头（收款人）记载的不同，可以分为：限制性抬头的汇票、指示性抬头的汇票和来人抬头的汇票。限制性抬头的汇票不能转让，收款人一般做成"仅付某公司"（Pay___Co. only）或"付某公司，不能转让"（Pay___Co.，not transferable）。②指示性抬头的汇票，一般做成"付某公司或其指定人"（Pay to the order of___Co. or Pay___Co. or order），这种抬头的汇票可以经过背书转让。国际上，指示性抬头的汇票使用最多。③来人抬头的汇票，一般做成"付给某公司或来人"（Pay___Co.or bearer）或"付给持票人"（Pay Bearer），这种抬头的汇票无须背书即可转让。

**3. 汇票的使用**

汇票的使用通常要经过出票（issue）、背书（endorsement）、提示（presentation）、承兑（acceptance）、保证（guarantee）和付款（payment）等手续。此外，如汇票遭到拒付，还会涉及做成拒绝证书（protest）和行使追索权（right of recourse）等法律问题。

（1）**出票**

出票人签发票据并将其交付给收款人的行为。

（2）**背书**

背书是指汇票的收款人或持票人在汇票的背面签字加批，将汇票权利转让给受让人（被背书人）的行为。对于受让人来说，在他（她）以前的背书人和出票人都是"前手"；而对于出让人来说，在他（她）让与以后的受让人都是"后手"。"前手"对"后手"负有担保汇票必然会被承兑或付款的责任。如果远期汇票的持有人欲提前取得票款，可以将经过背书的汇票转让给受让人（一般是银行或贴现行或金融公司），由受让人扣除利息后将票款给出让人，这种行为称为"贴现"（discount）。

（3）**提示**

提示是指持票人将汇票提交受票人，要求其付款或承兑的行为。如是即期汇票，要求受票人见票后立即付款；如为远期汇票，提示在受票人见票后办理承兑手续，并到期付款。

（4）**承兑**

承兑是指远期汇票的受票人在汇票正面写上"承兑"（acceptance）字样、注明承兑日期并签字，然后交还持票人。汇票一经承兑，表示承兑人承担到期付款的责任。远期限汇票若遭到受票人拒绝承兑，拒付发生。

（5）**付款**

即期汇票的受票人在持票人提示时即付；远期汇票的受票人在办理承兑手续后，在汇票到期日付款。汇票一经付款，出票人、汇票的"前手"和"后手"与付款人，在汇票上的债权债务关系全部得以清偿。

（6）**拒付**

如持票人在法定期限内向受票人提示付款或承兑，受票人逃避不见或明确表示拒付或

拒绝承兑，拒付事实发生。汇票的善意持有人有权向其所有的"前手"追索，直止追索到出票人。如果汇票是在承兑后遭受拒付的，则出票人可以凭承兑汇票向付款人进行追索。

持票人为了行使追索权，通常必须在法定时间内做成"拒付通知"和"拒绝证书"后才可行使追索权。拒绝证书一般由拒付地点的法定公证机构做出。持票人请求公证人做成拒绝证书时，应将汇票交出，由公证人持票向付款人再作提示，如仍遭拒付，即由公证人按规定格式做成拒绝证书，连同汇票交还持票人。持票人凭拒绝证书，向其"前手"行使追索权。

## （二）本票

《英国票据法》关于本票的概念："本票是一人向另一人开出的，由出票人签字，保证对某一特定的人或其指定人或持票人即期或固定的，或在可以确定的未来某一日期支付一定货币金额的书面的无条件支付承诺"（A Promissory Note is a an unconditional promise in writing made by one person to another signed by the maker engaging to pay on demand or a fixed or determinable future time a sum certain in money to or to the order of a specified person or to bearer.）。而根据中国《票据法》第七十三条规定："本票是指出票人签发的，承诺自己在见票时无条件支付给持票人或收款人一定金额的票据"。

### 1. 本票的内容

本票的绝对必要项目内容有：①标明"本票"字样。②无条件支付承诺。③出票人签章。④出票日期。⑤支付金额。⑥收款人或其指定人。这6项内容欠缺其一，本票无效。

本票的相对必要项目有：①付款地点。如未记载，以出票人的营业场所为付款地。②出票地。如未记载，也以出票人的营业场所为付款地。③付款期限。如果没有写清楚，可以视为"见票即付"本票。

### 2. 本票的分类

本票可分为商业本票和银行本票。商业本票由工商企业或个人签发。按照付款时间的不同，商业本票又可分为即期、远期两种。即期商业本票为"见票即付"，而远期商业本票则由出票人承诺于未来某一规定日期付款。因本票的付款人与出票人为同一人，因而远期本票不需要承兑。商业本票因为是商业信用，一般很难流通，在国际贸易中使用不多，除非该商业本票能获得银行保证。银行本票是由银行签发的本票，按照中国《票据法》的规定，银行本票只能由中国人民银行审定的银行或其他金融机构签发。银行本票一般都是即期本票，在国际贸易结算中使用的本票大多是银行本票。

### 3. 本票与汇票的主要区别

本票与汇票的主要区别在于：①本票是无条件的自我支付承诺，汇票是无条件的委付命令。②票据的当事人不同。本票的票面有两个当事人：出票人和收款人；汇票则有三个当事人：出票人、受票人和收款人。③远期本票无须承兑，远期汇票需要承兑。④出票人的责任不同。本票在任何情况下，出票人都是主债务人；远期汇票在承兑前，出票人是主债务人。承兑后，承兑人是主债务人；即期汇票在付款前，出票人是主债务人。⑤本票一般是单张签发，汇票一般是成套签发。如一套汇票有两份正本，则在第一份正本上，注明"付一不付二"，在第二份正本上，注明"付二不付一"。

### （三）支票

按照《英国票据法》关于支票的定义："简单地说，支票是以银行为付款人的即期汇票。详细地说，支票是银行客户开出的，由银行客户签字，授权银行对某一特定的人或其指定人或者持票来人即期支付一定货币金额的书面的无条件支付命令"（Briefly speaking, a Cheque is a bill of exchange drawn on a bank payable on demand. Detailed speaking, a Cheque is an unconditional order in writing addressed by the customer to a bank signed by that customer authorizing the bank to pay on demand a sum certain in money or to the order of a specified person or to bearer.）。而根据中国《票据法》第八十二条规定："支票是出票人签发的，委托办理支票存款业务的银行或其他金融机构在见票时无条件支付确定的金额给收款人或持票人的票据"。

出票人签发支票时，应在付款行存有不低于票面金额的存款或在付款行允许透支的额度内。如存款不足或超出透支额度，持票人会遭到拒付，这种支票称为空头支票。开出空头支票的出票人要负法律责任。

#### 1. 支票的必要内容

支票的必要内容有：①加注"支票"字样。②无条件支付命令。③付款银行的名称。④出票日期和地点。⑤付款地点。⑥支付金额。⑦付款人的名称。⑧收款人或其指定人的名称。其中，以①、②、③、⑦为绝对必要项目。而支票的出票日期、付款金额、收款人或其指定人的名称等可以在提示支票前加以补记。

#### 2. 支票的种类

支票按收款人不同，支票可以分为记名支票和不记名支票。按支票是否保付，可分为保付支票（certified check）和普通支票。保付支票是由付款银行在支票上加具"保付"字样并签字，以表明在支票提示时付款行一定付款。保付支票的付款行是支票的主债务人，出票人和背书人都可免除责任，免予追索。保付支票在一般情况下不会遭受退票，不会有止付通知。因此，保付支票的信用程度很高，有利于支票的流通，而普通支票的出票人是支票的主债务人；支票按是否划线，可分为划线支票和非划线支票。支票不带划线者称为现金支票或非划线支票（open cheque）。持此类支票既可提取现金，也可通过往来银行代收转账。支票带有划线者称为划线支票（crossed cheque），这种支票在支票上划有两道平行线，可分为一般划线支票（general crossing）和特别划线支票（special crossing）两种。一般划线支票是在平行线中不注明收款行名称的支票，收款人可通过任何一家银行代收转账；特别划线支票是在平行线中具体写明收款银行名称，付款银行只能将票款划付给划线中指定的银行，而不能像一般划线支票那样只要付给银行就行。非划线支票在由出票人、收款人、持票人加划横线后，或加注银行名称后，可成为一般划线支票或特别划线支票。但是不允许将划线支票转化成非划线支票，或将特别划线支票转化成一般划线支票。付款银行对划线支票和非划线支票所承担的责任是不同的。对划线支票，付款银行必须对真正的所有人付款或按划线的要求付款。

### 3. 支票与汇票的区别

支票与汇票的主要区别有：①支票的出票人是银行客户，付款人是开立账户银行，支票是授权书；汇票的出票人、付款人是没有限定的任何人，汇票是委托书。②支票是支付工具，只有即期付款，没有承兑，也没有到期日的记载；汇票是支付和信用工具，它有即期、远期等几种期限，有承兑行为，也可能有到期日的记载。③支票的主债务人是出票人；远期汇票的主债务人在承兑前是出票人，在承兑后是承兑人。④支票可以保付，汇票没有保付的做法。⑤支票的出票人和付款人之间要有资金关系；而汇票的出票人和付款人之间不必先有资金关系。⑥支票可以划线；汇票一般不能划线。⑦支票可以止付，而汇票在承兑后，付款是不可撤销的。⑧支票只能开出一张；汇票可以开出一套。

# 二、货款收付方式

国际货物买卖的货款收付，主要采用汇付、托收和跟单信用证三种方式。然而，近年来，银行保函、备用信用证等方式的使用比例也逐步上升。

## （一）汇付

汇付（remittance）又称汇款，是指买方主动通过银行将货款汇交卖方，它是买卖双方支付货款的一种最简便的方式。一笔汇款业务，一般涉及四个当事人：① 汇款人（remitter），指汇出款项的人，在国际贸易中通常为买方。②收款人（payee），指收取款项的人，在国际贸易中通常为卖方。③汇出行（remitting bank），指受汇款人的委托汇出款项的银行，通常是在进口地的银行。④汇入行（paying bank），指受汇出行委托解付汇款的银行，通常是出口地的银行。一般来说，汇款人与汇出行之间、汇出行与汇入行之间有一定的契约关系。

### 1. 汇付种类及其业务程序

办理汇付，需要由汇款人向汇出行填交汇款申请书，汇出行收妥款项后，有义务根据汇款申请书的指示向汇入行发出付款委托书；汇入行收到付款委托书后，有义务向收款人解付货款（见图6-1）。但是，汇出行和汇入行对不属于自身过失而造成的损失（如付款委托书在邮递途中遗失或延误等，致使收款人无法或迟期收款）不承担责任，而汇出行对汇入行工作上的过失也不承担责任。根据不同的汇款方法，汇付方式可分为信汇、电汇和票汇。

图6.1　汇付方式的一般业务流程

（1）信汇

在国际贸易中，如选择信汇（mail transfer，M/T），买方将货款交给本地银行（汇出行），该行以航空挂号信的方式向出口地的汇入行寄出付款委托书，委托汇入行将款项解付给卖方。信汇方式的费用低廉，但汇款在途时间长，卖方收款时间较晚，银行可短期占用资金。

（2）电汇

电汇（telegraphic transfer，T/T）与信汇不同的是：汇出行是采用电讯方式（电报、电传、SWIFT等）快捷方式，将付款委托书传递给汇入行，然后由出口地的汇入行解付货款给卖方。电汇方式具有收款速度快、便于卖方加速资金周转、避免汇率风险和安全可靠等优势，但是汇款费用相对较高。目前，在实际业务中，电汇使用最多。

（3）票汇

在国际贸易中，如选择票汇（banker's demand draft，D/D）付款，其作法是买方向本地银行购买银行汇票后，将汇票直接寄给卖方，卖方向汇票的付款银行提示汇票，然后由汇票的付款行将票款支付给卖方。

### 2. 汇付的特点

汇付属于商业信用。在国际贸易中使用汇付方式收付货款，其特点是：①手续简便，费用少。相比其他货款收付方式（如托收、信用证等），汇付方式的手续最简单，银行收取的手续费也最少。②使用灵活。可用于"预付"和"到付"。如"预付"，买方风险大；如"到付"，卖方风险大。买卖双方能否安全收货或收款，完全依赖对方的信用。如果相对方信用欠佳，很可能造成"货、款两空"。③资金负担不平衡。采用预付货款，买方资金负担较重，整个交易过程中需要的资金，几乎全由买方来提供；采用到付货款，卖方资金负担较重，整个交易过程中需要的资金，几乎全由卖方来提供。

### 3. 汇付在国际货物买卖中的具体运用

鉴于汇付方式的以上特点，买卖双方在交易磋商和合同签订环节，在确定采用"汇付"的前提下，往往需要就汇付的种类、付款时间、"货、单、款"的具体衔接及风险分担等方面进行具体的协商。以电汇为例，结合不同的运输方式、货物特点，来具体说明汇付在国际货物买卖中的具体运用。

（1）预付

预付是针对买方而言，对卖方来说是在装运货物前或在交出货运单据前收取货款，具体细分为以下3种：①随订单付现（cash with order）。合同签订后，买方就将全部货款预付给卖方。卖方收取预收款后，开始生产。买方需要承担买方是否能按期交货或质量等方面的全部风险，而卖方几乎不承担任何经营风险。②装运前若干天付款。买卖双方合同签订后，卖方开始安排生产。货物生产包装完毕后，将发货清单和预装运期通知买方，请其付款。货款收妥后，卖方才将货物装运出去。合同条款可规定为：100% payment should be made by T/T at least 10 days before shipment date（在合同规定的装运期前至少提前10天，买方应将货款全部电汇给卖方）。③装运后若干天付款，但必须付款赎单。买卖双方合同签订后，卖方先安排生产，然后将货物装运出去。在买方付清货款后，卖方再将全套商业单据（包括全套海运提单）寄交买方。合同条款可规定为：Payment made with ___days(such as 15/30 days)after the date of Bill of lading. The buyer will release full set of commercial documents, including shipping documents to the buyer on receipt of 100% payment（提单日后___天比如15天或30天付款，卖方在收到买方100%货款后，将全套商业单据（包括运输单据）寄交给买方。以上（1）、（2）、（3）预付的共同点是在买方付清货款前，卖方掌握货物或货运单据。但是卖方面临的风险还是有一定的差异。对卖方来说，风险（1）最小，（3）比较大，而（2）折中。

（2）到付

相对预付而言，到付是指买方在先得到货物后再进行付款的方式，具体有两种：①售定（be sold out/up）。卖方装运货物后，将全套货运单据寄交买方，以便买方提取货物进行销售。在合同规定的付款期限内，不管买方是否已将货物售罄，应将全部货款支付给卖方的结算方式。合同条款可规定为：Payment made within___days after shipment（装运后___天付款）。②寄售（consignment）。在合同规定的付款期限内，买方可以仅付给卖方销售完毕的货物价款。对未销售的部分货物，买方可以退货，也可以与卖方协商继续销售。相对售定来说，寄售项下卖方承担的风险进一步加重。

从上可知，"预付"和"到付"项下买卖双方承担的风险不一样。如，随订单付现，买方承担全部风险；而寄售则由卖方承担全部风险。在实践中，汇付除用于货款结算外，还广泛用于运保费、佣金、样品费和索赔、理赔款项及退补款结算。

## （二）托收

所谓托收（collection），是指卖方（或债权人）开立票据或商业单据或两者兼有，委托托收行通过其联行或代理行向买方（或债务人）收取货款或劳务费用的结算方式。票据可以是汇票、本票、支票或付款收据；商业单据为商业发票、运输单据、所有权单据或其他类似单据。托收体现商业信用。

### 1. 托收业务的当事人

托收业务有4个基本的当事人：委托人（principal）、托收行（remitting bank）、代理行（collecting bank）、付款人（drawee）。根据业务需要，还可能出现另两个当事人：提示行和需要时的代理。

### （1）委托人

委托人即是委托银行办理托收的当事人。委托人一般是卖方（出口商），根据票据法即为出票人。在托收业务中，委托人的责任和义务为：①根据合同规定交付货物，这是卖方最基本的义务，也是跟单托收的前提条件。②提交符合合同规定的单据。买方提货前必须取得单据，包括物权单据。③填写托收申请书，开立汇票，并将托收申请书和汇票连同商业单据一并交给托收行。托收委托申请书的内容，包括：委托人的名称、地址、有权印鉴；付款人的名称、地址，或开户行的名称、地址、账号；托收随附单据的名称和份数；托收交单方式；款项的收账要求；托收拒付或者拒绝承兑时应采取的必要措施，如是否要做成拒绝证书、货物抵港后是否代办存仓保险等；托收费用由谁承担及有关托收的其他要求。

（2）托收行

托收行是接受委托人的委托并通过国外代理行办理托收的银行。托收行一般是卖方的往来银行，根据委托人的指示办理，并对自己的过失负责。

托收行的责任和义务为：①缮制托收委托书。根据托收申请书的内容制作托收委托书，并将委托书和单据寄给国外的代理行，指示其向付款人收款。在实践中，托收委托书与托收申请书内容基本一致，只是函头名称不一样。托收申请书为"LETTER OF INSTRUCTION FOR OUTWARD COLLECTION"，而委托书是"COLLECTION ORDER"；②核验单据。托收行应当核实单据的名称和份数是否与申请书填写相同，但除此之外没有进一步审核单据的义务。托收行照常规处理业务，对自己的过失承担责任，选择代收行的费用和风险由委托人承担。

（3）代收行

代收行是指接受委托行的委托向付款人办理收款并交单的银行。代收行在托收业务中所承担的责任与托收行基本相同，如核对单据的份数和名称，如有不符应立即通知托收行；代收行在未经托收行同意前不得变更委托书上的任何条件，否则责任自负。除此以外，代收行还有以下责任：①保管好单据。代收行在买方按规定付款或承兑前不可以将单据放给买方。若买方拒付，代收行应当通知托收行，若发出通知后90日仍未收到指示，将单据退回托收行。②谨慎处理货物。代收行原则上无义务处理货物，只有在买方拒付时，才会根据委托人指示办理存仓、保险手续。若代收行为了保护货物，在遇到天灾人祸等紧急情况下，即使未得到委托人的指示也可以对货物采取行动。

（4）付款人

付款人是根据托收委托书的要求，被提示单据要求付款的当事人，一般是买方，依据票据法即为受票人。付款人有权审查单据并决定是否付款或承兑。如选择拒付，则必须经得起委托人的抗辩，否则会遭受信誉和经济上的损失。

（5）非基本当事人

托收业务还可能出现其他当事人。主要有：提示行、需要时的代理。提示行（presenting bank）是指向付款人提示单据，要求付款人付款或承兑的银行。若代收行与付款人无账户关系或者两者不在同一城市，代收行须转托另一家银行提示单据；需要时的代理（representative in case of need），是指委托人指定的代表。付款人在拒付后，需要时的代理可代理委托人办理货物存仓、保险、转售、运回或改变交单条件等事宜。委托人在托收指示中应明确完整地规定其权限，否则银行将不接受该代理的任何指示。

**2. 托收种类**

按托收项下是否随附商业单据，托收分为光票托收与跟单托收。光票托收（clean bill for collection）是指卖方仅开立汇票而不附任何商业单据，委托银行收取货款的一种托收方式。一般用于收取货款尾数、代垫费用、佣金、样品费或者其他贸易从属费用。光票托收的汇票有即期和远期之分。采用即期汇票，代收行收到汇票后应立即向受票人提示并要求付款；采用远期汇票，代收行收到汇票后，应立即向受票人提示，先要求承兑，以确定到期付款的责任。承兑后，代收行收回汇票，于到期日再做提示要求付款。若受票人拒付或拒绝承兑，除托收委托书另有规定外，应由代收行在法定期限内及时将拒付情况通知托收行转知委托人。

跟单托收按所需单据的不同，分为两种：①既有金融票据，又有商业单据的托收。这种托收是凭汇票付款，商业单据是汇票的附件，起"支持"汇票的作用；②没有金融单据，仅凭商业单据的托收。有些国家如日本、德国对汇票要征收印花税，为了减免税收负担而在信誉和信任度较高的公司之间采用。跟单托收按其交单方式，可分为付款交单与承兑交单：

**（1）付款交单**

付款交单（documents against payment）是指代收行必须在买方付清票款后，才将商业单据包括提单交给买方的一种交单方式。按卖方开立汇票的付款期限不同，付款交单分为即期付款交单与远期付款交单。所谓即期付款交单（D/P at sight）是指代收行提示跟单汇票给受票人要求其付款，而受票人见票即付后，代收行才交单给付款人的一种交单方式。合同条款可规定为：Upon first presentation, the buyer shall pay against documentary draft drawn by the seller at sight. The shipping documents are to be delivered against payment only.（买方应凭卖方开具的即期跟单汇票于见票时即期付款，付款后交单。）而远期付款交单（D/P at___ days after sight）是指代收行提示跟单汇票给受票人要求承兑，受票人承兑后由代收行保管全套商业单据，并于到期日提示付款，受票人付款后才能取得单据。合同条款可规定为：The Buyers shall pay against documentary draft by the Sellers at ... days after date of draft. The shipping documents are to be delivered against payment only.（买方应凭卖方开具的跟单汇票，于汇票出票后××天付款，付款后交单。）如果买方在远期付款交单条件下欲先取得单据、后付款，可凭信托收据（trust receipt，T/R）向代收行借取单据，先行提货，于汇票到期日再付清货款。所谓信托收据，就是买方借单时提供的一种书面信用担保文件，用来表示愿意以代收行的受托人身份代为提货、报关、存仓、保险、出售并承认货物所有权仍属银行。这种做法如果是代收行自己向买方提供的信用便利，则如代收行借出单据后，到期不能收到货款，应由代收行对委托人负全部责任。

**（2）承兑交单**

承兑交单（documents against acceptance）是指代收行在付款人承兑远期汇票后，把商业单据交给付款人，于汇票到期日时由付款人付款的一种交单方式。这种方式对卖方来讲风险较大，应慎重使用。合同条款可规定为：The Buyers shall duly accept the documentary draft drawn by the Sellers upon presentation and make payment at ... days after date of B/L. The shipping documents are to be delivered against acceptance.（买方对卖方开具的跟

单汇票，于提示时承兑，并应于提单日后××天付款，承兑后交单。）

### 3.托收的具体运用及应注意事项

托收是商业信用，卖方与托收行之间、托收行与代收行之间都是委托代理关系。买方是根据买卖合同付款，买方与代收行之间也不存在任何法律关系。银行办理托收业务时，只是按委托人的指示办事，并无承担买方必然付款的义务。

光票托收一般用于贸易从属费用的结算以及佣金、样品费的结算等，金额较小。对卖方来说，跟单托收中以即期付款交单风险最小，而以承兑交单风险最大。但是，买方的选择则刚好相反。相对于货到付款，托收有比较强的安全性。托收业务中买卖双方资金负担不平衡，卖方的资金负担较重，但托收项下的卖方比较容易控制单据。按照URC522，买方要在付款或承兑汇票后，才能取得单据。同时，托收项下的卖方可以利用单据向银行融通资金。

托收项下的买卖双方面临的政治风险与商业风险与在汇款项下基本相同。为防止买方拒收货物，卖方应该注意贸易术语的选择、货物的特点等。相对于汇款，托收项下的卖方还应注意以下事项。

（1）谨慎选择代收行

托收项下，卖方是在装运货物后备齐单据，委托银行向买方收取货款。银行的行为直接关系到卖方收汇的成功与否。按照URC522，托收行必须完全按照卖方的指示，依据URC522的相关规定办理业务，不得越权或擅自变更卖方的要求。而代收行必须完全遵照托收行的指示，并妥善保管好单据。在必要的情况下，谨慎处理好货物。例如，在即期付款交单条件下，托收行必须指示代收行在货款收妥的情况下才能将单据交给买方，否则单据将仍然控制在代收行手中。如代收行在收妥货款前，将单据先放给买方，买方到期拒付的风险要由代收行承担。代收行要为自己的过失承担责任。

（2）D/A的风险

由于D/A风险太大，卖方一般不应该接受D/A。如采用D/A，应采用取一定的控制风险措施，如采用D/A与银行保函相结合，或要求进口银行在汇票上保证，或办理出口信用保险、保理或包买票据等办法，以转嫁一定的风险。

（3）单据质量

托收项下银行只是核验单据，而非审核单据。买方为降低自己的风险，一般会仔细审核单据，以判定"单、货""单、同""单、单"是否一致。买方从这三个"一致"来判定卖方装运的货物是否符合合同要求。因此，卖方在制作单据时必须十分谨慎，以免出错，从而导致买方拒收货物。

（4）远期D/P的不规范性

远期付款交单的买方在承兑汇票后，受票据法制约，成为汇票的主债务人，但买方的承兑未能取得物权凭证（即对价）而有欠公平，卖方也没有获得相应的资金融通。如果在货物到达目的港（地）后，汇票的付款期限未到，那么货物在目的港（地）未及时办理进口清关会产生大量的滞港费用，最终有可能导致买方拒付货款或要求降价。因此，远期付款交单被国际商会视为"极不规范"的支付方式，卖方在实践中也应尽量避免接受远期付款交单。

### （三）跟单信用证

信用证有跟单信用证和备用信用证之分。因备用信用证同时具有跟单信用证和银行保函的性质，为便于说明，本部分内容以跟单信用证为主。以下的"信用证"，除非特别说明，即为"跟单信用证"。信用证付款是当今国际货物买卖中最重要的货款收付方式之一。按照UCP600第2条有关信用证的定义："信用证指一项不可撤销的安排，无论其名称或描述如何，该项安排构成开证行对相符交单予以承付的确定承诺"。所谓"相符交单"，指与信用证条款、本惯例的相关适用条款以及国际标准银行实务一致的交单。因此，信用证是开证行有条件的付款承诺。只要交单相符，卖方即能凭信用证安全收款。买卖合同中的信用证付款条款一般可规定为：The buyer shall open through a bank acceptable to the seller a documentary credit to reach the seller 15 days before the month of shipment。The credit shall be available with issuing bank (or xxx bank) by negotiation/sight payment /acceptance/deferred payment at____days after shipment and valid until 15th days after the date of shipment。（买方应通过卖方所认可的银行，于装运月份前提前15天开立一份装运日后×××天议付/即期付款/承兑/延期付款的信用证，并将信用证送达卖方，有效期为装运月份后15天在中国兑用有效。）

#### 1. 信用证的特点

##### （1）开证行负第一性付款责任

不管买方破产或拒付，只要交单相符，开证行必须付款。因此，开证行的资信是能否安全收汇的重要因素。信用证与汇付、托收的区别在于，信用证属于银行信用，而汇付、托收属于商业信用；

##### （2）信用证是一项自足的文件

信用证条款虽然是根据买卖合同开立的，但一经开立，它就成为独立于买卖合同以外的另一种契约，不受买卖合同的约束。信用证项下的所有银行只按信用证的规定处业务；

##### （3）信用证属于纯单据买卖

银行处理信用证业务时仅凭单据表面上判定交单是否符合信用证条款，不管单据真伪、不管合同、更不管货物。

#### 2. 信用证业务的当事人

信用证的当事人有：①申请人（applicant），指要求开立信用证的一方，一般为买方。②开证行（issuing bank），指应申请人要求或者代表自己开出信用证的银行，一般是买方所在地银行。③通知银行（advising bank），指应开证行的要求通知信用证的银行，一般是卖方所在地的银行。④受益人（beneficiary），指接受信用证并享受权益的一方，一般为卖方或实际供货人。⑤被指定银行（nominated bank），是指信用证可在其处兑用的银行，如信用证可在任何银行兑用，则任何银行均为被指定银行；⑥保兑行

（confirming bank），是根据开证行的授权或要求对信用证加具保兑的银行。信用证一经保兑，保兑行即对信用证独立负责，承担第一性的付款责任。保兑行可以由通知行或第三家银行来担当。⑦交单人（presenter），指实施交单行为的受益人、银行或其他人。其中，开证行与受益人是信用证不可缺少的两个基本当事人。

### 3. 信用证的基本内容

信用证的基本内容包括：①对信用证本身的说明，包括信用证的种类、性质、金额、信用证号码、开证日期、有效期和到期地点等。②货物说明，包括货物的名称、规格、数量、包装、价格等。③运输说明，包括装运的最迟期限、装运港（地）和目的港（地）、运输方式、可否分批装运和可否中途转船等。④对单据的要求，包括单据的种类和份数。⑤附加条款。视具体交易情况，可做出不同的规定，如银行费用、不符点扣费等。⑥责任文句。开证行对受益人及汇票持有人保证付款的责任文句、交单说明等。

### 4. 信用证样例

SEQUENCE OF TOTAL　　*27 : 1/1

FORM OF DOC. CREDIT　*40 A : IRREVOCABLE

DOC. CREDIT NUMBER　*20 : TCAM507846

DATE OF ISSUE　　1 C : 210709

EXPIRY　　　　　*31 D : DATE 210808 PLACE CHINA

APPLICANT　　　　*50 : URTA INDUSTRIES SDN BHD, NO.5 JALAN 3,

BANDAR SULTAN SULEIMAN, CHINESE

INDUSTRIAL PARK 42005 PORT KLANG,

SELANGOR, MALAYSIA

BENEFICIARY　　　*59 : B.F.TEXTILES (HANGZHOU) CO., LTD. NO.6,

LANE 10 LINTIAN ROAD, LINAN, ZHEJIANG

311300, P.R.CHINA

AMOUNT　　　　　*32 B : CURRENCY USD AMOUNT 20.533,69

AVAILABLE WITH/BY　*41 D : ISSUING BANK BY PAYMENT

DRAFTS AT…　　42 C : 30 DAYS AFTER SIGHT

DRAWEE　　　　42 D : DRAWN ON RHB BANK BERHAD, PORT KLANG

BRANCH FOR 100 PERCENT OF THE

INVOICE VALUE

PARTIAL SHIPMENTS　　43 P : ALLOWED

TRANSSHIPMENT　　　43 T : ALLOWED

LOADING IN CHARGE　44 A : SHANGHAI, CHINA

FOR TRANSPORT TO …　44 B : PORT KLANG, MALAYSIA

LATEST DATE OF SHIP.　44 C : 080728

DESCRIPT. OF GOODS　45 A : YARN DYED FABRICS-WIDTH 58/59"

AS PER PURCHASE CONTRACT NO:790040

(CIF) SUBJECT TO INCOTERMS 2000

DOCUMENTS REQUIRED    46 A :

+SIGNED COMMERCIAL INVOICE IN TRIPLICATE

+3/3 SET OF CLEAN OCEAN BILL OF LADING

+CERTIFICATE OF ORIGIN IN DUPLICATE

+PACKING LIST IN TRIPLICATE

+INSURANCE POLICY OR CERTIFICATE IN TRIPLICATE BLANK ENDORSED IN THE CURRENCY OF THE CREDIT FOR NOT LESS THAN 110 PERCENT OF INVOICE VALUE WITH CLAIMS PAYABLE IN KUALA LUMPUR COVERING FIRE, MARINE RISKS, INSTITUTE CARGO CLAUSES（CLAUSE A）,INSTITUTE WAR CLAUSES, STRIKES CLAUSES AND TPND FROM POINT ORIGIN TO APPLICANT'S WAREHOUSE IN PORT KLANG, MALAYSIA

ADDITIONAL COND     47 A :

+DRAFTS CLAUSED ´DRAWN UNDER DOCUMENTARY CREDIT NO. TCAM507846 DATED O9TH JULY 2008 OF RHB BANK BERHAD, PORT KLANG BRANCH´

+ALL DOCUMENTS MUST INDICATE OUR CREDIT NUMBER TCAM507846

+ALL DOCUMENTS PRESENTED MUST BE IN ENGLISH

+THE REIMBURSEMENT FEE OF THE ISSUING BANK ACCOUNTING TO USD30-00 IS STRICTLY FOR THE AMOUNT OF BENEFICIARY

+FULL SET CLEAN ON BOARD OCEAN BILL OF LADING MUST BE MADE OUT TO THE ORDER OF RHB BANK BERHAD, PORT KLANG BRANCH MARKED FREIGHT PREPAID AND NOTIFY APPLICANT

+THE AMOUNT OF EACH DRAFT NEGOTIATED MUST BE ENDORSED ON THE REVERSE OF THIS CREDIT

DETAILS OF CHARGES    71 B : ALL CHARGES INCLUDING ADVISING CHARGES AND NEGOTIATION CHARGES OUTSIDE MALAYSIA ARE FOR ACCOUNT OF BENEFICIARY

PRESENTATION PERIOD  48  : DOCUMENTS TO BE PRESENTED WITHIN 21 DAYS AFTER THE DATE OF ISSUANCE OF THE TRANSPORT DOCUMENTS BUT WITHIN THE VALIDITY OF THE CREDIT

CONFIRMATION          *49 : WITHOUT

INSTRUCTIONS          78 :

+DRAFTS AND DOCUMENTS MUST BE FORWARDED TO RHB BANK BERHAD, SHAH ALAM TRADE SERVICES CENTRE, NO.23 JALAN TENGKU AMPUAN ZABEDAH 9J/9 SECTION 9 40100 SHAH ALAM, MALAYSIA IN ONE LOT BY COURIER SERVICE

+UPON RECEIPT OF THE RELATIVE DOCUMENTS IN FULL COMPLIANCE WITH THE TERMS AND CONDITIONS OF THE CREDIT, WE SHALL COVER YOU AS PER YOUR INSTRUCTION ON MATURITY

+A DISCREPANCY FEE OF USD50-00 WILL BE DEDUCTED FROM THE PROCEEDS IF DOCUMENTS ARE PRSENTED WITH DISCREPANCY（IES）AND ACCEPTANCE OF SUCH DISCREPANT DOCUMENTS WILL NOT IN ANY WAY ALTER THE TERMS AND CONDITIONA OF THIS CREDIT

+NEGOTIATION OF DISCREPANT DOCUMENTS UNDER RESERVE OR GUARANTEE IS STRICTLY PROHIBITED

### 5. 信用证的分类

UCP600规定，凡是信用证都是不可撤销的。将信用证从不同的角度进行分类，可分为以下几种主要类型。

（1）保兑信用证与非保兑信用证

非保兑信用证即为一般的不可撤销信用证；保兑信用证是指开证银行开出的信用证，经另一家银行加以保兑，保兑行通常由通知行担任。保兑费归谁支付，以信用证约定的条款为准。若开证行授权另一家银行对信用证予以保兑，该银行有选择权。如该银行不准备照办，则其必须毫不迟疑地通知开证行，并在通知此信用证时对信用证不加具保兑；若该银行同意对信用证加以保兑，并且在信用证上真实加具保兑，才成为保兑银行，只要规定的单据提交给保兑行并且构成交单相符，保兑行必须承付或议付，而保兑行的议付不享有追索权。

（2）即期付款、延期付款、承兑和议付

信用证必须规定其是以即期付款、延期付款、承兑还是议付的方式兑用。UCP600将信用证付款方式分为两种：承付和议付。所谓承付是指：①如果信用证为即期付款信用证，则即期付款。②如果信用证为延期付款信用证，则承诺延期付款并在承诺到期日付款。③如果信用证为承兑信用证，则承兑受益人开出的汇票并在汇票到期日付款。议付是指被指定银行在相符交单下，在其应获偿付的银行工作日当天或之前向受益人预付或者同意预付款项，从而购买汇票（其付款人为被指定银行以外的其他银行）及/或单据的行为。对于即期付款、延期付款或承兑的信用证，信用证的兑用银行可以是被指定银行，也可以是开证行本身；而议付信用证一般规定有被指定银行。

信用证的兑用方式、兑用地点规定举例：①自由议付信用证（This credit is available with any bank by negotiation.）；②限制在通知行议付的信用证（This credit is available with advising bank by negotiation.）；③即期付款信用证，付款行为开证行（This credit is available with issuing bank by sight payment.）；④承兑信用证，承兑行为开证行，付款期限为见票后45天（This credit is available with issuing bank by acceptance at 45 days after sight.）；⑤延期付款信用证，付款行为开证行，付款期限为提单日后30天（This credit is available with issuing bank by deferred payment at 30 days after the date of bill of lading.）。

（3）可转让信用证和不可转让信用证

可转让信用证（transferable letter of credit）是指特别注明"可转让（Transferable）"字样的信用证。可转让信用证可应受益人（第一受益人）的要求转为全部或部分由另一受益人（第二受益人）兑用。没有特别注明"可转让（Transferable）"字样的信用证，即为不可转让信用证（non-transferable letter of credit）。

（4）循环信用证

循环信用证（revolving credit）是指信用证被全部或部分兑用后，能重新恢复原金额继续使用，直至规定的次数或金额用完为止的信用证。买卖双方订立长期合约，而货物采用分批装运的情况下，开立循环信用证可以使买方减少开证押金、降低重复开证的次数、简化开证手续。循环信用证按其循环方式的不同，又可分为3类：①自动循环信用证。信用证兑用后的一定时间内，无须开证行通知，信用证自动恢复原金额。②半自动循环信用证。信用证兑用后的一定时间内，如开证行未提出不能恢复原金额的通知，信用证就可自动恢复原金额。③非自动循环信用证。信用证兑用后，必须等待开证行通知，信用证才能恢复原金额。

### 6. 信用证业务的基本流程

以在出口国有一家被指定银行的信用证为例，来说明信用证业务的基本流程。信用证业务的基本流程，可细分为3个环节：开证环节、修改环节和兑用环节。

（1）开证环节

开证环节主要包括申请人申请开立信用证、开证行开立信用证、通知行通知信以及受益人审核信用证用证4个环节。

①申请人申请开立信用证。申请人（一般是买方）应按合同规定的开证时间要求，向开证行提出开证申请。开证行的资信应事先获得卖方认可。申请人申请开立信用证，应填写开证申请书，并提供若干押金或其他担保。开证申请书的内容应符合国际货物买卖合同的规定。

②开证行开立信用证。开证行根据开证申请书开立信用证，将信用证通过一定的方式传递给通知行。通知行一般为开证行在卖方所在地的代理行。信用证的传递方式有电开、信开两种。如果是电开，则开证行用电报、电传或SWIFT等电迅方式将信用证的内容传递给通知行；如果是信开，则开证行用航空挂号信的方式将信用证邮寄给通知行。信用证一经开出，开证行即承担不可撤销的付款责任。一般来说，若开证行拟开立一张在出口国有一家被指定银行的信用证，通常会指定通知行来担当承付、议付的责任；若开证行拟找一家银行对信用证加具保兑，惯常也会指定通知行来担当保兑行。要注意的是，该被指定银行在通知信用证的环节为通知行，但在信用证的兑用环节，按不

同的兑用方式，可能为即期付款行、议付行或承兑行。通知行与即期付款行、议付行或承兑行的责任是不一样的。

③通知行通知信用证。通知行在收到开证行的来信后，立即核对信用证的密押或印鉴。核实后，立即将信用证全文通知受益人。

④受益人审核信用证。受益人收到信用证后，立即审核信用证。审核的依据是买卖合同。在实践中，审核信用证时经常会发现"证、同"不一致。但要注意的是，并非所有的"证、同不一致"均要修改。"证、同"不一致是否需要修改，应视具体情况而定。如必须修改，则可以修改合同，也可以修改信用证。例如，若买卖合同规定在7月15日前装运，而开来的信用证规定在6月30日前装运，假如卖方（受益人）有把握能在6月30日前装运货物，那么信用证就不需要修改；假如卖方没有把握在6月30日前装运货物，但可以保证在7月15日前装运货物，那么一定要修改信用证，将信用证的装运期限从"6月30日前"修改为"7月15日前"。若买卖合同规定在7月15日前装运，而开来的信用证规定在7月30日前装运，假如卖方（受益人）有把握能在7月15日前装运货物，卖方只要在7月15日前将货物装运出去即可，信用证不需要修改；假如卖方没有把握在7月15日前装运货物，但可以保证在7月30日前装运货物，卖方应要求修改买卖合同而不是修改信用证，将买卖合同的装运期限从"7月15日前"修改为"7月30日前"。

（2）修改环节

受益人在审核信用证后，若判定信用证必须修改，信用证修改的路径与开证路径必须一致，即受益人向申请人提出修改；申请人填写信用证修改申请书交给开证行。如修改内容涉及金额增加，申请人还要补交开证押金；开证行修改信用证，并将信用证修改以同样的方式传递到同一通知行；通知行审核修改书的密押后，向受益人通知信用证修改的全部内容。受益人收到信用证修改后，仍然要仔细审核，并给予通知行有关接受或拒绝的通知（UCP600第10条c款）。受益人对信用证修改的内容，只能是全部接受或全部拒绝，不能对其内容部分接受、部分拒绝。若受益人未能给予接受或拒绝的通知，当交单与信用证以及尚未表示表示接受的修改要求一致时，视为受益人已做出接受，从此时起，该信用证被修改。

（3）兑用环节

如受益人认可信用证或其修改的内容，即按信用证规定条件装运货物。然后：

①受益人缮制单据。受益人按信用证规定装运货物后，备妥信用证规定的所有单据。

②受益人向被指定银行交单。受益人将信用证规定的单据，在信用证规定的交单期限和有效期限内，送交银行办理收款。如信用证有被指定银行，则交单路线一般推荐为：

受益人→被指定银行→保兑银行（如有的话）→开证行。

如果信用证在出口国既没有被指定银行，又没有保兑行，则受益人可以在本国委托一家银行代为交单。但在任何情况下，受益人均可以直接向开证行交单。要注意的是，受益人向被指定银行、保兑行、非信用证指定的银行交单所获得的保障是不一样的。若单据在被指定银行、保兑行寄往开证行的途中遗失，单据遗失的风险由开证行承担，最终由买方承担；若单据在由非信用证指定的银行寄往开证行的途中遗失，单据遗失的风险由卖方承担。

③被指定银行审单。被指定银行、保兑行（如有的话）、开证行在收到单据后，都有最多不超过5个银行工作日的审单时间，按照信用证内容审核单据，判定交单是否相符。如果受益人选择向被指定银行交单，在交单相符的条件下，被指定银行可以接受开证行的授权，对受益人的交单予以承付或议付，也可以选择拒绝。被指定银行对受益人承付不享有追索权，而议付享追索权。在拒绝承付或议付的情况下，受益人也可以向被指定银行提出押汇要求。所谓押汇，是指银行有追索权地购进受益人的汇票和所附单据，扣除若干利息和手续费，将款项交给受益人。被指定银行审单后，如发现交单不符，根据不符点的性质，对不符单据有3种处理方式：对于可修改的不符点，退回单据给受益人进行修改。修改完毕后，在信用证规定的交单期限内再次交单；若单据存在不符点但已不能修改，如不符点的性质比较严重，如晚装运、金额超支、信用证过期等，被指定银行先保留不符单据，然后电提不符点给开证行，若开证行接受"电提的不符点"，被指定银行再将单据寄往开证行收款；单据尽管存在不符点并且不能修改，但单据金额不大，不符点性质并不十分严重，如数量略微低于允许装运的数量，被指定银行采用表提不符点的方式，连同单据一块寄往开证行，由开证行决定是否付款。

④被指定银行寄单索偿。被指定银行将单据寄往保兑行（如有的话）、开证行索偿。如果是保兑信用证，被指定银行一般选择向保兑行寄单索偿。保兑行在收到单据后的最多不超过5个银行工作日的独立审单时间内，如判定交单相符，无追索权地向被指定银行承付或议付。要注意的是，保兑行的议付是不享有追索权的。然后，保兑行向开证行寄单索偿。对开证行来说，若判定交单相符或与被指定银行的"电提不符点"一致，无追索权地承付保兑银行或被指定银行；若判定交单不符或与被指定银行的"电提不符点"不一致，开证行可以拒绝承付，也可以自行决定联系申请人放弃不符点。如果开证行决定拒付，开证行必须发出拒付通知（按照UCP600第16条的规定）。拒付通知应以电讯方式发出。若不可能，则以其他快捷方式，在不迟于自交单日之次日起第五个银行工作日结束前发出。拒付通知的内容，必须申明银行拒绝承付，表明拒绝承付所依据的每一个不符点以及单据的处理方式。

⑤开证行通知申请人付款赎单。开证行承付后，通知申请人付款赎单。申请人独立审单，若交单相符，向开证行付款赎单；若交单不符，申请人自行决定付款或拒付。若申请人付款，申请人与开证行之间因开立信用证所构成的权利和义务关系告终。

⑥申请人付款提货。申请人付款取得单据后，凭运输单据向承运人提货。如发现货物不符，只能向受益人、承运人或保险公司等有关负责方索赔。

### （四）银行保函

银行保函（letter of guarantee，L/G），是指银行应委托人的申请向受益人开立的一种书面凭证，保证申请人按规定履行合同，否则由银行负责偿付款项。银行保函在实践中应用较为广泛，在进出口业务中，有时因交货时间较长，或交货条件比较复杂，难以用信用证进行结算，而且当事人的一方对于另一方所做出履行合同的承诺又感到不够安全，这时，便可要求对方提供银行保函，使货款的收付得到更确切的保障。

### （五）备用信用证

备用信用证（standby L/C），是指开证行根据申请人的请求对受益人开立的承诺承担某项义务的凭证。备用信用证属于银行信用，开证行保证在开证申请人未履行其义务时，即由开证行付款。备用信用证与跟单信用证的区别在于：①跟单信用证下，受益人只要履行信用证所规定的条件，即可要求开证行付款；备用信用证下，受益人只有在开证申请人未履行义务时，才能行使信用证规定的权利，备用信用证往往备而不用。②跟单信用证一般只适用于货物的买卖；备用信用证可适用于货物以外的多方面的交易。③跟单信用证一般以符合信用证规定的单据为付款依据；备用信用证一般凭受益人出具的说明开证申请人未履约的证明，让开证行保证付款。

### （六）不同结算方式的结合使用

#### 1. 信用证与汇付结合

在一笔交易中，部分货款用信用证方式支付，部分货款采用汇付方式结算。信用证结算方式是"先装运、后收款"，而汇付可以"预付"或"到付"。对于处于卖方市场的商品，在卖方不能争取到货款100%预付的情况下，可争取采用"预付+信用证"的收款方式；对于允许交货数量有一定机动幅度的某些初级产品买卖，或进口国家规定必须经其法定检验机构检验合格后才允许进口的货物，经买卖双方同意，采用"信用证+到付"的方式，如"货款的70%采用信用证付款，余款30%到付"，卖方在装运货物后，先凭信用证收取70%的款项，货物到达目的地（港）后检验合格后，用汇付方式支付30%。因此，使用这种结合形式，必须订明采用何种信用证、信用证支付的比例、汇付方式、汇付金额的比例和汇付的时间。

#### 2. 信用证与托收结合

在一笔交易中，部分货款采用信用证方式支付，余额采用托收方式结算。信用证和托收都是"先装运、后收款"的方式。因此，这种结合方式的通常做法是：卖方在装运货物后开立两张汇票，属于信用证项下的部分货款凭光票支付，而其余额则采用跟单汇票，即将运输单据随附在托收的汇票项下，按即期或远期付款交单方式托收。这种做法，卖方收汇较为安全，而买方可减少资金占用，提高资金的使用效率，因而易被买卖双方所接受。但是，在合同条款中，必须订明信用证的种类、信用证的支付金额、托收的交单方式、单据的处理等。

#### 3. 汇付与银行保函结合

汇付与银行保函结合使用，常用于成套设备、大型机械和大型交通运输工具如飞机、船舶等的货款结算。这类产品，交易金额大，生产周期长，往往要求买方以汇付方式预付部分货款或定金，其余大部分货款则由买方以开立银行保函的方式分期付款或延迟付款。

### 4. 汇付、托收与信用证结合

汇付、托收和信用证结合的方式一般用于成套设备的进出口。在成套设备买卖中，由于成交的金额较大，产品生产周期较长，无法一次付清所有的货款，故必须采取分期付款的方式或延期付款的方式。例如，在分期付款方式下，买卖双方首先订立合同条款，规定买方在产品投产前，先采用汇付方式，交纳合同金额的20%作为定金，其余货款按不同阶段分期支付。在分期阶段，买方开立信用证，支付每一笔分期应付的款项，信用证支付的总金额为70%。在交付使用时，买方开立银行保函给卖方，银行保函的金额为成交价的10%，买方向卖方承诺，在卖方承担质量保证期届满时，买方必须将最后一笔货款（10%）付清。

## 思考题

1. 如买卖双方约定"货物从上海运往香港，海运，付款方式为装运30天后电汇付款"，从上海到香港的海运时间一般是3天，请问：卖方收汇是否有风险？
2. 如买卖双方约定"货物从上海运往巴西，海运，付款方式为D/A 45天"，请问：卖方和买方存在怎样的风险？
3. 如买卖双方约定采用信用证方式付款，请问：买卖双方方应具备的信用证业务操作技能有哪些？
4. 试问在国际工程承包业务或国际货物买卖中如何运用银行保函或备用信用证？
5. 跨境电商中通常采用的付款方式分别类似于汇款中的哪种付款方式？

# Chapter 6

# Term of Payment

☞ Case 6.1

An export enterprise in Zhejiang province, China had concluded several small transactions with a Chinese-American businessman. The payment mode was cash in advance and the transaction was very smooth. Later, the customer said that the market had been opened and the quantity had increased, but the capital turnover was rather tight, so he asked the export enterprise to accept mode of payment as "D/P AT SIGHT. The export enterprise considered that under the "D/P at sight", the buyer could only get the documents by paying for the redemption. If the buyer refused to pay for the redemption, the ownership of the goods was still in the hands of the seller, so it accepted the buyer's request and shipped 1×40'FCL goods.After loading the goods, the buyer delayed payment on the pretext of lack of funds. Charges were incurred ten days after the arrival of the goods at the port of destination. The buyer requested to change the payment terms from "D/P at sight" to "D/A 30 days", otherwise the goods would be rejected.Considering that the variety and design of this batch of goods were customized for the customer. The goods were  transferred back to stock. The seller was forced to agree to the buyer's requirements. While, the export enterprise had never heard from the buyer after he picked up the goods against D/A. Therefore, we can learn a lesson from this case: In the buyer's market, mode of payment is changed to be more and more benefit for the buyer, the seller should never accept credit sales without understand the customer's credit enough, should not accept mode of payment with high-risk such as D/A or O/A (Open Account), unless can do enough to prevent the risk. If the buyer proposed to change mode of payment in the process of the transaction, the seller has reason to believe that the buyer is poor of credit. The seller should not accept the high-risk payment method for the products customized by the customer.

Payment is the most difficulty of business negotiation as both parties wish to obtain more security on payment of the goods. International trade presents a spectrum of risk, causing uncertainty over the timing of payments between the seller and the buyer. To the seller, the most secure and best method of payment is payment in advance or obtain payment guarantee of bank in order to realize receiving proceeds of sales in safety, speedy and timely. To the buyer, it's best to make payment after receipt of the goods or obtain the document title to the goods. The parties pay more attention on terms of payment and strive for beneficial conditions during business negotiation and contract signed.

Payment is very complicated as it is concerning to the banking institutions of both parties and/or third party's country, constrained by laws and regulations for foreign exchange, financial control rules and various common international practices and rules, as well as be influenced by international economics, trade, finance and currency, etc. Credit basis is very important on payment negotiation including commercial standing, bank standing and state standing. Based on this, the parties begin to discuss where/when/what/how to pay, such as mode of payment, payment tenor, payment place, payment currency and credit instrument. The terms of payment concluded have impact on the parties' turnover of capital, accommodation of funds, risks and expenses directly.

# 6.1 Negotiable Instruments

Proceeds can be settled by cash or non-cash. Payment in cash is limited to be used for buy sample, down payment and small amount of compensation, etc. Non-cash payment is widely used in international trade. To succeed in today's global marketplace, the seller must offer their customers attractive sales terms supported by the appropriate payment method to win sales against foreign competitors. The seller has to provide credit transaction to the buyers in order to keep or increase market shares. Negotiable bill is the credit instrument for settlement of debtor-creditor relationship between the seller and the buyer from cash to non-cash payment. It is the most important credit instrument in international trade and can transfer business standing relationship of the parties into debtor-creditor relationship of the bill. It include bills of exchange, promissory notes and checks·

## 6.1.1 Bill of Exchange

### 1. Definition

A bill of exchange is a unconditional order of writing , addressed by one person to another, signed by the person give it, requiring the person to whom it is addressed to pay on demand or at a fixed or determinable future time a sum certain in money  to or to the order of a specified person or to bearer. According to article 19 of Negotiable Instruments Law of the People's Republic of China adopted at the 13th Session of the Standing Committee of the Eighth National People's Congress on May 10th, 1995 and Revised at the 11th Session of the Standing Committee of the 10th National People's Congress of the People's Republic of China on August 28th, 2004, a draft is a bill signed by the drawer, requiring the entrusted payer to make unconditional payment in a fixed amount at the sight of the bill or on a fixed date to the payee or the holder·

### 2. Essentials of a Draft

The essentials of a draft include absolute necessary items, relative necessary items and random items. A draft must bear absolutely necessary items completely; lacking one of the absolutely necessary items is invalid. Although the relative necessary items are also very important, lacking one of them has no impact on the effectiveness of a draft. The random items are not important, whatever stated or none stated, are not influenced on the effectiveness of a draft.

(1) Absolute Necessary Items

In international trade, a valid draft is measured by the relating negotiable instruments law of issuing place. It should be noticed that the stipulating of absolute necessary items has some difference between negotiable instruments laws under civil law system and common law system. Generally, the stipulating under civil law system is relatively strict, whereas under common law is relatively flexible. A valid draft under civil law system must be equipped with seven absolute necessary items.

① Indicating "draft" so as to be known from promissory note or check. While, the British Negotiable Instruments Law hasn't this requirement.

② Unconditional written order for payment. Payment must be neither under restrictions, nor attach conditions.

③ A sum certain in money including determinate or may determinate amount of value. If the draft is stated payment terms of interest, the payment terms of interest must be indicated completely with definite interest rate and interest accrual period of the beginning and the end.

④ The drawer's name and signature. In drafting negotiable instruments, a drawer shall put his/her signature or seal to the instruments according to the legal conditions and bear the liabilities for the negotiable instruments in compliance with the items recorded on them. If the signature or seal is forged or unauthorized, the draft is invalid.

⑤ Name of the drawee. The drawee may be the payer of the draft. He/she acts as an acceptor and becomes the primary debtor if he/she accepted a usance draft. He/she acts as the payer if he/she made payment to a sight draft or an accepted draft.

⑥ Payee. He/she is primary creditor of the bill and must be indicated properly.

⑦ Date of issue. It must be stated on the draft so as to confirm legal capacity of drawer, to determine due date for payment, presentation, acceptance and the beginning date of interest calculating, etc. Article 22 of Negotiable Instruments Law of China stipulates: a draft shall bear the following items: Chinese characters denoting "draft", commission on unconditional payment, the amount of money fixed, name of the payer, name of the payee, date of draft and signature of the drawer. So, the stipulating of absolutely necessary items of Negotiable Instruments Law under China and civil law system are almost the same.

(2) The Relative Necessary Items

The relative necessary items of a draft include date of payment (tenor), place of payment and place of issue. The date of payment, place of payment and place of drawing recorded on the draft shall be clear and definite. If a draft does not bear the date of payment, it is a draft payable at sight. The place of draft is normally shown on the upper right of a draft and connected with the date of issue. If a draft does not bear the place of payment, the place of payment shall be the business site or the residence of the payer or the place where the payer often lives. If a draft does not bear the place of draft, the place of draft shall be taken as the business site or residence of the drawer or the place where the drawer often lives.

## ☞ Case 6.2

The date of payment may be recorded by one of the following forms: (a) Pay at sight/on demand. (b) Pay at a future determinable date. If the goods shipped on July 20, 2018, the draft drawn on July 25, 2018 and payment period was 30 days, the payment date of the draft can ne indicated as: (b1) Payment made 30 days after shipment (shipment date: July 20, 2018). (b2) Payment made 30 days after date hereof (The issuing date of draft). (b3) Payment made 30 days after sight. (b4) Payment made on Aug 19, 2018. This method was same as "payment made 30 days after shipment".

(3) The Random Items

The items other than absolute and relative necessary items are called as the random items, such as serial number, drawing clause, non transferable, protest or notice of dishonor waived, pay the first exchange/second being unpaid, pay the second exchange/first being unpaid, terms of interest accrual, may be recorded on a draft, but such items do not have the draft effect.

**3. Classification of a Draft**

There are many methods to classify a bill of exchange.

① As per difference of the drawers, a draft can be a bank draft or commercial drafts. The drawer and drawee of a bank draft are both banks. The drawer of a commercial bank must be a firm, a commercial firm or a person; the drawee may be a firm, a person or a bank.

②As per difference of the drafts attached commercial documents or not, a draft can be a documentary bill or clean bill. A documentary bill must be attached the commercial documents, such as commercial invoice, packing list, bill of lading, depot bill, insurance policy. A clean bill isn't attached any commercial documents. A commercial bill is normally the documentary bill.

③As per the date of payment, a draft can be a sight bill (demand bill) or usance bill. The drawee of the sight bill (demand bill) shall pay promptly (pay at sight) when the holder presents the draft to him/her. The drawee of the usance bill (time bill) shall accept the bill on first presentation and make payment on due on second presentation.

④As per difference of the acceptors, a time bill can be a commercial accepted bill or a bank accepted bill. A commercial accepted bill posses double business standings of the drawer and the acceptor. A bank accepted bill posses the drawer's business standing and the acceptor's bank standing. Generally, the holder would like more to own a bank accepted bill than a commercial accepted bill as it is easier to be transferred in the financial market. The drawer is the principal debtor of usance commercial draft before it is accepted. While, after it was accepted, the acceptor becomes the principal debtor instead of the drawer. The drawer is the second debtor of the bill after it was accepted.

⑤As per the methods of the payee stated, a draft can be a restrictive bill, indicative bill or bearer bill. The restrictive bill cannot be transferred as per the negotiable instrument laws. The payee on a restrictive bill is normally indicated as "Pay to xx Co only" or "Pay to xx Co., not transferable". The indicative bill can be transferred through endorsement and is used most widely. It is generally indicated as "Pay to the order of xx Co" or "Pay to xx Co or order. The bearer bill is indicated as "Pay to xx Co or bearer"or "Pay to bearer" and can be transferred without endorsement.

### 4. The Acts and Parties of a Draft

Acts of negotiable instruments shall be in conformity with the relating negotiable instrument laws, and shall not in any way infringe upon the public interests. Throughout a draft life cycle, it may go through drawing, endorsement, discounting, presentation, acceptance, guarantee and payment (see Figure 6.1). In addition, if the draft is dishonored, protest or recourse may be concerned.

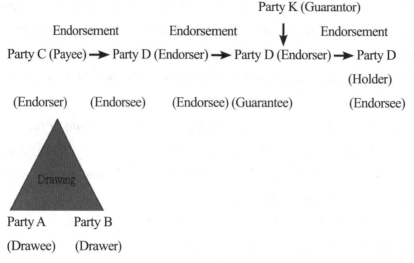

Figure 6.1 The Acts and Parties of a Draft

(1) Drawing

The drawing of a draft refers to the act of a drawer to sign and deliver the draft to the payee. The drawer of a draft shall have real authorized payment relations with the payees and have reliable sources of fund to pay the draft amount. It is forbidden to sign drafts without corresponding prices for the purpose of acquiring funds from banks or other parties to the negotiable instrument by deception. After signing the draft, the drawer shall bear the responsibility of ensuring the acceptance and payment of the draft. If a drawer has failed to get the draft accepted or paid, the drawer shall undertake to pay the amount and expenses to the holder who applies for recourse as per the credit instruments law. The holder of a draft may transfer the rights associated with the draft or authorize others to exercise some of the rights. If the drawer writes the meaning "Not Transferable" on a draft, the draft shall not be transferred. In exercising the rights provided for in the above mentioned the holder shall endorse it and deliver the draft.

(2) Endorsement

Endorsement refers to the recording of items concerned on the backside of a draft or on the allonge to the draft with a signature or seal. If a draft is endorsed over to another person entirely or in part, the draft shall bear the name of the endorser. The endorsement which transfers part or the entire amount on the draft to two or more persons is invalid. An endorsement shall not have conditions attached. If an endorsement has conditions attached, the conditions do not have the effect on the draft. If an endorsement bears the word "Collection", the endorsee has the right to exercise the rights to the draft commissioned on behalf of the endorser, but the endorsee shall not re-endorse over a draft to others. A draft may be mortgaged. In mortgaging a draft, the word "Hypothecation" shall be written in the form of endorsement. When having acquired the hypothecation according to law, the endorsee may exercise the rights to the draft.

After an endorser has endorsed over a draft to others, the endorser shall be liable to ensure the draft in the hands of the subsequent holder are accepted or paid. In endorsing a draft to others, the subsequent endorser shall be responsible for the authenticity of the endorsement by the immediate prior endorser. The subsequent endorser refers to the other debtors involved in the draft signed after the signer of the draft. If an endorser cannot get the draft accepted or paid, the endorser shall undertake to claim payment in the amount of the draft plus expenses from the holder same as the drawer.

A draft shall not be endorsed over to others when it has been refused to pay or accepted or the time of payment as indicated is overdue. If such a draft is endorsed over to others, the endorser shall bear the liability of the draft. If an endorser writes the words "Not Transferable" on a draft and the draft is transferred by the subsequent endorser, the original endorser shall not bear the liability of guarantee to the subsequent endorsee. If a draft has not enough space to satisfy the needs of writing, an allonge may be attached. The first person who writes on the allonge shall put his/her signature or seal to the sticking line of the allonge. An endorsement shall be signed by the endorser, with the date of endorsement.

An endorsement without date shall be regarded as an endorsement before the due date. In endorsing over a draft to others, the endorsement shall be in uninterrupted series. The holder shall prove the rights associated with the draft by an uninterrupted series of endorsement. The term "uninterrupted series" used in the preceding paragraph refers to the sequential consistency in the signatures or seals by the endorser and the endorsee in the transfer of negotiable instruments. If a draft is not endorsed over to another person, the holder shall put to the proof the right on the draft according to law.

(3) Discounting

The holder of a usance draft may acquire the amount of draft before due date through discounting. Discounting refers to the holder sell an accepted draft to others such as banks, discounting house or financial institutions before due date at a price less than its determined amount value.

(4) Presentation

Presentation is the premise of acceptance or payment of a draft. A draft must be duly presented for payment if it is a sight bill or duly presented for acceptance first and then presented for payment at maturity if it is a usance bill. A draft payable at sight need not be presented for acceptance. A holder of a draft shall make presentation for payment or acceptance according to the time limits stipulated in the relating negotiable instruments laws.

As per the negotiable instruments law of China, the presentation for payment of a draft payable at sight or for acceptance of a draft payable on a fixed future determinable date, shall be made to the payer within one month starting from the date of draft. Presentation for payment of a draft payable on a fixed future determinable date shall be made to the acceptor within 10 days starting from the due date. If a holder has failed to make presentation for acceptance according to the prescribed time limit, that holder shall lose the right of recourse against the prior holder. If the presentation for payment is made through banks entrusted with collection or through negotiable instruments exchange system, it shall be regarded as presentation for payment made by the holder. A payer shall accept or refuse to accept a draft presented for acceptance within time limit after receiving the draft. The Negotiable Instruments Law of China stipulates that the payer shall decide within three days.

In accepting a draft, the payer shall write "Accepted" across the face of the draft and the date of acceptance and fix the seal. For a draft payable on a fixed date after sight, the date of payment shall be recorded in acceptance. If no date of acceptance is recorded on a draft, the last day of the time limit prescribed in the first paragraph of the preceding article shall be taken as the date of acceptance. There shall be no conditions attached in accepting a draft. If there are conditions attached in acceptance, it shall be regarded as refusal of acceptance.

After receiving the draft for which presentation for acceptance is made, the payer may keep the accepted bill or return the accepted draft to the presenter. If the payer selects to keep the draft, he shall sign an acknowledgment for receiving the draft. The acknowledgment shall specify the date of the presentation for acceptance and shall be signed. After accepting a draft, the payer shall be liable to pay when the draft is due.

(5) Guarantee

A guarantor shall be some person other than the debtor of the draft and undertake the liabilities of guaranty for the debt involved in the draft. He shall record the following items on the draft or allonge: the word "Guarantee", name and residence of the guarantor, name of the guaranteed party, date of guaranty, signature or seal of the guarantor. If he has failed to record the name of the guaranteed party on the draft or allonge, the acceptor shall be the guaranteed party of the accepted draft, and the drawer shall be the guaranteed party for the draft not accepted. If he has failed to record date of guaranty, the date of draft shall be the date of guaranty. A guarantor shall guarantee that there are no conditions attached. If conditions have been attached, they shall not affect the liability of guaranty for the draft.

Further, a guarantor shall undertake the liability of guaranty for the right to the draft enjoyed by the holder who has acquired the draft according to law, except cases when the debt guaranteed has become invalid due to inadequate recording in the draft. He shall undertake several liabilities together with the guaranteed for the draft under guarantee. If the draft is not getting paid on due, the holder has the right to demand the guarantor for payment and the guarantor shall pay the full amount.

If there are two or more guarantors, the guarantors shall undertake a joint and several liabilities. After the draft debt is cleared, the guarantor may exercise the right of recourse of the holder against the guaranteed and the prior holder.

(6) Payment

If a holder presents for payment according to the provisions of the relating credit instruments law, the payer shall pay in the full amount of the draft on the same day. In making payments, the payer or its entrusted payer shall examine the consistency of the endorsement and check the legal identification or valid documents of the person who makes presentation for payment. If a holder has got the payment, the holder shall sign the draft and hand the draft to the payer.

If a holder has entrusted a bank for the collection, the bank entrusted shall enter into the account of the holder the amount of the draft collected and that shall be regarded as signed and accepted. The liabilities of a bank entrusted with collection by the holder are confined to transferring of the amount of the draft into the account of the holder according to the recordings on the draft.

If a payer or its entrusted payer makes the payment out of malicious motives or out of major blunder, the payer or its entrusted payer shall bear the liabilities on their own. If a payer makes the payment before the due date for draft payable on a fixed date or on a fixed date after the date of draft or on a fixed date after sight, the payer shall bear the responsibilities arising there from on his own.

If the parties to a draft have agreements concerning the currencies for payment, the provisions of the agreement shall apply. After the payer has paid the draft amount in full, the liabilities of all debts shall be relieved.

(7) Dishonor

Upon a refusal of payment to a draft, the holder may exercise the right of recourse against the endorser, drawer or other debtors of the draft. The holder may also exercise the right of recourse before the due day of a draft in one of the following cases: the acceptance of a draft is refused, or the acceptor or payer has died or fled, or is living in hiding, or the acceptor or payer has been declared bankrupt according to law or whose business operations have been suspended due to violations of the law.

In exercising the right of recourse, the holder shall provide the certificates relating to the refusal of acceptance or dishonor. In refusing the presentation for acceptance or for payment by the holder, the acceptor or payer shall produce certificates of dishonor or the statement on the ground for protest. If the acceptor or payer has failed to produce the certificate of dishonor or the statement on the ground for protest, the acceptor or payer shall bear all the civil responsibilities arising there from.

If no certificate of dishonor can be obtained due to the death, flee or hiding of the acceptor or payer or other reasons, other related certificates may be obtained according to law. If an acceptor or a payer has been declared bankrupt according to law, the related judicial documents of the court have the effect of certifying the dishonor. If an acceptor or a payer whose business operations have been suspended due to law violations, the related decisions on punishment by related administrative department in charge have the effect of certifying the dishonor.

If a holder is unable to present certificates of dishonor, the statement on the ground for protest or provide other legal certificates within the prescribed time limit, the holder shall lose the right of recourse against the prior holder.

However, the acceptor or payer shall continue to undertake the liabilities to the holder. A holder shall within time limit starting from the date of receiving the certificates relating to refusal of acceptance or dishonor, notify in writing the prior holder of the dishonor. The prior holder shall within time limit of receiving the notice, notify in writing the still preceding prior holder of the dishonor. The holder may also issue written notices to all the debtors of the draft all the same time.

As per the Negotiable Instruments Law of China, the time limit for notify in writing shall be within three days. The holder may continue to exercise the right of recourse even if notification is not made within the time limit prescribed in the preceding paragraph. If the holder has delayed the notification to the prior holder or drawer and caused losses thereby, the parties that have failed to make the notification within the prescribed time limit shall be liable to compensate for the losses, with the amount of compensation being the draft amount.

If the notice has been sent out according to the legal address or the addresses agreed upon within the prescribed time limit, the notification is regarded as having been issued. The written notice served according to the provisions of the first paragraph of the preceding article shall contain the main recordings of the draft and clearly indicates that the draft has been dishonored.

The drawer, endorser, acceptor and guarantor shall bear a joint and several liabilities with regard to the holder. A holder may exercise the right of recourse against one person or several persons or all the draft debtors in disregard of the sequential order of the debtors. After a holder has exercised the right of recourse against one person or several persons involving in the draft, the holder may also exercise the right of recourse over others involved in the draft. The person against whom the right of recourse has been exercised will enjoy the same right as the holder after the debt has been cleared. In the case in which the holder is the drawer, the holder has no right of recourse to the prior holder. In the case in which the holder is the endorser, the holder has no right of recourse against the subsequent holders.

In exercising the right of recourse, the holder may request the person subject to recourse to pay the following money and expenses: the amount of the draft dishonored, the interests calculated according to the rate fixed on the draft amount from the due date or the date of presentation for payment to the date of liquidation, the expenses incurred in obtaining the related certificates of dishonor and the issuing of notification.

When the person subject to recourse is clearing his debt, the holder shall deliver the draft and related certificates of dishonor and produce the receipts for the interests and expenses received. After debt clearance according to the provisions of the preceding article, the person against whom the right of recourse has been exercised may exercise the right of re-recourse against other draft debtors and request other debtors to pay the following amount and expenses: the complete amount cleared, the interests on the amount cleared , calculated according to the rate fixed on the draft from the date of liquidation to the date of liquidation for re-recourse and expenses on issuing notifications. When the person who exercises the right of re-recourse is getting paid, that person shall deliver the draft and the related certificates of dishonor and produce the receipts for the interests and expenses received.

## 6.1.2 Promissory Note

### 1. Definition

A promissory note is a an unconditional promise in writing made by one person to another signed by the maker engaging to pay on demand or a fixed or determinable future time a sum certain in money to or to the order of a specified person or to bearer. Article 73 of the negotiable instruments law of China stipulates: "A promissory note is an instrument written and issued by a drawer, promising to pay unconditionally a fixed amount of money to a payee or holder at the sight of the instrument. A promissory note may be a bank note or a commercial note. While, the term "promissory note" used in the negotiable instruments law of China refers to the bank note.

### 2. Essentials of a Promissory Note

A promissory note shall record the following items: "Promissory Note" indicated, unconditional promise to pay, amount of money fixed, name of the payee, date of issue and signature of the drawer. A promissory note is invalid if one of the above items is missing. The place of payment, the place of issue and other items recorded on the promissory note shall be clear and definite. If the instrument does not bear the place of payment, the business site of the issuer shall be taken as the place of payment. If the instrument does not bear the place of issue, the business site of the issuer shall be taken as the place of issue. If a promissory note does not bear the date of payment, it is payable at sight.

While, the negotiable instruments law of China stipulates "The maximum time limit of payment shall not exceed two months starting from the date of issue". When the holder of a promissory note presents the instrument, the drawer shall be liable to pay. If a holder has failed to present the instrument within the date of payment, the holder shall lose the right of recourse against the prior holders other than the drawer. The acts of a promissory note include drawing, endorsement, guaranty, payment and the exercise of the right of recourse, except for acceptance.

### 6.1.3 Check

#### 1. Definition

In briefly speaking, a check is a bill of exchange drawn on a bank payable on demand. In details speaking, a check is an unconditional order in writing addressed by the customer to a bank signed by that customer authorizing the bank to pay on demand a sum certain in money or to the order of a specified person or to bearer. Article 81 of the Negotiable Instruments Law of China stipulates " A check is an instrument issued by a drawer, at the sight of which the check deposit bank or other financial institutions unconditionally pay the fixed amount to the payee or holder."

#### 2. Essentials

A check must record the following items: "Check" denoted commission to pay unconditionally, amount fixed, name of the payee, date of drawing, signature of the drawer. A check shall be invalid if one of the above items is missing. The amount on a check may be filled in afterwards by the holder with the authorization of the drawer. The check with the amount not filled in shall not be used. If a check does not bear the name of the payee, it may be recorded afterwards with the authorization of the drawer. If a check does not bear the place of payment, the business site of the payer shall be taken as the place of payment. If a check does not bear the place of issue, the business site, residence of the drawer or the place where the drawer often lives shall be taken as the place of issue.

The amount of the check issued by the drawer shall not exceed the actual amount deposited by the payer at the time of payment. If the amount of the check issued by the drawer has exceeded the actual amount deposited by the payer at the time of payment, the check is a dishonorable check, which is strictly forbidden. The drawer shall not issue a check with the signature or seal that does not tally that submitted for counter-checking. A drawer shall undertake the liabilities to ensure the payment to the holder according to the amount of the check issued. If the deposit of the drawer at the place of payee is enough to pay the full amount of the check, the payer shall pay the full amount on the day.

### 3. Key Points for Using a Check

A check is payable at sight. The holder of a check shall make presentation for payment within time limit. For example, the relating laws of China stipulate "ten days starting from the date of draft". In the case when the time limit on the presentation for payment expires, the payer may refuse to pay. In the case when the payer refuses to pay, the drawer shall still bear the responsibility on the instrument to the holder. If a payer has paid the amount of a check, the payer shall no longer bear the liability for payment to the drawer and shall not bear the liability for payment to the holder, except the cases when payment is made out of ulterior motives or due to major blunder. A check can be endorsement, payment and with the exercise of the right of recourse. In opening a check deposit account and using checks, an applicant shall use the true name and present the legal document that certifies his/her identification, leave samples of the signature or seal in the true name of the applicant and there must be a reliable credit ability and a certain amount of money deposited in the bank. A check can be cashed or transferred into other accounts. For account transfer, a clear indication shall be made across the face of the check. If a check is used especially for cashing, the cash check can be made separately. A cash check can only be used for cashing. A transfer check can only be used in account transfer and cashing is not allowed.

# 6.2 Methods of Payment

Mode of payment refers to the channel of proceeds paid and received, including remittance, collection, documentary credit, letter of guarantee and standby credit, etc. Remittance, collection and documentary credit are three kinds of main and traditional modes of payment, the ratio of letter of guarantee and standby credit used are increasing gradually.

## 6.2.1 Remittance

Remittance means that the buyer remits money to the seller through a bank on his own initiative. Normally, four parties are involved in remittance including remitter, payee, remitting bank and paying bank. The remitter and the payee are generally the both parties of international trade, the remitter is the buyer and the payee is the seller. The remitting bank is the bank who accepts a commission from the remitter to remit a sum certain money to the nominated payee. The paying bank is usually located at the place of payee and accepts a commission from the remitting bank to pay the sum certain money to the nominated payee. A certain contractual relationship is existed between the paying bank and the remitting bank, such as sister banks and correspondent banks.

The Remitter shall fill application form for outward remittance and give it to the remitting bank together with the full funding of remitting money. The remitting bank shall make a payment order according to the application form for outward remittance issued by the remitter, send it to the paying bank through a certain method of communication and indicate the paying bank how to get the remitting money. Then, the paying bank pays the relating money to the nominated payee. The remitting bank or the paying bank is not responsible for any lost or delay of the remittance caused by faults out of his own negligence. Furthermore, the faults caused by the paying bank are also not for account of the remitting bank.

Remittance can be divided into T/T (telegraphic transfer), M/T (mail transfer) and D/D (Banker's Demand Draft). If T/T is applied, the remitting bank sends the payment order to the paying bank by telecommunications, such as swift, telex or cable, whereas M/T applied is by registered airmails. On the contrast, the paying bank receives the payment order under T/T is much faster than by M/T and the payee gets the funds more quickly. An international wire transfer is commonly used and has the advantage of being almost immediate. The sellers should provide clear routing instructions to the buyer when using this method, including the name and address of the receiving bank, the bank's SWIFT, Telex, and ABA (American Bankers Association) numbers, and the seller's name and address, bank account title, and account number. This option is more costly to the buyer than other options of CIA method, as the fee for an international wire transfer is usually paid by the sender. SWIFT is most popular and safety between banks communication. "One day global remittance" can be reached by many international banks. M/T is less used presently. D/D refers to the remitter purchases a banker's demand draft from the remitting bank and sends it to the payee for payment. The payee presents the draft to the paying bank and gets the draft value. D/D is less convenient than T/T.

Remittance is fallen into business firm standing. It depends on the adverse party's business firm standing if the seller can get payment or the buyer can get the goods of delivery safety. Among of all modes of payment, remittance is the basic and most flexible, convenient one. It can be used as Cash in advance (CIA) and open account (O/A).

The buyer bears more risks than the seller if cash in advance is applied, whereas on the opposite if open account is applied. If business firm standing of the adverse party is lacking or not good enough, the losses of goods and money together may be occurred. Meanwhile, remittance is easy to cause imbalance of funds obligation. The buyer shall provide part or full of the funds for the business and bear almost all the relating risks under cash in advance. On the contrary, the seller shall provide part or full of the funds for the business and bear almost all the relating risks under open account.

When CIA is applied, the seller can avoid credit risk or the risk of nonpayment, since payment is received prior to the transfer of owner¬ship of the goods. Wire transfers and credit cards are available for the seller for CIA options. However, requiring payment in advance is the least attractive option for the buyer, as this method creates cash flow problems. The foreign buyers are also concerned that the goods may not be sent if pay¬ment is made in advance. Thus, if the seller insists on CIA, he may lose out business as his competitors may be willing to offer more attractive payment terms.

An open account transaction means that the goods are shipped and delivered before payment is due, usually in 30 to 90 days. Obviously, this is the most advantageous option to the buyer in cash flow and cost terms, but it is consequently the highest risk option for the seller. Because of the intense competition of export markets, the foreign buyers often press the sellers to accept open account terms. In addition, the extension of credit by the seller to the buyer is more common abroad. Therefore, the sellers who are reluctant to extend credit may face the possibility of the loss of the sale to their competitors. However, while this method of payment will definitely enhance export competitiveness, the sellers should examine the political, economic, and commercial risks, as well as cultural influences to ensure the proceeds will be received in full and on time. It is possible to substantially mitigate the risk of nonpayment associated with open account trade by using export credit insurance and factoring. Sellers may also wish to seek export working capital financing to ensure that they have access to financing for export and for any credit while waiting to be paid.

The key points for CIA used as following at the seller's side.

① Full or significant partial payment is required, usually via credit card or bank/wire transfer, prior to the transfer of ownership of the goods.

② CIA, especially a wire transfer, is the most secure and favorable method of international trading for seller and, consequently, the least secure and attractive option for buyers. However, both the credit risk and the competitive landscape must be considered.

③ Insisting on these terms ultimately could cause sellers to lose customers to competitors who are willing offer more favorable payment terms to the buyers in the global market.

④ The creditworthy foreign buyers, who prefer greater security and better cash utilization, may find CIA terms unacceptable and may simply walk away from the deal.

⑤ The sellers may select credit cards as a viable method of CIA payment, especially for consumer goods or small transactions. The sellers should check with their credit card company(s) for specific rules on international use of credit cards. As international credit card transactions are typically placed via online, telephone, or fax methods that facilitate fraudulent transactions, proper precautions should be taken to determine the validity of transactions before the goods are shipped. Although the sellers must endure the fees charged by credit card companies, this option may help the business grow because of its convenience.

⑥The sellers may also select checks as a method of CIA payment. While, an international check may result in a lengthy collection delay of several weeks to months. Therefore, this method may defeat the original intention of receiving payment before shipment. If the check is in a foreign currency or drawn on a foreign bank, the collection process is likely to become more complicated and can significantly delay the availability of funds. Moreover, there is always a risk that a check may be returned due to insufficient funds in the buyer's account.

The key points for Open Account (O/A) used as following at the seller's side.

①The goods, along with all the necessary documents, are shipped directly to the buyer who agrees to pay the seller's invoice at a future date, usually in 30 to 90 days.

②The seller should be absolutely confident that the buyer will accept shipment and pay at agreed time and that the importing country is commercially and politically secure.

③Open account terms may help win customers in competitive markets, if used with one or more of the appropriate trade finance techniques that mitigate the risk of nonpayment.

④Open account terms may be offered in competitive markets with the use of one or more of following trade finance techniques: export working capital financing, government-guaranteed export working capital programs, export credit insurance, export factoring and forfaiting.

As for the above features of remittance and the key points of CIA and O/A payment, the remittance clauses in a sales contract normally include method of remittance, time of payment, how to link up the goods, documents and money, risks allocation, etc. It is suggested that the relating remittance clauses is stipulated further combine with mode of transportation, characteristics of the goods, etc.

The following examples cited are with shipment made by waterway transportation, remittance clauses may be adopted.

①Cash with order. 100% payment made by T/T within 7 days after contract signed.

②100% payment made by wire transfer at least 10 days before shipment. Shipment made on/before Sept 08, 2018.

③10% of price value by payment in advance by T/t, 90% of amount shall be paid within 18 months in installment after shipment.

④30% payment made by SWIFT 10 days before shipment, the balance shall be made within 15 days after shipment. Full set of shipping documents will be released to the buyer on the basis of 100% payment. Shipment made by sea freight on/before Sept 08, 2018.

⑤The Supplier agrees that the Buyer will effect payments under the term of T/T within 30 days against receipt of the original B/Ls.

⑥10% of price value is made as advance payment by T/T 15 days before shipment, 90% of amount shall be paid within 18 months by equal monthly installment after shipment.

Transport documents except for bill of lading, such as airway bill, railway bill and ocean bill, are not title to the goods. If the seller need to control the ownership of the goods before get payment and the payment term is remittance, the following examples cited are with shipment made by non-waterway transportation, remittance clauses may be adopted.

①The seller agrees that the Buyer will effect payments under the term of CAD (Cash against

documents). The seller shall deliver the contractual goods to the

warehouse_____ (Name) located at_____ (place) on/before Sept 08, 2018 and get

Payment at _____ (Bank name) located at_____ (place) against the following original

Documents: commercial invoice, packing lists, warehouse receipt, etc.

②Cash on Delivery(COD). Shipment made by airfreight on/before Sept 08, 2018. 100%

Payment shall be made by the buyer within 3 working days on receipt of the notification of arrival to the account of the seller's nominated forwarding agent.

## 6.2.2 Collection

Collection means the banker (collecting bank), in accordance with instructions received from the principal, in order to: obtain payment or acceptance from the payer, or deliver documents against payment and/or against acceptance or deliver documents on other terms and conditions. It includes clean collection and documentary collection. Documentary collection (D/C) means collection made against the financial documents and commercial documents together or against the commercial documents only. Commercial documents include invoices, transport documents, insurance documents, certificate of origins, etc. Clean collection means collection made against financial documents only, such as checks, bill of exchanges, promissory notes, payment receipts.

A documentary collection (D/C) is a transaction whereby the seller entrusts the collection of payment to the remitting bank (seller's bank), which sends docu¬ments to a collecting bank (buyer's bank), along with instructions for payment. Funds are received from the buyer and remitted to the seller through the banks involved in the collection in exchange for those documents. D/Cs involve the use of a draft that requires the buyer to pay the face amount either on sight (document against payment at sight—D/P at sight) or on a specified date in the future (document against payment at a future determinable date—usance D/P, or document against acceptance—D/A). As usance D/P has deficiencies in the payment mechanism, a lot of commercial bankers located in different countries refuse to accept usance D/P or regard it as D/A. It is suggested that the seller doesn't accept usance D/P as terms of payment, he can select D/P at sight or D/A. D/Cs concerns four basic parties including principal, remitting bank, collecting bank and payer. Sometimes, collection may concern presenting bank and agent in case of need.

The principal is usually the seller who entrust collection to the remitting banker. If a bill of exchange is need for collection, the principal is generally the drawer. The principal shall deliver the goods according to the contract, present the documents in conformity with the contract, make out the application form for outward collection (or called Letter of Instruction for Outward Collection), drafting bill of exchanges and hand over the documents, application forms and bill of exchanges to remitting bank together. The contents of application form for collection includes name, address, signatures of the principal, name & address of the drawee or his deposit bank's name, address and account number, kinds and copies of documents enclosed for collection, method of documentary collection, requirements for proceeds collected, requisite measures applied in case of dishonor, protest, warehouse insurance, charges and other requirements.

The remitting bank refers to the bank that is entrusted by the principal to handle collection through his sister banks or correspondent banks. He is usually the correspondent bank of principal (seller), settles collection as per the instructions received from the principal. He shall draft collection order according to application form for collection issued by the principal, send it to the collecting bank abroad together with the commercial documents and instruct him to collect proceeds as per the collection order.

The collecting bank refers to the bank that is authorized by the remitting bank to collect proceeds from the payer (the drawee) and deliver documents to the payer in case of payment or acceptance as per the instructions of collection order. His obligation for collection is greater than the remitting bank. He shall: ① Check documents received and notify each discrepancy to the remitting bank if any. ② Without change any instructions on the collection order beyond agreed by the remitting bank, otherwise be responsible for any fault by him. ③ Keep the documents carefully and rationally. The collecting bank can't deliver the documents to the buyer before acceptance or payment as per the instructions.

The drawee refers to the party who is presented the documents and asked for acceptance or payment by the collecting bank. Normally, the drawee is the buyer and become the potential payer. He has right to examine the documents and decide if payment or acceptance made or not. If he decided to make dishonor, he should stand up any demurrer from the principal, or would suffer reputation and financial losses.

The presenting bank refers to the bank that present documents to the drawee and ask him to make acceptance or payment. If the collecting bank is located in the different city with the drawee or the drawer doesn't open an account in the collecting bank, the collecting bank shall entrust another bank for presentation.

Representative in case of need is the agent nominated by the principal. If the drawee dishonored, the representative in case of need can hand over storage, insurance, return, transfer sales or change delivery conditions instead of the principal, etc. The principal shall specify right limitation of the representative in case of need on the instructions for outward collection; otherwise the collecting bank may refuse any instructions from the representative.

In practice, the contents of the application form for collection and collection order is almost same except for the name. Before send the relating documents to the collecting bank, the remitting bank shall check the documents, verify the name of documents and their copies in order to judge if they are in conformity with the application form for collection. It should be noticed that "checking documents" doesn't equal to "examining the documents". The remitting bank has no obligation to examine the contents of documents. He handles collection as common practice and if any, in charge for any defaults caused by himself. While, the relating charges and risks for the collecting bank selected are borne by the principal.

If the buyer refuses to accept or pay, the collecting bank shall notify the remitting bank as soon as possible. He can return documents to the remitting bank if he didn't get any instruction form the remitting bank 90 days after he sent the refusal notification. Meanwhile, he shall deal with the goods cautious. In principle, the collecting bank has no obligation to handle the goods. When the buyer made dishonor, the collecting bank may manage storage and insurance as per instructions received. In case of the urgent situations such as natural disasters occurred, in order to protect the goods, the collecting bank may take action to the goods even if no information received from the remitting bank.

A documentary collection is recommended for use in established trade relationships and in stable export markets. Under D/C transactions, the seller has little recourse against the buyer in case of nonpayment. The seller is exposed to more risk as D/C terms are more convenient and cheaper than an LC to the buyer. The process is simple, fast, and less costly than LCs. The bank assists in obtaining payment, but not guarantees payment. Banks do not verify the accuracy of documents. Thus, the D/C mechanism should only be used under the following conditions: The seller and buyer have a well-established relationship. The seller is confident that the importing country is stable politically and economically. When an open account sale is considered too risky, but an LC is also too expensive for the buyer, the parties may select to D/Cs. The following is the key points for D/C use.

①D/Cs is less complicated and less expensive than LCs.

②Under a D/C transaction, the buyer is not obligated to pay for goods prior to shipment.

③The seller retains title to the goods until the buyer either pays the face amount on sight or accepts the draft to incur a legal obligation to pay at a specified later date.

④Banks that play essential roles in transactions utiliz¬ing D/Cs are the remitting bank (seller's bank) and the collecting bank (buyer's bank).

⑤ While the banks control the flow of documents, they do not verify the documents nor take any risks, but can influence the mutually satisfactory settlement of a D/C transaction.

⑥ The instructions for outward collection lists instructions that specify the documents required for the transfer of title to the goods.

⑦ Although banks do act as facilitators for their clients under collections, documentary collections offer no verification process and limited recourse in the event of nonpayment.

The typical simplified flow of D/C transaction is as follows.

① The seller ships the goods to the buyer and receives in exchange the documents.

② The seller presents the documents with instructions for obtaining payment to its bank.

③ The seller's remitting bank sends the documents to the collecting bank.

④ The collecting bank releases the documents to the buyer upon receipt of payment, or

⑤ The collecting bank releases the documents on acceptance of draft from the buyer.

⑥ The buyer then presents the documents to the carrier in exchange for the goods.

⑦ Having received payment, the collecting bank forwards proceeds to the remitting bank.

⑧ Once payment is received, the remitting bank credits the exporter's account.

The features of documents against payment (D/P) collection at sight as following: Under a D/P collection, the exporter ships the goods, and then gives the documents to his bank, which will forward them to the importer's collecting bank, along with instructions on how to collect the money from the importer. In this arrangement, the collecting bank releases the documents to the importer only on payment for the goods. Upon receipt of payment, the collecting bank transmits the funds to the remitting bank for payment to the exporter. So, time of payment is between after shipment and before documents is released. The goods are transferred from the seller to the buyer after payment made on sight. For the exporter's risk, if the draft is unpaid, the goods may need to be disposed.

The features of documents against acceptance (D/A) Collection as following: Under a D/A collection, the exporter extends credit to the importer by using a time draft. In this case, the documents are released to the importer to receive the goods upon acceptance of the time draft. By accepting the draft, the importer becomes legally obligated to pay at a future date. At maturity, the collecting bank contacts the importer for payment. Upon receipt of payment, the collecting bank transmits the funds to the remitting bank. So, payment is made on maturity of draft at a specified future date. The goods are transferred from the seller to the buyer before payment but upon acceptance of draft. The exporter bears risks for having no control of the goods and may not get paid at due date

Terms of payment for collection can be stipulates as following.

① D/P at sight. Upon first presentation, the buyer shall pay against documentary draft drawn by the seller at sight. The shipping documents are to be delivered against payment only.

②D/P at 30 days after sight (or date of B/L, date of draft). The Buyers shall duly accept the documentary draft drawn by the Sellers at 30 (or 45, 60, 75, 90,) days after sight (or date of B/L, date of draft) upon first presentation and make payment on its maturity. The shipping documents are to be delivered against payment only.

③D/A at 30 days after sight (or date of B/L, date of draft). The Buyers shall duly accept the documentary draft drawn by the Sellers at 30 (or 45, 60, 75, 90,) days after sight (or date of B/L, date of draft) upon first presentation and make payment on its maturity. The shipping documents are to be delivered against acceptance.

## 6.2.3 Documentary Credit

### 1. Definition

The Uniform Customs and Practice for Documentary Credits, 2007 Revision, ICC Publication No. 600 ("UCP") are rules that apply to any documentary credit ("credit") (including, to the extent to which they may be applicable, any standby letter of credit) when the text of the credit expressly indicates that it is subject to these rules. They are binding on all parties thereto unless expressly modified or excluded by the credit. L/Cs includes documentary credit and standby credit.

Credit (Letter of credit, L/C) means any arrangement, however named or described, this is irrevocable and thereby constitutes a definite undertaking of the issuing bank to honor a complying presentation. Complying presentation means a presentation that is in accordance with the terms and conditions of the credit, the applicable provision of these rules and international standard banking practice. In briefly, L/C is a conditional acceptance of payment by a banker.

### 2. Functions

Credits are among the most secure instruments available to international traders. A documentary credit is a commitment by a bank on behalf of the buyer that payment will be made to the seller provided that the terms and conditions have been met, as verified through the presentation of all required documents. The buyer pays its bank to render this service.

A L/C is useful when reliable credit information about a foreign buyer is difficult to obtain, but you are satisfied with the creditworthiness of your buyer's foreign bank. When L/Cs are applicable, sellers will obtain the undertaking of conditional payment from the issuing bank as long as sellers can guarantee the quality of documents which are completely under control of the exporter. The banking charges such as opening charges are usually for the buyer's account. Seller has no awareness of or confidence in the credit status of the buyer and needs additional undertaking from the buyer's bank.

A L/C also protects the buyer since no payment obligation arises until the goods have been shipped or delivered as promised. This method also protects the buyer, since no payment obligation arises until the documents proving that the goods have been shipped or delivered as promised are presented. Credits can help the buyers to improve their credit and negotiating status. The importer provides conditional payment commitment of the bank to the exporter in addition to commercial credit so may be able to negotiate for a lower purchase price and better terms and ensure that the goods supplied are the goods ordered.

Risk is evenly spread between seller and buyer provided all terms and conditions are adhered to. The beneficiary collects payment after shipment. There are a variety of payment, financing and risk mitigation options under credit transactions While, process is complex, labor intensive and relatively expensive in terms of transaction costs. The seller enjoy lower risks as bank credit of the issuing bank replaces commercial credit of the buyer, the issuing bank provides undertaking of conditional payment to seller;

However, since L/Cs has many opportunities for discrepancies, they should be prepared by well trained persons or the function may need to be outsourced. Discrepant documents, literally not having an "I-dotted and T-crossed", can negate payment.

The following is the key points for credits use.

①A L/C, also referred to as a documentary credit, is a contractual agreement whereby a bank in the buyer's country, known as the issuing bank, acting on behalf of its customer (the buyer or importer), authorizes a bank in the seller's country, known as the advising bank, to make payment to the beneficiary (the seller or exporter) against the receipt of stipulated documents.

②The L/C is a separate contract from the sales contract on which it is based and, therefore, the bank is not concerned whether each party fulfills the terms of the sales contract.

③The bank's obligation to pay is solely conditional upon the seller's compliance with the terms and conditions of the L/C. In L/C transactions, banks deal in documents only, not goods.

### 3. Characteristics of a Letter of Credit

A L/C places a bank's credit instead of a commercial credit. It is guaranteed by the issuing bank's creditworthiness. Its main characteristics contain independence and abstraction.

(1) Independence

①A L/C stands independent of the sales contract. A credit by its nature is a separate transaction from the sale or other contract on which it may be based. Banks are in no way concerned with or bound by such contract, even if and reference whatever to it is included in the credit. Consequently, the undertaking of a bank to honor, to negotiate or to fulfill any other obligation under the credit is not subject to claims or defenses by the applicant resulting from its relationship with the issuing bank or the beneficiary. A beneficiary can in no case avail itself of the contractual relationships existing between banks or between the applicant and the issuing bank.

②The issuing bank undertakes to effect payment, quite independent of whether the applicant is bankrupt or in fault or not, provided the documents presented are in compliance with the terms and conditions of the credit.

③Banks deal with L/C business assume no responsibility for the acts of third parties taking part in one way or another in the credit transaction. For example, a bank assumes no liability or responsibility for the consequences arising out of the interruption of its business by Acts of God, riots, civil commotions, insurrections, wars, acts of terrorism, or by any strikes or lockouts or any other causes beyond its control. A bank will not, upon resumption of its business, honor or negotiate under a credit that expired during such interruption of its business.

(2) Abstraction

①In L/C business, banks deal with documents and not with goods, services or other performances to which the documents may relate.

②Banks engaged in L/C business assumes no responsibilities for the form, sufficiency, accuracy, genuineness, falsification or legal effect of any documents presented. Their main responsibility in this respect is to examine each document presented to see whether it appears on the face to be in compliance with the credit terms.

**4. Parties to a Credit**

A credit transaction concerns too many parties, including:

①Issuing bank means the bank that issues a credit at the request of an applicant or on its own behalf.

②Applicant means the party on whose request the credit is issued.

③Beneficiary means the party in whose favor a credit is issued.

④Advising bank means the bank that advises the credit at the request of the issuing bank.

⑤Confirming bank means the bank that adds its confirmation to a credit upon the issuing bank's authorization or request. Confirmation means a definite undertaking of the confirming bank, in addition to that of the issuing bank, to honor or negotiate a complying presentation.

⑥Nominated bank means the bank with which the credit is available or any bank in the case of a credit available with any bank.

⑦Presenter means a beneficiary, bank or other party that makes a presentation. Presentation means either the delivery of documents under a credit to the issuing bank or nominated bank or the documents so delivered.

**5. Processing of a Credit**

①The applicant (buyer) arranges for the issuing bank to open a L/C in favor of the seller (beneficiary).

②The issuing bank transmits the LC to the advising bank, which forwards it to the beneficiary (seller).

③ The beneficiary forwards the goods to a freight forwarder.

④ The freight forwarder dispatches the goods and the seller submits documents to the nominated bank or confirming bank.

⑤ The nominated bank or confirming bank checks documents for compliance with the LC and pays the beneficiary.

⑥ The applicant's account at the issuing bank is debited.

⑦ The issuing bank releases documents to the applicant to claim the goods from the carrier.

### 6. Forms of Credits

Except for irrevocable, confirmation, by negotiation, by sight payment, by acceptance or by deferred payment, LCs can take many forms, including anticipatory credit, revolving credit, transferrable credit and reciprocal credit.

(1) Irrevocable Credits

L/Cs is irrevocable, which means they may not be changed or cancelled unless both the buyer and seller agree. If the L/C does not mention whether it is revocable or irrevocable, it automatically defaults to irrevocable. The undertaking of issuing bank is as following.

① Provided that the stipulated documents are presented to the nominated bank or to the issuing bank and that they constitute a complying presentation, the issuing bank must honor if the credit is available by:

(a) Sight payment, deferred payment or acceptance with the issuing bank.

(b) Sight payment with a nominated bank and that nominated bank does not pay.

(c) Deferred payment with a nominated bank and that nominated bank does not incur its deferred payment undertaking or, having incurred its deferred payment undertaking, does not pay at maturity.

(d) Acceptance with a nominated bank and that nominated bank does not accept a draft drawn on it or, having accepted a draft drawn on it, does not pay at maturity.

(e) Negotiation with a nominated bank and that nominated bank does not negotiate.

② An issuing bank is irrevocably bound to honor as of the time it issues the credit.

③ An issuing bank undertakes to reimburse a nominated bank that has honored or negotiated a complying presentation and forwarded the documents to the issuing bank. Reimbursement for the amount of a complying presentation under a credit available by acceptance or deferred payment is due at maturity, whether or not the nominated bank prepaid or purchased before maturity. An issuing bank's undertaking to reimburse a nominated bank is independent of the issuing bank's undertaking to the beneficiary.

(2) Credits by Negotiation, Sight Payment, Acceptance or Deferred Payment

A credit shall be by negotiation, by sight payment, by acceptance or by deferred payment. A credit must state the bank with which it is available or whether it is available with any bank. It available with a nominated bank is also available with the issuing bank. A credit must not be issued available by a draft drawn on the applicant. By nominating a bank to accept a draft or incur a deferred payment undertaking, an issuing bank authorizes that nominated bank to prepay or purchase a draft accepted or a deferred payment undertaking incurred by that nominated bank.

For a complying presentation, the issuing bank must honor, while the nominated bank may honor or negotiate.

①Honour means: (a) To pay at sight if the credit is available by sight payment. (b) To incur a deferred payment undertaking and pay at maturity if the credit is available by deferred payment. (c) To accept a bill of exchange ("draft") drawn by the beneficiary and pay at maturity if the credit is available by acceptance.

②Negotiation means the purchase by the nominated bank of drafts (drawn on a bank other than the nominated bank) and/or documents under a complying presentation, by advancing or agreeing to advance funds to the beneficiary on or before the banking day on which reimbursement is due to (to be paid the nominated bank. Banking day means a day on which a bank is regularly open at the place at which an act subject to these rules is to be performed.

Unless a nominated bank is the confirming bank, an authorization to honor or negotiate does not impose any obligation on that nominated bank to honor or negotiate, except when expressly agreed to by that nominated bank and so communicated to the beneficiary. Receipt or examination and forwarding of documents by a nominated bank that is not a confirming bank does not make that nominated bank liable to honor or negotiate , not does it constitute honor or negotiation.

Normally, the available clause of a credit is indicated the available method, place and time as following: ①This credit is available with any bank by negotiation at sight. ②This credit is available with advising bank by sight payment. ③This credit is available with advising bank by deferred payment at 30 days after date of bill of lading. ④This credit is available with issuing bank by acceptance against beneficiary's draft at 30 days after sight drawn upon issuing bank.

If the seller and buyer signed a contract with payment by a sight credit, while a usance credit is applied for and stipulated: "The usance drafts are payable on a sight-basis, discount charges and acceptance commission are for applicant's account. Drawer bank's discount or interest charges, stamp duty and acceptance commission are for account of the applicant and therefore the beneficiary is to receive value for term draft as if drawn at sight."We called it as a usance credit with payable at sight.

(3) Confirmed Credits

Credits include confirmed credits or non-confirmed credits. A confirmed letter of credit refers to a greater degree of protection afforded to the seller when a LC issued by a foreign bank (the buyer's issuing bank) and confirmed by a bank, generally the seller's advising bank. Sellers should require confirming letter of credits if they are concerned about the credit standing of foreign bank, or when they are operating in a high-risk market, where political upheaval, economic collapse, devaluation or exchange controls could put the payment at risk.

If the issuing bank nominated a bank to act as the confirming bank and the bank confirmed on the credit, the credit became a confirmed credit, otherwise not. Confirmation means that the confirming bank adds its guarantee to pay the beneficiary.

The confirming bank undertaking is as following.

①Provided that the stipulated documents are presented to the confirming bank or to any other nominated bank and that they constitute a complying presentation, the confirming bank must: (a) Honor, if the credit is available by: (i) sight payment, deferred payment or acceptance with the confirming bank. (ii) sight payment with another nominated bank and that nominated bank does not pay. (iii) deferred payment with another nominated bank and that nominated bank does not incur its deferred payment undertaking or, having incurred its deferred payment undertaking, does not pay at maturity. (iv) acceptance with another nominated bank and that nominated bank does not accept a draft drawn on it or, having accepted a draft drawn on it, does not pay at maturity. (v) negotiation with another nominated bank and that nominated bank does not negotiate. (b) Negotiate, without recourse, if the credit is available by negotiation with the confirming bank.

②A confirming bank is irrevocably bound to honor or negotiate as of the time it adds its confirmation to the credit.

③A confirming bank undertakes to reimburse another nominated bank that has honored or negotiated a complying presentation and forwarded the documents to the confirming bank. Reimbursement for the amount of a complying presentation under a credit available by acceptance or deferred payment is due at maturity, whether or not another nominated bank prepaid or purchased before maturity. A confirming bank's undertaking to reimburse another nominated bank is independent of the confirming bank's undertaking to the beneficiary.

④If a bank is authorized or requested by the issuing bank to confirm a credit but is not prepared to do so, it must inform the issuing bank without delay and may advise the credit without confirmation.

(4) Anticipatory Credits

An anticipatory credit is a special kind of credits that the issuing bank authorizes the advising bank to give an advance payment to the beneficiary in case of need. It means that the beneficiary under an anticipatory credit can apply for a pre-shipment financing from the advising bank. The shipped cargo proceed of this credit can be used for repayment. Such kind of financing is guaranteed by the issuing bank.

The stipulating in the credit is stated as: "We, Issuing bank hereby authorize you (advising bank) at your discretion to grant to the beneficiary an advance or advance to the extent of xxx (value), any interest accrued thereon should be charged to him from the date of each advance to the date of repayment at the current rate of interest in xxx (mainly, exportation place). The proceeds of any draft negotiated under this credit may at your discretion be applied by you in the repayment to you of the whole or any part of such advance together with interest as aforesaid. In consideration of your bank making such advance to the beneficiary who will eventually fail to effect shipment covered by the credit, we guarantee repayment and undertake to pay you on demand any sum owing by the beneficiary in respect of such advance together with interest thereon."

(5) Revolving Credits

If consecutive monthly shipment is stipulated in a sales contract and payment is made by a documentary credit. In order to decrease margin, a revolving credit can be used, such as " The amount of this letter of credit USD100,000 is revolving on a monthly basis for the first time in March, 2018, for the last time in October, 2018. The maximum amount payable under this credit is USD800,000." The buyer applied for a credit with total amount USD800,000 to the issuing bank, each month could draw USD100,000. The buyer deposited margin calculated by USD100,000 instead of USD800,000. The buyers can have a transaction with leverage effect under a revolving credit.

With a revolving LC, the issuing bank restores the credit to its original amount once it has been drawn down. After the first drawing, the credit amount can be renewed according to amount or time. According to the amount, the revolving credits can be sub-divided into non-cumulative revolving credit and cumulative revolving credit, such as: "The amount of this credit is revolving on a monthly non-cumulative basis for six times and commending on may 18, 2016." According to time, the revolving credits can be sub-divided into non-automatic revolving credit and automatic revolving credit, such as: "The amount of this credit is USD100,000 revolving 5 times to maximum USD600,000."

(6) Transferable Credits and Transferred Credits

When a LC is issued as transferable, the payment obligation under the original credit can be transferred to one or more "second beneficiaries."Transferable credit means a credit that specifically states it is "transferable". A transferable credit may be made available in whole or in part to another beneficiary ("second beneficiary") at the request of the beneficiary ("first beneficiary"). Transferring bank means a nominated bank that transfers the credit. An issuing bank may be a transferring bank. A bank is under no obligation to transfer a credit except to the extent and in the manner expressly consented to by that bank.

A credit may be transferred in part to more than one second beneficiary provided partial drawing or shipments are allowed. Transferred credit means a credit that has been made available by the transferring bank to a second beneficiary. The transferred credit must accurately reflect the terms and conditions of the credit, including confirmation, if any, with the exception of the amount of the credit, any unit price stated therein, the expiry date, the period for presentation, or the latest shipment date or given period for shipment, any or all which may be reduced or curtailed. The percentage for which insurance cover must be affected may be increased to provide the amount of cover stipulated in the credit of these articles.

Unless otherwise agreed at the time of transfer, all charges (such as commissions, fees, costs or expenses) incurred in respect of a transfer must be paid by the first beneficiary. Any request for transfer must indicate if and under what conditions amendments may be advised to the second beneficiary. The transferred credit must clearly indicate those conditions. If a credit is transferred to more than one second beneficiary, rejection of an amendment by one or more second beneficiary does not invalidate the acceptance by any other second beneficiary, with respect to which the transferred credit will be amended accordingly. For any second beneficiary that rejected the amendment, the transferred credit will remain amendment.

Presentation of documents by or on behalf of a second beneficiary must be made to the transferring bank. The name of the first beneficiary may be substituted for that of the applicant in the credit. If the name of the applicant is specifically required by the credit to appear in any document other than the invoice, such requirement must be reflected in the transferred credit. The first beneficiary has the right to substitute its own invoice and draft, if any, for those of a second beneficiary for an amount not in excess of that stipulated in the credit, and upon such substitution the first beneficiary can draw under the credit for the difference, if any, between its invoice and the invoice of a second beneficiary. The first beneficiary may, in its request for transfer, indicate that honor or negotiation is to be effected to a second beneficiary at the place to which the credit has been transferred, up to and including the expiry date of the credit.

If the first beneficiary is to present its own invoice and draft, if any, but fails to do so on first demand, or if the invoices presented by the first beneficiary create discrepancies that did not exist in the presentation made by the second beneficiary and the first beneficiary fails to correct them on first demand, the transferring bank has the right to present the documents as received from the second beneficiary to the issuing bank, without further responsibility to the first beneficiary.

(7) Reciprocal Credit

Under processing trade, both parties are mutual importer and importer. For example, party

A may purchase equipment(s) or materials from party B and sell the manufactured products to him. If party A shall apply for a documentary credit in favor of party B for purchasing equipment or materials firstly, then party B apply for a documentary credit in favor of party A for purchasing manufacturing products later. As the outgoing credit was opened earlier than the incoming credit, in order to avoid the incoming credit isn't opened finally, the reciprocal credit can be used.

The reciprocal credit can be stipulated as: ① This credit is reciprocal credit against xx bank credit no. xx favoring xx covering shipment of xx. Or ② This credit shall not be available unless and until the reciprocal credit is established by ×× bank in favor of ×× for a sum of ×× covering shipment from ×× to ××. The reciprocal credit in effect shall advise by telex from ×× bank to beneficiary. ③ This credit is available by draft drawn on us at 180 days after bill of lading date. Payment will be effected by us on maturity of the draft against the above-mentioned documents and our receipt of the credit opener's advice stating that a reciprocal credit in favor of applicant issued by xx bank for account of beneficiary available by sight draft has been received by and found acceptable to them.

**7. Essential of a Documentary Credit**

The essentials of a documentary credit include basic information, drawing clause, shipment clause, documents required, additional conditions, etc.

(1) Basic Information

Basic information includes: ① Form of a credit, such as irrevocable, transferable. ② Credit number and advising bank's reference number. ③ Issuing date and place. ④ Expiry date and place. A credit must state an expiry date for presentation. An expiry date stated for honor or negotiation will be deemed to be an expiry date for presentation. The place of the bank with which the credit is available is the place for presentation. The place for presentation under a credit available with any bank is that of any bank. A place for presentation other than that of the issuing bank is in addition to the place of the issuing bank. Generally, a presentation by or on behalf of the beneficiary must be made on or before the expiry date. ⑤ Applicant's name and address. Applicant may be the end buyer, if any, the contracted buyer is agent. ⑥ Beneficiary's name and address. Normally, the beneficiary is the contracted seller. ⑦ Advising bank. It is best that the advising bank is nominated and located at the export country. ⑧ Credit amount. Normally, it contains the standard currency code plus amount both in word and figure.

If a credit stipulates tolerance in credit amount, quantity and unit prices, article 30 of UCP 600 stipulates: ① The words " about" or "approximately "used in connection with the amount of the credit or the quantity or the unit price stated in the credit are to be construed as allowing a tolerance not to exceed more or less than the amount, the quantity or the unit price to which they refer. ② A tolerance not to exceed 5% more or less than the quantity of the goods is allowed, provided the credit does not state the quantity in terms of a stipulated number of packing units or individual items and the total amount of the drawings does not exceed the amount of the credit. ③ Even when partial shipment are not allowed, a tolerance not to exceed 5% less than the amount of the credit is allowed, provided that the quantity of the goods, if stated in the credit, is shipped in full and a unit price, if stated in the credit, is not reduced or that sub-article 30(b) is not applicable.

(2) Drawing Clauses

Drawing clause is normally including where/when/how to be available for a documentary credit. A credit with a nominated bank in the exporting country is better for the exporter. The drawing clause is indicated as following: "Credit available with □ issuing bank □ Name and address of the nominated bank □ any bank By □ sight payment □ acceptance □ deferred payment □ negotiation against the documents detailed herein and □ beneficiary's draft (s) for _____% of invoice value at____ days after □ sight/ □shipment date drawn on_____".

When filling the application form for issuing a documentary credit, precautions shall be noticed: the name and addr of the nominated bank cannot be shown as you or your bank, the drawee cannot be indicated as applicant. When issuing bank is selected as the available place, the available method cannot be selected by negotiation. If deferred payment is selected, beneficiary's draft (s) cannot be selected. Also the tenor can not be selected as "after sight".

(3) Shipment Clauses

The shipment clauses include: ① Partial shipment. When applicable, select one from "□ allowed" or "□ not allowed". ② Transshipment. When applicable, select one from "□ allowed" or "□ not allowed". ③ Place of shipment. It is shown as "Loading on board/dispatch/taking in charge at/from_____". ④ Place of destination. It is shown as "For transportation to_____". ⑤ Time of shipment. It is shown as "not later than_____". (vi) Description of the goods/service

(4) Documents Required

Documents required includes commercial invoice, packing list, transport documents, insurance documents, certificate of origin, inspection certificated, etc. It must be shown as which kind of documents, its original and copies required. In general, transport documents are including bill of lading, seaway bill, airway bill, railway bill, cargo receipt, depot bill, inland waterway transport document, combined transport documents, etc. Please be noticed that cover notes will not be accepted as insurance documents.

(5) Additional Conditions

The Additional conditions include presentation period, discrepancies charges, reimbursement indication, bank to bank reimbursement arrangement and indications to the advising bank, such as request the advising bank to add confirmation, pages of credit and authorized signature of the issuing bank.

### 8. Tips for exporters to use documentary credits

The documentary credits are recommended for use in new or less-established trade relationships when you are satisfied with the creditworthiness of the buyer's bank. Standby LCs can be used in lieu of security or cash deposits as a secondary payment mechanism. Tips for Exporters to use credits include: ① Consult with your bank before the importer applies for a LC. ② Consider whether a confirmed LC is needed. ③ Negotiate with the importer and agree upon detailed terms to be incorporated into the L/C. ④ Determine if all terms can be compiled within the prescribed time limits. ⑤ Ensure that all the documents are consistent with the terms and conditions of the L/C. ⑥ Beware of many discrepancy opportunities that may cause nonpayment or delayed payment.

### 9. Specimen of Payment Term in a Sales Contract and a Documentary Credit

(1) Specimen of Payment Terms in a Contract

① 100% payment made by a documentary credit. The buyer shall open through a bank acceptable to the seller a documentary credit to reach the seller 15 days before the month of shipment. The credit shall be available with any bank by negotiation/sight payment / acceptance/deferred payment at_____days after shipment and valid until 15th days after the date of shipment.

② 100% payment made by combined a credit with documentary collection. 50% payment of the invoice value is available against clean draft at sight and be held against payment under a sight credit. The remaining 50% payment is available against documentary draft at sight and be held against payment under D/P at sight. The full set of shipping documents shall accompany the collection item and shall only be released after full payment of the invoice value. If the importer fails to pay full invoice value, the shipping documents shall be held by the issuing bank (or paying bank) at the seller's disposal.

③ 100% payment made by combined a credit with remittance. 80% of invoice value by an irrevocable L/C, available by sight draft against surrender of full set of shipping documents to the negotiating bank at port of shipment, the remaining 20% by remittance after arrival of cargo and re-inspection of cargo up to the stipulated standard.

(2) Specimen of a Documentary Credit

SEQUENCE OF TOTAL　*27 　: 1/1

FORM OF DOC. CREDIT *40 A : IRREVOCABLE

DOC. CREDIT NUMBER　*20 　: TCAM507846

DATE OF ISSUE　　　 31 C : 210709

EXPIRY　　　　　*31 D : DATE 210808 PLACE CHINA

APPLICANT        *50 : URTA INDUSTRIES SDN BHD, NO.5 JALAN 3, BANDAR SULTAN SULEIMAN,CHINESE INDUSTRIAL PARK 42005 PORT KLANG, SELANGOR, MALAYSIA

BENEFICIARY      *59 : B.F.TEXTILES (HANGZHOU) CO., LTD. NO.6, LANE 10 LINTIAN ROAD, LINAN, ZHEJIANG 311300, P.R.CHINA

AMOUNT        *32 B : CURRENCY USD AMOUNT 20.533,69

AVAILABLE WITH/BY    *41 D : ISSUING BANK BY PAYMENT

DRAFTS AT…      42 C : 30 DAYS AFTER SIGHT

DRAWEE        42 D : DRAWN ON RHB BANK BERHAD,PORT KLANG BRANCH FOR 100 PERCENT OF THE INVOICE VALUE

PARTIAL SHIPMENTS      43 P : ALLOWED

TRANSSHIPMENT      43 T : ALLOWED

LOADING IN CHARGE    44 A : SHANGHAI, CHINA

FOR TRANSPORT TO …   44 B :  PORT KLANG, MALAYSIA

LATEST DATE OF SHIP.    44 C : 180728

DESCRIPT. OF GOODS    45 A : YARN DYED FABRICS-WIDTH 58/59"

AS PER PURCHASE CONTRACT NO:790040

(CIF) SUBJECT TO INCOTERMS® 2010

DOCUMENTS REQUIRED    46 A :

+SIGNED COMMERCIAL INVOICE IN TRIPLICATE

+3/3 SET OF CLEAN OCEAN BILL OF LADING

+CERTIFICATE OF ORIGIN IN DUPLICATE

+PACKING LIST IN TRIPLICATE

+INSURANCE POLICY OR CERTIFICATE IN TRIPLICATE BLANK ENDORSED IN THE CURRENCY OF THE CREDIT FOR NOT LESS THAN 110 PERCENT OF INVOICE VALUE WITH CLAIMS PAYABLE IN KUALA LUMPUR COVERING FIRE, MARINE RISKS, INSTITUTE CARGO CLAUSES (CLAUSE A) ,INSTITUTE WAR CLAUSES, STRIKES CLAUSES AND TPND FROM POINT ORIGIN TO APLICANT'S WAREHOUSE IN PORT KLANG, MALAYSIA

ADDITIONAL COND      47 A :

+DRAFTS CLAUSED ´DRAWN UNDER DOCUMENTARY CREDIT NO. TCAM507846 DATED O9TH JULY 2008 OF RHB BANK BERHAD, PORT KLANG BRANCH´

+ALL DOCUMENTS MUST INDICATE OUR CREDIT NUMBER TCAM507846

+ALL DOCUMENTS PRESENTED MUST BE IN ENGLISH

+THE REIMBURSEMENT FEE OF THE ISSUING BANK ACCOUNTING TO USD30-00 IS STRICTLY FOR THE AMOUNT OF BENEFICIARY

+FULL SET CLEAN ON BOARD OCEAN BILL OF LADING MUST BE MADE OUT TO THE ORDER OF RHB BANK BERHAD, PORT KLANG BRANCH MARKED FREIGHT PREPAID AND NOTIFY APPLICANT

+THE AMOUNT OF EACH DRAFT NEGOTIATED MUST BE ENDORSED ON THE

REVERSE OF THIS CREDIT

DETAILS OF CHARGES   71 B : ALL CHARGES INCLUDING ADVISING

CHARGES AND NEGOTIATION CHARGES

OUTSIDE MALAYSIA ARE FOR ACCOUNT

OF BENEFICIARY

PRESENTATION PERIOD 48   : DOCUMENTS TO BE PRESENTED WITHIN

21 DAYS AFTER THE DATE OF ISSUANCE

OF THE TRANSPORT DOCUMENTS BUT

WITHIN THE VALIDITY OF THE CREDIT

CONFIRMATION          *49 : WITHOUT

INSTRUCTIONS          78 :

+DRAFTS AND DOCUMENTS MUST BE FORWARDED TO RHB BANK BERHAD, SHAH ALAM TRADE SERVICES CENTRE, NO.23 JALAN TENGKU AMPUAN ZABEDAH 9J/9 SECTION 9 40100 SHAH ALAM, MALAYSIA IN ONE LOT BY COURIER SERVICE

+UPON RECEIPT OF THE RELATIVE DOCUMENTS IN FULL COMPLIANCE WITH THE TERMS AND CONDITIONS OF THE CREDIT, WE SHALL COVER YOU AS PER YOUR INSTRUCTION ON MATURITY

+A DISCREPANCY FEE OF USD50-00 WILL BE DEDUCTED FROM THE PROCEEDS IF DOCUMENTS ARE PRSENTED WITH DISCREPANCY · IES · AND ACCEPTANCE OF SUCH DISCREPANT DOCUMENTS WILL NOT IN ANY WAY ALTER THE TERMS AND CONDITIONA OF THIS CREDIT

+NEGOTIATION OF DISCREPANT DOCUMENTS UNDER RESERVE OR GUARANTEE IS STRICTLY PROHIBITED

## 6.2.4 Letter of Guarantee

### 1. Definition

A bank guarantee is used as an instrument for securing performance or payment especially in international business. It is a writing promise issued by a bank at the request of its customer, undertaking to make payment to the beneficiary within the limits of a stated sum of money in the event of default by the principal. A bank guarantee may also be defined as an independent obligation where the guarantor (a bank/financial instruction/surety) has to make a special agreement with its customer, ensuring that it will be refunded by him for any payment to be effected under the contract of guarantee.

### 2. Functions

Guarantees are used widely and flexibility especially in international business, complicated transactions and the transactions without a documentary credit, etc.

①Guarantee does not consist in assuming the debtor's liability (by the guarantor) in the latter's interest, but in recouping the beneficiary for any damage caused by faulty performance.

②Guarantee is used as secure mechanism for payment of the contract amount.

③A contractor uses a guarantee as default instrument that covers the risk of non-performance or defective performance by the contractor

### 3. Parties to a Bank Guarantee

Four parties are involved in a bank guarantee transaction, including beneficiary, principal, guarantor and the instructing party.

(1) Beneficiary

Beneficiary refers to the party in whose favor the guarantee is issued. He is secured against the risk of the principal's not fulfilling his obligations towards the beneficiary in respect of the underlying transaction for which the demand guarantee is given. He will not obtain a sum of money if the obligations are not fulfilled.

(2) Principal

Principal refers to the party at whose request the guarantee is issued. The principal will be claimed if he is in breach of his obligations.

(3) Guarantor

Guarantor refers to the party issues a guarantee undertaking to make payment to the beneficiary in the event of default of the principal against the presentation of a written demand and other specified documents. He is not required to decide whether the beneficiary and the principal have or have not fulfilled their obligations under the underlying transaction with which the guarantor is not concerned. The guarantor is willing to meet its commitment in terms of guarantee, without becoming involved in possible disputes between beneficiary and principal regarding to correct performance by the principal of his obligations.

(4) Instructing Party

Instructing party refers to a bank or a financial institution or any other body acting as instructing party issues a counter guarantee acting on the instruction of a principal in favor of a bank or a financial institution located in the beneficiary's country.

### 4. Forms of Bank Guarantees

Bank guarantees are widely used in international trade and international construction or engineering contract. In international trade, bank guarantees contains tender guarantee, performance guarantee, advance/down payment guarantee, quality guarantee, maintenance guarantee, payment guarantee and deferred payment guarantee, etc. In international construction/engineering contract, there are bid (tender) guarantee, duty free guarantee, retention money guarantee, overdraft guarantee, payment guarantee, performance guarantee, maintenance guarantee, customs guarantee, etc

(1) Tender Guarantee

Tender guarantee is a written undertaking issued by the Bank at the request of tenderee in projects of construction works or material procurement subject to bidding, guaranteeing that the tenderer will not withdraw or modify his tender within the validity period, and, if awarded the tender, will sign the contract or submit the performance guarantee within a specified period.

It is applicable to public bidding or tender evaluation, when the employer requires the tenderer to submit tender security. It is used to avoid losses resulted from render's modification or withdrawal of tender during tender evaluation or rejection of contract conclusion after the award, the tenteree usually asks the tenderer to submit tender security to bind the tenderer. Tender guarantee is a substitute of cash security.

It is convenience provided by the product to the client.① To the tenderer: reduce the overstock of funds that have to be submitted as cash security; optimize the allocation of limited funds in comparison with the payment of cash security; simple procedures to meet time restraint.② To the tenderee: judiciously bind the contractor or supplier to fulfill contractual obligations and protect his own interests; circumvent the tedious procedures of collecting and returning the security and thereby improve efficiency.

(2)Performance Guarantee

Performance guarantee is a written undertaking issued by the guarantor to the employer or buyer at the request of the contractor or supplier, guaranteeing that the latter will strictly perform his contractual obligations. It is applicable to providing guarantee for the performance of contractual obligations by the principal; common cases including projects involving construction contracting or material procurement.

In such construction or procurement projects, the employer or buyer, to avoid losses incurred by the failure of the contractor or supplier to perform contractual obligations, often asks the contractor or supplier to submit performance security to bind the latter. Performance guarantee is a substitute of cash security.

It is convenience provided by the product to the client. ① To the contractor or supplier: reduce the overstock of funds that have to be submitted as cash security; optimize the allocation of limited funds in comparison with the payment of cash security. ② To the employer or buyer: judiciously bind the contractor or supplier to fulfill contractual obligations and protect his own interests; circumvent the tedious procedures of collecting and returning the cash security and thereby improve efficiency.

(3) Advance Payment Guarantee

Advance payment guarantee is a written undertaking issued by the guarantor to the employer or buyer at the request of the contractor or supplier, guaranteeing that the latter will perform his contractual obligations after the employer or buyer has affected the advance payment. It is applicable to providing guarantee for the performance of contractual obligations by the principal; common cases including projects involving construction contracting or material procurement.

In such construction or procurement projects, the employer or buyer, to avoid the loss of advance payment incurred by the failure of the contractor or supplier to perform contractual obligations after the latter has obtained the advance payment, asks the bank to make the guarantee for the repayment of the advance if the contractor or supplier fails to perform contractual obligations.

It is convenience provided by the product to the client. ① To the employer or buyer: ensure that the advance payment will be recovered smoothly when the contractor or supplier fails to perform contractual obligations; enhance the binding force on the contractor or supplier to perform the contract. ② To the contractor or supplier: facilitate the timely payment of the advance; timely obtain the funds to launch the project and to facilitate the smooth execution of the contract.

(4) Retention Money Guarantee

It is a written undertaking issued by the guarantor to the employer or buyer at the request of the contractor or supplier, guaranteeing that the latter will perform his contractual obligations after the latter has drawn the final payment in advance. Retention money guarantee is also called "final payment guarantee". It is applicable to the later stage of contract execution when the employer or buyer retains the final payment and the contractor or supplier has to draw the final payment in advance with the bank's letter of guarantee.

It is convenience provided by the product to the client. ① To the contractor or supplier: take back the final payment in advance to make up for the insufficient working capital; improve fund turnover. ② To the employer or buyer: gain guarantee for the performance of follow-up obligations; achieve the same effect as the retained final payment.

(5) Warranty Guarantee

It is a written undertaking issued by the guarantor to the employer or buyer at the request of the contractor or supplier, guaranteeing that the latter will perform his contractual obligations during the warranty or maintenance period. Warranty guarantee is also called "maintenance guarantee". It is applicable to the warranty or maintenance period of the contract on construction contracting or goods supply, when the employer or buyer requires the contractor or supplier to perform the warranty obligation.

After contracting or supply projects enter the warranty or maintenance period, the employer or buyer, in order to prevent the in conformity of the quality of works or goods with the contractual stipulations, or the reluctance or failure on the contractor or supplier's part to carry out repair, replacement or maintenance, often asks the contractor or supplier to provide warranty guarantee before the performance guarantee expires, thereby binding the contractor or supplier to the obligations in the warranty period.

It is convenience provided by the product to the client. ① To employer or buyer: guarantee the contractor or supplier to perform warranty or maintenance obligations. ② To contractor or supplier: improve the market competitive power of the contractor or supplier.

(6) Customs Guarantee

It is a written undertaking issued by the guarantor to the customs at the request of the importer (including processing trade enterprises), guaranteeing that the latter will perform his obligation of duty payment. The customs guarantee mainly includes two types, they are guarantee for payment of customs duty and guarantee for payment of taxes on processing trade.

It is applicable to import of commodities and goods before related sate policies on tax reduction or exemption become definite; temporary entry of equipment and instruments into the customs boundary of other countries for ongoing overseas contract construction, overseas exhibition or promotion; import of materials and spare parts by processing trade enterprises; clearance first and taxation later for some goods by the customs.

It is convenience provided by the product to the client: reduce overstock of funds that have to be submitted by the enterprises as security for customs duty; the practice of "clearance first and taxation later" expedites the customs clearance for goods and avoid additional cost due to the detention of good at ports; reduce the procedures of tax refund for articles entering customs boundary of other countries on a temporary basis.

(7) Payment Guarantee

It is a written undertaking issued by the guarantor to the seller at the request of the buyer, guaranteeing that the buyer will perform his payment obligations under contracts for purchase of commodity, technology, patent or labor. It is applicable to commodity trade, technical service trade, or construction projects involving payment. In construction project, payment guarantee serves as the guarantee for the employer's timely and full payment for construction progress to the contractor under terms of construction contracting.

In commodity trade, it serves as the guarantee for the buyer's timely payment after the seller has delivered goods as agreed in the contract. In commodity trade, the functions of payment guarantee is similarly as the letter of credit, but has simpler procedures, flexible formats to fit different needs. Letter of credit has to follow fixed format and conventions while the format of payment guarantee can be tail or made for specific project or customer. Meanwhile, payment guarantee has a wider application scope than the letter of credit because it can be used for both commodity trade and construction project.

Payment guarantees are convenience provided by the product to the client. ① To the seller or contractor: gain adequate guarantee for the collection of payment for goods and construction to facilitate his goods delivery, construction and progress of the trade. ② To the buyer or employer: protect the interests of the buyer or employer since payment terms in the payment guarantee can bind the behavior of the seller or contractor to a certain extent.

(8) Financing Guarantee

Financing guarantee is a written undertaking issued by the guarantor to the lender at the request of the borrower, guaranteeing that the borrower will perform his obligation of repaying the loan fund. Financing guarantee mainly covers loan guarantee, overdraft guarantee, guarantee for securities issuance and credit line guarantee. It is applicable when the borrower intends to gain all forms of financing from banks or other financial institutions, or when the borrower intends to issue securities in the financial market.

It is convenience provided by the product to the client. ① To the borrower: lower financing cost and help the borrower gain financing; raise the borrower's credit rating which is instrumental in the sales of securities. ② To the lender or buyers of securities: spread financing risks and improve the security of loan fund; gain sufficient guarantee for the redemption of securities.

(9) Leasing Guarantee

It is a written undertaking issued by the guarantor to the lesser at the request of the lessee, guaranteeing that the lessee will timely pay the rent. Leasing guarantee can be divided into guarantee for financing leasing and guarantee for operating leasing by leasing mode. In leasing projects, the leaser often asks the bank to make guarantee for the timely payment of rent by the lessee to safeguard against the failure of the lessee to make timely rent payment (especially under financial leasing, when the lease term is long, and object of leasing is of specific nature, the leaser has to take big risk).

It is convenience provided by the product to the client. ① To the leaser: facilitate the execution of leasing contract; gain guarantee for timely collection of rent. ② To the lessee: help the lessee gain the right to use the equipment; gain funds accommodation and accelerate fund turnover.

(10) Guarantee for Compensation Trade

Under terms of contract on compensation trade, guarantee for compensation trade is a written undertaking issued by the guarantor to the licensor of equipment and technology at the request of the licensee, guaranteeing that the licensee will pay for the equipment or technology with products or spot exchange.

It is applicable in projects of compensation trade when the licensee needs to pay for the equipment or technology introduced with products or spot exchange, or in compensation trade when the licensor of equipment and trade asks the bank to make guarantee for the licensee's payment with products or spot exchange to protect against the licensee's failure to produce as per the contract or to make payment with proceeds from product sales.

It is convenience provided by the product to the client. ① To the licensor of equipment and technology: gain adequate guarantee for the recovery of payment for equipment and technology. ② To the licensee of equipment and technology: facilitate the conclusion and performance of the contract for compensation trade and solve the problem of insufficient funds.

## 6.2.5 Standby credits

### 1. Definition

Standby credit is originated in USA for banker's restrictions to issue L/G outward. A Standby Letter of Credit is any letter of credit, or similar arrangement however named or described, which represents an obligation to the beneficiary on the part of the issuer. ① To repay money borrowed by or advanced to or for the account of the account party. ② To make payment on account of any indebtedness undertaken by the account party. ③ To make payment on account of any default by the account party

### 2. Functions

Standby credits can be regards as the letter of credits with functions of letter of guarantees or letter of guarantees with functions of letter of credits. A letter of guarantee can be acted as an independent guarantee and a financial tool.

Standby credits are also the independent documents. The issuing bank engages payment on the first position. Payment is made against the representing documents in compliance with the terms and conditions of standby credit.

## 6.2.6 Conclusion

Mode of Payment decides time & place of payment, documents transferring & financing costs. The seller wants get payment as soon as possible, preferably as soon as an order is placed or before the goods are sent to the buyer. The buyer wants to receive the goods as soon as possible, but to delay payment as long as possible, preferably until after the goods are resold to generate enough income to make payment to the seller. To succeed in today's global marketplace, sellers must offer their customers attractive sales terms supported by the appropriate payment method to win sales against foreign competitors. Sellers have to provide credit transaction to the buyers in order to maintain or enlarge market shares.

The seller and buyer own different market power. An appropriate payment mode must be chosen carefully to minimize the payment risk at the seller's end while also accommodating the needs of the buyer. New ways of International payment shall be designed and/or further subdivision of each kind of payment mode and/or fusion two or more kinds of payment modes in a business contract. For example, the payment terms in a sales contract is stipulated as following: ① The Supplier agrees that the Buyer will effect payments under the term of T/T（Telegram Transfer）against receipt of B/L by fax. ② Hong Kong Suppliers agree that the Buyer will effect payments under the term of CAD (Cash against Documents). ③ Only in case of new Suppliers and first order to them, the Buyer might agree to effect payments under L/C terms. The L/C charges on the Buyer side will be borne by the Buyer and the L/C charges on Suppliers side will be borne by the Supplier. The Bill of Lading made out to order and notify the buyer. ④ In case that the Supplier still insist on L/C terms even after the first order, the Supplier agree to take over all L/C charges on him as well as the Buyers side. In those cases we request a Bill of Lading.

## Questions

1. If the seller and the buyer agree that the goods shall be shipped from Shanghai to Hong Kong by sea, and payment shall be made by telegraphic transfer within 30 days after the shipment. While, shipment from Shanghai to Hong Kong is generally 3 days. Please have an analysis on the seller's risk to collect payment.

2. If the seller and the buyer agree that the goods shall be shipped from Shanghai to Rio Grande, Brazil by sea, and payment made by open account within 45 days after shipment. Please have an analysis on the seller's risk and buyer's risks.

3. If the seller and the buyer agree to make payment by letter of credit, which basic skills that the seller and buyer shall own under credit transaction?

4. How can the letter of guarantees or standby credits be used in international engineering projects or international commodities sales?

5. What kinds of payment mode are used in cross-border e-commerce ?

# 第七章

# 国际货物买卖争议的预防与处理

☞ **案例 7.1**

2003年1月23日，宁波市工艺品进出口有限公司(简称宁波工艺品公司)与瑞士DUFERCO S.A.(简称瑞士公司)在宁波订立了买卖冷轧钢的合同，合同的仲裁条款规定："一切因执行本合同或与本合同有关的争执，应由双方通过友好协商解决。如经协商不能得到解决时，应提交设在中国北京的国际商会仲裁委员会，按照《联合国国际货物销售公约》进行仲裁。"

合同在履行中发生争议，2005年9月12日瑞士公司将争议提交到ICC，新加坡独任仲裁庭书面审理了此案，在案件审理过程中，仲裁庭向宁波工艺品公司送达了《审理事项书》和《临时时间表》，这些文件均送达给宁波工艺品公司，后者签收了文件，但没有提交任何答辩，也未对仲裁庭的管辖权提出任何异议。独任仲裁庭于2007年9月21日在北京作出了编号为14006/MS/JB/JEM号裁决(以下简称ICC裁决)。宁波工艺品公司未能执行此裁决，2008年2月27日，宁波市中级人民法院受理了瑞士公司执行该ICC裁决的申请。法院经审理后认为，宁波工艺品公司未在有效期限内对仲裁协议的效力提出异议，且ICC仲裁院已在仲裁裁决中作出仲裁条款有效的认定，根据《最高人民法院关于适用<中华人民共和国仲裁法>若干问题的解释》第13条的规定，当事人在仲裁庭首次开庭前没有对仲裁协议的效力提出异议，而后向人民法院申请确认仲裁协议无效的，人民法院不予受理。仲裁机构对仲裁协议的效力作出决定后，当事人向人民法院申请确认仲裁协议效力或者申请撤销仲裁机构的决定的，人民法院不予受理，故宁波工艺品公司关于仲裁协议无效的主张不能成立。法院认为本案裁决属于《纽约公约》项下的非国内裁决，法院经审理后认为不存在公约规定的不予执行的情形，并于2009年4月22日裁定承认与执行该ICC裁决。

本案系ICC仲裁庭适用其规则在我国北京作出的裁决，也是一起向我国法院申请承认与执行ICC仲裁院依据其仲裁规则在我国境内作出的裁决案例。我国法院在对该裁决的承认与执行，适用了《纽约公约》规定的条件。但是，对于外国裁决究竟是裁决地国的裁决，还是ICC所在地法国的裁决，理论与实践中仍存在着不同的看法。（本案摘自于：赵秀文.从相关案例看ICC仲裁院裁决在我国的承认与执行[J]法学，2010（3）：69-70.）

商品的检验、索赔、仲裁、不可抗力虽非合同订立的主要交易条件，但与预防和处理争议有关，因而也是合同中的重要交易条件。

# 一、商品的检验

在国际货物买卖中，买卖双方分处不同的国家或地区，一般不能当面交接货物。进出口货物需要经过长途运输、多次装卸，货物的品质、数量等容易出现问题并引起争议。为了保障买卖双方的利益，避免争议的发生，或发生争议以后便于分清责任和进行处理，就需要由一个有资格的、有权威的、独立于买卖双方以外的公正的第三者，即专业的检验检疫机构负责对卖方交付的货物的质量、数量、包装进行检验，或对装运技术、货物残损等情况进行检验或鉴定。检验机构检验或鉴定后出具相应的检验证书，作为买卖双方交接货物、支付货款和进行索赔、理赔的重要依据。因此，进出口货物检验是买卖双方交接货物过程中不可少的重要环节。国际货物买卖合同中的商品检验条款内容，一般包括检验时间和检验地点、检验内容、检验机构、检验标准、检验证书等。

## （一）有关货物检验的法律规定

《联合国国际货物销售合同公约》和英美法系的法律都认为，除买卖双方另有约定外，买方有权对自己所购买的货物进行检验，而卖方应予以配合。《联合国国际货物销售合同公约》规定："买方必须在按情况实际可行的最短时间内检验货物或由他人检验货物；如果合同涉及到货物的运输，检验可推迟到货物到达目的地后进行；如果货物在运输途中改运或买方须再发运货物，没有合理机会加以检验，而卖方在订立合同时已知道或理应知道这种改运或再发运的可能性，检验可推迟到货物到达目的地后进行。"英国《货物买卖法》规定："除另有约定外，当卖方向买方交货时，根据买方的请求，卖方应向其提供一个检验货物的合理机会，以便能确定该货物是否符合合同规定。"中国法律也认可买方对收到的货物有检验权。

但是，买方对货物拥有检验权并不是买方对货物接受的前提条件，买方对收到的货物可以进行检验，也可以不进行检验，假如买方没有利用合理的机会对货物进行检验，就等于放弃了检验权，也就丧失了拒收货物的权利。美国《统一商法典》规定，凡属下列情况均表明买方接受货物：①在有合理机会对货物进行检验之后，买方向卖方表示货物符合合同，或表示尽管货物不符合合同，他们将收取或保留货物；②在买方有合理机会对货物检验之后，未做出有效的拒收；③买方做出任何与卖方对货物的所有权相抵触的行为。

### （二）商品检验的方式与内容

#### 1. 商品检验方式

商品检验可以分为：卖方检验（第一方检验）、买方检验（第二方检验）和检验机构检验（第三方检验）。在实际业务中，一般以检验机构检验为主。对于卖方交付的货物，买方是接受还是拒收，主要依据有关检验机构的公正的检验结果而定。

#### 2. 商品检验的内容

商品检验的内容因货物的特性、相关法律法规、买卖合同的具体规定、技术标准和申请人的申请意愿不同而不同，一般有质量检验、数量和重量检验、包装检验、出口商品装运技术检验和进出口商品鉴定等。

（1）质量检验

质量检验（quality inspection）又称为品质检验，是货物检验的主要项目。质量检验的内容主要包括：①外观质量。检查商品外观的形态、尺寸、规格、式样、花色、造型、表面缺陷、表面加工装饰水平等；②内在质量，主要包括成分检验和各种性能检验等。成分检验包括有效成分的种类、含量、杂质及有害物质的限量等；性能检验包括商品应具备的强度、硬度、弹性、伸缩率、耐热性等物理性能，以及耐酸/碱性、抗腐蚀性、溶解性、化学相容性等；机械性能检验包括抗压、抗拉、冲击、振动、跌落等；使用性能检验包括完成规定非动作、特定的使用效果，比如汽车的刹车、车速要求，电视机的声响和图像效果，机器生产的产品完好率等；③特定质量检验项目。特定质量检验项目是指为了安全、卫生、环境保护等目的，针对不同商品而进行的特别要求的质量检验，如食品卫生质量的检验（一般检验食品的有害生物、食品添加剂、农药残留量、重金属含量等）；动植物检验；对危险物品的安全性能检验；对飞机、船舶、车辆安全防护检验；对废气、噪声、废水的限量检验等。

（2）数量或重量检验

数量（quantity）或重量（weight）条款是国际货物买卖合同的重要内容，因此数量或重量检验是检验的主要内容之一。

（3）包装检验

包装检验是对进出口货物的外包装和内包装以及包装标志进行检验。

（4）出口装运技术检验

是对装运出口的粮油食品、冷冻品等易腐食品的船舱和集装箱实施强制性检验。其中，船舱检验包括干货舱检验、油舱检验、冷藏舱检验、以确认其对所装货物的适载性；集装箱鉴定包括监视装箱、监视卸箱、承租鉴定、退租鉴定，以及集装箱的清洁、温度、风雨密固性等单项鉴定。

（5）进出口商品鉴定

检验机构根据买卖合同、运输合同和保险合同等相关方的申请或国外检验机构的委托，办理进出口商品鉴定业务，签发各种鉴定证书，供申请单位作为办理货物交接、结算、计费、通关、计税、索赔或举证等有效凭证。进出口商品鉴定业务范围包括：进出口商品质量鉴定、装运技术条件鉴定、集装箱鉴定、外商投资财产鉴定和其他鉴定业务。

### （三）货物检验的时间、地点、检验机构与检验证书

国际公约与大多数国家的法律都规定了买卖双方对货物检验的权利与义务。但是对于买方双方应在何时、何地进行检验，各国法律并无统一规定。货物检验的时间和地点关系着买卖双方的切身利益、检验权的行使、检验机构的指定以及日后有关索赔的法律依据问题，所以买卖双方应在买方合同中明确规定检验的时间与地点。

#### 1. 货物检验的时间和地点

在国际货物买卖合同中，有关货物检验时间和检验地点的规定一般有4种。

**（1）出口国检验**

出口国检验可分为产地检验和在装运港（地）检验。产地检验是指在货物离开生产地点如工厂、农场或矿山之前，由卖方或其委托的检验机构人员，会同买方检验人员对货物进行检验或验收。卖方只对货物离开产地前的品质负责，货物离开产地后的风险由买方负责。装运港（地）检验是指以离岸质量、重量（或数量）为准。按此规定，货物在装运港或装运地，在装运前或装运时经由双方所约定的检验机构对货物的质量、重量或数量进行检验，并由该机构出具相应的检验证书作为决定交货质量、重量或数量的依据。货物运抵目的港或目的地后，如买主对货物进行复验并发现问题，无权再表示拒收或提出异议和索赔。

**（2）进口国检验**

进口国检验是指在货物运抵目的港（地）卸货后检验，或在买方营业处所或最终用户的所在地检验。目的港（地）检验以到岸质量、重量（或数量）为准。在货物运抵目的港（地）卸货后的一定时间内，由双方约定的检验机构进行检验，并由该机构出具的检验证书作为确认交付货物的质量、重量或数量的依据。如检验证书证明货物与合同规定不符系属卖方责任，卖方应予负责。"买方营业处所或用户所在地检验"，一般适用于那些密封包装、精密复杂的商品，不宜在使用前拆包检验，或对于那些需要安装调试才能进行检验的成套设备、机电仪表产品，将检验延伸和推迟到货物运抵买方营业所或最终用户的所在地后的一定时间内进行，并以双方约定由该地的检验机构所出具的检验证书作为决定交货质量和数量的依据。

**（3）出口国检验、进口国复验**

所谓出口国检验、进口国复验，其作法是以在装运港或装运地出具的检验证书作为卖方收取货款的必要单据之一，但是货物运抵目的地后买方有复验权。如经双方约定的检验机构复验后发现货物不符合合同规定，且这种不符情况确系属于卖方责任而不属于承运人或保险公司的责任范围，买方有权在规定的时间内凭复验证书向卖方提出异议和索赔，或拒收货物。

（4）出口国装运前预检验、进口国最终检验

由买方自行派人或委托检验机构人员在出口国装运前对货物进行预检验，待货物运抵目的港（地）后，买方再进行最终检验，以此检验结果作为索赔依据。

以上四类规定方法，各有特点，应视具体的货物买卖性质决定。其中，以"出口国检验、进口国复验"的做法使用最多，因为这种做法既肯定了卖方提交的检验证书是有效的交接货物和结算凭证，同时又确认了买方的复验权。

### 2. 检验检疫机构

检验检疫机构分为官方检验机构和民间检验机构。例如，美国食品药物管理局（FDA）、法国国家实验室检测中心、日本通商产业检查所等为官方检验机构。除政府设立的官方商品检验机构外，世界上许多国家中还有由商会、协会、同业公会或私人设立的半官方或民间商品检验机构，对国际货物进行检验和鉴定。国际上比较有名望、有权威的民间商品检验机构有：①瑞士通用公证行（SGS）；②英国英之杰检验集团（IITS）；③日本海事检定协会（NKKK）；④新日本检定协会（SK）；⑤日本海外货物检查株式会社（OMIC）；⑥美国保险商安全试验所（UL）；⑦美国材料与试验学会（ASTM）；⑧加拿大标准协会（CSA）；⑨国际羊毛局（IWS）；⑩中国商品检验公司（CCIC）。例如，UL是一个独立的、非营利的、从事公共安全试验和鉴定的非政府机构。UL制定的安全标准是UL进行产品测试和安全认证的依据。目前，UL安全标准的影响已远远超出美国的国界，全世界约有50多个国家和地区开展按UL安全标准进行测试和认证的工作。

### 3. 检验证书

检验证书在国际货物买卖中具有重要的法律地位。中国检验检疫机构签发的检验证书种类有：品质检验证书、重量或数量检验证书、包装检验证书、兽医检验证书、卫生/健康证书、消毒检验证书、熏蒸证书、残损检验证书、温度检验证书、船舱检验证书、货载衡量检验证书、价值证明书、生丝品级及公量检验证书、舱口检视证书、监视装/卸载证书等。检验证书，尽管类别不一，但其作用是基本相同的，主要表现在下列几个方面：①作为证明卖方所交货物的品质、重量（数量）、包装及卫生条件等是否符合合同规定的依据；②作为买方对品质、重量、包装等条件提出异议、拒收货物、要求索赔、解决争议的凭证；③作为卖方向银行交单的单据之一；④作为海关验放、征收关税和优惠减免关税的必要证明。

☞ **案例7.2**

根据肯尼亚媒体2018年10月的最新报道，肯尼亚标准局（Kenya Bureau of Standards）宣布暂停与中国检验认证集团(CCIC)和SGS远东地区的合作，并将处以数百万先令的罚款，原因是认为该两家认证公司放任不合格产品流入肯尼亚市场。目前，肯尼亚标准局已不认可中国检验认证集团及SGS远东地区包括日本、韩国、朝鲜、印度尼西亚、马来西亚、菲律宾、泰国、新加坡、越南、柬埔寨所签

发的COC证书。肯方认为，为了方便不合标准和非法的货物入境，这两家公司在中国、印度尼西亚、马来西亚、越南和泰国检查货物，未能对已检验的集装箱做好封签，然后将货物装船运往肯尼亚市场。在中国检验认证集团和SGS远东地区被暂停相关业务后，目前出口肯尼亚的商品，只接受Cotecna Inspection SA、Veritas Bureau、Intertek International Ltd这几家机构出具的检验COC证书。

# 二、索赔

## （一）违约及其法律责任

国际货物买卖合同明确规定了买卖双方的权利和义务，对贸易双方均有约束力。任何一方当事人都必须按照合同规定严格履行其合同义务，否则即构成违约。一方违约不仅会使买卖双方发生争议，而且也会给另一方造成经济损失。因而，违约的一方当事人应承担相应的违约责任。在国际货物买卖过程中，违约事件时有发生，一般集中在交货的品质、数量（或重量）、交货期等问题上。例如，在国际市场价格波动频繁的时候，卖方会不交货或不按时发货，或交货的品质、数量（重量）不符合合同要求；而买方会不按时开立信用证或不付款、不按时付款。索赔是指受到损失的一方当事人向违约方提出损害赔偿的要求，而理赔是指违约方当事人受理受损方提出的索赔要求。

不同性质的违约，所承担的法律责任不同。《联合国国际货物销售合同公约》将违约分为"根本性违约"和"非根本性违约"。根本性违约是指"一方当事人违反合同的结果，致使另一方当事人蒙受损失，以至于实际上剥夺了他根据合同规定有权期待得到的东西，即为根本违反合同。"如违约行为属于根本性违约，受损害方有权向违约方要求损害赔偿，并可宣告合同无效。如违约的情况尚未达到根本性违约的程度，则受损害方只能要求损害赔偿而不能宣告合同无效。美国法律将违约分为"重大违约"和"轻微违约"。重大违约是指一方当事人违约，指使另一方当事人无法取得这项交易下他本应得的主要利益，受损害方可以要求解除合同，同时要求损害赔偿。对于"轻微违约"，受损方只能要求赔偿而不能解除合同。英国法律将违约分为"违反要件"和"违反担保"。"要件"是指合同中的重要和根本性条款，如合同中与商品直接有关的品质、数量（重量）、交货期等。"担保"是指合同中的次要和附属性条款，是与商品无直接关联的条件。在合同的一方当事人违反要件的情况下，另一方当事人（受损方）有权解除合同，并有权提出损害赔偿。而在违反担保的情况下，受损方只能提出损害赔偿，而不能解除合同。

## （二）国际货物买卖合同中的索赔条款

为了进出口交易的顺利履行，国际货物买卖合同中往往订有索赔条款。索赔条款通常有以下两种规定方法。

### 1. 异议与索赔条款

异议与索赔条款（discrepancy and claim clause）主要用于国际货物买卖合同，一般适用于对卖方交付货物的品质、数量或包装等方面提出索赔。该条款的内容，除规定一方如违反合同，另一方有权索赔外，还包括索赔期限、索赔依据和索赔办法等。其中：

索赔依据是指受损方在提出索赔时必须提供的、证明对方有违约事实真相的书面材料，主要是检验机构出具的检验证书。值得注意的是，该检验机构必须是买卖双方均认可的，该出证机构一般在合同中加以规定。

索赔期限是指受损方当事人向违约方提出索赔的有效时限。逾期索赔，违约方可不予受理。在索赔期限内，买方可就货物的品质、数量、包装等与合同规定不相符合之处向卖方提出索赔。买卖双方一般在合同中规定索赔时效，即约定索赔时效。除约定索赔时效外，还有法定索赔时效，即根据有关法律和惯例的规定，受损方有权向违约方提出索赔的期限。合同中约定的具体索赔期限，应根据货物品种、特性及检验所需时间等决定。约定索赔期限规定不宜过长或过短，过长会使卖方承担过重的责任，而过短会使买方无法行使索赔权。约定索赔时效的效力，一般高于法定索赔时效。

在国际货物买卖合同中，交易双方一般将检验条款和索赔条款结合起来订立，称为"检验与索赔条款"，索赔期限实际上是检验条款中的复验期限。如买卖合同约定了索赔期限，买方应抓紧检验，一旦发现货物有不符合合同规定的情况，应立即请检验机关复验出证，并严格按约定的期限索赔。如买卖合同中订有货物的品质保证期，万一在质量保证期内出现质量问题，买方应立即向卖方提出索赔。

☞ **案例7.3**

2000年1月20日，香港甲公司和上海乙公司签订了一份合同，由甲公司向乙公司提供韩国生产的手机零配件，货物最迟不得晚于2月10日发运，甲公司在合同中承诺对产品的质量保证期为货物抵达目的地后12个月。2月7日，甲公司向乙公司提供合同规定的货物。2001年3月25日，乙公司在使用过程中发现部分产品有质量问题，要求甲公司换货。如不能换货，则要求退货，并要求甲公司承担有关费用损失。甲公司答复乙公司，因货物在入库前已详细检查、核对并已投入使用，因而拒绝赔偿。因乙公司对合同项下的货物的品质存在异议，2001年4月2日，即在收货后第13个月，乙公司将合同项下的货物送交中国商品检验机构检验。检验机构出具的检验证书证明，该批货物存在5项缺陷，系制造不良所致。4月5日，乙公司据此提起仲裁，要求甲公司赔偿5万美元。甲公司认为，乙公司不能证明第二次送检的产品系交货时的产品，且第二次商检的时间已经超过索赔有效期，商检证书不能发生效力。仲裁庭经审理后认为，乙公司未在规定时间内检验货物质量，失去索赔权，驳回了乙公司的请求，裁定甲公司没有赔偿责任。

### 2. 罚金条款

罚金条款又称为"违约金条款"，一般适用于卖方延期交货，或者买方延迟开证、延期接货、延期付款等情况。当一方当事人未能履行合同义务时，应向另一方支付一定数额的违约金以补偿其损失。罚金数额的大小应根据违约时间的长短而定，并规定出最高金额，由买卖双方事先商定。一般来说，罚金数额以不超过货物总金额的5%为宜。各国法律对合同中的罚金条款有不同的解释，一些大陆法国家（如德国）一般都承认合同中的罚金条款；而英美法则将合同中的罚金条款按其性质分为补偿性的"预约赔偿金"和惩罚性的"罚金"两种。英美法国家的法律只承认损害赔偿，不承认对于带有惩罚性的罚金。

# 三、不可抗力

不可抗力（force majeure）即人力不可抗拒，它是指买卖合同签订后，不是由于合同任一方当事人的过失或疏忽，而是发生了当事人在订立合同时不能预见、不能预防，对其发生不能避免、不能克服的事件，以致合同不能履行或不能如期履行。遭受意外事件的一方，可以据此免除履行合同的责任或延期履行合同，对方无权要求赔偿。目前，国际社会对不可抗力的定义及其并不统一，各国法律的解释差别较大。例如，法国法律称为"不可抗力"、英美法系称为"合同落空"、大陆法系称为"情势变迁"或"契约失效"，而《联合国国际货物销售合同公约》称之为"履行合同的障碍"。

### （一）不可抗力的法律后果

对于不可抗力事件的法律后果，各国的分歧较大。例如，英美法国家认为，一旦出现"合同落空"，合同即告终结，从而自动解除了当事人的履约义务，而有些国家法律认为，出现不可抗力事件不一定使合同得以全部解除，应根据不可抗力事件的发生原因、性质、规模、对履约的实际影响来加以区别对待。

中国对不可抗力事件规定了三种可能产生的后果：①如果发生不可抗力事件，致使合同义务不能全部履行，当事人可解除合同，并免除全部责任；②如果发生不可抗力事件，致使合同的部分义务不能履行，当事人可免除部分义务；③如果发生不可抗力事件，不是导致合同不能履行，而只是不能按约定的时间履行，则当事人可以延迟履行合同，并在该事件的后果影响持续的时间内，免除其延迟履行的责任。另外，中国还规定了不可抗力事件中要求免责的一方应承担的两项义务：①应及时通知另一方，以减轻可能给另一方所造成的损失。如果没有及时通知而给另一方造成损失，怠于通知的一方应对此承担责任；②应在合理的时间内向另一方提供有关机构出具的证明，以证明不可抗力事件的发生。在中国，公证机构、中国国际贸易促进委员会均可以出具不可抗力证明。

### （二）不可抗力事件的构成条件与范围

尽管各国法律和《公约》等对不可抗力的名称及解释存在差别，但都认为构成这类事件需要同时具备4项条件：①在订立合同后发生；②在订立合同时不能预见；③事件的发生不是当事人所能控制，是无法避免、无法预防的；④事件的发生不是任何一方当事人的疏忽或过失造成的。导致不可抗力事件发生的原因通常有以下2种情况：①由自然原因引起，如水灾、旱灾、暴风雪、地震、火灾、海啸、冰封等；②由社会原因引起，如战争、罢工、政府禁令、贸易政策调整等。一般来说，因自然原因引起的不可抗力事件，贸易双方容易达成共识。但是，对于因社会原因引起的不可抗力，各国的法律解释差别较大，买卖双方的争议更是经常发生。因此，贸易双方在签订国际货物买卖合同时，应在合同中约定不可抗力条款，并视事件的具体发生情况协商解决。

### （三）合同中的不可抗力条款

不可抗力条款是一种免责条款，可全部免除或部分免除因不可抗力事件而违约的一方当事人的履约责任。国际货物买卖合同中的不可抗力条款，其基本内容一般为：不可抗力事件的范围、事件发生后通知对方的期限、出具证明文件的机构以及不可抗力事件的后果。根据不可抗力事件的规定范围，不可抗力条款通常有3种规定办法：概括式、列举式和综合式。

#### 1. 概括式规定

该规定方法不在合同中罗列哪些事件属于不可抗力事件，而只是采用笼统规定。例如，由于公认的不可抗力的原因，致使卖方不能交货或延期交货，卖方不负责任，或"由于不可抗力事故使合同不能履行，发生事故的一方可据此免除责任。该方法过于笼统、含义模糊、解释伸缩性大，容易引起争议。

#### 2. 列举式规定

该规定方法是在合同中详列具体的不可抗力事件。例如，由于战争、地震、水灾、火灾、暴风雨、雪灾等原因，致使卖方不能全部或部分装运或延迟装运合同货物，卖方对于这种不能装运或延迟装运本合同货物不负有责任。但卖方须用电报或电传通知买方，并须在多少天（比如15天）以内，以航空挂号信方式向买方提交由中国国际贸易促进委员会出具的证明此类事件的证明书。该方法虽然明确具体，但文字繁琐，有可能出现遗漏情况

#### 3. 综合式规定

该规定方法是在合同中列明可能发生的不可抗力事故（如战争、洪水、地震、火灾等）的同时，再加上"以及双方同意的其他不可抗力事故"的文句。例如：由于战争、地震、水灾、火灾、暴风雨、雪灾或其他不可抗力的原因，致使卖方不能全部或部分装运或延迟装运合同货物，卖方对于这种不能装运或延迟装运本合同货物不负有责任。但卖方须用电报或电传通知买方，并须在多少天（如15天）内以航空挂号信件向买方提交由中国国际贸易促进委员会出具的证明此类事件的证明书。该方法既明确具体，又有

一定的灵活性。

### （四）订立不可抗力条款应注意的问题

①明确不可抗力发生后的通知方式和通知期限。发生不可抗力事件时，遭受不可抗力事件的一方应及时通知另一方，以便对方及时采取一些相应措施，如查明不可抗力的事实真相，对履行合同的影响程度等。另一方在收到通知后如有异议，应及时向对方提出。交易一方援引不可抗力条款免责时，另一方当事人应按合同规定严格进行审查，以确定其援引的内容是否属于不可抗力条款规定的范围。

②应规定出具不可抗力证明文件及其相应的出证机构。发生不可抗力事件时，一方面，遭遇不可抗力事件的一方应提供有效的证明文件。该证明文件的出具机构，可规定为发生不可抗力事件地区的合法的公证机构，或是当地的商会。

③规定不可抗力的法律后果。在合同中规定什么情况下可以撤销合同，什么情况下可以部分解除合同，或延期履行合同等。

# 四、仲　裁

国际货物买卖合同的双方应是一种平等互利的合作关系。合同签订后，贸易双方之间一旦发生争议，首先应通过友好协商的方式解决。如果友好协商不成功，当事人可按照合同约定，采用调解、仲裁或诉讼方式解决争议。

调解（conciliation）是指在争议发生后，买卖双方当事人自愿将争议提交选定的调解机构（法院、仲裁机构等），由该机构按调解程序进行调解。若调解成功，双方应签订和解协议，作为一种新的契约予以执行；若调解意见不为双方或其中一方接受，则该意见对当事人无约束力，调解即告失败。

诉讼（litigation）是在争议发生后，一方当事人向法院起诉，控告合同的另一方。起诉方一般要求法院判决另一方当事人以赔偿经济损失或支付违约金的方式承担违约责任，也有要求对方实际履行合同义务的。采用诉讼方式解决争议，其具有下列特点：①诉讼带有强制性，只要向有管辖权的法院起诉，另一方就必须应诉，争议双方都无权选择法官；②程序复杂，处理问题比仲裁慢；③诉讼解决争议时，双方当事人紧张，有伤和气，不利于今后贸易关系的继续发展；④诉讼费用较高。

仲裁（arbitration）又称公断。买卖双方在执行合同的过程中如发生争议，按协议将有关争议提交仲裁机构裁决。采取仲裁解决争议，与诉讼相比，仲裁方式的好处有：①采用仲裁是以双方自愿为基础，双方当事人自行选定仲裁员因而具有一定的灵活性；②仲裁程序较简单，且仲裁员一般是熟国际贸易业务的专家和知名人士等，故仲裁解决问题较快；③仲裁费用比诉讼费低；④仲裁对争议双方继续发展贸易关系的影响较小；⑤仲裁是终局性裁决，败诉方不得上诉，必须执行。

值得注意的是，采用诉讼和仲裁并不排除友好协商或调解。因采取仲裁解决争议有许多有利的方面，因而仲裁成为国际贸易中最为广泛采用的解决争议的重要方式。

☞ **案例7.4**

本案为仲裁案件。申请人为一家美国公司，被申请人为中国外贸公司。双方于1994年11月12日间先后签订了三份售货合同，由被申请人向申请人出售货物总价值468,000美元，价格术语CIF鹿特丹，最后交货期限为1994年12月31日。合同约定在中国国际经济贸易仲裁委员会仲裁。因市场发生剧烈变化，被申请人未能履行交货义务，申请人遂提起仲裁，请求仲裁庭裁决被申请人：①申请人遭受的利润损失567,000美元；②支付信用证费用计2,192.36美元；③赔偿申请人为此案支付的律师费；④承担全部仲裁费用。而被申请人在申辩时认为，因国内、国际市场价格飞涨，国内货源紧缺，到交货时价格已经上涨了1至2倍，双方订立合同时所期望的目的已经落空，因此被申请人按合同价格交货的义务，因履行合同时的环境与订立合同时的情况有本质的变化而得以免除。另外，根据《联合国国际货物销售合同公约》，被申请人应赔偿的损失为交货期满时交货地市场价格与合同价格的差价。申请人根据《公约》提出进一步申诉，损害赔偿的范围应包括申请人应得的利润。申请人通过多种方式证明了当时存在的国际市场价格，否认了交货地的时价。仲裁庭裁决意见：根据《公约》有关卖方义务的规定，被申请人的行为已经构成违约，申请人有权要求损害赔偿。被申请人援引合同落空理论来解释其不履行合同交货义务的行为是没有法律依据的，这是因为：①本案的适用法应为《公约》；②《公约》没有明示规定商品价格变化是不可抗力；③中国法律对于合同落空没有明示规定；④订立合同时双方可以预见到国际市场价格风险；⑤本案商品价格变动未达到"显失公平"的程度，而且被申请人未能合理证明交货地的时价，因此被申请人的抗辩被驳回。裁决被申请人赔偿申请人三份合同项下的利润损失共计550,800美元、被申请人向申请人支付其中两份合同项下的改证费和电传费通知费683.31美元。本案仲裁费，申请人分担10%，被申请人分担90%。

采取仲裁方式解决争议的前提是有书面的仲裁协议。书面仲裁协议有两类：一类是在争议发生之前订立，通常是买卖双方在合同中规定仲裁条款；另一类是在争议发生之后订立的，买卖双方在争议发生后，签署专门的仲裁协议，同意把已经发生的争议提交仲裁。这两类仲裁协议的法律效力是相同的，最常见的是合同中的仲裁条款。

仲裁协议的作用有：①约束双方当事人只能以仲裁方式解决其争议，不得向法院起诉；②排除法院对有关案件的管辖权，如果一方背仲裁协议，自行向法院起诉，另一方可根据仲裁协议要求法院不予受理，并将争议案件交仲裁庭裁断；③使仲裁机构取得对争议的管辖权。因此，买卖双方当事人如不愿将争议提交法院审理，最好在争议发生前，在合同中规定仲裁条款，以免对未来发生争议后，因不能提交仲裁而不得不诉诸于法院。

签订仲裁协议时，双方当事人当认真考虑仲裁协议的实质性问题。根据中国仲裁法及其他有关法律的规定，结合仲裁实践，当事人之间订立的仲裁协议在下列情况下无效：①以口头方式订立；②将不可仲裁的事项提交仲裁；③无行为能力人或限制行为能力人订立的仲裁协议；④通过胁迫手段订立的仲裁协议；⑤仲裁事项未约定或约定不明确，当事人不能达成补充协议的；⑥仲裁机构未约定或约定不明确，当事人不能达成补充协议的；⑦约定的仲裁事项超出法律规定的仲裁范围的；⑧仲裁协议明显地剥夺了双方当事人的平等仲裁权。

合同中的仲裁条款的具体内容，一般包括：提交仲裁的争议范围、仲裁地点、仲裁规则、仲裁程序、仲裁裁决的效力、仲裁费的负担等。

### （一）仲裁地点

仲裁地点所适用的程序法与合同所适用的实体法关系密切。按照西方国家的法律，凡属程序方面的问题，除非仲裁协议另有规定，一般都适用于审判地法律，即在哪个国家仲裁，就往往适用哪个国家的仲裁法规。而确定合同双方当事人权利、义务的实体法，如合同中未规定，一般由仲裁员根据仲裁地点所在国家法律冲突规则予以确定。因此，仲裁地点不同，适用法律可能不同，对买卖双方的权利、义务的解释就会有差别，其结果也会不同。

在国际货物买卖合同中，关于仲裁地点的约定，一般有3种规定办法：①规定在卖方所在国仲裁；②规定在买方所在国仲裁；③规定在双方同意的第三国仲裁。

### （二）仲裁机构

仲裁机构由买卖双方自主选择，其审理案件的管辖权完全取决于当事人的选择和授权。国际商事仲裁机构可分为临时仲裁机构和常设仲裁机构。临时仲裁机构是指根据当事人的仲裁条款或仲裁协议，在争议发生后由双方当事人推荐的仲裁员临时组成的，负责裁断当事人的争议，并在裁决后即行解散的临时性仲裁机构。常设仲裁机构是指依据国际条约或国内法成立的具有固定组织和地点、固定的仲裁程序规则的永久性仲裁机构。

目前国际上影响较大的几个常设商事仲裁机构是：①国际商会仲裁院，成立于1923年，总部设在巴黎；②瑞典斯德哥尔摩商事仲裁院，成立于1917年；③英国伦敦仲裁院，成立于1892年；④美国仲裁协会，成立于1926年，总部设在纽约；⑤瑞士苏黎世商会仲裁院，成立于1911年；⑥中国国际经济贸易仲裁委员会，成立于1956年，1980年、1988年两次调整，总部设在北京，在深圳、上海设有分会；⑦中国海事仲裁委员会，成立于1959年，1988年调整，总部设在北京。

### （三）仲裁程序

各国仲裁机构一般都有自己的仲裁程序规则。仲裁程序的主要内容大致如下：

### 1. 提出仲裁申请

这是仲裁程序开始的首要手续。各国法律对申请书的规定不一致，《中国国际经济贸易仲裁委员会仲裁规定》规定：当事人一方申请仲裁时，应向该委员会提交包括下列内容的签名申请书：申诉人和被诉人的名称、地址；申诉人所依据的仲裁协议；申诉人的要求及所据的事实和证据。申诉人向仲裁委员会提交仲裁申请书时，应附具本人要求所依据的事实的证明文件，指定一名仲裁员，预缴一定数额的仲裁费。如果委托代理人办理仲裁事项或参与仲裁的，应提交书面委托书。

### 2. 组织仲裁庭

根据中国仲裁规则规定，申诉人和被申诉人各自在仲裁委员会仲裁员名册中指定1名仲裁员，并由仲裁委员会主席指定1名仲裁员为首席仲裁员，共同组成仲裁庭审理案件；双方当事人亦可在仲裁委员名册共同指定或委托仲裁委员会主席指定1名仲裁员为独任仲裁员，成立仲裁庭，单独审理案件。

### 3. 审理案件

仲裁庭审理案件的形式有两种：一是不开庭审理，这种审理一般是经当事人申请，或由仲裁庭征得双方当事人同意，只依据书面文件进行审理并做出裁决；二是开庭审理，这种审理按照仲裁规则的规定，采取不公开审理，如果双方当事人要求公开进行审理时，由仲裁庭做出决定。

### 4. 做出裁决

裁决是仲裁程序的最后一个环节。裁决做出后，审理案件的程序即告终结，因而这种裁决被称为最终裁决。根据中国仲裁规则，除最终裁决外，仲裁庭认为有必要或接受当事人之提议，在仲裁过程中，可就案件的任何问题做出中间裁决或者部分裁决。中间裁决是指对审理清楚的争议所做的暂时性裁决，以利于对案件的进一步审理；部分裁决是指仲裁庭对整个争议中的一些问题已经审理清楚，而先行做出的部分终局性裁决。这种裁决是构成最终裁决的组部分。

仲裁裁决必须于案件审理终结之日起45天内以书面形式做出，仲裁裁决除由于调解达成和解而做出的裁决书外，应说明裁决所依据的理由，并写明裁决是终局的和做出裁决的日期地点，以及仲裁员的署名等。当事人对于仲裁裁决书，应依照其中所规定的时间自动履行，裁决书未规定期限的，应立即履行。一方当事人不履行的，另一方当事可以根据中国法律的规定，向中国法院申请执行，或根据有关国际公约、或中国缔结或参加的其他国际条约的规定办理。

### （四）仲裁裁决效力

根据中国仲裁规则规定，仲裁应当根据事实，依照法律合同规定，参照国际惯例，并遵循公平合理原则，独立公正地做出裁决。仲裁裁决是终局的，双方当事人均有约束力。任何一方当事人不得向法院起诉，也不得向其他任何机构提出变更裁决的请求。

但是，按照国际仲裁规则的一般规定，以下仲裁裁决结果无效，当事人可在法定期限内，请求仲裁地的管辖法院撤销仲裁裁决，并宣布其为无效：①仲裁裁决是在无仲裁协议的情况下做出的；②是以无效（或过期）的仲裁协议为据做出的裁决；③仲裁员行为不当或越权所做出的裁决；④以伪造证据为依据所做出的裁决；⑤裁决的事项属于仲裁地法律规定不得提交仲裁处理的裁决等。

### （五）仲裁费用

有关仲裁费用的承担问题，贸易双方应在仲裁条款中订明。一般规定由败诉方承担，也有的规定由仲裁庭酌情决定。根据中国仲裁规则规定，仲裁庭有权裁定败诉方补偿胜诉方因办理案件支出的部分合理的费用，但补偿金额最多不得超过胜诉方所得胜金额的10%。

仲裁裁决的执行，包括对本国仲裁裁决的执行与对外国仲裁裁决的执行。对本国仲裁裁决执行的手续较为简单，而对于外国仲裁裁决的执行就较为复杂。对外国的仲裁裁决执行不仅涉及买卖双方当事人的利益，而且还涉及两国之间的利害关系，故各国对执行外国的仲裁裁决，都规定了一些限制，存在许多分歧。

关于承认与执行外国仲裁裁决的国际公约有3个：①1923年缔结的《1923年日内瓦仲裁条款议定书》；②1927年缔结的《关于执行外国仲裁裁决的公约》；③1958年在纽约缔结的《承认和执行外国仲裁裁决 的公约》，简称纽约公约。中国于1986年12月2日正式加入了纽约公约，但有两项保留：①中华人民共和国只在互惠的基础上对在另一缔约国领土内做出的仲裁裁决的承认和执行适用该公约；②中华人民共和国只对根据中华人民共和国法律认定为属于契约性和非契约性商事法律关系所引起的争议适用该公约。中国政府对上述公约的加入和所作的声明，不仅为中国承认与执行外国仲裁裁决提供了法律依据，而且也有利于中国仲裁机构所做出的裁决在国外公约成员国内的执行。2018年6月26日，经过85个联合国成员与35个国际政府间组织、非政府组织的3年反复讨论，联合国贸易法委员会（UNCITRAL）第五十一届大会通过了关于执行调解所产生的和解协议的公约草案。该公约被命名为《新加坡调解公约》。下一步，将由联合国大会通过该公约草案和修订后的《联合国贸易法委员会国际商事调解示范法》（以下称"《示范法》"），再向成员开放签署。《新加坡调解公约》将在3个以上成员签署后生效。签署仪式预计将于2019年在新加坡举行。

☞ **阅读材料7.1**

## 世界各国的茶叶检验标准

茶叶检验标准分为茶叶生产国标准和非茶叶生产国标准两种类型。前者以出口检验为主，后者以进口检验为主。目前，世界各国茶叶检验标准逐渐趋向于制定国家标准。有些国家不仅将国际标准化组织的标准推荐转化为国家标准，而且同时还规定茶叶必须遵守各国的食品卫生标准和法规。

印度：印度是世界上茶叶生产、消费和出口数量最多的国家，95%以上是红茶。制定的茶叶检验国家标准有4种：茶叶规格（IS3633—72）、茶叶取样（IS3611—67）、茶叶术语（IS4545—66）以及茶叶包装规格（IS10—76）。印度早在1966年就把茶叶术语列为国家标准。根据茶叶化学成分的分析，制定了红茶品质规格。为了与ISO 3720保持一致，印度修订了本国的茶叶国家标准，政府用法令支持国家标准的实施。为了保证茶叶质量，印度政府设有茶叶质量监管机构"茶叶局"，并订有茶叶质量管理条例，在产地和出运港口实施检验，使规定的最低标准得到严格遵守。

斯里兰卡：订有红茶（CS：135—1979）、速溶茶叶（CS：401—1976）和禁止劣茶输出法标准。所有茶叶在生产过程中或出口时，茶叶质量都要受茶叶局监管。除经申请许可，用作提取咖啡碱、色素或其他工业用途（不包括提取速溶茶）者外，对不符合法令的低劣茶叶，不得出口。

日本：茶叶标准由农林、厚生、通商产业3省联合颁布。订有茶叶质量标准、检验方法、包装条件、取样方法等。质量标准包括形状、色泽、水色、香味、水分、茶梗、粉末及卫生指标等。订有最低标准样茶，每年由有关部门研究制定。

土耳其：土耳其的茶叶国家标准共有9种，均于1971年公布施行。其编号和标题如下：

TS 1561—71 茶叶已知物质含量的粉末状样品的制备；

TS 1562—71 茶叶在103摄氏度下重量损失的测定；

TS 1563—71 茶叶水浸出物的测验；

TS 1564—71 茶叶总灰分的测定；

TS 1565—71 茶叶水溶灰分的测定；

TS 1566—71 茶叶酸不溶灰分的测定；

TS 1567—71 茶叶水溶灰分碱度测定；

TS 1568—71 茶叶从大包装中取样；

TS 2948—71 茶叶从小包装中取样。

土耳其是以国际标准化组织推荐的茶叶国际标准作为他的国家标准的。

中国：中国茶叶出口标准《茶叶出口标准WMB48-8"茶叶"》是1981年修订的，其内容包括：①茶叶规格；②茶叶包装；③茶叶检验方法。同时，配套制定了《出口茶叶取样和检验暂行技术规程》《特种茶叶出口程序标准》《出口茶叶质量安全控制规范》。茶叶品质规格把出口茶叶分为红茶、绿茶、乌龙茶、花茶、白茶、紧压茶等6类。其规定：①各类各级茶叶必须符合中华人民共和国对外贸易部制定的标准样茶或出口合同规定的成交样茶；②各类各级茶叶必须品质正常，无劣变及其他异味；③茶叶须洁净，不得含有非茶类夹杂物。

美国：美国进口茶叶的最低标准是通过不同方式和评茶师的感官审评建立起来

的。在1987年制定的"茶叶进口法案"中规定，所有进入美国的茶叶，不得低于美国茶叶专家委员会制定的最低标准样茶。最低标准样茶计有7种：①中国红茶（包括台湾省）；②红茶；③乌龙茶（包括台湾省）；④绿茶；⑤中国包种茶（包括台湾省）；⑥香料茶（spiced tea）；⑦加香茶（flavored tea）。各类进口茶叶，根据美国《食品、药品和化妆品管理规定》，必须经美国卫生人类服务部、食品及药物管理局（Food and Drug Administration，简称FDA）抽样检验。品质低于法定标准，或污染、变质或纯度不符消费要求的产品，茶叶检验官有权禁止进口；对茶叶的农药残留量除非经出口国环境保护部门许可，或按规定证明残留量在允许范围内，否则属不合法产品。

澳大利亚：海关"进口管理法"1975年和1977年先后规定，绝对禁止进口的茶叶有：①泡过的茶叶；②掺有假茶或不适合人类饮用的茶叶；③有损于健康和不合卫生的茶叶。对一般进口茶叶，必须符合下列标准：水浸出物不少于30%（以干态计），总灰分不超过8%，水溶性灰分不超过3%（以干态计）。

巴基斯坦：巴基斯坦的茶叶国家标准有以下3种：ps 493—1965 茶叶标准–a；ps 18—1958 茶叶包装箱及制箱用胶合板；ps 784—1970 茶叶标准–b。茶叶标准规定红茶必须经过发酵、干燥而正常，不含非茶类夹杂物、茶灰或其他杂质。允许含茶梗，但不允许未发酵的，含梗量不得超过10%。绿茶必须经过干燥而正常，不含非茶类夹杂物、茶灰或其他杂质。茶叶理化标准有：①水浸出物不得低于33%；②总灰分含量应在3%—8%之间，其中水溶性灰分占总灰分的比例不低于45%；③水溶性灰分碱度，以k2o计应在重量的1.5%—2%；④酸不溶性灰分不得超过0.8%。⑤粗纤维含量不得超过15%；⑥咖啡碱含量不得少于2.5%。⑦茶多酚含量不得少于10%；⑧红茶水分不超过10%。以上限量标准均有其自己的检验方法。

英国：已把ISO3720红茶规格标准等，转换为英国的国家茶叶标准。规定从1981年4月1日起，凡在伦敦拍卖市场出售的茶叶，必须符合这个标准，否则就不能出售。将ISO1839—1980茶叶取样方法，转换为BS5987—1985英国标准。其他标准还有：

bs 6008—1985 茶—供感官检验用茶汤的制备；

bs 6048—1987 茶—红茶技术条件；

bs 6049/1—85 茶—已知干物质含量的磨碎试样的制备；

bs 6049/2—85 茶—在103摄氏度失重的测定；

bs 6049/3—85 茶—水浸出物的测定；

bs 6049/4—88 茶叶总灰分的测定；

bs 6049/5—81 茶叶水溶性灰分和水不溶性灰分的测定；

bs 6049/6—88 茶叶酸不溶灰分的测定；

bs 6049/7—71 茶叶水溶性灰公碱度的测定；

bs 6325—82 茶—红茶有关术语词汇；

bs 6986/1—88 速溶茶取样方法；

bs 6986/2—88 速溶茶松散密度和压实密度的测定方法。

智利：其茶叶国家标准有：①水分不超过12%；②粉末不超过5%；③含梗量不超过20%；④总灰分不超过8%；⑤10%盐酸不溶灰分不超过1%；⑥水浸出物红茶不少于24%、绿茶不少于28%；⑦咖啡碱不少于1%。

法国：赞成ISO3720，并十分重视标准中茶叶代用品的鉴别，其茶叶国家标准有下列10种：nfvo 3—001—1972 茶叶规格；nfvo 3—340—1972 茶叶取样；nfvo 3—341—1966 茶叶试验用粉末状样品的制备；nfvo 3—342—1966 茶叶水分和挥发性物质测定；nfvo 3—343—1968 茶叶水浸出物测定；nfvo 3—344—1968 茶叶总灰分测定；nfvo 3-345-1968 茶叶水溶灰分和水不溶灰分测定；nfvo 3—346—1968 茶叶水溶灰分碱度测定；nfvo 3—347—1968 茶叶酸不溶灰分测定；nfvo 3—355—1972 茶叶制备感官审评用的茶汤。

罗马尼亚：茶叶国家标准有以下4种：stas：968216—1975 红茶；stas：968217—1976 茶的灰分测定；stas：968214—1974 茶叶从大容器中取样；stas：968215—1974 茶叶从小容器中取样。

保加利亚：茶叶国家标准有：b.a.c 9808—1972 红茶；b.a.c 2757—1977 开胃茶；b.a.c 2758-1977 安神茶；b.a.c 2759—1977 利尿茶。

德国：该国赞成ISO3720，除有严格的茶叶卫生标准外，定有以下检验方法标准：din 10800-81 茶叶和茶叶制品的检验——干物质含量的测定；din 10801—86 茶咖啡碱含量的测定；din 10802—83 茶总灰分测定；din 10803—85 茶水浸出物的测定；din 10804—86 茶叶和茶叶制品的检验——茶鞣质含量的测定；din 10805—87 茶酸不溶灰分的测定；din 10806—83 茶试样制备；din 10809—88 茶感官审评方法。

其他：捷克和斯洛伐克的茶叶标准有：茶叶取样；（csn 58011—89）；茶叶词汇（csn 581303—88）；发酵红茶一般规定（csn 581350—74）。匈牙利的茶叶标准有：茶叶（msz 8170—80）。沙特阿拉伯的茶叶标准有：茶叶（ssa 275—82）。

☞ 阅读材料7.2

## 我国林产品出口贸易争端典型案例

我国林产品出口贸易争端案件数量显著增长。2000—2006年，全国林产品出口贸易争端28起，平均每年4起。2007—2012年，林产品出口纠纷重要案件50起，平均每年8.3起，其中2010年达11起；在所有对我发起林产品贸易救济调查案的国家或地区中，美国19起居首，其次是印度6起，第三是巴基斯坦4起，居第四的有欧盟、澳大利亚、韩国、阿根廷和土耳其等，均为3起。其中，美对华硬木装饰胶合板"双反"案是一个比较典型的案例。此案是继2010年11月美对华多层木地板"双反"案后的第二起美对华林产品"双反"案，共有74个10位税号的胶合板产品被纳入调查范围，涉案金额6.165亿美元，波及中国企业200多家。

2012年9月27日，美国硬木胶合板公平贸易协会代表美国内产业正式向DOC和ITC提出申请，请求对华硬木胶合板产品进行反补贴与反倾销调查并要求对涉案产品征收 298.36%—321.68%的反倾销税、征收微量反补贴税。2012年10月18日，DOC公告，决定对原产于中国的硬木装饰胶合板进行反倾销和反补贴调查。2012年11月9日，ITC公告，对原产于中国的硬木装饰胶合板做出反倾销和反补贴产业损害初裁。

2013年2月27日，DOC公告，对华硬木装饰胶合板做出反补贴初裁，裁定中国普遍补贴率为22.63%；亚洲创建河源木业有限公司等15家中国企业的补贴率为27.16%；只有3家企业获得微量补贴率裁定，低于1%。同年4月30日，DOC公告，对华硬木装饰胶合板做出反倾销初裁，裁定中国企业普遍倾销幅度为63.96%，101家单独税申请企业的倾销幅度为22.14%；只有两家企业被裁定为微量倾销，倾销幅度分别为0.62%和1.83%。9月17日，DOC 做出肯定性终裁，中国普通补贴率降至13.58%；反倾销税率大幅飙升，中国普通倾销幅度高达121.65%，105 家单独税申请企业的倾销幅度为59.46%，初裁微量倾销的临沂圣福源和江阳集团两家企业的终裁倾销幅度升至55.76%与62.55%。

2013年11月6日，ITC6名委员就硬木装饰胶合板双反案件的损害终裁进行投票，结果出席的5名委员均投否定票。ITC以无产业损害结案，意味着DOC的高额终裁税率将不会生效。

## 思考题：

1. 国际贸易解决争议的方式有哪些？其中，诉讼与仲裁有何异同？

2. 某夏天，中国南方发生特大洪水灾害，在此之前外贸企业与外商签订有3份大米出口合同，合同的商品名称分别为："太湖大米""在某仓库存放的江苏大米""中国大米"，7—8月份交货。请就以上情况，分别说明中国外贸企业如何向外商提出免责要求？

3. 中国某公司与外商签订一份出口合同，在合同中明确规定了仲裁条款，约定在履约过程中如产生争议，在中国仲裁。后来，外商对商品的品质发生争议，对方在其所在地法院起诉中方当事人，法院发来传票，要求中方公司出庭应诉。对此，你认为应如何处理？

4. 试问跨境电商中买家如何防范质量风险？

# Chapter 7

# General Terms of a Sales Contract

☞ Case 7.1

Ninbo Arts and Crafts Co Ltd (Hereafter called as Ningbo Company) and DUFERCO S.A. in Swiss (hereafter called as Swiss Company) entered into a contract on Jan 23, 2003 for buying and selling cold-rolled steel. The arbitration clause of the contract stipulated:"all dispute in connection with this contract or the execution thereof shall be settled by negotiation friendly. If no settlement can be reached, the case in dispute shall then be submitted to the Arbitration of the International Chamber of Commerce in Beijing,China,in accordance with the United Nations Convention on the International Sale of Goods.

The contract was disputed in the performance. On September 12, 2005, the Swiss company submitted the dispute to the ICC. The Singapore arbitral tribunal heard the case in writing. During the trial, the arbitral tribunal delivered the Trial Order and the Temporary Timetable to Ningbo Company. These documents were all delivered to Ningbo Company, the latter signed the documents, but did not submit any reply, nor did they raise any objection to the jurisdiction of the arbitral tribunal.The sole arbitral tribunal issued the ruling No. 14006/MS/JB/JEM (hereinafter referred to as the ICC ruling) in Beijing on September 21, 2007. Ningbo Company failed to implement this ruling. On February 27, 2008, the Ningbo Intermediate People's Court accepted the application of the Swiss company to enforce the ICC ruling.

After hearing the case, the court held that Ningbo Company did not raise any objection to the validity of the arbitration agreement within the validity period,and the ICC Court of Arbitration has made a valid determination of the arbitration clause in the arbitral award, according to the Supreme People's Court on the application of the arbitration of the People's Republic of China. Article 13 of the Law explains that if the parties do not object to the validity of the arbitration agreement before the first hearing of the arbitral tribunal and then apply to the people's court for confirmation that the arbitration agreement is invalid, the people's court will not accept it. After the arbitral institution makes a decision on the validity of the arbitration agreement, if the party applies to the people's court for confirmation of the validity of the arbitration agreement or applies for revoking the decision of the arbitral institution, the people's court shall not accept it.

Therefore, the claim of the Ningbo Company that the arbitration agreement is invalid cannot be established. The court held that the ruling in this case belonged to the non-international ruling under the New York Convention. After hearing the case, the court found that there was no non-implementation of the provisions of the Convention and ruled recognize and enforce the ICC ruling on April 22, 2009.

This case was the ICC arbitral tribunal applying the ruling made by its rules in Beijing, China, which had applied to the Chinese court for recognition and enforcement of the ruling made by the ICC Court of Arbitration in accordance with its arbitration rules. ( This case is taken from: Zhao Xiuwen. The Recognition and Implementation of ICC Ruling in China from the Perspective of Relevant Cases[J].  Law, 2010 (3) 69-70.)

As globalization continues to expand, so do international business relationships. Sustaining these relationships is essential for maintaining the flow of trade between nations. Strong relationships play a central role in all international trade, in the emerging markets context they are even more critical. This is due in great part to the weaker rule of law in emerging markets. Where commerce does not have as strong of a legal system to lean upon in managing disputes, companies must depend on other mechanisms to enable a productive environment for commerce and trade. So they do business with those they know and trust, not simply as a matter of preference, but as a matter of survival.

Dispute settlement is the central pillar of the multilateral trading system, and the WTO's unique contribution to the stability of the global economy. Without a means of settling disputes, the rules-based system would be less effective because the rules could not be enforced. The WTO's procedure underscores the rule of law, and it makes the trading system more secure and predictable. The system is based on clearly-defined rules, with timetables for completing a case. First rulings are made by a panel and endorsed (or rejected) by the WTO's full membership. Appeals based on points of law are possible.

Resolving trade disputes is one of the core activities during negotiating and performing a sales contract. A dispute aroused when one party believes another party is violating an agreement or a commitment that it has made. Commercial litigation is lengthy, costly, hard to enforce and, because of the adversarial nature of the proceedings, will often damage business relationships beyond compare. In order to avoid disputes happened or settle disputes, except for the subject matters, price, payment, transport and insurance clauses, a sales contract shall stipulate the methods how to settle disputes, including inspection of the goods, claims, arbitration and force majeure, etc.

# 7.1 Inspection of the Goods

In generally, both parties of international trade are located at two different nations/regions, the seller can not deliver the goods to the buyer on spot. The goods shall have to be transported in long distance and with several times of be loaded and unloaded on the different conveyances tools. Disputes are caused by the problems of quality and/or quantity of the goods. In order to protect interest, avoid controversy aroused, or identify responsibilities and deal with the disputes, how to inspect the goods shall be specified stipulate in the sales contract in advance. The relating inspection certificate is the important evidence for taking delivery of the goods, payment, lodging claims and making satisfaction. Inspection of the goods is an important link for delivery of the goods from the seller to the buyer.

## 7.1.1 Legal Provisions Relating to Inspection

Whatever the United Nations Convention on Contracts for the International sale of Goods or the Anglo-American Law recognizes that the buyer has right to inspect the goods purchased, unless otherwise agreed by the buyer and the seller. The seller shall give sufficient support to the buyer. The Contract Law of China also deems that the buyer has right to examine the goods received.

Article 38 of the United Nations Convention on Contracts for the International sale of Goods stipulates: ① The buyer must examine the goods, or cause them to be examined, within as short a period as is practicable in the circumstances. ② If the contract involves carriage of the goods, examination may be deferred until after the goods have arrived at their destination. ③ If the goods are redirected in transit or re-dispatched by the buyer without a reasonable opportunity for examination by him and at the time of the conclusion of the contract the Seller knew or ought to have known of the possibility of such redirection or re-dispatch, examination may be deferred until after the goods have arrived at the new destination".

Article 34 of Sale of Goods Act 1979[England] stipulates: ① Where goods are delivered to the buyer, and he has not previously examined them, he is not deemed to have accepted them until he has a reasonable opportunity of examining them for the purpose of ascertaining whether they are in conformity with the contract. ② Unless otherwise agreed, when the seller intends to deliver the goods to the buyer, he is bound on request to afford the buyer a reasonable opportunity of examining the goods for the purpose of ascertaining whether they are in conformity with the contract. However, the buyer's right to inspect the goods is not a prerequisite for the acceptance of the goods by the buyer. The buyer may inspect the goods received or may not inspect the goods. If the buyer does not take advantage of a reasonable opportunity to inspect the goods, it means that he give up the right to inspect the goods and has lost the right to reject the goods.

The Uniform Commercial Code of the United States stipulates that the buyer accepts the goods in all of the following situations: ①after a reasonable opportunity to inspect the goods, the buyer indicates to the seller that the goods are in conformity with the contract, or that they will receive or retain the goods, even the goods are not in conformity with the contract. ②In the event that the buyer has a reasonable opportunity to inspect the goods, it fails to make an effective rejection. ③The buyer shall act in violation of all rights of the seller to the goods.

## 7.1.2 Inspection Clauses in a Sales Contract

The inspection clauses in a sales contract generally include the time and place of inspection, the contents of inspection, inspection institutions, inspection standards and inspection certificates, etc.

### 1. Inspection Institutions

Inspection of the goods can be divided into seller's inspection (First party's inspection), buyer's inspection (second party's inspection) and the third party's inspection. It is necessary to have a qualified, authoritative and impartial third party independent of the buyer and the seller, that is, a professional inspection and quarantine institution shall be responsible for inspecting the quality, quantity and packaging of the goods delivered by the seller, or for inspecting or appraising the shipment technology and the damaged goods. In practice, inspection of the goods is generally performed by the inspection institutions. Whatever the buyer takes delivery of the goods or rejects the goods, it is mainly based on the impartial inspection result of the inspection institutions.

The relating institutions can be divided into official inspection institutions and private inspection institutions. For example, U.S. Food and Drug administration (FDA), the national laboratory testing center of France and The trade and industry inspection institute of Japan are official inspection agencies. In addition to the official commodity inspection institutions established by the government, many countries also have semi-official or private commodity inspection institutions established by Chambers of commerce, associations, trade unions or private organizations to inspect and identify the international goods.

The global renowned and authoritative private commodity inspection organizations include: ①SGS: Societe Generale de Surveillance. ②IITS: Inchcape inspection and testing services. ③NKKK: Japan marine surveyors & sworn measures association. ④SK: New Japan surveyors and sworn measures association.⑤OMIC: Japan overseas merchandise Inspection Company.⑥UL: Underwriter Laboratories Inc.⑦ASTM: American Society for Testing and Materials.⑧CSA: Canadian Standards Association.⑨IWS: International Wool Secretariat. ⑩CCIC: China Certification & Inspection (Group) Co., Ltd.

For example, UL is an independent, non-profit, nongovernmental organization that conducts public safety testing and certification. UL's safety standards are the basis for UL to conduct product testing and safety certification. At present, the impact of UL safety standards has gone far beyond the borders of the United States, and more than 50 countries and regions around the world have carried out testing and certification according to UL safety standards.

### 2. Time & Place of Inspection

The international conventions and the laws of most countries stipulate the rights and obligations of buyers and sellers to inspect the goods. However, there is no uniform regulation on when and where the buyer and the seller should conduct the inspection. The time and place for inspection of the goods is related to the vital interests of both parties, the exercise of inspection right, the designation of inspection institution and the legal basis of claim in the future. Therefore, both parties should specify the time and place of inspection in the buyer's contract. The time and place of inspection can be stipulated by four methods.

（1）Inspection in the Exporting Country

Inspection of the goods in the exporting country can be further divided into inspection at the place of origin and inspection at the place (port) of shipment. If the goods are inspected at the place of origin, the seller is only in charge for the quality and quantity of the goods before its leaving the origin place. The buyer bears the risks for the loss of damaged to the goods during transportation. If the goods are inspected in the place (port) of shipment, the inspected result of landing quality, weight or quantity indicated on the inspection certificate is as final. When the goods arrived at place (port) of destination, the buyer has no right to reject the goods or raise an objection and claim for the problem goods after re-inspection of the goods.

（2）Inspection in the Importing Country

Inspection of the goods in the importing country refers to inspect the goods when the goods unloaded from the arriving tools at place (port) of destination, or arrived at the business site of buyer, or the place of end-user. If the goods are inspected in the place (port) of destination, the inspected result of unloading quality, weight or quantity indicated on the inspection certificate is as final. The seller is responsible for the inspected result not conformity with the contract stipulated. Inspection of the goods in the buyer's business site or the end-user's place, is suitable for the sealed packaged cargo and sophisticated cargo. It is not in appropriate if they are performed unpacking inspection before use. For the complete sets of equipment and electrical instrumentation products need to be tested after installation and debugging, the goods can be inspected within a certain period of time after arriving at the buyer's business site or the end-user's place as agreed by the both parties.

(3) Inspection in the Exporting Country and Re-Inspection in the Importing Country

The inspection certificate of landing at place (port) of shipment is necessary for collecting payment, when inspection in the exporting country and re-inspection in the import country applicable, While, the buyer has right to re-inspect the goods when the goods arrived at the place (port) of destination. If the goods is not conformity with the contract stipulated after re-inspected by the inspection institutions agreed by the both parties, and the discrepancies is not fallen into the area of responsibilities of the carrier or the insurer, the buyer has right to reject the goods, raise an objection, or lodge a claim.

(4) Pre-Inspection in the Exporting Country and Final Inspection at the Importing Country

It refers to the buyer nominates a person or entrust a surveyor of inspection institution to have a pre-inspection of the goods before landing at the exporting country. When the goods arrived at destination, the buyer has a final inspection. The final inspect result is the evidence for the buyer to lodge a claim.

Each of the above four prescribed methods, with its own characteristics, shall be determined according to the specific nature of the goods. Among them, the practice of "inspection in the exporting country and re-inspection in the importing country" is the most used, because it not only affirms that the inspection certificate submitted by the seller is an effective delivery and settlement

### 3. Contents of Inspection

The content of inspection varies according to the characteristics of the goods, relevant laws and regulations, specific provisions of the sales contract, technical standards and the intention of applicant to apply for the inspection. Generally, there are quality inspection, quantity and weight inspection, packing inspection, shipping technical inspection and appraisal of import and export commodities.

(1) Quality Inspection

Quality Inspection is the main item for Inspection of the goods. The content of quality inspection mainly includes appearance and internal quality. Appearance quality contains morphology, size, specification, pattern, color, shape, surface defect, surface processing and decoration level of the goods, etc. There are many contents of internal quality inspection, including component inspection and performance tests. Among them:

① The composition inspection includes types, contents, impurities and limits of hazardous.

② Performance tests include physical properties inspections, such as strength, hardness, elasticity, shrinkage, solubility, heat resistance, acid/alkali resistance, corrosion resistance, chemical compatibility.

③Mechanical performance tests include pressure resistance, tension resistance, impact, vibration, drop, etc.

④Functional performance tests include the completion of specified non-action and specific use effects, such as the braking and speed requirements of the car, the sound and image effects of the TV set, and the completion rate of products produced by the machine.

⑤The specific items quality inspection refers to the quality inspection with special requirements for different commodities for the purposes of safety, hygiene and environmental protection, such as food hygiene quality inspection, animal and plant inspection, inspection for the safety performance of dangerous goods, safety protection and inspection of aircraft, ships and vehicles and limit testing of waste gas, noise, waste water. The food hygiene quality is generally inspected the harmful organisms, food additives, pesticide residues, and heavy metal content, etc.

(2) Weight/Quantity/Packing Inspection

The weight clauses or quantity clauses are main terms of a sales contract. So weight inspection or quantity inspection is one of main contends of inspection. Packing inspection includes the inspection of the outer packing, inner packing and packing marks of the import and export goods.

(3) Shipping Technical Inspection

The shipping technical inspection is a compulsory inspection of the cabins and containers of perishable food, such as grain, oil and food, frozen goods. Among them, the cabin inspection includes dry cargo hold inspection, oil tank inspection, and cold storage tank inspection to confirm the cargo's load ability. The Container identification includes container's monitoring of loading and unloading, rental appraisal, rent refund appraisal, as well as container cleaning, temperature, wind and rain tightness and other single identification.

(4) Appraisal of the Import and Export Goods

According to the application of relevant parties such as a sales contract, transport contract and insurance contract or the entrust of foreign inspection institutions, the inspection institution shall handle the appraisal business of import and export commodities and issue various appraisal certificates, which shall be used by the applying unit as valid certificates for the goods handover, payment settlement, billing, customs clearance, tax calculation, claim or proof. The business scope of appraisal of import and export commodities includes: quality appraisal of import and export commodities, technical condition appraisal of shipment, container appraisal, property appraisal of foreign investment and other appraisal services.

**5. Inspection Certificates**

The inspection certificate has an important legal position in the international sale of goods. The types of inspection certificate issued by the China inspection and quarantine institutions include: Inspection certificate of quality, inspection certificate of quantity/weight, inspection certificate of packing,veterinary inspection certificate, sanitary/health certificates, disinfection certificate,

fumigation certificate, inspection certificate on damaged cargo, inspection certificate of

temperture, inspection certificate of carbine hold/tank, inspection certificate on cargo weight and measurement, inspection certificate of value, inspection certificate of quality and quantity of raw silk, certificate of hatch examine, certificate of monitor loading/unloading and certificate of hatch sealing

The inspection certificates with different types but basically have the same function mainly as following: ① As a basis for proving that the quality, weight (quantity), packing and sanitary conditions of the goods delivered by the seller are in conformity with the provisions of the contract. ② As the buyer's certificate of objection to quality, weight, packing and other conditions, refusal of goods, claim for compensation and settlement of disputes. ③ As one of the documents to be presented to the bank by the seller. ④ As a necessary certificate for customs examination and release, tariff collection and preferential tariff reduction and reduction.

# 7.2 Claims

The international sales contract clearly stipulates the rights and obligations of both parties and is binding on both parties. Either party must strictly perform its contractual obligations in accordance with the provisions of the contract. A default by one party not only causes disputes between buyers and sellers, but also causes economic losses to the other party. Therefore, the party in breach shall bear the corresponding liability for breach of contract. In the course of international goods trading, the event of breach of contract occurs from time to time, generally focusing on the quality, quantity (or weight) of delivery, delivery time and other issues. For example, when the international market price fluctuates frequently, the seller will not deliver the goods or deliver the goods on time, or the quality, quantity (weight) of the goods delivered will not meet the requirements of the contract. The buyer will not open the L/C on time or make payment on time. The party who has suffered a loss may lodge a claim to the breaching party for damages, and the breaching party shall settle the claim.

## 7.2.1 Breach of Contract and Its Legal Liability

The breach of contract with different nature has different legal liability. Fundamental breach and non-fundamental breach are classified by the United Nations Convention on

Contracts for the international sale of goods. A fundamental breach of contract is in which one party breaches the contract, causing the other party to suffer losses, thereby effectively depriving him of what he is entitled to expect under the contract. If a fundamental breach is happened, the damaged party shall have the right to claim damages from the breaching party and may declare the contract null and void. If the case of breach has not reached the level of fundamental breach, the damaged party can only claim damages and cannot declare the contract invalid.

The relating raw of United States divides default into material default and minor default. A material breach is a breach of contract by one party, which causes the other party unable to obtain the principal benefits due to the transaction. For minor breach, the damaged party can only ask for compensation but cannot cancel the contract.

The British law divides breach of contract into breach of essentials and breach of guarantee. Essentials refers to the important and fundamental clauses in a contract, such as the quality, quantity (weight), delivery time, etc. that are directly related to the goods in the contract. Guarantee refers to the secondary and subsidiary clauses in the contract, which are not directly related to the goods. The other party (the damaged party) shall have the right to terminate the contract and to claim damages if one party breaches the essential .In the case of breach of the guarantee, the damaged party can only claim damages and cannot terminate the contract.

## 7.2.2 Claim Clauses in a Sales Contract

In order to carry out the import and export business smoothly, the claim clauses are generally stipulated in a sales contract, including discrepancy and claim clause and penalty clause.

### 1. Discrepancy and Claim Clause

Discrepancy and Claim clauses is mainly used in the international sales contract, generally for the claim related to the quality, quantity or packing of the goods that the seller delivers to the buyer. The content of this clause, besides stipulating that if one party violates the contract, the other party has the right to claim for compensation, it also includes the period of claim, basis of claim and method of claim. Among them:

① The claim basis refers to the written materials that must be provided by the damaged party when filing the claim, proving that the other party has the truth of the fact of breach of contract, mainly the inspection certificate issued by the inspection institution. It is worth noting that the inspection institution must be mutually acceptable to both the buyer and the seller. The certification body is generally stipulated in the contract.

② The claim period refers to the effective time limit for the injured party to lodge a claim with the breaching party. If a claim is overdue, the breach of contract may not be accepted. Within the time of claim, the buyer may lodge a claim against the seller for any discrepancy between the quality, quantity and packing of the goods and the provisions of the contract. Generally, the buyer and the seller stipulate the limitation of claims in the contract, namely the limitation of claims.

③ In addition to the time limit of claims, there is also a statutory limitation of claims, that is, in accordance with the provisions of relevant laws and practices, the damaged party has the right to lodge a claim with the breaching party. The specific claim period stipulated in the contract shall be determined according to the type of goods, characteristics and time required for inspection. The agreed claim period shall not be too long or too short, and the seller shall bear too much responsibility if it is too long, and the buyer shall not be able to exercise the right of claim if it is too short. The effectiveness of the prescribed limitation of claims is generally higher than that of the statutory limitation of claims.

④ In an international sales contract, the parties to the contract generally combine the inspection terms with the claim terms, which are called "inspection and claim terms". The claim period is actually the re-inspection period in the inspection terms. If the time limit for claim is stipulated in the sales contract, the buyer shall promptly inspect the goods. Once the goods are found to be in non-conformity with the provisions of the contract, the buyer shall immediately ask the inspection authorities to re-inspect the certificate and claim the goods in strict accordance with the agreed time limit. If the quality guarantee period of the goods is stipulated in the sales contract, in case of any quality problem during the period of quality guarantee, the buyer shall immediately lodge a claim with the seller.

## ☞ Case 7.2

on January 20, 2020, Hong Kong Company A and Shanghai Company B signed a contract whereby Company A provided mobile phone parts made in ROK to Company B, and the goods were shipped no later than February 10. Company A promised in the contract that the quality guarantee period of the products would be 12 months after the goods arrived at the destination. On February 7, Company A provided the goods stipulated in the contract to Company B. On March 25, 2021, Company B found some quality problems in the use of the products and required Company A to replace them ,or return money and bear the concerned losses and charges. Co. A refused to compensate and replied to Co. B that the goods had been inspected, checked and put into use in detail before warehousing.

Because Co. B disagreed with the quality of the goods , on April 02, 2021, that was, 13 months after receiving the goods, Co. B sent the goods to China Commodity Inspection Authorities for inspection. The inspection certificate issued by the inspection institution proved that there were 5 defects in this batch of goods, which were caused by defective manufacturing.On April 05, Co. B initiated arbitration to claim compensation of USD 50,000 from Co. A.

In the opinion of Co. A, Co. B could not prove that the products submitted for the second inspection were the products delivered at the time of delivery, and the second inspection time had exceeded the validity of the claim, and the inspection certificate could not take effect. After the hearing, the arbitration tribunal held that Co. B had lost the right to claim compensation for not inspecting the quality of the goods within the stipulated time, rejected the request of Co. B, and ruled that Co. A was not liable for compensation.

### 2. Penalty Clause

The penalty clause, also known as "liquidated damages clause", generally applies to cases where the seller delays the delivery of the goods, or the buyer delays in issuing the letter of credit, taking delivery of the goods or making payment. When one party fails to fulfill its contractual obligations, it shall pay a certain amount of liquidated damages to the other party to compensate for its losses. The amount of the fine shall be determined according to the length of the time of default and the maximum amount shall be set by both parties in advance.

Generally speaking, the fine should not exceed 5% of the total value of the goods. Each country's laws have different interpretations on the penalty clauses in the contract. Some continental law countries (such as Germany) generally recognize the penalty clauses in the contract. However, in Anglo-American countries, the penalty clauses in the contract can be divided into the compensatory appointment compensation and punitive penalty according to their nature. In Anglo-American countries, the law only recognizes damages and does not recognize punitive fines.

# 7.3 Force Majeure

Force Majeure refers to the event(s) happened after the contracts conclude and causes the contract unable to be performed or not be performed as scheduled. Force majeure is not due to the fault or negligence of contract party, but at the time of the conclusion of contract that the parties cannot foreseeable, preventable and the event happened is unavoidable and insurmountable. The party suffering from the event(s) may be exempted from the obligation to perform the contract or postpone the performance of the contract, and the other party shall not have the right to claim compensation.

At present, the definition of force majeure by the international community is not unified, and the interpretation of the laws of various countries is quite different. For example, the French law called it as force majeure. The Anglo-American law system called it as contract failure. The continental law system called as situation change or contract failure. And the United Nations convention on the international sale of goods called it as the obstacles to the performance of contracts.

## 7.3.1 The Legal Consequences of Force Majeure

The legal consequences of force majeure event are different between countries. For example, the countries of Anglo-American law system believe that once appear failed contract, the contract came to an end, and automatically remove the performance obligations of the parties. Some other countries believe that a force majeure event does not necessarily make the contract to remove all. It shall be treated differently according to the reason, nature, scale, the actual impact on the performance.

In addition, China has stipulated two obligations of the party exempted from liability in the event of force majeure: ① The other party shall be notified in a timely manner to mitigate any losses that may be incurred to the other party. If the other party is not notified in time and causes losses to the other party, the party who fails to notify shall be liable for such losses. ② The other party shall, within a reasonable time, submit to the other party a certificate issued by the relevant authorities to prove the occurrence of a force majeure event. In China, the notary public and the China council for the promotion of international trade may issue a certificate of force majeure.

## 7.3.2 The Constitutive Conditions and Scope of the Force Majeure Events

Despite the differences in the names and interpretations of force majeure in national laws and the convention, it is considered that such events are structured in a manner that requires four conditions: ① Occur after the conclusion of a contract. ② Cannot be foreseen when a contract is concluded. ③ Cannot be controlled by the parties concerned, they cannot be avoided or prevented. ④ Shall not be caused by the fault or negligence of any party.

The reasons for the occurrence of force majeure events usually include the following two situations: ① Nature causes, such as flood, drought, blizzards, earthquakes, fires, tsunamis, ice storms. ② Civil affairs, such as war, strikes, government bans, trade policy adjustments.

Generally, due to natural causes of force majeure events, the trade parties are easy to reach consensus. However, regarding to the force majeure caused by social reasons, the legal interpretation of various countries is quite different, and disputes between buyers and sellers are more frequent. Therefore, when signing an international sales contract, both parties shall stipulate the terms of force majeure in the contract and solve the problem through negotiation according to the specific circumstances of the event.

### 7.3.3 Force Majeure Clauses in the Contract

The force majeure clause is a kind of disclaimer clause, which can completely or partially exempts the party who breaches the contract due to the force majeure event from the performance of the contract. The basic contents of the force majeure clauses in the international sales contract generally include the scope of force majeure events, the time limit for notifying the other party after the occurrence of event, the institution issuing the supporting documents and the consequences of the force majeure event. According to the scope of force majeure events, the force majeure clause usually has three methods of stipulations.

**1. General Provisions**

This method does not list which events are force majeure events in the contract. For example, the seller shall not be held liable for the failure or delay in delivery of the goods due to a recognized force majeure event, or for the failure to perform the contract due to a force majeure event. This method of stipulation is too general, vague meaning, with large interpretation scalability and easy to cause controversy.

**2. Examples**

The prescribed method is to specify specific force majeure events in the contract. For example, due to war, earthquake, flood, fire, storm and snow disaster, the seller shall not be liable for the failure or delay in shipping the contracted goods in whole or in part. However, the seller shall notify the buyer by telex or telex and shall submit to the buyer by registered airmail a certificate of such event issued by the China council for the promotion of international trade within 15 days. Although this method lists the force majeure events one by one is clear and specific, it is complicated and may lead to omission

**3. Comprehensive Provisions**

This method is to include the possible force majeure events (such as war, flood, earthquake, fire.) in the contract, together with the words "and other force majeure events agreed by both parties". For example, due to war, earthquake, flood, fire, storm, snowstorm or other force majeure events, the seller shall not be liable for the failure or delay in shipping the contracted goods in whole or in part. However, the seller shall notify the buyer by telex or telex and shall submit to the buyer by registered airmail within 15 days a certificate issued by the China council for the promotion of international trade certifying such events. This approach to stipulate is both specific and flexible.

## 7.3.4 Matters for Attention in the Conclusion of Force Majeure Clauses

The first is to define the notification method and notification period after the occurrence of force majeure. In case of a force majeure event, the party suffering from the force majeure event shall promptly notify the other party, so that the other party may take appropriate measures in a timely manner, such as finding out the facts of the force majeure event and its impact on the performance of the contract. If the other party has any objection after receiving the notice, it shall raise such objection to the other party in time. When one party of the transaction refers to the exemption of the force majeure clause, the other party shall conduct a strict review in accordance with the provisions of the contract to determine whether the quoted content falls within the scope prescribed by the force majeure clause.

The second is to stipulate the certificate of force majeure and its corresponding issuing institutions. When a force majeure event occurs, on the one hand, the party suffering from the force majeure event shall provide the valid supporting documents. The issuing authority of the certification document may stipulate that it is a legal notary institution in the area of force majeure or a local chamber of commerce.

The third is to provide for the legal consequences of force majeure. In the contract, it is stipulated under which circumstances the contract can be revoked, under which circumstances the contract can be partially rescinded, or the contract can be extended.

# 7.4   Methods of Disputes Settlement and Arbitration

## 7.4.1 The Methods of Disputes Settlement

The two parties of an international sales contract have an equal and mutually beneficial cooperation. After the signing of the contract, any dispute between the two parties shall be settled through friendly negotiation. If the friendly negotiation fails, the parties may settle the dispute through mediation, arbitration or litigation as agreed in the contract.

Conciliation means that after a dispute arises, the parties voluntarily submit the dispute to a selected mediation institution (a court or an arbitration institution, etc.) for mediation in accordance with the mediation procedures. If the mediation is successful, both parties shall enter into a settlement agreement and execute it as a new contract. If the mediation opinion is not accepted by either parties or one of them, it is not binding on the parties and the mediation will fail.

### 1. Litigation

Litigation is in dispute happens, one parties to the court, the accused of the contract the other party.The prosecution party generally requires the court to order the other party to assume the liability for breach of contract in the form of compensation for economic losses or payment of liquidated damages.The settlement of disputes by means of litigation has the following characteristics: ① It is mandatory to bring a lawsuit to a competent court, and the other party must answer the case, and neither party in dispute has the right to choose a judge.② The procedures are complex and problems are handled more slowly than arbitration. ③ When solving a dispute through litigation, the parties concerned are nervous and angry, which is not conducive to the further development of trade relations in the future.④ The costs of litigation are higher.

**2. Arbitration**

In case of any dispute arising between the buyer and the seller during the execution of the contract, the relevant dispute shall be submitted to the arbitration institution for arbitration according to the agreement. The advantages of arbitration over litigation are that: ① Arbitration is conducted on a voluntary basis and the parties have the flexibility to select their own arbitrators.② The arbitration procedure is relatively simple, and the arbitrators are generally experts and familiar with the international trade business, so arbitration solves problems quickly.③ The arbitration costs are lower than litigation costs.④ Arbitration has less impact on the continued development of trade relations between the parties.⑤ The arbitration award is final and the losing party shall not appeal and must perform.

It is noteworthy that the use of litigation and arbitration does not preclude friendly consultation or mediation. Because there are many advantages to settle disputes by arbitration, arbitration has become the most widely used important way to settle disputes in international trade.

## 7.4.2 Arbitration Agreement

A written arbitration agreement is a prerequisite for the settlement of disputes by arbitration. There are two types of written arbitration agreement: one is that it is concluded before the occurrence of a dispute, usually the buyer and the seller stipulate the arbitration clause in the contract. The other is concluded after the occurrence of disputes. After the occurrence of disputes, the buyer and the seller sign a special arbitration agreement and agree to submit the disputes that have already occurred to arbitration. The legal effect of these two kinds of arbitration agreements is the same; the most common is the arbitration clause in the contract.

The arbitration agreement has the following functions: ① It constrains both parties to settle their disputes only by arbitration and shall not bring a lawsuit to the court.② If one party, in violation of the arbitration agreement, brings a lawsuit to the court by itself, the other party may, according to the arbitration agreement, request the court to reject the case and submit the case in dispute to the arbitration tribunal for adjudication. ③Attach the arbitral body to obtain jurisdiction over the dispute. Therefore, if the buyer and the seller are unwilling to submit the dispute to the court for trial, it is better to stipulate the arbitration clause in the contract before the dispute occurs, so as not to submit the dispute to the court for arbitration in the future.

When signing an arbitration agreement, both parties should seriously consider the substantive issues of the arbitration agreement. In accordance with the provisions of the Chinese arbitration law and other relevant laws and in combination with the practice of arbitration, the arbitration agreement concluded between the parties shall be null and void in the following circumstances.

①The arbitration agreement is concluded orally.

②Any non-arbitral matter is submitted to arbitration.

③The arbitration agreements concluded by persons with disabilities or persons with limited capacity.

④The arbitration agreement concluded under duress.

⑤The arbitration matters have not been agreed upon or are not clearly agreed upon, where the parties fail to reach a supplementary agreement to clarify the arbitration matters.

⑥The arbitral institution fails to specify or stipulate clearly, and the parties fail to reach a supplementary agreement.

⑦The matter under review is beyond the scope of arbitration prescribed by law.

⑧Arbitration agreement concluded in such a way as to deprive both parties of the equal right of arbitration obviously.

## 7.4.3 Contents of Arbitration Clauses

The specific contents of the arbitration clauses in the contract generally include: the scope of disputes submitted for arbitration, the place of arbitration, the arbitration rules, the arbitration procedures, the validity of the arbitration award, and the burden of the arbitration fee.

**1. Arbitration Place**

The procedural law applicable to the arbitration site is closely related to the substantive law applicable to the contract. According to the laws of western countries, all procedural matters, unless otherwise provided for in the arbitration agreement, generally apply to the law of the place of trial, that is, in which country the arbitration is conducted, the arbitration laws of which country are usually applied. The substantive law determining the rights and obligations of the parties to a contract, if not specified in the contract, shall be generally determined by the arbitrator in accordance with the law conflict rules of the country where the arbitration is located.

Therefore, the interpretation of the rights and obligations of the buyer and the seller will be different and the result will be different depending on the location of the arbitration and the applicable law. In an international sales contract, generally there are three ways to specify the place of arbitration: governing the arbitration in the country of the seller, the buyer or in a mutually agreed third country.

### 2. Arbitration Institution

The arbitration institution is a private institution chosen by the buyer and the seller to settle the disputes. Its jurisdiction is entirely dependent on the choice and authorization of the parties. The international commercial arbitration institutions can be divided into temporary arbitration institutions and permanent arbitration institutions.

The provisional arbitration institution refers to a temporary arbitration institution which, in accordance with the arbitration clauses or arbitration agreement of the parties, is temporarily composed of arbitrators recommended by both parties after the occurrence of a dispute, shall be responsible for adjudicating the disputes between the parties and shall be dissolved immediately after the award.

A permanent arbitration institution is a permanent arbitration institution established in accordance with international treaties or domestic law with fixed organization, place and fixed rules of arbitration procedure. At present, the most influential permanent international commercial arbitration institutions are:

①ICC International Court of Arbitration established in 1923 and headquartered in Paris.

②Stockholm commercial arbitration institute, Sweden, founded in 1917.

③British institute of arbitration, London, founded in 1892.

④American arbitration association, founded in 1926 and headquartered in New York

⑤Arbitration court of Zurich chamber of commerce, Switzerland, founded in 1911.

⑥China international economic and trade arbitration commission , established in 1956, adjusted twice in 1980 and 1988, with its headquarters in Beijing and branches in Shenzhen and Shanghai.

⑦China maritime arbitration commission, founded in 1959, revised in 1988 and headquartered in Beijing.

### 3. The Arbitration Procedure

The arbitration institutions of various countries generally have their own rules of arbitration procedure. The main contents of the arbitration procedure are as follows:

(1) Submit an Application for Arbitration

This is the first procedure to start the arbitration process. The arbitration rules of China international economic and trade arbitration commission stipulate that when one party applies for arbitration, it shall submit a signed application including the name and address of the applicant and the defendant to the commission, the arbitration agreement on which the complainant is based, the complainant's claim and the facts and evidence against it. When submitting an application for arbitration to the arbitration commission, the complainant shall attach to the documentary evidence of the facts on which he has requested, designate an arbitrator and prepay a certain amount of arbitration fee. If an agent is entrusted to handle or participate in the arbitration, a written power of attorney shall be submitted.

(2) Organizing an Arbitration Tribunal

According to the rules of arbitration in China, the applicant and the respondent respectively designate one arbitrator in the list of arbitrators of the arbitration commission, and one arbitrator shall be appointed as the chief arbitrator by the chairman of the arbitration commission. The parties may jointly decide or entrust the chairman of the arbitration commission to designate one arbitrator as the sole arbitrator in the list of arbitrators, establish an arbitration tribunal and hear the case separately.

(3) Hearing Cases

There are two ways for an arbitral tribunal to hear a case: first, it does not hold a court session. Such a hearing is usually applied by the parties concerned or approved by the parties concerned, only based on the written documents and the tribunal hears the case and makes an award. Second, the hearing shall be held in court. Such hearing shall be conducted in private according to the arbitration rules. The arbitral tribunal shall make a decision if the parties require a public hearing.

(4) Make a Decision

The award is the last link in the arbitration procedure. After a decision is made, the process of hearing the case is concluded, so this decision is called final decision. According to China's arbitration rules, in addition to the final award, the arbitral tribunal may, in the course of arbitration, make an intermediate award or partial award on any issue of the case, if it deems it necessary or accepts the proposal of the parties concerned. The intermediate award refers to the temporary award made for the trial of a clear dispute in order to facilitate the further trial of the case. Partial award means that the arbitral tribunal has heard clearly some issues in the whole dispute and made some final decisions in advance. Such a decision is a component of the final decision.

The arbitral award shall be made in writing within 45 days from the end of the case. In addition to the award made by conciliation and settlement, the arbitral award shall state the reasons on which the award is based and specify the place where the award is final and the date on which the award is made and the signature of the arbitrator. The parties shall perform the arbitration award automatically according to the time stipulated in the arbitration award. If one party fails to perform, the other party may, in accordance with the provisions of Chinese law, apply to a Chinese court for enforcement, or in accordance with the relevant international conventions or other international treaties concluded or acceded to by China

### 4. Validity of Arbitration Award

According to China's arbitration rules, arbitration shall be conducted independently and fairly in accordance with the facts, the provisions of legal contracts, international practices and the principle of fairness and rationality. The arbitral award shall be final and binding upon both parties. Neither party may bring a lawsuit to the court or make a request to change the award to any other body.However, in accordance with the general provisions of the international arbitration rules, the following arbitral awards shall be null and void, and the parties may, within the statutory time limit, request the competent court of the place of arbitration to revoke the arbitral award and declare it null and void.

① The arbitral award is made without an arbitration agreement.

② The verdict is based on an invalid (or expired) arbitration agreement.

③ An award made by the arbitrator for misconduct or exceeding his authority.

④ A decision made on the ground of falsifying evidence

⑤ Where the matter under the jurisdiction of arbitration belongs to the case where the law of the place of arbitration stipulates that it shall not be submitted for arbitration.

### 5. The Arbitration Fee

The parties shall specify in the arbitration clause the payment of the arbitration fee. Generally, it shall be borne by the losing party, or decided at the discretion of the arbitration tribunal. According to China's arbitration rules, the arbitration tribunal has the power to determine that the losing party compensates the winning party for some reasonable expenses incurred in handling the case, but the maximum amount of compensation shall not exceed 10% of the winning party's winning amount.

### 6. International Convention of Arbitration

The execution of the arbitration award includes the execution of the domestic arbitration award and the execution of the foreign arbitration award. The procedures for the execution of domestic arbitral awards are relatively simple, while those for foreign arbitral awards are more complicated.

The enforcement of foreign arbitral awards involves not only the interests of both parties, but also the interests between the two countries. Therefore, all countries have set some restrictions on the implementation of foreign arbitral awards, and there are many differences.

There are three international conventions on the recognition and enforcement of foreign arbitral awards:① The Geneva protocol on arbitration articles of 1923, concluded in 1923.② The convention on the implementation of foreign arbitral awards, concluded in

1927.③The New York convention for the recognition and enforcement of foreign arbitral awards, concluded in New York in 1958.China officially acceded to the New York convention on 2 December 1986, but has two reservations:①The declaration and implementation of arbitral awards made in the territory of another state party on the basis of reciprocity only. ②The People's Republic of China shall apply the convention only to disputes arising out of contractual and non-contractual commercial legal relations as determined by the laws of the People's Republic of China.The accession and declaration of the Chinese government to the aforesaid convention not only provide legal basis for China to recognize and implement foreign arbitral awards, but also facilitate the implementation of the decisions made by Chinese arbitration institutions in the countries of foreign member states of the convention.

On June 26, 2018, after three years of repeated discussions between 85 member states of the United Nations, 35 international intergovernmental and non-governmental organizations, the United Nations Trade Law Commission (UNCITRAL), at its fifty-first session, adopted the draft convention on the implementation of reconciliation agreements resulting from mediation. The convention is called the Singapore Mediation Convention.Next, the draft convention and the revised UNCITRAL model law on international commercial conciliation (hereinafter referred to as the "model law") will be adopted by the general assembly of the United Nations and open for signature by member states.The Singapore Convention on Mediation will enter into force after being signed by more than three member states.The signing ceremony is expected to take place in Singapore in 2019.

## 7.5 Conclusion

The trend toward using alternative dispute resolution methods as a means of disputes settlement without resorting to national or regional court systems. The alternative dispute resolution aims to resolve disputes in a way that is less expensive, faster and more predictable than adversarial judicial proceedings. Assessing your options, there are several forms of alternative dispute resolution.

①Arbitration. This is a legal form. The disputing parties refer the problem to an arbitrator or an arbitral tribunal and agree to be bound by its findings.

②Conciliation. This is a form in which the disputing parties use a conciliator, who meets with each party separately to determine their issues and help resolve their conflicts. It is different from mediation because the main goal is to conciliate, usually by seeking concessions.

③Mediation.This is a process that sues a neutral third party to help the disputing parties resolve their disagreement. The mediator assists communication between the parties and generates options that might help resolve the conflict. A mediator helps the parties form their own solution, rather than making a decision.

④ Fact finding. This form uses an impartial group of experts to determine what the facts are in a dispute. The fact finders might be requested to investigate or evaluate the matters under dispute and present a report that establishes the facts. In some circumstances, the fact finder might also be asked to prepare a situation assessment or a recommendation for resolution.

## ☞ References 7.1

### 5 Tips for Managing Troubled Relationships in Emerging Markets

How to manage commercial relationships in emerging markets, even through difficult waters.

An ounce of prevention beats a pound of cure. Investing in healthy, strong commercial relationships is the best way to avoid having to manage difficult situations later. Be conscientious to always communicate respect for local culture and the company. Make sure to visit people with whom you have key business relationships in person at least once a year, and preferably more frequently. When your international trading partners have not seen you, they may start making business decisions without taking you into account. They may simply forget about you, or more insidiously, figure that you will never find out about some of their decisions. Sometimes even the most proactive, positive relationship management does not result in harmonious relationships. However, that does not mean that you cannot work towards a turnaround.

Do not "evergreen". Evergreening in this context means spending money in an attempt to hide or ineffectually fix the problems of a troubled investment that has already been made. This is also known colloquially as 'throwing good money after bad'. Don't invest more resources to fix a problem unless you're sure the benefits will exceed the costs. For instance, before bringing in lawyers, consider whether the time and legal expenses will be worth the likely recovery. Cross-border ligation procedures can be very lengthy, cumbersome, and ineffective, especially in the emerging markets context.

Always point to the common benefit in moving forward. Anyone who has been in international trade long enough has been in situations that are not going smoothly or even in accordance to contracts. In such a situation, it is better to focus on future positive outcomes of turning around the situation rather than taking a threatening or adversarial tone. This could be as simple as pointing out that a smooth working relationship will lead to an expanded trading relationship in the future from which both companies will greatly benefit.

Take a long-term view and keep things positive. Avoid taking a narrow transaction perspective in any relationship. Understand that the potential value creation is not limited to the transaction at hand, but is also in the ten or one hundred transactions that can follow if a great relationship is put in place.

Bring in an external perspective. Sometimes, outsiders can broaden your perspective about the issue at hand, and find outside-of-the-box solutions that can solve your problems. They can also intervene in situations where the two parties are no longer able to have a conversation together without further disintegration of the situation.

## Questions

1. What are the ways in which international trade can settle disputes? Among them, what are the differences and similarities between litigation and arbitration?

2. One summer, southern China was hit by a devastating flood. Before that, the export company signed three contracts of rice exports. The commodity names of the contracts were "Taihu rice," "Jiangsu rice stored in a warehouse", and "China rice". Please explain how can the Chinese export company claim exemption from liability for the above situations.

3. Co A in China has signed an export contract with a foreign Company, which clearly stipulates arbitration clauses and stipulates that any dispute arising from the performance of the contract shall be arbitrated in China. Later, when a dispute arose over the quality of the goods, the other party sued the Chinese party in the court where it was located. The court issued a subpoena, requesting the Chinese company to appear in court to answer the lawsuit. What do you think should be done about it?

4. How can the buyers in cross-border e-commerce prevent quality risks?

# 第八章
# 国际货物买卖的交易磋商与合同订立

☞ **案例8.1**

某年11月4日顺达公司应瑞典TG公司的请求报价："报实盘，可供棉花500公吨，每公吨340欧元CIP斯德哥尔摩，即期装运，发盘有效期至11月24日。"TG公司收到报盘后要求顺达公司："降低价格；延长要约有效期"。顺达公司遂将价格每公公吨减至320欧元，延长要约有效期至11月30日。TG公司又请求顺达公司："增加数量；再次延长要约有效期"。顺达公司再将数量增至800公吨，延长要约有效期至12月10日。TG公司于12月6日来电表示接受。顺达公司在接到TG公司承诺电报时，发现国际市场因受灾影响，棉花市场价格暴涨。顺达公司不愿意成交，复电称："由于世界市场价格变化，在接到承诺电报前已将货物售出，不能提供货物"。TG公司不同意这一说法，认为承诺是在要约有效期内做出因而有效，坚持要求顺达公司按要约的条件履行合同，并提出执行合同或者赔偿差价损失6万欧元，否则将起诉于法院。本案的关键在于交易是否达成。交易磋商的一般程序包括询盘、发盘、还盘、接受和签订合同等环节，其中发盘和接受是交易达成的两个必不可少的基本环节。在本案中，经过推迟的发盘有效期是12月10日，TG公司的承诺于12月6日到达，属于有效接受，合同应于12月6日成立。顺达公司以"由于世界市场价格变化，货物在接到承诺电报前已售出"为由不履行合同已构成违约，因为双方间的买卖合同已经成立。

☞ **案例8.2**

美国A公司10月4日向中国B公司以传真发盘，出售电子元器件，规定于当天下午5时复到有效。B公司于当天下午4时以传真答复，对发盘中的价格及检验索赔条件提出了不同意见。10月5日，A公司与B公司通过电话进行洽商，双方各作了让步，B公司同意接受A公司的价格，A公司同意B公司提出的检验索赔条件。至此，双方口头达成了一致意见，并一致同意两公司的代表在广交会上签署合同。10月20

日，A公司的代表去广交会会见了B公司的代表，并交给他一份A公司已签了字的合同文本，B公司的代表则表示要审阅后再签字。三天后，A公司的代表再次会见B公司的代表，而B公司的代表仍未在合同上签字。A公司的代表索回了未签字的合同。11月，A公司致电B公司要求开证履约，B公司不同意，双方当事人发生争议。本案的关键在于合同的形式是否有效。合同相识是买卖双方当事人就确立、变更、终止民事权利义务关系达成一致的方式，是合同当事人内在意思的外在表现形式。根据《公约》和《中华人民共和国合同法》的有关规定，当事人订立合同，有书面形式、口头形式和其他形式。合同的上述形式均具有相同的法律效力，都是合同的法定形式。当事人通常可以根据需要进行选择。但应该注意，在法律做出强制性规定和当事人做出约定的情况下，应该根据法律的规定和当事人的约定。可见当事人在订立买卖合同时，要根据国际公约或者国内法是否对其做出规定及双方当事人的合意或意愿，来确定买卖合同的具体形式。本案中，双方当事人在前期的书面传真中并没有达成交易，而随后在口头磋商中虽达成协议，但又保留了条件，即决定在10月广交会上达成书面合同。后来由于种种原因，双方最终并未达成书面协议，因此，买卖合同所要求的具体形式没有完成，双方的交易也就没有成立。

交易磋商是指买卖双方以买卖某种商品为目的，通过一定的程序就交易的各项条件进行洽商并最后达成协议的全过程。交易磋商以订立合同为目的，一旦双方对各项交易条件协商一致，买卖合同即告成立。交易磋商的过程，即是合同订立的过程。磋商是合同的根据，合同是磋商的结果。交易磋商决定交易的成败与合同质量的高低，直接关系到买卖双方的经济利益。

# 一、交易磋商

交易磋商的一般程序包括四个环节：询盘、发盘、还盘和接受。其中，发盘和接受是交易磋商的两个基本环节，属于法律行为，因而必须符合法律，才能订立法律上有效的合同。

## （一）询盘

询盘（enquiry）又称询价，是指买方或卖方为了购买或销售某种商品，向对方询问有关交易条件。其内容可以是询问价格，也可询问其他交易条件（如数量、包装、付款条件、装运期等）中的一项或几项。询盘的目的是邀请对方发盘。询盘可由买方做出，也可由卖方做出。询盘按发送对象的不同，可分为买方询盘、卖方询盘。买方询盘习惯上被称为"邀请发盘"（Invitation to make an offer），如"Please offer Chinese North-east Rice, First Grade, Crop Year 2009, 1000 M/T, November shipment CIF London."（求购中国2009年产一级东北大米1000公公吨，10月份装船，请报CIF伦敦价）。卖方询盘又被称为"邀请递盘"（Invitation to make a bid），如"Can supply Chinese North-east Rice, First Grade，Crop Year 2009，1000 M/T，October shipment，please bid."（可供中国2009年产一级东北大米1000公公吨，11月份装船，请递盘。"

询盘可以向多个人发出，以便"货比三家""价比三家"，了解国外行情，争取有利的贸易条件。但是，询盘应注意以下几个问题：①询盘对于询盘人和被询盘人均无法律上的约束力，而且不是交易磋商的必经步骤；②询盘往往是一笔交易的起点，且是进行调查研究、试探市场动态的一种手段，故不应忽视；③在实际业务中，不能滥发询盘，以免引起不良后果，影响企业在国际市场的信誉。

### （二）发盘

发盘（Offer）又称发价，在法律上称为"要约"，是买方或卖方向对方提出各项交易条件，并愿意按照这些条件达成交易、订立合同的一种肯定表示。发出发盘的当事人被称为"发盘人"（要约人），发盘指向的对方当事人被称为"受盘人""被发价人"（受要约人）。发盘是买卖双方达成交易必不可少的基本环节，可以由卖方提出，也可以由买方提出，可以是一方在收到对方询盘后提出，也可以不经对方询盘而提出。在实际业务中，如交易条件由卖方提出，则该发盘被称为"卖方发盘"（Selling Offer）；如交易条件由买方提出，则称为"买方发盘"（Buying Offer）、订货（Order）或递盘（Bid）。在发盘有效期内，发盘人不得任意撤销或修改其内容。发盘一经对方在有效期内表示接受，发盘人则受其约束，并承担按发盘条件与对方订立合同的法律责任。

#### 1. 发盘的构成要件

发盘（Offer）被称为"发价"或"要约"。构成一项法律上有效的发盘，必须同时具备以下4个条件。

（1）**发盘必须表明订立合同的意旨**

按照《联合国国际货物销售合同公约》（后简称《公约》）规定，发盘人必须在发盘中表示出订立合同的意旨（contractual intent）或订约的意图。如果被发盘人接受发盘，合同即告成立，双方就确立了合同关系。

（2）**必须向一个或一个以上特定的人提出**

《公约》规定，订立合同应向一个或一个以上特定的人（specific persons）提出订约建议。公约所指"特定的人"是指定具体的企业、公司或个人，如A企业、B公司或C个人。这一规定的目的是将向特定对象做出发盘的行为，与在报刊上刊登广告、向国外客商寄发的商品目录、价目单和其他宣传品的行为区分开来。是否向特定的人发出邀请也是"发盘"与"邀请发盘"的重要区别。

（3）**订立合同建议的内容十分确定**

发盘是一种订立合同的建议，在法律上把这种订立合同的建议称为意思表示。发盘人的意思表示是意欲订立一项合同，而此项订立合同的建议，其内容应十分确定。

根据《公约》第14条第一款的规定："向一个或一个以上特定的人提出的订立合

同的建议，如果十分确定并且表明发价人在得到接受时承受约束的意旨，即构成发价。一个建议如果写明货物并且明示或暗示地规定数量和价格或规定如何确定数量和价格，即为十分确定"。 因此，一项订约建议只要列明货物、数量和价格三项条件，即可被认为其内容"十分确定"，并构成一项有效的发盘。如该发盘为受盘人所接受，即可成立合同。至于货物的包装、交货和支付条件等内容，可在合同成立后，按照双方已确定的习惯做法、惯例或按《公约》有关买卖双方义务的规定，予以补充。但是，如果一项建议缺少货物、数量和价格三个方面的任何一个内容，就不是一个确定的发盘，即使对方接受也不构成合同。为了防止误解或争议的发生，在实际工作中，最好能明示或暗示规定至少6项主要交易条件，即货物的品名和质量（品质）、数量、包装、价格、交货和支付条件。这样，一旦受盘人表示接受，双方即可明白无误地了解双方协商一致的主要合同条款，而无须借助于任何可能引起意见分歧的补救措施。

**（4）发盘必须传达到受盘人**

按照《公约》第15条第一款又规定："发价送达被发价人时生效"；中国也采用类似规定。发盘无论是以口头或是书面形式做出，只有被传达到受盘人时才生效。

**2. 发盘的有效期**

发盘的有效期是指可供受盘人对发盘做出接受的期限。该期限具有两层意思：①发盘人在发盘有效期内受约束。如果受盘人在有效期内将"接受通知"送达发盘人，发盘人承担按发盘条件与之订立合同的责任。②超过有效期，发盘人将不再受约束。发盘的有效期是对发盘人的一种限制，也是对发盘人的一种保障。在国际货物买卖中，发盘人对发盘有效期可作明确的规定，也可不作明确的规定。

**（1）明确规定发盘有效期**

明确规定有效期，并不是构成发盘不可缺少的条件。明确规定有效期的发盘，从发盘被传达到受盘人时开始生效，到发盘规定的有效期届满时失效。发盘有效期限的长短，一般取决于商品的种类、市场情况和交易额等诸因素。常见的明确规定有效期的主要方法有：

①规定最迟接受的期限。发盘人在发盘中明确规定受盘人表示接受的最迟期限。为了避免争议，最迟接受的期限应予以"最明确的限定"。例如："实盘限7月10日复"（Firm offer subject to reply 10th July）。但是，这种有效期的规定方法存在一个问题，即该截止期（7月10日）是指受盘人所在地发出接受通知的期限，还是指接受通知必须送达发盘人的期限？为了明确发盘的截止期，在规定最迟接受的期限时，可同时限定以接受送达发盘人或以发盘人所在地的时间为准。如："Subject reply reaching here 10th July"（发盘限7月10日复到）；"Offer subject reply 10th July in our time"（发盘限我方时间15日复）；"Offer valid until this Friday our time"（发盘有效至我方时间本星期五）。

②规定一段接受的期间。发盘人可规定发盘在一段时间内有效。例如，"Offer valid three days"（发盘有效期三天）；"Offer reply in seven days"（发盘七天内复）。但是，采

用这种规定有效期的方法，存在一个如何计算"一段接受期间"的起算时间问题。根据《公约》第20条规定：发盘人在电报或信件中订定的一段接受期间，从电报交发时刻或信上载明的发信日期起算。如信上未载明发信日期，则以信封上所载日期起算。发盘人以电话、电传或其他可立即传达到对方的通信方法订定的一段接受期间，从发盘到达到受盘人时起算。在计算一段接受期间时，这段时间内的正式假日或非营业日应计算在内。但是如果接受通知在接受期间的最后一天未能送达发盘人的地址，因为那天在发盘人的营业所在地是正式假日或非营业日，则这段时间应顺延至下一个营业日。

（2）**不明确规定发盘有效期**

不明确规定有效期的发盘，按法律规定在合理时间内有效。但"合理时间"在国际上并无统一明确的解释。有些国家的法律虽有规定，但彼此之间有很大差异。例如，美国《统一商法典》2—205条规定："一个商人的发盘有效期的合理时间不超过3个月"。按《公约》第18条第二款规定，衡量"合理时间"的长短，须适当考虑交易的情况，包括发价人所使用的通信方法的快捷程度"。因此，"合理时间"并无很确切的标准，具有很大的伸缩性。同时，《公约》第18条第二款还规定："对口头发价必须立即接受，但情况有别者不在此限。"所谓"立即接受"，可理解为：在双方口头磋商时当场有效，受盘人不在磋商当场表示接受，发盘随即失效。对"情况有别者"，则可理解为：发盘人在口头发盘时，明确规定了有效期，例如"有效三天，"则该发盘不在"立即接受"之列。

**3. 发盘的生效**

发盘于送达被发盘人时生效。怎样才算"送达"（Reaches）？从法律或业务上来说，当发盘投递到被发盘人的营业地或通讯地址时即为"送达"。如果发盘通过电子商务网络，根据《联合国贸易法委员会电子商务示范法》的规定，收件人指定特定系统接收发盘的，该发盘进入该特定系统的时间视为到达时间，发盘开始生效；未指定特定系统的，发盘进入被发盘人的任何系统的首次时间，视为到达时间，发盘开始生效。

**4. 发盘的撤回和撤销**

当一项发盘发出后，发盘人可否改变想法将发盘收回？这不仅仅是一个业务作法上的问题，而且还关系到买卖合同可否订立。《公约》对此作了两种区分，即发盘生效前是撤回问题；而发盘生效后是撤销问题。

（1）**发盘的撤回**

发盘的撤回（withdrawal）是指发盘人将尚未为受盘人收到的发盘予以撤销。按《公约》第15第二款规定："一项发价，即使是不可撤销的，得予撤回，如果撤回通知于发价送达被发价人之前或同时送达被发价人"。这一规定是建立在发盘尚未生效的基础上的。"撤回"的实质是阻止发盘生效。但是，《公约》要求"撤回通知"应先于发盘到达对方或至少要求是同时到达，否则发盘不能撤回。在实际业务中，发盘的撤回只有在使用信件或电报向国外发盘时方可适用，因为使用信件或电报发盘，从信件投邮或电报交发到信件或电报送达收件人有一段时间间隔。在发盘信件投邮或电报交发后，发盘人发现市场情况有重大变化或发盘内容有误，可采用更快捷的通信方法（如电话、电传、电子邮件等），在发盘信件或电报送达受盘人前通知受盘人撤回发盘。如果发盘是采用电话、电传或电子邮件等数据电文做出，因这些信息随发随到，就不存在撤回发盘的可能性。

（2）发盘的撤销

发盘的撤销是指发盘人将已经为受盘人收到的发盘予以取消的行为。对于一项已送达受盘人的发盘是否可以得以撤销，各国法律的规定存在较大差异，关键在于一项已生效的发盘对发盘人是否具有约束力。大陆法主张发盘原则上对发盘人具有约束力。一项发盘一经送达受盘人就不得撤销，除非发盘人在发盘中注明不受约束。而英美法主张发盘在被接受之前得予撤销，即使发盘人在发盘中明确规定了可以接受的期间，该发盘对发盘人也不具约束力，除非受盘人为使该发盘保持可供接受而付出某种"对价"，如支付一定金额或做出其他行为或给付了一定物品。

《公约》第16条对大陆法和英美法在此问题上的分歧，进行了协调并做出了折中的规定：已为受盘人收到的发盘，如果撤销的通知在受盘人发出接受通知前送达受盘人，可予撤销。但是，在下列情况下不得撤销：①发盘是以规定有效期或以其他方式表明为不可撤销的；或②如受盘人有理由依赖该项发盘是不可撤销的，并已本着对该发盘的信赖采取了行动。《公约》规定的以上①②两种情况，又可细分为3种情形：第一种情形是在发盘中规定了接受的期限，如"1月20日前复到我方有效"；第二种情形是在发盘中明确声明该发盘是不可撤销的。究竟怎样的发盘才算是不可撤销的，这要从发盘的内容和用语来判断；第三种情形是被发盘人有合理的理由认为该项发盘是不可撤销的，并已依赖该项发盘的信赖行事。因此，《公约》在实质上倾向于大陆法的规定，即已为受盘人收到的发盘基本上是不得撤销的。

**5. 发盘的终止**

发盘的终止是指发盘法律效力的消失，它含有两方面的含义：①发盘人不再受发盘的约束；②受盘人失去了接受该发盘的权利。发盘在以下情况下终止：①受盘人明确表示拒绝发盘，只要该拒绝通知送达发盘人，发盘效力自动终止；②受盘人没有明确表示拒绝，但对发盘的某些条件做了"实质性变更"，发盘效力即告终止；③发盘规定的接受有效期限届满或合理期限届满，发盘即告终止；未明确规定有效期的发盘，因在合理时间内未被接受而失效；④发盘人在受盘人做出接受前对发盘进行了有效的撤销；⑤适用法律所规定的其他条件成就。例如，当发盘人或受盘人为自然人时，在发盘被接受前该自然人丧失行为能力（如死亡或精神失常）；当发盘人为法人（例如公司）时，在发盘被接受前，该法人被依法宣告破产；特定的标的物毁灭，如一件珍贵的独一无二的、不可替代的艺术品，在发盘做出后在火灾中焚毁；发盘中的商品被贸易国政府宣布禁止出口或进口。在这些情况下，发盘将依据法律而终止有效。

## （三）还盘

还盘（counter-offer），又称还价，是受盘人对发盘内容不完全同意而提出修改或变更的表示。还盘可以针对价格，也可以针对支付方式、交货期、争议的解决方式等提出修改意见。一方接到对方的还盘后，可以表示接受，也可以进行再还盘，即针对对方的还盘再提出修改意见。因此，有时一笔交易要经过多次回合才能完成。还盘可采用口头或书面形式表示。在还盘时，贸易双方已经同意的条件一般无须重复列出。还盘应注意：①一旦发生还盘，原发盘自动失效，发盘人不再受其约束。②还盘被视为一项新的发盘。③还盘，可以还实盘，也可以还虚盘。

### （四）接受

接受（acceptance）在法律上称"承诺"，是买方或卖方同意对方在发盘中提出的各项交易条件，并愿按这些条件与对方达成交易、订立合同的一种肯定表示。《公约》第18条第一款规定："被发价人声明或做出其他行为表示同意一项发价，即为接受。缄默或不行动本身不等于接受"。接受于表示同意的通知送达发盘人时生效。如未在发盘规定的时间内或在合理的时间内送达，接受无效，但必须适当地考虑交易情况；而《公约》第19条第一款还规定：对发盘表示接受但载有添加、限制或其他更改的答复，即为拒绝该项发盘并构成还盘。因此，接受是指被发盘人在发盘有效期限内无条件地同意发盘的意思表示。一方发盘经另一方接受，交易即告达成，合同即告订立，双方就应分别履行其应承担的合同义务。表示接受，一般用"接受"（accept）、"同意"（agree）和"确认"（confirm）等术语。

#### 1. 接受的构成条件

根据以上定义以及《公约》第18条第二、三款和第19条的规定，构成一项法律上有效的接受，必须具备以下4个条件。

（1）**接受必须由特定的受盘人做出**

一项有效的发盘必须是向一个或一个以上的特定的人做出的。因此，对发盘表示接受，也必须是发盘中所指明的特定的受盘人，而不能是其他人。如果其他人通过某种途径获悉非向他做出的发盘，而向发盘人表示接受，该"接受"只是其他人向原发盘人做出的一项发盘，除非原发盘人表示同意，合同不能成立。

（2）**受盘人必须以一定的方式表示接受**

按《公约》第18条第一款的规定，受盘人表示接受的方式有两种：①用"声明"做出表示。即受盘人用口头或书面形式向发盘人表示同意发盘。这是国际贸易中最常用的表示方法。受盘人可用词简明，以"接受"或"确认"来明确地表达受盘人同意发盘的意思；②用"做出行为"来表示。所谓用"做出行为"来表示接受，通常是指由卖方发运货物或由买方支付价款来表示；也可用"做出其他任何行为"来表示，如开始生产所买卖的货物、为发盘人采购有关货物等。如果受盘人在思想上愿意接受对方的发盘，但以"默不作声"或"不做出任何其他行动"表示其对发盘的同意，在法律上并不承认。

（3）**接受必须在发盘的有效期内传达到发盘人**

接受必须在发盘的有效期内被传达到发盘人方能生效，这是法律的一般要求。但是，接受何时生效，各国法律解释不同。英美法系的国家采用"投邮生效"原则："如以信件或电报传达时，当信件投邮或电报交发，接受即告生效"。按此原则，如果接受的函电在邮递途中延误或遗失，导致发盘人未能在有效期内收到，甚至根本没有收到，也不影响合同成立。因此，传递延误或遗失的风险，由发盘人承担。但是，如果发盘人在发盘中规定，接受必须于有效期内传达到发盘人，则接受的函电必须传达到发盘人时，接受方能生效。大陆法系的国家采用"到达生效"原则，即表示接受的函电必须在发盘有效期内到达发盘人，接受才能生效。如果表示接受的函电，在邮递过程中延误或遗失，合同不能成立。也就是说，传递延误或遗失的风险由受盘人承担。《公约》采用"到达生效"原则。

**（4）接受必须是对发盘实质性内容的同意**

如要达成交易，成立合同，受盘人必须无条件的、全部同意发盘的条件。但在实际业务中，受盘人表示接受时，往往会对发盘内容做出某些添加、限制或其他更改。为了适应现代商业的需要，尽量促进交易的达成，《公约》将接受中对发盘条件所作的变更分为"实质性变更"和"非实质性变更"。

凡对货物的价格、付款、质量和数量、交货地点和时间、赔偿责任范围或解决争端等添加、限制或更改，均视为实质上变更发盘的条件。如受盘人表示接受但含有实质变更，则构成还盘。如发盘人对此不予确认，合同不能成立。

至于非实质性变更，例如，要求提供重量单、装箱单、商检证和产地证等单据，要求增加提供装船样品或某些单据的份数，更改分批装运的次数，或要求在包装上刷制指定的标志等。附有这类非实质性变更的接受，除非发盘人及时向受盘人表示反对，否则仍构成有效接受，合同得以成立，并且合同的条件以该项发盘的条件以及在接受中所载的变更为准。

**2. 逾期接受**

如果接受通知超过发盘规定的有效期限，或在发盘未具体规定有效期限的情况下超过合理时间才传达到发盘人，就构成一项"逾期接受"（late acceptance）或称为"迟到的接受"。逾期接受在一般情况下无效。但是，为了保护无过失的受盘人利益，同时兼顾发盘人的利益，《公约》对两种情况下的逾期接受，做出了规定：①发盘人表示愿意"接受"逾期接受时，该逾期接受仍有接受的效力。《公约》第21条第一款规定，逾期接受仍有接受的效力，如果发盘人毫不迟延地用口头或书面将此种意见通知被发盘人；②因传递延误的逾期接受，仍具有接受的效力。《公约》第21条第二款规定：如果载有逾期接受的信件或其他书面文件表明，它是在传递正常、能及时送达发盘人的情况下寄发的，则该逾期接受具有接受的效力，除非发盘人毫不迟延地用口头或书面通知受盘人，他认为他的发盘已经失效。

**3. 接受的撤回**

接受于表示同意的通知送达发盘人时生效。在接受通知送达发盘人之前，受盘人可随时撤回接受，阻止接受生效，但以撤回通知先于接受或与接受通知同时到达发盘人为限。接受通知一经到达发盘人即不能撤销。接受一经生效，合同即告成立。如要撤销接受，实质上已属毁约行为。由于《公约》关于接受生效的时间，采用了"到达生效"的原则，因此在接受未到达发盘人前，该接受尚未发生法律效力，因而可以撤回。但是，在实践中真正能做到把一项已发出的接受撤回是很困难的，因为目前大多数交易都采用快捷的数据电文，如电传、传真、Email等发送接受通知。

询盘、发盘、还盘和接受是交易磋商的一般程序。在实际业务中，询盘并不是每笔交易磋商不可缺少的环节，买方或卖方都可不经对方提出询盘，而直接向对方作出发盘。还盘也不是交易磋商的必经环节，受盘人接到发盘后，可以立即接受；即使受盘人做出还盘，它实际上是对原发盘的拒绝而做出的一项新发盘。对还盘做再还盘，同样是拒绝还盘后的一项新发盘。因此，在法律上，发盘和接受是达成交易不可缺少的两个基本环节。

# 二、国际货物买卖合同的签订

在交易磋商过程中，一方发盘经另一方确认后，交易即告成立，买卖双方就构成了合同关系。按照《公约》第11条的规定："销售合同无须以书面订立或书面证明，在形式方面也不受任何其他条件的限制。销售合同可以用包括人证在内的任何方法证明"。贸易双方在交易磋商过程中的往返函电，可以作为合同成立的书面证明。但是，根据国际贸易习惯，在从事国际货物买卖活动过程中，买卖双方一般要签署书面的买卖合同，以进一步明确双方的权利和义务。

## （一）签订书面合同的作用

在国际货物买卖合同中，卖方的基本义务是交付货物的所有权，买方的基本义务是支付货款。签订书面合同具有三方面的重要意义：①作为合同成立的证据。②作为合同生效的条件。③成为合同履行的依据。

## （二）国际货物买卖合同的形式

在国际上，对货物买卖合同的形式，没有特定的限制。买卖双方可采用正式的合同、确认书、协议，也可采用备忘录等形式。此外，还有意向书、订单和委托订购单等。

### 1. 合同和确认书

在实际工作中，企业采用的书面合同形式，主要有合同和确认书两种形式。其中，合同有销售合同（sales contract）和购货合同（purchase contract）；确认书有销售确认书（sales confirmation）和购货确认书（purchase confirmation）。企业一般都印有固定的格式，成交后，由业务员按双方谈定的交易条件逐项填写即可。合同和确认书虽然在格式、条款项目的设立和措词上有所不同，但作为合同双方协商一致的交易条件，都应完整、明确地加以拟定。经买卖双方签署的合同和确认书是法律上有效的文件，对买卖双方有同样的约束力。

### 2. 协议

货物买卖合同如冠以"协议"或"协议书"的名称，只要它的内容对买卖双方的权利和义务已作了明确、具体和肯定的规定，它就与"合同"一样对买卖双方有约束力。如果买卖双方所洽谈的交易比较复杂，经过谈判后，商定了一部分条件，还有一部分条件有待进一步商洽，在此情况下，双方可先签订一个"初步协议"（preliminary agreement）或"原则性协议"（agreement in general），把双方已商定的条件确定下来，其余条款待后再行洽谈。在这种协议内，应订明"本协议属初步性质，正式合同有待进一步洽商后签订"（This Agreement is of preliminary nature, a formal contract will be signed after further negotiation），或做出其他类似意义的声明，以明确该协议不属正式有效的合同性质，防止引起误解。

### 3. 备忘录

备忘录（memorandum）也可作为书面合同的形式之一。如果买卖双方商定的交易条件，明确、具体地在备忘录中一一作了规定，并经双方签字，那么这种备忘录的性质与合同无异。但是，如果贸易双方在洽谈后，只对某些事项达成一定程度的理解或谅解，并将这种理解或谅解以"备忘录"的形式记录下来，作为双方今后交易或合作的依据，或作为初步协议供将来进一步洽谈的参考，这种备忘录可以"理解备忘录"或"谅解备忘录"（memorandum of understanding）为名，它在法律上不具有约束力。

### 4. 意向书

在交易磋商尚未最后达成协议前，买卖双方为了达成某项交易，将共同争取实现的目标、设想和意愿，有时还包括初步商定的部分交易条件，记录于一份书面文件上，作为今后进一步谈判的参考和依据，这种书面文件称为"意向书"（letter of intent）。意向书只是双方当事人为了达成某项协议所作出的一种意愿的表示（expression of intentions），它不是法律文件，对有关当事人没有约束力。意向书的有关当事人彼此负有道义上的责任，在进一步洽谈时，一般不应与意向书中所作的规定偏离太远。

### 5. 订单和委托订购单

订单（order）是指由进口商或实际买方制作的货物订购单。委托订购单（indent）是指由代理商或佣金商制作的代客购买货物的订购单。对于订单或委托订购单，卖方应仔细审核其内容。对于经过交易磋商成交后寄来的订单或委托订购单，可理解为买方的购货合同或购货确认书。若发现其中有些条款与双方磋商协议一致的条件不符或另有添加、更改的，则应分情况处理。若不符或添加、更改的情况并不严重、性质轻微，卖方可以接受；如涉及实质性改变、出入较大，卖方不能接受的，应及时向对方明确提出异议，而不能保持沉默，置之不理。对于未进行过交易磋商，买方径自寄来的订单或委托订购单，卖方应按照其具体内容，判定是发盘或是发盘邀请。认真研究其内容后，决定是否与之交易，并及时答复买方。

**思考题**

1. 构成一项有效的发盘、接受必须具备什么条件?

2. 在国际货物买卖合同中,哪些货物不适用《联合国国际货物销售合同公约》?

3. 国际货物买卖合同包括哪些内容?

4. 请用一个具体的例子来说明跨境电商如何开展询盘、发盘、还盘与接受。

# Chapter 8

# Business Negotiation and Contract Signed

☞ Case 8.1

on November 4, 2010, Shunda Company made a firm offer at the request of TG Company in Sweden: Firm offer for 500 metric tons of cotton at Euros 340 per metric ton CIP Stockholm, prompt shipment, offer valid until November 24. TG Company asked Shunda Company to reduce the price and extend the validity of the offer . Then, Shunda reduced the price to Euros 320 per metric ton, extending the offer until November 30. While, TG Company requested Shunda Company to increase the quantity and renew the offer .Shunda increased the quantity to 800 metric tons and extended the offer until December 10.

On December 6, TG company called to accept. When Shunda Company received the promise telegram from TG Company, it found that the international market was affected by the disaster and the cotton market price soared.Shunda company was unwilling to close a deal and replied: Due to the change of world market price, the goods had been sold before receiving the promised telegram and could not be supplied. TG Company did not agree with this statement, believing that the acceptance was made within the validity period of the offer and therefore valid, and insists that Shunda Company should perform the contract according to the terms of the offer, and propose to execute the contract or compensate for the difference loss of 60,000 Euros, otherwise it would sue the court.

The key to the case was whether a deal had been reached.The general procedure of business negotiation includes inquiry, offer, counter-offer, acceptance and contract signing, among which offer and acceptance are two essential basic links for the transaction.In this case, the delayed offer was valid for December 10, the commitment of TG Company arrived on December 6, which was a valid acceptance, and the contract should be established on December 6. The failure to perform the contract on the ground of Shunda Company that the goods had been sold before receiving the acceptance telegram due to the change of world market price constituted a breach of contract because the sales contract between the two parties had been established.

In international trade, a business contract normally refers to the agreement concluded by both parties and enforceable by law, by which they mutually promise to sell or buy some particular commodity, transfer or acquire a certain industrial property or know-how, or render or accept a certain service. Business negotiation refers to the entire process regarding to terms and conditions of a Sales (or Purchase) contract and finally reach an agreement for the purpose of buy & sell some or particular commodity(ies). Business negotiation aims to conclude a transaction. The process of business negotiation is that of conclude a transaction. The concluded transaction is based on the mutual agreement on various terms and conditions by both parties. In case of a transaction concluded, as usual, both parties need sign a Sales (Purchase) Contract.

# 8.1 Forms and Contents of a Business Contract

## 8.1.1 Forms of a Business Contract

Business contract may be concluded in formal or informal, in oral or in written, and in sealed or unsealed. The relating stipulations vary from country to country in the world. The business contract generally adopted in import or export business is usually the formal written contract, i.e. the sales contract or purchase contract. In some cases, it may take the form of sales confirmation or purchase confirmation. "Contract", as distinguished from "agreement", means the total legal obligation that results from the parties' agreement as determined by (the Uniform Commercial Code) as supplemented by any other applicable laws (§1-201 General Definitions, The Uniform Commercial Code).

Article 11 of The United Nations Convention on Contracts for the International Sales of Goods (CISG) stipulates: "A contract of sale need not be concluded in or evidenced by writing and is not subject to any other requirement as to form. It may be proved by any means, including witnesses."

Article 4 of Sales of Goods Act 1979 (England) stipulates: "A contract of sale may be made in writing (either with or without seal), or by word of mouth, or partly in writing and partly by word of mouth, or may be implied from the conduct of the parties."

§ 2-201 (1) of The Uniform Commercial Code (UCC) stipulates: "Except as otherwise provided in this section, a contract for the sale of goods for the price of $500 or more is not enforceable by way of action or defense unless there is some writing sufficient to indicate that a contract for sale has been made between the parties and signed by the party against whom enforcement is sought or by his authorized agent or broker. Writing is not insufficient because it omits or incorrectly states a term agreed upon but the contract is not enforceable under this paragraph beyond the quantity of goods shown in such writing".

Article 10 of Contract Law of the People's Republic of China stipulates: "The parties may use written, oral or other forms in entering into a contract. A contract shall be in written form if the laws or administrative regulations so provide. A contract shall be concluded in written form if the parties so agree." Written form refers to a form such as a written contractual agreement, letter, electronic data text (including a telegram, telex, fax, electronic data exchange and e-mail) that can tangibly express the contents contained therein.

## 8.1.2 Contents of a Sales Contract

Article 12 of Contract Law of the People's Republic of China (1999) stipulates: "The contents of a contract shall be agreed upon by the parties, and shall generally contain the following clauses: titles or names and domiciles of the parties, subject matter, quantity, quality, price or remuneration, time limit, place and method of performance, liability for breach of contract, and method to settle disputes." Contents of a sales contract include preamble, body and witness clause.

### 1. Preamble

The preamble includes Buyer/Seller's name & address, contact methods, contract number, signed date & place, the enforced law and normally state "The sellers are willing to sell & the buyers are willing to buy the listed commodity & terms and agree between the parties". The enforced law refers to the laws which exert a great influence over the international sales of goods, should be studied and grasped especially, such as: ① CISG: The United Nations Convention on Contracts for the International Sale of Goods(1980); ② Sales of Goods Act 1979 (England); ③ UCC, the Uniform Commercial Code in the United States (2004); ④ Contract Law of the People's Republic of China (1999) ; ⑤ The Warsaw-oxford Rules (1932).

### 2. Body

The body includes: ① name of the commodity and its quality; ② quantity; ③ unit price & total amount; ④ packing & shipping marks; ⑤ delivery (place/port of shipment/destination, mode of transport, time of shipment, transport documents, partial shipment & transshipment, transport insurance, shipment advice, etc); ⑥ terms of payment; ⑦ the general terms and conditions, such as inspection of the goods, claims and discrepancies clauses, penalty clauses, arbitration and force majeure.

### 3. Witness

The witness clauses include the versions applied and the buyer/seller's signature, such as

"The contract is made out in Chinese and English, Both versions being equally authentic."

# 8.2 Methods of Business Negotiation

Under normal circumstances, business negotiation may be carried out through correspondence. Telecommunication such as emails, faxes, cables, telexes and QQ are often used for business negotiation in written, especially emails. Oral business negotiation may be occurred at exhibitions, visiting with face to face or by telephone and Skype, etc. Normally, business negotiation to conclude a deal will combine both above. The parties may conclude a contract by reference to a model text of each kind of contract.

Business negotiation exists anywhere, anytime, anybody and aims to conclude a Sales (Purchase) Contract. In order to prioritize and process of business negotiation, six main trade terms and conditions including name of the commodity and its quality, quantity, price, packing, delivery and payment usually need negotiate each time. While, Inspection, claims, force majeure and arbitration can be fixed or format as general terms.

# 8.3 Procedure of Business Negotiation

Business negotiation includes four steps generally, named enquiry, offer, counter-offer and acceptance. Offer and acceptance are two basic legal acts of transaction concluded and therefore must be conformity with the relating laws and regulations in order to sign an effective contract.

## 8.3.1 Enquiry

In foreign trade, an enquiry is usually made by the buyer without engagement to get information about the goods to be ordered, such as quality, quantity, price, delivery time and other terms. Enquiry can be made by the buyer or the seller. According to the different objectives, enquiry can be divided into two categories. If the enquiry is made by the buyer, it is called as "invitation to make an offer". If the enquiry is made by the seller, it is called as "invitation to make a bid".

An enquiry can be made to one or more suppliers simultaneously and may ask more information. Its contents shall be not essential and will not bind upon both parties. It should be brief, specific, courteous and reasonable. The contents of the enquiry can be taken as evidence to handle the disputes arises in the performance of the contract.

## ☞ Case 8.2

Specimens for Invitation to Make an Offer and Invitation to Make a Bid

Invitation to make an offer: Please offer China North-east Rice, First Grade, Crop Year 2015, 1000 M/Ts, CIF Pusan Incoterms ®2010.

Invitation to make a bid: Can supply China North-east Rice, First Grade, Crop Year 2015, 1000 M/Ts, Please bid."

## ☞ Case 8.3

Specimen of "Invitation to Make an Offer" Sent by Email

From: K & L Co., Ltd.

TO: Hangzhou Tenglong Weaving Co., Ltd.

Attn: Sales Department

Subject: Enquiry

Date: May 12, 2015

Dear Sirs,

We are interested in buying Chenille Upholstery Fabrics. It would be very appreciated if you could give us an offer on the basis of CIF Liverpool, UK and send some new designs for our reference.

We are looking forward to hearing from you by E-mail.

Best Regards

Carl Clifton

Manager of Purchasing Department

K & L Co., Ltd.

The subject for an enquiry may be used to get the most favorable trade terms & conditions by "shop around" and be familiar with the foreign market. However, an enquiry is not a necessary step of business negotiation, it should be noticed that: Firstly, it shall not binding upon the parties; Secondly, it is normally the beginning of business negotiation and become one kind of main measures for market investigation and research as well as dynamics adjustment, so that it should not be ignored; Thirdly, to over-issue enquiry is not allowed in practice in order to avoid negative effect on corporate reputation in the international market.

## 8.3.2 Offer

The answer to an enquiry may become an offer. In return, the answer to an enquiry should be prompt, definite and helpful. An offer is a promise conditioned on acceptance which, no matter whether from a seller or a buyer, must be communicated to the offeree and must clearly undertake a performance definite as to all essential terms. The party who issues an offer is called as "Offeror" and the opposite party that the offer addressed is called as "Offeree". If the offer is issued by the seller, it is a "selling offer". Vice versa, it is caller as "buying bid".

### 1. Effectiveness of an Offer

The precondition of an offer valid in legal have to meet the following four criteria simultaneously.

①The offer should be made and presented to one or more specific persons. "Specified persons" is designated specific firms, companies or individuals, such as companies A, B or individual C. The purpose of this provision is to distinguish the differences between make an offer to specific persons and the advertising in the press, send business e-catalogs, price lists and other promotional materials behaviors. Make an offer to specific persons is an important distinction between "the offer" and "invite the offer.

②The offer has to display the Contractual intent. The offer shall indicate the intention of the offeror to be bond in case of acceptance. The offeror expresses that he shall conclude the transaction on the terms and conditions stipulated in the offer. If the offer accepted, a contract will be formed and then the two sides establish a contractual relationship.

③The contents of the offer shall be definite. The offer is a proposal for concluding a contract. This kind of proposal is called an intention in law. The offeror's intention indicates that they want to enter into a contract, and its content of the recommendation concluded in the contract should be very determined.

④An offer must be communicated to the offeror. An offer becomes effective when it reaches the offeree. If it loses during the transmission, the offer will not take effect. It's the effective principle of an offer. Whether the offer made in oral or in writing form, the offer will enter into force only when it goes into the offeror.

### 2. Firm Offer & Non-Firm Offer

An offer must clearly undertake a performance definite as to all essential terms. It means that the offer must be a firm offer instead of non-firm offer. For a firm offer, its contents must be clear and definite and with engagement to the offeror. Otherwise, it becomes a non-firm offer.

Normally, the offer shall contain six main trade terms completely, definitely and clearly, including name of the goods and its quality, quantity, packing, price, delivery and terms of payment. Sometimes, it need not contain six main trade terms and conditions based on some of them are fixed through general terms and conditions in advance, or from previous letters, cables, telexes, or as per certain trade practices by two parties. Thus, the two parties can precisely understand the main terms of the contract being made after their negotiation and finally it is unnecessary to refer to any remedial measures that may lead to some controversy.

As per Clause 1, article 14 of The United Nations Convention on Contracts for the International Sales of Goods (UNCISG)"A proposal for concluding a contract addressed to one or more specific persons constitutes an offer if it is sufficiently definite and indicates the intention of the offeror to be bound in case of acceptance. A proposal is sufficiently definite if it indicated the goods and expressly or implicitly fixes or makes provision for determining the quantity and the price.

## ☞ Case 8.4

Specimen of a "Firm Offer" Sent by Email

To: K & L Co., Ltd., UK

Attn: Mr. Karl Clifton

From Hangzhou Tenglong Weaving Co., Ltd.

Subject: Offer

Date: May 15, 2020

Dear Mr. Clifton,

Thank you very much for your email regarding to the enquiry of Chenille Upholstery Fabrics. As per your requirement, we offer as following and attachment you will find the relative photos of three quoting designs.

Design: Ritzi, Intimo, Flamenco with pattern Jacquard/Stripe/allover/plain

Colorways: Gold/Champagne/Sky/Sage/Candlelight/Antique/Taupe/Walnut/Espresso/Forest

Specification: $150D \times 3.5N + 7S$, 162x64, width 280 cm

Composition: 70% of Polyester, 30% of Cotton

Weight: 1,080 grams/square yard

Price: USD6.30 per yard CIF Liverpool, UK Incoterms®2010.

Packing: Single piece in a poly bag, outer packing is a plastic woven bag, piece length is 50 yards with 5 yards more or less is acceptable.

Quantity: Minimum order with 500 yards per color per pattern per design.

Payment: Payment shall be made by Letter of credit be available with any bank by negotiation at sight valid for negotiation until 15 days after shipment.

Delivery: Shipment will be made within 45 days after receipt of L/C.

The above offer is valid till May 20, 2020.

We are looking forward to receiving your reply by email with thanks.


Best Regards

Yanhong Yang


A non-firm offer is without engagement. In most cases, the contents of a non-firm offer are not clear and definite, the main terms and conditions are not completely. In a non-firm offer, it always states as "The price is only for your reference", "Delivery may be made in August or in September", "Subject to our final confirmation", "Subject to prior sale" or "Without engagement".

## ☞ Case 8.5

Specimen of a "Non-Firm Offer": We offer China Northeast Rice, Crop Year 2020, 1,000 M/Ts with our reference price at USD1,280.00 per metric ton FOB Dalian subject to our final confirmation.


It's better to stipulate a period of validity in an offer for acceptance. The offer is terminated until the date of validity stipulated in the offer. If an offer does not stipulate the time of validity, it will be effective within a reasonable time. An oral offer must be accepted immediately, unless otherwise agreed & unless the circumstances indicated otherwise. The period of validity can be stipulated as: "Offer reply by email on or before May 20, 2020", or "If I do not hear from you on/before May 20, 2020, I shall assume your answer is negative." It is recommended that you'd better not use "Offer reply immediately", "promptly", or "as soon as possible".

## ☞ Case 8.6

How to understand "Offer valid for five days" if an offer sent on 12:15 PM, May 12, 2020 (Tuesday, Chinese Beijing Time) by email and reached the offeree at 0:15 AM, May 12, eastern summer time of the USA. The offeror was located at Shanghai, China; the offeree was located at New York, the USA.

Article 20 of The United Nations Convention on Contracts for the International Sales of Goods (UNCISG) stipulates: "A period of time for acceptance fixed by the offeror in a telegram or a letter begins to run from the moment the telegram is handed in for dispatch or from the date shown on the letter or, if no such date is shown, from the date shown on the envelope. A period of time for acceptance fixed by the offeror by telephone, telex or other means of instantaneous communication begins to run from the moment the offer reaches the offeree. Official holidays or non-business days occurring during the period for acceptance are included in calculating the period. However, if a notice of acceptance cannot be delivered at the address of the offeree on the last day of the period because that day falls on an official holidays or a non-business day at the place of business of the offeror, the period is extended until the first business day which follows".

As per Article 20 of UNCISG, as the offer sent by email ( apply instantaneous communication), the effective time will be calculated from the commencement moment that the offer reached the offeree (00:15 AM, May 12, eastern summer time of the USA) and till 0:15 AM, May 17, eastern summer time of the USA (12:15 PM, May 17, 2020, Sunday, Chinese Beijing Time). If the offeree sent an acceptance notice on 12:15 PM, May 16, eastern summer time of the USA, the offeror received it on 00:15 AM, May 17, Beijing Time. As Sunday is the non-business day in China, the period is extended to May 18 (Monday). In this case, if the offer was sent by airmail instead of email, the offer may be terminated during its transmission from Shanghai to New York, as the period of time for acceptance is calculating from the date shown on the letter or, if no such date is shown, from the date shown on the envelope. The offer was terminated if the airmail didn't reach the offeree on/before May 15 (Friday) and receive it on May 18 (Monday), as the official holidays or non-business days occurring during the period for acceptance are included in calculating the period.

### 3. Withdrawal and Revocation of an Offer

An offer, even if it is irrevocable, may be withdrawn if the withdrawal reaches the offeree before or at the same time as the offer. As to whether an offer can be revoked or not, different laws have different explanations. As per The British laws and American Laws, an offer can be revoked at any time before acceptance, except the offer which is made with a consideration or signed and sealed by the offeror. While, the Law of the Continental countries stipulate that an offer cannot be revoked within the time of validity

Article 16 of UNCISG stipulates: "Until a contract is concluded, an offer may be revoked if the revocation reaches the offeree before he has dispatched an acceptance. However, an offer cannot be revoked, if it indicates, whether by stating a fixed time for acceptance or otherwise, that it is irrevocable; or if it was reasonable for the offeree to rely on the offer as being irrevocable and the offeree has acted in reliance on the offer. China Contract Law stipulates the same.

**4. Termination of an Offer**

In the following cases, an offer is terminated: ① the time of validity stipulated in the offer becomes due. ② The offeree rejects or makes a counter offer. ③ The offeror revokes the offer effectively before acceptance d. As per application of law, such as Force majeure happen or lost act including died, bankrupt.

## 8.3.3 Counter-Offer

After the offeree received the firm offer, he may accept it, refuse it, or may not accept it wholly and put forward some additions, modifications, limitations, etc as to the basic terms and conditions contained in the offer. If the offeree accepts the offer, it means that a deal concluded between the offeror and the offeree. If the offeree refuses it expressly, the offer is terminated at once. If the offeree put it aside, the offer is terminated due to maturity of period for acceptance fixed in the offer or in the reasonable time. If the offeree didn't accept it in wholly and put forward some additions, modifications, limitations, it may become a counter offer or an acceptance. Once a counter-offer made, the original offer loses its effectiveness and the counter offer becomes a new offer.

Article 19 of UNCISG stipulates: "A reply to an offer which purports to be an acceptance but contains additions, limitations or other modifications is a rejection of the offer and constitutes a counter-offer. However, a reply to an offer which purports to be an acceptance but contains additional or different terms which do not materially alter the terms of the offer constitutes an acceptance, unless the offeror, without undue delay, objects orally to the discrepancy or dispatches a notice to that effect. If he does not so object, the terms of the contract are the terms of the offer with the modifications contained in the acceptance. Additional or different terms relating, among other things, to the price, payment, quality and quantity of the goods, place and time of delivery, extent of one party's liability to the other or the settlement of disputes are considered to alter the terms of the offer materially".

A reply to an offer contains non-materially alteration still constitutes an effective acceptance if the additions, limitations or other modifications to an offer is relating to documents, shipping samples, shipping lots (times), shipping marks, or packing's new & old. A reply to an offer contains materially alteration constitutes a counter-offer if alteration made direct to the price, payment, quality and quantity of the goods, place and time of delivery, extent of one party's liability to the other or the settlement of disputes.

☞ Case 8.7

How to separate materially alteration from non-material alteration for an answer to the offer sent on May 12, 2020 in Case 3?

Reply 1: If Mr. Karl Clifton replied as following on May 19 ,2020: We accept your offer on May 15, 2020 if the price is USD 6.10 per yard CIF Liverpool instead of USD6.30 per yard. Shipment shall be made within 30 days after S/C concluded.

Reply 2: If Mr. Karl Clifton replied as following on May 19, 2020: We accept your offer on May 15, 2020. Outer packing uses double plastic woven bag.

Answer: For reply 1, the offeree made a counter offer as he aimed to change price and time of shipment that belong to materially alteration. For reply 2, the offeree made an effective acceptance as he aimed to remind the offeror to use "double" plastic woven bag especially as the offeror only indicated in the offer as "packed in woven bag". The addition belonged to non-materially alteration. Unless the offeror, without undue delay, objects orally to the discrepancy or dispatches a notice to that effect. If he does not so object, the relating terms of the contract are the terms of the offer with the modifications contained in the acceptance. The goods should be packed in double woven bags.

## ☞ Case 8.8

If Hangzhou Tenglong Weaving Co Ltd didn't reply the email in reply 1, Mr. Clifton sent an email on May 22, 2015 and stated: We accept your offer on May 15, 2015. The purchase contract is attached, please sign back. How can the seller do? Why?

Answer: Whatever the seller accept the contract or not was based on his option. As usual, the original lost his effectiveness as the buyer made a counter offer in order to change price of the goods and time of shipment. The counter offer became a new offer. The seller need not be binding upon the original offer. The email sent on May 22, 2015 by the buyer could be regard as one another new offer. As the offeree of the new offer, the seller may accept it or refuse it. If the deal was profitable or the seller looked very important on build a new trade relationship with the buyer, he may accept it and conclude a transaction.

Normally, a reply to an offer contains additions, limitations or other modifications aims to state one or more main trade terms more clearly, definitely and without ambiguity. For example, if the incoming message on Aug 15, 2018 stated: " Please offer China North-east Rice (First Grade) Crop Year 2018, 1,000 M/TS, CIF Busan Incoterms ®2010". The outgoing message on Aug 17, 2018 stated: "Offer firm China North-east Rice (First Grade) Crop Year 2018, 1,000 M/TS, packed in gunny bag Sept/Oct equal shipment, USD 1,280.00 per MT CIF Busan Incoterms ®2010, Pay by Irrevocable sight L/C Reply here before 24th".

However, there was several understanding for "Sept/Oct equal shipment", such as: Shipment made in September, 2018 by six equal lots., Shipment made in October, 2018 by two equal lots., Shipment made in September and October by monthly equal lots. If the buyer wants the goods could be shipped by 500 MTs in September and the balance shipped in October, he could reply to the offeror as: "Aug/Sept monthly equal shipment". If he wanted to set shipment lots, he may reply as: "Sept/Oct monthly equal shipment, 2 equal lots per month." If he wanted to set shipment schedule in most details, he may reply as: Sept/Oct monthly equal shipment, 2 equal lots per month, the first lot shipped between 05th—10th of each month, the second lot shipped between 20the—25th of each month, total 4 equal shipment lots, or 250 MTS shipped between 05th—10th of September, 250 MTS shipped between 20th—25th of September, 250 MTS shipped between 05th—10th of October, 250 MTS shipped between 20th—25th of October.

### 8.3.4 Acceptance

An acceptance shall be made by a specific offeree. The acceptance made by the third party will not be effective. It should be declared in certain ways, either orally or in a written form, silence or inactivity do not itself amount to acceptance. Acceptance shall reach the offeror within the time of validity. The acceptance shall be in conformity with the offer (Mirror-image rule for British Law, pure, totally conform for the Continent Law). It means that an acceptance shall be unconditional and without any modify clause (s).

How to understand "Acceptance shall reach the offeror within the time of validity"? If the parties are in presence, when the offeree says "I ACCEPT", no problems arises. If the parties deal with the acceptance without face to face, an exception will be created to the rule that acceptance takes effect only when communicated. If the offeree sending his acceptance uses the means authorized by the offeror, the acceptance takes effect at the moment it is placed in the process of communication by that means. On the other hand, if the offeree use varies means authorized by the offeror, the acceptance becomes effective and the contract is concluded only when it is actually communicated.

When an acceptance takes effect from, The British Law and The American Law are applied to DESPATCH THEORY. It means that an acceptance cannot be withdrawn. The Law of the Continental countries, UNCISG and China apply to RECEIPT THEORY. It means that acceptance can be withdrawn. With popularization and development of telecommunication, Dispatch Theory lost its material meanings. An offer, declaration of acceptance or any other indication of intention "reaches" the addressee when it is made orally to him or delivered by any other means to him personally, to his place of business or mailing address or, if he does not have a place of business or mailing address, to his habitual residence.

Late acceptance may be caused fewer than two circumstances. The first is that an acceptance made after maturity or out of the time validity fixed in an offer. The second is that an acceptance made within the time of validity but reach the offeror out due time. If it has been normal, it would be reached the offeror in due time. Accept or not accept a late acceptance is on the option of the offeror but with different operations. Article 21 of UNCISG stipulates: "A late acceptance is nevertheless effective as an acceptance if without delay the offeror orally so informs the offeree or dispatches a notice to that effect. If a letter or other writing containing a late acceptance shows that it has been sent in such circumstances that if its transmission had been normal it would have reached the offeror in due time, the late acceptance is effective as an acceptance unless, without delay, the offeror orally informs the offeree that he considers his offer as having lapsed or dispatches a notice to that effect. Under the first circumstance, if the offeror wishes to accept the late acceptance, a statement should be made as "I accept your late acceptance", while silence means refusal. Under the second circumstance, if the offeror wishes to refuse the late acceptance, a statement should be made as "I refuse to accept your late acceptance", while silence means accept.

## 8.3.5 Contract Signed

A contract is concluded at the moment when an acceptance of an offer becomes effective. It is recommended that both parties shall sign a written contract (confirmation).The contract in writing can be used as evidence for the conclusion of the contract. Sometimes it is a necessary condition for the effectiveness of the contract. In accordance with international trade practices, in the process of engaging in international sales of goods, the seller and the buyer generally need to sign a written sales contract to further clarify the rights and obligations of both parties.

In international trade, there are no specific restrictions on the form of contracts for the sale and purchase of goods.The buyer and seller may use formal contracts, confirmations, agreements, memorandam and other forms.In addition, there are letters of intent, orders and purchase orders. The contract in writing may be used as a foundation for performance of the contract.

### 1. Contract and Confirmation

In practice, the written contract form that the traders use, basically have contract and confirmation, including sales contract, purchase contract, sales confirmation and purchase confirmation. The contracts or confirmation are generally printed with a fixed format and can be filled according to the agreed terms of transaction that the two parties concluded after business negotiation. Although the contract and confirmation differ in terms of format, their items establishment and wording should be completely and clearly stipulated as the terms of transaction agreed upon by both parties through business negotiation.The contract and confirmation signed by the seller and the buyer are legally valid and are equally binding upon the seller and the buyer.

### 2. Agreement

If a contract for the sale and purchase of goods is entitled with the name"Agreement", as long as its contents have made clear, specific and affirmative provisions on the rights and obligations of both parties, it will be binding on both parties like "Contract".

If business negotiation between the seller and the buyer is more complex. After negotiations, agreed to the terms of part, part of this condition remains to be further negotiation, both parties can signed a preliminary agreement firstly or an agreement in general. The two parties have agreed conditions determine down, the rest shall be negotiated further. In order to avoild misunderstanding, this Agreement shall state that it is of the preliminary nature, a formal contract will be signed after further negotiation so as to clarify that this agreement is not a formal and valid contract.

### 3. Memorandum

Memorandum is one of the forms of a written contract. If the terms of the transaction agreed upon by the seller and the buyer are clearly and specifically set forth in a memorandum and signed by both parties, such memorandum shall have the same nature as a contract. However, if both parties only reach a certain degree of understanding or understanding some of the items, and this kind of understanding or understanding recorded in the form of "Memorandum", as the basis of the two parties trading or cooperation in the future, or as a preliminary agreement for further negotiation, this Memorandum can be regarded as memorandum of understanding, it is not legally binding upon both parties.

### 4. Letter of Intent

Before the business negotiation has been finally reached an agreement, in order to reach a deal, the goals, vision and will that the buyer and the seller will work together to strive for , sometimes including preliminary agreed part of the deal, will be recorded in a written document, as a basis and reference for future negotiations, the written document is called as Letter of intent.

A letter of intent is just an expression of intentions made by the two parties to an agreement. It is not a legal document and is not binding upon the parties concerned.The concerned parties of the letter of intent bear moral responsibilities to each other. Generally, they should not deviate too far from the provisions of the letter of intent in further negotiation.

### 5. Orders and Intent

Order means a purchase order for the goods made by the importer or the actual buyer. Indent means the purchase order for the goods made by an agent or commission agent on behalf of his principal. The seller shall carefully review the contents of an order or an authorized purchase order. An order or purchase order sent after negotiation may be construed as a purchase contract or purchase confirmation.

If the order is found that some of the terms are inconsistent with the terms agreed upon by the two parties through negotiation, or are added or changed, it shall be dealt with separately. The seller may accept the non-conformity or the non-serious or minor nature of the addition or modification. In case of material change , if the seller cannot accept it, it shall raise an objection to the other party without delay and shall not keep silent and ignore it.

The seller shall determine whether an offer or an invitation for an order or an authorized purchase order sent directly by the buyer without negotiation is an offer or an invitation for an offer according to the specific content thereof. After carefully studying its contents and decide whether to deal with it or not, and timely reply to the buyer.

## Questions

1. What basic conditions must be constitute in a valid offer or acceptance?
2. In the international transactions, which kinds of goods does not in "United Nations Convention on contracts for the International Sale of Goods, 1980"?
3. What contents must be have in an International sales contract of goods?
4. Please use a specific specimen to state how to make an enquiry, offer, counter-offer and acceptance in cross-board e-commerce.

# 第九章

# 国际货物买卖合同的履行

☞ **案例9.1**

日本商人和犹太商人签订了10000箱蘑菇罐头合同，合同规定每箱20罐，每罐100克。但在出货的时候，日本人却装了10000箱150克/罐的蘑菇罐头，货物的重量比合同多了50%，但是犹太商人拒绝收货。日本出口商无奈地表示，愿意超出合同的重量不收钱，但是犹太商人还是不同意，并要求赔偿，理由是日本商人违反了合同。最后几经谈判，日本商人无可奈何，赔了犹太商人10多万美元，还要把货物另作处理。这件事情传出后，各国的商人都开始"理解"犹太商人这一做法的用意。一位英国律师对此事件的解释是："从国际贸易规则和国际惯例来讲，合同的品质条件是一项很重要的条件，英国法把它称为要件。合同规定的商品规格是每罐100克，而出口商实际交付的却是150克，虽然重量增加了50克，但是卖方没有按规定条件交货是违反合同的。按国际惯例，犹太商人完全有权拒收货物并提出索赔"。一些消费者分析："犹太商人购买这样规格的商品，是有自己特定的商业目的的，包括消费者的爱好和习惯、市场需求情况、对付竞争对手的策略等。如果出口方装运的150克罐头不适应市场消费习惯，那犹太商人是不会接受的。最简单的问题就是，如果这次150克罐头的价格与100克罐头的价格一样，那下一次重量回到100克，消费者怎么看待？"还有一些熟悉市场的人士分析："犹太商人拒收货物的原因，很有可能是在一些进口管制比较严格的国家申请进口的许可证是100克的，而实际是150克的货物很容易遭到有关部门的质疑，被怀疑为有意逃避进口管理和关税，以少报多，是要受到罚款的处罚或者被追究责任的"。而犹太商人听了哈哈大笑："我们并没有考虑这么多啊！"原来犹太人极为注重合同，信任合同，相信签约的双方都是会严格遵守。他们认为合同是生意成功与否的关键，人的存在本身也是在履行合同，一切买卖强调要守约。

　　履行合同是买卖双方的共同责任。合同履行是当事人实现合同内容的行为，只有履行了合同，才能使合同签订所寄予的愿望和目的得以实现。履行合同的重要性不亚于合同的磋商和签订。履行合同义务，不仅仅是经济行为，也是法律行为。合同一经有效订立，绝不能因考虑不周，疏忽失职或因为避免或减少损失而任意地片面地修改或撕毁，也决不能因货源、资金、运输等方面不落实而将应尽的义务任意减免。对卖方来说，履行合同的基本义务是按合同规定交付货物，移交一切与货物有关的单据，并转移货物的所有权；买方的基本义务是按照合同规定，支付货款和收取货物。如果买卖双方各自严格按照合同规定履行义务，一笔交易就得以圆满实现。

　　在对外经济活动中，树立和维护信誉是至关重要的。重合同的目的在于守信用，守信用的意义绝非履行一份合同后所体现出来的经济目的和效益所能衡量，它关系到对外信誉，包括企业信誉、国家信誉。在实际业务中，有时会发生一方当事人不履行或不完全履行合同义务而导致另一方受到损害的情形，受损害的一方有权按照法律和国际惯例采取提出包括损害赔偿要求在内的适当措施。

　　当事人如期望顺利履行合同，必须认真做好内、外协调工作。其中，外部协调工作除涉及另一方当事人外，还涉及银行、检验机构、海关、运输、保险、政府机构等相关部门；内部要涉及研发设计、生产、质检、财务、销售、用货、单证与储运等部门。因国际货物买卖合同的某些特定条款内容与这些内部部门密切相关，这些内部部门的相关人员应对各自负责的合同条款内容进行认真审核。

# 一、国际货物买卖合同履行的流程

　　国际货物买卖合同的履行涉及面广，各环节之间具有密切的联系。在实际业务中，由于交易对象不同、合同采用的贸易术语、付款条件、交货方式等不同，买卖双方履行合同的具体做法也有所差异，其业务环节和内容有所不同。在具体业务中，各环节常常需要前后交叉或齐头并进开展活动。下面分别以出口贸易和进口贸易为例，简要介绍其各自的基本流程和主要内容。

## （一）卖方履行合同的基本流程

　　卖方履行合同面临的环节很多、涉及面广。以出口贸易采用CIF贸易术语和采用跟单信用证付款为例，卖方履行合同的基本流程见图9.1。卖方采用其他贸易条件和付款方式成交的合同，合同履行除某些细节有所差异外，基本做法大致相同。卖方在履行合同时，一般要经过货（备货）、证（催证、审证、改证）、运（托运、保险、报验、通关）、款（制单、收款）四个基本环节。其中，CIF贸易合同的"运"是海上运输。在履行每个环节时，卖方应注意各环节与其他环节的相互配合与协调，防止"货""证""运"脱节以及在装运后的出现"交单不符"等现象，以免最终影响安全收款。卖方在安全收款后，按照中国的实际，还需按照国家有关规定办理出口收汇核销和出口退税。

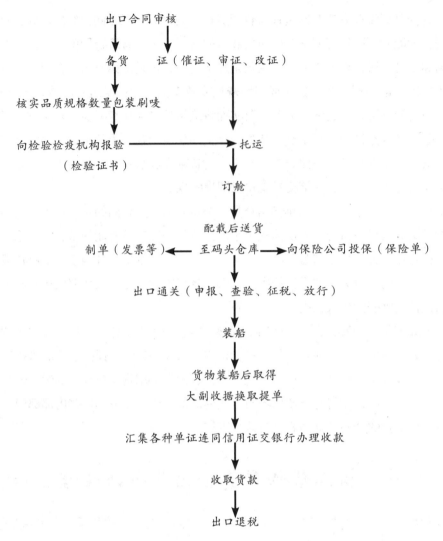

（合同以CIF贸易术语成交，采用跟单信用证付款）

图9.1 卖方履行合同的基本流程

### （二）买方履行合同的基本流程

以进口贸易采用FOB贸易术语和跟单信用证付款为例，买方履行该类合同的一般程序是：评审合同、开立信用证、租船订舱、装运、办理保险、审单付款、办理清关、报检和货物在国内的运输、转运和拨交，以实现进口货物按时、按质、按量顺利到达。如发现国外卖方有违法行为，应及时提出异议和索赔。图9.2是买方履行FOB条件+跟单信用证结算合同的基本流程。

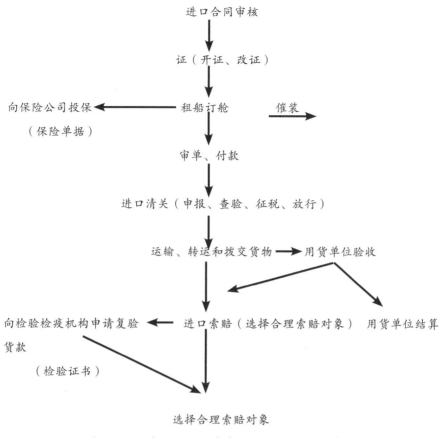

进口合同审核

证（开证、改证）

向保险公司投保 ← 租船订舱 → 催装

（保险单据）

审单、付款

进口清关（申报、查验、征税、放行）

运输、转运和拨交货物 → 用货单位验收

向检验检疫机构申请复验 ← 进口索赔（选择合理索赔对象） 用货单位结算
货款

（检验证书）

选择合理索赔对象

（向承运人索赔 向出口商索赔 要求保险理赔等）

（合同以FOB贸易术语成交，采用跟单信用证付款）

图9.2 买方履行合同的基本流程

# 二、国际货物买卖合同条款的审核

## （一）国际货物买卖合同审核的作用

买卖双方在正式签署或正式履行国际货物买卖合同之前，应就合同条款的内容进行仔细审核。审核国际货物买卖合同的具体作用有：①判定合同条款的内容是否清楚明确，防止贸易双方因就某条款内容理解不一致而导致的纠纷；②对于明显不合理的条款内容，在合同履行之前或签署之间提请对方修改，以促进履约顺利进行；③便于合同履行各环节的相关人员明白各自的工作职责，了解各条款之间的相互关系，防止履约环节脱节；④判定各条款间的内容是否相互呼应衔接，有否出现彼此矛盾的内容。合同内容应从实际出发，体现公平合理的原则，对贸易双方均有约束力。

## （二）国际货物买卖合同的审核

国际货物买卖合同的内容一般包括3个部分：约首、本文和约尾。其中，约首部分包括合同名称、合同编号、合同签订的日期和地点、订约双方名称和地址、适用的法律等；本文部分是合同的主要组成部分，由基本条款和格式化条款组成。基本条款包括商品名称、品质规格、数量、包装、价格、交货、付款等；格式化条款，即一般交易条款、通用条款，包括商品检验、索赔、不可抗力、仲裁等；约尾部分包括合同的有效期、合同使用的文字及其效力，买卖双方的签字等。

### 1. 约首部分的审核

合同名称应正确体现合同的内容，买方制作的合同通常称为购货合同（purchase contract）或购货确认书（purchase confirmation）；卖方制作的合同通称售货合同（sales contract）或售货确认书（sales confirmation）。双方当事人的名称和详细地址应在合同中正确载明，除了便于识别当事人之外，在发生纠纷时可作为决定诉讼管辖的重要依据，也便于在必要的时候进行联系；订约日期应为接受生效日期。合同成立、履行及解释所依据的法律，对双方当事人都十分重要。根据多数国家的法律，当事人可以选择处理合同争议所适用的法律，并在合同中加以规定。如在合同中没有约定适用的法律，则约首部分的订约地点规定非常关键，因为订约地点有时可决定合同适用的法律。

### 2. 约文部分的审核

约文部分的审核内容包括基本条款和格式化条款。

#### （1）审核商品的名称和质量条款

商品的名称与质量条款内容的重点审核要求：①合同的品名与质量条款内容应明确、具体，既要避免做空洞、笼统的规定，又要防止将做不到或不必要的描述性语句加入。很多商品在不同的国家有不同的名称，在询盘和签订合同时，所使用的商品名称应采用国际上的通用名称，能代表拟订购或出售的商品。②选用合适的品名，以便降低关税、方便进出口和节省运费。③在凭样品买卖时，由于各国对凭样品买卖的法律规定不尽相同，在合同上必须订明交货品质是与样品"完全相符"或是"大体相似"，并注明样品寄送日期。④对凭说明书或商品目录买卖时，为防止交货时鱼目混珠，以假乱真，应详细列明生产国别、生产厂家、产品规格型号以及使用目的，并订明最低的品质保证条款及检验方法，以排除"免责条款"。⑤商品的使用目的应尽可能具体，并在合同中做出明文规定。

#### （2）审核数量条款

在买卖合同中应明确规定数量、计量单位与确定数量的时间和地点。计量单位有重量、个数、长度、面积、体积与容积等。重量的计量方法有：毛重、净重、公量、理论重量、法定重量和净净重等。如选择以毛重计量与计价，应在合同中明确规定"以毛作净"（gross for net）。如果合同中未明确重量的计量方法，则理解为以净重计量。由于货物在仓储、运输环节会发生损耗，买卖双方最好事先在合同中规定确定数量的时间与地点，如以装运时的数量为准，或以目的港卸货时的数量为准，或以进入进口地仓库或工厂时核定的数量为准等。对于一般的商品特别是初级产品，其数量条款内容除规定数量、计量单位、确定数量的时间与地点外，还可以规定溢短装幅度和明确溢短装的选择权。如数量规定有溢短装条款，在采用信用证结算的情况下，信用证可兑用的金额也应有相应的增减幅度。

（3）审核价格条款

在国际货物买卖中，计价货币与支付货币通常为同一种货币。买卖双方可协商决定是否采用出口国货币、进口国货币或第三国货币。买卖双方在选择计价货币和支付货币时，应将该货币可能上浮或下浮的幅度考虑进去，压低进口价格、抬高出口价格或采用国际上通用的外汇保值条款。不同的价格条件包含不同的费用和责任。如采用CIF贸易术语，卖方要办理货物运输和保险；而FOB贸易术语，卖方则不需要办理货物运输和保险。

（4）审核交付条款

货物的交付条款，通常包括运输方式、装运时间（到货时间）、装运港（地）、目的港（地）、运输单据、装运通知、分批装运和转运等。买卖双方在货物交接过程中应承担的责任，由采用的贸易术语所决定。以象征性交货的贸易术语为例，来说明如何审核货物的交付条款：①FOB、CFR、CIF只适合水上运输，以这三种贸易术语成交的买卖合同属于装运合同。在货物的交付条款中，只需规定装运时间，不应规定货物到达时间；货物从装运港运到目的港，全程采用水上运输。②FCA、CPT、CIP适合于各种运输方式，以这三种贸易术语成交的买卖合同也属于装运合同。在货物的交付条款中，只要规定装运时间，不应规定货物的到达时间；可采用任何运输方式，将货物从装运地运到目的地。③以CFR、FOB、FCA、CPT贸易方式成交，合同的保险条款应订明"保险由买方自理"。④以CIP、CIF贸易条件成交的合同，由卖方负责办理保险，合同中的保险条款应订明"由卖方负责办理保险，并规定保险金额、投保险别、保险条款、赔付地点和货币名称等"。

同时，以CFR、CIF、CPT、CIP成交的合同，由卖方办理运输，应在合同中对卖方的运输责任做出约束规定。例如："卖方负责将本合同所列货物由装运港装上直达班轮到目的港，中途不得转船。货物不得用悬挂买方不能接受的国家的旗帜的船只装运"。对于签约后可能发生的额外费用，如运价上涨、港口封航产生的绕港费用等，可在合同中明确规定由谁负担。在CFR、CPT条件下，卖方在装船后立即发出装船通知就显得格外重要，在合同中还应订立装运通知和风险划分的条款；在FCA、FOB条件下，由买方负责运输。卖方在备妥货物后应向买方发出通知，以便买方安排运输；买方安排好船只或指定承运人后，应发装运通知给卖方，以便卖方安排装运。为了便于买方既按合同又按卖方的要求安排运输，合同中除应指定装运港（地）外，还应规定合理的装运时间、卖方发出货物备妥的通知期限、通知内容、未按要求发出通知应承担的责任，以及买方应给予卖方装运信息的充分通知等。除此之外，合同中还应规定卖方不能按时交货或买方不能按时安排运输应承担的责任。

（5）审核付款条件

付款条件直接关系到买卖双方的利益。稍有不慎，不仅会增加费用支出，而且还会发生卖方出货后收不到货款，或买方付款后而拿不到货物及/或进口需要的凭证和单据的情况。国际货物买卖合同中采用的付款方式有汇款、托收、信用证、银行保函和备用信用证等。无论采用哪种付款方式，买卖双方应在"货""单""款"上加以平衡，以降低风险。

（6）审核包装条款

包装条款一般包括包装材料、包装方式、包装容量、唛头等。如果合同约定"唛头由买方指定"，则应具体规定唛头指定的最后期限，并订明若到时未收到有关唛头通知，卖方可自行决定。如买卖双方约定"包装材料的全部或部分由买方负责提供"，则合同中应规定包装材料到达卖方的最迟时间和延期到达的责任。该"最迟时间"应与合同规定的"装运期限"相衔接。包装费用一般含在货价内。如买方要求特殊包装，除非事先明确，否则超出的包装费用原则上应由买方负担，并在合同中规定具体的包装费用金额和支付办法。另外，在合同中要避免对包装条款做笼统的规定，例如"适合海运包装"（seaworthy packing）和"习惯包装"（customary packing）或"卖方惯用包装"（seller's usual packing）等术语，除非买卖双方对包装方式的具体内容事先充分交换了意见，或由于长期的业务交往已取得一致的认识。否则此类规定缺乏统一认识，容易引起纠纷与争议。

（7）审核格式条款

格式条款是当事人为了重复使用而预先拟定，并在订立合同时未与对方协商的条款。凡已在格式条款中订明的事项，在合同的基本条款中可以不再另作规定。格式条款和非格式条款不一致的，应以非格式条款为准。当事人对格式条款的理解发生争议的，应当按照通常理解予以解释。对格式条款有两种以上解释的，应当做出不利于提供格式条款一方的解释。合同条款的共性部分都可列入格式条款中。例如：品质条款中的品质机动幅度的规定；数量条款中溢短装比例的规定；运输条款中是否允许转船、分批、提供运输单据的种类、份数的规定；信用证支付方式中关于信用证的类别及开证日期的规定；商品检验、索赔、仲裁、不可抗力等条款，等等。

由于标准合同中一般印有这些内容，加上业务操作流程中的习惯性操作较多，格式条款的内容容易被忽视，可能导致日后履行合同难度的增加。因此，应重视和仔细斟酌格式条款内容。为了应对贸易实践的不断变化，应对格式条款的内容根据实际需要加以适当调整。例如，对于商品检验条款，可经过慎重选择，改变检验机构，灵活确定检验方式、确定检验内容及标准、明确检验费用由谁承担等。

### 3. 约尾部分审核

贸易双方经交易磋商达成协议后，通常由一方当事人缮制正本合同书一式两份，经签署后寄送另一方当事人，要求对方签署后寄回一份存查，并作为履约和处理争议的依据。对于对方寄来或签退的合同要进行审查，确保合同内容未经修改或添加。如有与达成的协议不符或加注未取得协议的文句，应视具体情况酌情处理。经双方签署的合同书内容如与磋商一致的条款有出入时，就应以经签署的合同书为准。

# 三、卖方履行合同的主要环节

## （一）备货

备货是指买卖合同订立后，卖方为了保证按时、按质、按量履行合同的交货义务，根据合同规定的品质、包装、数量和交货时间等的要求，着手货物的准备工作。

### 1. 备货环节的主要内容

备货是卖方履行合同的重要环节。《联合国国际货物销售合同公约》第37条明确规定："卖方必须按照合同和本公约的规定交付货物，移交一切与货物有关的单据并转移货物所有权"。因此，按照合同交付货物、移交单据、转移货物所有权是卖方的三项基本义务。而交付货物是最基本的义务，因为交付货物是移交单据并转移货物所有权的前提。做好备货工作是履行交货义务的物质基础。备货环节的工作内容，包括：①落实相应的配套资金。②按合同和信用证的要求进行生产、加工或仓储。③组织货源或催交货物。④核实货物加工、整理、包装和刷唛情况。有的货物即使已经验收进仓，还需要根据合同的规定进行再次的整理、加工和包装，并在外包装上加刷运输标志和其他必要的标志。⑤对货物进行验收和清点。

### 2. 备货环节应注意的事项

卖方必须严格按照合同或信用证要求备货。在备货时须对以下问题予以高度重视。

①货物的名称、规格必须与合同规定一致，货物应进行严格挑选、加工和整理。如凭规格、等级、标准等文字说明买卖，交付货物的品质必须和合同规定的规格、等级、标准等文字说明相符；如凭样品买卖，交付货物的品质必须与样品一致；如既凭文字说明又凭样品买卖，则两者均应相符。同时，货物的品质还须符合同一规格货物通常使用的目的和在订立合同时买方通知卖方的特定目的。

②货物的数量必须符合合同的规定。如发现货物数量不符合合同要求，应及时采取必要措施，在规定期限内补足。考虑到商品的自然损耗和储运过程中的货损，以及合同中的溢短装条款，备货数量一般以略多于合同规定的数量为宜。根据UCP600的规定：凡"约""大约"或类似意义的词语用于数量时，应解释为允许有不超过10%的增减幅度。而该惯例还规定：除非信用证规定所列的货物数量不得增减，在支取金额不超过信用证金额的条件下，即使不许分批装运，货物数量也允许有5%的伸缩。但信用证规定货物数量按包装或个数计数时，此项伸缩不适用。因此，合理运用信用证的溢短装条款，或在合同中明确规定溢短装数量，并且规定溢短装数量的选择权归卖方，卖方合理利用允许的溢短装比例，不仅备货数量比较灵活，而且可以在市场波动情况下创造可观的效益。

③货物的包装必须符合合同与信用证规定以及运输要求。如合同未对包装做具体规定，卖方应按照同类货物通用的方式进行包装。如果没有通用的包装方式，则应按照足

以保全和保护货物的方式进行包装；应认真核对货物内外包装的装潢设计；如发现包装不良或破损等情况，应及时进行修整或更换，以免在装运时取得"不清洁提单"，造成收款困难；对于包装标志，如合同有规定或另有指定，则按合同规定或指定办理；如合同未做规定或客户对此无要求的，则由卖方自行选定办理；如进口国当局规定包装标志必须使用特定文字，一般应予以照办。标志的刷写部位和文字大小要适当，图案字迹清楚并且不易褪色。在保证质量和不违反合同规定前提下，可尽量压缩包装体积或降低货物包装的重量，以节约运输费用。

④货物备妥的时间应符合合同和信用证规定的装运期限要求，并结合船期进行安排。为防止发生意外，造成延误装运，从而引起纠纷或经济损失，在时间掌握上，一般还要适当留有余地。

⑤抓紧落实信用证或预付款。对于情况不够了解或资信欠佳的客户，以及是按客户要求定制的货物，一般应按合同规定，在收到对方开来的信用证，审核无误后再进行生产，以防对方不履行合同，造成商品积压等问题；如合同规定买方应支付一定比例预付款的，则应在预付款入账后将货物装运出去。

⑥凡属法定检验或合同约定由检验检疫部门进行检验检疫的出口货物，应按规定的手续向出入境检验检疫机构申请报检，检验合格后取得相应的合格证书。

⑦货物必须是第三方不得提出任何权利或请求的。卖方应保证对所售货物享有合法的所有权。准备交付的货物，还必须是第三方不能根据工业产权或其他知识产权主张任何权利和请求的。但按照《联合国国际货物销售合同公约》规定，此项权利或请求以卖方在合同订立时已经知道或不可能不知道的权利或要求为限。

### （二）催证、审证和改证

凡规定以信用证付款的合同，买方必须按照合同规定及时开立信用证，信用证的内容应与合同相符，或者虽有不符，但其不符内容能为卖方接受。因此，以信用证方式付款的合同，催证、审证、改证就成为卖方履行合同的重要环节。原则上，卖方应在收到买方开来的信用证后开始备货。如果买方没有及时开证，卖方应酌情考虑一边催证、一边备货。

#### 1. 催证

为保证合同的顺利履行，卖方在必要的、适当的时候，可通过信件、电报、电传或其他方式，提醒和催促买方按照合同规定的时间开立信用证。对于大宗交易或按买方要求特别定制的商品，买方按时开立信用证非常重要，因为卖方一般是在收到信用证后开始备货。如果买方延期开证或者拒绝开证，轻者造成卖方不能准时装运货物，或因市场行情发生变化造成损失；重者造成卖方不能将货物销售出去，严重影响卖方的可持续经营。一般情况下，买方应在货物装运期前至少提前15天，将信用证开到卖方。对于资信情况不很了解的客户，卖方原则上应坚持在装运期前30天（或以上），配合生产加工期限和客户的要求，要求买方开出信用证。

在实际业务中，买方如遇到市场行情变化或缺乏资金，往往拖延开证。在下列情况下，卖方应催促买方按时开立信用证：①在合同规定装运期限较长（如3个月或以上），并且规定买方应在装运期前一定期限（如30天）开证的情况下，卖方在通知买方预期装运期时，应同时催促买方按约定时间开证。②结合船期情况，如有可能提前装运，可与买方商议要求提前开证。③如买方未在合同规定的期限内开立信用证，卖方有权向买方要求损害赔偿。在此之前，仍可催促买方开证。④开证期限未到，但发现客户资信不佳，或市场情况有变，也可催促买方开证。

### 2. 审证

收到买方开来的信用证后，卖方应对照合同，依据UCP600审核信用证。审证的基本原则是"证、同一致"，即信用证的内容必须与合同规定一致。但在实际业务中，经常会发现信用证内容并不完全与合同规定相符。为了确保安全收款，卖方在收到信用证后，应立即对其内容进行认真地核对和审查。信用证审核的项目一般包括：

（1）**审核信用证的种类**

UCP600规定，信用证必须规定其是以即期付款、承兑、延期付款还是议付的方式兑用。因此，卖方应审核信用证的兑用方式是否与合同规定相符；如合同规定开立保兑信用证，则审核信用证是否按照合同约定加以保兑。如是保兑的信用证，卖方还需对保兑行的资信、保兑费用的规定进行审核。

（2）**审核申请人和受益人**

申请人、受益人的名称和地址经常会与合同上显示的名称或地址不一样。按照UCP600的规定，申请人与受益人的名称，必须与合同规定一致，但他们的具体地址可与合同规定不尽相同，但其国别（或地区）名称必须一致。

（3）**审核信用证的支付货币和金额**

信用证的金额和支付的货币名称应与合同规定一致，总金额的大小写必须一致。如果合同订有溢短装条款，信用证金额应包括溢短装部分的金额；如果信用证采用的支付货币与合同规定的货币不一致，应按一定的外汇牌价折算成合同货币，在不低于或相当于原合同货币总金额时才可接受。

（4）**审核货物描述与装运规定**

信用证的品名、质量、规格、数量、包装、单价、装运港、卸货港、目的地、保险等内容应与合同规定一致。

（5）**审核信用证的交单地点与截止日**

根据UCP600号的规定，所有信用证必须规定一个交单的截止日。信用证规定的承付或议付的截止日期被视为交单的截止日，信用证规定的被指定银行所在地即为交单地点，但开证行的所在地也可作为交单地点。对于卖方来说，交单应在截止日当天或之前完成。为了避免过期交单，交单截止日与实际装运日期的间隔不能太短，一般以15天或21天为宜。为了方便交单和信用证兑用，卖方应争取让买方开立有"被指定银行的信用证"比较有利。

（6）审核装运期和有效期

装运期是对货物装运时间的规定，原则上必须与合同一致。因开证延误而导致不能按期装运，或因生产或船期安排等原因，造成货物不能在装运期内按期装运，可与买方协商延期装运。信用证的有效期与装运期应有一定的合理间隔，以便卖方在货物装运后有足够的时间进行制单和交单。信用证的有效期限，一般规定为最迟装运日后15天（或21天）。信用证的到期地点，对卖方来说，规定在出口国家到期比较有利。如信用证规定在国外到期，那么到期地点一般规定为开证行的所在地，单据必须在到期日（或之前）寄达开证行。

为此，卖方有可能承担单据邮寄延误或遗失的风险。

（7）审核转船和分批装运条款

货物中途转船，不仅延误时间，增加费用开支，而且还有可能出现货损。因此，买方一般不愿意允许货物转船。但是，允许转船对卖方比较有利。卖方在审核信用证的转船条款时，应注意其是否与合同规定一致。如果允许转船，还应注意允许转船的内容是否具有特殊要求，如转运地点、船名或船公司是否特别指定。而卖方需考虑这些特殊要求是否有把握控制。如不能加以控制，则应要求买方改证；如信用证规定分批、定期、定量装运，应注意每批装运的时间间隔是否合理。按照UCP600，如信用证规定在指定的时间段内分期发运或分期支款，任何一批未按信用证规定期限发运或支取时，信用证对该期及以后各期均告失效。因此，审证时要认真对待。

（8）审核单据

卖方要仔细审核信用证要求提供的单据种类、份数及填制要求等。如信用证对某种单据提出特别要求，如要求提供证实的商业发票或经进口国的领事签证等，应视具体情况判断是否接受或提请修改。

（9）审核其他条款和特殊条款

对在信用证的空白处、边缘处加注的字句和戳记应特别注意。这些内容往往是信用证内容的重要补充或修改，稍不注意就可能造成事故或损失。对于信用证上的特殊要求条款，如不能做到或不合理的要及时提出修改。

3. 改证

如在审证时发现一些问题，卖方应根据问题的性质采用不同的处理方法。如出现违反卖方所在国的对外贸易政策，影响合同履行和安全收款的情况，卖方可要求买方必须修改；对于不违反对外贸易政策，经过努力可以做到，不增加太多费用的情况，卖方可以酌情处理。而信用证的修改，应由申请人向开证行提出。未经开证行、保兑行（如有的话）及受益人同意，信用证既不得修改，也不得撤销。受益人对同一修改的内容不允许部分接受，部分接受被视为拒绝修改。因此，卖方对信用证的审核和修改，是保证合同顺利履行和安全收款的重要前提，卖方应予以足够的重视。

### （三）货物装运

备妥货物和落实信用证后，出口合同履行进入到租船订舱、出货装柜和装船环节。货物装运涉及的环节很多，包括托运、报检、投保、通关、装船、发送装运通知等，每个环节都十分重要。以6种象征性的贸易术语成交，卖方负责办理出口清关手续。如合同要求办理货物检验，或属于出口国规定的法定检验产品，卖方在办理出口清关手续之前还应申请检验。如以CFR、CIF、CPT、CIP贸易术语成交，由卖方负责运输，签订运输合同；如以FCA、FOB贸易术语成交，卖方应在合理时间内向买方发出备货完毕的通知，以便买方即使安排运输。货物装运后，卖方应及时向买方发出装运通知。发送装运通知，在CFR、CPT贸易术语下尤其重要。如以CIF、CIP贸易术语成交，卖方在货物装运前，还应办妥运输保险。

### （四）制单、结汇

货物装运后，卖方应按照合同或信用证的规定，正确缮制各种单据。在信用证规定的交单截止日或之前，将各种单据和必要的凭证递交银行办理收款。根据UCP600，只有"交单相符"，开证行才承担付款责任。因此，卖方应正确、完备地提交信用证所规定的单据。

#### 1.单据

在FOB、FCA、CFR、CFP、CIF和CIP贸易合同项下，单据是卖方履行货物买卖合同的证明。卖方凭提交的单据来证明其是否履行了合同的义务以及履行的程度。卖方只要在规定的时间内交付了货物并提交了合乎要求的单据，就已履行了自己在合同项下的义务，而不必亲自交付实际的货物。

单据包括汇票、运输单据、保险单据、商业发票和其他单据等。按照单据作用的不同，单据可分为基本单据和附属单据。基本单据是国际贸易不可缺少的单据；附属单据是根据不同业务需要或规定，要求卖方特别提供的单据。随着贸易实践的发展，商业发票依然被认定为基本单据，而运输单据、保险单据已逐渐从基本单据退居为非基本单据（附属单据）。附属单据一般因进口国家（或地区）、产品性质、数量、运输方式的不同而异，主要包括海关发票、领事发票、产地证、检验证、船运公司证明以及附属于商业单据的装箱单、受益人证明、电报抄本等。根据单据签发人的不同，单据还可分为商业单据、运输单据、保险单据和政府单据。商业单据一般由卖方签发、运输单据由承运人或者其代理签发、保险单据由承保人签发、政府单据则由相关的政府职能部门签发。

#### 2.制单的基本要求

单据制作力求做到"正确、完整、及时、简明、整洁"。"正确"是指制作的单据只有做到"交单相符"，才能够保证及时收汇；"完整"是指必须按照信用证的规定提供各项单据。单据的份数和单据本身的项目也必须完整无缺；"及时"是指应在信用证规定的有效期内，及时将单据送交被指定银行或开证银行，以免信用证过期或延期交单；"简明"是指单据的内容应按照信用证的要求填写，力求简明，切勿加列不必要的内容，以免弄巧成拙；"整洁"是指单据的布局要美观大方，缮写或打印的字迹要清楚，单据表面要清洁，对更改的地方要加盖校正章。有些单据，如提单、汇票以及其他一些单据的主要项目，如金额、件数、重量等，一般不宜修改。

# 四、买方履行合同的主要环节

## （一）申请开立信用证

买方应按合同规定填写"开立跟单信用证申请书"，选择从事国际结算的商业银行办理申请开立信用证。买方在申请开证时，应注意以下问题：

①如果合同规定有开证时间，买方应在规定的期限内开立信用证；如果合同中只规定了装运期而未规定开证日期，买方应在合理时间内开证。一般情况下，买方应在合同规定的装运期前30～45天申请开证，以便卖方收到信用证后，开始备货，并在装运期内安排装运货物。如果合同规定在卖方确定交货期后开证的，买方应在收到卖方上述通知后再办理申请开证手续。如果合同规定在卖方领到出口许可证或支付履约保证金后开证的，应在收到卖方出口许可证复印件或收到保证金后再申请开证。

②信用证条款应与合同一致，信用证中要详细列明合同中规定的有关条款。

③单据条款要明确。买方在申请开证时，必须列明需要卖方提供的各项单据及份数，并对单据的内容提出具体要求。

④通知行的指定应由开证行决定，不应同意由卖方指定。

⑤特殊条款的利用。在有些特殊情况下，可以利用信用证中的特殊条款做出规定。

⑥对于卖方要求修改信用证的要求，买方应慎重考虑。

## （二）租船订舱、保险和审单付款

### 1．租船订舱

以FOB贸易术语成交的合同，买方应负责租船订舱。按合同规定，卖方应在装运前的一定时期内，将预计装运日期通知买方。买方在收到通知后，应及时办理租船订舱手续。在办妥租船订舱后，应按规定的期限通知卖方船名、航次及船期，以便卖方备货装船。买方应随时了解和掌握卖方的备货和装船准备情况，必要时催促卖方按时装运。对成交数量巨大或重要的进口物资，在一定情况下，买方应派人到出口地点监督装运。卖方装船后，应及时用电报、传真或电子邮件向买方发出装船通知，以便买方办理保险和办理进口报关接货等事宜。

在CFR或CIF价格条件下，由卖方负责租船订舱。买方也应随时了解和掌握卖方的备货和装船准备情况，催促对方按时装运。装船后，卖方应及时用电报、传真或电子邮件向买方发出装船通知，通知买方船名、航次及船期和其他装运信息，以便买方及时办理运输保险、进口清关、接货等事宜。

### 2．办理运输保险

以FOB、CFR贸易术语成交的合同，一般由买方自行选择办理货物运输保险。针对每批装运货物，在收到装船通知后，买方应将船名、提单号、开航日期、商品名称、数量、装运港、目的港等项内容通知保险公司，向保险公司办理投保。买方可以就每批进口货物单独投保，也可与保险公司签订一定时期的进口预约保险，并对保险险别做相应的具体规定。

### 3．审单付款

在信用证项下，卖方装运货物后，根据信用证的规定，可向被指定银行或开证行直接办理交单。而被指定银行收单和审单后，会将全套单据寄交给开证行。然后，开证行向买方提示单据。买方在付款前，要对单据进行认真审核。如"交单相符"，同意办理付款赎单；如"交单不符"，则选择全部拒付、部分支付或者货到检验合格后付款。在托收项下，代收行在收到国外单据和汇票以后，向买方提示单据。买方在规定的期限内，通知银行是否同意付款或承兑。如果买方拒绝付款或承兑，代收银行一般无权提出疑问。在汇付项下，买方在收到卖方自行提交或由他人转交的单据后，按发票金额和合同规定的付款方式，向卖方付款。

## （三）进口商品报检

申请进口商品检验时，买方（申报人）必须填写进口商品检验申请单，在提供合同、商业发票、装箱单、提单副本件和进口到货通知书外，还需分别提供以下有关资料：①申请品质检验的，加附国外品质证书（质保书），使用说明书及有关标准和技术资料。如凭样成交的，要提供成交小样。②申请重量（数量）鉴定的，须附重量（数量）明细单、磅码清单、装箱单或实货清单等。③申请残损鉴定的，须附理货凭证，残损或短缺单，或铁路商务记录，或空运事故等记录有关证明残损的单证。④申请复验，应提供买方自行验收情况的详细验收记录、磅码单或检验结果单。⑤对结合成分纯度或公量计价的进口商品，报检人（买方）在申请品质检验时，还应同时申请重量鉴定。

## （四）进口清关

按照中国海关的规定，一般商品的进口监管，包括接受申报、查验货物、征收关税、清关放行四个环节。

### 1．进口货物申报

进口货物申报，是指货物入境后，由收货人或其代理人向海关申报，交验规定的单据，请求办理进口手续的过程。中国《海关法》对进出口货物的申报时限作了规定。进口货物的收货人（买方）应当自运输工具申报进境之日起14天内向海关申报。进口货物的收货人超过14天期限未向海关申报的，由海关征收滞报金。对于超过3个月还没有向海关申报进口的，其进口货物由海关依法提取变卖处理。如果属于不宜长期保存的货物，海关可以根据实际情况提前处理。变卖后所得价款扣除运输、装卸、储存等费用和税款后，尚有余款的，自货物变卖之日起一年内，经收货人申请，予以发还。逾期无人申请的，上缴国库。

进口清关除应提交进口货物报关单外，还应随附进口许可证和其他批准文件、提货单、发票、装箱单、减税或免税证明文件，海关认为必要时，应交验合同、产地证明和其他有关单证。如为《种类表》内的商品，应受动植物检疫管制的进口货物或受其他管制的进口货物，在报关时还要交验有关部门签发的证明。

**2．进口货物查验**

海关以报关单、许可证等为依据，对进口货物进行实际的核对和检查，以确保货物合法进口。海关查验货物时，进口货物的收货人（买方）或其代理人应当在场，并负责搬运货物、开拆和重封货物的包装。海关认为必要时，可以径行开验、复验或提取货样。查验后，海关在有关集装箱或者包装上加封，并做好检验记录备查。

海关通过对货物的查验，检查核对实际进口货物是否与报关单和进口许可证相符，确定货物的性质、成分、规格、用途等，以便准确依法计征关税，进行归类统计。

进口货物的查验，一般是在海关规定的时间、场所，即海关的监管区域内的仓库、场所进行。但为了方便合法进出，对进口的散装货物、大宗货物和危险品等，海关可以结合装卸环节，在现场直接验放。对于成套设备和"门到门"运输的集装箱货物，经申报人申请，海关可以派员到监管区域外的地点，就地查验放行，但海关需按规定收取费用。

**3．进口货物征税**

根据《中华人民共和国进出口关税条例》的规定，海关税则的进口税率分为普通税率和优惠税率两种。对产自与中国没有签订贸易互惠条约或协定的国家的进口货物，按普通税率征税；对产自与中国有贸易互惠条约或协定的国家进口的货物，按优惠税率征收。《关税条例》规定，进口货物以海关审定的货物运抵我国的到岸价格作为完税价格。

为了保证关税及时入库，进口货物的纳税人应在海关填发税款交纳的次日起7日内（星期日或节假日除外）缴纳税款。

**4．进口货物的放行**

进口货物在办理完向海关申报、接受查验、缴纳税款等手续后，由海关在货运单据上签印放行。收货人（买方）或其代理人必须凭海关签印放行的货运单据才能提取进口货物。货物放行是海关对一般进口货物监管的最后一个环节，放行就是结关。对于担保放行货物、保税货物、暂时进口的货物和海关给予减免税进口的货物，放行不等于办结海关手续，还要在办理核销、结案或者补办进出口和纳税手续后，才能结关。

**（五）接货、验收和拨交**

进口货物到港后，由港方负责卸货。在卸货时港方应该对货物进行检查，如发现短缺，及时填写"短缺报告"交船方签字，并根据短缺情况向船方提出保留索赔权的书面声明。卸货发现残损，应将货物存放在海关指定仓库，待保险公司会同商检机构验放后做出处理。货物经检验、报关和海关放行后，买方可以提取货物。

### （六）进口索赔

合同一般都规定：在货物到达后，如发现存在质量、数量、残损等问题，可凭合同规定的检验检疫机构出局的检验证书作为索赔依据。在检验证书上，一般均详细列明检验结果并判明责任归属：①属于卖方责任，如货物原装数量不足、品质规格与合同规定不符、包装不良致使货物受损，买方凭检验证书向卖方索赔。②属于承运人责任，如货物短卸、货物残损，均可凭船方"短卸报告"、国境站铁路商务记录或航空、邮电部门签发的事故签证和检验证书，买方可向外运公司、铁路、航空、邮电部门等提出索赔。③属于保险公司责任。由于自然灾害、意外事故或运输中其他事故的发生，致使货物受损，并且属于承保险别范围内的；或因承运人不予赔偿或赔偿金额不足抵补损失的部分，并且属于承保险别承保责任范围内的，买方凭检验证书、保险单向保险公司提出索赔。

买方在办理对外索赔时，一般应注意以下几个问题：①索赔金额。除受损货物价值外，检验费、装卸费、银行手续费、仓储费用、利息等费用也可包括在索赔金额内。②索赔证据。首先应填制索赔清单，随附检验证书、发票、装箱单、提单副本。另外，面对不同的索赔对象，还要另附相应的有关证件。③凡已向国外提出索赔的货物，应妥善保管足够数量，且具有代表性的复验样品，并注意保持现状。对外提出退货换货的部分货物，在未结案前不能动用。对不需退货换货的，可以只保留一定数量的不合格品，保留期限应与索赔期相同。④买方提出索赔后，国外责任方要求看货或修理的，买方应事先与检验机构取得联系并做好准备工作。

☞ **阅读材料8.1**

## 中国特种茶出口的标准程序

中国出口茶分绿茶、红茶和特种茶。其中，特种茶包括乌龙茶、花茶、黄茶、白茶、普洱茶、紧压茶和其他茶。特种茶是我国独有的出口商品，出口主要集中在日本、美国、加拿大、法国、英国、德国和东南亚市场，消费区域较为固定，经营企业也相对集中。加入WTO后，乌龙茶成为我国在国际贸易中具有强竞争力的优势农产品之一。

1.商务洽谈：贸易双方先进行洽谈。中方茶叶出口企业首先向客户邮寄茶叶小样，由客户进行全面的检测，当检测合格后，可以进一步签订正式合同。

2.准备货物：因国际市场对特种茶的品种需求各不相同，但单一品种需求量会较大。中方茶叶出口企业应提前准备好货物，并且保证货物的品质稳定一致。为保障货物质量，可委托国内权威技术检测部门进行检测，以确保茶叶产品符合出口标准。

3.申请许可证：中方茶叶出口企业如果是生产加工型企业，长期从事进出口贸易，并有独立的进出口权，可以到当地商检局进行备案，直接向国内大型外贸公司申领进出口许可证（注：国家对茶叶出口仍实行计划配额和出口许可证管理，同时需出口合同），同时可以依客户要求申请FORM A（普惠制产地证）。FORM A可以在当地海关的出入境检验检疫部门办理。凡有茶叶出口经营权的部委直属公司，其茶叶出口许可证由商务部配额许可证事务局核发。各省、自治区、直辖市及计划单列市茶叶出口企业的茶叶出口许可证由商务部各特派员办事处核发。

4. 报检：中方茶叶出口企业应该完成报检工作。企业依客户要求提供材料（包括国内权威技术检测单位的检测报告），申请海关的出入境检验检疫部门完成各项检测。如果茶叶出口企业在当地出海关入境检验检疫部门有备案，可以直接申请当地海关出入境检验检疫部门进行商检，商检放行即可出口。

5. 报关：中方茶叶出口企业应该完成报关工作。报关需要茶叶出口企业向有关部门提供进出口许可证、报关委托书、报关单、发票、装箱单等。

6. 定舱：完成上述申报和检测工作后，中方茶叶出口企业就可以向货运公司发出海运或空运定舱委托定舱。

7. 提单确认：由合同双方确认提单各细节，以确保提单无任何遗漏。

8. 货物投保：如果货值比较高，可以根据实际需要向保险公司投保。

9. 货物出运：针对客户需要，采用海运或空运出口。茶叶出口企业向货运公司发出货物。

10. 装船通知：在货物出运后，通知客户货物已经出运。同时，将提货单邮寄给客户。

11. 交单结算：一般采用银行交单，买卖双方完成收汇（银行水单）、付货款（增值税票认证）、付运费等过程。同时，涉及到外汇交易的可以向国家外汇管理局进行外汇申报。

12. 收尾工作：中方茶叶出口企业收回报关单，申报出口退税。

专家建议：对于长期从事茶叶生产加工的出口型企业要选择正规渠道，如果没有独立出口的能力和条件，可以申请国内大型外贸公司（如：中国茶叶股份有限公司）进行合作形式的出口贸易，一般国内大型外贸公司在国际茶叶市场都有较高的信誉，可以大大降低出口贸易中的风险，减少不必要的损失。详情可与中国茶叶股份有限公司各省茶叶分公司联系。

☞ 阅读材料8.2

## 中国进口食品的基本清关流程

第一：资质审核。中国进口商应具有进口资质，通常需做食品收货人备案。食品进口资质并不是指进口企业一定要具备食品流通许可证资格。食品流通许可证主要用于国内市场销售的环节，属于工商监督管理。如果进口企业需要在国内销售食品和开具发票，需要申请办理食品流通许可证。因此，没有食品流通许可证的进口企业，也能进口食品。

第二：海关预申报。食品进口分海运、空运和陆运方式进口。因海运和空运涉及到法定商检，货物无法提前进行预申报，但陆运可以提前进行货物预申报。提前申报是指货物没到目的港（地）之前就可以向海关申报进口。对于海关总署规定须重点审核的进口商品，海关一般会进行核价。待海关核价且货到目的港（地）后，基本可以不交保证金就可交税提货。

办理特殊食品预审核证明（只限营养食品）需提供：

1.《进出口特殊食品预审申请表》1份；

2.申请单位和进出口代理商的有效工商营业执照副本复印件1份（原件备查）

3.贸易合同书或协议书复印件1份；

4.产品质量标准；

5.产品说明书及5R彩色照片1张；

6.属预包装的进出口特殊食品，需提交标签样张3份及原标签样张翻译件3份，或《进出口预包装食品标签审核证书》复印件，原件备查；

7.生产工艺流程；

8.企业在生产当地的卫生许可证明或生产销售证明（进口特殊食品需提供）；

9.具有中国国家实验室认证资格(CNAL)或省级计量认证资格（CMA）的实验室出具的产品成分、卫生指标检验报告或产品检验合格证明；

10.保证函(保证在进出口和经营各环节不宣传任何保健功效)；

11.生产企业、经销商可委托进出口商办理预审，属委托办理的，需提交委托人出具的委托书原件。

如为普通食品进口，则需提供资料1即可。

第三：中文标签审核。进口企业应提供货物的包装图片和翻译文档，参照我国的食品标签通则和相关食品标准，办理标签审核。办理中文标签备案需提供：中文销售标签样式、原标签样张及中文翻译、原产地证或自由销售证明、申请单位营业执照复印件。很多食品进口还需要国外提供健康证书等。

第四：将备案好的标签或者经海关出入境检验检疫部门审核过的标签连同报检资料向商检机构申报检验。海运和空运进口是先抽样后出具通关单，而陆运则可以先出通关单后进行抽样。货物需存放到指定的仓库，化妆品和橄榄油需申领CIQ标志。加贴完中文标签经海关出入境检验检疫部门检验。如检验合格，则出具卫生合格证书，不合格则出具不合格证书。

第五：缴税放行。持标签备案证书、预审证明、贸易合同、商业发票、装箱单、原产地证或自由销售证等向海关申报食品进口。待海关出税单后缴税放行，然后通知运输公司办理通关手续并持报检单在商检查车场办理抽样送检，递交保函先办理通关手续，货物暂存放在仓库不得销售或使用，一般出结果要7个工作日。检验合格后，由海关出入境检验检疫部门出具卫生检验证书，准予货物销售和使用，如不合格则办理退运手续。

## 思考题

1.进出口合同的履行程序一般包括哪些方面？

2.在出口合同的履行中如何审核信用证？

3.合同成立的时间和地点分别是怎样确定的？

4.合同买卖双方的主要义务分别是什么？

5.跨境电商卖方履约的基本流程是怎样的？

# Chapter 9

# How to Perform an International Sales Contract

☞ Case 9.1

A contract was signed between a Japanese seller and a Jewish buyer for 10,000 cartons of mushrooms, each carton should contain 20 cans and 100 grams each can. At the time of shipment, the Japanese packed 10,000 cartons of 150grams/can of mushrooms, the actual weight of which was 50% higher than the contract. The Jewish buyer refused to accept the goods. The Japanese seller said reluctantly that he would accept no payment for the exceeding weight, but the Jewish buyer did not agree. He demanded a compensation on the grounds that the Japanese had violated the contract. Finally, after several negotiations, the Japanese had no alternative but to compensate the Jewish buyer more than 100,000 dollars, and deal with the goods. As the story spread, businessmen from all over the world began to "understand" what the Jewish merchants were doing.

A British lawyer explained the incident: "In terms of international trade rules and international practices, the quality condition of a contract is an important condition. The specification of the goods is 100 grams per can, while the exporter actually delivers 150grams. Although the weight is increased by 50 grams, the seller's failure to deliver the goods on the stipulated terms and conditions is a breach of contract. According to international practice, Jewish merchants are entitled to reject the goods and claim compensation." Some consumer analysis: "Jewish merchants buy goods of this size for their own specific business purposes, including consumer tastes and habits, market demands, and strategies for dealing with competitors. Jewish merchants would not accept a 150-gram can shipped by the exporter if it did not adapt to market consumption. The simplest question is, if the price of a 150-gram can is the same as the price of a 100 grams can, then the next time the weight goes back to 100 grams, what do consumers think?"There are some people who are familiar with the market analysis: "The cause of the Jewish businessman rejected goods, is likely to be in some countries of import control more strictly apply for import license is 100 grams, and the actual is 150 grams of goods easily was questioned by authorities, suspected of being deliberately escape import management and tariff, with few too many, is punished by fines or be held accountable."

The Jewish merchant laughed. "We didn't think about that much."It turned out that the Jews were highly contract minded, trusted the contract, and believed that both parties to the contract would strictly abide by it. They believe that the contract is the key to the success of the business, the existence of the person is also in the performance of the contract, and all the sales emphasize to keep the contract.

It is the common responsibility of both the buyer and the seller to perform the contract. The performance of the contract is the action of the parties to realize the content of the contract. It is no less important to perform a contract than to negotiate and sign it. Fulfilling contractual obligations is not only economic but also legal. Once the contract is concluded effectively, it shall not be unilaterally amended or torn up arbitrarily due to poor consideration, neglect of duty or loss avoidance or reduction, nor shall it be arbitrarily exempted from due obligations, due to failure to implement the contract in aspects such as supply, site and transportation of funds. For the seller, the basic obligation to perform the contract is to deliver the goods according to the contract, hand over all documents related to the goods and transfer the ownership of the goods. The basic obligation of the buyer is to make payment and collect the goods in accordance with the contract. If both the buyer and the seller fulfill their obligations strictly in accordance with the contract, a transaction will be consummated. In foreign economic activities, it is crucial to establish and maintain credibility. The purpose of abiding by a contract is to keep promise, and the meaning of keeping promise is far from the economic purpose and benefit reflected after the performance of a contract can be measured. In the actual business, sometimes one party fails to perform or fully performs its contractual obligations, thus causing damage to the other party, and the injured party is entitled to take appropriate measures including claim for damages in accordance with laws and international practices.

If the parties expect to perform the contract smoothly, they must do a good job of internal and external coordination. Among them, the external coordination work involves not only the other party, but also related departments such as Banks, inspection agencies, customs, transportation, insurance and government agencies. Internal to involve the departments including R& D design, production, quality inspection, finance, sales, goods, documents, storage and transportation. Due to the close connection between certain clauses of international sales contract and these internal departments, the concern parties of these internal departments should carefully review the contents of contract terms they are responsible for.

# 9.1 The Processing to Perform an International Sales Contract

The performance of an international sales contract involves a wide range of aspects. There are close links between the various links. The business links and contents are different due to different trading objects and different trading conditions. In specific operations, the links often need to be intersected or coordinated to carry out activities. The basic procedures of export and import are introduced respectively.

## 9.1.1 The Basic Procedures of the Seller's Performance of the Contract

The specific practice of the seller to perform the contract is different due to the different trade term and conditions of payment and delivery. Figure 9.1 indicates the basic process of the seller's performance of the contract under CIF term and by a documentary letter of credit. The performance practice is basically same except for some details if the seller uses other trade terms and payment method to conclude the contract. The seller shall, when performing the contract, generally go through four basic steps: goods (preparation of goods), Letter of credit (reminders, examination and alteration), transportation (consignments, insurance, application for inspection, customs clearance) and payments (making documents and receiving payments). Among them, the "transport" of CIF contract is by sea or inland waterway transport. In performing each link, the seller shall pay attention to the mutual coordination and coordination between each joint and other links to prevent the disconnection of "goods", "credit", "shipment" and "payment", as well as the occurrence of "non-complying presentation" after shipment, so as to avoid the ultimate impact on the safety collection. According to China's actual situation and the concerned regulation, after the seller gets payment safely, he still need to deal with verification of foreign exchange collection and export drawback.

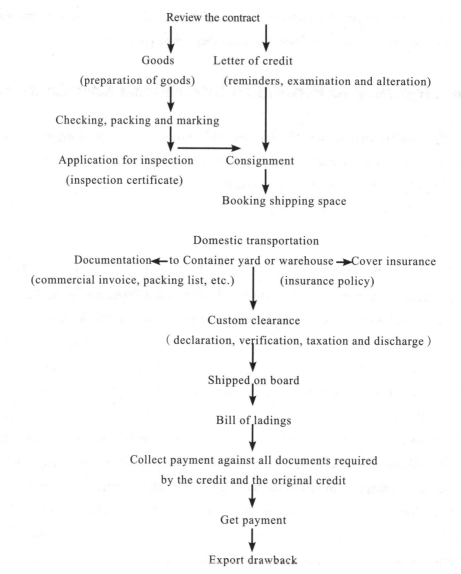

(The contract reached under CIF term and by a documentary credit)
Figure 9.1 Basic Procedures of the Seller's Performance of the Contract

## 9.1.2 The Basic Procedures for the Buyer to Perform the Contract

As an example, Figure 9.2 indicated the basic process for the buyer to perform the FOB contract by a documentary letter of credit. The general procedure to perform the contract by the buyer are: review the contract and open the L/C, charter booking, shipment, insurance, payment, examination of documents, customs clearance, commodity inspection and the domestic transportation of the goods, transshipment and delivery, in order to realize the import goods arrived on time, and the goods including quality, volume reached in good properly. If the foreign seller is found to have illegal acts, the buyer shall promptly raise objections and claims.

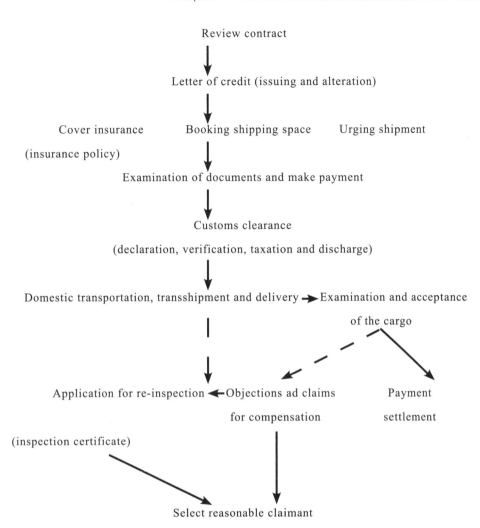

(The contract reached under FOB term and by a documentary credit)
Figure 9.2 Basic Procedures of the Seller's Performance of the Contract

# 9.2 Examination of the International Sales Contract

The buyer and seller shall carefully review the terms and conditions of the sales contract before signing or performing the contract. The specific role of examining the international sales contract is as follows: ①To determine whether the terms and conditions of the contract are clear or not to prevent disputes caused by the inconsistency of the understanding between the two parties of a certain clause. ②To ask the other party to amend the apparently unreasonable terms before or between the execution of the contract to facilitate the smooth implementation of the contract. ③To make it easy to understand their respective job duties, the mutual relations between the terms, and prevent the disconnection of the performance link for the personnel involved in the performance of each link of the contract. ④ To determine whether the content between the terms of the agreement, whether there are contradictory content. The content of the contract shall proceed from reality, reflect the principle of fairness and reasonableness, and be binding on both parties.

The international sales contract generally consists of three parts: the preamble, the body and the end. The preamble of the contract includes the contract name, contract number, date and place of signing the contract, name and address of both parties, applicable law, etc. This body is the main part of the contract including the basic terms and formatting terms. The basic terms include commodity name, quality specification, quantity, packing, price, delivery, payment, etc. Format terms, i.e. general trade terms and general terms, including commodity inspection, claim, force majeure, arbitration, etc. The end includes the term of validity of the contract, the language used in the contract and its validity, and the signature of both parties.

## 9.2.1 How to Examine the Preamble

The contract name shall reflect the contents of the contract correctly. The contract made by the buyer is usually called purchase contract or purchase confirmation. The contract made by the seller is called sales contract or sales confirmation. The names and detailed addresses of both parties shall be clearly stated in the contract. In addition to facilitating identification of the parties, the names and detailed addresses of both parties may serve as an important basis for determining the jurisdiction of the litigation in the event of a dispute, as well as facilitating communication when necessary. The date of contract shall be the effective date of acceptance. The law on which the contract is formed, performed and interpreted is of great importance to both parties. According to the laws of most countries, parties may choose the laws applicable to the settlement of a contract dispute and specify them in the contract. Where applicable law is not agreed in the contract, the location of the first part of the contract is critical, as the location can sometimes determine the law applicable to the contract.

## 9.2.2 How to Examine the Body

The content of review includes the basic clauses and formatting clauses.

**1. How to Review the Name and Quality Terms of the Goods**

Key requirements for the review of the name of the commodity and the contents of the quality clause include: ① The content of the brand name and quality clause should be clear and specific. It should avoid making empty and general provisions, and avoid adding descriptive sentences that are unfeasible or unnecessary. Many commodities have different names in different countries. The name of the commodity used in enquiry and contract should be the international common name, which can represent the goods to be ordered or sold. ② Use appropriate names to reduce tariffs, facilitate imports and exports and save freight. ③When selling by sample, the contract must specify that the delivery quality is "exactly the same" or "substantially similar" to the sample and indicate the date of delivery of the sample, as the legal requirements for the sale by sample are different in each country. ④When buying and selling by instruction or catalogue, in order to prevent the false and true in delivery, the country of production, manufacturer, product specification and model as well as the purpose of use should be specified in detail, and the lowest quality guarantee clause and inspection method should be specified to exclude the "disclaimer clause". ⑤The use purpose of commodities shall be as specific as possible and shall be expressly stipulated in the contract.

**2. How to Review the Quantity Terms**

The quantity, unit of measurement and time and place of determination shall be clearly specified in the sales contract. The unit of measurement includes weight, number, length, area, volume and dimension, etc. The measurement methods of weight are: gross weight, net weight, conditioned weight, theoretical weight, legal weight and net net weight, etc. "Gross for net" shall be clearly defined in the contract if gross weight measurement and valuation is chosen. If the measurement method of weight is not specified in the contract, it shall be understood as net weight measurement. As the goods will be damaged in the process of storage and transportation, it is better for the buyer and seller to specify the time and place of quantity in the contract in advance, such as the quantity at the time of shipment, the quantity at the port of destination for unloading, or the quantity at the time of entering the warehouse or factory at the place of import. For general commodities, especially the primary products, the quantity clause shall not only stipulate quantity, unit of measurement, time and place to determine quantity, but also specify the range of overfill and short-pack and the choice of overfill and short-pack. If the quantity is stipulated in terms of excess or shortage, the amount of the letter of credit payable shall be increased or decreased accordingly in the case of settlement by letter of credit.

**3. How to Review the Price Terms**

In the international sale of goods, the currency of account and the currency of payment are usually the same currency. The buyer and seller may decide through consultation whether to use the currency of the exporting country, the importing country or the third country. Buyers and sellers should take into account the extent to which the value of the currency may rise or fall in their choice of the currency to be denominated in and to be paid in, either by driving down the price of imports or by driving up the price of exports or by adopting internationally accepted currency hedging provisions. Different price terms include different fees and responsibilities .In the case of CIF terms, the seller shall arrange for transportation and insurance of the goods. For FOB trade terms, the seller does not need to handle cargo transportation and insurance.

### 4. How to Review Delivery Terms

Delivery terms of the goods shall normally include mode of transport, time of arrival (time of arrival), port of shipment (place), port of destination (place), transport documents, advice of shipment, partial shipment and transshipment, etc. The responsibilities of the buyer and seller during the delivery of the goods shall be determined by the trade terms used. An example of how to review the terms of delivery of goods is the trade term for symbolic delivery:

（1）Time of Shipment and Time of Arrival

FOB, CFR and CIF are only suitable for shipping on sea or inland waterway. Therefore, in the terms of delivery of the goods, as long as the time of shipment is stipulated, the time of arrival should not be specified. The mode of transport of goods shall be by sea or inland waterway transport from the port of loading to the port of destination. FCA, CPT and CIP are suitable for all kinds of transportation. Therefore, in the terms of delivery of the goods, as long as the time of shipment is specified, the time of arrival should not be specified. The transport may be carried from the place of shipment to the destination.

（2）Transport Insurance

In the case of CFR, FOB, FCA and CPT, the insurance clauses in the contract shall stipulate that "insurance shall be covered by the buyer"; If a contract is concluded on CIP and CIF terms, the seller shall be responsible for the insurance. The insurance clauses in the contract shall stipulate that the seller shall be responsible for the insurance and stipulate the amount of insurance, the type of insurance, the insurance clauses, the place of indemnity and the name of currency.

（3）Contract of Carriage

The contract which is concluded by CFR, CIF, CPT and CIP shall be delivered by the seller. The seller's liability for transport shall be governed by the contract. The seller is responsible for loading the contracted goods from the port of loading on a direct liner to the port of destination without transshipment. The goods shall not be carried by vessels flying the flags of countries not acceptable to the buyer. For the additional costs that may occur after signing the contract, such as the increase of freight rate and the cost of circumventing the port due to the closure of the port, the contract can clearly stipulate who shall bear the additional costs.

（4）Shipping Advice

Under CFR and CPT conditions, it is very important for the seller to give the shipping notice immediately after shipment. Therefore, the contract should also include the terms of shipping notice and risk division. Under FCA and FOB conditions, the buyer is responsible for transportation. The seller shall give notice to the buyer when the goods are ready, so that the buyer can arrange the transportation. After the buyer has arranged the vessel or named carrier, the buyer shall send the shipping notice to the seller so that the seller can arrange the shipment. In order to facilitate the buyer in accordance with the contract and arrange transportation according to the requirement of the seller, the contract should specify the port of shipment (ground), also should set a reasonable time of shipment, the seller send cargo ready notice period, responsibility, did not notice as required, and the buyer shall give the seller sufficient notice of shipment information, etc. In addition, the contract shall also stipulate the seller's failure to deliver the goods on time or the buyer's failure to arrange the transportation on time.

（5）How to Review the Payment Terms

Payment terms are directly related to the interests of both buyers and sellers. A little carelessness will not only increase the expense, but also result in the seller's failure to receive payment for goods after shipment, or the buyer's failure to get the goods and/or the necessary documents and documents for import after payment. Payment methods used in international sales contracts include remittance, collection, letter of credit, bank guarantee and standby credit. Either way, the buyer and seller should balance the "goods", "documents" and "payments" to reduce the risk.

**6. How to Review the Packing Terms**

Packing terms generally include packing materials, packing methods, packing capacity, shipping mark, etc. If the contract stipulates that "marks shall be specified by the buyer", it shall specify the deadline specified by the shipping marks and specify that the seller may, at its sole discretion, if no notice of the marks is received at that time. If the buyer and the seller agree that "all or part of the packing materials shall be provided by the buyer", the contract shall stipulate the latest time for the arrival of the packing materials to the seller and the responsibility for the delay of their arrival. The "latest time" shall be linked to the "time for shipment" stipulated in the contract. Packing charge is generally included in the price. If the buyer requests special packing, the extra packing charge shall, in principle, be borne by the buyer unless specified in advance. In addition, to avoid the packing clause in the contract for general provisions, such as "seaworthy packing" (seaworthy packing) and "customary packing" (customary packing) or idiomatic packaging "the seller" (the seller's usual packing) terms, unless the buyer and Seller with respect to the manner of packing details fully exchanged views in advance, or due to the understanding of the long-term business relationship has been agreed. Otherwise this kind of regulation lacks unified understanding, easy to cause dispute and controversy.

**7. How to Review the Format Terms**

A standard clause is a clause prepared in advance for repeated use by the parties and not negotiated with the other party at the time of conclusion of the contract. Any matter already specified in the standard terms may not be otherwise provided in the basic terms of the contract. If the standard terms and non-standard terms are inconsistent, the non-standard terms shall prevail. Where the parties dispute over the interpretation of the standard terms, they shall interpret them in accordance with the usual understanding. Where there are two or more interpretations of the standard terms, an interpretation against the party providing the standard terms shall be made. The common parts of the contract terms can be included in the standard terms. For example: The requirement of flexible range of quality in the quality clause; The proportion of excess or shortage in the quantity clause; The provisions on whether transshipment, partial shipment or the type and number of copies of the transport documents are allowed in the transport terms; The type of credit and the date of issuance stipulated in the payment method of letter of credit; Commodity inspection, claim, arbitration, force majeure clause, etc.

Because these contents are generally printed in standard contracts, and there are many habitual operations in business operation process, the content of format terms is easy to be ignored, which may lead to the increase of difficulty in fulfilling the contract in the future. Therefore, consideration should be given to the content of the format clause. In order to cope with the constant changes in trade practices, the content of format clauses should be adjusted according to actual needs. For example, the terms of commodity inspection can be carefully selected, the inspection institution can be changed, and the inspection methods, contents and standards can be determined flexibly.

### 9.2.3 How to Examine the End Part of Contract

After the two parties have negotiated and reached an agreement, the original copy of the contract is normally prepared by one party in duplicate, and the signed copy is sent to the other party, and the signed copy is required to be sent back to the other party for deposit, which will be the basis for the performance and settlement of disputes. The other party shall review the sent or returned contract to ensure that the contents of the contract are not modified or added. Any language which is inconsistent with the agreement concluded or in which no agreement has been entered into shall be dealt with as the case may be. In case of any discrepancy between the contents of the contract signed by both parties and the terms agreed upon in the consultation, the contract signed by both parties shall prevail.

## 9.3 The Main Link of the Seller's Performance of the Contract

### 9.3.1 Preparation of Goods

Preparation of goods means that, after the conclusion of the sales contract, the seller shall, in order to guarantee the performance of the delivery obligation of the contract on time, quality and quantity, prepare the goods according to the requirements of quality, packing, quantity and delivery time stipulated in the contract.

### 1. Main Content of Preparation of Goods

Preparation of goods is an important part of the seller's performance of the contract. Article 37 of the United Nations convention on the international sale of goods expressly states: "The seller must deliver the goods in accordance with the contract and the provisions of this convention, hand over all documents relating to the goods and transfer title to the goods." Accordingly, deliver goods according to the contract, hand over documents and transfer the ownership of goods is fundamental obligation of the seller. And the delivery of goods is the most basic obligation, because the delivery of goods is the transfer of documents and the premise of the transfer of ownership of goods. Preparation of goods is the material basis for fulfilling the delivery obligation.

The content of goods preparation includes:

① Follow up the corresponding supporting funds.

② Make processing or warehousing according to the requirements of the contract and letter of credit.

③ Organize the supply of goods or to urge the delivery of goods;

④ Check the processing, packing and brushing of the goods, even if some goods have been checked and accepted into the warehouse, they still need to be sorted, processed and packed again according to the provisions of the contract.

⑤ Check and accept the goods.

### 2. Attention Matters for Preparation of Goods

The seller must prepare the goods strictly in accordance with the contract or letter of credit. In the process of goods preparation, the following issues should be emphasized:

① The name and specification of the goods must be in accordance with the contract. If they are inconsistent, they should be selected, processed and sorted until they meet the requirements. If the goods are bought and sold according to specifications, grades and standards, the quality of the goods delivered must conform to the specifications, grades and standards specified in the contract. If the goods are sold by sample, the quality to be delivered must be in accordance with the sample. If both by written description and by sample, both should be consistent. In addition, the quality of the goods must be applicable to the purpose for which they are commonly used in the same specification and to the specific purpose for which the buyer notifies the seller at the time of the conclusion of the contract.

② The quantity of the goods must comply with the contract. If the quantity of goods is found not in conformity with the requirements of the contract, necessary measures shall be taken in time and made up within the prescribed time limit. Taking into account the natural wear and tear of the goods and the damage during storage and transportation, as well as the excess and short loading clauses in the contract, the quantity of goods in stock is generally a little more than the quantity specified in the contract. According to the UCP600 regulation, words of "approximately", "approximately" or similar meaning shall be interpreted as allowing a margin of increase or decrease of not more than 10 per cent in number. The practice also stipulates that the quantity of goods listed in the L/C shall not be increased or decreased, and the quantity of goods shall be allowed to vary by 5%, even if partial shipments are not allowed, provided that the amount of withdrawals shall not exceed the amount of the L/C. However, this expansion is not applicable when the L/C stipulates that the quantity of goods shall be counted in terms of package or number. Therefore, the reasonable use of the L/C's terms of excess and shortage, or the contract clearly stipulates the quantity of excess and shortage, and stipulates that the option of excess and shortage shall belong to the seller. The seller's reasonable use of the allowable proportion of excess and shortage not only makes the quantity of goods more flexible, but also can create considerable benefits in the case of market fluctuation.

③Packing of the goods must be in conformity with the contract and letter of credit and transport requirements. If the contract does not specify the packing, the seller shall pack the same kind of goods in the usual way. If there is no general way of packing, the goods shall be packed in a manner sufficient to preserve and protect them. In the process of goods preparation, the interior and exterior packaging decoration design, should be carefully checked and examined. If any package is found to be defective or damaged, it shall be repaired or replaced in time to avoid the "unclean bill of lading" being obtained at the time of shipment, which may cause difficulty in receiving payment. For the packaging marks, if the contract is specified or otherwise specified, it shall be dealt with in accordance with the contract or specified. If the contract is not specified or the customer does not require it, the seller shall make the choice. If the authorities of the importing country stipulate that the packaging marks must use specific characters, they should generally comply. The mark should be brushed and the size of the text appropriate, the pattern is clear and does not fade easily. On the premise that the quality of the goods is guaranteed and the contract is not violated, the volume of the packages or the weight of the packages can be reduced as far as possible to save transportation costs.

④The time for goods to be ready shall be in conformity with the time limit for shipment stipulated in the contract and letter of credit, and shall be arranged in accordance with the shipping date. In order to prevent the occurrence of accidents, delay in shipment, and thus cause disputes or economic losses, there should be a proper time control.

⑤The letter of credit or prepayment shall be implemented earliest. For the customers who are not familiar with the situation or have poor credit standing, and the products are customized according to the customer's requirements, the production shall be carried out according to the contract provisions after receiving the letter of credit from the other party and checking it without error. If the contract stipulates that the buyer shall pay a certain percentage of the advance payment, the goods shall be shipped after the advance payment is entered into the account.

⑥ All exported goods that are subject to legal inspection or agreed upon in the contract for inspection and quarantine by the inspection and quarantine department shall apply to the entry-exit inspection and quarantine organization for inspection according to the prescribed procedures, and obtain the corresponding certificate of conformity after passing the inspection.

⑦ Goods must be from a third party without any right or claim. The seller shall guarantee lawful title to the goods sold. The goods to be delivered must also be goods that a third party cannot claim any rights and claims under industrial or other intellectual property rights. However, in accordance with the United Nations convention on contracts for the international sale of goods, this right or request is limited to rights or claims that the seller knew or could not have known at the time of the conclusion of the contract.

## 9.3.2 Urging, Examination and Alteration of L/C

Where a contract stipulates payment by letter of credit, the buyer must open the L/C in time as stipulated in the contract. Accordingly, the contract that pays by letter of credit, how to urge , examine and ask for modifying the letter of credit become the important link that the seller fulfils a contract. In principle, the seller should prepare the goods after receiving the letter of credit from the buyer. If the buyer fails to open the L/C in time, the seller shall consider as appropriate and prepare the goods while urging the L/C.

**1.To remind and Urge the Buyer to Open the L/C**

In order to guarantee that the contract can be performed smoothly , the seller may, when necessary and appropriate, remind and urge the buyer to open the L/C by letter, cable, telex or other means. It is very important for the buyer to open the L/C on time for bulk transactions or specially customized commodities as required by the buyer, as the seller usually begins to prepare the goods after receiving the L/C. If the buyer delays opening the L/C or refuses to open the L/C, it will cause the seller to fail to ship the goods on time or cause losses due to changes in the market. The heavy causes the seller to be unable to sell the goods, which seriously affects the sustainable operation of the seller. Generally, the buyer shall open the L/C to the seller at least 15 days in advance of the time of shipment. The seller shall, in principle, insist that the buyer open the L/C 30 days (or more) before the time of shipment, in accordance with the time of production and processing and the requirements of the customer.

In practice, if the buyer encountered market changes or lack of funds, often delay the opening of the L/C.In the following circumstances, the seller shall urge the buyer open the L/C on time.

①A longer shipping time limit prescribed by the contract (e.g., 3 months or more), and the buyer shall be in a certain period (e.g., 30 days) before the shipment time under the condition of open the L/C, the seller notify the buyer of the anticipated in shipment, should also urge the buyer open the L/C according to the agreed time.

②If shipment is possible in advance, the seller may discuss with the buyer to ask for the opening of L/C in advance.

③In case the buyer fails to open the L/C within the time limit specified in the contract, the seller shall be entitled to claim damages against the buyer. Before that, the buyer can still be urged to open the L/C.

However, if the customer's credit is not good or the market situation changes, the buyer shall be urged to open the letter of credit

### 2. Examination of Letter of Credit

Upon receipt of the letter of credit from the buyer, the seller shall review the letter of credit under UCP600 in accordance with the contract. The basic principle of review is that the content of the letter of credit must be consistent with the contract provisions. However, in actual business, it is often found that the content of the letter of credit is not completely consistent with the contract provisions. In order to ensure the safe collection of payment, the seller shall check and examine the contents of the letter of credit immediately after receiving it. The items for the review of L/C generally include:

①Examine the type of letter of credit. Under UCP600, a credit must specify whether it is to be used against payment at sight, by acceptance, deferred or negotiation. Therefore, the seller should check whether the method of exchange of the letter of credit is consistent with the contract. If a confirmed letter of credit is issued as stipulated in the contract, it shall be checked whether the credit is confirmed as agreed in the contract. If the credit is confirmed, the seller should also check the bank's credit and confirmation fee.

②Examine the applicant and beneficiary.The name and address of the applicant and beneficiary will often differ from the name or address shown on the contract. According to UCP600, the name of applicant and beneficiary must be consistent with the contract, but their specific address may be different from the contract, but their country (or region) name must be consistent.

③Check the payment currency and amount of the letter of credit. The amount of the credit and the currency of payment shall be in accordance with the contract and the case of the total amount shall be in accordance with the contract. If the contract contains terms of excess shipment, the credit amount shall include the amount of excess shipment. If the payment currency adopted by the letter of credit is inconsistent with the currency specified in the contract, it shall be converted into the contract currency at a certain foreign exchange rate and accepted when the amount is not less than or equal to the total amount of the original contract currency.

④Review the description and shipping instructions of the goods. The content of the L/C, quality, specification, quantity, packing, unit price, loading port, unloading port, destination, insurance and so on shall be consistent with the contract.

⑤Check the place and deadline of the letter of credit. According to UCP600, L/C must specify a deadline for presentation of documents. The closing date for the acceptance or negotiation of the L/C shall be deemed to be the closing date for the presentation of the l/c. The location of the nominated bank specified in the L/C shall be the place of presentation, but the location of the issuing bank may also be the place of presentation. For the seller, the documents shall be delivered on or before the deadline. In order to avoid overdue documents, the time between the deadline and the actual date of shipment should not be too short. In order to facilitate the exchange of documents and letters of credit, the seller should strive to let the buyer open a letter of credit with the designated bank.

⑥Review shipment date and validity. The time of shipment stipulated must be consistent with the contract. In principle, shipment cannot be effected due to delay in issuing of L/C, or due to production or shipment arrangement, etc. The validity of the L/C should be reasonably spaced from the time of shipment so that the seller has sufficient time to prepare and deliver the documents after shipment. The expiry date of the L/C is normally 15 (or 21) days after the latest date of shipment. Where the letter of credit expires, it is advantageous for the seller to stipulate the expiry date in the exporting country. If the L/C is to expire in a foreign country, the place of expiry is generally to be the place of the issuing bank, and the documents must reach the issuing bank on (or before) the expiry date. For this reason, the seller may bear the risk of delay or loss of the documents.

⑦Review transshipment and partial shipment terms. If the goods are to be transshipped in the middle of the journey, it will not only delay the time and increase the expenses, but also cause damage to the goods. Therefore, buyers are generally unwilling to allow transshipment of the goods. However, it is more advantageous for the seller to allow transshipment. The seller shall check whether the terms of transshipment in the letter of credit are consistent with the contract. If transshipment is allowed, please note whether the content of transshipment is subject to special requirements, such as the name of the vessel to be transferred at the place of transshipment or whether the vessel company is specifically designated. And the seller needs to consider whether these special requirements are sure to control. If it cannot be controlled, the buyer shall be required to alter the letter of credit. If the L/C stipulates that the shipment shall be made in installments at fixed intervals, it shall be noted whether the time interval for each shipment is reasonable. According to UCP600, if the L/C stipulates shipment or payment by installments within the specified period of time, if any batch fails to be shipped or withdrawn within the stipulated period of the L/C, the L/C will become invalid for that period and for subsequent periods. Therefore, the L/C should be taken seriously.

⑧Review documents required. The seller should carefully check the type of documents required by the letter of credit, the number of documents and filling requirements. If letter of credit puts forward special requirement to some kind of document, if the commercial bill that asks to provide proof or the consular visa of classics country, wait, should judge whether accept or request to revise according to specific circumstance.

⑨Review other terms and special terms. Particular attention should be paid to the wording and marking in the margins and margins of the letter of credit. These contents are often important additions or amendments to the contents of the letter of credit. The special requirements on the letter of credit shall be amended in time if they cannot be fulfilled or are unreasonable.

### 3. Alteration of Letter of Credit

If some problems are found during the examination, the seller shall adopt different treatment methods according to the nature of the problems. The seller may require the buyer to amend the contract if it violates the foreign trade policy of the country where the seller is located and affects the performance of the contract and the safe collection of payment. In cases where there is no violation of foreign trade policy, which can be achieved through efforts and without too much cost increase, the seller may deal with it at his discretion. Amendments to the L/C shall be made by the applicant to the issuing bank. The credit shall not be amended or cancelled without the consent of the issuing bank, confirming bank (if any) and the beneficiary. The beneficiary does not allow partial acceptance of the same amendment and partial acceptance is deemed to reject the amendment. Therefore, the examination and amendment of the letter of credit by the seller is an important prerequisite for the smooth performance of the contract and the safe collection of payment, and the seller should pay enough attention to it.

## 9.3.3 Shipment of Goods

After the goods are ready and the L/C is implemented, the export contract will be performed in the stages of space booking, loading and unloading. There are many links involved in the shipment of the goods, including shipment, inspection application, insurance, customs clearance, loading, and sending of the shipping notice. Each link is of great importance. If the deal is closed with any of 6 kinds of symbolic trade terms, the seller is responsible for the export clearance formalities. If the contract requires the goods to be inspected or the products to be legally inspected as specified by the exporting country, the seller shall apply for inspection before going through the export clearance procedures. If the transaction is concluded in terms of CFR, CIF, CPT and CIP, the seller shall be responsible for the transportation and sign the transport contract. In case of a transaction concluded in FCA, FOB trade terms, the seller shall, within a reasonable time, give the buyer notice of the completion of the preparation of the goods so that the buyer can arrange the transportation. The seller shall advise the buyer of shipment in time after shipment. The shipping advice is especially important under CFR, CPT trade terms. In the event of a transaction concluded on CIF or CIP terms, the seller shall, before the shipment of the goods, arrange for transportation insurance.

## 9.3.4 Documentation

After shipment, the seller should make all kinds of documents according to the contract or letter of credit, submit all documents and the necessary documents to the bank for collection at or before the date of presentation of the L/C. According to UCP600, the issuing bank is liable for payment only if the documents are in conformity. Therefore, the seller shall present the documents stipulated in the letter of credit in a correct and complete manner.

**1. Documents**

Contracts under FOB, FCA, CFR, CFP, CIF, and CIP term, the documents are the evidence of the seller's performance of the contract for the sale of goods. The seller shall present the documents to prove whether it has performed its obligations under the contract and the extent of its performance. As long as the seller has submitted the required documents within the specified time, the seller has fulfilled its obligations under the contract without having to deliver the actual goods in person.

Documents include bills of exchange, transport documents, insurance documents, commercial invoices and other documents. According to the different functions of documents, documents can be divided into basic documents and subsidiary documents. Basic documents are indispensable documents for international trade. The subsidiary documents are required to be specially provided by the seller according to different business requirements or regulations. With the development of trade practice, commercial invoices are still recognized as basic documents, while transport documents and insurance documents have gradually retreated from basic documents to non-basic documents (subsidiary documents). Subsidiary documents generally vary according to the country (or region) of import, product nature, quantity and mode of transport, mainly including customs invoice, consular invoice, certificate of origin, inspection certificate, certificate of shipping company and packing list, beneficiary certificate, copy of telegram attached. Documents can also be divided into commercial documents, transport documents, insurance documents and government documents, depending on who issued them. Commercial documents are generally issued by the seller, transport documents are issued by the carrier or its agent, insurance documents are issued by the insurer, and government documents are issued by relevant government departments.

**2. Basic Requirements for Documentation**

Documentation shall be achieved as "correct, completeness, timely, conciseness and neat". "Correct" means that only a complying presentation can secure getting payment timely. "Completeness" means that all documents must be presented in accordance with the terms of the credit. The number of copies of the documents and the items of the documents themselves must also be complete. "Timely" means that documents shall be delivered to the nominated bank or issuing bank in time within the validity period stipulated in the credit to avoid the expiry or delay of the L/C. "Conciseness" means that the contents of the documents should be filled in accordance with the requirements of the letter of credit. "Neat" means that documents should be arranged in a beautiful and elegant way, written or printed clearly, documents should be clean, and corrections should be stamped. Some documents, such as bill of lading of draft and other documents of the main items, such as the amount of call number of call weight, generally should not be modified.

# 9.4 The Main Link of the Buyer's Performance of the Contract

## 9.4.1 Application for Issuing a Credit

The buyer should fill in the application form for issuing a documentary letter of credit according to the contract, and choose the commercial bank engaged in international settlement to apply for opening letter of credit. The buyer should pay attention to the following problems when applying for opening a letter of credit.

①If the contract stipulates the issuing time, the buyer shall open the L/C within the specified time limit. If the contract specifies only the time of shipment and does not specify the date of opening L/C, the buyer shall open L/C within a reasonable time. Generally, the buyer should apply for opening L/C 30 to 45 days before the time of shipment stipulated in the contract so that the seller can start preparing the goods after receiving the L/C and arrange the shipment within the time of shipment. If the contract provides for the issuance of l/c after the date of delivery is determined by the seller, the buyer shall apply for the issuance of L/C after receiving the above notice from the seller. If the contract provides for the issuance of the credit after the seller has received the export license or paid the performance security, the application shall be made after the seller has received the copy of the export license or received the security.

②The terms and conditions of the L/C should be consistent with the contract.

③ The terms of the document should be clear. When the buyer applies for the opening of the L/C, it must specify the documents and the number of copies to be provided by the seller, and put forward specific requirements on the contents of the documents.

④The appointment of the advising bank shall be decided by the issuing bank and shall not be agreed by the seller.

⑤Utilization of special clauses. In some special cases, the special terms of the letter of credit can be used to make provisions.

⑥Buyer should think carefully about seller's request to amend L/C.

## 9.4.2 Shipment, Insurance, Examination of Documents, and Payment

### 1. Shipment

For a contract concluded under FOB terms, the buyer shall be responsible for chartering the ship or booking the shipping space. As stipulated in the contract, the seller shall inform the buyer of the expected date of shipment within a certain period before shipment. Upon receipt of the notice, the buyer shall promptly go through the procedures for booking the shipping space. After booking the space, the seller should be informed of the name of the vessel, the voyage and the sailing date within the prescribed time limit so that the seller can prepare for shipment. The buyer shall keep abreast of the seller's stockpiling and shipping preparations and shall urge the seller to ship the goods on time if necessary. The buyer shall, under certain circumstances, send a person to the place of export to supervise the shipment of imported materials of great quantity or importance. The seller shall send the shipping notice to the buyer by cable, fax or E-mail in time after loading the goods, so that the buyer can handle the insurance and import declaration and other matters.

Under CFR or CIF terms, the seller is responsible for chartering the ship and booking the space. The buyer should also keep abreast of the seller's stock and shipping readiness to urge the seller to ship the goods on time. After shipment, the seller shall send the shipping notice to the buyer by cable, fax or E-mail in a timely manner, informing the buyer of the name of the vessel, the voyage and the date of shipment and other shipping information, so as to enable the buyer to deal with the matters of transportation, insurance, import customs clearance and goods receiving timely.

### 2. Transport Insurance

For a contract concluded on the basis of FOB or CFR terms, the transport insurance shall generally be covered by the buyer at his option. For each shipment, the buyer, upon receipt of the shipping advice, shall notify the insurance company of the name of the vessel, bill of lading number, date of departure, name of commodity, quantity, port of shipment, port of destination and so on, and apply to the insurance company for insurance. The buyer can insure the goods of each batch of imports separately, also can sign with insurance company the entrance that has certain period is sure, make corresponding specific regulation to insurance particular.

### 3. Examination of Documents and Making Payment

Under the letter of credit, in accordance with the stipulations of the L/C, after loading the goods, the seller need prepare all documents required by the credit and present to the nominated bank or issuing bank. The nominated bank will send the full set of documents to the issuing bank after receiving and reviewing the documents. The issuing bank then presents the documents to the buyer. The buyer should carefully examine the documents before making payment. If the documents constitutes a complying presentation, the buyer agree to handle payment redemption. In the case of "non-conformity of documents", the payment shall be refused in full, paid in part or paid after the goods have passed the inspection.

Under collection, the collecting bank will present the documents to the buyer upon receipt of the foreign documents and drafts. The buyer notifies the bank within the specified period whether the payment or acceptance is agreed. The collecting bank generally has no right to ask questions if the buyer refuses payment or acceptance.

Under remittance, the buyer shall, upon receipt of the documents submitted by the seller or delivered by others, pay to the foreign seller in accordance with the invoice value and the payment method specified in the contract.

### 4. Apply for Inspection of Import Goods

When applying for import commodity inspection, besides the contract, commercial invoice, packing list, a copy of the bill of lading and the arrival of notice, the buyer (applicants) must fill in the import commodity inspection application form and provide the following information.

①Applying for quality inspection, and foreign quality certificate (warranty), instruction manual and the relevant standards and technical data. If a deal is concluded by sample, should offer a small sample.

②Where the application for weight (quantity) certification is submitted, a weight (quantity) list, , or a physical cargo list shall be attached.

③In case of an application for a damage identification, a receipt for tallage, a form for damage or shortage, or a railway business record, or an air transport accident, or a document certifying the damage.

④Prior to the application for re-inspection, the buyer shall provide detailed acceptance record, weight (quantity) list or inspection result sheet of its own acceptance situation.

⑤As for the imported goods with purity of combined components or public price, the applicant (buyer) should also apply for weight identification at the same time when applying for quality inspection.

## 9.4.3 Customs Clearance

According to the provisions of the Chinese customs, four links are included for import clearance of the generl cargo.

### 1. Declaration of Imported Goods

Declaration of import goods refers to the process in which the consignee or its agent declares to the customs after the entry of goods, delivers the documents specified for inspection, and requests the handling of import procedures. China's customs law stipulates the time limit for declaration of import and export goods.The consignee (buyer) of the imported goods shall declare to the customs within 14 days from the date of declaration of the means of transport entering the country.Where the consignee of the imported goods fails to declare to the customs within the period of 14 days, the customs shall collect the overdue declaration. If the import has not been declared to the customs for more than 3 months, the import goods shall be extracted and sold by the customs according to law. If the goods are not suitable for long-term storage, the customs can deal with them in advance according to the actual situation. The proceeds of the sale, after deducting the expenses for transportation, handling, storage and other taxes and duties, shall be returned to the consignee within one year from the date of the sale of the goods. If no application is made after the time limit, it shall be turned over to the state treasury.

Import customs clearance shall be accompanied by import license, other approval documents and  documentation of tax reduction or exemption for archival bill of lading and packing list. The import goods subject to the animal and plant quarantine control or other control shall be submitted for inspection by the relevant authorities at the time of customs declaration.

### 2. Inspection of Imported Goods

The customs shall carry out actual check and inspection of the imported goods on the basis of registration of customs declaration forms to ensure the lawful import of the goods. When the goods are inspected by the customs, the consignee (buyer) or its agent of the imported goods shall be on the spot and be responsible for carrying, opening and sealing the goods. If the customs deems it necessary, they may conduct a preliminary survey and re-examine the goods or take samples. After inspection, the customs seals the relevant containers or packages, and makes inspection records for reference.

Through the inspection of the goods, the customs shall check whether the actual imported goods are consistent with the customs declaration and import license, determine the nature of the goods, specification and use, etc., so as to calculate and collect the duties according to the law.

The inspection of import goods is generally carried out in the place where the time is specified by the customs, that is, the place where the warehouse is located in the area under the supervision of the customs. However, in order to facilitate the legal entry and exit, the customs can directly inspect the imported bulk goods and dangerous goods by combining loading and unloading links. For the complete sets of equipment and container goods transported "door to door", upon the application of the declarer, the customs may send officers to inspect the goods at the places outside the surveillance area and release them on the spot, but the customs shall charge fees according to the regulations.

### 3. Import Duties

According to the regulations of the People's Republic of China on import and export tariffs, the import tax rate of customs tariff is divided into ordinary tax rate and preferential tax rate. The import goods from countries which have no reciprocal trade treaties or agreements with China, shall be taxed at ordinary rates. The goods imported from countries which have reciprocal trade treaties or agreements with China shall be subject to preferential tax rates.The customs regulations stipulate that the customs value of imported goods shall be the CIF value of the goods examined and approved by the customs. In order to guarantee the timely entry of customs duties into the warehouse, the taxpayers of imported goods shall pay the duties within 7 days (except Sunday or holiday) from the day after the customs declaration and payment of duties.

### 4. Release of Imported Goods

The customs shall sign and seal the shipping documents and release the imported goods after completing the procedures such as declaration to the customs, accepting the customs declaration and payment of duty. The consignee (buyer) or its agent must present the shipping documents signed and released by the customs before taking delivery of the imported goods. The release of goods is the last step of the customs supervision of the general import goods, and the release is the clearance. For the goods released under guarantee, bonded goods, goods temporarily imported and goods subject to duty reduction or exemption by the customs, release is not equivalent to the completion of customs formalities, and clearance can be achieved only after verification and cancellation, settlement of cases or completion of import and export and tax formalities.

### 5. Domestic Transport, Delivery and Acceptance

When the imported goods arrive at the port of destination, upon discharge, the port shall inspect the goods. If any shortage is found, the port shall fill in the "shortage report" and submit it to the ship for signature in time.If the goods are found damaged in discharging, they shall be stored in a warehouse designated by the customs and dealt with after inspection by the insurance company and the commodity inspection authorities.The buyer may take delivery of the goods after inspection, customs clearance and customs clearance.

### 6. Import Claim

The contract stipulates generally: After the goods arrives, if there is problem on quality, quantity or  damage to the goods, a claim may be lodged against the inspection certificate issued by the inspection and quarantine body stipulates in the contract. The inspection results are generally specified in detail on the inspection certificate, and the responsibility is determined.

①The seller shall be responsible for the damage caused by the shortage of the original quantity of the goods, the non-conformity of quality specifications with the contract provisions, and the poor packing. The buyer shall claim for damages against the seller with the inspection certificate.

②The carrier shall be responsible for unloaded damaged with the ship's "short-landed report", the railway business record of frontier station or the accident visa and inspection certificate issued by the aviation and postal departments.

③The insurance company is responsible for the goods damaged and fall within the scope of covered insurance as a result of natural disasters, accidents or other accidents during transport.

④If the part of the loss is not indemnified by the carrier or the amount of indemnity is insufficient to cover the loss, and falls within the scope of liability covered by the undertaking, the buyer shall make a claim against the inspection certificate to the insurance company.

The buyer should pay attention to the following problems when handling external claims.

①The amount of the claim is available. In addition to the value of damaged goods, inspection fee, handling fee, bank handling fee, storage fee, interest and other expenses can also be included in the claim amount.

②Proof of claim.The claim should be made out firstly, accompanied by inspection certificate, commercail invoice, packing list, copy of bill of lading. Additional, different object of claim need  attach the concerned certificate additionally.

③Where claims have been made abroad, the representative re-inspection samples shall be properly kept sufficiently and the status quo shall be maintained. Part of the goods for return and exchange shall not be used before the case is closed. If the goods do not need to be returned or replaced, only a certain amount of non-conforming products can be kept, and the retention period should be the same as the claim period.

④The buyer shall get in touch with the inspection organization and make preparations in advance, if the foreign responsible party asks to see the goods or repair after the buyer raises the claim.

## Questions

1. Please describe the basic procedures of performing an international sales of contract for the seller and buyer.

2. If the international sales contract is stipulated with 100% payment made by a documentary credit, how to examine the relating credit?

3. How to determine the date and place of contract signed?

4. Please explain the general obligations of the contractual parties of an international sales contract.

# 第十章

# 国际贸易主要方式

☞ **案例10.1**

　　江苏弘业股份有限公司成立于1979年，于1997年在上交所挂牌上市，是全国工艺品行业和江苏省外经贸系统第一家上市企业，现为江苏省苏豪控股集团有限公司的重要成员企业，注册资本24676.75万元。公司先后通过了ISO9001质量管理体系、ISO14001环境管理体系和OHSAS18001职业健康安全管理体系认证，是"中国质量诚信企业""南京市总部企业""南京市外贸综合服务试点培育对象"，自主品牌"爱涛Artall"连续多年荣获"江苏名牌产品"和"江苏省重点培育和发展的国际知名品牌"称号。通过不断的投入和建设，公司持续增强市场开拓、技术研发、生产制造、质量保障等核心能力，进出口总额连年攀升，多次入选全国进出口企业500强。出口商品包括机电产品、船舶、玩具、休闲礼品、纺织服装、鞋帽服饰和家居用品等，进口商品涵盖化工、矿产、煤炭、医疗器械、机电设备、食品等领域，产品主要出口北美、英国、欧盟、日本和东盟等海外地区。

　　公司自成立以来，每年都参加华交会、广交会。在每届交易会上，该公司的玩具、箱包、礼品、鞋帽、服装、体育休闲用品、家具等产品摊位均在品牌展区展出，吸引了国内外广大客商。同时，该公司常年组织业务部门到国外参展，走到世界各地去推销自己的产品。在德国科隆五金展、日本国际礼品展、美国拉斯维加斯国际礼品及消费品展、美国拉斯维加斯鞋展、法兰克福秋季消费品展、美国纽约玩具展等国际博览会上都能看到HOLLY（ARTALL）产品的展示。2016年公司对"一带一路"沿线国家的出口额为9879.5万美元，占出口总额的31.93%。在其15个控股企业和业务部中，除国际贸易有限公司、进出口有限公司、海外业务部外，还拥有国际技术工程有限公司、电商部、金融投资部和环保科技、文化产业、化肥工业、工艺品等有限公司；在其7个重点投资企业中，包括了期货、文化产权交易、融资租赁、信用再担保、投资创业等新型公司。

当前，国际贸易范围不断扩大，交易类型日趋复杂，贸易方式多样化发展。除逐笔售定外，还有包销、代理、寄售、拍卖、招标与投标、期货交易、加工贸易、对等贸易、租赁贸易等。同时，电子商务对国际贸易的影响不断向深层次扩展，中国跨境电商发展势头迅猛，跨境电商已成为带动我国外贸发展的中坚力量。2017年中国出口跨境电商交易规模为6.3万亿元，同比2016年增长14.5%，其中B2B为5.1万亿元，同比增长13.3%。跨境电商出口能高效满足海外需求，已成为传统贸易出口的有效补充。

# 一、经 销

## （一）经销的概念及分类

经销是指企业或个人为另一个企业或个人按照双方签订的合同销售商品。根据经销商权限的不同，经销可分为包销和一般经销。包销是指经销商在规定的期限和地域内，对指定的商品享有独家专营权。出口方为达到在别国推销自己产品的目的，可以和国外的某家经销商达成包销（exclusive sale）或独家（sole sale）经销协议，把某产品种或某类别产品在某地区的独家经营权利在一定期限内授予对方，即包销商。一般经销是指经销商不享有独家专营权，供货商可在同一时间、同一地区委派几家经销商来经销同类商品。如果出口企业通过协议只是把某种或某类商品在某地区的经营权在一定期限内授予一家企业，且无排他性，这家出口企业还可以把该经营权授予其他企业，这些企业就是一般经销商。经销属于售定，供货方与经销商之间是一种买卖关系，但又与通常的单边逐笔售定不同。当事人双方除签有买卖合同外，通常须事先签订有经销协议，确定双方对等的权利和义务。

## （二）包销

包销是国际贸易中习惯采用的方式之一，是指出口方与国外经销商达成协议，把指定商品在指定地区在一定时间内的独家经营权授予该经销商，而经销商须承诺不经营其他来源的同类或可替代商品。双方通过签订包销协议，建立起一种稳定的长期的买卖关系。具体的每笔交易，以包销协议为基础，须另行订立买卖合同。包销的一般做法如图10.1所示。出口方与包销商之间的权利与义务由包销协议、买卖合同确定，但买卖合同必须符合包销协议的规定。

包销有利于出口方利用包销商的资金和销售能力，在特定的区域建立起稳定发展的市场；有利于包销商取得专卖的机会，在指定商品的销售中处于有利的地位，避免多头竞争而导致降价减盈。因此，包销商有较高的经营积极性，能在广告促销和售后服务中做较多的投入。但是，包销商须买断商品自行销售，需投入一定的资金，并承担销售风险。若包销商资金不足或缺少销售能力，有可能形成"包而不销"。如何选择一个合适的包销商是出口方采用包销方式的关键所在。

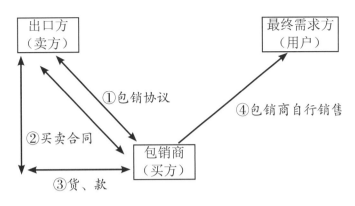

图10.1　包销的基本做法

### （三）包销协议的内容

经销协议是供货方和经销方订立的明确双方法律关系的契约，其内容的繁简可根据经销商品的特点、经销地区的差异，以及双方当事人的意图加以确定。经销协议中一般只规定双方当事人的权利义务和一般交易条件，而每批货物的交付需依据经销协议订立具体的买卖合同，以进一步明确价格、数量、交货期和付款方式等具体交易条件。因此，经销协议本身不是买卖合同。包销商品的价格可作一次性规定，也可以在订立买卖合同时按市场行情商定。一般贸易条件如检验、索赔、保险、不可抗力等，可在包销协议中予以规定。包销协议的主要内容及其注意事项，包括：

①包销协议的名称、签约日期与地点。

②包销协议的前文，如明确规定出口方与包销商间的关系是本人与本人的关系（principal to principal），即买卖关系。包销商自筹资金买断商品进行销售，自负盈亏。

③包销商品的范围。如出口方经营的商品种类繁多，或同类（种）商品有不同的品牌与规格，双方当事人可在包销协议中明确约定包销商品的具体范围。在确定包销商品的范围时，要结合出口方的经营意图与包销商的经营能力、资信状况加以考虑。在包销协议中最好进一步规定：停止生产的产品或新推出的产品是否适用于该包销协议。

④包销地区，即包销商行使销售的地理范围，可以为一个国家或几个国家，或一个国家中的几个城市，或一个城市等。在确定包销地区时，应考虑下列因素：(a)包销规模及包销商的能力；(b)包销商能控制的销售网络；(c)包销商品的性质及种类；(d)市场的差异程度；包销地区的政治、地理和交通条件等。经销地区可根据业务发展的需要由双方协商后加以调整。在包销方式下，出口方在包销区域内不得再指定其他经销商经营同类商品，以维护包销商的专营权。为维护出口方的利益，有的包销协议也规定包销商不得越区销售。

⑤包销期限。包销期限可长可短，通常为一年，经销期限届满协议终止；也可在包销协议中不规定期限，只规定中止条款或续约条款等。为防止一方利用对方履约中的一些微不足道的差异作为撕毁协议的借口，可在协议中规定终止条款，明确什么情况下可解除协议。另外，还可在合同中规定延期条款，如规定经双方协商后予以延期，或规定

在协议到期前若干天如没有发生终止协议的通知，可自动延长一期。

⑥专营权。专营权包括专卖权和专买权。前者指出口方承诺在协议有效期内不向包销地区内的其他客户出售包销商品；后者指包销商承诺只向协议的出口方购买该商品，不得向第三者购买同类商品或有竞争性的替代商品。专卖权是区别一般经销协议的主要条件。

⑦最低包销数量或金额。如在协议中规定了数量与金额，包销商必须向出口方购买该规定数量和金额，出口方也必须向包销商出口上述数量和金额，因而对双方具有同等约束力。包销数额一般是规定最低承购额及其计算办法，即一定时期内经销商须承购的数额下限。为防止经销商订约后拖延履行，可以规定最低承购额以实际装运数为准。

⑧作价办法。包销商品的作价办法有：a)在规定期限内一次性作价，即以协议价格为准。采用这种作价方法，交易双方要承担价格变动的风险，故采用较少；b)在规定的包销期限内，分批作价。由于国际商品市场的价格变化多端，因此采用分批作价较为普遍。

⑨广告、宣传、市场报道和商标保护。经销商要负责做好广告宣传、市场调研，维护供货人权益。尽管出口方不实际涉足包销地区的销售业务，但其十分关心开拓海外市场。协议可规定：a)经销商有促进销售和广告宣传的义务，而供货商应提供必要的样品和宣传资料。广告宣传方式及其相关费用，一般在经销协议中规定由经销商承担；b)承担市场调研的义务，以供出口商参考制定销售策略和改进产品质量；c)如供货商的商标权或专利权在包销地区内受到侵害，包销商要及时采取保护性措施规定。同时，出口方还可要求包销商负责为其商品刊登广告，如在包销协议中规定包销商应出资在其包销地区为出口方产品举办展览、招揽订单，在当地报刊上登载广告；访问有希望达成交易的客户；尽量提供市场报道等。

除上述主要内容外，还应规定不可抗力及仲裁条款等一般交易条件，其规定方法与一般买卖合同大致相同。

### （四）经销利弊及其应注意事项

经销是出口方稳固市场、扩大销售的有效途径之一。出口方通常在价格、支付条件等方面给予经销商一定的优惠，以调动经销商的积极性，利用其经销渠道为其推销产品；还可要求经销商提供售后服务、开展市场调研。如采用独家经销，因经销商在经销区域内对指定的商品享有专营权，可在一定程度上可避免或减少自相竞争；如采用一般经销，则在同一市场上可能有多个经销商同时经营供货商的同一类（种）商品。当销路不好时，有些经销商会因资金周转困难而削价抛售，而消费者是"买涨不买落"，可能形成连锁反应。采用独家经销，只要经销商选择得当，就可以利用经销商熟悉所在国或地区的消费习惯、政府条例、法规等方面的便利条件，及时为出口方提供市场供需、消费者反映等情况，以做到适销对路，减少不必要的法律纠纷。经销商一般也愿意按协议规定为所经销的商品刊登广告、做宣传，或者承担其他义务，促使双方在合作中共同受益。但是，许多实践经验也表明，采用经销出口时，应注意以下问题。

①慎重选择经销商。如果经销商的信誉好，能够重合同、守信用，且经营能力强，即使在市场情况不好时，也能充分利用自己的经验和手段，努力完成推销定额。如果经销商选择不当，会使供货商作茧自缚。比如，有些包销商在市场不利时，会拒绝完成协议中规定的承购数额，导致出口计划无法完成，且失掉其他客户；也有的包销商凭借自己独家专营的特殊地位，反过来在价格及其他条件上要挟供货商，损害对方利益。为防止这类情况发生，出口商在选择经销商时，应先做认真的资信调查，了解对方的口碑、信誉和经销能力。

②注意当地的相关法律规定。独家经销协议中有关专营的规定有时会构成"限制性商业惯例"，即滥用市场支配地位，限制其他企业进入市场，或以其他不正当的方式限制竞争，这在许多国家的立法中属于管制之列。有些包销协议在规定包销商品的种类及经销区域时，做出了下列限制性规定：包销商不得经营其他厂家的同类产品，或禁止将包销的产品销往包销区域以外的地区等。这类规定有可能违反某些国家管制"限制性商业惯例"的条例和法令，如反托拉斯法(antitrust law)。在签订独家经销协议时，应当了解当地的有关法规，并注意使用文句，尽可能避免与当地的法律发生抵触。

# 二、代理

## （一）代理的概念及分类

除经销外，出口方也可以通过和国外企业达成代理协议，委托代理商在市场上招揽生意，或从事其他委托的事务。代理是指代理人（agent）按照本人（principal）的授权，代本人同第三者订立合同或做其他法律行为，由此而产生的权利与义务直接对本人发生效力。代理人与委托人属于委托买卖关系。国际贸易中的代理（agency），主要是指销售代理。出口商作为委托人，授权代理人代表出口商推销商品、签订合同，由此产生的权利和义务直接对委托人发生效力。委托商对由此产生的权利与义务负责，代理商只收取约定的佣金。代理的基本做法如图10.2所示。

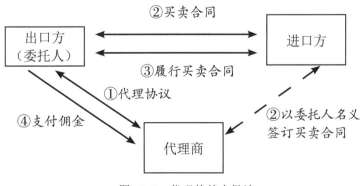

图10.2　代理的基本做法

根据委托人授予代理人权限的不同，销售代理可分为下列几种。

①总代理（general agent）。作为委托人的全权代表，在指定地区内，代表委托人从事销售活动和其他范围的广泛商务活动。他除有权代表委托人签订买卖合同、处理货物外，也可进行一些非商业性的活动。他有权指派分代理，并可分享代理的佣金。

②独家代理(exclusive agent / sale agent)。在代理协议规定的时空内，对指定商品享有专营权。委托人不得在以上时空范围内自行销售或通过其他代理销售。

③一般代理（agent），又称为佣金代理，是不享有独家代理专营权的代理商。委托人可同时委托若干个代理在同一地区推销相同商品。佣金代理商根据推销商品的实际金额，向委托人计收佣金。委托人可直接与该地区的实际买主成交，且无须支付佣金给佣金代理商。

### （二）独家代理协议

独家代理协议的主要内容包括：

①双方的基本关系。出口方与代理商之间是委托代理关系。代理人在委托人的授权范围内谨慎行事。委托人对代理人在上述范围内的代理行为，承担民事责任。

②代理的商品、地区和期限。代理协议中应明确说明代理销售商品的类别和型号。独家代理则必须进一步明确代理的地理范围，并约定代理协议的有效期限，或规定中止条款。

③专营权。在规定的商品、地区和期限范围内，授权该独家代理为唯一同买主进行交易的中间商。若委托人与买主直接发生交易，仍应按交易金额向独家代理支付佣金。

④佣金条款。代理协议中必须规定佣金率、支付佣金的时间和方法。佣金率可与成交金额或数量相联系。

⑤最低成交额。独家代理通常承诺最低成交数量或金额。若未能达到该数额，委托人有权中止协议或按协议规定调整佣金率。

⑥商情报告。代理人有义务向委托人定期或不定期提供商情报告，以使委托人了解当地的市场情况和代理人的工作业绩。能否提供合理的商情报告是考核代理人的重要依据。

### （三）代理的使用

出口商委托代理人销售商品，主要是利用代理商熟悉销售地市场、有广泛销售渠道的优势。特别需要指出的是，代理人的商誉对商品销售乃至出口企业的形象有举足轻重的作用。选择一个代理商，不仅仅着眼于他的销售能力，也应重视代理商已有的商誉。

# 三、寄售

## （一）寄售的概念

寄售（consignment）是一种委托代售的贸易方式，有别于代理，是出口商委托国外代销商向用户进行现货买卖的一种交易方式，也是国际贸易中习惯采用的做法之一。出口商可在寄售地区选定代销人，签订寄售协议，然后将货物运往国外的寄售地点，委托当地的代销商按照寄售协议规定的条件在当地市场上销售。商品售出后，代销商扣除佣金和其他费用后，将货款交付给寄售人。为扩大出口、促进成交，可适当运用寄售。寄售基本做法如图10.3所示。

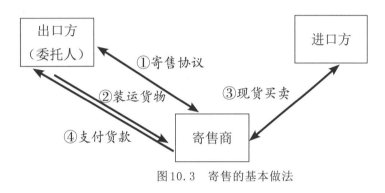

图10.3　寄售的基本做法

## （二）寄售的特点、作用与风险

寄售与逐笔成交的国际贸易相比，具有下列几个特点：①寄售属于典型的凭实物买卖的现货交易方式。寄售人需要先将货物运至目的地市场（寄售地），然后由代销人在寄售地向当地买主销售。①寄售人与代销人之间是委托代售关系，而非买卖关系。代销人只根据寄售人的指示处置货物，货物的所有权在出售之前仍属寄售人。②所寄售的货物在售出之前，包括运输途中和到达寄售地后的一切费用和风险，均由寄售人承担。寄售货物装运出口后，当货物尚在运输途中，如有条件也可成交出售。如中途出售不成功再运至原定目的地。

对于逐笔成交的国际贸易，国外买方往往对产品有所了解，一般采用批量成交、远期交货的方式。采用寄售，可以让商品在市场上与用户直接见面，按需要的数量随意购买、现货现买，从而有利于抓住销售时机，开拓新市场。但是，采用寄售，出口商须承担一定的风险和费用：

①货物需要先装运，待售后才能收回货款，出口商的资金负担较重。

②货物需在寄售地区安排存仓、提货，而代销商不承担任何费用和风险。

③如代销商不遵守寄售协议、不能妥善代管货物，或出售后不能及时汇回货款，都将给出口商带来损失。

④如果货物滞销，需要运回货物或转运其他口岸，出口商将遭受损失。

### （三）寄售协议

寄售协议的主要内容包括：

①双方的基本关系。货物在出售前所有权仍属寄售人；代销人以代理人身份出售商品、收取货款、处理争议等，风险和费用由寄售人承担。

②寄售商品的价格。寄售商品价格有三种规定方式：其一，规定最低售价；其二，由代销人按市场行情自行定价；其三，由代销人向寄售人报价，征得寄售人同意后确定价格，这种做法较为普遍使用。

③佣金条款。通常规定佣金的比率，有时还可增加佣金比率增减额的计算方法。佣金可由代销人在货款中自行扣除。

④代销人的义务。包括保管货物，代办进口报关、存仓、保险等手续并及时向寄售人通报商情。代销人应按协议规定的方式和时间将货款交付寄售人。有的寄售协议中还规定代销人应向寄售人出具银行保函或备用信用证，保证承担寄售协议规定的义务。

⑤寄售人的义务。须按协议规定时间出运货物，偿付代销人所垫付的代办费用。

### （四）寄售方式的应用

①着眼于开拓新市场、建立客户关系。既要销售商品，又要树立企业形象，应选择优质适销的产品。

②选择合适的寄售地点。寄售地应选择交通便捷的贸易中心或自由港、自由贸易区，以方便货物的进出转运，降低费用。

③选择合适的代销人。代销人应在当地具有良好的商誉，有相关商品的营销经验和推销能力，有能力代办报关、存仓等业务。

④重视安全收汇。可在寄售协议中明确规定要求代销人开立银行保函、备用信用证或凭银行承兑汇票发货。

## 四、拍卖

### （一）拍卖的概念

拍卖（auction）是指拍卖行接受货主的委托，按照一定的规则和程序在拍卖场所以公开叫价的方法，把货物卖给出价最高的买主的一种交易方式。拍卖是一种通过众多买主竞价，实现现货交易的方式。国际贸易中采用拍卖方式进行交易的商品，往往是一些品质难以标准化或难以久存，或传统上有拍卖习惯的商品，如艺术品、古董、茶叶、烟叶、兔毛、皮毛、木材、水果、花卉、羊毛等。拍卖程序不同于一般的出口交易，其交易过程大致要经过准备、看货、出价成交和付款交货等四个阶段。

### （二）拍卖的竞价方式

#### 1. 增价拍卖

增价拍卖又称"英格兰式拍卖"（English auction）、买方叫价拍卖，这是最常见的拍卖方式。拍卖时，由拍卖人宣布预定的最低价，然后竞买者（bidder）相继出价竞购。拍卖行可规定每次加价的金额限度，直至某一价格，经拍卖人（auctioneer）三次提示而无人加价时，则为最高价，由拍卖人击槌表示成交。按照拍卖章程规定，在拍卖人落槌前，叫价人可以撤销出价；如果货主与拍卖人事先商定了最低限价，而竞买人的叫价低于该价，拍卖人可终止拍卖。

#### 2. 减价拍卖

减价拍卖又称荷兰式拍卖（Dutch auction），源于世界上最大的荷兰花卉拍卖市场，由拍卖人先开出最高价格，然后渐次降低价格，直到有人表示接受，即达成交易。这种拍卖方式，买主之间无反复竞价的过程，且买主一旦表示接受，不能再行撤销。由于减价拍卖成交迅速，特别适合于数量大，批次多的鲜活商品。

#### 3. 密封递价拍卖

密封递价拍卖又称招标式拍卖。采用该方法，先由拍卖人公布每批商品的具体情况和拍卖条件等，由买主在规定的时间内将密封的报价单（也称标书）递交拍卖人，供拍卖人进行审查比较，决定将该货物卖给哪一个竞买者。这种拍卖方式，和上述两种方式相比较，有以下两个特点：

①除价格条件外，还可能有其他交易条件需要考虑。

②可以采取公开开标或不公开开标方式。有些国家的政府或海关在处理库存物资或没收货物时，往往采用该拍卖方法。

### （三）拍卖的一般程序

#### 1. 准备阶段

货主与拍卖行达成拍卖协议，规定货物品种和数量、交货方式与时间、限定价格以及佣金等事项。货主把货物运至拍卖地点，存放于拍卖人指定的仓库，由拍卖人进行分类、分批编号。拍卖人印发拍品目录，并刊登拍卖通告。买主在正式拍卖前可至存放拍卖商品的仓库查看货物，必要时可抽取样品供分析测试。

#### 2. 正式拍卖

在规定的时间和地点，按拍品目录规定的顺序逐批拍卖。以增价方式拍卖，买方出价相当于要约，拍卖人落槌相当于承诺。在落槌之前，买方有权撤销出价，卖方也有权撤回拍卖商品。以减价方式拍卖，拍卖人报价相当于要约，而买方一旦表示接受，即为承诺，交易成立，双方均受约束。

#### 3. 付款和交货

成交后，买方签署成交确认书，并支付部分货款作定金，待买方付清全部货款后，拍卖行开出提货单，买方凭单提货。拍卖行从货款中提取一定比例的佣金，作为提供拍卖服务的报酬，并扣除按合同应由货主承担的费用后，将货款交付货主。

### （四）拍卖的注意事项

#### 1. 关于商品的品质

由于参加拍卖的商品往往难以用具体规格加以描述，且买主在拍卖前有权查验货物，拍卖行通常在拍卖章程中规定"卖方对品质概不负责"。所以，在拍卖后，买方对商品没有复验权，也不存在索赔的问题。对于某些货物可能存在隐蔽的缺陷，凭一般的查验手段难以发现，有的拍卖章程中也规定了买方的索赔期限。

#### 2. 关于公开和公平的原则

拍卖和招标投标一样，是一种按公平竞争的原则，进行公开交易的贸易方式。为保证公开和公平的原则不被违反，拍卖行制定了拍卖章程。买卖双方都必须严格遵守、买方不得互相串通，以压低报价；卖方也不得由代理人出价竞买，以哄抬价格、这些均构成违规违法行为。

# 五、招标投标

### （一）招标和投标的概念

招标和投标（invitation to tender & submission of tender）是一种贸易方式的两个方面。该方式既适用于物资设备采购，也适用于发包工程项目。当招标单位需要采购商品或兴办某工程时，可以发出招标公告或招标单，邀请有兴趣的企业在指定期限内按照一定程序报价，即投标。投标人可应招标人的邀请，根据招标公告或招标单的规定条件，在规定的时间内向招标人递盘的行为。投标后，由招标人开标与评标，选择最满意的投标人进行交易，这种方式在国际贸易中经常采用。

招标投标和拍卖，是国际和国内贸易中两种常见的方式，买卖双方并不直接进行交易磋商。招标投标是卖主之间的竞争，而拍卖是买主之间的竞争。标的公开，竞争公开，成交迅速，是这两种方式的特点。由于招标和投标方式具有公平竞争的特点，使得许多大中型工程项目和物资采购，特别是国与国之间的政府贷款项目和国际金融组织的贷款项目，都规定采用国际竞争性招标（ICB）的方式进行采购或发包。

### （二）招标和投标的一般程序

#### 1. 准备工作

招标的准备工作一般包括：

①刊发招标通告。通常在权威报刊或专业刊物上公布招标通告，如世界银行出版的援助项目招标月刊等。

②资格预审。投标人应填写"资格预审表"，包括投标人的经营规模、人员设施概

况、工程记录等，并提供有关证明文件和资料。由招标人确认其是否具有投标能力。资格预审是保证招标工作顺利进行的关键步骤。

③编制招标文件（bidding documents）。招标伊始，招标人即组织有关人员制订招标书，说明采购商品或发包工程的技术条件和贸易条件。

投标的准备工作一般包括：

①评判标书。投标人取得标书后，应严格按照招标条件对商品或工程所要求的质量、技术标准、交货期限、工程量和进度安排等进行核算，并结合自身的条件和市场竞争态势，估计能否完全满足招标要求和能否提出有竞争性的报价。

②编制投标书和落实担保。投标书是投标人对招标人的一项不可撤销的发盘。其主要内容包括对招标条件的确认、商品或各个项目的有关指标和工程进度、技术说明和图纸、投标人应承担的责任，以及总价和单价分析表。招标人为防止投标人中标后拒不签约，通常要求投标人提交投标保证金，一般为总价的3%～10%，或以银行保函或备用信用证代替现金作保。投标人应在投标前落实担保人。

**2. 递送投标文件**

投标文件包括投标书、投标保函或备用信用证、投标书中单项说明的附件，以及其他必要文件。投标文件应密封后在规定时间内送达指定地点，可以专人递交，也可以挂号邮寄。

**3. 开标**

招标人在预先公布的时间和地点，当众开启密封的投标文件，宣读内容，允许在场的投标人作记录或录音。开标后，投标人不得更改投标内容。开标是对外公开标书内容，以保证招标工作公正进行的一种形式，并不当场确定中标人。

**4. 评标和决标**

招标人必须对投标进行审核、比较，然后择优确定中标人选，具体包括：①审查投标文件，判定其内容是否符合招标文件的要求，计算是否正确，技术是否可行等；②比较投标人的交易条件，可逐项打分或集体评议或投票表决，以确定中标人选。初步确定的中标人选，可以是一个或若干个替补人选；③对中标人选进行资格复审。如果第一中标人经复审合格，即成为该次招标的中标人选。否则，依次复审替补中标人选。凡出现下列情况之一者，招标人可宣布招标失败，重新组织第二轮招标：参加投标人太少，缺乏竞争性所有投标书和招标要求不符；投标价格均明显超过国际市场平均价格。

**5. 中标签约**

确定中标人后，招标人以书面通知中标人在规定的期限内到招标人所在地签订合同，并缴纳履约保证金或以银行保函作履约担保。

### （三）招标方式

国际上采用的招标方式归纳起来有3类，共4种方式。

### 1. 竞争性招标

竞争性招标（international competitive bidding，ICB）指招标人邀请几个乃至几十个投标人参加投标，通过投标人竞争，选择其中最有利的投标人达成交易。政府采购物资，大部分采用竞争性的公开招标办法。国际性竞争投标，通常有两种做法：

①公开投标（open bidding）。公开投标是一种无限竞争性招标(unlimited competitive bidding)。采用这种做法时，招标人要在国内外主要报刊上刊登招标广告，凡对该项招标内容有兴趣的人均有机会购买招标资料进行投标。

②选择性招标（selected bidding）。选择性招标又称邀请招标，它是有限竞争性招标（limited competitive bidding）。采用此做法时，招标人不在报刊上刊登广告，而是根据自己具体的业务关系和信息资料由招标人对客商进行邀请，进行资格预审后，再由他们进行投标。

### 2. 谈判招标

谈判招标（negotiated bidding）又叫议标，它是非公开的、非竞争性的招标。这种招标由招标人物色几家客商直接进行全同谈判，谈判成功，交易达成。

### 3. 两段招标

两段招标（two-stage bidding）是指无限竞争招标和有限竞争招标的综合方式。采用此方式时，先是用公开招标，再用选择招标分两段进行。

# 六、国际展览会

## （一）展览会的相关概念、含义及其分类

### 1. 展览会的相关概念

展览会是一种综合运用各种媒介、手段，推广产品、宣传企业形象和建立良好公共关系的大型活动，是一种复合、直观、形象和生动的传播方式，是一种高度集中和高效率的沟通方式。各社会组织都非常重视利用展览会来塑造和展现自己的最佳形象。参加展览会，可以帮助企业开拓国内国外市场，在实施"引进来、走出去"发展战略中发挥至关重要的作用。

在现代展览业中，广义的展览会可以包括所有形式的展览，而狭义的展览会专指贸易和宣传性质的展览。具有贸易性质的展览会，可以定义为"在固定的某个地点或一系列地点与特定的日期和期限里，通过展示达到产品、服务、信息交流的社会形式，包括宣传成就、宣传政策、普及科技知识、建立公司形象、了解市场发展趋势等"。它可以帮助商人在最短时间内、在最小的空间里，用最小的成本，做出最大的生意。

### 2. 展览会的名称含义

在实际应用中，展览会名称相当繁杂。英语国家主要用fair、exhibition、show、mart、display等来表示展览会。在中文里，展览会名称也有博览会、展览会、展览、展销会、

博览展销会、看样订货会、展览交流会、交易会、贸易洽谈会、展示会、展评会、样品陈列、庙会、集市、墟、场等。有一些展览使用非专业名词，如：日、周、市场和中心等。例如，澳大利亚全国农业日（Australian National Field Days）、柏林国际绿色周（Berlin International Green Week）、亚特兰大国际地毯市场（International Carpet and Rug Market）、电信世界中心（World Center for Office-Information-Telecommunication）等。

在英文中，fair是指传统形式的展览会，即集市与庙会。"exhibition"是指在集市和庙会基础上发展起来的具有贸易性质的、专业的、现代展览会，通常被作为各种展览会的总称，规模庞大的、内容繁杂的综合性展览，在英文中仍被称为"fair"，在中国被称为"博览"。因此，外国"博览会"要加以区别：是属于现代化的大型综合展览会，还是传统的乡村集市。"show"在英文中的原意是展示，但在美国、加拿大等国家，show已替代exhibition。在这些国家，贸易展览会大多被称作show，而宣传展览会则被称作exhibition。exposition源于法国，是法文的展览会。因这种展览会不做贸易，主要是为了宣传，exposition便有了"宣传性质的展览会"的含义。因其他国家纷纷举办宣传性质的展览会，且由于法语的世界影响，以及世界两大展览会组织"国际博览会联盟"和"国际展览会局"的总部均设在法国，不仅在法语国家，而且在北美等英语地区，exposition也被广泛地使用。

**3. 展览会的分类方法**

根据其举办的性质、内容、规模、时间和场地的不同，展览会的具体分类有：

①展览性质通常由展览组织者决定，可通过参观者的成分反映出来：对工商界开放的展览，一般是贸易性质的展览；对公众开放的展览，主要是消费性质的展览。

②展览分为综合展览和专业展览两类。综合展览是指包括全行业或数个行业的展览会，也被称作横向型展览会，如工业展、轻工业展；专业展览是指仅展示某一行业甚至某一产品的展览会，如钟表展。专业展览会常常同时举办讨论会、报告会，用以介绍新产品、新技术。

③展览会分为国际、国家、地区、地方展，以及单个公司的独家展。这里所指的规模是指展出者和参观者的所代表的区域规模，而不是展览场地规模。不同规模的展览有不同的特色和优势，应根据企业自身条件和需要来选择。

④展览会有定期举办和不定期举办两种。定期的有一年四次、一年两次、一年一次，或两年一次等；不定期展会则是视需要和条件举办，分长期和短期。长期展可以是三个月、半年、甚至常设，而短期展一般不超过一个月。发达国家的专业贸易展览会一般是三天。

⑤大部分的展览会是在专用的展览场馆内举办的。展览场馆有室内场馆和室外场馆之分。其中，室内场馆多用于展示常规展品，比如纺织展、电子展；室外场馆多用于展示超大、超重展品，比如航空展、矿山设备展。而在几个地方轮流举办的展览会被称作巡回展。

### （二）企业参展的目标与定位

参展企业应具备较高的参展素质和参展能力，准确判断展览会的价值。成熟的参展商由于在精神和价值观上与所选择的展览会一致，更容易获得参展的成功感，实现企业参展目标，圆满完成国际市场营销计划。企业参展的目标与定位，可通过以下五方面内容来设定：

①一个国际知名的展览会实际上就是一次行业年会，从行业协会到产业链的各个环节均被聚集在一个时空里，是行业信息的大潮到来之际，市场信息反馈快、效率高、质量高。世界一流的品牌展览会，能够聚集行业最有影响力的媒体参与。大部分的展览会都有市场政策发布新闻会和行业市场宏观走势分析与专题论坛，50%以上的企业会通过展览会把最新的产品信息发布给目标消费群体。传播信息、收集行业信息是企业参展的最基本目标。

②展览会是一个公平买卖的市场，是提供企业进行商业交易的特定场所，其所处地位就是一个独立的第三方，其对展览产品的认证相当于第三方认证，具有一定的客观权威性。例如，贵州的茅台酒，之所以在20世纪70年代被周恩来总理点名定为"国宴酒"招待美国总统尼克松，是由于贵州茅台酒厂在1915年参加美国旧金山举办的巴拿马世界博览会期间被评选为金奖。因此，产品在展览会上评奖和认证，是企业参展营销的主要目的之一。

③展览会作为一个行业盛会，将行业各方人士在短短的3~5天内汇集到一个展览场馆中，大家平等交流，联络老客户，结识新客户，发现潜在客户，刺探竞争对手，观摩新产品，所有活动均以个人调动五官全力体验为基础，与他人进行平等沟通为纽带，成为企业决策者的最直接的、对各类信息加以综合分析的第一手资料依据。这样的价值体验具有唯一性、时效性和前瞻性，是展览会作为国际贸易方式区别于其他贸易方式最重要的不可替代特征之一，一次参展常常能成为一次深刻难忘的体验。

④国际知名的展览会似乎像人一样，有自己的"灵魂"，能倡导、传播一种理念，而这种理念能够左右消费行为，在消费市场上可能引爆流行，在生产资料市场上可能引起生产方式的革命。例如，汉诺威工业博览会能够给予参观者带来强烈体验，能使参观者在心灵上形成一种"极化""磁化"作用。而这种作用足够强烈，并能固化为一种"观念"，形成参展企业的独特"理念价值"：只要该企业能参加这个展览会，就足以说明该企业能紧跟消费市场，有足够能力与本行业竞争对手展开竞争。

⑤成熟的参展企业懂得如何利用展览会去影响自己的消费群体，与竞争对手进行较量，成为一个消费者群体的"精神领袖"。一个达到精神领袖境界的展览，就是按照已经设定的一套清晰的价值观念，成为某种生活方式的鉴定者和护卫者。通过展览会及其举办的多种相关活动，促进人们对所倡导概念的理解，为广大参展商"制造"一个通用型的价值观念或价值信仰平台，从而带来巨大的商业效果。例如，法兰克福照明展览会被称为"世界照明行业的麦加"，是全球照明行业毕生追求的

圣地，是反映世界照明行业最新动态和市场的晴雨表。成熟的参展商为能参加这样的展览会而自豪和骄傲，既体现了企业的实力，又能令参展商拥有一种精神上的归属感。

### （三）参展规定与要求

#### 1. 展位设计

展览会对展架及展品都有限制规定，尤其对双层展台、楼梯、展位顶部向外延伸的结构等限制更严。限高往往不是禁止超高。如果办理了有关手续，并达到技术标准，有可能获准构建超高展台、布置展品。同时，很多展览会禁止全封闭展台。如果展台封闭，展览会就失去了展示作用，参观者就会有抱怨。但是，参展商可以封闭办公室、谈判室和仓库等。因此，展位一般规定有一定比例的面积必须朝外敞开，该部分面积一般要求高于70%，而其余30%以下的面积允许封闭。

#### 2. 展览用具

展架、展具材料必须使用经防火处理的材料，限制使用塑料和危险化学品。绝大部分国家的展览会对电器使用也有严格的规定，所用电器的技术指标必须符合当地规定和要求。

#### 3. 展位过道

为保证人流的畅通，展览会一般会规定走道宽度，禁止展出者的展台、道具、产品占用走道，同时规定电视不得面向走道、柜台必须离走道一定距离等。

#### 4. 消防设施

如果是大面积的展位，必须按展馆面积和预计的观众人数，按比例设紧急通道或出口并设标志，配备消防器材。有些展览会要求参展企业指定消防负责人，并要求全体参展人员知道消防规定和紧急出口等。

#### 5. 展品规定

对于超高、超重展品，一般需要先于其他展品进馆，要尽早与展览会组织者或展馆所有者商量。只要采取适当措施，一般都可以解决。对于超高展品，只要展馆高度足够，就可以与展馆商量解决；对于超重展品，可以使用地托，分散单位负荷；对于超宽展品，最难解决的问题是展馆卸货大门的尺寸，但展览组织者一般会愿意积极协助。因考虑安全，有些展览会会限制操作机器；对于武器，一般都有专门的规定，且手续都很麻烦。

#### 6. 展览环境

背景音乐由展览会组织者安排，参展商的声像设备音量必须控制在不影响周围展出者的范围内；若展览会组织者想取得协调效果，往往会提出色彩要求，要求展出者使用某种基本色调或标题色调。另外，展览会还可能会提出对标题字型、大小的规定，但这方面规定大多比较宽松。参展商只要遵守规定，且不干扰周围展台（比如噪声太大），一般都可以任意设计展台形状、摆置展品、使用颜色。

### 7. 展场劳工

很多国家（尤其是发达国家）规定，展场劳工必须是工会注册工人，不允许参展商自己动手。在美国纽约，如果参展商自己拿起锤子想钉根钉子，当地工人就会夺下锤子阻止你干活。美国人剥夺你的"劳动权"，听起来很荒唐，但是却是事实，还必须遵守。

### 8. 布展手续

展览会大多要求参展商将设计送审，并要求参展商在施工前办理手续。

## （四）中国的国际会展业

中国会展业在各城市发展迅速，尤其以北京、上海、广州、大连、成都五大会展城市最为活跃，形成了"环渤海、长三角、珠三角、东北、中西部"5个会展经济产业带。

### 1. 环渤海会展经济带

环渤海会展经济带以北京为中心，以天津、廊坊等城市为重点，其会展业发展早、规模大、数量多、专业化、国际化程度高、门类齐全、知名品牌展会集中、辐射广。

### 2. 长三角会展经济带

长三角会展经济带以上海为中心，以南京、杭州、宁波、苏州等城市为依托。该产业带起点高、政府支持力度大、规划布局合理、贸易色彩浓厚，受区位优势、产业结构影响大，发展潜力巨大。

### 3. 珠三角会展经济带

珠三角会展经济带以广州为中心，以广交会为助推器，以深圳、珠海、厦门、东莞等会展城市群为依托，形成了国际化和现代化程度高、会展产业结构特色突出、会展地域及产业分布密集的会展经济带。

### 4. 东北会展经济带

东北会展经济带以大连为中心，以沈阳、长春等城市为重点，依托东北工业基地的产业优势及东北亚的区位优势，形成了长春汽博会、沈阳制博会、大连服装展等品牌展会。

### 5. 中西部会展经济带

中西部会展经济带以成都为中心，以重庆、西安等城市为重点，通过不断发展，现已形成了成都的西部国际博览会、重庆的高交会、西安的东西部洽谈会等品牌展会。

☞ 案例10.2

## 中国进出口商品交易会

中国进出口商品交易会，又称广交会，创办于1957年春，每年春秋两季在广州举办，由商务部和广东省人民政府联合主办，中国对外贸易中心承办，是中国目前历史最长、规模最大、商品种类最全、到会采购商最多且分布国别地区最广、成交效果最好、信誉最佳的综合性国际贸易盛会。自2007年4月15日第101届起，广交会由中国出口商品交易会更名为中国进出口商品交易会，由单一出口平台变为进出口双向交易平台。中国进出口商品交易会贸易方式灵活多样，除传统的看样成交外，还举办网上交易会。广交会以出口贸易为主，也做进口生意，还可以开展多种形式的经济技术合作与交流，以及商检、保险、运输、广告、咨询等业务活动。来自世界各地的客商云集广州，互通商情，增进友谊。

　　截至2020年，广交会已历经了63年的改革创新发展，经受住了各种严峻考验，从未中断，加强了中国与世界的贸易往来，展示了中国形象和发展成就，是中国企业开拓国际市场的优质平台，是贯彻实施我国外贸发展战略的引导示范基地。已成为中国外贸第一促进平台，被誉为中国外贸的晴雨表和风向标，是中国对外开放的窗口、缩影和标志。截至第122届，广交会累计出口成交约12937亿美元，累计到会境外采购商约822万人次。目前，每届广交会展览规模达118.5万平方米，境内外参展企业近2.5万家，210多个国家和地区的约20万名境外采购商与会。

　　2016年10月第120届广交会开幕之际，中共中央总书记、国家主席、中央军委主席习近平致贺信，中共中央政治局常委、国务院总理李克强做出批示表示祝贺，充分肯定了广交会在我国改革开放和经济社会发展中的重要地位和积极贡献，指明了新时期广交会的工作重点和努力方向，对广交会进一步扩大对外开放、培育外贸竞争新优势、加快建设经贸强国、推动广交会改革创新具有十分重大的意义。广交会正以习近平新时代中国特色社会主义思想为指导，深入学习贯彻落实党的十九大精神，以新发展理念为统领，积极创新体制机制和商务模式，持续提升国际化、专业化、市场化、信息化水平，建设"智慧广交会"和"绿色广交会"，积极推进从出口贸易单一功能平台向结识客户、展示洽谈、行业交流、信息发布、产品推介等综合功能平台转变，更好发挥全方位对外开放平台作用，把广交会打造成国际一流的"卖全球买全球"的新时代全方位对外开放平台，为推动经贸强国建设和开放型经济发展做出新的贡献。

# 七、商品交易所

## （一）商品交易所的概念

　　商品交易所（commodity exchange）是指按照一定规章程序买卖特定商品的有组织的市场。只有正式会员可以进入商品交易所交易，其他人或企业通过正式会员或经纪人交易。商品交易所经营的商品，一般是标准化的原材料，且按照标准化的合同交易。商品交易所里有现货交易和期货交易，但以期货交易为主。许多农产品、有色金属原料等，主要在商品交易所里交易。期货交易（futures transaction）是众多的买主和卖主，在商品交易所内按照一定的规则，用喊叫并借助手势进行讨价还价，通过激烈竞争达成交易的一种贸易方式。

### （二）期货交易与现货交易的区别

期货交易不同于商品中的现货交易。在现货交易的情况下，买卖双方可以任何方式，在任何地点和时间达成实物交易。卖方必须交付实际货物，买方必须支付货款。而期货交易则是在一定时间、在特定期货市场上，即在商品交易所内，按照交易所预先制订的"标准期货合同"进行的期货买卖。成交后买卖双方并不移交商品的所有权。

期货交易具有以下几个特点。

①期货交易不规定双方提供或者接受实际货物。

②交易的结果不是转移实际货物，而是支付或者取得签订合同之日与履行合同之日的价格差额。

③期货合同是由交易所制订的标准期货合同，并且只能按照交易所规定的商品标准和种类进行交易。

④期货交易的交货期是按照交易所规定的交货期确定的，不同商品的交货期不同；期货合同都必须在每个交易所设立的清算所进行登记及结算。

### （三）期货交易的种类

期货交易，根据交易者的目的，有两种不同性质的种类：①利用期货合同作为赌博的筹码，买进卖出，从价格涨落的差额中追逐利润，开展投机活动，在商业习惯上称为"买空卖空"。它是投机者根据自己对市场前景的判断而进行的赌博性投机活动。所谓"买空"，又称"多头"，是指投机者估计价格要涨，买进期货；一旦货期涨价，再卖出期货，从中赚取差价。②真正从事实物交易的人做套期保值，又称为"海琴"。

# 八、加工贸易

加工贸易主要包括来料加工、来件装配、进料加工、出料加工和补偿贸易。它与通常所说的"三来一补"（即来料加工、来件装配、来样加工和中小型补偿贸易）的区别在于：来样加工属于一般出口贸易，不属于加工贸易的范围；来料加工和来件装配，统称为加工装配。加工贸易的主要内容包括：在"三来一补"中去掉来样加工，再加上进料加工和出料加工。

### （一）来料加工装配贸易

#### 1. 来料加工装配贸易的概念

来料加工装配贸易是指由外商提供全部或部分原材料、辅料、零部件、元器件、配套件和包装物料，必要时提供设备，由我方按对方的要求进行加工装配，成品交对方销售，我方收取工缴费。对方提供的作价设备价款，我方可用工缴费偿还的交易形式。

**2. 来料加工装配贸易的分类**

来料加工装配贸易可分为：

①全部来料来件的加工装配。国外委托方提供全部原辅材料和元器件，由承接方企业加工后，将成品交国外委托方，制件和成品均不计价，承接方按合同收取工缴费。

②部分来料来件的加工装配。国外委托方要求加工装配的成品中有部分料件需由承接方提供，故承接方除收取工缴费外，还应收取所提供的料件的价款。

③对口合同，各作各价。国外委托方和承接方签署两份对口合同：一份是委托方提供的原辅材料和元器件的销售合同，一份是承接方出口成品的合同。对于全部来料来件，两份合同的差价即为工缴费；对于部分来料来件，两份合同的差价，既包括工缴费，也包括国内承接方所提供的料件的价款。以对口合同方式进行的加工装配贸易，必须在合同中表明。承接方无须支付外汇。

加工装配业务，对于委托方来说，是利用承接方的劳务，降低产品成本；对于承接方来说，则是以商品为载体的一种劳务输出。目前，承接对外加工装配贸易的企业有两种类型。

①承接方为我国企业或合资企业，和委托方之间是单纯的委托加工关系，通过承接加工业务，企业得以利用国外资金，发挥生产潜力，扩大出口，增加收入，并能获得国际市场信息，加快产品升级换代，改善管理水平和改进工艺技术。

②国外委托方在国内直接投资设厂，然后以委托加工装配的方式充分利用我国的政策优惠和低廉的劳动力，并在一定程度上与我国原来的出口贸易争夺市场。尽管目前这种"前店后厂"的方式对发展我国经济利大于弊。但从长远来看，应采用合理的政策，引导其转向技术密集型和资本密集型产业，同时加强税务管理。

我国自20世纪70年代末至80年代初，就把对外加工装配业务作为利用外资的一种形式，在政策上加以保护和支持，因而发展迅速。加工装配贸易额，在我国进出口总额中，已占有相当大的比重。

**3. 来料加工装配贸易合同**

对外加工装配业务是一种劳务贸易，有关合同的当事人是委托方和承接方。与一般货物买卖合同有许多不同之处，其主要内容如下。

①合同标的。买卖合同的标的是商品，而加工装配合同的标的是劳务，即为将原材料和元器件加工装配成指定的产品而付出的劳动以及一定的技术或工艺。为说明所提供劳务的性质，应具体规定加工装配业务的内容和要求。

②对来料来件的规定。料件是实现提供劳务的物质基础。合同中应规定料件的品质、数量，还必须规定委托方送交制件的时间、地点。为了明确责任，对委托方不能按质、按量、按时提供料件的情况，应在合同中规定处理方法。

③对交付成品的规定。所要交付成品的规格、质量、交货数量和交货期限，应在合同中明确规定。例如，万一承接方不能按合同规定交付成品，应承担相应的损害赔偿责任。

④关于耗料率和残次品率的规定。耗料率是指单位产品所要消耗的原材料或元器件的数额。残次品率是指不合格产品在全部产品中的所占比率。这两项指标，与产品成本直接相关，又受到加工方的技术水平和生产条件的限制，所以双方应协商规定一个合理的标准，超过规定的比率，应由加工方承担责任。

⑤关于工缴费的规定。加工装配业务本质上是一种劳务贸易，工缴费即体现了劳务的价值。工缴费的规定，应以国际劳务价格作为参照标准、对我国来说，则以东南亚地区的工资水平作为计算标准，参照加工企业所提供的劳务质量和生产效率，计收的工缴费应既有利可图，又有竞争力。

⑥运输和保险。在加工装配贸易过程中，不转移料件和成品的所有权，其所有权归委托方所有，运输和保险的责任由委托方承担。在具体业务中，对出口成品的运输和保险，以及料件进口和存仓的保险，均可由承接方代办，费用由委托方另行支付或者计入工缴费内。

⑦付款方式。委托方向承接方支付工缴费的方式有两种：①料件和成品均不计价，由委托方通过信用证或汇付方式，向承接方支付工缴费；②料件和成品分别计价，其差额即为工缴费，对此承接方应掌握"先收后付"的原则，具体的做法可以采用：①料件用D/A，，成品用 D/P 即期；②料件用 D/A，成品用即期信用证；③对开信用证方式，料件用远期信用证，成品用即期信用证。必须注意远期和即期的时间间隔应考虑加工全过程所需时间以保证先收妥成品货款，再支付料件货款。

**4. 我国对加工装配贸易的管理**

①合同报批。对外加工装配合同，须经商务部、国务院有关部委或者省、自治区、直辖市的商务部门，或由它们授权的机关审批。报批时应填写"加工装配贸易申报表"一式四份，并附合同副本。

②海关登记备案。自合同批准之日起一个月内，向海关提交批准文件和合同副本。如有必要，应随附料、件和设备清单。经审核后，由海关核发"对外加工装配进出口货物登记手册"，其进出口货物凭"登记手册"办理报关手续。对没有办理"登记注册"的单位，其进出口货物，海关不予放行。

③进出口货物的监管。料件、设备和成品进出口时，有关单位或其代理人应填写进出口货物专用报关单一式四份和发票、装箱单等有关单证，以及"登记手册"向进出口地海关申报。海关接受申报后，经查验认可后放行。加工装配贸易进口的料件，属海关保税货物。自进口之日起至加工成成品出口之日止，应接受海关监管，有关单位必须将进口料件的使用和加工成品出口的情况列入海关认可的专门账册，海关有权随时检查。

④核销。加工装配合同执行完成之后，有关单位应于最后一批成品出口之日起一个月内，持"登记手册"和进出口货物报关单向海关办理核销手续。对剩余的料件，根据不同情况予以征、免税。若进口料、件或成品因种种原因转为内销，必须经原审批机关批准和海关核准，并按一般进口货物征收关税和进口增值税

### （二）进料加工与、出料加工和带料加工出口

进料加工贸易是指我方用外汇购买进口的原料、材料、辅料、元器件、零部件、配套件和包装物料，加工成品或半成品后再外销出口的交易形式。进料加工装配贸易也可采取对口合同的交易形式，即买卖双方分别签订进口和出口对口合同。我方在料件进口时先付料件款，加工成品出口时再向对方收取成品款。

进料加工贸易与加工装配贸易的共同之处在于原材料和元器件来自国外，加工后成品也销往国外市场。但两者有本质上的区别：

①进料加工贸易的进口料件和出口成品是两笔独立的交易，进料加工企业需自筹资金从国外购入料件，然后自行向国外市场销售，而装配加工贸易的进、出为一笔交易的两个方面，料件和成品的所有权均同委托方所有，承接方无须支付进口费用，也不承担销售风险。

②从事进料加工贸易的企业，获得的是出口成品的利润，利润的大小取决于出口成品的市场行情；而加工装配贸易的承接方收取的是工缴费，工缴费的大小以劳动力的费用，即工资水平作为核算基础。进料加工贸易的收益一般大于加工装配贸易，但风险也较大。

③进料加工贸易的企业拥有自主权，可根据自身的技术、设备和生产能力，选择市场上的适销商品从事进料加工；加工装配贸易由委托方控制生产的品种、数量和销售地区。

出料加工贸易是指将我国境内的原辅料、零部件、元器件或半成品交由境外厂商按我方要求进行加工或装配，成品复运进口，我方支付工缴费的交易形式，不包括"带料加工出口"。

"带料加工出口"是指我方在境外投资开办企业，将我境内的原辅料、零部件、元器件或半成品运至境外加工或装配，成品在境外销售。带料加工出口项下运出境的货物，应按实际贸易方式统计。例如，机械设备、原材料等出口，按一般贸易统计；来、进料加工成品出口，按来、进料加工贸易统计；租赁出口按租赁贸易统计。

### （三）补偿贸易

补偿贸易（compensation trade）又称为产品返销，是指交易一方在对方提供信用的基础上，进口设备技术，以该设备技术所生产的产品，分期抵付进口设备技术的价款及利息。

#### 1. 补偿贸易的使用

早期的补偿贸易主要用于兴建大型工业企业。例如，苏联从日本引进价值8.6亿美元的采矿设备，以1亿吨煤作为偿还；波兰从美国进口价值4亿美元的化工设备和技术，以相关工业产品返销抵偿。后期的补偿贸易趋向多样化，不但有大型成套设备，也有中小型项目。例如，20世纪80年代，在波兰向西方出口的电子和机械产品中，属于补偿贸易返销的占比为40%—50%。同期，我国也曾广泛采用补偿贸易方式，引进国外先进技术设备，但规模不大，多为小型项目。近年来，因外商普遍以设备技术作为直接投资

进入我国,故补偿贸易更趋减少。但是,随着我国市场经济的发展,补偿贸易在利用外资、促进产品销售方面的优越性不容忽视。

**2. 补偿贸易的作用**

①对设备技术进口方的作用:企业通过补偿贸易引进设备技术,可解决因资金短缺、进行设备更新和技术改造的难题,使产品得以升级换代,增强其市场竞争能力(包括国际市场和国内市场)。设备技术进口方将产品返销,在抵偿设备技术价款的同时,也利用了设备出口方在国外的销售渠道,使产品进入国外市场。以进口设备技术来带动产品的出口,即"以进带出",是当代中小型补偿贸易的一大特点。尽管以补偿贸易方式引进的设备技术,往往并不十分先进,甚至是二手设备。但是,如果产品能够运销且市场前景良好,设备价格合理,对发展中国家增加产品出口,扩大国内就业机会,提高地区经济发展水平仍是有利的。

②对技术出口方的作用:出口方可在提供信贷的基础上,扩大设备和技术的出口。出口方出于转移产业的需要,通过补偿贸易方式将产业转移至发展中国家,既获得了转让设备和技术的价款,又从返销商品的销售中获取利润,可谓是一举两得。

**3. 现代补偿贸易的特点**

①跨国公司把补偿贸易作为扩大销售资本性货物的手段,通过开展补偿贸易扩大设备技术出口,并以此获取双重利润。补偿贸易是一种易货贸易,以设备技术和相关产品做交换,供方既要承担所需要的设备技术,又需要承担相关抵偿产品的销售。如果供方是单一的设备制造商,就难以接受这种贸易方式。随着跨国公司多种经营的迅速发展,生产企业前向经济一体化已日臻完善。跨国公司在国内外建立了广泛的销售代理或自己的销售公司,从而有能力销售相关的返销产品。

②国际产业转移的纵深发展成为补偿贸易的有力促进因素。随着世界分工的进一步发展,一些发展中国家的经济已具有长足的进步,良好的投资环境使发达国家将部分技术和资本密集型产业向发展中国家转移。尽管大部分产业转移是为了占领国外市场,但也有相当一部分产品是返销或者是用来装配整机的零部件。设备技术出口方主要从返销产品中牟取利润,而不是主要从出口设备技术中牟利。而设备技术进口方则通过信贷方式,引进较为先进的设备技术,既建立了生产基地,又出口了产品,成为可能达成补偿贸易的又一基础。

③设备技术的先进性是补偿贸易双方的主要矛盾。为了加强对先进技术和设备的控制,面对市场的激烈竞争,身处发达国家的部分企业在产业转移中采取了不同的方式,常见的是直接投资。仅利用东道国的土地、劳动力、原料与动力资源,而把生产技术和设备的所有权、使用权都掌握在自己手中。因补偿贸易对设备技术出口方具有双重利润的吸引力,使得进口方也具有了争取引进先进设备技术的能力。双方达成交易的关键是:①技术设备出口方之间的竞争态势;②返销产品(或零部件)的市场前景;③设备技术进口方的配套能力;④偿付条件。

#### 4. 补偿贸易的注意事项

开展补偿贸易业务，必须重点明确以下三方面内容。

①引进设备技术的先进性、适用性及其保障措施。对引进的设备技术，必须就其质量保证和技术合作方式做出明确规定，技术上至少应该是领先于国内水平，并在国际上也较为先进的、设备供应方并应对涉及工业产权的问题做出保证。

②返销产品抵偿设备技术价款的规定。回购是设备出口方的基本义务。我国在补偿贸易中，通常用直接产品补偿。但在具体交易中，有不同做法：(a)全额补偿。全部设备技术价款由等额的返销产品抵偿。(b)部分补偿。由设备进口方支付部分现汇，其余大部分价款通过返销产品补偿。(c)超额补偿、要求设备出口方承诺回购超过补偿金额的返销商品。(d)以相关劳务补偿。这是一种来料加工相结合的补偿贸易，即引进设备技术后，接受对方的来料来件加工业务，以工缴费抵偿设备技术价款。

③偿还期限和结算方式。偿还期限和返销商品的数量和价格直接相关。必须对返销商品的作价原则、定价标准和方法做出规定，并应通过约定返销商品的数量或金额，安排偿还期限。补偿贸易虽然是以产品抵偿设备，但并非直接的易货贸易，双方仍要通过货币进行计价支付。设备进口方必须掌握先收后付的原则，选择适当的结算方式。

采用补偿贸易方式，引进先进的技术设备，同时"以进带出"。设备进口方利用设备出口方的销售能力，进入国外市场，是利用外资的一种有效途径。当前，国际经济合作发展迅速，产业转移的范围已突破了劳动密集型产业，并延伸至技术密集型和资本密集型产业。我国企业应抓住这一契机，充分利用自身的优势，使得补偿贸易方式在利益分配、市场控制和自主经营上独特的优势为我所用。

# 九、租赁贸易

## （一）租赁贸易的概念

租赁贸易（leasing trade）是指承办租赁业务的企业与外商签订国际租赁贸易合同，租赁期为一年及以上的租赁进出口货物。租赁贸易是当代经济交易中最为活跃的一种贸易方式。发达国家的固定资产投资，有三分之一以上是通过租赁贸易方式实现的，无论在国内或国际贸易中，租赁市场是一个对供需双方均有十分吸引力的市场。租赁贸易的设备拥有者与承租人订立租约，把设备交付给承租人使用，收取一定的租金。

租赁对象主要是资本货物，包括机电设备、运输设备、建筑机械、医疗器械、飞机船舶和各种大型成套设备及设施等。出租人一般为准金融机构，即附属于银行或信托投资公司的租赁公司，也有专业租赁公司或生产制造商兼营自己产品的租赁业务；承租人通常为生产或服务企业。出租人向承租人提供所需设备，承租人则按租赁合同向出租人定期支付租金、设备的所有权属于出租人，承租人取得的是使用权。

### （二）租赁贸易的分类

租赁贸易可分为融资租赁、经营租赁、转租租赁和回租租赁。

#### 1. 融资租赁

融资租赁（financial lease）的标的物主要是由租赁公司出资购买、并由用户选定的设备。融资租赁的租期较长，通常租赁期结束（接近设备的使用期）、待全部租金付清后，设备所有权就转移给承租人，或者由用户支付残值后拥有设备。相当于承租人分期付款买到了设备。租赁期内由用户自行维修保养，租赁期满，设备归用户所有。在整个设备使用期内，只租给一个用户。租赁公司按照设备成本、利息加上费用，分摊成租金向承租人收取，故又称为"完全支付租赁"或"一次性租赁"。融资租赁是最基本的租赁形式。

#### 2. 经营租赁

经营性租赁（operating lease）的租赁期较短，设备拥有者须通过多次出租，才能收回设备投资及其他费用。在设备使用的有效期内，不仅仅租给一个用户，每个用户所缴付的租金只相当于设备投资的一部分，故又称为"不完全支付"租赁。在租赁期内，由出租人提供设备维修保养服务，以期保持设备的良好状态供再次出租。对承租人来说，这种租赁方式和提供的服务，使他获得了始终保持正常运转的高新技术设备，但租金也比较高。经营租赁的标的物一般是通用设备。当承租人只需短期使用某种通用设备时，往往采用这种租赁方式。经营租赁的出租人通常是生产制造商兼营的租赁公司或者专业租赁公司。

#### 3. 转租租赁

我国在以租赁方式引进国外设备时，往往由我国的租赁公司作为承租人向国外租赁公司租用设备，然后再将该设备转租给国内用户。经营转租业务的租赁公司，一方面为用户企业提供了信用担保，即以自己的名义承担了支付租金的责任；另一方面又为用户承办涉外租赁合同的洽谈和签订，以及各项进口手续和费用。我国租赁公司除办理转租赁外，也作为中介机构为国内用户企业介绍国外租赁公司，由用户企业与国外公司直接签约。我国租赁公司开立保函，为国内承租人定期支付租金作保。

#### 4. 回租租赁

承租人向出租人租赁原来属于自己的设施。其做法是先由承租人和出租人签订租赁协议，然后再签订买卖合同，由出租人购进标的物，将其租给承租人，即原物主。这种租赁方式主要用于不动产，由于承租人缺少资金而出售不动产以筹措所需资金。回租租赁属于融资租赁，标的物的售价将分摊在各期租金中。但在回租租赁业务中，标的物的售价往往并不反映真正的市场价，而更多取决于承租人所需资金的数额。当然也不可能超过其真正的市场价。

### （三）租赁贸易的当事人

租赁贸易往往是三边贸易，即有3个当事人：出租人、承租人和供货商。承租人选定所需设备和供应商后，由租赁公司洽谈购买。租赁贸易的一般程序见图10.4。

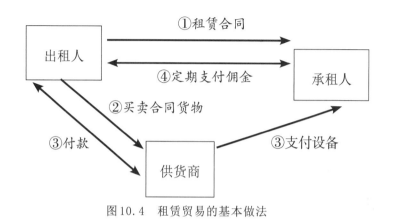

图10.4　租赁贸易的基本做法

### （四）租赁贸易的作用

租赁贸易是一种通过融物的形式实现中长期资金融通的贸易方式，其实质是出租人向承租人提供信贷式。租赁贸易是在信贷基础上进行的。在租赁贸易中，除非承租人自身有足够好的信誉，经租赁公司评估后，可在一定额度内实现租赁。但在通常情况下，租赁公司要求承租人提供经济担保，如银行、投资信托公司、保险公司等出具的保函。从利用外资、引进设备的角度看，租赁与一般的中长期信贷和延期付款有相似之处。对供需双方来说，有其特有的优越性。

对承租人而言：

①如利用中长期信贷或延期付款方式购入设备，将记录在企业的资产负债表内。而租赁的设备，则不作为企业的负债记录，不影响企业的举债能力。即使企业能以自有资金购入设备。若改用租赁方式，则可增强流动资金的周转能力，改善企业的资产质量。承租人支付的租金可列入生产或经营成本从而降低了企业应税收入的数额。

②承租人可按自身需要选择生产厂商和所需设备，确定技术指标。而租赁公司作为市场中的大买家，往往拥有优越的谈判地位，能以相对优惠的价格购进设备，从而降低承租人支付的租金。

③以租赁方式引进设备，承租人只须和租赁公司达成协议，而落实资金和采购设备均由租赁公司负责，故而业务环节减少，设备到位所需时间较短。

④承租人可以分享租赁公司所享受的减免税优惠以及所具有的资金运作优势，从而降低租金支出。承租人所支付的租金，包括设备价款、利息和租赁手续费，在租赁期内一般固定不变，而中长期贷款的利率往往是浮动的，有上升的趋势。

⑤国际市场是买方市场，承租人作为用户具有一定的优势。充分利用这一优势，在

一定条件下，比起直接获得国外出口信贷，更具现实性和更为经济，比起外商直接投资，在收益分配和经营控制上更有利于设备引进方。

对出租人而言：

①出租人购买设备进行租赁业务，作为设备所有人、可享受投资减税待遇，以及折旧或按政策加速折旧的优惠。

②金融租赁公司作为出租人，租赁贸易也是一种金融业务，由此扩大了资金投放市场。由于拥有设备所有权和应收租主的承诺贷款风险较小，专业租赁公司作为出租人，一般只需支付所购设备款项的20%～40%，其余部分则以设备所有权和租金受让权作为抵押，由银行等金融机构提供贷款，但出租人仍享有全部减税利益。

一些大型制造公司往往附设租赁公司，通过以租代销扩大出口业务。对售价高，相对陈旧老化的设备，租赁是行之有效的促销方式。

### （五）租赁贸易的租金和租期

构成租金的主要项目包括租赁标的物的购置成本、租赁期间的利息和费用、经营开支、税收和利润。租金的计算公式一般为：租金＝[（标的物的购置成本−估计残值）+利息+税收+费用+利润+经营开支]/租期其中，利息最为关键，它和租期有关。租期愈长，相应的利率就愈高。租金也和租赁公司的资金来源以及所享受的减免税优惠有关。融资租赁是一次性租赁，故租期最长可与设备使用的有效期一致。但是，如果承租人有足够的支付能力，在不造成企业负担过重的情况下，缩短租期，有利于减少利息负担。

### （六）国际租赁贸易的一般做法

以融资租赁为例，说明国际租赁贸易的一般做法。

①委托租赁。用户企业将已选定的租赁物品向租赁公司提示，并填写租赁委托书。租赁委托书中应包括企业资产负债状况及经营指标。如有必要，应表明可以提供的担保。

②洽购标的物。由用户企业或租赁公司或双方联合，与租赁标的物的制造厂或供应商磋商购买标的物的贸易条件。

③签订租赁合同。当购买标的物的贸易条件已商定，租赁公司即出具租赁费估价单。双方然后就租期、租金、租赁标的物的交接验收、维修保养以及保险等条件达成一致，并签署租赁合同。

④签订购货合同。租赁公司与制造商就事先谈妥的贸易条件，正式签订购货合同。

⑤交货验收。制造商按合同规定直接向用户交货。我国企业以租赁方式引进设备，其手续等同于一般进口贸易。用户企业验收合格，以承租人身份向租赁公司出具验收收据。

⑥支付租金和履行合同义务。承租人应按合同规定定期支付租金，履行合同中规定

的其他义务。租赁公司应按合同规定，承担保险和维修责任。融资租赁一般由用户自行维修。

⑦期满留购。融资租赁期满后，通常标的物所有权即归承租人所有。租赁合同也可规定由用户支付一定数额的设备残值后，才拥有所有权。

# 十、跨境电子商务

## （一）跨境电子商务定义及特征

目前，在相关政策领域、国际组织、咨询公司和学术研究领域尚未就跨境电子商务给出明确的定义。联合国在2000年关注到了国际贸易和电子商务的关系；欧盟在其电子商务统计中最早出现了跨境电子商务（cross border e-commerce）的名称和有关内容；国际邮政组织（IPC）在2010年的《跨境电子商务报告》中分析了2009年的跨境电子商务状况，但也没有明确界定跨境电子商务的概念，而是采用了"Internet shopping""online shopping""online cross-border shopping"等多个不同的说法；E bay、尼尔森等著名公司及诸多学者的表述中也运用了不同的表达方法，如跨境在线贸易、外贸电子、跨境网购、国际电子商务等。但是，综合起来，可以将跨境电子商务的概念做如下的表述：跨境电子商务是指分属不同关境的交易主体，通过电子商务平台达成交易、进行支付结算，并通过跨境物流送达商品、完成交易的一种国际商业活动，它是一种利用现代信息技术进行各类跨境领域的以数字化交易为主要方式的一种新型贸易活动和模式，涵盖了营销、交易、支付、服务等各项商务活动。

这种新型的贸易模式融合了国际贸易和电子商务两方面的特征，具有更大的复杂性，主要表现在：一是信息流、资金流、物流等多种要素流动须紧密结合，任何一方面的不足或衔接不够，就会阻碍整体商务活动的完成；二是流程繁杂且不完善，国际贸易通常具有非常复杂的流程，牵涉到海关、检疫检验、外汇、税收、货运等多个环节，而电子商务作为新兴交易方式，在通关、支付、税收等领域的法规目前还不太完善；三是风险触发因素较多，容易受到国际经济政治宏观环境和各国政策的影响。从技术层面看，跨境电子商务具有以下特点：一是渠道上的现代性，即以现代信息技术和网络渠道为交易途径，二是空间上的国际性，即由一个经济体成员境内向另一个经济体成员境内提供的贸易服务，三是方式上的数字化，即以无纸化为主要交易方式。

跨境电子商务与贸易便利化（trade facilitation）、无纸贸易（paperless trade）紧密相连，但具有一定的区别。无纸贸易、贸易便利化和跨境电子商务是不同发展阶段和发展侧面的概念。贸易便利化是指国际贸易流程的简化与协调，更多是从贸易环境和政府管理的角度来看，不仅包括电子商务，也包括电子政务。无纸贸易至今还没有统一的定义，但一般认为其是以EDI为核心和基础的贸易活动，即通过计算机系统实现标准化的电子化的贸易流程和数据传送和处理，以完成贸易活动的全过程。贸易便利化是跨境电子商务发展的基础环境，无纸贸易是跨境电子商务的发展基础和早期主要途径。无纸贸易和电子商务都是世界贸易便利化的主要途径和核心内容之一。

### （二）跨境电子商务的主要经营模式

电子商务提供的交互式运行机制为国际贸易提供了一种信息较为完备的市场环境，通过国际贸易这一世界经济运行的纽带，达到跨国界资源和生产要素的最优配置，使市场机制在全球范围内充分有效地发挥作用。按照交易对象、交易渠道、货物流通、监管方式、资金交付、信息和单据往来等的不同，可以将跨境电子商务分为不同的类型。

按照交易对象的不同，跨境电子商务可以分为B2B、B2C、C2C和B2G。B2B为企业与企业之间的跨境电子商务，主要应用于企业之间的采购与进出口贸易等；B2C为企业与消费者个人之间的跨境电子商务，主要应用于企业直接销售或消费者全球购活动；C2C为消费者之间的跨境电子商务，主要应用于消费者之间的个人拍卖等行为；B2G主要是企业与政府之间的跨境电子商务，主要应用于政府采购，但目前进行跨境采购要受到各国诸多法规的限制。目前，中国跨境电子商务主要分为企业对企业（即B2B）和企业对消费者（即B2C）两种贸易模式。在B2B模式下，企业运用电子商务以广告和信息发布为主，成交和通关流程基本在线下完成，本质上仍属传统贸易，已纳入海关一般贸易统计。在B2C模式下，我国企业直接面对国外消费者，以销售个人消费品为主，物流方面主要采用航空小包、邮寄、快递等方式，其报关主体是邮政或快递公司，目前大多未纳入海关登记。

按照交易渠道的不同，当前主要有EDI、互联网两种方式。EDI是以电子数据交换的方式进行跨境电子商务。自20世纪70年代以来，国际组织一直在致力推动有关数据传输标准和安全等技术的发展，目前已较为成熟。EDI主要应用于企业与企业之间的电子商务活动。由于EDI对企业数据的标准化程度及软硬件的要求较高，必须租用专线进行，因而随着互联网的普及，利用互联网进行跨境交易越来越普遍，尤其是在中小企业中。但在大型企业中，EDI还广泛存在，欧盟统计局数据显示，2012年欧盟28国中有33%的企业采用EDI方式，80%的企业采用互联网方式。

按照货物流通方向的不同，可以分为进口跨境电子商务和出口跨境电子商务；按照海关监管方式的不同，又可主要分为一般跨境电子商务和保税跨境电子商务。一般跨境电子商务主要用于在一般进出口货物，大多是小额进出口货物，保税跨境电子商务主要是用于在保税进出口货物，二者在通关手续等方面有明显不同。

### （三）跨境电商在国际贸易中的创新表现

跨境电子商务突破了传统贸易以单向物流为主的运作模式，建立起了以资金流为形式、信息流为核心、商品流为主体的全新物流体系，提供全方位、多层次、多角度的互动式服务。近年来，作为国际贸易的一种新渠道，出口跨境电商保持快速增长。

①虚拟经营：跨国公司的新型合作竞争方式，开启了信息社会的公司组织及运作

方式变革的序幕，打破了传统公司的组织机构层次和界限，使跨国公司成为一个开放系统。这种外部资源"虚拟"内部化的形式，使公司的经营向柔性化、弹性化方向发展。所有生产环节都被纳进网络，利用网上"虚拟现实"的技术在世界范围内进行直观的协调。

②虚拟公司：国际贸易的新型经营主体，通过开放系统的动态网络组合寻找资源和同盟，以适应瞬息万变的经济竞争环境和消费需求向个性化、多样化方向发展的趋势，给跨国经营者带来分工合作、资源互用、利益共享的好处。

③虚拟市场：国际贸易新的运行环境。通过网上"虚拟"信息的交换，突破传统市场以一定的地域为存在条件的局限性，在全球范围内形成以信息网络为纽带的一个统一的大"市场"，促进经济全球化的进程和新型世界市场的形成。信息活动加速了资本、商品、技术等生产要素的全球活动，带动了全球"网络经济"的崛起。在这种网络贸易的环境下，各国间的经贸联系与合作也大大加强。

### （四）跨境电子商务对国际贸易的影响

电子商务将通过提供比电话传输更快、更方便、更便宜的信息交换平台，进一步促进贸易的增长和发展。在电子商务条件下，信息成为最重要的生产要素和资源，即国与国之间对信息的生产、反馈与使用能力上的差异。信息资源在国际贸易中的地位越来越重要。跨境电子商务已成为国际贸易发展的新推动力。电子商务突破了时空限制，使得信息跨国界传递和资源共享得以实现，满足了国际贸易快速增长的要求，促进了国际贸易的发展。当前，电子商务对国际贸易的影响不断向深层次扩展，在国际贸易、国际贸易治理、国际贸易运行机制、国际贸易营销手段及国际贸易运输方式等方面都带来了深刻的变革，具体表现为：

①改变了传统国际贸易方式，促进了国际贸易的发展。电子商务通过网络虚拟信息的交换，开辟了一个开放、多维、立体的市场空间，突破了传统市场必须以一定的地域空间存在为前提的束缚，全球贸易市场以信息网络为纽带形成一个统一的"大市场"，促进了世界经济市场全球化的形成。

②改变了国际贸易的运作方式，极大地提高了国际贸易的效益和效率。电子商务提供的交互式网络运行机制为国际贸易提供了一种信息较为完备的市场环境，使得信息跨国界传递和资源共享得以实现，满足了国际贸易快速增长的要求，从而促进了国际贸易的发展。并且，电子商务能够降低交易价格，让那些成本过高或执行困难的交易变得可能。

③改变了国际贸易运行机制。电子商务改变了传统的流通模式，减少了中间环节，大大缩短了生产厂家与消费者之间供求链的距离，改变了传统的市场结构，使得生产者和消费者的直接交易成为可能，大幅度降低了企业的经营管理成本。

④增加了国际贸易的新型经营主体：虚拟公司。现代信息通信技术通过单个公司在各自的专业领域拥有的核心技术，把众多公司相互连接为通过公司群体网络运作的"虚

拟公司"，完成一个公司不能承担的市场功能可以更加有效地向市场提供商品和服务。这种虚拟公司能够适应瞬息万变的经济竞争环境和消费需求向个性化、多样化方向发展的趋势，给跨国公司带来分工合作、优势互补、资源互用、利益共享的好处。

⑤改变了国际贸易的竞争态势，促使企业更好地适应市场变化。首先，电子商务的应用与企业生产制造活动相结合，使企业的产品和服务更贴近市场的需求，有助于提高企业生产的敏捷性和适应性。其次，电子商务成本低、快捷等特点使实力较差的中小企业也有机会参与到大的国际贸易中来，开拓国际市场，并且发挥其灵活机动的竞争优势，有利于中小企业的发展。再次，网络强大的通信能力和电子商务系统便利的商品交易环境，缩短了与消费者之间的实际间隔，同时也促使营销者和消费者的沟通方式进一步发生变化。企业可以直接面对消费者，和消费者进行沟通、交流，从而共同创造新的市场需求。

⑥给予了消费者更多的选择性。企业通过电子商务手段，将信息以多媒体方式在网上传播，通过智能搜索和查询的方式，方便消费者通过互联网了解更多的商品与服务信息，比如：同类商品的种类更多、产品之间的替换性更强、消费者有更多的选择余地。消费者可以亲身参与产品的设计、生产与评测，成为企业经营全过程中的重要的、积极的参与者。

同时，网络贸易也给与小额消费提供了便利，节约了消费者的购物时间，最大限度地缩短了生产与消费间的间隔，使得按需消费在技术上将成为可能。

### （五）跨境电子商务发展面临的问题

电子商务的兴起，使得信息技术因素在国际贸易中成为贸易参与国或企业国际竞争力的构成要素。国家或企业的信息处理效率成为其参与国际竞争的基础和条件，信息基础设施的发达程度和信息产业的规模比重，都极大地影响了一国在国际贸易其至世界经济中的竞争实力和竞争地位。但跨境电子商务发展还面临一系列的问题，主要体现在技术层面和法律层面。

#### 1. 技术层面

①EDI报文标准不统一。在EDI作为电子化外贸的主要载体时期，EDI所需的专用硬件线路和各国不统一的报文标准是主要问题。只有使用统一"报文标准"（即发送方与接受方的计算机都能识别的通用语言）的买卖双方，通过EDI传输的数据才会被对方解码，进而使用。进入2000年之后，iEDI对传统EDI的取代逐渐解决了这个问题。iEDI将传统电子数据交换移植到internet上来，使数据交换摆脱了专用网络VAN的束缚。然而，目前主要适用于北美国家的美国EDI标准和主要在欧洲和亚洲国家使用的联合国EDI标准并不统一，这对国际贸易信息的传输带来许多不便。

②EDI硬件成本高，而且应用程序存在安全问题。EDI必须使用专用的网络硬件，即VAN网络（value-added network），这不但需要企业或政府机关从电信营运部门申请专线，而且即使大型进出口企业在使用EDI的过程中，EDI的应用程序即电子商务所直接

依存的计算机操作系统均不同程度地存在安全隐患。

### 2. 法律层面

①数据电文的法律承认问题。传统上的贸易合同一般采用书面方式，通过手写签名或印章来辨别身份。在电子商务中，贸易双方主要依靠数据电文的交换来达成合同，包括电子货币和电子签名等形式。如果要承认通过数据电文订立的合同合法有效，首先就要承认数据电文的法律地位。由于数据电文是存储在硬盘上的无形物，所以在实际应用中对其是否有充分的法律地位的认识是不统一的，尚待进一步明确规定。

②要约的撤回、撤销及承诺的撤回。关于要约及承诺的撤回，法律在时间上的要求是"送达之前"或"同时送达"。而在EDI电子商务之下，要约和承诺的送达只需几秒钟，所以这种"撤回"是完全不可能实现的。同样，要约的撤销在电子商务中也是不可能的。

③电子签名的法律问题。传统的合同、单据大都需要双方当事人的签章，才会具有法律效力，相应的电子商务的合同单据则需电子签名，而在当前条件下，电子签名的技术还不完善，制作伪造电子签名远远易于伪造实际合同的签名。因而我国法律对电子签名的应用目前还有许多限制。这就大大妨碍了正常贸易的进行。

此外，还存在网络信息的隐私权与知识产权保护问题，无形产品的网络交易对征收海关进出口关税和国内其他财政贸易政策与市场准入等问题。这些由电子商务带来的新问题都要求在贸易立法上做出相应的调整和变更，使之有利于保护贸易当事人的合法权益。

# 十一、其他贸易方式

## （一）市场采购贸易

市场采购贸易方式是指由符合条件的经营者在经国家商务主管等部门认定的市场集聚区内采购的、单票报关单商品货值15万（含15万）美元以下、并在采购地办理出口商品通关手续的贸易方式。市场采购贸易相比一般贸易，具有以下特点：①在报关方面采用分类通关、简化归类；②在报检方面采用备案管理、口岸检验；③在出口收汇方面，采用主体监管、总量核查；④在退税方面，采用免税备案、免征免退。市场采购贸易方式出口的货物直接免征增值税（包括以增值税为计税依据的城建税、教费附加和地方教育附加等），在征收方式上采取不征不退的方式，即市场集聚区的市场经营户未取得或无法取得增值税发票的货物均可以市场采购贸易方式出口。

市场采购模式通过享受国家支持的主体准入、出口通关、免税模式、外汇管理等一系列独有的相关政策，极大地提高了对外贸易的便利化程度：一是准入门槛更低，凡在产业集聚区内的商户、贸易公司经备案后都可以参与试点；二是通关出口更快，允许组柜拼箱，实行简化归类申报，对超过10种商品的单只货柜，报关单只需要列一票商品；三是税收政策更优，实施增值税免征不退政策；四是外汇管理更活，允许开立经常项目外汇账户，支持跨境人民币结算。其最核心的优势是外贸出口的产品可以在"家门口"实现"一次申报、一次查验、一次放行"；其最根本的保证是产品质量可实现"源头可溯、责任可究、风险可控"；其最巨大的潜力是辐射带动周边市场，实现国内外两个市场的同频互动与深度融合。

截至2019年2月，中华人民共和国商务部公布的3批市场采购贸易方式共包括8个试点单位，其中：第一批市场采购试点是浙江义乌市场采购试点；第二批市场采购试点包括：江苏海门叠石桥国际家纺城和浙江海宁皮革城；第三批市场采购试点包括：江苏省常熟服装城、广东省广州花都皮革皮具市场、山东省临沂商城工程物资市场、湖北省武汉汉口北国际商品交易中心和河北省白沟箱包市场。

市场采购贸易方式试点不仅激发了市场主体活力、扩大了市场规模、提升了国际化水平、推动了外贸增长，而且在推进外贸新业态试点工作和促进外贸创新发展方面取得了积极成效。除推动通关便利化，实现可追溯之外，通过市场采购集聚区的打造，推动内外贸一体化发展，加快产业集聚，推动跨境电子商务发展。作为一种高效、快捷、低成本的新型外贸方式，有利于吸引国际采购商集聚，推动专业市场经营者实现自有品牌设计的小批量、多批次出口，快速应对国际市场变化。

### （二）对等贸易

对等贸易（counter trade）是指贸易双方采用某种协议，达到进出口平衡的一种贸易方式，包括易货贸易、互购（counter purchase）等，在我国又译为"反向贸易""互抵贸易"等。我们一般可以把对等贸易理解为以进出结合、出口抵补进口为特征的各种贸易方式的总称，包括易货、记账贸易、互购、产品回购、转手贸易等。其中，易货贸易是指不通过货币媒介而直接用出口货物交换进口货物的贸易。易货贸易双方的交易值相等，通常不涉及现汇支付；而互购贸易通常使用现汇结算，但并不要求互购价值相等。补偿贸易也可被列为是对等贸易的一种形式。

### （三）边境小额贸易

边境小额贸易是指我国沿陆地边境线经国家批准对外开放的边境县（旗）、边境城市辖区内（以下简称边境地区），经批准有边境小额贸易经营权的企业，通过国家指定的陆地口岸，与毗邻国家边境地区的企业或其他贸易机构进行贸易活动，包括易货贸易、现汇贸易等。

### （四）对外承包工程出口货物

对外承包工程出口货物是指经商务部批准，有对外承包工程经营权的公司，为承包国外建设工程项目和开展劳务合作等对外合作项目而出口的设备、物资，但不包括边境地区经商务部批准有对外经济技术合作经营权的企业与我国毗邻国家开展承包工程和劳务合作项下出口的工程设备、物资。

## （五）外商投资企业进口货物

外商投资企业作为投资进口的设备、物品，是指外商投资企业以投资总额内的资金（包括中方投资）所进口的机器设备、零部件和其他物料。其他物料包括建厂（场）以及安装、加固机器的所需材料，以及根据国家规定进口本企业自用合理数量的交通工具、生产用车辆和办公用品（设备）。

## （六）保税仓库进出境货物

保税仓库进出境货物，包括从境外直接存入保税仓库的货物、从出口监管仓库运出境的货物，但不包括保税区的仓储、转口货物。

## （七）保税区仓储、转口货物

保税区仓储、转口货物是指从境外存入保税区的仓储、转口货物和从保税区运出境的仓储、转口货物，不包括从境外存入非保税区和从非保税区运出境的仓储、转口货物。

**思考题**

1.试分析国际贸易独家经销、独家代理、寄售之间的区别。
2.试举例说明国际贸易招投标、国际拍卖的作用
3.关注并对比分析中国出口商品交易会和中国进口商品博览会。
4.跟踪跨境电商的发展趋势并分析其在国际贸易中的作用
5.加工贸易在我国的发展情况及其作用

# Chapter 10

# Types of International Trade

☞ Case 10.1

Jiangsu Holly Co., Ltd was founded in 1979 and listed in the Shanghai Stock Exchange in 1997. She is the first listed company of national handicraft industry and economic and foreign trade cooperation system in Jiangsu province. Now, she is one of the important member enterprises of Jiangsu Suhao Holding Group Co., Ltd. She owns registered capital of 246.7675 million yuan, has passed the ISO9001 quality management system, ISO14001 environmental management system and OHSAS18001 occupational health and safety management system certification. She is the quality credit enterprise of China, Nanjing headquarters enterprises and the cultivating object of Nanjing foreign trade comprehensive service pilot. The owned brand "Artall" has been awarded the title of "Jiangsu famous brand products" and "international famous brand of Jiangsu key cultivation and development" for many years.

Through continuous investment and construction, she continues to enhance its core capabilities of market development, technology research and development, production and manufacturing, quality assurance, and so on, the total amount of import and export has been increasing by years, and has been listed in the top 500 national import and export enterprises for many times. The export goods include mechanical and electrical products, ships, toys, leisure gifts, textiles, clothing, shoes, hats and the household items. The import goods include chemical, mineral, coal, medical equipment, mechanical and electrical equipment, food and other fields. Products are mainly exported to North America, the United Kingdom, the European Union, Japan, ASEAN and other overseas regions.

She attends China fair, Canton fair every year.In each session of the trade fair, the company's toys, bags, gifts, shoes, hats, clothing, sports leisure supplies, furniture and other products are displayed in the brand exhibition area, attracting domestic and foreign merchants. She also participate in foreign exhibitions to promote sales.The display of HOLLY (ARTALL) products can be seen at the hardware show in cologne, Germany, the international gift show in Japan, the international gift and consumer goods show in Las Vegas, the USA shoe show in  Las Vegas, the autumn consumer goods show in Frankfurt, the USA toy show in New York and other international fairs. In 2016, the company's exports to countries along "the Belt and Road" were $98.795 million, accounting for 31.93% of the total exports. In addition to international trade co limited, import & export co limited and overseas business departments, she also owns international technical engineering co limited, e-commerce department, financial and investment department and environmental science & technology, cultural industry, fertilizer industry, handicraft co limited. Her seven key investment enterprises include futures, cultural property transactions, financial leasing, credit guarantee, investment and entrepreneurship, and other new companies.

Trade patterns are increasingly diversified with the expansion and of international trade and the complexity of trade types. In addition to the mode of order and sale of specific deal, there are distribution, agency, consignment, auction, invitation to tender & submission of tender, futures trading, processing trade, reciprocal trade, leasing trade, etc.At the same time, the impact of e-commerce on international trade continues to expand deeply. Cross-boarder e-commerce has been developing rapidly in China and become the backbone of China's foreign trade development.The volume of China's export by cross-border e-commerce was 6.3 trillion yuan in 2017, more than 14.5% in 2016. Of which, B2B was 5.1 trillion yuan, higher than 13.3 of in 2016. Cross-border e-commerce exports can effectively meet the needs of overseas consumers and become an effective supplement to traditional trade exports.

# 10.1 Distribution

## 10.1.1 Concept and Classification of Distribution

Distribution refers to the economic behavior of an enterprise or individual selling goods for another enterprise or individual in accordance with the contract signed by both parties. Distribution can be divided into exclusive sale and general distribution according to the different authority of the distributor. Exclusive sale refers to the distributor enjoys the exclusive franchise rights for the designated goods within the prescribed time limit and territory. For the general distribution, the  distributor does not have the exclusive franchise, and the supplier may appoint  several companies to distribute the similar products in the same territory at the same time.

Therefore, in order to promote sale of the products in other countries, an export firm may enter into an exclusive sale or exclusive sale agreement with a foreign firm, granting the exclusive operation right of a certain commodity or a certain category to the foreign firm ( exclusive distributor ) in a certain territory within a certain period. If the agreement is no exclusivity, the export firm can also give the management right to the other firms ( general distributors). Distribution is a kind of special sale that the relationship of supplier and distributor is buying and selling. In addition to sign a sales contract, both parties shall usually sign a distribution agreement in advance to determine the rights and obligations.

### 10.1.2 Exclusive Sales

Exclusive sales is one of customary pattern in international trade. Exclusive Sales refers to the export firm and the foreign distributor reach an agreement, grant the exclusive right of the designated goods to the distributor in the designated territory within a certain period, and the distributor undertakes not to operate the same kind or substitute goods from other sources. By signing an exclusive sales agreement, both parties establish a stable long-term relationship of purchase and sale.For each specific transaction, a separate sales contract shall be concluded on the basis of an exclusive sales agreement.The general practice of exclusive sales is shown in Figure 10.1. The rights and obligations of both parties are determined by the exclusive sale agreement.The sales contract signed by both parties must also comply with the provisions of the exclusive sales agreement.

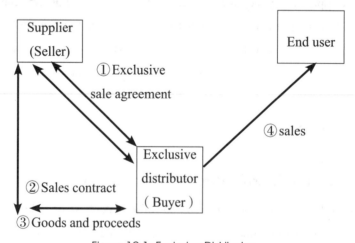

Figure 10.1  Exclusive Distributor

The export firm can take advantage of the exclusive distributor's funds and sales ability to establish a stable developing market in the specific territory. The exclusive distributor can obtain the opportunity of exclusive sales and are in a favorable position in the sales of designated commodities, avoiding the situation of price reduction and profit reduction caused by long competition. Accordingly, the exclusive distributor has higher management enthusiasm and  make more investment in advertisement promotion and after-sale service.However, since the exclusive distributor buys the goods and sells them by himself, he needs to invest some money and take the risk of selling the goods. If he is short of funds or lack of sales capacity, it is possible to be exclusive "without sales". How to choose a suitable distributor for the export firm is the key to a successful approach to exclusive distributor.

## 10.1.3 Clauses of the Exclusive Sales Agreement

The exclusive sales agreement is the contract concluded by the export firm and the distributor. Its contents can be simplified or complicated according to the characteristics of the goods, the situation of the distribution territory and the intention of the parties. In practice, it may be only stipulated the rights and obligations of both parties and the general conditions. Each subsequent delivery of goods shall conclude a specific sales contract according to the distribution agreement, so as to further clarify the specific conditions, including price, quantity, delivery time and payment method.Therefore, the distribution agreement itself is not a sales contract.The price of an exclusive sale of goods may be stipulated in a lump sum, or may be agreed upon the market situation in a sales contract. The general terms refer to the terms applicable to each transaction during the term of distribution agreement, such as payment method, inspection, claim, insurance, force majeure and other terms and conditions.

Except for the name, date and place of the agreement, main contents of the exclusive sales agreement and the matters needing attention include:

**1. The Preamble**

Generally, the preamble is used to clear the relationship of both parties are principal to principal, i.e. the buying and selling relation.The exclusive distributor shall raise funds to buy the commodities and sell them at their own profit and loss.

**2. Scope of Exclusive Sales**

If the supplier owns a wide range of commodities, both parties shall clearly stipulate the specific scope of the exclusive sales of commodities, the different brands and specifications of the same type in the exclusive sales agreement. When determine the scope of the exclusive sales of goods, the exporter shall consider the intention of sales, the sales capacity and the credit status of distributor. If all the commodities are covered in the scope of exclusive sales, in order to avoid disputes, it is better to specify in the agreement whether a product is stopped production or a new products are introduced to the exclusive sales agreement.

**3. Territory of Exclusive Sales**

The territory of exclusive sales refers to the geographical scope of the distributor's exercise of sales. It can be stipulated by the following ways:①to identify a country or countries,②to identify several cities in a country, or③to identify a city, etc. In determining the territory of exclusive sales, size of an underwriting area, the following factors should be taken into account.

①The scale and ability of the distributor.

②The distribution network controlled by the distributor.

③The nature and type of goods sold exclusively.

④The degree of market differentiation.

⑤The political regions, geography and traffic conditions of exclusive sales.

The provisions of the distribution territory may be adjusted according to the specific situation of business development agreed by both parties.Under the exclusive sales, the supplier shall not designate another distributor to operate similar products in the territory of exclusive sale to maintain the exclusive right of the distributor.In order to protect the interests of the distributor, some exclusive sales agreements stipulate that the distributor shall not sell the exclusive sales in the other territory.

**4. Period of Exclusive Sales**

The period of exclusive sales may be long or short. In practice, the time limit may be one year, or not specified in the agreement, but only the suspension clause or renewal clause. The agreement shall terminate upon expiration.In order to prevent one party using some trivial differences in the performance of the other party as an excuse to tear up the agreement, the termination clause can be provided in the agreement to clarify when the agreement can be terminated.In addition, the term of extension can be set forth in the contract. If the term of extension can be agreed upon by both parties, or if no notice of termination has been given several days prior to the expiration of the agreement, the term of extension can be extended automatically.

**5. Franchise**

Franchises include exclusive selling and exclusive buying.The former indicates that the supplier undertakes not to sell the exclusive sale goods to the other customers in the territory of exclusive sale during the period of this agreement.The latter means that the distributor undertakes to purchase only such goods from the supplier under the agreement and shall not purchase similar or competitive alternatives from a third party.The exclusive right is the essential content of the exclusive sale agreement, and is the main condition different from the general distribution agreement.

**6. Minimum Quantity or Amount of Goods Sold Exclusively**

If quantity and amount are specified in the agreement, the distributor must bear the obligation to purchase the specified quantity and amount from the supplier, and the supplier must bear the responsibility to export the said quantity and amount to the distributor.This quantity or amount shall be equally binding upon the parties hereto. The distribution amount is generally stipulated as the minimum purchase amount within a certain period and clarifies the calculation method. In order to prevent the distributor from delaying the implementation of the contract, the minimum purchase amount can be specified based on the actual shipment.

### 7. Pricing Method

The pricing method for the exclusive sale of goods is as follows.

①The price shall be done in one time within the prescribed time limit.That is to say, the price specified in the agreement shall prevail regardless of whether the price of the goods is increased or not. By adopting this pricing method, both parties shall bear the risk of price changes, so it is less adopted in practice.

②The price shall be fixed in batches within the stipulated time limit for exclusive sales.As the price of international commodity market is variable, it is more common to adopt batch pricing.

### 8. Advertisement, Publicity, Market Report and Trademark Protection

The distributor shall do well in advertising publicity, market research and maintenance of the rights and interests of suppliers.The parties to an exclusive sales agreement are buyers and sellers.Although the consignor (the exporter) does not actually set foot in the sales business in the exclusive territory, he concerns to explore the overseas markets.Therefore, the agreement may stipulate that:

①The distributor shall have the obligation to promote sales and advertising, while the supplier  shall provide necessary samples and publicity materials.The way of publicity and its related expenses shall generally be applied and borne by the distributor.

②To undertake the obligation of market research for exporters' reference to develop sales strategies and improve product quality.

③If the supplier's trademark right or patent right is found to be infringed in the territory, the distributor shall promptly take protective measures.

In order to promote the brand used in the exclusive sale of products, the supplier often asks the distributor to be responsible for placing certain advertisements for his products.The distributor may be stipulated in the sole sale agreement that he shall be responsible for and contribute to the holding of exhibitions, solicitation of orders, and advertising in the local press for the products in the exclusive sale territory, visit customers with prospects for a deal and try to provide market coverage, etc.

In addition to the main contents mentioned above, the general conditions, such as force majeure and arbitration clauses, shall be stipulated in the same method as the general sales contracts.

### 10.1.4 Advantages of Distribution

For suppliers, the distribution is one of the effective ways to stabilize the market and expand sales. The supplier usually gives the distributor a certain preferential in terms of price and payment conditions, which is conducive to arousing the distributor's enthusiasm and using its distribution channels to promote the sales. In some cases, the distributors may be required to provide after-sales services and conduct market research. Different ways of distribution are not exactly the same for export promotion. In the case of exclusive distribution, the distributor shall, to a certain extent, avoid or reduce losses caused by self-competition, by having exclusive rights to the designated goods in the territory.

In the same market, if there are many firms operating the same products, when the market is not good, some businessmen will sell at reduced prices because of the difficulty of capital turnover. It has the potential to create a ripple effect that other merchants will follow. The psychology of many consumers is buy up and not buy down, compete to depreciate and may destroys the market.

In addition, under the exclusive distribution, as long as the distributor is selected properly, as they are familiar with the consumption habit of the territory, and own the convenience of the respect such as government regulations, rules and regulations, they can provide the necessary information to suppliers in a timely manner, such as the situation of supply and demand, the reflection of consumers on product, and help the suppliers to improve the products, accomplish marketable, and reduce the unnecessary legal disputes.

Generally, the distributor is also willing to advertise, publicize, or undertake other obligations for the products distributed in accordance with the provisions of the agreement, so that the business amount of the products is constantly expanded and both parties can benefit from the cooperation.

### 10.1.5 Matters Needing Attention for Distribution

However, many practical experiences indicate that the following issues should be noted when exporting by means of distribution.

**1. To Choose the Distributor Carefully**

The Supplier and distributor have a relatively long-term cooperative relationship. If the distributor is selected with good reputation, who can abide the contract, keep the promise, and has strong management ability, even if the market situation is not good, the distributor can make full use of his experience and means to complete the sales quota. If the distributor is selected improperly, their operation ability is not good or the credit is not good, then the supplier will become self-tied.This problem is particularly pronounced in the context of exclusive distribution.Some distributors, when market conditions are not favorable, refuse to fulfill the purchase amount specified in the agreement, resulting in the failure of the supplier's original export plan and loss of other customers.Also there are some  distributors who, by virtue of their exclusive special status, in turn hold the supplier hostage in terms of price and other conditions to gain profits for themselves, but to the detriment of the suppliers.In order to prevent this kind of situation from happening, when the supplier chooses the distributor, should do serious credit investigation first, understand the other party's reputation, reputation and distribution ability.

### 2. Pay Attention to the Relevant Local Laws and Regulations

The exclusivity provisions of the agreement sometimes constitute "restrictive business practices" in the form of exclusive distribution.The general interpretation of "restrictive business practices" is that the development of trade or commerce is adversely affected by the abuse of the dominant position of market forces, by restricting the entry of other firms into the market, or by other improper means restricting competition.The central issue is the restriction of competition and the operation of markets, which are regulated in the legislation of many countries.

In some exclusive sales agreements, where the type of goods to be sold and the territory to be sold is specified, the following restrictions are sometimes made: the distributor shall not operate similar products of other manufacturers or sell the products to areas outside the territory. Such regulations might violate regulations and laws that regulate "restrictive business practices", such as the antitrust law. Therefore, when signing the exclusive distribution agreement, the parties should understand the relevant local laws and regulations, and pay attention to the use of language, as far as possible to avoid conflict with local laws.

# 10.2 Agency

## 10.2.1 Concept and Classification of Agency

In addition to distribution, the export firm may enter into an agency agreements with the foreign agent and entrust the agent to solicit business or engage in other entrusted affairs. Agency refers to the agent enters into a contract with a third party or performs other legal actions according to the authorization of the Principal. The rights and obligations arising therefrom are directly valid for the principal.

The agent acts within the scope authorized by the principal, does not bear the sales risks and costs, does not have to advance the funds, and is usually paid a commission of the agreed proportion of the amount of the transaction concluded, regardless of the profit or loss of the transaction. The agent only acts on behalf of the principal, such as soliciting customers, soliciting orders, signing sales contracts on behalf of the principal, handling the principal's goods, accepting payment for goods, and he does not participate in the transaction as a party to the contract.

The agency in international trade is usually the sales agent. The supplier entered into an agreement with a foreign agent. The supplier shall act as the principal and authorize the agent to promote commodities sales and sign contracts on behalf of him, and the rights and obligations arising therefrom shall have direct effect on the principal. The agent is responsible for the rights and obligations arising therefrom and the agent only receives the agreed commission. The general practice of an agent is shown in Figure 10.2.

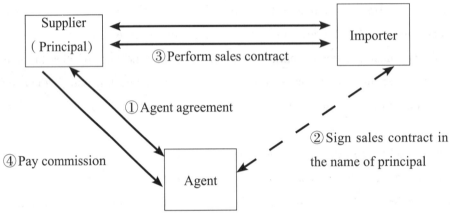

Figure 10.2 The Basic Approach of Agency

Sales agents can be divided into the following types according to the different authorization granted by the principal:

(1) General Agent

As the exclusive representative of the supplier, he conducts sales activities and other extensive business activities on behalf of the supplier in the designated area.He has the right to sign sales contracts, handle goods and other commercial activities on behalf of his principal, as well as some non-commercial activities. He has the right to appoint sub-agents and to share the commission of the agents.

(2) Exclusive Agent

The agent who has the exclusive right to sell the specified commodities within the time and area specified in the agency agreement. The principal shall not sell the commodities by himself or through other agents within the above scope.

(3) Commission Agent

An agent who is not entitled to exclusive agency rights. A principal may entrust several agents to sell the same goods in the same area at the same time. The commission shall be charged on the basis of the actual amount of the goods sales as per the method and percentage provided in the agreement. The principal may conclude the transaction directly with the actual buyer in the area without paying commission to the commission agent.

## 10.2.2 Exclusive Agency Agreement

Exclusive agency means that the agent has exclusive rights in the agreed area and period, that is, the consignor shall not sell the goods directly or indirectly to other buyers in the agent area. The main contents of the exclusive agency agreement include:

①Basic relationship between the parties. The relationship between the exporter and the agent is a principal-agent relationship. The agent shall act within the scope authorized by the principal and shall act in good faith and faithfully. The principal shall bear civil liability for the agent's acts within the above scope.

②Commodities, regions and period of agency. In the authorization of the principal to the agent, the type and specification of the commodity to be sold by the agent shall be clearly stated, while the exclusive agent must specify the geographical scope of its business, and agree on the validity period of the agency agreement, or stipulate the suspension clause.

③Franchise. To the extent indicated above, the principal undertakes to appoint an exclusive agent as the sole agent dealing with the buyer. In the event of a direct transaction between the principal and the buyer, the principal shall pay commission to the sole agent for the amount of the transaction.

④Commission clause. The commission rate, the time and method to pay the commission must be specified in the agency agreement. The commission rate may be related to the amount or quantity of the transaction.

⑤Minimum turnover. A sole agent usually promises a minimum quantity or amount. If this amount is not achieved, the principal is entitled to terminate the agreement or adjust the commission rate as agreed herein.

⑥Business report. The agent is obliged to provide regular or irregular business reports to the principal so that the principal may know the local market conditions and the performance of the agent. Whether can provide reasonable commercial situation report is the important basis that inspects agent.

## 10.2.3 Application of Agency

The exporter entrusts an agent to sell goods, basically is to use the advantage that the agent is familiar with the market of the place of sale, have extensive sale channel. It should be pointed out that the goodwill of the agent plays an important role in the sales of goods and even the image of export enterprises. Choosing an agent should not only focus on his sales ability, but also on his existing goodwill. At present, many multinational companies have entered the field of sales agents in the international market. How to exploit the market with the good reputation of multinational companies is a subject worth studying for Chinese enterprises

# 10.3 Consignment

### 10.3.1 Concept of Consignment

Different from agency, consignment is a trade mode in which an exporter entrusts a foreign firm to buy and sell goods from the spot to the user. It is also one of the practices used in international trade. By means of consignment, the exporter shall select a consignee in the consignment area, sign a consignment agreement, and then consign the goods to a foreign consignment place and entrust the local seller to sell the goods in the local market according to the conditions specified in the consignment agreement. When the merchandise is sold, the distributor delivers the payment to the consignor after deducting commissions and other fees. In China's import and export business, the use of consignment is not universal. However, in the transaction of certain commodities, in order to facilitate the transaction, the need to expand exports can also be flexible and appropriate use of consignment. The basic practice of consignment is as shown in Figure 10.3.

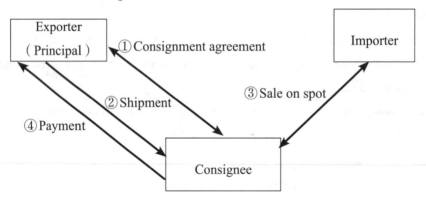

Figure 10.3 Basic Practices of Consignment

### 10.3.2 Characteristics, Functions and Risks of Consignment

Compared with the normal way of selling out, the way of consignment in international trade has the following characteristics.

①It is a typical way of dealing in physical goods. The consignor shall ship the goods to the destination market (place of consignment) and then sell them to local buyers at the place of consignment by the consignee.

②not a sales relationship. The consignee only handles the goods as directed by the consignor and the title to the goods remains with the consignor until it is sold on the consignment.

③The consignor shall bear all costs and risks of the consigned goods before they are sold, including during transit and after arrival at the place of consignment. When the goods are still in transit, they may be sold on condition that they are in transit. If the sale is unsuccessful, the goods will be transported to the original destination.

Consignment is a method of selling goods on hand after shipment. For the specific sales of international trade, the foreign buyer often has the understanding to the seller's product, conclude a deal with quantities and delivery in a determinable future date. Consignment can let the consumers meet the commodities directly on the market and purchase at will. It is an effective way to seize the opportunity of sales and open up new markets, especially for the consumer goods.

However, the exporter must bear certain risks and expenses.

①The goods need to be shipped before getting payment, so the exporter's financial burden is heavy.

②The goods shall be stored and picked up in the consignment area, and the distributor shall not bear any costs and risks.

③If the distributor fails to comply with the consignment agreement, fails to properly take care of the goods, or fails to timely remit the payment after the sale, it will bring losses to the exporter.

④If the goods are not marketable and need to be transported back to another port, the exporter will suffer.

## 10.3.3 Consignment Agreement

The consignment agreement shall stipulate the conditions and specific practices related to consignment, and the main contents are as follows:

**1. Basic Relationship Between the Parties**

The relationship between the consignor and the consignee is a principal-agent relationship. The ownership of the goods remains with the consignor until they are sold. The consignee shall sell the goods as an agent, collect payment, settle disputes, etc., and the risks and expenses thereof shall be borne by the consignor.

**2. Price of the Consigned Goods**

There are three ways to set the price of goods on consignment. First, to stipulate the lowest price. Second, to sell the goods according to the market price. Third, to determine the price with the consignor's consent. The third pricing method is used more commonly.

**3. Commission Clause**

Calculating the rate of commission and, in some cases, increase or decrease. Commission is usually deducted by the consignee from the payment for goods.

### 4. Obligations of the Consignee

Obligations of the consignee includes the custody of goods, import customs declaration, storage, insurance procedures and other procedures and timely notify the consignor of business. The consignee shall deliver the payment to the consignor in the manner and time specified in the agreement. Some consignment agreements also stipulate that the consignee shall issue its bank guarantee or standby letter of credit to the consignor to guarantee that it will assume the obligations specified in the consignment agreement.

### 5. Obligations of the Consignor

The goods shall be shipped within the time stipulated in the agreement to reimburse the commission charges advanced by the consignee.

## 10.3.4 Application of Consignment

① To focus on exploring new markets. In order to establish customer relation and want to sell commodity already, the consignor shall choose the product with high grade and marketable.

② To select the appropriate place for consignment. The place of consignment shall be the trade center with convenient transportation or free port, free trade zone to facilitate the entry and exit of goods and reduce the cost.

③ To select a suitable consignee. The consignee shall have a good reputation in the local area, have relevant marketing experience and marketing ability, have the ability to handle customs declaration, warehousing and other business.

④ To pay attention on safe collection of foreign exchange. The consignment agreement may specify that the consignee be required to issue a bank guarantee, a standby letter of credit or deliver goods against a banker's acceptance draft.

# 10. 4 Auction

## 10.4.1 Concept of Auction

Auction is a method of dealing in which an auction house accepts a consignee to sell the goods to the highest bidder at the auction house in accordance with certain rules and procedures. Auction is a way of trading spot goods through lots of bids from buyers. The commodity that uses auction to undertake trading in international trade, it is normally hard to standardize or be hard to save for a long time, or the commodity that has auction habit on tradition, be like artwork, antique, tea, tobacco, rabbit hair, fur, lumber, fruit, flowers, wool. Auction procedure is different from the general export transaction, its transaction process to go through the preparation, look at the goods, bid to conclude the transaction and payment delivery and other four stages.

## 10.4.2 The Method of Bidding at an Auction

### 1. Mark-up Auction

Mark up auction, also known as "English auction," the buyer bid auction.This is the most common type of auction.At an auction, the auctioneer announces the intended price and the bidder bids one after another.The auction house may set a limit on the amount of each mark-up until a certain price is reached. When no one raises the price after being prompted three times by the auctioneer, the highest price shall be indicated by the auctioneer's hammer.According to the auction articles, the bidder may revoke the bid before the auctioneer drops the hammer;The auctioneer may terminate the auction if the buyer's bid is lower than the minimum price agreed between the seller and the auctioneer.

### 2. Descending Price Auction

Descending price auction also known as dutch auction, it comes from the world's largest Dutch flower auction market, where the auctioneer bids the highest price and then lowers it gradually until a deal is agreed.In this auction, there is no process of repeated bidding among buyers, and once the buyer expresses acceptance, it cannot be withdrawn.

### 3. Sealed Bid Auction

Sealed bid auction, also known as tendering auction.The auctioneer shall first announce the specific conditions and auction conditions of each batch of goods, and the buyer shall submit the sealed quotation (also known as tender) to the auctioneer within the specified time for the auctioneer to review the comparison and decide which bidder to sell the goods to.Compared with the above two methods, this method has the following two characteristics: First, in addition to the price conditions, there may be other trading conditions to consider. Second, can adopt open bid, also can adopt not open bid.This auction method is often used by the governments or customs of some countries in the processing of goods in stock or in the confiscation of goods;It is also possible to auction large facilities or large quantities of inventory.

## 10.4.3 General Procedure of Auction

### 1. Preparation Stage

The consignor and the auction house reach an auction agreement, stipulating the goods type and quantity, delivery method and time, limited price and commission and other matters. The owner delivers the goods to the auction site and stores them in the warehouse designated by the auctioneer.The auctioneer issues a catalogue of lots and publishes an auction notice. The buyer can check the goods at the warehouse where the auction goods are stored before the official auction and, if necessary, take samples for analysis and testing.

**2. Official Auction**

At the specified time and place, the auction shall be conducted in the order specified in the catalogue.In a bid auction, the buyer's bid is equivalent to an offer, and the auctioneer's hammer is equivalent to an acceptance.Before dropping the hammer, the buyer has the right to withdraw the bid and the seller has the right to withdraw the auction item.In a reduced price auction, the auctioneer's quotation is equivalent to an offer, and once the buyer expresses acceptance, it is an acceptance, and the transaction is established, both parties are bound.

**3. Payment and Delivery**

Upon completion, the buyer signs the sales confirmation and pays a deposit for part of the purchase price. After the buyer has paid all the purchase price, the auction house issues the bill of lading and the buyer takes delivery of the goods.The auction house takes a percentage of commission from the payment for goods as a reward for providing auction services, and delivers the loan to the owner after deducting the fees that should be borne by the owner according to the contract.

## 10.4.4 Matters Needing Attention to the Auction

**1. Quality of Goods**

The auction house usually stipulates in its articles of association that "the seller is not responsible for the quality", as the goods to be auctioned are often difficult to describe with specific specifications and the buyer has the right to inspect the goods before the suction. Therefore, after the auction, the buyer has no right to reinspect the goods, and there is no claim. Some goods may have hidden defects, it is difficult to find by ordinary means of inspection, some auction articles also stipulate the buyer's claim period.

**2. Principles of Openness and Fairness**

Auction and bidding are the same, is a fair competition in accordance with the principle of open trade.To ensure that the principles of openness and fairness are not violated, the auction house has a charter for the sale. Both the buyer and the seller must strictly observe, and the buyer shall not collude with each other to drive down the price. The seller shall not bid by the agent to bid up the price, which constitutes violation of the law.

# 10.5 Invitation to Tender & Submission of Tender

## 10.5.1 Concept of Tendering and Bidding

Invitation to tender & submission of tender are two aspects of a trade. This mode of trade applies to both the purchase of materials and equipment, as well as contract projects.

Tendering is an act by which the tenderer (purchaser or project owner) issues a tender notice specifying the specific content of the commodity or contract project to be purchased, invites the bidder (seller or project contractor) to bid at the specified time and place, and contracts with the bidder whose conditions are most favorable to the tenderer. Tender is the behavior that the bidder (seller or engineering contractor) should be invited by the tenderee, according to the conditions specified by the tenderee, offer offer to the tenderee at the specified time and place to try to clinch a deal.

When a tendering unit needs to purchase commodities or initiate a project, it may put forward the variety, quantity and relevant buying and selling conditions of the commodities to be purchased, and may issue a tender notice or tender sheet, inviting interested enterprises to offer prices within a specified period according to a certain procedure, that is, to bid. The bidder may, at the invitation of the tenderer, submit his offer to the tenderer within the prescribed time according to the requirements prescribed in the tender announcement or tender list. After bidding, the tenderer shall open and evaluate the bid and select the most satisfied bidder for the transaction, which is often used in international trade.

Bidding and auction are two common methods of international and domestic trade. Bidding is a competition among sellers, while auction is a competition among buyers. The characteristic of these two kinds of modes includes: the subject matters are open, the competitions are open and reach deals are quickly. Due to tendering and bidding has the characteristics of fair competition, international competitive bidding (the ICB ) are adopted by many large and medium-sized projects and materials procurement, especially the international government loan project and international financial organizations loan project.

## 10.5.2　General Procedures of Tendering and Bidding

### 1. Preparation

The preparation of tenders generally includes:①Publish the tender notices. The tender notices of international public bidding are usually published in authoritative newspapers or relevant professional publications, such as *People's Daily* in China, the bidding monthly published of the world bank for aid projects.②Pre-qualifying. The bidder shall fill in the pre-qualifying form prepared by the tenderer, including the bidder's business scale, personnel and facilities profile, project records, etc., and provide relevant supporting documents and materials. The tenderer shall confirm whether he or she has the bid ability. Oversimplification is the key step to ensure the successful bidding.③Prepare bidding documents. At the beginning of the bid invitation, the tenderer shall organize relevant personnel to prepare the bid invitation and state the technical and trade conditions for the purchase of goods or contract works.

Preparation of bidding generally includes: ① Bid evaluation. After the bidder acquires the bid, it shall calculate the required quality, technical standard, delivery term, project quantity and schedule according to the bidding conditions strictly, and estimate whether it can fully meet the bidding requirements and submit competitive quotation based on its own conditions and market competitive situation. ② Prepare the tender and implement the guarantee. The tender is an irrevocable offer made by the bidder to the tenderer. The main contents include the confirmation of the bidding conditions, the related indicators and project progress, technical specifications and drawings, the responsibilities of the bidder, and the total price and unit price analysis table. If the bidder refuses to sign the contract after winning the bid, the bidder is usually required to submit the bid security, which is usually 3%—10% of the total price, or the bank guarantee letter or standby letter of credit is used instead of cash. The bidder shall implement the guarantor before bidding.

### 2. Submit Tender Documents

The tender documents include the tender, tender bond or stand-by letter of credit, annexes to the individual instructions in the tender, and other necessary documents. The tender documents shall be delivered to the designated place within the specified time after being sealed. They can be submitted by hand or sent by registered post.

### 3. Open the Bid

The sealed tender documents shall be opened in public at a pre-announced time and place, read out the contents, and allow the bidders present to record or record. After the bid opening, the bidder shall not alter the contents of bid. Bid opening is the content of public tender, to ensure the fair conduct of bidding work in a form, not on the spot to determine the winning bidder.

### 4. Bid Evaluation and Award

In addition to the price conditions, technical quality, project schedule or delivery time, the services provided will affect the quality of the tender. The tenderer must review and compare the bid, and then select the best candidate to win the bid. Its main work is as follows.

① Examining the tender documents, determining whether their contents meet the requirements of the tender documents, calculating correctly, and whether the technology is feasible, etc.

② To compare the conditions of the bidder's transaction, the bid winner can be determined by grading or collective evaluation or voting. The initially identified bid winner may be one or several alternate candidates.

③ To review the qualifications of the successful candidate. If the first winning bidder is qualified through review, he will be the successful candidate for the bidding.

Otherwise, review the alternate bid winners in turn.

Where any of the following situations occur, the tenderer may declare the bidding failure and reorganize the second round of bidding.

①Too few bidders are participating in the bidding and all tenders are not competitive and do not meet the bidding requirements.

②The bidding price is obviously higher than the average price in the international market.

**5. Sign the Contract**

After determining the winning bidder, the tenderer shall notify the winning bidder in writing to sign the contract at the place where the tenderer is located within the prescribed time limit, and shall pay the performance guarantee or the bank guarantee as the performance guarantee.

## 10.5.3 Mode of Bidding

There are three types and four kinds of bidding adopted internationally.

**1. Competitive Bidding**

International competitive bidding (ICB) refers to a tenderer inviting several or even dozens of bidders to participate in bidding, and selecting the most favorable bidder for the bid through competition from most bidders. The government purchases materials mostly through competitive bidding. International competitive bidding is usually done in two ways:①Open bidding. An open bid is an unlimited competitive bidding. When adopting this practice, the tenderer shall publish tender advertisements in major domestic and foreign newspapers and shall have the opportunity to purchase tender materials for bidding by anyone interested in the contents of the tender.②Selected bidding. Selective bidding, also known as invitation bidding, is a limited competitive bidding. When adopting this practice, the tenderer does not publish advertisement on the newspaper, but according to oneself specific business relation and intelligence data are invited to the travelling trader by the tenderer, after conducting pre-qualifying examination, by them again undertake bidding.

**2. Negotiation and Bidding**

Negotiated bidding, also called negotiation, it is an open, competitive bidding. This kind of tender looks for a few merchant to negotiation. If negotiation is successful, trade is reached.

**3. Two-Stage Bidding**

Two-stage bidding is a comprehensive way of bidding for unlimited competition and limited competition. When adopting this method, first use open tender, use again choose tender to undertake in two paragraph.

# 10.6 International Exhibitions

## 10.6.1 Concepts of the Exhibition

The exhibition is a large-scale event that uses all kinds of media and means to popularize products, publicize corporate image and establish good public relations. It is a complex, intuitive, and vivid way of communication, providing opportunities for direct two-way communication with the public. It is a highly focused and efficient way of communication, and a comprehensive large-scale public relations thematic event. All social organizations attach great importance to using exhibitions to shape and present their best images. Participating in exhibitions can help enterprises to explore domestic and foreign markets and play a vital role in the development strategy.

In the modern exhibition industry, exhibitions in the broad sense can include all forms of exhibitions, while in the narrow sense, exhibitions specifically refer to trade and publicity exhibitions. Exhibition, with characteristics of trade, can be defined as "in a series of fixed location or location with a specific date and time limit, by showing to achieve social form of products, services, information exchange, including propaganda, propaganda policy achievement, popularize knowledge of science and technology, set up the company image, understand market trends, such as". It can help the businessmen make the biggest deals in the shortest time, in the smallest space, at the least cost.

## 10.6.2 Classification of the Exhibition

In practice, exhibition name is quite complex, such as fair, exhibition, show, mart, display, export. Other exhibitions use non-technical terms, such as day, week, market and center, such as the Australian National Field Days, Berlin International Green Week, the International Carpet and Rug Market in Atlanta, the World Center for office-information and Telecommunication.

In English, fair is a traditional form of exhibition, fair and temple fair. Exhibition refers to the modern exhibition of trade nature developed on the basis of fairs and temple fairs, which is usually used as the general term of various forms of exhibitions. Those comprehensive exhibitions with large scale and complex contents are still called fair in English. In China, expositions should be distinguished between large and modern comprehensive exhibitions or traditional rural fairs. In English, the original meaning of "show" is "display". But in the United States, Canada and other countries, "show" has been replaced by "exhibition". In these countries, trade fairs are mostly called "show" and propaganda exhibitions are called exhibition. Exposition originated in France and is an exhibition of French. Since this kind of exhibition does not trade, mainly for the purpose of publicity, exposition has the meaning of "publicity exhibition". Since exhibitions of a promotional nature are held in many other countries and because of the influence of the francophone world, as well as the headquarters of the world's two major exhibition organizations, the league of international fairs and the bureau of international fairs, are located in France.

## 10.6.3 Classification of Exhibitions

Exhibitions can be classified according to their nature, content, scale, time and venue. For example:

### 1. Nature of Exhibition

The nature of the exhibition is usually determined by the exhibition organizers and can be reflected by the visitors' ingredients. Trade exhibitions are open to business and industry. Exhibitions open to the public are mainly consumer exhibitions.

### 2. Exhibition Contents

There are two types of exhibitions, namely comprehensive exhibition and professional exhibition. The comprehensive exhibition refers to the exhibition covering the whole industry or several industries, also known as horizontal exhibition, such as industrial exhibition, light industry exhibition. The professional exhibitions are exhibitions that show only a certain industry or even a certain product. The professional exhibitions often hold seminars and lectures at the same time to introduce new products and technologies.

### 3. Exhibition Scale

Exhibitions are divided into international, national, regional and local exhibitions as well as exclusive exhibitions by individual companies. Exhibitions of different sizes have different features and advantages and should be selected according to the conditions and needs of enterprises.

### 4. Exhibition Time

There are two kinds of exhibition, including regular and irregular, such as four times a year, twice a year, once a year, or once every two years. Non-scheduled exhibitions are held according to needs and conditions, both long-term and short-term. The long run can be three months, six months, or even permanent, while the short run usually does not exceed one month. The professional trade fairs in developed countries are usually three days.

### 5. Exhibition Area

Most exhibitions are held in special exhibition venues. The exhibition venue is divided into indoor and outdoor venues. Among them, indoor venues are mainly used for displaying regular exhibits, such as textile exhibitions and electronic exhibitions. Outdoor venues are mainly used to display super large and overweight exhibits, such as air shows and mine equipment exhibitions. Exhibitions held in several places are called tour exhibitions.

## 10.6.4 The Object and Orientation of Enterprises' Participation

Exhibitors should have high quality and capacity to participate, be able to accurately judge the value of the exhibition, and make wise and scientific decision to participate. The exhibitors should try their best to achieve: the purpose of the exhibition is clear, the effect of the exhibition is obvious, and the satisfaction of the exhibition is high.

Mature exhibitors are more likely to achieve the success of the exhibition, achieve the enterprises' participation goals, and successfully complete the international marketing plan, because they are consistent with the selected exhibition in spirit and values. The objectives and orientation of enterprises' participation can be set through the following five aspects.

① An internationally renowned exhibition is actually an industry annual conference. Every link from the industry association to the industry chain is gathered in a space-time, which is a spring tide of industry information coming, and the market information feedback is fast, efficient and high quality. The world class brand expo can gather the most influential media in the industry to participate. Most of the exhibitions have press conferences on market policies and industrial market macro trend analysis and special topics BBS. Over 50% of the enterprises will release the latest product information to target consumers through the exhibition. Disseminating information and collecting information is the most basic goal for enterprises to participate in the exhibition.

② The exhibition is a fair market for buying and selling, a special place for enterprises to conduct business transactions, and its position is an independent third party. Its certification of exhibition products is equivalent to third-party certification and has certain objective authority. For example, Guizhou Moutai Liquor was named as "state banquet wine" by Premier Zhou En-lai in the 1970s for President Nixon, because it was selected as a gold award during the Panama World Exposition in San Francisco of the United States in 1915. Therefore, product evaluation and certification at the exhibition is one of the main purposes for enterprises to participate in marketing.

③ The exhibition as an industry event, within 3—5 days, the industry parties come together in an exhibition venues, equal communication with others, contact customers, meet new customer, find potential clients, spying on competitors, to inspect the new product. All activities are based on the personal experience, became the most direct resources of first-hand information for the corporate decision makers. The experience is unique, timely and forward-looking, and it is one of the most important irreplaceable features of the exhibition as the international trade mode is different from other trade modes. A single exhibition can often be a profound and memorable experience.

④ The internationally renowned exhibition seems to have its own "soul", and can advocate and spread a kind of idea, which can control consumption behavior, may explode popularity in the consumption market, and may cause revolution in production mode in the production data market. For example, the Hanover industrial expo can give visitors a strong experience and enable them to form a "polarization" and "magnetization" in their hearts. And this function is strong enough, and can solidify into a kind of "idea", forming the unique "idea value" of the exhibitors: as long as the enterprises can participate in this exhibition, it is enough to show that the enterprises can keep up with the consumer market and have enough ability to compete with the competitors of this industry.

⑤ The mature exhibitors know how to use the exhibition to influence their consumer groups, compete with competitors and become the "spiritual leader" of a consumer group. An exhibition of spiritual leadership is a kind of life style appraiser and guardian according to a set of clear values. Through the exhibition and various related activities held by it, the understanding of the concept advocated is promoted, and a universal value concept or value belief platform is "made" for the vast number of exhibitors, thus bringing huge commercial effects. For example, the Frankfurt lighting exhibition is called "the Mecca of the world lighting industry". It is the holy land of the whole life of the global lighting industry and a barometer of the latest development of the world lighting industry and the market. The mature exhibitors are proud to attend such an exhibition, which not only reflects the strength of the enterprise, but also makes the exhibitors have a sense of belonging.

## 10.6.5 Rules and Requirements for Participation

### 1. Booth Design

The exhibition has restrictions on the exhibition stands and exhibits, especially on the double-deck exhibition stands, staircases, and the structure extending outward from the top of the booth. The height limits are often not a prohibition on super elevation. If you go through the procedures and meet the technical standards, you may be allowed to build super-high booths and arrange exhibits. At the same time, many exhibitions have banned completely closed booths. If the booth is closed, the exhibition will lose its usefulness and visitors will complain. However, exhibitors can close their offices, negotiating rooms and warehouses, etc. Therefore, a certain proportion of the booth area must be open to the outside, and the area of this part is generally required to be more than 70%, while the remaining area under 30% is allowed to be closed.

### 2. Exhibition Equipment

The materials for exhibition racks and fittings shall be of materials treated with fire prevention, and the use of plastics and hazardous chemicals shall be restricted. Most of the national exhibitions also have strict regulations on the use of electrical appliances, and the technical indicators of the appliances must comply with local regulations and requirements.

### 3. Aisle of Booth

In order to guarantee the smooth flow of people, the width of footpath shall meet the requirement of regulation, the exhibition stand and its displayed products are prohibited to occupy the footpath, the TV can't face to the footpath and the counter must leave footpath a certain distance.

### 4. Fire Protection Facilities

If it is a large area of the booth, it must be proportional to the size of the pavilion and the expected number of visitors, emergency access or exit, and signs, with fire equipment. Some exhibitions require exhibitors to appoint fire chief and require all exhibitors to know fire regulations and emergency exits.

### 5. Exhibit Requirements

For super high and overweight exhibits, they generally need to enter the museum before other exhibits, and to discuss with the exhibition organizers or exhibition owners as soon as possible. As long as appropriate measures are taken, they can generally be solved. For the ultra high exhibits, as long as the height of the exhibition hall enough, can discuss with the exhibition hall. For overweight exhibits, the floor holder can be used to disperse the unit load. For the ultra-wide exhibits, the most difficult problem to solve is the size of the unloading gate of the exhibition hall, but exhibition organizers are generally willing to help. Due to safety concerns, some exhibitions limit the operation of machines. For weapons, there are usually special regulations and procedures are cumbersome.

### 6. Exhibition Environment

Background music is arranged by the organizer of the exhibition. The sound volume of the exhibitor's audio and video equipment must be controlled within the scope that does not affect the exhibitors around. If the exhibition organizers want to achieve a coordinated effect, they will often put forward color requirements, requiring exhibitors to use some basic tone or title tone. In addition, the exhibition may also put forward on the title font, size of the provisions, but this is mostly relaxed. As long as the exhibitors abide by the regulations and do not disturb the surrounding booth (such as too much noise), they can generally design the shape of the booth, place the exhibits and use colors at will.

### 7. Exhibition Labor

Many countries, particularly developed ones, require workers to be registered in trade unions and do not allow exhibitors to do their own work. In New York, if an exhibitor picks up a hammer to hammer a nail, local workers will grab the hammer to stop the exhibitor from working. It may sound ridiculous, but it is true and must be obeyed.

**8. Arranging Exhibition Procedures**

Most exhibitors are required to submit their designs for review and to go through formalities before construction.

## 10.6.6 China's Exhibition Industry

China's exhibition industry has been developing rapidly in various cities. Beijing, Shanghai, Guangzhou, Dalian and Chengdu are the five most active exhibition cities, forming five exhibition economic industrial belts, including "Bohai Rim, Yangtze River Delta, Pearl River Delta, Northeast China and Central & Western China".

### 1. Bohai Exhibition Economic Belt

With Beijing as the center and Tianjin, Langfang and other cities as the focus, has early development, large scale and large quantity of exhibition industry, high degree of specialization and internationalization, complete categories, and concentrated and extensive exhibition of well-known brands.

### 2. Yangtze River Delta Exhibition Economic Belt

With Shanghai as the center and Nanjing, Hangzhou, Ningbo, Suzhou and other cities as the support.This industrial belt has a high starting point, strong government support, reasonable planning and layout, and rich trade, which is greatly influenced by regional advantages and industrial structure and has huge development potential.

### 3. Pearl River Delta Exhibition Economic Belt

With Guangzhou as the center, Canton Fair as the booster, and Shenzhen, Zhuhai, Xiamen and Dongguan as the support, forms an exhibition economic belt with high degree of internationalization and modernization, prominent features of exhibition industrial structure, and dense distribution of exhibition area and industry.

### 4. Northeast Exhibition Economic Belt

With Dalian as the center, Shenyang, Changchun and other cities as the focus, forms brands exhibition like Changchun automobile expo,Shenyang manufacturing expo and Dalian garment exhibition by relying on industrial advantages of the northeast industrial base and regional advantages of northeast Asia.

### 5. Central and Western Exhibition Economic Belt

With Chengdu as the center and Chongqing, Xi'an and other cities as the focus, has formed brand exhibitions such as Chengdu western international fair, Chongqing hi-tech fair and Xi 'an east and west fair through continuous development.

## ☞ Case 10.2

### China Import and Export Commodities Fair

China import and export commodities fair, also called Canton fair, founded in the spring of 1957, held in Guangzhou during the spring and autumn every year. It is undertaken by China foreign trade center and jointly organized by Ministry of Commerce and Guangdong People's Government. Currently, it is the oldest, largest and best comprehensive international trade event with most complete variety of commodity, numbers of distribution and purchasers of nationality, clinch deals with best effect and credibility.

Since the 101st session of April 15, 2007, Canton fair has been renamed as China import and export fair by China export commodities fair, and changed from a single export platform to a two-way trading platform. China's trade in import and export commodities fair is flexible and diversified. In addition to traditional sample transaction, Virtual Expo (Online Exhibition) is also held. The Canton fair is mainly engaged in export trade, but also in import business. It can also carry out various forms of economic and technological cooperation and exchanges, as well as business activities such as commodity inspection, insurance, transportation, advertising and consultation. Businessmen from all over the world gathered in Guangzhou to exchange business and enhance friendship.

By 2020, Canton fair has experienced 63 years of development, reform and innovation have withstood all kinds of severe test, never interrupt, strengthened the trade of China and the world, display the image and development achievements of China. It is also a good platform for Chinese enterprises to exploit the international market, to implement the guiding demonstration base of China's foreign trade development strategy. It has become the first platform for promoting China's foreign trade and is honored as the barometer and weathervane of China's foreign trade. It is the window, epitome and symbol of China's opening up to the outside world. By the end of the 122nd session, the Canton fair had a total export volume of about 129.37 billion US dollars, with a total of about 8.22 million overseas buyers. At present, the exhibition scale of each session of Canton fair reaches 1,185,000 square meters, with nearly 25,000 domestic and overseas exhibitors, and about 200,000 overseas buyers from over 210 countries and regions attending the conference.

Mr. Xi Jinping, the General Secretary of the CPC, the State President and Chairman of central military commission sent a message at the opening of the 120th Canton fair in October 2016. Premier Li Keqiang fully affirmed the important position and active contribution of Canton fair in the direction of China's reform, opening up and economic and social development. In the new period, it owns great significance for the Canton fair to promote reform and innovation for further expand the opening to the outside world , cultivating new foreign trade competitive advantage, speed up the construction of economic power. Canton fair will continue to be a world-class platform for all-round opening-up in the new era of "selling the world and buying the world", and make new contributions to the development of China's economic and trade powers and its open economy.

# 10.7 Commodities Exchange

## 10.7.1 Concept of Commodities Exchange

Commodities exchange is an organized market in which a specific commodity is bought or sold according to certain regulatory procedures. Only members can trade on the commodities exchange, while others or businesses can trade through regular members or brokers. Commodities traded on commodity exchanges are generally standardized raw materials and are traded on standardized contracts. Commodity exchanges offer spot and futures trading, but mainly futures trading. Many agricultural products, non-ferrous metal raw materials, etc. are mainly traded in commodity exchanges. Futures transaction is a type of trade in which buyers and sellers, under certain rules, bargain with shouts and gestures and compete fiercely to complete a transaction.

## 10.7.2 Differences Between Futures Trading and Spot Trading

Futures trading is different from spot trading in commodities. In the case of spot transactions, buyers and sellers can, in any way, make physical transactions at any time and place. The seller must deliver the actual goods and the buyer must pay for the goods. Futures trading, on the other hand, is the buying and selling of futures at a certain time in a particular futures market, that is, in a Commodity Exchange, in accordance with the "standard futures contract" prepared by the exchange. The buyer and seller do not transfer ownership of the goods after the transaction.

Futures trading has the following characteristics.

①Futures trading does not require both parties to provide or accept actual goods. The result of the transaction is not the transfer of actual goods, but the difference in price between the date of signing the contract or the date of execution of the contract and the date of performance.

②A futures contract is a standard futures contract established by an exchange and can only be traded according to the commodity standards and categories specified by the exchange. The delivery date of futures trading is determined according to the delivery date specified by the exchange. Futures contracts must be registered and settled at clearing houses set up on each exchange.

### 10.7.3 Types of Futures Trading

Futures trading, according to the purpose of the trader, has two kinds of different natures: ①Using the futures contract as the gambling. Through buying and selling, chasing profits from the difference of price fluctuation. ②Hedging, refers to the speculators estimate that the price will rise, buying futures. Once the delivery price rises, then sell the futures, from which earn the difference.

## 10.8 Processing Trade

### 10.8.1 Concept

Processing trade mainly includes processing of supplied materials and assembling of supplied parts. Processing and assembling trade of supplied materials means that all or part of raw materials, auxiliary materials, spare parts, components, parts and packages are provided by foreign merchants. If necessary, equipment should be provided, which shall be processed and assembled by one party according to the requirements of the other party. The price of the equipment provided by the other party shall be paid in the form of payment of wages.

### 10.8.2 Classification

Processing and assembling trade of supplied materials can be divided into:

①Processing and assembling of all incoming materials and parts. The foreign consignor shall provide all raw and auxiliary materials and components. After being processed by the undertaking enterprise, the finished products shall be delivered to the foreign consignor, and the manufactured products and finished products shall not be priced.

②Processing and assembling of some supplied materials and parts. Part of the finished products to be processed and assembled by the foreign entrusting party shall be provided by the receiving party. The government receiving party shall collect the price of the materials provided in addition to the payment for work.

③The corresponding contract shall be made at each price. The foreign consignor and the contractor sign two counterpart contracts: one is the sales contract of raw materials and components provided by the consignor and the other is the contract of the contractor's export of finished products. For all incoming materials, two contract price difference is pay. For some pieces of incoming materials, the price difference between the two contracts shall include both the payment for work and the price of materials provided by domestic receivers. The processing and assembling trade conducted by means of counterpart contract shall be indicated in the contract. The receiver does not have to pay foreign exchange.

Processing and assembling business, for entrusting party, is to use the labor service of the receiver to reduce product cost. For the receiver, it is a kind of labor service output with goods as the carrier.

## 10.8.3 Contract for Processing and Assembling of Supplied Materials

Foreign processing and assembling business is a kind of labor service trade, the party concerned about the contract is entrusting party and accepting party. There are many differences from general contract of sale of goods. The main contents are as follows:

**1. Subject Matter of the Contract**

The object of the sales contract is commodity, while the object of the processing and assembling contract is labor service, that is, labor and certain technology or technology paid for the processing and assembling of raw materials and components into specified products. In order to explain the nature of the labor services provided, the content and requirements of processing and assembling business should be specified.

**2. Regulations on Incoming Materials**

The quality and quantity of materials shall be stipulated in the contract, and the time and place of delivery by the consignor shall be specified. In order to clarify the responsibility, the consignor shall specify the treatment method in the contract for the failure of the consignor to provide materials in accordance with quality, quantity and time.

**3. Provisions for the Delivery of Finished Products**

The specifications, quality, delivery quantity and delivery time of the finished products to be delivered shall be clearly stipulated in the contract. For example, in case the contractor fails to deliver the finished product as stipulated in the contract, it shall be liable for damages accordingly.

**4. Provisions on Consumption Rate and Defective Rate**

Consumption rate refers to the amount of raw materials or components to be consumed per unit product. Defective rate refers to the proportion of unqualified products in all products. These two indicators are directly related to the product cost and are limited by the technological level and production conditions of the processing party. Therefore, both parties shall set a reasonable standard through consultation, and the processing party shall bear the responsibility for exceeding the specified ratio.

### 5. Regulations on Wage Payment

Processing and assembling business is a kind of labor service trade essentially, pay cost embodies the value of labor service namely. The regulation of pay cost of work, should take international labor service price as reference standard, to our country, take the salary level of southeast Asia as computation standard, consult the labor service quality that processing enterprise provides and production efficiency, the pay cost of work that collect should be both profitable, have competition ability again.

### 6. Transportation and Insurance

In the process of processing and assembling trade, the ownership of materials and finished products shall not be transferred, and the ownership shall be owned by the entrusting party, and the liability of transportation and insurance shall be borne by the entrusting party. In the specific business, the transportation and insurance of exported finished products, as well as the import and storage of materials and materials, can be handled on behalf of the recipient, the cost will be paid by the entrusting party or included in the payment of wages.

### 7. Payment Method

There are two ways of payment by the entrusting party to the receiving party: the payment of goods and finished products is not priced, and the entrusting party shall pay the payment to the receiving party through letter of credit or remittance. The difference between the parts and the finished products shall be the payment of labor fee. Attention must be paid to the time interval between forward and spot to take into account the time required in the whole process of processing so as to ensure payment for finished goods is received before payment for materials.

## 10.8.4 The Management of Processing and Assembling Trade in China

### 1. The Contract Submitted for Approval

Foreign processing and assembling contracts must be examined and approved by the ministry of foreign economic relations and trade, the relevant ministries and commissions under the state council, or the departments of foreign trade and economic cooperation of provinces, autonomous regions and municipalities directly under the central government, or by agencies authorized by them. The "processing and assembling trade declaration form" should be completed in quadruplicate and attached with a copy of the contract.

### 2. Customs Registration and Filing

Submit approval documents and copy of the contract to the customs within one month from the date of approval of the contract. List of materials, parts and equipment, if necessary. After examination and verification, the customs will issue a "registration manual for foreign processing and assembling import and export goods". The customs shall not release the import and export goods of a unit that has not been registered.

**3. Supervision of Import and Export Goods**

When materials, equipment and finished products are imported or exported, the related units or their agents should fill out the declaration form for import and export goods in quadruplicate, invoice, packing list and other relevant documents, and the "registration manual" should be declared to the customs at the place of import and export. After the customs accepts the declaration, it will be released after inspection and approval. Processing and assembling trade imports of materials, customs bonded goods. The customs shall accept the supervision and control from the date of import to the date of export of finished products. The relevant units must include the use of imported materials and the export of processed finished products in special accounts approved by the customs, and the customs has the right to inspect them at any time.

**4. Cancel after Verification**

After the completion of the processing and assembling contract, the unit concerned shall, within one month from the date of the export of the last batch of finished products, handle the verification and cancellation procedures with the customs with the "registration manual" and the import and export goods declaration form. The remaining materials shall be levied and exempted according to different circumstances. If the imported materials, parts or finished products are converted to domestic sales for various reasons, they must be approved by the original examination and approval authority and the customs, and customs duties and import VAT shall be levied on the general imported goods

## 10.8.5 Compensation Trade

Compensation trade is also known as product resale, which refers to the equipment technology imported by one trading party on the basis of credit provided by the other party. Products produced by the equipment technology are deducted by stages for the price and interest of imported equipment technology.

Early compensation trade was mainly used to build large industrial enterprises. For example, the Soviet union imported $860 million worth of mining equipment from Japan in return for 100 million tons of coal. Poland imported $400 million worth of chemical equipment and technology from the United States, which was offset by the resale of related industrial products. In the later stage, compensation trade tends to be diversified. There are not only large complete sets of equipment, but also small and medium-sized projects. In the 1980s, for example, 40 to 50 per cent of Poland's exports of electronics and machinery to the west were resold as compensation. In the same period, China has widely adopted the method of compensation trade and introduced foreign advanced technology and equipment, but the scale is small, mostly for small projects. In recent years, as foreign direct investment in equipment and technology is widely used in China, compensation trade is decreasing. However, with the development of China's market economy, the advantages of compensation trade in utilizing foreign capital and promoting product sales cannot be ignored.

### 1. Role of Equipment Technology Importers

The enterprises can introduce equipment technology to solve the problems caused by capital shortage, equipment update, technological transformation, upgrade products and enhance their market competitiveness, including the international market and the domestic market. The equipment technology importer resells the products, making use of the overseas sales channels of the equipment exporter while offsetting the technical price of the equipment to bring the products into the foreign market. Although techniques of equipment introduced in the form of compensation trade are often not very advanced, or even second-hand equipment, if the products can be sold and the equipment price is reasonable, it will be beneficial for developing countries to increase the export of products, expand domestic employment opportunities and improve the level of regional economic development.

### 2. Role of the Technology Exporter

The exporter may expand the export of equipment and technology on the basis of providing credit. For the need of transferring industry, the exporter transfers the industry to the developing countries through compensation trade, which not only gains the price of transferring equipment and technology, but also makes profits from the sales of returned commodities. The multinational corporations take compensation trade as a means to expand the sales of capital goods, expand the export of equipment and technology through compensation trade, and obtain double profits.

Compensation trade is a barter trade. In exchange of equipment technology and related products, the supplier shall not only assume the required equipment technology, but also undertake the sales of related compensation products. If the supplier is a single equipment manufacturer, it is difficult to accept this way of trade. With the rapid development of of multinational companies, the forward economic integration of production enterprises has been perfected day by day. The multinational companies have established a wide range of sales agents or their own sales companies at home and abroad, thus having the ability to sell the relevant resale products.

The in-depth development of international industrial transfer has become a strong promoting factor of compensation trade. With the further development of the division of labor in the world, the economies of some developing countries have made considerable progress. The sound investment environment enables developed countries to transfer some technology and capital-intensive industries to developing countries. Although most of the industry transfers are to capture foreign markets, a significant proportion of the products are resold or used to assemble the parts of the machine. The exporter of the equipment technology shall profit mainly from the resale of the products, not mainly from the export of the equipment technology. The equipment and technology importers, by means of credit, introduced relatively advanced equipment and technology, which not only established the production base, but also exported the products, becoming another basis for the possibility of compensation trade.

The advanced equipment technology is the main contradiction between the two sides in compensation trade. In order to strengthen the control of advanced technology and equipment and face the fierce market competition, some enterprises in developed countries have adopted different ways in industrial transfer, and direct investment is common. Only use the land, labor, raw materials and power resources of the host country, but control the ownership and use right of production technology and equipment in their own hands. Because compensation trade has double profit attraction to equipment technology exporter, it also makes importer have the ability to strive for the introduction of advanced equipment technology.

### 3. Notices to Compensation Trade

To carry out compensation trade business, three aspects must be focused on:

①Advanced, applicable and supporting measures of imported equipment technology. The imported equipment and technologies must be clearly defined in terms of their quality assurance and technical cooperation. The technology should be at least ahead of the domestic level, and the equipment supplier, which is also relatively advanced internationally, should also guarantee the industrial property rights.

②Provisions for the resale of products to offset the technical price of equipment. Buyback is the basic obligation of equipment exporter. China usually compensates with direct products in compensation trade. But in a specific deal, there is a different approach:

(a) Full compensation. All equipment technical costs shall be offset by equal amount of resale products.

(b) Partial compensation. The equipment importer shall pay part of the cash, and the rest of the price shall be compensated by the resale of the products.

(c) Excessive compensation, requiring the equipment exporter to promise to buy back the returned goods in excess of the compensation amount.

(d) Compensation for relevant labor services. This is a kind of compensation trade that combines the processing of supplied materials, that is, after the introduction of equipment technology, accepting the processing business of incoming parts from the other side, offsetting the technical cost of equipment with the payment of wages.

③Repayment term and settlement method. The repayment period is directly related to the quantity and price of the returned goods. The price setting principles, pricing standards and methods of the resale goods must be specified, and the repayment period shall be arranged by stipulating the quantity or amount of the resale goods. Although compensation trade is the product of compensation equipment, but is not direct barter trade, both sides still have to pay through currency. The equipment importer must master the principle of first collection and second payment, and choose an appropriate settlement method.

Compensation trade is an effective way to make use of foreign capital to import equipment by utilizing the sales capacity of the equipment exporter and entering the foreign market. At present, international economic cooperation is developing rapidly, and the scope of industrial transfer has broken through labor-intensive industries and extended to technology-intensive and capital-intensive industries. Chinese enterprises should seize this opportunity and make full use of their advantages to make use of the unique advantages of compensation trade in profit distribution, market control and independent operation.

# 10.9 Leasing Trade

## 10.9.1 Concept of Leasing Trade

Leasing trade is one of the most active trade modes in contemporary economic transactions. More than one-third of the fixed asset investment in developed countries is realized through leasing trade. Whether in domestic or international trade, leasing market is a very attractive market for both supply and demand parties. The owner of the leased equipment shall enter into a lease with the lessee to deliver the equipment to the lessee for use at a rent.

The leasing objects are mainly capital goods, including electronic equipment, transport equipment, construction machinery, medical equipment, aircraft and ships and various large complete sets of equipment and facilities. The lessor generally shall be the financial institution, namely the leasing company attached to the bank or the trust investment company, or the professional leasing company or the production manufacturer to concurrently operate the leasing business of its own products. The tenant is usually a production or service business. Where the lessor provides the lessee with the necessary equipment, the lessee shall pay the lessor the rental on a regular basis and the ownership of the equipment belongs to the lessor. The lessee shall obtain the right of use.

## 10.9.2 Classification of Leasing Trade

Leasing trade can be divided into financing lease, operating lease, sublease and back lease.

### 1. Financial Lease

The subject matter of financial leasing is mainly equipment purchased by the leasing company and selected by the user. The lease term of the finance lease is long, and usually the lease term ends (close to the use period of the equipment). After the full rent is paid, the ownership of the equipment is transferred to the lessee, or the equipment is owned after the user pays the residual value. The lessee bought the equipment in installments. During the lease term, the equipment shall be owned by the user. Only one user will be hired during the whole equipment life. The leasing company collects the rent from the lessee according to the cost of equipment, interest and fees, so it is also called "full payment lease" or "one-time lease". Financial leasing is the most basic form of leasing.

### 2. Operating Lease

The lease term of an operating lease is relatively short, and the owner of the equipment must rent it out several times to recover the equipment investment and other expenses. During the term of validity of the equipment, not only one user is leased, but each user only pays a part of the equipment investment, so it is also known as "incomplete payment" lease. During the lease term, the lessor shall provide equipment maintenance services to keep the equipment in good condition for re-lease. For the lessee, this way of leasing and the services provided enables him to obtain the high-tech equipment which is always in normal operation, but the rent is also relatively high. The subject matter of operating lease is general equipment. When the lessee only needs to use some general equipment for a short period of time, this rental method is often adopted. The lessor of operating lease is usually a leasing company or a professional leasing company operated by the manufacturer.

### 3. Sublease

When China introduces foreign equipment in the way of leasing, the leasing company in China usually leases the equipment to foreign companies as the lessee, and then sublets the equipment to domestic users. On the one hand, the leasing company, which operates the sublease business, provides the user enterprise with credit guarantee, that is, it bears the responsibility of paying the rent in its own name. On the other hand, it undertakes the negotiation and signing of foreign-related lease contract for users, as well as import procedures and costs. In addition to transacting lease, leasing companies in China also serve as intermediary agencies to introduce foreign leasing companies to domestic user enterprises and directly sign contracts with foreign companies. China's leasing companies issued a letter of guarantee for domestic lessee regular payment of rent.

### 4. Lease Back

The lessee shall lease to the lessor its own facilities. Its practice is signed lease agreement first by tenant and lessor, sign buy and sell a contract again next, buy by lessor content, lease its to tenant, namely original owner. This lease is mainly used for real estate, and the tenant is short of funds to sell the real estate to raise the required funds. Leaseback belongs to finance lease, the price of the subject matter will be Shared among the rent of each period. However, in the leaseback business, the price of the subject matter does not reflect the true market price, but more depends on the amount of money needed by the lessee. Of course, it is impossible to exceed the actual market price.

Leasing trade usually has three parties: lessor, lessee and supplier. After the lessee selects the required equipment and the supplier, the leasing company will discuss the purchase. General procedures for leasing trade are shown in Figure 10.4.

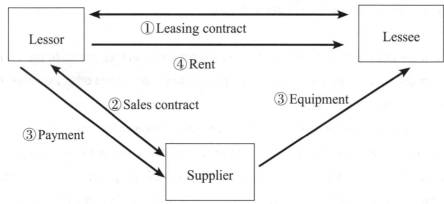

Figure 10.4  Basic Practices of Leasing Trade

Leasing trade is a trade way to realize medium and long term financing through the form of financial materials. Its essence is that the lessor provides credit to the lessee. Leasing trade is conducted on a credit basis. In the leasing trade, unless the lessee himself has a good enough reputation, after being evaluated by the leasing company, the leasing may be realized within a certain amount. However, under normal circumstances, the leasing company requires the lessee to provide financial guarantee, such as the letter of guarantee issued by the bank, investment trust company, insurance company. From the perspective of utilizing foreign capital and introducing equipment, leasing is similar to medium - and long-term credit and deferred payment in general. There are unique advantages for both parties.

If the equipment is purchased with medium and long term credit or deferred payment, it will be recorded in the balance sheet of the enterprise. The leased equipment, on the other hand, does not serve as the liability record of the enterprise and does not affect the debt capacity of the enterprise. Even if companies can buy equipment with their own money. If the leasing mode is changed, the working capital turnover capacity can be enhanced and the asset quality of the enterprise can be improved. The rent paid by the lessee may be included in the cost of production or operation, thus reducing the amount of the enterprise's tax payer;

The lessee may select the manufacturer and the required equipment according to its own needs and determine the technical indicators. As a big buyer in the market, the leasing company usually has a superior negotiating position and can purchase equipment at a relatively favorable price, thus reducing the rent paid by the lessee. The lessee only has to reach an agreement with the leasing company to import the equipment by way of leasing, while the money to implement and purchase the equipment are all taken care of by the leasing company. As a result, business links are reduced and the time required for the equipment to be put in place is relatively short. The lessee can share the tax relief and operational advantages enjoyed by the leasing company, so as to reduce rent expenditure. The rent paid by the lessee, including equipment price, interest and rental fee, is generally fixed during the lease term, while the interest rate of medium and long-term loan is usually fluctuating and tends to rise.

The international market is the buyer's market, the lessee as the user has certain advantages. Taking full advantage of this advantage, under certain conditions, it is more realistic and economical than direct access to foreign export credit, and more advantageous to the equipment importer in terms of income distribution and operation control than foreign direct investment.

The lessor purchases equipment for leasing business, as the owner of equipment, can enjoy investment tax reduction, as well as depreciation or accelerated depreciation policies preferential.

As a lessor, leasing trade is also a kind of financial business, thus expanding the funds to the market. Due to have the ownership of the equipment and should produce the pledge loan risk is lesser, professional leasing company as a lessor, generally only need to pay for the purchased equipment of 20% — 40%, and the rest to the ownership of the equipment and rent the transfer rights as collateral by Banks and other financial institutions to provide loans, but the lessor still enjoys all tax benefits. Some large manufacturing companies are setting up rental companies to expand their export business through leasing. Leasing is an effective way to promote expensive and relatively old equipment.

The main items constituting the rent include the purchase cost of the subject matter of the lease, interest and expenses during the lease term, operating expenses, taxes and profits. Generally, the following formula can be used: Rent =(Acquisition Cost — Estimated Residue Value of the Subject Matter+ Interest + Taxes + Expenses + Profits + Operating Expenses)/ Lease period.

Among them, interest is the most important. It is related to the lease term. The longer the lease term, the higher the corresponding interest rate will be. The rent is also related to the capital source of the leasing company and the preferential tax exemption. Financial leasing is a one-off lease, so the longest lease term can be consistent with the validity of the equipment. However, if the lessee has sufficient capacity to pay, shortening the lease term without causing too much burden on the enterprise will help reduce the interest burden.

Take financial leasing as an example to illustrate the general practice of international leasing trade.

①Entrusted lease. The user enterprise shall notify the leasing company of the selected articles and fill in the leasing authorization letter. The letter of authorization shall include the assets and liabilities status and operating indicators of the enterprise. If necessary, state the guarantees available.

②Subject matter to be purchased. The terms of trade for the purchase of the subject matter shall be negotiated with the manufacturer or supplier of the subject matter by the user's business or leasing company or both parties.

③Sign the lease contract. When the terms of trade for the subject matter have been agreed upon, the leasing company will issue the rental valuation. The parties then agree on the terms and conditions of the lease term, rent, handover and acceptance of the subject matter of the lease, maintenance and insurance, and sign the lease contract.

④Sign a purchase contract. The leasing company signs the purchase contract with the manufacturer on the agreed terms of trade.

⑤Delivery and acceptance. The manufacturer delivers the goods directly to the customer according to the contract. The enterprise imports equipment by means of leasing, its procedure is equal to general import trade. Upon acceptance, the user enterprise shall issue the acceptance receipt to the leasing company as the lessee.

⑥Payment of rent and performance of contractual obligations. The lessee shall pay the rent regularly according to the provisions of the contract and perform other obligations specified in the contract. The leasing company shall be liable for insurance and maintenance in accordance with the contract. Financial leasing is generally maintained by users themselves.

⑦Stay for purchase upon expiration. After the expiry of a finance lease, the ownership of the subject matter normally belongs to the lessee. The lease contract may also stipulate that the user shall pay a certain amount of residual value of the equipment before taking ownership.

## 10.10 Cross-Border E-Commerce

The interactive operation mechanism provided by e-commerce provides a market environment with complete information for international trade. Through the link of the world economic operation, international trade reaches the optimal allocation of cross-border resources and production factors, enabling the market mechanism to play a full and effective role in the global scope. Cross-border e-commerce has broken through the operation format of traditional trade dominated by one-way logistics, established a new logistics system with capital flow as the form, information flow as the core and commodity flow as the main body, and provided all-round, multilevel and mufti-angle interactive services.

## 10.10.1 Innovative Performance of Cross-Border E-Commerce in International Trade

### 1. Virtual Management

The new cooperative and competitive mode of transnational corporations starts the reform of corporate organization and operation mode of the information society, breaks the organizational level and boundary of traditional corporations, and makes transnational corporations an open system. This kind of "virtual" internalization of external resources makes the company's operation develop to a flexible direction. All production links are incorporated into the network, and the technology of "virtual reality" is utilized to make intuitive coordination in the world.

### 2. The Virtual Corporation

The new type of international trade management, through the open system of dynamic network combination, looking for resources and the alliance, to adapt to the rapidly changing economic and competitive environment to develop in the direction of personalized, diversified consumer demand trend, bring multinational operator division of labor cooperation, resource interoperability, benefit sharing of benefits.

### 3. Virtual Market

It is the new operating environment for international trade. Through the exchange of online "virtual" information, the traditional market has broken through the limitations of the existing conditions in a certain region, and a unified large "market" linked by information network has been formed worldwide, which has promoted the process of economic globalization and the form ation of a new world market. Information activities have accelerated the global activities of production factors such as capital, goods and technology, and led to the rise of the global "network economy". In such an environment of Internet trade, economic and trade ties and cooperation among countries have been greatly strengthened.

## 10.10.2 The Impact of E-Commerce on International Trade

E-commerce will further boost the growth and development of trade by offering information exchange platforms that are faster, more convenient and cheaper than telephony. In the context of e-commerce, information becomes the most important production factors and resources, that is, the differences between countries in the production, feedback and use of information. Information resources play an increasingly important role in international trade. Cross-border e-commerce has become a new driving force for the development of international trade. E-commerce has broken through the time and space constraints, enabling information to be transmitted across borders and resource sharing, meeting the requirements of rapid growth of international trade and promoting the development of international trade. At present, the impact of e-commerce on international trade is constantly expanding in a profound way, which has brought profound changes in such aspects as international trade, international trade governance, international trade operation mechanism, international trade marketing means and international trade transportation mode. The specific manifestations are as follows.

### 1. Change the Traditional Mode of International Trade and Promoted Its Development

Through the internet virtual information exchange, electronic commerce opened up an open, multidimensional, three-dimensional market space, break the traditional market on the premise of a certain geographical space, and form a unified "big market" by the linkage of global information network.

### 2. Change the Operation Mode of International Trade and Greatly Improved Its Efficiency

The interactive network operating mechanism provided by e-commerce provides a relatively complete market environment for international trade, enabling information to be transmitted across borders and resource sharing, meeting the requirement of rapid growth of international trade, and thus promoting the development of international trade. E-commerce can lower transaction prices, making it possible for transactions that are too costly or difficult to execute.

### 3. Change the Operating Mechanism of International Trade

E-commerce has changed the traditional circulation mode, reduced the intermediate links, greatly shortened the distance between the supply chain and the demand chain between manufacturers and consumers, changed the traditional market structure, made the direct transaction between producers and consumers possible, and greatly reduced the operating and management costs of enterprises.

### 4. Add a New type of Operation Subject of International Trade

Modern information and communication technology, through the core technology possessed by a single company in their professional fields, connects many companies to each other as "virtual companies" operating through the company's network of groups. The completion of a market function that a company cannot undertake can provide goods and services to the market more effectively. This kind of virtual company can adapt to the rapidly changing economic competition environment and the trend of personalized and diversified consumption demands, and bring the benefits of labor division cooperation, complementary advantages, resource mutual utilization and benefit sharing to multinational companies.

**5. Change the Competitive Situation of International Trade**

First of all, the application of e-commerce is combined with the production and manufacturing activities of enterprises, which makes the products and services of enterprises closer to the market demand and helps improve the agility and adaptability of enterprise production. Secondly, the low cost and high speed of e-commerce make it possible for small and medium-sized enterprises with weak strength to participate in the large international trade, expand the international market, and give play to their flexible competitive advantages, which is conducive to the development of small and medium-sized enterprises. Thirdly, the powerful communication capability of the network and the convenient commodity transaction environment of e-commerce system shorten the actual gap between consumers and the marketers, and further change the communication mode between them. Enterprises can directly face consumers and communicate with them, thus jointly creating new market demands.

**6. More Choices Are Given to Consumers**

By means of e-commerce, enterprises spread information on the Internet in a multimedia way, and through intelligent search and inquiry, consumers can learn more information about goods and services through the Internet, such as more kinds of similar goods, stronger substitutability between products, and more choices for consumers. Consumers can personally participate in the design, production and evaluation of products, and become an important and active participant in the whole process of enterprise operation.

At the same time, online trade also provides convenience for small consumption, saves consumers' shopping time, and minimizes the gap between production and consumption, making on-demand consumption technically possible.

## 10.10.3 Problems Faced by Cross-Border E-commerce Development

With the rise of e-commerce, information technology has become an important factor in international trade. The information processing efficiency of a country or enterprise has become the basis and condition for it to participate in international competition. The development degree of information infrastructure and the scale proportion of information industry have greatly affected the competitive strength and competitive position of a country in international trade and even the world economy. However, cross-border e-commerce development also faces a series of problems, which are mainly reflected in the technical and legal aspects.

**1. Technical Level**

①EDI standard is not unified. In the period of EDI as the main carrier of electronic foreign trade, EDI required special hardware lines and different countries' different standard of message is the main problem. Data transmitted via EDI can only be decoded and used by buyers and sellers using uniform "message standards" (common language that both sender and receiver computers can recognize). After entering 2000, the replacement of traditional EDI by iEDI gradually solved this problem. IEDI has transplanted the traditional electronic data exchange to the Internet, which makes the data exchange free from the bondage of the special network VAN. However, the us EDI standard, which is mainly applicable to north American countries, is not unified with the United Nations EDI standard, which is mainly used in European and Asian countries, which brings a lot of inconvenience to the transmission of international trade information.

② EDI hardware cost is high and the application has security problems.EDI must use a dedicated Network hardware, namely VAN Network (Value - added Network), it not only need from telecom operating companies or government authority departments to apply for special line, and even if large import and export enterprises in the process of using EDI, e-commerce EDI applications that are directly dependent computer operating system are the varying degree existence safe hidden trouble.

**2. Legal Level**

① Withdrawal of offer, revocation and withdrawal of acceptance. With regard to the withdrawal of offer and acceptance, the legal requirement in time is "before" or "at the same time". Under EDI e-commerce, the delivery of offer and acceptance only takes a few seconds, so such "withdrawal" is completely impossible. Likewise, the withdrawal of an offer is not possible in e-commerce.

② Legal issues of electronic signature. Most of the traditional contracts and documents need to be signed by both parties before they can have legal effect. The corresponding contract documents of e-commerce need to be signed electronically. However, under the current conditions, the technology of electronic signature is still not perfect. Therefore, there are still many restrictions on the application of electronic signature in Chinese law. This greatly impedes normal trade.

In addition, there are also problems of privacy and intellectual property protection of online information, as well as problems of online transaction of intangible products on the imposition of customs import and export tariffs and other domestic financial and trade policies and market access. These new problems brought by e-commerce require corresponding adjustments and changes in trade legislation, which is conducive to protecting the legitimate rights and interests of trade parties.

# 10.11 Market Procurement Trade

The mode of market procurement trade refers to the qualified business operators purchase goods under the value of USD 150,000 (including USD 150,000) in the market agglomeration zone recognized by the state department of commerce and other departments, and go through the customs clearance procedures for exports at the place of purchase. Compared with general trade, market procurement trade has the following characteristics:①Classify customs clearance and simplified classification.②Record filing for management and inspect at port. ③Subject supervision and adopt total verification.④Tax-free record filing, exemption and refund. The mode of market procurement trade of export goods is exempted from VAT directly (including VAT tax basis of city building duty, education surtax, etc.). If the enterprise in the market concentration area has not obtained or unable to obtain the VAT invoice of goods, the enterprise can apply for market procurement trade to export the goods.

Market procurement mode greatly improves the facilitation of foreign trade through a series of unique policies, such as subject access, export clearance, tax exemption mode and foreign exchange management supported by the state.

First, the entry threshold is lower. All merchants and trading companies in the industrial cluster area can participate in the pilot project after being put on record.

Second, the export customs clearance is faster, allowing group container consolidation and implementation of simplified classification declaration. If a container contains more than 10 kinds of goods, the customs declaration only need list one kind of goods.

Third, the tax policy is better and value-added tax exemption policy is implemented.

Fourth, the management of foreign exchange is more flexible, allow the opening of current account foreign exchange accounts, and support cross-border CNY settlement. Its core advantage is that the export products can be achieved one declaration, one check and one release at home. The most fundamental guarantee is that the quality of product can be realized "traceable source, traceable responsibility and controllable risk" The greatest potential of market procurement trade is to radiate the surrounding market and realize the same frequency interaction and deep integration of the two markets at home and abroad.

By February 2019, the ministry of commerce of the People's Republic of China announced three batches of market procurement trade pilot including eight pilot units. The first pilot is Yiwu China International Commodity City. The second batch includes Haimen Diedaishiqiao International Home-textile city in Jiangsu and Haining leather city in Zhejiang. The third batch of pilot market procurement includes Changshu garment city of Jiangsu, Guangzhou Huadu leather and leather goods market of Guangdong province, Linyi engineering materials market of Shandong, Wuhan hankou north international commodity trading center of Hubei and Baigou box and bag market of Hebei province.

The pilot project of market procurement trade has not only stimulated the vitality of market subjects, expanded the market scale, enhanced the level of internationalization and promoted the growth of foreign trade, but also achieved positive results in promoting the pilot work of new forms of foreign trade and promoting the innovative development of foreign trade. In addition to facilitating customs clearance and achieving trace-ability, it promote the integrated development of domestic and foreign trade, accelerate industrial agglomeration and promote the development of cross-border e-commerce by building a market procurement agglomeration zone. As an efficient, fast and low-cost new foreign trade mode, it is conducive to attract international buyers to gather, promote professional market operators to realize small batch and multi-batch export of private brand design, and quickly respond to changes in the international market.

# 10.12 Counter Trade

Counter trade refers to the two parties adopt some kind of agreement to achieve balance between import and export, including barter trade, counter purchase, etc. Among them, barter trade refers to the direct exchange of export goods for import goods without monetary media. The value of barter trade of the two sides is equal, usually does not involve cash payment. Counter purchase trade is usually settled in spot exchange, but does not require the counter purchase to be of equal value. Compensation trade can also be classified as a form of counter trade.

## Questions

1. Please have an analysis on the differences between exclusive distribution, sole agent and consignment in international trade.
2. Please try to illustrate the role of international bidding and auction.
3. Please compare China Export Fair with China Import Fair.
4. Please track the trend of cross-border e-commerce development and have an analysis on its functions in the area of international trade.
5. Please have analysis on the situation of processing trade development in China.